OXFORD STUDIES ON THE ROMAN ECONOMY

General Editors

ALAN BOWMAN ANDREW WILSON

OXFORD STUDIES ON THE ROMAN ECONOMY

This innovative monograph series reflects a vigorous revival of interest in the ancient economy, focusing on the Mediterranean world under Roman rule (*c.*100 BC to AD 350). Carefully quantified archaeological and documentary data is integrated to help ancient historians, economic historians, and archaeologists think about economic behaviour collectively rather than from separate perspectives. The volumes include a substantial comparative element and thus will be of interest to historians of other periods and places.

The Indo-Roman Pepper Trade and the Muziris Papyrus

FEDERICO DE ROMANIS

OXFORD
UNIVERSITY PRESS

OXFORD
UNIVERSITY PRESS

Great Clarendon Street, Oxford, OX2 6DP,
United Kingdom

Oxford University Press is a department of the University of Oxford. It furthers the University's objective of excellence in research, scholarship, and education by publishing worldwide. Oxford is a registered trade mark of Oxford University Press in the UK and in certain other countries

First Edition published in 2020

Impression: 1

Published in the United States of America by Oxford University Press
198 Madison Avenue, New York, NY 10016, United States of America

British Library Cataloguing in Publication Data
Data available

Library of Congress Control Number: 2019949287

ISBN 978–0–19–884234–7

Printed and bound by
CPI Group (UK) Ltd, Croydon, CR0 4YY

To my daughters,
and all the women in my life

Acknowledgements

This book is a late repayment for two undeserved blessings that I received quite early in my career. One has been, of course, the publication of the Muziris papyrus; the other, still earlier, the visionary and charismatic mentorship of Santo Mazzarino, who directed me to the subject of Roman trade with South India even before the Muziris papyrus had been heard of.

In all the years I have been struggling with this project, I have been helped by an endless number of people, one way or another. I am afraid it would be impossible to thank them all here. However, I feel it indispensable to express my gratitude to Prof. B. Palme, Direktor der Papyrussammlung und des Papyrusmuseums, Österreichische Nationalbibliothek, to Prof. D. Freedberg, Director of the Italian Academy for Advanced Study in America, to Prof. A. Jördens, Direktor of the Institut für Papyrologie, Universität Heidelberg, to Prof. K.N. Panikkar, Chairman of the Kerala Council for Historical Research, and to Prof. J. Trinquier, of the École Normale Supérieure (Paris) for the support provided by their institutions. Moreover, I would like to acknowledge S. Abraham, the late N. Athiyaman, C.J. Boyajian, B. Borell, K. Butcher, P.J. Cherian, M.R. Falivene, H. Falk, P. Heilporn, C. Intartaglia, R.K. Jayasree, F. Morelli, A. Orengo, K. Rajan, A. Roque, V. Selvakumar, A. Sirinian, Y. Subbarayalu, C. Tavolieri, and L.F. Thomaz.

Selected chapters have been presented in (and have profited from) seminars held at the Kerala Council for Historical Research (Thiruvananthapuram), the Italian Academy for Advanced Study in America, Columbia University (New York), the Collège de France (Paris), the Institute of Archaeology (Oxford University), the Institut für Papyrologie (Universität Heidelberg), and at the École Normale Supérieure (Paris). I thank all the participants for their precious suggestions.

R. S. Bagnall has closely followed the writing of this book: to him I owe an enormous debt of gratitude. Drafts have also been read by R. Ast, A. Bowman, A. Wilson, and three anonymous referees. I thank them for their constructive criticism and recommendations. The style greatly improved under the care and attention of J. B. Johnson. The maps have been drawn by C. Cady (Fig. 1.6 and 1.7) and F. Rizzo (all the others); the reconstruction of the papyrus (Fig. 0.2) has been sketched by M. Chighine. Needless to say, for what is printed here, I am the only one responsible.

I thank A. Bowman and A. Wilson for accepting my book in their series.

In this *tour de force*, my partner, Shinu Anna Abraham, has been a constant, funny, and loving support.

Contents

List of Figures xiii
List of Tables xvii
List of Abbreviations xix

Introduction and Synopsis 1
P. Vindob. G 40822: Text and Translation 9

Part I. Contextualizing the Muziris Papyrus

1. Bridging Disconnected Seas 31
   1.1. Challenges 32
   1.2. The Northern Passages 35
   1.3. The Southern Passages 46
   1.4. Multifaceted Complementarity 54

2. Riding the Monsoons 59
   2.1. Direct Sea Routes 61
   2.2. Multi-stage Sea Routes 67
   2.3. Heading for India 76
   2.4. The Pleiades in the Middle of the Yard 80

3. Pepper Lands 84
   3.1. Kottanarike, the Southern Pepper-producing Land 84
   3.2. Male, the Northern Pepper-producing Land 93
   3.3. Early Modern Quantitative Dimensions 98
   3.4. Ancient Prices 101

4. South Indian Perspectives 107
   4.1. Gatherers 108
   4.2. Traders 115
   4.3. Kings 119
   4.4. The Pepper Pendulum 120

5. Supporting Sources 125
   5.1. Strabo: The Customs Duties on Indian Commodities 125
   5.2. The *Periplus*: The Ships and Cargoes of the South India Trade 135

5.3. Pliny: The Timetable of the Commercial Enterprises to South India 141
5.4. Ptolemy: The Evolution of the South Indian Context 150

Part II. Let Him Look to His Bond: A Loan Contract for Muziris (*P. Vindob.* G 40822 Recto)

6. Deadline and Whereabouts 159
6.1. A Debated Contract 159
6.2. Time and Maritime Loans 162
6.3. The Deadline for the Repayment of the Muziris Loan Contracts 168
6.4. In the Beginning Was the Loan Contract 170

7. Selling and Repaying 173
7.1. Repaying a Maritime Loan in Fourth-century BC Athens 174
7.2. Under the Lender's Power and Seal 179
7.3. Earnings and Benefit of Assumption 181
7.4. Outstanding Loans 184

8. Loan and Logistics 188
8.1. What the Loan Was All About 188
8.2. Prudent Loans for Maritime Trade 193
8.3. Caravans from Berenice 198
8.4. The Coptos Ships 203
8.5. Late Medieval *Comparanda* 206

Part III. The Assessment of a Cargo from Muziris (*P. Vindob.* G 40822 Verso)

9. Three Minor Cargoes 211
9.1. Three-quarters of an Indiaman's Cargo 211
9.2. Gangetic Nard 215
9.3. *Schidai* 217
9.4. Straightforward and Circuitous Evaluations 222
9.5. Cargoes, Quarters, and the Arabarchs' Additional Shares 229

10. The Other Cargo Items 231
10.1. Col. ii, ll. 14–30: An Overview 231
10.2. Pepper: Col. ii, ll. 20–30 (and ll. 1–3) 236
10.3. Tortoise Shell (?) and Malabathron: Col. ii, ll. 14–19 245

11. Contrasts 251
11.1. Ancient and Early Modern Pepper Carriers 252
11.2. Another Pepper Trade 260
11.3. Conspicuous Absences 263
11.4. Indian and African Tusks 268

Part IV. The Red Sea Tax and the Muziris Papyrus

12. *Maris Rubri Vectigal* 277
12.1. Payments in Kind and Payments in Money 277
12.2. Double Customs Duties on Different Tax Bases 283
12.3. Rates 288
12.4. Fiscal Values 291
12.5. Weight Standards 294

13. *Dramatis Personae* 298
13.1. Arabarchs, *Paralemptai*, and *Grammateis* 298
13.2. A Lender/Customs Collector 308
13.3. A Borrower/Ship Owner 312
13.4. The Imperial Administration 317

Epilogue 321

Appendices

1. Exchanging Coins at Barygaza 327
2. Axum and Silis in the *Kephalaia*: Trade and Powers in the Late Antique Indian Ocean 333

References 335
Index of Sources 361
Geographical Index 373
Subject Index 378

List of Figures

0.1 a) and b) *P.Vindob.* G 40822 recto and verso. 12
http://data.onb.ac.at/rec/RZ00001642/Austrian National Library.

0.2 Hypothetical reconstructions of the missing columns of *P.Vindob.* G 40822. 24

1.1 Red Sea and Gulf of Aden July winds. From *Red Sea and Gulf of Aden Pilot*, twelfth edition. 32
© Crown Copyright and/or database rights. Reproduced by permission of the Controller of Her Majesty's Stationery Office and the UK Hydrographic Office (www.GOV.uk/UKHO). Further copying or reproduction without permission strictly prohibited.

1.2 Red Sea and Gulf of Aden January winds. From *Red Sea and Gulf of Aden Pilot*, twelfth edition. 33
© Crown Copyright and/or database rights. Reproduced by permission of the Controller of Her Majesty's Stationery Office and the UK Hydrographic Office (www.GOV.uk/UKHO). Further copying or reproduction without permission strictly prohibited.

1.3 Connections between Red Sea ports and the Nile in Ancient and Medieval times. 35

1.4 Nile Gauge at Cairo. 40
From W.Willcocks and J.I.Craig, *Egyptian irrigation*, London 1913[3], 182, pl. 8.

1.5 Major Ancient and Medieval north Red Sea ports. 43

1.6 Eastern Desert caravan roads. 50

1.7 Coptos–Berenice caravan road between Phoinikon and Aphrodites Oros. 52
(©JAXA) ALOS World 3D–30m (AW3D30) Version 2.2
https://www.eorc.jaxa.jp/ALOS/en/aw3d30/index.htm downloaded in August 2019.

1.8 The Bi'r Minayḥ passage. 53
(©JAXA) ALOS World 3D–30m (AW3D30) Version 2.2
https://www.eorc.jaxa.jp/ALOS/en/aw3d30/index.htm downloaded in August 2019.

1.9 Timetable of the sea routes to Adulis and Muza. 57

2.1 Open-water routes to India. 63

2.2 Normal end dates for the southwest monsoon. From *West Coast of India Pilot*,1986, 11 edn, 47; Diagram 22. 65
© Crown Copyright and/or database rights. Reproduced by permission of the Controller of Her Majesty's Stationery Office and the UK Hydrographic Office (www.GOV.uk/UKHO). Further copying or reproduction without permission strictly prohibited.

2.3 Provenances of the Red Sea ships anchored at Adulis in winter AD 524/5. 69

2.4 Distribution of the find spots for ʿAqaba pottery (based on a map by P. Yule). 71

2.5 Timing of the *dīmānī, ṣā'iḥ,* and *kārim* sailing seasons. 73

2.6 Timing of the *tīrmāh* and *lāḥiq* sailing seasons. 73

2.7 Islands of the Arabian Sea and places mentioned by the *Periplus.* 78

3.1 The major Early Roman (Muziris), Late Antique (Mangalore), and Late Medieval (Calicut) pepper emporia. 85

3.2 Ports and landmarks of the ancient *Tamiḻakam.* 87

3.3 Pepper trade centres according to *Cousas da India e do Japão* (AD 1548). 90

3.4 Pepper collection/trade centres according to a note in da Costa's *Relatório* (AD 1607). 91

3.5 Cosmas Indicopleustes' splendid emporia of India. 95

3.6 Landmarks for Portuguese pepper productivity estimates. 99

3.7 Early Modern estimates or partial data regarding South Malabar's pepper productivity (in tons). 101

4.1 Pepper garden drawn by Peter Mundy. 109
From *The Travels of Peter Mundy in Europe and Asia, 1608–1667.*
Courtesy of the Biblioteca della Società Geografica.

4.2 Places mentioned by Fra Paolino as venues for pepper woods and encounters with the Maler. 111

4.3 Ancient, Late Antique, and Medieval South Indian emporia. 122

5.1 Distribution of pendants and moulds imitating the reverse of Tiberius' PONT MAX. 128
Courtesy B. Borell.

5.2 Denarius of Tiberius *RIC* I[2] 95, no. 30. British Museum number 1988,0917.50. 129
© The Trustees of the British Museum.

5.3 Stone mould from Khlong Thom (southern Thailand), Wat Khlong Thom Museum. 129
Courtesy B. Borell.

5.4 Pliny's South India sea route return journey. 147

5.5 *Carreira da Índia* return voyage. 148

5.6 Ptolemy's world map (Harleian MS 7182, ff 58–59). 150
© The British Library.

6.1 Timing of Roman trade with South India. 170

7.1 Lender's options in case of an outstanding loan. 186

8.1 The sequence of the phrases at recto col. ii, ll. 8–16. 191

8.2 The sequence of the phrases at recto col. ii, ll. 8–16 as it should be, if the borrower meant to assume the desert and river transport expenses. 191

9.1 Evaluation of the sound ivory cargo's three-quarter portion. 226

9.2 Evaluation of the *schidai* cargo's three-quarter portion. 226

10.1 *P.Vindob.* G 40822 verso col. ii, ll. 25–6. 237
P.Vindob. G 40822. Austrian National Library. http://data.onb.ac.at/rec/RZ00001642.

10.2 *P.Vindob.* G 40822 verso col. ii, ll. 20–21. 242
P.Vindob. G 40822. Austrian National Library. http://data.onb.ac.at/rec/RZ00001642.

10.3 Evaluation of the pepper three-quarter portion. 244

10.4 Values of the *Hermapollon* cargo's three-quarter portions. 247

10.5 Weight of the *Hermapollon*'s cargo. 249

11.1 South Malabar's pepper productivity (Early Modern estimates or partial data) and the *Hermapollon*'s pepper cargo (in tons). 254

11.2 Bartolomeu Velho, Portolan Atlas (ca. 1560) Huntington Library HM 44 f 7. 263
Courtesy of the Huntington Library, San Marino, California.

11.3 Average weight per tusk of seven sixteenth-century lots and the *Hermapollon*'s cargo (in kg). 271

11.4 Availability of ivory according to the *Periplus* (small circles 'little ivory', medium circles 'ivory', big circle 'great amount of ivory'). 273

The publisher and the author apologize for any errors or omissions in the above list. If contacted, they will be pleased to rectify these at the earliest opportunity.

List of Tables

2.1 Timetable of the direct Egypt–India sea routes. 67
2.2 Timetable of the India–Aden sea routes. 72
2.3 Timetable of the Egypt–Aden sea routes. 72
2.4 North Indian direct and multi-stage sea routes. 74
2.5 South Indian direct and multi-stage sea routes. 75
3.1 Gold : pepper ratios. 102
3.2 Prices and fiscal values for some commodities imported from the Indian Ocean. 103
9.1 Layout of verso col. iii. 223
10.1 Cargoes and values evaluated on verso col. iii. 232
10.2 Layout of verso coll. ii–iii. 233
10.3 Endings of verso col. ii, ll. 14–30. 235
10.4 Hypotheses of the pepper weight number before recalculation. 241
10.5 Values of the six cargoes' three-quarter portions. 246
10.6 Quantities and values of the six cargoes. 249
11.1 Ships and cargoes of the *Carreira da Índia*, 1501–85 (in *quintais*). 257
11.2 Average weight per tusk in the lot in *DPMAC* 3.572–9, first the whole cargo (385 tusks), then its fourteen sublots. 271
12.1 Pepper purchases by guilds at Edfu (AD 649). 278
12.2 Reconstructed layout of *P. Vindob.* G 40.822 verso coll. i–iv. 285
12.3 Verso col. ii, ll. 1–13: factorization of the pepper, Gangetic nard, sound ivory, and *schidai* cargoes. 286
12.4 Formulae for the evaluation of the three-quarter portions of the *Hermapollon*'s cargoes. 288
12.5 Prices and fiscal values of black pepper and frankincense (in drachmas per mina). 293
12.6 Pepper fiscal values in the Muziris papyrus and in *BM Or.* inv. 8903, approximations for Alexandria market prices in the second and seventh centuries AD, and the ratio between the two data. 294
12.7 Weight unit standards in Roman Egypt. 296
13.1 Hypothetical balance of the *Hermapollon*'s enterprise. 324

List of Abbreviations

Abbreviations follow the *Checklist of Greek, Latin, Demotic and Coptic Papyri, Ostraca and Tablets* for papyrological texts and the fourth edition of the *Oxford Classical Dictionary* for ancient literary and epigraphical texts. Exception is made for the *Periplus Maris Erythraei,* which is referred to as *PME.* Abbreviated references to documents that are not included in these systems are explained in the list below.

Abū al-Fidāʾ	Abū al-Fidāʾ, *Kitāb Taqwīm al-buldān, Géographie d'Aboulféda. Texte arabe publié d'après les manuscrits de Paris et de Leyde . . . par M. Reinaud et M. le Bon Mac Guckin de Slane.* Paris, 1840 (Fr. transl. *Géographie d'Aboulféda* traduite de l'arabe en français et accompagnée de notes d'éclaircissements par M. Reinaud et Stanislas Guyard. 2 vols. Paris, 1848–83).
Aḫbār al-Ṣīn wa 'l-Hind	Abū Zayd al-Sīrāfī, *Accounts of India and China,* edited and translated by T. Mackintosh-Smith, in Ph.F. Kennedy, Sh.M. Toorawa, *Two Arabic Travel Books.* New York, 2014.
Al-Balāḏurī	Ahmad bin Yahya bin Jabir al Biladuri, *Liber Expugnationis Regionum,* ed. M. J. de Goeje, Leiden: Brill, 1863–66. (Engl. transl. *The Origins of Islamic State,* vol. 1., transl. Ph. Hitti, New York: Columbia University Press, 1916. Vol. 2, transl. F. C. Murgotten. New York: Columbia University Press, 1924.)
Al-Dimašqī	Al-Dimašqī, *Nuḫbat al-dahr fī ʿaǧāʾib al-barr wa-al-baḥr,* ed. A. Mehren. Leipzig, 1923.
Al-Muqaddasī	Al-Muqaddasī, *Kitāb aḥsan al-taqāsīm fī maʾrifat al-aqālīm,* ed. M.J. de Goeje, *Descriptio Imperii Moslemici.* Leiden: Brill, 1906. (Engl. transl. Shams al-Dīn al-Muqaddasī, *The Best Divisions for Knowledge of the Regions. Aḥsan al-Taqāsīm fī Maʾrifat al Aqālīm, translated by Basil Anthony Collins, reviewed by Mohammad Hamid Altaʾī.* Reading, 1994.)
Al-Qalqašandī	Al-Qalqašandī, *Ṣubḥ al-aʿšā fī kitābat al-inšāʾ.* 14 vols. Cairo, 1913–19.
Al-Ṭabarī	*Taʾrīkh al-rusul wa-l-mulūk,* ed. M.J. de Goeje et al., Leiden, 1879–1901 (Leiden, 1964–5). (Engl. transl. *The History of al-Tabarī (Taʾrīkh al-rusul wa 'l-mulūk).* 39 vols. Albany, 1985–99 [+ Index, 2007].)
ANTT	*Arqívo Nacional da Torre do Tombo.*

Barbosa	Duarte Barbosa, *Livro em que dá relação do que viu e ouviu no Oriente Duarte Barbosa, Introdução, e notas de Augusto Reis Machado*, Lisbon, 1946 (Engl. transl. *The Book of Duarte Barbosa. An Account of the Countries Bordering on the Indian Ocean and their Inhabitants, written by Duarte Barbosa, and completed about 1518 A.D.* Translated... edited and annoted by M. Longworth Dames. 2 vols. London, 1921).
Buchanan	Buchanan, F. *Journey from Madras through the Countries of Mysore, Canara, and Malabar.* 2 vols. London, 1807.
CAA	R. A. de Bulhão Pato and H. Lopes de Mendonça (eds). *Cartas de Affonso de Albuquerque, seguidas de documentos que as elucidam.* 7 vols. Lisbon, 1884–1935.
Caderno 1518	G. Bouchon. *Navires et cargaison: Retour de l'Inde en 1518. Caderno dos oficiaes da India da carreguacam das naos que vieram o anno mdxviij*, Paris, 1977.
Ca' Masser	'Relazione di Leonardo da Ca' Masser alla serenissima Repubblica di Venezia in sopra il commercio dei portoghesi nell'India dopo la scoperta del Capo di Buona Speranza 1497–1506,' *Archivio Storico Italiano* II. Florence, 1845, 13–51. (*Relatione de Lunardo da Cha Masser*, ms. Bibl. Marciana, IT VII 877 [8651], miscellaneo: Relazioni di ambasciatori [...], cc. 298 r-318 v.)
Caminha	L. de Albuquerque and M. Caeiro. *Cartas de Rui Gonçalves de Caminha.* Lisbon, 1989.
Castanheda	Castanheda, Fernão Lopes de. *História do descobrimento e conquista de India pelos Portugueses.* 8 vols. Coimbra, 1552–61.
CIS	*Corpus Inscriptionum Semiticarum.* Paris, 1881–.
Correa	Correa, G. *Lendas da India.* 8 vols. Lisbon, 1858–66.
Costa	Costa, F. da. *Relatório sobre o trato da pimenta*, in *Documentação Ultramarina Portuguesa*, iii. Lisbon 1963, 293–379.
Cousas da India	*Livro que trata das cousas da India e do Japão*, introd. e notas Adelino de Almeida Calado, *Boletim da Biblioteca da Universidade de Coimbra* 24 (1960), 1–138.
CVR	*Cartas dos Vice-Reys da Índia.*
DPMAC	*Documentos sobre os Portugueses em Moçambique e na África Central.* 9 vols. Lisbon, 1962–89.
DPP	A. da Silva Rego, *Documentação para a História das Missões do Padroado Português do Oriente. Índia.* 12 vols. Lisbon, 1948–58.
DUP	*Documentação ultramarina portuguesa.* Lisbon, 1960–.

FHN	Eide, T., Hægg, T., Pierce, R. H. and Török, L., *Fontes Historiae Nubiorum*. Bergen, 1994.
Figuéiredo Falcão	Figuéiredo Falcão, L. de, *Libro em que se contém toda a fazenda e real patrimonio dos reinos de Portugal, India e ilhas adjacentes e outras particularidades*. 1607. [ed. Lisbon, 1859].
Fitch	Horton Ryley, J. *Ralph Fitch: England's Pioneer to India and Bruma, his Companions and Contemporaries with his remarkable narrative told in his own words*. London, 1899.
Fra Paolino	Paolino da S. Bartolomeo, *Viaggio alle Indie orientali*. Rome, 1796.
Gollenesse	*Memorandum* by Julius Valentyn Stein Van Gollenesse in A. Galletti, A.J. Van der Burg, P. Groot, *The Dutch in Malabar*. Madras, 1911, 43–97.
Gomes de Brito	Gomes de Brito, B. *Historia tragico-maritima*. 2 vols. Lisbon, 1735–6.
HAG	Historical Archives, Goa (Panaji).
Ḥudūd al-ʿālam	Ḥudūd al-ʿālam. *'The Regions of the World'—A Persian Geography 372 A.H.-982 A.D. Translated and Explained by V. Minorsky*. Cambridge, 1970^2.
Ibn ʿAbd al-Ḥakam	Ibn ʿAbd al-Ḥakam, *The history of the conquest of Egypt, North Africa and Spain. Known as Futūḥ Miṣr of Ibn ʿAbd al-Ḥakam edited... by Ch.C. Torrey*. Yale, 1922.
Ibn Baṭūṭah	*Voyages d'Ibn Battoutah. Texte Arabe, accompagné d'une traduction par Ch. Defrémery et B.R. Sanguinetti*. Paris, 1854 (Engl. transl. *The Reḥla of Ibn Baṭṭūṭa (India, Maldive Islands and Ceylon), Translation and Commentary by Mahdi Husain*. Baroda, 1976 (repr.)).
Ibn Ǧubayr	*The Travels of Ibn Jubayr by W. Wright, revised by M.J. De Goeje*. Leiden and London, 1907; (Engl. transl. *The Travels of Ibn Jubayr, translated from the original Arabic by R.J.C. Broadhurst*. London, 1952).
Ibn Ḫurradāḏbih	*Kitāb al masālik wa-l-mamālik*, ed. M.J. de Goeje. Leiden, 1889 (Engl. transl. *Arabic classical accounts of India and China. Translated from original Arabic with Commentaries by S. Maqbul Ahmad*. Shimla, 1989).
Ibn Māǧid	G.R. Tibbetts, *Arab Navigation in the Indian Ocean before the Coming of the Portuguese, being a translation of Kitāb al-Fawāʾid fī uṣūl al-baḥr waʾl-qawāʾid*. London, 1971.
I.Eph	*Inschriften von Ephesos, (Inschriften Griechischer Städte aus Kleinasien 11–17)*. Bonn, 1979–1984.
IGLS	*Les inscriptions grecques et latines de la Syrie*. Paris, 1929–.

I.Kanaïs	Bernand, A. *Le paneion d'el-Kanaïs: les inscriptions grecques.* Leiden, 1972.
I.Ko.Ko.	Bernand, A. *De Koptos à Kosseir.* Leiden, 1977.
I.Memnon	Bernand, A. and Bernand, É. *Les inscriptions grecques et latines du Colosse de Memnon*, Le Caire 1960.
I.Pan	Bernand, A. *Pan du désert.* Leiden, 1977.
I.Philae	Bernand, A. and Bernand, É. *Les inscriptions grecques et latines de Philae.* 2 vols. Paris, 1969.
I.Portes	Bernand, A. *Les portes du désert. Recueil des inscriptions grecques d'Antinooupolis, Tentyris, Koptos, Apollonopolis Parva et Apollonopolis Magna.* Paris, 1984.
Letter of D. Manuel	*Carta de El-Rei D. Manuel ao Rei Catholico, narrando-lhe as viagens portuguezas á India desde 1500 até 1505, reimpressa sobre o prototypo romano de 1505 vertida em linguagem e annotada por Prospero Peragallo.* Lisbon, 1892.
Linschoten	Van Linschoten, J.H. *The Voyage of John Huygen Van Linschoten to the East Indies. From the old English Translation of 1598.* 2 vols. London, 1885.
Livros das Monções	R. de Bulhão Pato (ed), *Documentos remettidos da India ou Livros das Monções.* 5 vols. Lisbon, 1880–1935.
Magno	Magno, Alessandro. *Voyages (1557–1565). Traduction et notes de Wilfred Naar, préface de A. Tenenti.* Paris, 2002.
Ma Huan	Ma Huan, *Ying-yai sheng-lan. 'The overall survey of the ocean's shores' [1433]. Translated from the Chinese text edited by Feng Ch'eng-Chün with introduction, notes and appendices by J. V. G. Mills.* London, 1970.
Marignolli	Marignolli, Giovanni de' = J. Emler (ed), *Fontes rerum Bohemicarum*, III. Pragae, 1882: 492–604.
Mendes	Mendes, R. *Prática d'Arismética.* Lisbon, 1540.
Milne	Milne, J.G. *Catalogue Général des antiquités du Musée du Caire. Greek Inscriptions.* Oxford, 1905.
MSR	Hultsch, F. *Metrologicorum Scriptorum Reliquiae.* 2 vols. Lipsiae, 1864/6.
Mun	Mun, Th. *A discourse of trade, from England vnto the East-Indies answering to diverse obiections which are vsually made against the same.* London, 1621.
Mundy	*The Travels of Peter Mundy in Europe and Asia, 1608–1667. Edited by L. M. Anstey, R.C. Temple*, 3 vols. Cambridge, 1907–36.
Murchio	Murchio, V.M. *Il viaggio all'Indie orientali.* Rome, 1672.
Orta	Orta, G. de. *Colóquios dos simples e drogas da India. Edição publicada por deliberação da Academia Realdas Sciencias de Lisboa pelo Conde de Ficalho.* 2 vols. Lisbon, 1891–1895; English translation *Colloquies on the simple and drugs of*

	India [1563], edited and annotated by the Conde de Ficalho, transl. Clements Markham. London, 1913.
PAT	Hillers, D.R. and Cussini, E. *Palmyrene Aramaic Texts.* London, 1996.
Piloti	*L'Égypte au commencement du quinzième siècle d'après le Traité d'Emmanuel Piloti de Crète (Incipit 1420) avec une introduction et des notes par P.-H. Dopp.* Cairo, 1950.
Pires	Pires, Tomé. *The Suma Oriental of Tomé Pires: An Account of the East, from the Red Sea to Japan, Written in Malacca and India in 1512–1515 and the Book of Francisco Rodrigues, Pilot-Major of the Armada that Discovered Banda and the Moluccas, Rutter of a Voyage in the Red Sea, Nautical Rules, Almanack and Maps, Written and Drawn in the East before 1515 edited by A. Cortesão.* 2 vols. London, 1944 (Port. text, 2.323–511; Engl. transl. 1.1–228; 2.229–89).
Pires de Távora	Carta de Lourenço Pires de Távora a el-Rei. 1560 Novembro 30 in *Corpo diplomatico portoguez contendo os actos e relações politicas e diplomaticas de Portugal com as diversas potencias do mundo desde o seculo xvi até os nossos dias.* Lisbon, 1886, 9.108–12.
Polo	Polo, Marco. *Milione. Le divisament dou monde. Il Milione nelle redazioni toscana e franco-italiana.* A cura di G. Ronchi; introduzione di C. Segre. Milano, 1982.
Quirini	Quirini, V. 'Relazione', in E. Albèri (ed). *Relazioni degli ambasciatori veneti al Senato; raccolte, annotate ed edite da E. Albéri.* Florence, 1863, 5–19.
Relaçaõ 1568	Wicki, J. (1961). 'Duas relações sobre a situação da Ĩndia portuguesa nos anos 1568 e 1569', *Studia* 8: 133–220.
RES	*Répertoire d'épigraphie sémitique.*
Santa Cruz	Santa Cruz, Alvaro de Baçan. 'Parecer al Rey Don Felipe segundo sobre la navegacion de la India de Portugal', in J. Gentil da Silva (ed.), *Alguns elementos para a história do comércio da Ĩndia de Portugal existentes na Biblioteca Nacional de Madrid.* Lisbon, 1959, 53–9.
Sanuto	Sanuto, M. *I diarii di Marino Sanuto (mccccxcvi–mdxxxiii) dall'autografo Marciano ital. cl. vii codd. cdxix–cdlxxvii,* 58 vols. Venezia, 1879–1903.
Sassetti	Sassetti, F. *Lettere da vari paesi, 1570–88. Introduzione, testo e note a cura di Vanni Bramanti.* Milan, 1970.
Sebastião	*Leis, e Provisões, que El Rei Dom Sebastião nosso senhor fez depois que começou a governar.* Coimbra, 1816^2.

Seure	Seure, Chevalier de (1895), 'Lettre au Roy (30/1/1559)', in E. Falgairolle, 'Le chevalier de Seur ambassadeur de France en Portugal au xvie siècle', *Mémoires de l'Académie de Nîmes* 18: 49–85.
SII	*South Indian Inscriptions.* Madras 1890–.
UMTL	*University of Madras Tamil Lexicon.* Madras, 1926–39.
Urk.	K. Sethe, *Hieroglyphische Urkunden der griechisch-römischen Zeit.* Leipzig, 1904.
Varthema	*Itinerario de Ludovico de Varthema Bolognese nello Egypto, nella Surria, nella Arabia deserta & felice, nella Persia, nella India, & nella Ethiopia. La fede, el uiuere, & costume de tutte le prefate Prouincie.* Rome, 1510 (Engl. transl. *The travels of Ludovico di Varthema in Egypt, Syria, Arabia Deserta and Arabia Felix, in Persia, India, and Ethiopia, A.D. 1503 to 1508 translated... by George Percy Badger.* London, 1863).
Yāqūt	Yāqūt al-Ḥamawī al-Rumī, *Kitāb Mu'ğam al-buldān. Geographisches Wörterbuch... herausgegeben von* F. Wüstenfeld, 5 vols. Leipzig, 1866–73.

necessità di scrivere, libertà, autenticità, rischio

(P.P. Pasolini)

Introduction and Synopsis

The aim of this book is to offer an interpretation of the two texts of the *P. Vindobonensis* G 40822, now widely referred to as the Muziris papyrus. It is not often that two papyrological texts require an entire book for elucidation. These two certainly do, in part because their fragmentary status and technical nature make the process of understanding them somewhat laborious, and in part because evaluating their relevance calls for both extensive commentary and numerous intersecting paths of in-depth research.

It would be incorrect to say that without these two texts, we would have no knowledge of the Indo-Roman trade practices referred to therein. On the contrary, thanks to the information provided by a variety of literary sources, Roman Egypt's South India trade has always ranked among the best-known chapters of Roman trade—and the recent or ongoing archaeological excavations in Egypt (Myos Hormos, Berenice, the Eastern Desert), Arabia ('Aynunah, al-Wajh, Qan'i, Khor Rori), East Africa (Adulis), and India (Pattanam) have greatly enriched and still continue to enrich the corpus of evidence.

Still, by themselves, all these data would fail to produce a sufficiently vivid picture of this ancient phenomenon, one that is detailed and nuanced enough to enable close comparisons with Medieval and Early Modern successors. Without the Muziris papyrus texts, our current evidence regarding South Indian trade would be like a *partitura* of a *concerto*—but minus the soloist parts. Conversely, these two esoteric and fragmentary texts would be hopelessly enigmatic, if no other sources were available to add depth to a host of related matters, such as the commercial and political geography of ancient South India, the sailing schedule and the size of the ships plying the South India sea route, the commodities exchanged in the South Indian emporia, and the taxes imposed on the Indian commodities en route from the Red Sea to the Mediterranean.

On the other hand, remarkable as it is, all this information would not be quite so significant if it could not be contrasted with analogous trade evidence from the Middle and Early Modern Ages. It is the dialogue between internal and external clues, and between contemporaneous and non-contemporaneous evidence, that enables us to exploit the enormous informative potential of the

The Indo-Roman Pepper Trade and the Muziris Papyrus. Federico De Romanis, Oxford University Press (2020).
 DOI: 10.1093/oso/9780198842347.001.0001

Muziris papyrus. When viewed against the twin backdrops of ancient sources on South Indian trade and of Medieval and Early Modern documents on pepper commerce, the two texts become foundational resources for the history of commercial relationships between South India and the West.

Of course, this does not mean that the Rome–South India trade has no more secrets. Quite the opposite—in its *partitura*, several soloist parts remain missing. For instance, the papyrus texts reveal nothing about the exports from the Roman Empire to India; hence, they contribute very little to the age-old question about the flow of Roman coinage to India. Moreover, with regard to imports from India, we will see that the cargo evaluated on the verso of the Muziris papyrus fails to follow the trade model exemplified in the *Periplus of the Erythraean Sea* in every detail. As a consequence, one is left wondering whether the discrepancies point to an evolution in the trade with South India from the mid-first (the time of the *Periplus*) to the mid-second (approximately the time of the Muziris papyrus) century AD, or whether they merely stem from the different nature of the documents—one a synthetic overview of the whole South India trade, and the other a detailed description of a single commercial enterprise.

Despite these and other drawbacks, one cannot deny that the publication of the Muziris papyrus texts—and the slow, tedious process of their interpretation and explanation—mark a turning point for studies on Indo-Roman trade specifically,[1] and on the Roman economy more broadly. On the Roman side, apart from showing the impressive organizational and financial potential of ancient mercantile communities, the Muziris papyrus clarifies some of the routine practices associated with Greco-Roman maritime loan agreements, and demonstrates how such practices were adapted to the peculiarities of the South India trade. It also details how customs duties on imported Indian items were assessed and collected, and hints at the intriguing interplay among the state, the financial élites (tax-collectors and lenders), and the merchants. Finally, the texts of the Muziris papyrus disclose the workings of the administrative division that managed the collection of customs duties, showing how it financially and logistically supported the India-bound merchants.

On the Indian side, the cargo of the *Hermapollon*—the Roman Indiaman whose imports are itemized and evaluated on the verso of the Muziris papyrus—highlights the commercial importance of a region and of an emporion strategically poised between the Arabian Sea and the Bay of Bengal. It introduces us to the socio-economic ties between the coastal plains and inland hills of South India, and to the maritime links between the northern and southern parts of the subcontinent. It enables approximations of the local

[1] Despite Gurukkal (2016), I still think it appropriate to use the formula 'Indo-Roman trade'. For my position regarding Gurukkal's point of view, cf. De Romanis (2019) and chapter four of this volume.

production of pepper and ivory and allows a glimpse of the military strength of the Cēra kingdom.

Furthermore, since trade relations between South India and the West have been an enduring feature of Indian Ocean history, the importance of the Muziris papyrus texts extends beyond the chronological confines of Indo-Roman trade. Indeed, the texts become key documents for building a *longue durée* perspective of Indian Ocean trade. Unquestionably, these texts are among the most valuable gifts from papyrology to the histories of the world.

Such fundamental documents deserve to be studied from a variety of angles, examined under the microscopes of different specializations, and collated with the widest range of documents. It is beyond my ability to recount the interactions between the Mediterranean and Indian Ocean in all their diachronic and geographic complexity, but in this book I have tried my best to compare and contrast the texts of the Muziris papyrus with other documents pertinent to Indo-Mediterranean (or Indo-European) trade in Ancient, Medieval, and Early Modern times. The important points I may have missed—or misunderstood—are left to others to determine.

This book is not a line-by-line, word-by-word commentary, but instead an interpretation of the two fragmentary texts of the Muziris papyrus. The first five chapters (Part I) contextualize the documents, clarifying various fundamentals: the logistical aspects of the communication between the Mediterranean and South India; the geography and anthropology of pepper production and trade in ancient India; and the contributions of certain Greek and Latin writers towards understanding the papyrus texts. The next three chapters (Part II) address questions pertaining to the recto text, which is a loan contract between a merchant and a financier for a commercial venture to the South Indian emporion of Muziris. These chapters attempt to clarify when and for how long the loan was granted, how the loan was to be repaid, and which expenses the loan was expected to cover. The first two chapters of Part III deal with the verso text, a fiscal assessment of Indian commodities transported on a cargo ship named the *Hermapollon*. The third chapter presents four contrasts. In the first two the tonnage of the *Hermapollon* is contrasted with the ships of the sixteenth century, both the carracks of the *Carreira da Índia* and the ships of the Moorish trade of the Red Sea route. The third contrast is between the *Hermapollon*'s cargo and the commodities available in Limyrike's emporia during the mid-first century AD. The fourth is between the ivory tusks carried by the *Hermapollon* and those exported from East Africa by the Portuguese ships in the sixteenth century. Finally, Part IV comprises two chapters. One details the structure and technicalities related to the customs duties charged on Indian commodities as they moved from the Red Sea to the Mediterranean; the other characterizes the two co-signatories of the loan contract.

It is customary to summarize the conclusions of a book at its end. In this case, it is preferable to state them at the outset, so that the arguments laid out in the text may be more easily followed and checked. Specifically, I will argue that:

1. From the Augustan age until perhaps the beginning of the third century AD, trade between Egypt and South India was characterized by certain specific features that are recognizable in the Muziris papyrus texts:
   a. a particular strategy for transferring cargoes between the Mediterranean and the Red Sea—a Nile voyage between Alexandria and Coptos in combination with a desert crossing between Coptos and a Red Sea port (most probably Berenice);
   b. direct round-trip voyages between a Red Sea port and the South Indian emporia located around Vembanad Lake;
   c. the use of very large transoceanic vessels to convey considerable quantities of pepper and malabathron;
   d. precisely scheduled departures (around 20 July for the outward journey, and between 9 December and 13 January for the return);
   e. commercial enterprises that lasted less than one year;
   f. commodities subject to double, heavy customs duties during their passage from the Red Sea to the Mediterranean.
2. The text on the recto side of the Muziris papyrus was a loan contract for a commercial enterprise to the South Indian emporion of Muziris. The contract was signed in Alexandria before the merchant/borrower departed for India, for a loan that was valid for one year. Unless unexpected circumstances delayed the return to Egypt, the money had to be repaid by the deadline traditionally established for Muziris loan contracts, which started in June and expired the same day of the following year.
3. The loan covered all the expenses inside Egypt: the river voyages between Alexandria and Coptos, the desert crossings between Coptos and Berenice, and other minor expenses for the unloading and loading of the cargo and its storage in the fiscal warehouses of Coptos and Alexandria. The money was not delivered in a single consignment nor was it a precisely fixed sum, and since most of it was delivered when the cargo was safely ashore, the yield must have been lower than those usually given by loans that were solely maritime in nature.
4. The caravans conveying South Indian commodities from Berenice to Coptos were deemed an 'imperial service', and the prefect of Egypt had to ensure that enough camels were available for ships returning from South India. The borrower promises to transfer the pledged cargo from the Red Sea to Coptos in a single voyage. Since the pledged cargo is the

entire cargo of the *Hermapollon* (more than 650 tons), the caravan comprised several thousand camels.

5. Next, the borrower promises to transfer the pledged cargo from Coptos to Alexandria, again in a single voyage. Therefore, the river ship should have had the same cargo-carrying capacity as the ocean-going vessel.
6. Precisely because of their size, the river ships that moved Indian commodities from Coptos to Alexandria did not sail through the Schedia canal, nor did they anchor in the Lake Harbour. Instead, they sailed down the Canopic branch of the Nile and docked at Iuliopolis/Nicopolis.
7. In Mediterranean maritime loan contracts, once the ship arrived at its destination, the creditor could take control of the cargo, but the borrower was not prevented from selling it as he wished. Nor was the borrower compelled to repay his entire debt with his first sale. It was the borrower who determined what, to whom, and at what price the goods were to be sold, whereas the lender (or his representatives) appropriated the earnings of these partial sales and provided receipts until the borrower's debt was fully repaid.
8. The loan contract of the Muziris papyrus anticipates the same procedure. The Indian cargoes were put on sale first at the emporion of Coptos, where many Egyptian retailers convened, and then at the Mediterranean emporion of Alexandria. The borrower decided what, to whom, and at what price to sell. The lender (or his representatives) appropriated the proceeds of the sales and provided the borrower with acknowledging receipts until the debt was repaid.
9. While transiting from the Red Sea to the Mediterranean, Indian commodities were subject to customs duties twice, once upon entering Egypt and again upon leaving it. The tariff rate of the import duties was 25 per cent, and it applied to 100 per cent of the cargo. The tariff rate of the export duties was also 25 per cent, but it was levied on only 75 per cent of the cargo. On top of the import customs duties, some Indian commodities—among those imported by the *Hermapollon*, pepper and ivory—were subject to a surcharge said to be taken in addition by the arabarchs. The same commodities were granted a discount on the export customs duties calculated through a reduction of the nominal weight.
10. The verso text, which comprised at least three columns, presented the assessment of both the import and export customs duties of a cargo that arrived (most likely from Muziris) on an Indiaman named the *Hermapollon*. Its surviving columns (coll. ii, very partially, and iii, almost entirely) present an assessment of the three-quarter portions of six

cargoes (Gangetic nard, 'sound' ivory tusks, fragments of ivory tusks, malabathron, pepper, and, perhaps, tortoise shell). The considerable total of the calculated values—1,151 monetary talents and 5,852 drachmas—was the tax base for the export customs duties.

11. In the missing col. i, the import customs duties were assessed. There was probably also a col. iv, with the sum of the import and the export customs duties.
12. Of course, the goods sold and consumed in Egypt were not subject to export duties, which is why portions of three of the six items—pepper, malabathron, and tortoise shell (?)—were not evaluated for the export round.
13. The evaluations of the *Hermapollon*'s six cargoes were not recorded randomly, but according to an order. First, the three commodities (tortoise shell (?), malabathron, and pepper) which had been partly sold in Egypt, then the three (Gangetic nard, ivory tusks, ivory trimmings) that were transported in their entirety outside Egypt. In each group, the commodities that were subject to the surcharge on the import customs duties and enjoyed the discount on the export customs duties (pepper, ivory tusks, ivory trimmings) were evaluated last.
14. The merchant was free to choose whether to pay in money or in kind. However, since each cargo item was assessed based on fiscal values that were much lower than the usual market prices, those customs duties were paid more often than not in money. At any rate, the customs duties on the cargo evaluated in the Muziris papyrus were meant to be paid in money. By contrast, Late Antique evidence suggests that customs duties on Indian commodities were paid, at least occasionally, in kind.
15. Unsurprisingly for an Indiaman returning from Muziris, the major cargo carried by the *Hermapollon* was pepper, whose three-quarter portion is evaluated at verso col. ii, ll. 20–30. Its two monetary values at col. ii, ll. 25–6 and 30 (771 talents and 4,632 drachmas and at l. 30 a subtotal ending with 3 obols) imply that its fiscal value per mina was an even number of drachmas that is a submultiple of twenty-four, but not a multiple of four. Since any number below six would give an impossibly huge cargo, its fiscal value was six drachmas per mina.
16. The weight number at verso col. ii, l. 20 quantifies the three-quarter portion of the pepper cargo. It must be restored as *μ(υριάδος) α]'Γφ[* (1]3,5[??). The entire pepper cargo weighed more than 18,000 talents (*c.*552 tons).
17. The weight number at verso col. ii, l. 18 approximates the three-quarter portion of the second main cargo. Its fiscal value was 12 drachmas per

mina and may be identified as malabathron. The entire cargo weighed more than 2,480 talents (*c.*76 tons).

18. Quite remarkably, the *Hermapollon*'s cargo did not include any pearls or precious stones.
19. The task of collecting customs duties on Indian commodities entering the Roman Empire via Egypt (i.e., the Red Sea tax) was contracted out to a *societas publicorum* called the *arabarchia*, which was presided over by a *manceps* called the arabarch, and supported by associates and guarantors, also called arabarchs.
20. Under the terms of the contract, the arabarchs kept a share of the Red Sea tax revenue for themselves. Depending on the contract they had with the imperial treasury, they were also permitted to collect small surcharges on the import customs duties. The treasury compensated the merchants for these surcharges by granting them a discount on the export customs duties.
21. The *paralemptes tes Erythras thalasses* (or *Berenikes*) was to the *arabarchia* what the *magister* was to the *societas publicorum*. Probably appointed by the arabarch(s), he was the leader of the team that collected the Red Sea tax. The *grammateis* at Myos Hormos and Berenice were subordinates of the *paralemptes*.
22. The lender of the Muziris papyrus loan contract was the *paralemptes* of the Red Sea tax, which means that the financier who supports the India trader in the loan contract on the recto is the same man as the customs officer who collects the duties assessed on the verso. His agents and representatives in the Red Sea port, at Coptos, and at Alexandria comprised the personnel of the Red Sea tax department.
23. The designated borrower in the loan contract was also the owner of the *Hermapollon*. Most probably, he alone co-signed the loan contract in his capacity as chief representative of the group of merchants whose cargoes were being carried on the *Hermapollon*.

P. Vindob. G 40822

Text and Translation

Introductory Notes

The *P.Vindob.* G 40822 is a fragment of a papyrus 38 cm high and 27 cm wide, written on both sides. The blank space on the top and at the bottom shows that no line is missing on top or at the bottom of recto col. ii and verso col. iii. First edition by Harrauer/Sijpensteijn (1985). Afterwards, Thür (1987); Casson (1990); *SB* 18. 13167; De Romanis (1998) (verso col. iii only); Morelli (2011) (emendations on both texts, but transcription of verso only). A transcription of both recto and verso is also available at http://papyri.info/ddbdp/sb;18;13167. No transcription, but relevant emendations were suggested by Rathbone (2000) and De Romanis (2011 [2012]). Pictures both of recto and verso are available online (open access) at the website of the Papyrussammlung of the Österreichische Nationalbibliothek: http://aleph.onb.ac.at/F/?func=find-c&ccl_term=WID%3DRZ00001642&local_base=ONB08. At the time of the first edition, a fragment pertaining to verso col. ii, ll. 17–20 had been positioned upside down, with obvious consequences.

The recto side preserves almost in its entirety one column consisting of 26 lines, with 45 to 55 letters in each line, written in a clear and elegant hand. The preserved column was preceded and followed by portions of the text that are missing. The analysis of the verso text (cf. pp. 211–250; 283–288) strongly suggests that on the recto side just one column followed the surviving fragment. Therefore, the text on the recto side comprised at least three columns, of which only the second to last survives. For convenience's sake, the surviving column will be referred to as 'col. ii', even if more than one column could be missing on the left. Except for l. 22, which is all preserved, a variable number of letters—from one to more than a dozen—are missing on the left margin. More often than not, the restoration of the lacunae is quite straightforward, but in three instances (ll. 2, 10, 23) it is not; the reading of l. 2 is further complicated by a few uncertain letters (cf. pp. 198–200).

Written by a more cursive, but not less skilled hand, the text on the verso had narrower columns with a greater number of lines. The extant fragment preserves few letters of the right end of a column and the entire subsequent column. The last preserved column counts 29 lines. The preceding column was longer; although it keeps traces of only 28 lines, it will be argued (cf. p. 239) that once it had 30 lines. The editors posited that the text of the verso comprised only the two columns that somehow survive. Accepted so far, this assumption turns out to be inaccurate. The width of the columns and the analysis of both texts show that on the left of the only partially extant column of the verso, there was another one (cf. pp. 283–7). Consequently, in the present book what have been previously called col. i and col. ii will be called col. ii and col. iii, respectively. Moreover, it will be argued (cf. p. 287) that after verso col. iii, one or more columns followed.

The English translation incorporates the restorations adopted in the Greek text. They are discussed in Parts II and III. In the apparatus, Morelli will stand for Morelli (2011), Rathbone for Rathbone (2000), and Thür for Thür (1987).

Fig. 0.1a *P.Vindob.* G 40822 recto.
http://data.onb.ac.at/rec/RZ00001642/Austrian National Library.

Fig. 0.1b *P. Vindob.* G 40822 verso.
http://data.onb.ac.at/rec/RZ00001642/Austrian National Library.

Text and Translation of the Extant Columns

Recto
i

\- - - - - - - - - - -

ii

1 [- - -] . μένων σου ἑτέρων ἐπι̣[τ]ρόπων ἢ φροντιστῶν καὶ στήσας
2 [- - -] . . σω καμηλείτηι α . . . . ρ . . . πρὸς ἐπίθ̣εσιν τῆς εἰς Κόπτον
3 [- - -]υ̣ καὶ ἀνοίσω διὰ τοῦ ὄρους μετὰ παραφυλακῆς καὶ ἀσ̣φ̣α̣λε̣ίας
4 [εἰς τὰ]ς ἐπὶ Κόπτου δημοσίας παραλημπτικὰς ἀποθήκας καὶ ποι-
5 [ήσω ὑ]π̣ὸ τὴν σὴν ἢ τῶν σῶν ἐπιτρόπων ἢ τοῦ παρόντος αὐτῶν
6 [ἐξουσία]ν καὶ σφραγεῖδα μέχρι ποταμοῦ ἐμβολῆς καὶ ἐμβαλοῦμαι
7 [τῶι δέ]οντι καιρῶι εἰς ποτάμ̣ιον ἀσφαλὲς πλοῖον καὶ κατοίσω εἰς τὴν
8 [ἐν Ἀλε]ξανδρείᾳ̣ τῆς τετάρτης παραλημπτικὴν ἀποθήκην καὶ ὁ-
9 [μοίω]ς ποιήσω ὑπὸ τὴν σὴν ἢ τῶν σῶν ἐξουσίαν καὶ σφραγεῖδα ταῖς
10 [ἐκ δανε]ί̣ου ἀπὸ τοῦ νῦν μέχρι τεταρτολογίας δαπάναις πάσαις καὶ φο-
11 [ρέτρω]ν̣ ὄρους καὶ ναύλων ποταμίων καὶ τῶν ἄλλων κατὰ μέρος ἀνα-
12 [λωμά]τ̣ων πρὸς τὸ ἐνστάντος τοῦ ἐν ταῖς κατὰ Μουζεῖριν τοῦ δα-
13 [νείου σ]υνγραφαῖς τῆς ἀποδόσεως ὡ̣ρισμένου χρόνου ἐὰν μὴ δικαί-
14 [ως τότ]ε̣ χρεολυτῶ τὸ προκείμενον ἐν ἐμοὶ δάνειον τότε εἶναι
15 [πρὸς σ]ὲ̣ καὶ τοὺς σοὺς ἐπιτρόπους ἢ φροντιστὰς τὴν ἐγλογὴν καὶ ὁλο-
16 [σχερῆ] ἐξουσίαν ὡς ἐὰν αἱρῆσθε ποιήσασθαι τὰ τῆς πράξεως χωρὶς
17 [διαστ]ολῆς καὶ προσκρίσεως (*l.* προσκλήσεως) κρατεῖν τε καὶ κυριεύειν
τὴν προκε̣ι̣-
18 [μένη]ν ὑποθήκην καὶ τεταρτολογεῖν καὶ τὰ λοιπὰ ἐσόμενα μέρη
19 [τρία μ]εταφέρειν οὗ ἐὰν αἱρῆσθε καὶ πωλεῖν καὶ μεθυποτίθεσθαι
20 [καὶ] ἑ̣τ̣[έ]ρωι παραχωρεῖν ὡς ἐὰν αἱρῆσθε καὶ τὰ καθ' ἑαυτὴν διοικονο-
21 [με]ῖσθαι καθ' ὃν ἐὰν βούλησθε τρόπον καὶ ἑαυτῶι ὠνεῖσθαι τῆς ἐπὶ \τοῦ/
22 καιροῦ φανησομένης τιμῆς καὶ ἐκκρού[ει]ν καὶ ἐνλογεῖν τὰ πεσούμενα
23 [ἀπ' ὠνίων εἰς ἔκτεισιν τ]οῦ δανείου τῆς πίστεως τῶν πεσουμένων
24 [οὔσης π]ερὶ σὲ καὶ τοὺς ἐπιτρόπους ἢ φροντιστάς, ὄντων ἡμῶν ἀσυκοφαν-
25 [τήτ]ω̣ν κατὰ πάντα τρόπον τοῦ δὲ περ̣ὶ τὴ̣ν ἐνθήκην ἐνλείμματός
26 [τ]ε καὶ πλεονάσματος πρὸς ἐμὲ τὸν δεδανεισμένον κα̣ὶ̣ ὑποτεθει-

Recto
i

– – – – – – – – – – –

ii

...your other agents or managers and having weighed
I will...to...cameleer...for the shipment of the...to Coptos
and I will bring [sc. the cargo] through the desert with vigilance and precaution
up to the public customs warehouses in Coptos and I will
put [sc. the cargo] under the power and seal of yourself or your administrators
or whoever of them is there up to the loading [sc. of the cargo] on the river and I will load
at the required time in a safe river ship and I will convey [sc. the cargo] downstream up to the
customs warehouse of the quarter-tax in Alexandria and likewise
I will put [sc. the cargo] under your or your people's power and seal for
all the expenses from [= met with] the loan from now until the payment of the quarter-tax —the
costs of the desert transports, the river freights and the other due outlays—
so that, if, on the occurrence of the time established for the repayment in the loan contracts for
Muziris, I do not properly pay the aforesaid loan in my name,
then you and your agents or managers shall have the choice and complete power, if you choose, to carry out execution
without notification or summons and to get possession and own the aforesaid
security and levy the quarter-tax and transfer the three parts that will
remain to whomever you choose and sell and re-hypothecate
and cede to another, if you choose, and handle the security
whichever way you want and buy for yourself at the then
current price and subtract [sc. its value] and reckon the future proceeds from the goods
for the payment in full of the loan, with the benefit of assumption regarding the proceeds
being on you and your agents or managers, and us being absolutely free from
misrepresentation; the shortfall or surplus with respect to the capital will be on me, the borrower and mort-

iii

1 [*μένον ὄντος - - -*

– – – – – – – – – – –

ii 1 [- - -]̣ *μένων ego …ο.̣μένων edd. ἐπι̣[τ]ρόπων ego ἐπ[ι]τρό̣πων edd. ἐπ[ι]τρ̣όπων Thür* 2 [- - -]̣ ̣*σω ego* [*δώσω τ*]*ῷ̣ σῷ̣ edd.* [- - -]*δ̣ώσω Morelli παρα*]*δώσω Gonis apud Morelli; l. καμηλίτηι; α….ρ… ego ἄλλα (τάλαντα) ρο (δ̣ρ̣α̣χμ̣ὰ̣ς̣) ν̣ edd. ἄλλα (τάλαντα) ε̣*[*ἴ*]*κ̣ο̣σ̣ι̣ Harrauer apud Casson (1990) ἀξ̣ιοχρέ̣ωι Morelli* 3 [*εἰσόδο*]*υ̣ edd.* [*ἀνόδο*]*υ̣ Casson (1986)* [*συνόδο*]*υ̣ Thür* 6 *l. σφραγῖδα* 7 *ποτάμ̣ιον Morelli ι postea addito ποτάμ<ι>ον Koenen apud Casson (1990), ποταμὸν edd.* 8 *Ἀλε*]*ξ̣ανδρείᾳ Morelli Ἀλεξ*]*ανδρείᾳ edd.* 9 *l. σφραγῖδα* 10 [*ἐκ δανε*]*ί̣ου vel sim. De Romanis (1998) (cf. pp. 188–93)* [*τοῦ πλο*]*ί̣ου edd.* [*ἐκ τοῦ ἰδ*]*ίου Morelli;* 10–11 *φο | ρέτρω*]*ν̣ ὅρους Morelli, φο | ρέτρου*] *ὅρους edd. φο | ρέτρων*] *ὅρους Thür* 11 *ποταμίων Morelli ποταμίταις edd.* 12 *post πρός lacunam postulaverunt edd., qui in commentario exempli gratia suppleverunt πρὸς <ἐμέ τὸν ναύκληρον ὄντων. ὁμολογοῦμεν συμπεφωνηκέναι τὰ προγεγραμμένα πρὸς> τὸ ἐνστάντος (cf. p. 189, n.5)* 13 *l. σ*]*υγγραφαῖς* 14. *l. χρεωλυτῷ* 15 *l. ἐκλογὴν* 17 *διαστ*]*ολῆς Thür προσβ*]*ολῆς edd.; l. προσκλήσεως Thür; προκε̣ι̣- Morelli πρ̣ο̣κ*[*ει- edd.* 22 *l. ἐλλογεῖν* 23 *ἀπ᾽ ὠνίων εἰς ἔκτεισιν τ*]*οῦ δανείου exempli gratia ego (cf. pp. 181–4) τοῦ προγεγραμμέν*]*ο̣υ̣ δανείου edd., ὑπὲρ τοῦ προκειμέν*]*ο̣υ̣ δανείου Thür* 25 *ἐνλείμματός (l. ἐλλείμματός) Morelli ἐνλείματός edd.*

iii

1 [gager . . .

\- - - - - - - - - - -

Verso

i

\- - - - - - - - - -

ii

1 [ ] μν(αῖ) νθ

2 [ ] μν(αῖ) ι̣δ L´δ´

3 [ ] . μν(αῖ) νη

4 [Νάρδου Γανγιτικῆς κιστῶν π τετάρτη κίσ]τ̣α̣ι̣ κ

5 [Ἐλέφαντος ὑγιοῦς ἐν μὲν ὀδ]ο̣ῦ̣σ̣ι ρξζ ὁλ(κῆς) (ταλάντων) ρε μν(ῶν) ιγ

6 [ ] . . (τάλαντα) κϛ μν(αῖ) λ

7 [ ]ν̣τ̣ω τῆς τετάρτης

8 [ὁμ]ο̣ίως ὁλ(κῆς) μν(αῖ) ια L´δ´

9 [ ] . (τάλαντα) κϛ μν(αῖ) ιη δ´

10 [ἐν δὲ σχίδαις] ὁ̣λ̣κ̣(ῆς) (ταλάντων) ιζ μν(ῶν) λγ

11 [ ] (τάλαντα) δ μν(αῖ) μ̣ϛ

12 [ ] . . . . . π..ικω

13 [ ] (τάλαντα) δ μν(αῖ) κγ δ´

14 [Χελώνης? - - - μν(ῶν)] λα̣ L´

15 [ ] . . κ̣α

16 [ ]η̣

17 [Μαλαβάθρου] . . [μν(ῶν)] . δ´

18 [ὧν ὁμοίως τιμὴ λογίζεται ὁλκ(ῆς) (ταλάντων)] Ἀωξ [? μν(ῶν) ??] Ḷ´δ´

19 [ὡς τῆς μν(ᾶς) (δραχμῶν) ιβ ἀργ](υρίου) (τάλαντα) σ̣κ[? (δραχμαὶ) ?,??θ]

20 [Πιπέρεως ὁλκ(ῆς) (ταλάντων) μ(υριάδος) α] Ἀφ [?? μν(ῶν) μδ δ´]

21 [ὧν ὁμοίως τιμὴ λογίζεται ὁλκ(ῆς) μὲν (ταλάντων) μ(υριάδος) α] Ἀσκγ μν(ῶν) β̣

22 [ ]κα̣ ἐξ ὧν̣ ἀ̣ν̣τ̣ι̣

23 [ ]ται η . . . υ . . .

24 [ ] . . . . . . ριων

25 [ὁλκ(ῆς) (ταλάντων) μ(υριάδος) α Ἀβωξβ μν(ῶν) νβ ὡς τῆς μν(ᾶς) (δραχμῶν) ϛ] ἀ̣ρ̣γ(υρίου) (τάλαντα) ψοα

26 (δ̣ρ̣α̣χ̣μ̣α̣ὶ̣) Ἀχλβ

27 [ ] μ̣ν̣(ῶ̣ν̣) μδ̣ δ´

28 [ ] . . . ν

29 [ὡς τῆς μν(ᾶς) (δραχμῶν) ϛ (τάλαντα) ? (δραχμαὶ) ?,??ε𐅵]

30 [γίν(εται) ἐπὶ τὸ αὐτὸ (τάλαντα) ψ?? (δραχμαὶ) ?,??ζ𐅵]

Verso

i

– – – – – – – – – –

ii

1 [ ] 59 minas
2 [ ] 14 ½ ¼ minas
3 [ ] 58 minas
4 [Of **Gangetic Nard** 80 containers, quarter-tax contai]ners 20
5 [Of **Sound Ivory** in] 167 **Tusks** of 105 talents of weight 13 minas
6 [ ] 26 talents [of weight] 30 minas
7 [ ] of the quarter-tax
8 [ ] likewise 11 ½ ¼ minas of weight
9 [ ] 26 talents [of weight] 18 ¼ minas
10 [in ?? *Schidai*] of 17 talents of weight 33 minas
11 [ ] 4 talents [of weight] 46 minas
12 [ ]…
13 [ ] 4 talents [of weight] 23 ¼ [minas]
14 [Of **Tortoise shell?**]31 ½ [minas]
15 [ ]21 [minas]
16 [ ]8 [drachmas]
17 [Of **Malabathron**] ¼ [minas]
18 [ ] 1,86̣? [talents of weight, ??] ½ ¼ [minas]
19 [ ]2̣2? talents of money [?,??9 drachmas]
20 [Of **Pepper**, 1]3,5?? [talents of weight 44¼ minas]
21 [of which likewise the value is reckoned thus: 1]3,223 [talents of weight] 2̣ minas
22 [ ] from which…
23 [ ]…
24 [ ]…
25 [12,862 talents of weight 52 minas at 6 drachmas per mina:] 771 talents of money
26 4,632 drachmas
27 [ ] 44̣ ¼ minas
28 [ ]
29 [for each mina 6 drachmas makes ?? talents of money ?,??5 drachmas 3 obols]
30 [All together makes 7?? talents of money ?,??7 drachmas 3 obols]

iii

1 Νάρδου Γανγιτικῆς κιστῶν ξ ὧν ὁμοίως
2 τιμὴ λογίζεται ὡς τῆς κίστης (δραχμῶν) ʼΔφ ἀργυρί-
3 ου (τάλαντα) με
4 Ἐλέφαντος ὑγιοῦς μὲν ὁλκ(ῆς) (ταλάντων) οη μν(ῶν) νδ Ḷ´δ̣´
5 ὧν ὁμοίως τιμὴ λογίζεται ὁλκ(ῆς) μὲν (ταλάντων) οη μν(ῶν) μγ
6 τῶν γινομένων σταθμίοις τῆς τετάρτης τοῦ
7 ταλάντου λογιζομένο̣υ̣ πρὸ̣ς̣ λί(τρας) ϙ̄ε̄ λι(τρῶν) ʼΖυοη
8 ἐξ ὧν αἱρεῖ λογιζομ̣έ̣ν̣ων εἰς τὸ τάλαντον λι(τρῶν) ϙ̣̄[ζ̄ L´
9 ὅσῳ συνήθως πρὸς τοὺς ἐμπόρους λογίζεται ὁλ[κ(ῆ̣ς)
10 (τάλαντα) οϛ μν(αῖ) μα̣ ὡς τῆς μν(ᾶς) (δραχμῶν) ρ (τάλαντα) οϛ
(δραχμαὶ) ʼΔρ̣
11 τῶν δὲ λοιπῶν ὑπὸ τῶν ἀραβαρχῶν πλείω ὑπὲρ
12 τῆς τεταρτολο̣γίας ἀρθέντων ἐν ἀ̣ριθμῷ̣ ὀδόντων
13 παρὰ τὸ αἱροῦν [---]λων ὀδόντων μν(ῶν) ια Ḷ´[δ̣´
14 ὡς τῆς μν(ᾶς) τῶ̣ν̣ ἴ̣σ̣ω̣ν (δραχμῶν) ρ (δραχμαὶ) ʼΑ̣ροε̣
15 γίν(εται) ἐπὶ τὸ α̣ὐ̣τ̣ὸ̣ (τάλαντα) οϛ (δραχμαὶ) ʼΕσο̣ε̣
16 σχιδῶν̣ δ̣ ὁλκ(ῆς) (ταλάντων) ιγ μν(ῶν) θ Ḷ´δ´
17 ὧν ὁμοίως τιμὴ λογ̣ί̣ζεται ὁλκῆς μὲν (ταλάντων) ιβ μν(ῶν) μ[ζ
18 τῶν ὡς πρόκ̣ε̣ι̣τ̣α̣ι̣ ὁ̣μοίοις̣ σταθμ̣ί̣ο̣ις μὲν τετάρτης
19 λι(τρῶν) ʼΑσιδ καθὼς ⟦καὶ⟧ δὲ πρὸς τοὺς ἐμπόρους λογί-
20 ζεται ὁλκ(ῆς) (ταλάντων) ιβ μν(ῶν) κζ ὡ̣ς τῆς μν(ᾶς) (δραχμῶν) ο
21 ἀργ(υρίου) (τάλαντα) η (δραχμαὶ) ʼΔσϙ
22 τῶν δὲ λοιπῶν πλείω ὑπὲρ τῆς τεταρτολογίας ἀρθει-
23 σῶν ὡς πρόκειται μν(ῶν) κβ <L´> δ´ ὡς τῆς μνᾶς τῶν
24 ἴσων (δραχμῶν) ο ἀργ(υρίου) (δραχμαὶ) ʼΑφϙβ𐅵
25 γίν(εται) σχιδῶν (τάλαντα) η (δραχμαὶ) ʼΕωπβ𐅵
26 γίνεται τιμῆς ἐλέφαντος ἀργ(υρίου) [(τάλαντα) πε (δραχμαὶ) ʼΕρνζ𐅵]
27 ἐπὶ τὸ αὐτὸ τιμῆς μερῶν γ̄ τῶν ἐκπεπλευκότων
28 ἐν τῷ ⟦εμ⟧ Ἑρμαπόλλωνι πλοίῳ φορτίων ἀργυ-
29 ρίου (τάλαντα) ʼΑρνα (δραχμαὶ) ʼΕωνβ

iii

1 Of **Gangetic nard**, 60 containers, of which likewise
2 the value is reckoned per container at 4,500 drachmas:
3 45 talents of money.
4 Of **'sound' ivory**, 78 talents of weight 54 ½ ¼ minas,
5 of which likewise the value is reckoned thus: Of the 78 talents of weight 4[3] minas
6 which – since, for the weight standard of the quarter-tax,
7 the talent is reckoned at 95 lbs. – are 7,478 lbs.;
8 from which, being reckoned 97.5 pounds to talent,
9 as it is usually reckoned for the merchants, is derived
10 76 talents of weight 41 minas, at 100 drachmas per mina: 76 talents 4,100 drachmas
11 Of the remaining (*sc.* tusks), taken in addition by the arabarchs for
12 the the payment of the quarter-tax, in the number of tusks
13 together with the result of the...tusks, 11 ½ [¼] minas,
14 at the same 100 drachmas per mina: drachmas 1,175.
15 Makes the total 76 talents 5,275 drachmas.
16 Of ***schidai***, 13 talents of weight 9 ½ ¼ minas,
17 of which likewise the value is reckoned thus: Of the 12 talents of weight 47 minas,
18 which, as above, for the same weight standard of the quarter-tax, are
19 1,214 lbs., in the way they are reckoned for the merchants,
20 12 talents of weight 27 minas, at 70 drachmas per mina:
21 8 talents of money 4,290 drachmas
22 The remaining (sc. *schidai*), taken in addition for the the payment of the quarter-tax,
23 as above, 22< ½>¼ minas at the
24 same 70 drachmas per mina: 1,592 drachmas of money 3 obols.
25 Total for *schidai*: 8 talents 5,882 drachmas 3 obols
26 Total for the value of ivory: [85 talents of money 5,157 drachmas 3 obols].
27 Grand total of the value of the 3 (*sc.* out of four) parts of the cargo
28 shipped out on the vessel *Hermapollon*:
29 1,151 talents of money 5,852 drachmas.

iv

\- - - - - - - - -

i cf. pp. 283–8

ii 4 [Νάρδου Γανγιτικῆς κιστῶν π τετάρτη κίσ]τ̣α̣ι̣ κ Morelli]κ edd. 5 (ταλάντων) ρε Morelli (ταλάντων) ρκ edd. 11 μν(αῖ) μ̣ϛ Morelli μν(αῖ) κ̣ϛ edd. 12] . . . . . . π..ικω edd.]…. ω̣ (μ̣έ̣τ̣ρ̣ω̣ in commentario) ἐμ̣π[ο]ρ̣ικῷ̣ Morelli 13 (τάλαντα) δ Morelli (τάλαντα) κ̣δ edd. 14 λα̣ L′ ego (cf. pp. 232–5) . ὁλ(κῆς) α̣ L′ edd. μα̣ L′ Morelli 15 . . κ̣α Morelli . . σα edd. 17 - - -] .. [μν(ῶν)]. δ′ ego ὁ]λ̣κ(ῆς) [μν(ῶν)] κ̣γ δ′ Morelli . ϛδ′ edd. 18 Ἀωξ̣ [? μν (ῶν) ??] Ḷ′δ′ De Romanis (2011 [2012]) Ἀ̣σ̣. [- - -] δ̣. Morelli 19 ϙ̣κ De Romanis (2011 [2012]) σκ̣ Morelli 20 πιπέρεως ὁλκ(ῆς) (ταλάντων) μ(υριάδος) α] Ἐφ̣ [. . μν(ῶν) μδ δ′] ego (cf. pp. 242–4) πιπέρεως ὁλκ(ῆς) (ταλάντων) μ(υριάδος) α] Ἐτ̣η De Romanis (2011 [2012]) πιπέρεως ὁλκ(ῆς) (ταλάντων)] Ἐτ̣η [μν(ῶν) Morelli 21 ὧν ὁμοίως τιμὴ λογίζεται ὁλκ(ῆς) (ταλάντων) μ(υριάδος) α] Ἐσκγ μν(ῶν) β̣ De Romanis (2011 [2012]) (cf. p. 241) ὁλκ(ῆς) (ταλάντων)] Ἐσ̣ιε μν(ῶν). γ Morelli 22]κα̣ ἐξ ὧν̣ ἀ̣ν̣τ̣ι̣ Morelli κ ἐξ ὧν [ἀ]ντ̣ι edd.; 25–6 ὁλκ(ῆς) (ταλάντων) μ(υριάδος) α Ἐωξβ μν(ῶν) νβ ὡς τῆς μν(ᾶς) (δραχμῶν) ϛ] ἀ̣ρ̣γ(υρίου) (τάλαντα) ψοα | (δ̣ρ̣α̣χμ̣α̣ὶ̣) Ἀχλβ De Romanis (2011 [2012]) (cf. pp. 239–241)] . . ἀ̣ρ̣γ(υρίου) (τάλαντα) ψοα |] (δ̣ρ̣α̣χμ̣α̣ὶ̣) Ἀχλβ Morelli, μ̣ν̣(ῶν) (δραχμῶν) ψοα | - - - (ταλάντων)] δ (δραχμῶν) λβ edd. 27 μ̣ν̣(ῶ̣ν̣) . μ . δ′ δ′ Morelli . μ . δ′ edd. 28] ... ν Morelli].[.]τον edd. 29–30 [ὡς τῆς μν(ᾶς) (δραχμῶν) ϛ (τάλαντα) ? (δραχμαὶ) ?,??ε∫] | [γίν(εται) ἐπὶ τὸ αὐτὸ (τάλαντα) ψ?? (δραχμαὶ) ?,??ζ∫] ego (cf. p. 244)

iii 1 l. Γαγγιτικῆς, 4 νδ Ḷ′δ̣′ Harrauer apud Thür, νδ Ḷ′ edd., 5 μν(ῶν) μγ Morelli, μν(ῶν) μ[γ] edd., 7 λί(τρας) ϙε̅ λι(τρῶν) De Romanis (1998), λί(τρας) (γίνονται) ϙε̅ λί(τραι) edd.; 8 ϙ̣̅[ζ̅ L′ Bagnall (epistula electronica 02.03.2018), ο̅[edd. 10 μν(αῖ) μα̣ De Romanis (1998) μν(αῖ) με edd., (δραχμαὶ) Ἀρ̣ De Romanis (1998) (δραχμαὶ) Ἀφ edd. 13 [- - -]λων ego καὶ τεταρτολογουμένων edd. διπ̣ή̣χ̣ε̣ω̣ν̣ ὅ̣λων Morelli; ια Ḷ[δ′ Thür, ια Ḷ edd., 14 ρ (δραχμαὶ) Morelli, ρ [ἀργ(υρίου)] (δραχμαί) edd.; 15 Ἐσο̣ε̣ De Romanis (1998), Ἐσ̣οε̣ Morelli, Ἐ̣χο̣ε̣ edd.; 16 σχιδῶν .δ . ὁλκ(ῆς) Morelli σχιδῶν δ’ ὁλκ(ῆς) Rathbone σχιδῶν ν̣δ ὁλκ(ῆς) edd.; 18 ὡς πρόκ̣ε̣ιτ̣α̣ι̣ ὁμ̣οίοις̣ σταθμ̣ί̣ο̣ις̣ Morelli ὡς πρό̣κ̣(ειται) γιν̣(ομένων) ἐ̣κ̣ τ̣ου̣̂ μ̣έ̣ρους̣ σταθμίοις edd. 23 μν(ῶν) edd. μν(αῖ) Thür; κβ <L′> δ′ Morelli κβḶ′δ′ edd.; 26 (τάλαντα) πε (δραχμαὶ) Ἐρνζ∫] Rathbone 27 μερῶν γ̅ Rathbone μερῶν ϛ̅ edd.; 29 (τάλαντα) Ἀρνα (δραχμαὶ) Ἐωνβ Morelli (τάλαντα) Ἀρνδ (δραχμαὶ) Ἐωνβ edd.

iv

- - - - - - - - - -

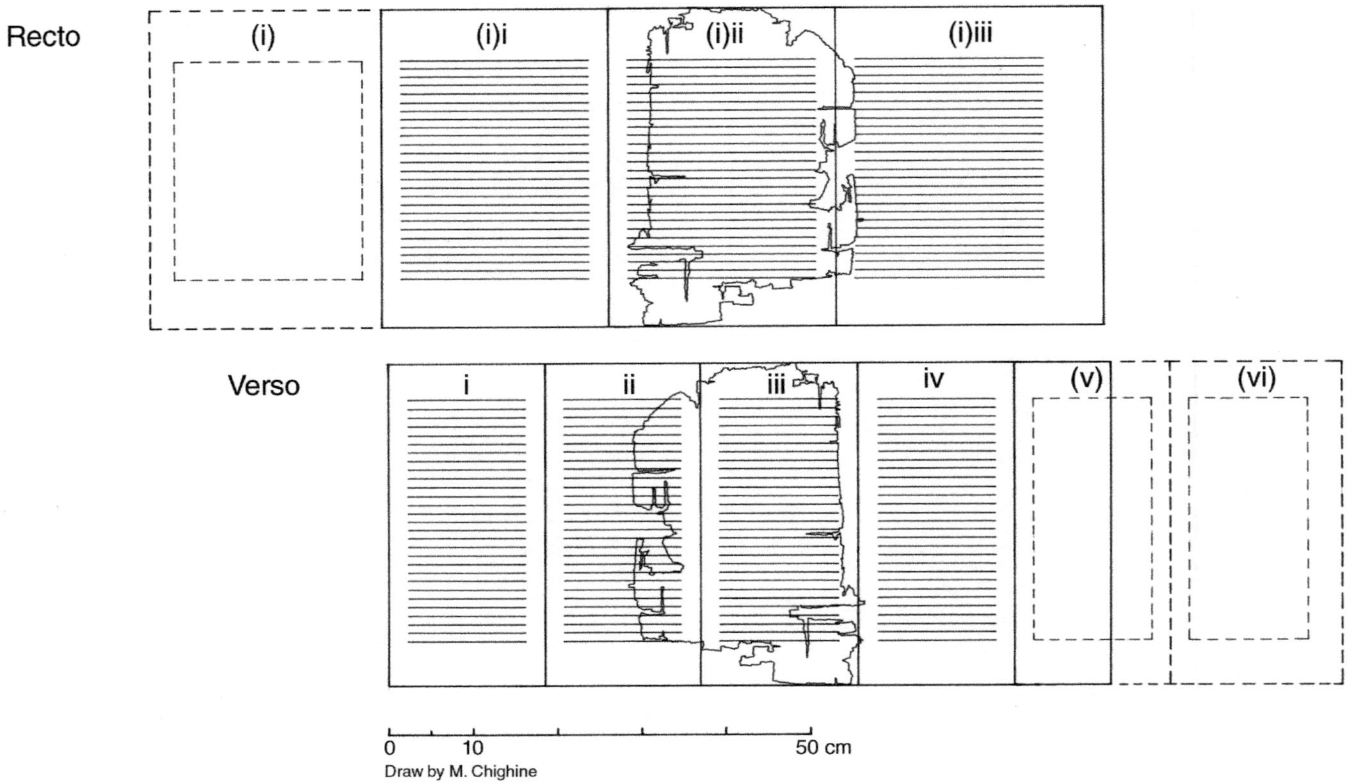

Fig. 0.2 Hypothetical reconstructions of the missing columns of *P.Vindob.* G 40822.

Content (and *Hypothetical Content*) of the Extant and Missing Columns

Recto. Loan contract in support of a commercial enterprise to Muziris

col. i(i) [or coll. (i) and i(i)]: *Names of the co-signatories; Specifics of the loan (value, extent, aim, yield, collateral, names of the ship and its captain); Terms for the outward journey (Nile sailing, desert crossing, sea voyage); Terms for the business in India; Terms for the return sea voyage; Unloading of the cargo;*

col. (i)ii: Terms for the desert crossing; Terms for the storage and sale of goods in Coptos; Terms for the Nile sailing; Terms for the storage and sale of goods in Alexandria; Consequences of failure to repay the loan.

col. (i)iii: *Consequences of failure to repay the loan; Consequences of failure to leave India on time; Consequences of damages to the cargo or the ship during the return journey; Acknowledgement of contract validity; Names of witnesses.*

Verso. Assessment of customs duties on the Indian cargo imported by the ship the Hermapollon (*and debit and credit balance?*)

col. i: *Reckoning of the import customs duties of the six items imported by the Hermapollon (ll. 1–21 ca.); Itemization of the first two commodities of the cargo (ll. 22–8 ca.); Beginning of the itemization of the third commodity of the cargo.*

col. ii: Itemization of the third commodity of the cargo (ll.1–3); Itemization of the other three commodities of the cargo (ll. 4–13); Value of the three-quarter portions of the first three items of the cargo (ll. 14–30).

col. iii: Value of the three-quarter portions of the other three items of the cargo (ll. 1–26); Total value of the three-quarter portions of the six items imported by the Hermapollon (ll. 27–9).

col. iv *[or* ***coll. iv, (v) and (vi)****]: Reckoning of the export customs duties; Total import and export customs duties; Itemization of the loan (travel expenses in Egypt and other minor disbursements); Sum of the customs duties and the loan; Recognition of the proceeds from the sales; Final balance.*

Part I

Contextualizing the Muziris Papyrus

1

Bridging Disconnected Seas

The trade documented on the two texts of the Muziris papyrus is part of a historical phenomenon in which the Mediterranean world and the southern portion of the Indian peninsula were closely intertwined. At least since the Hellenistic age, trade relationships with the Indian subcontinent have been an essential ingredient in the history of the ancient Mediterranean. Although the centripetal forces exerted by its internal connectivity encouraged its inhabitants to look inward, the Mediterranean was never a *hortus conclusus*. The passage to the Black Sea opened the Pontic regions to Greek and eventually to Byzantine interactions. The gate to the Atlantic produced the trade of Tartessos and Gades, as well as the explorations of Pytheas and the visions that foreshadowed the geographical discoveries of the Early Modern Age. The corridor of the Red Sea—the one of interest here—produced, among other things, the robust commercial intercourse that introduced the commodities of the Indian Ocean world to the societies of the Mediterranean.

The economic importance of the Red Sea corridor in Antiquity can hardly be exaggerated, and the extended ramifications of Roman trade in the Indian Ocean is best reflected by the impressive corpus of Greco-Roman knowledge about the Indian Ocean. Representing the synthesis of centuries of voyages and enquiries by Indian Ocean seafarers, Ptolemy's *Geography* remained the unrivalled description of that world until the Early Modern Age. The world view of medieval Arab geographers, with their land of Islam sandwiched between the 'Sea of the Romans' and the 'Sea of the Persians' (or the Ethiopians or the Chinese), was deeply rooted in the commercial horizons exposed by Indian Ocean trade in the first centuries of the Christian era.

However, the route to the Indian Ocean offered by the Red Sea was a laboured one. In this chapter, we will consider the environmental challenges to the interchange between the Mediterranean and Red Seas, and how they were overcome in particular during Antiquity.

The different transportation systems that were used, either in succession or simultaneously, to accommodate different commercial needs will be examined by distinguishing between the northern passages, which utilized ports located in the vicinity of the Gulf of Suez, and the southern passages, which were

The Indo-Roman Pepper Trade and the Muziris Papyrus. Federico De Romanis, Oxford University Press (2020).
 DOI: 10.1093/oso/9780198842347.001.0001

dependent upon Red Sea ports at around 26°, 24°, and 22° N. I will argue that the former were suitable only for very small ships, whereas the latter could accommodate vessels of medium or even large tonnage.

1.1. CHALLENGES

Apart from the lack of a natural connecting waterway, three severe environmental and meteorological challenges shaped the transport systems between the Mediterranean and the Indian Ocean before the invention of steam power. The first challenge was navigating the Red Sea north of 20° N. In itself, the fact that the northern part of the Red Sea is beset all year by northerly winds (Figs. 1.1 and 1.2) would not have been a severe hindrance,[1] but in a sea characterized by treacherous coral reefs and unfriendly arid shores, it was a major discouraging factor. Since navigation was more time-consuming, difficult, and dangerous the further north one sailed in the Red Sea, it became

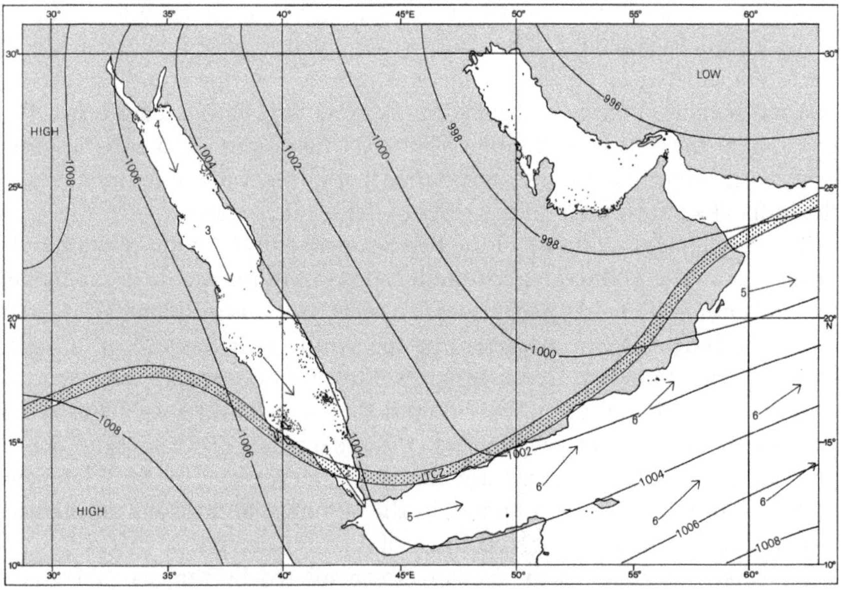

Fig. 1.1 Red Sea and Gulf of Aden July winds.

© Crown Copyright and/or database rights. Reproduced by permission of the Controller of Her Majesty's Stationery Office and the UK Hydrographic Office (www.GOV.uk/UKHO). Further copying or reproduction without permission strictly prohibited.

[1] On the Red Sea wind pattern, see Davies and Morgan (2000: 29–30); Whitewright (2007: 78–83); Kotarba-Morley (2015: 79–82); *Red Sea and Gulf of Aden Pilot* (2015: 30–9).

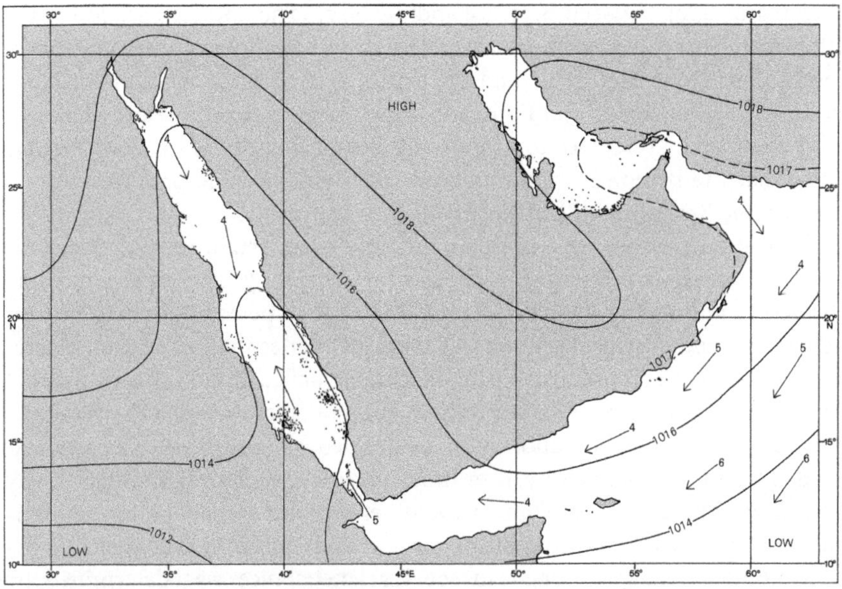

Fig. 1.2 Red Sea and Gulf of Aden January winds.

preferable, under certain circumstances, to land south of the Gulf of Suez, traverse overland through the Eastern Desert, and then sail the Nile.[2]

However, the further south one docked in the Red Sea, the longer, more laborious, and more expensive the desert and river legs became. This leads us to the second and third challenges. There is no need to emphasize the hardship of transferring a ship's cargo on hundreds or thousands of camels, and crossing the desert for hundreds of kilometres, either on the Arabian or on the Egyptian side. It may be worthwhile, instead, to point out that during the (early) summer—in time for the merchants leaving Alexandria to reach the Red Sea ports of Upper Egypt—the Etesian winds support upstream navigation on the Nile, but only up to the bend of Qena, beyond which they drop.[3] It is therefore not a coincidence that Coptos in late Hellenistic and Roman times and Qūṣ in the Middle Ages were the spots where the river journey and desert crossing most often intersected.[4] Alternative meeting points such as Apollonopolis Magna (Edfu) or Antinoupolis proved to be less suitable overall. Neither the Edfu-Berenice caravan road of the Ptolemies nor the *Via Hadriana* from Berenice to Antinoupolis were of great use to the Red Sea

[2] De Romanis (1996a: 19–31); Facey (2004). For the same problem in the Persian Gulf, see Potts (1990: 1.23).

[3] Cf. Cooper (2011: 197–201; 2014: 128–32). The deadlines for the departures for East African, Arabian, and Indian destinations are in *PME* 6, 14, 24, 28, 39, 49, 56.

[4] Garcin (1976: 96–111).

traders travelling between Berenice and the Nile.[5] The northern section of the latter may have played some commercial role in Late Antiquity, as a couple of inscriptions from Abū Šaʿār[6] and the presence of an *arabarches* in Antinoupolis in AD 568 suggest.[7] But Epiphanius' emphasis on Berenice (and silence on Abū Šaʿār) and a reference to Coptos and Berenice in the *Martyrium Arethae* show that the Berenice-Coptos caravan road remained the preferred way to connect the Red Sea with Upper Egypt.[8]

Over the centuries, the need to link the Mediterranean and Red Seas resulted in a series of different strategies for navigating the Red Sea, crossing the desert, and sailing the Nile (Fig. 1.3). Since each permutation had its own advantages and drawbacks, none was markedly better than any other. Therefore, it makes little sense to evaluate their convenience in the abstract, without regard to the specific vessels, sea routes, and schedules to which they related.[9] The fact that each combination could be deemed more suitable to a particular kind of business explains why, over time, one was chosen over another or why several were practised simultaneously. Whenever the available information is sufficient to determine the motives for a change in (or the coexistence of) transhipment strategies, one can see that the choice was determined by the effort to adjust to the requirements of different business forms. Thus, the various arrangements for connecting the Mediterranean and Red Sea shores may serve as an indicator of the polymorphous nature of Indo-Mediterranean trade.

Over time, the pepper trade also took different forms in Antiquity. We will see that at least two basic and consequential facts compel us to distinguish the pepper trade of the mid-first century AD, as represented by the *Periplus of the Erythraean Sea* (henceforth the *Periplus*), from that of the sixth century, as told by Cosmas Indicopleustes: first, the sea routes, which were direct in the first century and multi-stage in the sixth, and second, the location of the pepper emporia in southwestern India, which were in the Kottanarike region in the first century AD, and in the Male region in the sixth.

When the texts of the Muziris papyrus were written, Roman trade in the Indian Ocean was evolving from its Early Imperial forms to those of Late Antiquity. As in all transitional periods, there was a mix of old and new, of past and future. The past forms are attested by the Muziris papyrus itself, which still envisages a commercial enterprise involving a direct sea route to

[5] See p. 47, and p. 204, n. 68.

[6] The inscription of the Indicopleustes Andreas (*SEG* 44.1435): Bagnall and Sheridan (1994b: 112); and the fragment with the letters *]um mercator[*: Bagnall and Sheridan (1994a: 162). On the site, see Sidebotham (2011: 182–4).

[7] *P.Cair.Masp.* 2.67166, ll. 8–9.

[8] *Martyrium Arethae* 27. The passage by Epiphanius is quoted below, p. 38. Is the pepper sent to Philae by Tantani, phylarch of Nobades in Qasr Ibrim *c.*AD 450 (*FHN* III 322), a sign of an influence on Berenice?

[9] Whitewright (2007); Cooper (2011).

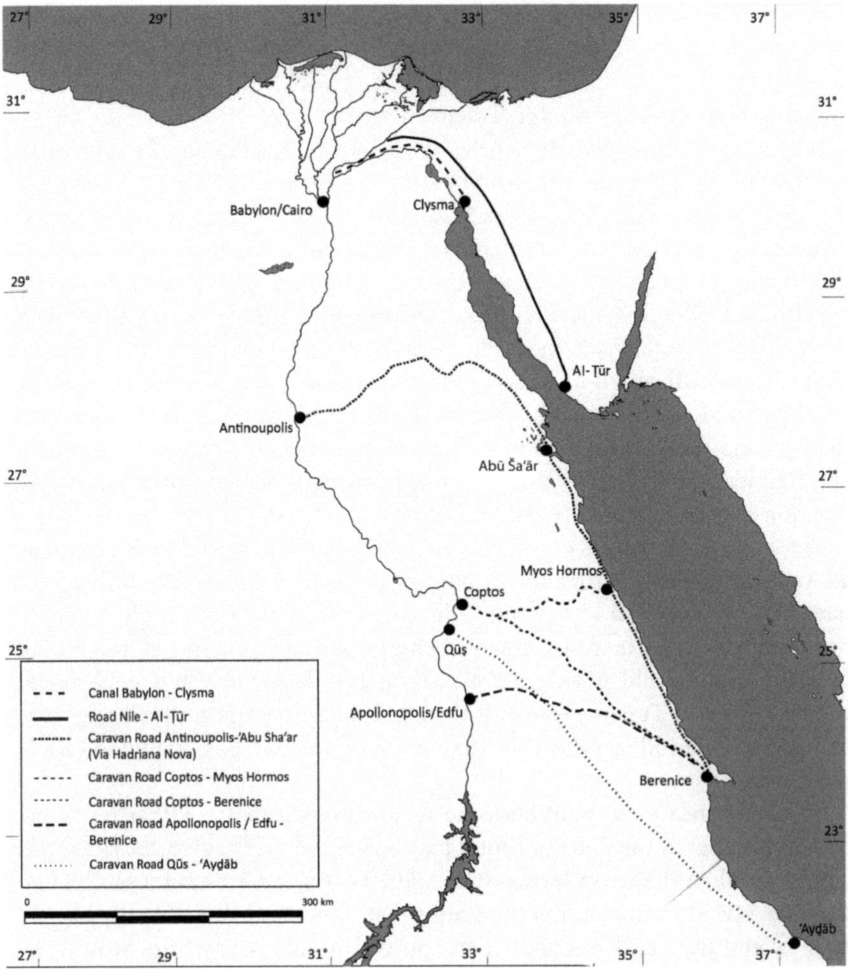

Fig. 1.3 Connections between Red Sea ports and the Nile in Ancient and Medieval times.

Muziris and a connection to the Mediterranean that included a limited Red Sea sailing, a desert crossing to Coptos, and a voyage down the Nile to Alexandria. The future forms were heralded by the opening of Trajan's Canal.

1.2. THE NORTHERN PASSAGES

As mentioned, by extending a voyage on the Red Sea to one of the northern passages, one either abolished or minimized the desert crossing and river sailing. During the late Middle Ages, the transhipments were based at the port of al-Ṭūr (at around 28° N, on the Sinai Peninsula). From there followed a caravan road to the Nile and a river voyage to Cairo.[10] During Late Antiquity and the Early Islamic period, transhipments pivoted to the port of Clysma/Qulzum (at around 30° N) and Trajan's Canal.[11]

It is difficult to say whether the construction under Trajan of a new canal joining the Nile delta and the Red Sea was a consequence of, or a driving force for, the transformation of Rome's trade with India.[12] Unlike its more or less ephemeral predecessors—the canals of Necho, Darius, and Ptolemy Philadelphus—Trajan's Canal provided a seasonally intermittent waterway between the Nile and the Red Sea until well after the Arab conquest. Such longevity is particularly remarkable because it was achieved by the imperial administration through annual *corvées* that ensured the maintenance of the canal bed and embankments.[13] Yet the shipping of commodities between the Red Sea and the Nile Delta is not often recognized as the reason for building and maintaining Trajan's Canal. Although the commercial relevance of Late Antique Clysma is generally acknowledged, opinions differ about the convenience for Clysma's traders of a canal such as Trajan's, which was not navigable all year round. In particular, it has often been claimed that the canal's navigability, restricted to the time when the river was at its height,[14] would have been of little use for commercial enterprises such as those of the Indian Ocean, which would have required premature departures and delayed returns.[15] But was Trajan's Canal navigable in fact only upon plenitude? Was its navigable period too short for the timing of *any* Red Sea or Indian Ocean sea route?

A few clarifications about both the seasonal navigability of Trajan's Canal and the timings of the Red Sea routes may be in order. Of course, the canal was navigable when the water level of the Nile was at its peak and unusable when the river was at its lowest. But the claims that, first, its navigability began only after plenitude, and second, that post-plenitude departure would be

[10] See pp. 206–8. [11] De Romanis (2015b); Gascou (2018).

[12] A tax for the new canal is attested by *SB* 6.9545.32 (2 September AD 112); *O.Marb. priv.* (15 September AD 112); and probably by *O.Cair.GPW* 99 (25 August AD 112); *O.Eleph.DAIK* 18 (8 August AD 114); 19 (19 August AD 114); *O.Wilck.* 89 (20 August AD 114); 90 (23 August AD 114); 91 (25 July–23 August AD 114); 92 (29 August AD 113–28 August AD 114); *O.Bodl.* 2.871 (29 September AD 114), cf. Jördens, Heilporn, and Duttenhöfer (2007: 469–85).

[13] Maintenance works are attested by *P.Oxy.* 60.4070 (*c.*AD 208); *P.Cair.Isid.* 81 (9 April AD 297); *P.Oxy.* 55.3814 (third–fourth cent. AD); *P.Oxy.* 12.1426 (AD 332); *PSI* 1.87 (29 June AD 423); 6.689a (AD 423); 6.689b (AD 423–4?); 6.689d (29 August AD 420–28 August AD 421); *P.Wash.Univ.* 1.7 (fifth–sixth centuries AD). Cf. De Romanis (2002: 31–3). On Clysma's relevance in Late Antiquity see, e.g., Mayerson (1996); Nappo (2018: 129–36).

[14] Redmount (1995: 134); Aubert (2004: 228); Jördens, Heilporn, P., and Duttenhöfer (2007: 477); Trombley (2009: 102); Cooper (2009: 204); Sidebotham (2011: 181).

[15] Cooper (2009: 205); Sidebotham (2011: 181); Aubert (2015: 38–41, especially 40).

unfeasible, are both questionable. Such notions are based on the assumption that both in Antiquity (when the canal was intermittently navigable) and in the Middle Ages (when the canal was continuously un-navigable), water was released into the canal only after the river had reached its maximum height.[16] Granted, during the Middle Ages earthen dams, annually destroyed and reconstructed, prevented the Nile from flowing into the canal before plenitude was reached.[17] But this management of Trajan's Canal, implemented to irrigate the villages of the lower Delta, need not have extended back to the Roman period, when the imperial administration may have had different priorities.[18] There is no compelling reason to assume that Trajan's Canal was not navigable in July or August, which was certainly early enough for ships bound for Adulis or South Arabia—indeed, even for a voyage to India. As a matter of fact, an indication that Trajan's Canal allowed vessels to reach Clysma in time for a voyage to India can be found in a well-known passage of Lucian's *Alexander or the False Prophet*.

> Indeed, he [*sc.* Alexander] seriously imperilled one of the Epicureans who ventured to expose him in the presence of a great crowd. The man went up to him and said in a loud voice: 'Come now, Alexander! You prevailed upon such-and-such a Paphlagonian to put his servants on trial for their lives before the governor of Galatia on the charge that they had murdered his son, a student at Alexandria. But the young man is living, and has come back alive after the execution of the servants, whom you gave over to the wild beasts.' What had happened was this. The young man had sailed upstream towards Egypt as far as Clysma, and as a vessel was just putting to sea, was induced to join others in a voyage to India (*ἀναπλεύσας ὁ νεανίσκος εἰς Αἴγυπτον ἄχρι τοῦ Κλύσματος, πλοίου ἀναγομένου ἐπείσθη καὶ αὐτὸς εἰς Ἰνδίαν πλεῦσαι*). Then because he was overdue, those ill-starred servants concluded that the young man either had lost his life during his cruise upon the Nile or had been made away with by brigands, who were numerous at the time; and they returned with the report of his disappearance. Then followed the oracle and their condemnation, after which the young man presented himself, telling of his travels.[19]

One ought not to minimize the value of this passage. Even if the story of the young Paphlagonian sailing up to Clysma and boarding a ship to India was, despite all appearances, entirely fictional,[20] we should assume that Lucian referred to real travel options, as he does in the definitely fictional dialogue *The Lover of Lies*, where Eucrates says that he desired (and managed) to listen to Memnon by sailing upstream (*ἀναπλεύσας*) to Coptos, and then going

[16] Trombley (2009: 102); Cooper (2009: 204; 2014: 118). The point of the practice was to achieve the highest levels and the swiftest ebbing of the river. Before Trajan, it was applied to other canals: Plin., *NH* 5.58.

[17] Popper (1951: 82–7); Ducène (2010: 72–5).

[18] Blouin (2014: 34).

[19] Luc., *Alex.* 44; transl. by A.M. Harmon, with modifications.

[20] Aubert (2015: 37). In general, on the historical reliability of Lucian's *Alexander or the False Prophet*, see Jones (1986: 133–48); Victor (1997: 8–26).

(ἐλθών) roughly 40 kilometres further up to Memnon's statue.[21] The credible backdrop for the story reported in *Alexander or the False Prophet* includes the once numerous brigands (πολλοὶ δὲ ἦσαν τότε), which a reader of Commodus' years (or later) would have understood as a clear reference to the revolt of the *Boukoloi*, repressed by AD 171.[22] Furthermore, *Alexander or the False Prophet* may have been written during or after Lucian's stay in Alexandria, when he could have easily ascertained how local merchants reached Clysma, and how they set sail from there.[23] In short, we have no reason to doubt the viability of sailing from Alexandria to Clysma early enough in the season to board ships bound southwards across the Red Sea. It can only be wondered whether the ship departing Clysma was really sailing all the way to India or, as they demonstrably did in later ages, only to an intermediate port in either East Africa or South Arabia (from which the young Paphlagonian would have transferred to an India-bound ship).[24]

There are also indications that when Clysma's ships returned to their home port, Trajan's Canal was still usable. A hint may be found in a passage about the Red Sea ports by Epiphanius, who lived for quite some time in Egypt and Palestine, and eventually, between AD 374 and 377, wrote his *Panarion*.

> There are excellent harbours on the Red Sea, separated one from another, at the different gates of the Roman realm. One of these is at Aila . . . Another harbour is at Castrum in Clysma, and another is in the far Upper Egypt, at a place called Bernice, through which place called Bernice they go to the Thebaid. And the various kinds of merchandise which arrive there from India are either diffused in the Thebaid or brought to Alexandria by way of the river Chrysorrhoas—I mean the Nile, which is called Gihon in the scriptures—and to all the land of the Egyptians and Pelusium. And this is how merchants from India who reach the other lands by sea make trading voyages to the Roman Empire.[25]

This passage requires elucidation. Epiphanius mentions three 'excellent harbours' at the 'gates of the Roman land'—Aila, Clysma, and Berenice—emphasizing that the last one is in far Upper Egypt, and connected to the Thebaid (ἄλλος δὲ ἀνωτάτω ἐπὶ τὴν Βερνίκην καλουμένην, δι' ἧς Βερνίκης καλουμένης ἐπὶ τὴν Θηβαΐδα φέρονται). Then, he remarks that the commodities which arrived *there* from India were *either* circulated in the Thebaid *or* directed, through the Nile, to Alexandria, the 'whole land of the Egyptians', and Pelusium (καὶ τὰ ἀπὸ τῆς Ἰνδικῆς ἐρχόμενα εἴδη ἐκεῖσε τῇ Θηβαΐδι

[21] Luc., *Philops.* 33.

[22] Blouin (2014: 267–97). *Alexander or the False Prophet* was written after Marcus Aurelius' death: Luc., *Alex.* 48.

[23] Lucian held office in Egypt while he was writing his *Apologia* in extreme old age: Luc., *Apol.* 4; 12. On his office, see vander Leest (1985).

[24] On the development of the multi-stage routes to India, see pp. 67–75.

[25] Epiph., *Adv. haeres.* 66; transl. by F. Williams, with modifications.

διαχύνεται ἢ ἐπὶ τὴν Ἀλεξανδρέων διὰ τοῦ Χρυσορρόᾳ ποταμοῦ, Νείλου δέ φημι, τοῦ καὶ Γεὼν ἐν ταῖς γραφαῖς λεγομένου, καὶ ἐπὶ πᾶσαν τῶν Αἰγυπτίων γῆν καὶ ἐπὶ τὸ Πηλούσιον φέρεται). In my view, the adverb *ἐκεῖσε* (there) refers to the two ports mentioned last, Clysma and Berenice (Aila is left aside). Epiphanius seeks to clarify the consequences of their different locations and transhipment systems: the commodities unloaded at Berenice were sent to the Thebaid, and those delivered at Clysma were shipped via the Nile (that is, via Trajan's Canal) to Alexandria, all of Egypt, and Pelusium.

Almost two centuries after Epiphanius, further evidence for the movement of Indian commodities through Trajan's Canal is provided by a pertinent passage in the commentary on Aristotle's *Meteorology* by Olympiodorus of Alexandria:

> The same ships carry more cargo on sea than on lake. And indeed, for this reason many Indian Ocean seafarers suffer shipwreck ignoring that. In the sea, they fill the ships with the cargo, and the sea, due to its earthy nature, pushes the ships up and carries them. Then, they go in the rivers or water bodies and suffer shipwreck, because rivers and water bodies do not have the same earthy nature due to the smoky exhalation and they cannot push the ships up.[26]

The reference to the accidents of the Indian Ocean seafarers (*ἰνδικοπλεῦσται*) —evoked to demonstrate that fresh water is less dense than sea water— confirms that Olympiodorus was familiar with the logistics of the transfer of Indian commodities from the Red Sea to the city in which he lived. Loaded to the maximum limit allowed by the seawaters, these ships sank when they entered canals or other water bodies (*ἔρχονται δὲ ἐν ποταμοῖς ἢ λίμναις καὶ ναυαγοῦσι*) due to the poorer buoyancy of fresh water. The uninterrupted navigation, first by sea and then by canal and other water bodies, shows that Olympiodorus was describing a shipment entirely by water from the Red Sea to the Nile Delta.[27]

In conclusion, it cannot be doubted that the canal primarily served the needs of Indian Ocean traders. Whatever the intentions of Trajan when he planned the excavation of the canal and the opening of the *Via Traiana Nova* between Bostra and Aila,[28] there is a thread that connects the creation of those facilities and the emergence of Clysma and Aila as excellent Red Sea ports in Late Antiquity.

However, the fact that Trajan's Canal was navigable long enough to allow both a timely departure and an easy return for *some* ships bound for *some* destinations does not mean that any Indian Ocean seafarer could take advantage of its navigability. As mentioned, Trajan's Canal was not navigable all year. It could not be sailed, for instance, when maintenance was underway.

[26] Olymp., *in met.* 81.
[27] For the term *λίμνη* denoting water bodies of the Nile Delta, see Blouin (2014: 135).
[28] Graf (1995); Bazou (1998); Abudanah et al. (2016).

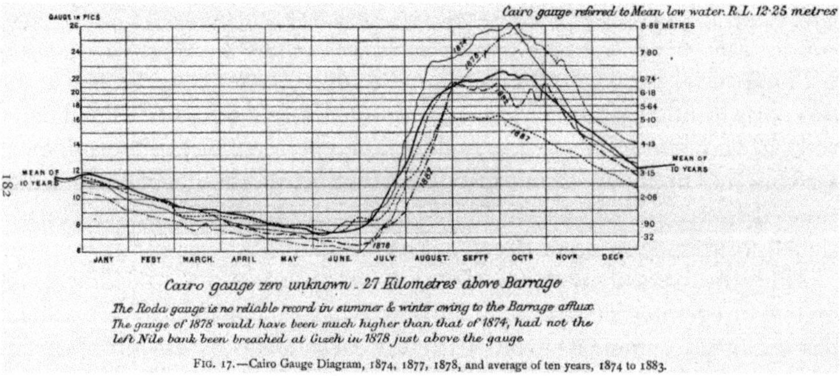

Fig. 1.4 Nile Gauge at Cairo.

From W.Willcocks and J.I.Craig, *Egyptian irrigation*, London 1913³, 182, pl. 8.

In AD 297, maintenance work lasted at least two months after 9 April.[29] In AD 424, work went on for three months, possibly starting from 26 March (1 Pharmouthi) or slightly later.[30] As shown by Fig. 1.4, during these months the Nile was at its shallowest in Lower Egypt.

In order to identify the sea routes for which Trajan's Canal could be of use, it is crucial to establish for how many of the remaining 275 days (roughly from July to February) the canal was navigable. In this respect, the clearest indication is provided by a papyrus dating to AD 710, documenting the use of the canal after it was reopened by ʿAmr b. al-ʿĀṣ. In this letter, the governor of Egypt, Qurra b. Šarīk, urges Basilios, *dioiketes* of Aphrodito,[31] to convey provisions requested for the ships in Clysma as soon as possible, before the waters of Trajan's Canal recede. Should Basilios fail to deliver what is due while the canal is still navigable, Qurra warns, Basilios will have to pay for the expensive land transport from Babylon (Cairo) to Clysma.

> If anything of what is required is in your administration, as soon as you receive the present letter, immediately, in that very same hour, send it without delaying or asking further instructions from us concerning this subject, if you understand and have any brain. You will know that if anything of those supplies or money comes too late and the subsidence of the waters occurs, you will convey it up to the same Clysma on the highway providing the cost for the land transport with your own substance.[32]

[29] *P.Cair. Isid.* 81.

[30] *PSI* 6.689a, l. 5: χρ(ε)ίαν τῆς τριμήνου; l. 10: ἐργάσασθαι ἐπὶ χρόνον μῆνας τρῖς. It is unclear if in 29 June AD 423 (*PSI* 1.87), the three-month service was over.

[31] In general, on the correspondence between Qurra and Basilios, see Papaconstantinou (2015).

[32] *P.Lond.* 4.1346, ll. 12–20, Cf. Cooper (2009: 204–5); Trombley (2009: 105–6); De Romanis (2015b: 130–1). A road from Babylon to Clysma is attested by the *Itinerarium Antonini* 169.2 and partially confirmed by *ILS* 657.

This letter, which was not the first (nor, probably, the last) to be sent from Qurra to Basilios on that matter in those months, is dated 3 January (7 Gregorian), and was received on 9 February (13 Gregorian) 710.[33] The phrase 'if the subsidence of the waters occurs' (*ἐὰν—γένηται ἀπόβασις τῶν ὑδάτων*) cannot refer to the beginning of the drop in water level (normally in October), but to the moment when the water level would become so low as to preclude any passage through Trajan's Canal.[34] The pressing overtones of the missive, urging prompt action, suggest that Qurra was aware that his letter might not be delivered as soon as was desirable. The thirty-seven days that elapsed between the writing and delivery of this letter are definitely more than the ten days of some of Qurra's letters, but also less than the forty-three or fifty-nine days of yet others.[35] Nothing suggests that Qurra's demand was preposterous or that the flood was exceptionally late that year. Thus we may safely assume that *P.Lond.* 4.1346 reflects the normal operational pattern connecting Clysma and the Nile, and conclude that under normal circumstances, Trajan's Canal ceased to be navigable well after 7 January (Gregorian) —probably in March. Certainly this was not sufficient time for everyone, but for those seafarers who were able to leave Clysma in July or August and return by January or even February, the canal was a safe choice.

The contract drawn up on the recto of the Muziris papyrus—most probably signed after Trajan's Canal was completed—expects the merchant returning from South India to transfer his cargo to Coptos. Such a destination implies that the port at which the merchant was supposed to land (most probably specified in the missing part of the papyrus) lay further south than Clysma.[36] Quite obviously, the canal did not work for the South India sea route. However, the pattern of trade illustrated by the papyrus represents only one—very particular—type of Roman trade on the Red Sea and Indian Ocean. The fact that the canal could not meet the requirements of that sea route does not mean that it would be of no use to others. The navigable season of Trajan's Canal was certainly long enough, during the Umayyad period, for the transfer of

[33] Previous dispatches are referred to in *P.Lond.* 4.1346, ll. 4–11. Fragments of other letters by Qurra on the same subject are *SB* 10.10459, *P.Lond.* 4.1465 and, in Arabic, *B.M.Or.* 6232 (2). *P.Lond.* 4.1465 l. 4: *τὸ τέταρτον ἐτάξαμεν διὰ τῆς δι[οικήσεώς σου* suggests that they may all belong to the same eighth *indictio* (709/710). It seems that Basilios did not succeed, cf. *P.Lond.* 1465 l. 1–2: *ἐγένετο ἀπόβασις τῶν ὑδάτων τοῦ Τραιανοῦ τοῦ βαστάξαι αὐτὰ διὰ γῆς ἕως το[ῦ] αὐτοῦ Κλ[ύσματος.*

[34] For a difference between the beginning of the drop and the end of the navigable period, *SB* 10.10459 l. 11–12: *ἤδη γὰρ ἤρξατο ἀποβαί[νειν τὸ ὕδωρ τοῦ Τραιανοῦ],|[ἐπ]εὶ ἐὰν ἀποβῇ τὸ ὕδωρ ὡς εἴρηται κτλ.*

[35] Ten days between the writing and delivery: *P.Lond.* 4.1351 and *P.Ross.Georg.* 4.16; forty-three days: *P.Lond.* 4.1341; fifty-nine days: *P.Lond.* 4.1379.

[36] Aubert (2015: 37–8).

grain provisions from Egypt to Ḥiǧāz, for instance.[37] But a more comprehensive assessment of the canal's functionality is better postponed to the second chapter, when the timings of the sea routes from India will be considered.

Qurra's letter shows that land transport from Babylon to Clysma was considerably more expensive than the transfer via canal. It goes without saying that a desert crossing further south, from the Thebaid to Quṣayr, Berenice, or 'Ayḏāb, would have been even more expensive. The reduction of the Red Sea leg exacted a heavy price in the form of a longer desert crossing and extended river sailing. Yet the northern passages, whether by Clysma and Trajan's Canal in Late Antiquity and the early Islamic period or by al-Ṭūr and the caravan to Cairo in the late Middle Ages, were never the only options connecting the Mediterranean and the Red Sea.

While considering the revenues of Mamluk Egypt, Al-Qalqašandī reviews the pros and cons of four different Red Sea ports (Fig. 1.5):

> First port: 'Ayḏāb. Most of the ship captains (*ru'asā' al-marākib*) who cross the sea from Jeddah to 'Ayḏāb headed to this port because its surroundings had plenty of water, and people who crossed that sea were safe. From this port, they travelled with the commodities to Qūṣ, and from Qūṣ to the *funduq* of the Kārim in Fusṭāṭ, on the Nile.
>
> Second port: al-Quṣayr is located north of 'Ayḏāb. Some boats headed to al-Quṣayr because it was closer to Qūṣ, whereas 'Ayḏāb was further away; from al-Quṣayr the commodities were transferred to Qūṣ, and from Qūṣ to the *funduq* of the Kārim, as we have already said, although most of the imports did not go beyond 'Ayḏāb.
>
> Third port: al-Ṭūr is a port near the Cape, inside Baḥr al-Qulzum (*fī ǧānib al-ra's al-dāḫil fī Baḥr al-Qulzum*), in the direction of Baḥr al-Qulzum, between the promontory of Aylat and the Egyptian shore. In the past, this port was visited by many people, who chose to come here for several reasons: because some ship captains (*ru'asā' al-marākib*) were keen to head for this place; because its ships were close to the land of Ḥiǧāz and the land never disappeared from sight during the navigation; and because there were several roadsteads. When a ship owner (*ṣāḥib al-markab*) wanted 'to change the sea' (to shift to land transport), he found a roadstead where he entered. Eventually, after the extinction of the Banū Budayr (Abbasid merchants), this destination and the sea routes from it were abandoned. The travellers were no longer interested in heading for this place, because there was a nation who frightened the crews, so they sailed only during the daylight time. The situation remained unchanged until AH 780 (AD 1378/9),

[37] Ibn 'Abd al-Ḥakam, 163–6; al-Ṭabarī, 1.2574–7; al-Balāḏurī, 216 (Engl. transl. 340–1). Mayerson (1996: 125–6); De Romanis (2002: 46; 67–70); Sijpesteijn (2007: 447–8); Cooper (2014: 230–2).

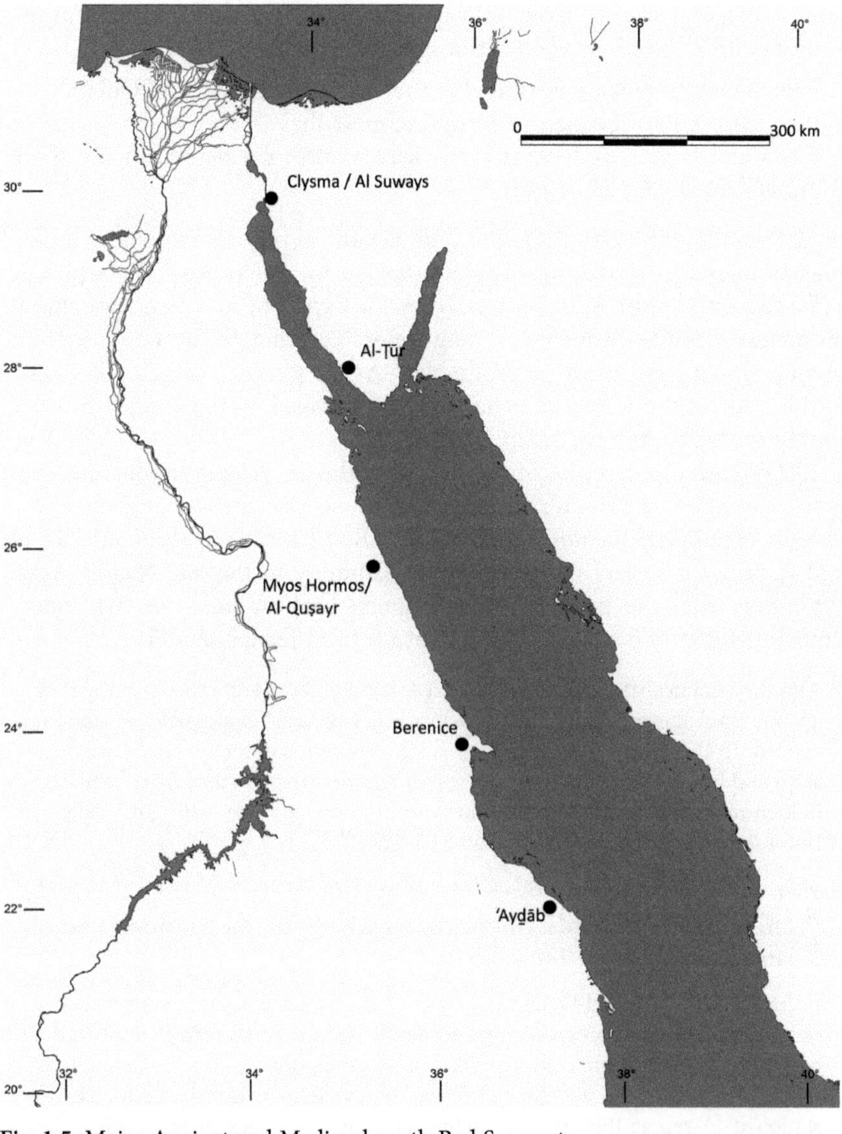

Fig. 1.5 Major Ancient and Medieval north Red Sea ports.

when emir Ṣalāḥ al-Dīn b. ʻArrām, who was then great chamberlain (*ḥāǧib al-ḥuǧǧāb*) of the Egyptian regions, ordered to make a ship in that place and to make it sail; he then ordered another ship to follow, and then he incited the men to use them for their travels. Then, people also restored boats in that place (*amarū al-marākib fī-hi*). Boats from Yemen (*marākib al-Yaman*) came with cargoes, while ʻAyḏāb and al-Quṣayr were abandoned.

> As a consequence, convoys of staple food (*ġilāl*) reached Ḥiǧāz and the profits from the wheat (*ḥinṭa*) transport were huge.
>
> Fourth port: al-Suways is located in the vicinity of the ruins of Qulzum, on the coast of the Egyptian regions. Amongst these places is the closest to Cairo and Fusṭāṭ, and yet it is the least visited: the base is in the shore (*ʿumda*) of al-Ṭūr, as we said.[38]

In al-Qalqašandī's view, al-Quṣayr and al-Suways play an entirely marginal role compared to ʿAyḏāb in earlier and al-Ṭūr in later times.[39] But while al-Ṭūr's success appears to be buttressed by the export of Egyptian agricultural products to Ḥiǧāz—which the long desert crossing to either Quṣayr or ʿAyḏāb would have made unprofitable—ʿAyḏāb's earlier primacy is linked to the trade of the Kārim merchants, and explained by the abundant water supply at ʿAyḏāb and the safety of its sea.[40]

Al-Qalqašandī's mention of the 'safety' of the sea around ʿAyḏāb deserves special attention, in particular because it contrasts with the warnings about the dangers of sailing in the northern part of the Red Sea that were reiterated again and again by a variety of writers from Antiquity to the late Middle Ages. Beginning from the most recent and going back in time, we may quote Emmanuel Piloti's description of the voyage from Jeddah to al-Ṭūr:

> And they sail near the coast and never lose sight of land, and every evening they anchor until the morning, and they proceed with sails, if possible, or oars, if needed. In this way of sailing, which is scarcely rational, they often break their ships and lose the ships and the spices—the reason being that they find shoals and hidden rocks and they bump into them without seeing them, with great danger. But if they are lucky, they reach Torre (al-Ṭūr).[41]

Earlier writers refer to the voyage in the opposite direction, from Clysma/al-Qulzum or Aila southwards. Although favoured by northerly winds, it was no less dangerous. This is al-Muqaddasī:

> In fact, reaching from al-Qulzum as far as al-Jār are dangerous rocks on account of which ships do not proceed except by day. The captain takes his position in the crow's nest, and is completely absorbed in observing the sea. If a rock should be sighted, he cries out: 'To the right!' or 'To the left!' Two cabin boys are so stationed to repeat the cry. The helmsman has two ropes in hand which he pulls right or left, according to the directions. If they are negligent about this, the ship may strike the rocks, and be wrecked.[42]

38 Al-Qalqašandī, 3.468–70; transl. by C. Intartaglia.

39 On al-Quṣayr, Whitcomb and Johnson (1979; 1982); Guo (2004); Blue (2007); Regourd (2011).

40 Al-Qalqašandī's appreciation is at odds with the complaints by Ibn Ǧubayr, 67; 70 (Engl. transl. 64; 66–7), but the Valencian pilgrim would have been even more dissatisfied with the alternative itineraries.

41 Piloti, 46. For the port of Jeddah, see Facey (2009).

42 Al-Muqaddasī, 12 (transl. by B.A. Collins, 11–13).

Then Procopius:

> And those who sail into this part of it no longer see the land on the right, but they always anchor along the left coast when night comes on. For it is impossible to navigate in the darkness on this sea, since it is everywhere full of shoals. But there are harbours there and great numbers of them, not made by the hand of man, but by the natural contour of the land, and for this reason it is not difficult for mariners to find anchorage wherever they happen to be.[43]

And finally, Jerome:

> Those who navigate the Red Sea... have to encounter many difficulties and dangers before they reach the city of Auxuma... so full are the waters of hidden reefs and impassable shoals that a look-out has constantly to be kept from the masthead to direct the helmsman how to shape his course. They may count themselves fortunate if after six months they make the port of the above-mentioned city. At this point the ocean begins, to cross which a whole year hardly suffices.[44]

Focused as they are on the peculiar sailing conditions in the northern Red Sea, these descriptions fail to point out one characteristic of those ships, which is indeed important if we are to understand how the traders from Clysma, Aila, or al-Ṭūr managed to overcome the difficulties and dangers of the long Red Sea navigation. When the ships that sailed up to the northern part of the Red Sea are compared with those that crossed the Arabian Sea, it becomes clear that the increased risk of a prolonged Red Sea leg was to some extent counterbalanced by a reduction in the tonnage of the ships.

For instance, Duarte Barbosa specifies that the spice cargoes were transferred from Calicut to Arabia by 1,000- to 1,200-*bahar* (166–199 tons) vessels, but forwarded from Aden or Jeddah to al-Ṭūr or Suez in small—that is, smaller—ships (*em pequenos nauios*).[45] The different size of the Red Sea ships compared to the Arabian Sea ships is also emphasized by Fernão Lopes de Castanheda. The Moorish merchants involved in the India trade used large vessels (*grãdes naos*) in the Jeddah–Calicut leg, but small *gelbas* (< Ar. *ǧilāb*)[46] in the Suez–Jeddah leg: 'and they sailed in these *gelbas* because they were safer, since in big ships they risked for the many shoals that are between Suez and Jeddah' (*hião nesta gelbas por irem mais seguras, porque em nauios grandes corrião perigo, por os muyto bayxos que ha de çuez a Iuda*).[47]

Castanheda's remarks are enlightening. They spell out a precautionary rule that was applicable at all times before the age of steam power: whenever it was

[43] Procop., *Pers.* 1.19.6–7 (transl. by H.B. Dewing).
[44] Jer., *Ep.* 125, 3; transl. by W. H. Fremantle.
[45] Barbosa, 160–1 (Engl. transl. 2.76–7); see also Pires de Távora 111, below pp. 261–2.
[46] On the *ǧilāb*, cf. Agius (2008: 316–20); Vallet (2010: 427–31).
[47] Castanheda, 2.150–1.

necessary to sail the northern part of the Red Sea, it was advisable to reduce the tonnage of the ships. Conversely, whenever it was necessary to carry huge cargoes in large vessels, it was prudent to break the Red Sea passage at more southern latitudes. Such a rule helps to explain the evolution of Red Sea port infrastructures during the Ptolemaic and Roman periods.

1.3. THE SOUTHERN PASSAGES

Erected in 264 BC, the Pithom stele triumphantly chronicles several achievements by Ptolemy Philadelphus in the Red Sea: the excavation in 269 BC of a canal between the Nile and Heroonpolis on the Red Sea; the founding in 264 BC of Ptolemais *ton theron* on the Sudanese coast; and the capture and shipment of elephants by sea from the same Ptolemais *ton theron* to Heroonpolis.[48] The canal was wide and deep enough for very large vessels,[49] but as for the arrival of ships at Heroonpolis, the optimism displayed by the Pithom stele turned out to be unjustified. Vessels as large as the 'elephant carriers' (*elephantegoi*) could not avoid enormous difficulties as they sailed up to the northernmost reaches of the Red Sea. The decision was quickly made to modify the elephant transport route.

Confronted with the repeated failures understandably ignored by the Pithom stele, Ptolemy Philadelphus adjusted to the geographic conditions: he founded the new port town Berenice on the Red Sea coast of Egypt at almost 24° N, and a caravan road was opened from there to Apollonopolis Magna (Edfu).[50] Strabo claims, in error, that the caravan road led to Coptos. In all likelihood, he mistook for Apollonopolis Parva (Qūṣ) *an* Apollonopolis—meant to be Apollonopolis Magna (Edfu)—indicated by his source as a starting point for the caravan road to Berenice.[51] The new port and caravan road may have already been functioning by 17 May 255 BC, when Ptolemaic soldiers were garrisoned at al-Kanā'yis, a watering station along the Edfu–Berenice caravan road.[52] The reason for this adjustment, as noted by

[48] *Urk.* 2.101–2 (l. 24). An English translation in Mueller (2006: 198).

[49] Strab. 17.1.26.

[50] Plin., *NH* 6.168; Strab. 17.1.44–5.

[51] The *quid pro quo* also explains Strabo's subsequent remark that there were two cities at each end of the same caravan road, Berenice and Myos Hormos on the Red Sea, and Coptos and Apollonopolis on the Nile (17.1.45). The phrase makes sense only if Strabo meant Apollonopolis Parva (Qūṣ), a dozen kilometres upstream from Coptos, and was unaware of the actual distance between Myos Hormos and Berenice (*c.*270 kilometres).

[52] *I.Kanaïs* 10. Other inscriptions from the same spot may go back to approximately the same period: the dedication of Satyros to Arsinoe, thea Philadelphos (*I.Kanaïs* 9), and the graffito by Dorion, a carpenter sent to the elephant hunts in East Africa under Eumedes, the explorer and founder of Ptolemais *ton theron* (*I.Kanaïs* 9bis). To the same period should belong the officer in

Strabo, echoes the passages quoted above regarding the sailing conditions in the Red Sea: 'the Red Sea is a difficult sea to sail in, especially for those who sail it from its (northern) recess.'[53] From this point on, the elephant carriers would land at Berenice and never again sail further north.[54]

The history of the site of Berenice is peculiar.[55] It turned out to be the most long-lived of the ancient Red Sea harbours of Ptolemaic and then Roman Egypt, but the site hosted no Medieval or Early Modern port. Moreover, during its long life throughout Antiquity its role changed, reflecting the evolving relationship between the Mediterranean and Red Seas. Founded to give an approachable landing point for the early Ptolemaic elephant carriers, the port declined in the second century BC, when elephant hunts ceased and the maritime trade in aromatics started to boom.

In contrast with the elephant hunters, the frankincense and aromatics merchants dealt with cargoes that were much easier to handle. Consequently, for them it was pointless to end their Red Sea navigation at Berenice and be subject to very expensive desert and river transports. A more agile system had to be set in place. Although smaller and swifter than the huge elephant carriers of the early Ptolemies, the ships of the frankincense and aromatics merchants were still too large to sail the Red Sea up to Suez. A suitable compromise was sought a couple of degrees latitude north of Berenice, at the port known as Myos Hormos, which enabled the transport of cargo directly to Coptos on the Nile River.

The choice of Coptos as the Nilotic hub for the Red Sea trade was recommended by at least two factors. Located at a confluence of wadis, Coptos was a natural point of departure for the caravan roads into the Eastern Desert of Egypt (not coincidentally known since pharaonic times as the 'Coptos desert'). Also, Coptos was close enough to the bend of Qena, made reachable during the summer by the Etesian winds.[56] The benefits of this logistical restructuring were substantial. Prolonging the Red Sea journey for a few days not only avoided some 180 kilometres of river sailing (unaided by the Etesian winds in the outward journey), but also ensured a much shorter and safer desert crossing along the well-established caravan routes of the 'Coptos desert'.

In 130 BC, a Ptolemaic official named Soterichos was sent to, among other things, 'ensure the safety of those who transfer aromatics and other foreign

charge, in the Thebaid, *πρὸς τῆι χορηγία[ι τ]ῶν ἐλεφάντω̣[ν* (*WChr* 435, l.79): see Fraser (1972: 1.178; 2.305–6 n. 365).

[53] Strab. 17.1.45: *τοῦτο δὲ πρᾶξαι διὰ τὸ τὴν Ἐρυθρὰν δύσπλουν εἶναι καὶ μάλιστα τοῖς ἐκ τοῦ μυχοῦ πλοϊζομένοις*. Strabo may have thought that the disastrous voyage of Aelius Gallus' fleet from Kleopatris to Leuke Kome (Strab. 16.4.23) confirmed the conclusions reached by the Ptolemaic navigators.

[54] *WChr* 452, ll. 22–3: *καὶ ἡ ἐλεφαντηγὸ[ς] ἡ ἐν Βερε|νίκηι τέλος ἔχει*. [224 BC]

[55] On Berenice, see Sidebotham (2011); Sidebotham and Zych (2012); Sidebotham et al. (2015); Sidebotham and Zych (2016).

[56] On Coptos as gate to the Eastern Desert, see recently Pantalacci (2018); on the wind regime in the Nile valley, see above n.3.

items from the Coptos desert'.[57] It was probably through the same Coptos desert that Ptolemaios and Tryphon were sent in 133 BC 'to receive (viz. on the Red Sea shore) and bring down (viz. to the Nile) all the foreign goods imported from the Aromatophoros Land'.[58] At the same time, Myos Hormos emerged as the main Ptolemaic port in what was becoming the 'Erythraean and Indian Sea'.[59] At the beginning of Roman rule, the Coptos–Myos Hormos route was the most travelled passage between the Red Sea and the Nile, and in 26 or 25 BC, as many as 120 ships set sail for India from Myos Hormos.[60]

Strabo knew of no ship sailing for India from Berenice, and such ignorance cannot be blamed on a lack of information. Although Berenice was not annihilated by Myos Hormos' triumph in the late Ptolemaic period, in Strabo's eyes Berenice was just 'a city without a harbour, but having convenient landing places for the opportunity of the passage (*sc.* to the Nile)',[61] whereas Myos Hormos was the city 'having the naval station of the seafarers' (*τὸ ναύσταθμον τῶν πλοϊζομένων*).[62] By contrast, Pliny indicates Berenice, and Berenice only, as the departure port of ships bound for South India.[63] This discrepancy has a simple explanation. The launch of a direct sea route to the pepper emporia of South India, the large volume of pepper available there, and the introduction of large-tonnage vessels to transfer very large cargoes compelled the traders to reduce the sea voyage in the Red Sea. The new pattern of trade gave Berenice an unprecedented boost. The old port of the elephant carriers, which barely survived the end of the elephant hunts, blossomed again as the port of the very large carriers of black pepper.

It is worth mentioning that Berenice's re-emergence as the departure point for South Indian trade coincides with a significant semantic shift. Familiar to Greek science since the fourth century BC, the word *peperi* is a loanword from middle Indian (cf. Skt. *pippalī*) through an Iranian intermediary.[64] In Indian languages, the term designates the *piper longum*. Theophrastus refers to two pepper species, neither of which indicates black pepper.[65] From the late first century BC onwards, Greek and Latin authors use the simple term *πέπερι*/*piper* to indicate the *piper nigrum*, whereas they rely on the formula *πέπερι μακρόν*/*piper longum* to designate the true *pippalī*.[66] This semantic sliding results from

[57] *I.Pan* 86, ll. 9–11. [58] *SEG* 49.2251, ll. 6–10.

[59] For the identification and excavations of the site, Peacock and Blue (2006; 2011). Myos Hormos is already mentioned as a 'great harbour' by Agatharchides 81 and Artemidorus (apud Strab. 16.4.5). The expansion of Ptolemaic trade in the Indian Ocean is reflected by the office *ἐπὶ τῆς Ἰνδικῆς καὶ Ἐρυθρᾶς θαλάσσης*, which appears at the latest in 14 May 62 BC: *I.Philae* 1.52, 53. Its occurrence in *SB* 5.8036 goes back to either 74/3 BC or, less probably, 45/4 BC: Ricketts (1982/3: 161–5); De Romanis (1996: 142–3). Hölbl (2000: 239–40).

[60] Strab. 2.5.12; 17.1.45. [61] Strab. 17.1.45. [62] Strab. 17.1.45.

[63] Plin., *NH* 6.103–4. [64] Hippoc., *Mul.* 205. [65] Theophr., *Hist. pl.* 9.20.

[66] It is uncertain whether the pepper sent by Sulla to the Athenian priestess (Plut., *Sull.* 13.3) was already black or still long pepper.

the success of the South Indian trade evidenced by the Muziris papyrus. In Latin literature, the stages of this shift are reflected in the occurrences of the word *piper* first in Varro,[67] then in Horace's second book of *Satires* and first book of *Epistles*,[68] in Vitruvius,[69] and then again in the second book of Horace's *Epistles*, where what was traditionally called the *vicus turarius* was referred to as the *vicus* where frankincense, aromatics, and pepper were sold.[70] Archaeologically, the surge in the pepper trade during the Augustan age is indicated by the remains of black pepper found in the Roman camp of Oberaden, occupied in Germany between 11 and 8 BC.[71] Thus, the process that much later led the storehouse of all the aromatic substances to be labelled *horrea piperataria* was already in motion in the Augustan age.[72]

In the desert between Coptos and Berenice, the new pattern of trade becomes apparent in the inscription engraved by C. Numidius Eros upon his return from India.[73] The place and time of his stop—the Paneion of Wādī Minayḥ (Fig. 1.6) on a day between the end of February and the end of March in 2 BC—strongly suggests, as we will see, that he was returning from South India with a very large cargo.

Apart from the revival of Berenice, the new pattern of trade had an impact on the transhipment logistics between the Mediterranean and the Red Sea. In what seems to be an addition to a first draft of the seventeenth book of his *Geography*, Strabo contrasts old and new methods for crossing the desert:

> In earlier times the camel merchants travelled only by night, looking to the stars for guidance, and, like the mariners, also carried water with them when they travelled; but now they have constructed wells (*hydreia*), having dug down to a great depth, and, although rain water is scarce, still they have made cisterns (*dexamenai*) for it.[74]

Actually, along the Coptos-Berenice road, the caravans continued to travel by night, at least in the summertime. But the stages of the voyage and the location

[67] Varro, *Sat. Men.* 581.

[68] Hor., *Sat.* 2. 4.74–5; 8.49; *Epist.* 1.14.23. The second book of the *Satires* may go back to about 30 BC; the first book of the *Epistles* to around 20 BC: Nisbet (2007: 12; 15).

[69] Vitruv. 8.3.13.

[70] [Ascon.], *ad Cic. II Verr.* 1.154, 170 Stangl; Hor., *Epist.* 2.1.269–70: see Lega (1999). Horace's epistle to Augustus goes back to 11 BC, see Nisbet (2007: 18–20).

[71] Kučan (1984; 1992: 245–6). For peppercorns in Pompeii see Ciaraldi (2007: 102; 114–15; 125; 139), but the fourth-to-second-century BC chronology assigned to the two corns found in the Casa delle nozze di Ercole is perplexing.

[72] See Houston (2003).

[73] *AÉ* 1999, 1722; 1723.

[74] Strab. 17.1.45; translation by H. L. Jones, with modifications. Jones translates *hydreia* as 'watering places', but Strabo's distinction between *hydreia* dug down to a great depth and *dexamenai* that collected rare rain waters clarifies that the *hydreia* are groundwater containers—that is, wells.

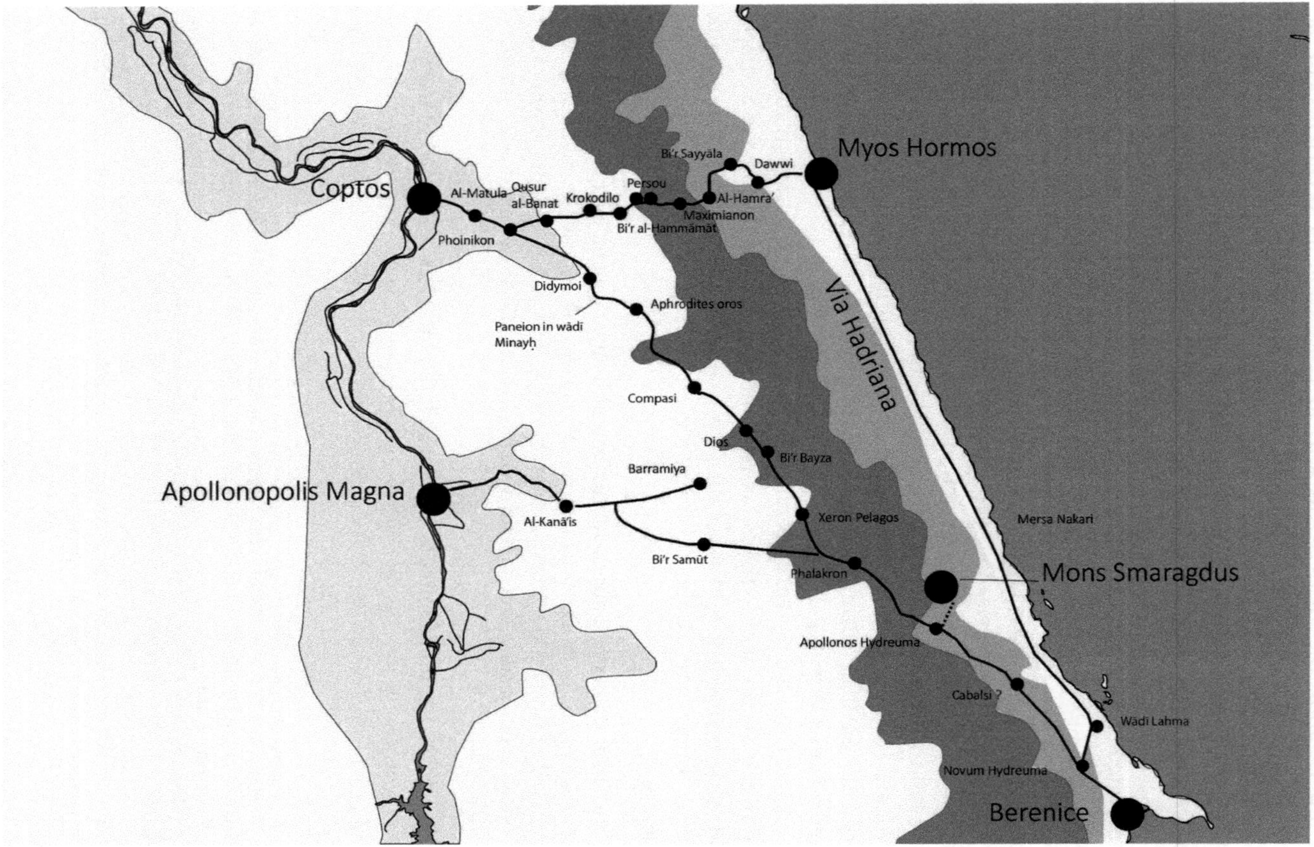

Fig. 1.6 Eastern Desert caravan roads.

of the stops were now reshaped by the location of the new watering points. Strabo's *hydreia* are hardly different from the *lacci* built in the Eastern Desert by more than 1,400 Roman soldiers in a year that the fragmentary inscription from Coptos fails to disclose.[75] Of the four wells mentioned in the inscription, one is at Myos Hormos and three are along the Coptos–Berenice caravan road: at Compasi, at Apollonos Hydreuma, and in the region of Berenice.

Apparently, the (re)construction of these wells was decisive in shaping the way that the distance between the Red Sea and the Nile was covered. As described by Pliny, the voyage from Coptos to Berenice included seven stops: the first was at the *hydreuma* of Phoenicon, which was the closest to Coptos and served both the Myos Hormos and the Berenice caravan roads. No *laccus* was (re)built there by the Roman army. Of the six stops that followed, three were at *hydreumata* provided with the new *lacci*, and the other three were in the open desert (*in monte*), approximately halfway between one well and another.[76]

Between the first (Phoinikon) and the second (Compasi) watering points, the layout of the caravan road as described by Pliny is revealed by the al-Bouweib inscriptions,[77] the Wādī Minayḥ inscriptions,[78] the Wādī Minayḥ al-Ḥīr inscriptions,[79] and the AD 77/78 *praesidia* of Didymoi and Aphrodites Oros, erected under Vespasian (Fig. 1.7).[80]

The inscription of the Minaean Yḏkrʾl—most probably a trader in aromatics from the late Ptolemaic period—at the well of Bi'r Minayḥ (25° 33' 29.51" N; 33° 36' 19.90" E) shows how the desert between Coptos and Berenice was traversed before the wells were (re)built by the Roman army.[81] Remarkably,

[75] *ILS* 2483. The legionaries from Galatia or nearby cities were probably former soldiers of the Galatian kingdom who had been absorbed into the Roman army. A *terminus ante quem* earlier than the completion of Strabo's *Geography* may be suggested by the inscriptions at Wādī Minayḥ (the earliest dated one goes back to 4 BC), if they imply that the well at Compasi was then already functional: see De Romanis (1996: 219–24).

[76] Plin., *NH* 6.102–3. *Hydreuma* means groundwater: De Romanis (2006a: 633–42).

[77] 25° 48' 13" N, 33° 20' 55" E. The earliest dated inscription is Augustan: *I.Ko.Ko.* 141, cf. Cuvigny, Bülow-Jacobsen, and Bosson (2000: 245).

[78] 25° 39' 41.05" N, 33° 29' 8.94" E; the earliest is also Augustan: *SEG* 46.2176, cf. Cuvigny, Bülow-Jacobsen, Nehmé and Robin (1999: 137).

[79] 25° 39' 1.00" N, 33° 32' 12.24" E; the earliest dated is Tiberian: *SEG* 46.2176.1,2,3= *SEG* 48.2035, cf. Cuvigny, Bülow-Jacobsen, Nehmé and Robin (1999: 170 nn. 71, 72; 173 n. 81).

[80] *AÉ* 2005, 1626; 1627. Cf. Bagnall, Bülow-Jacobsen, and Cuvigny (2001: 327–9). I understand the toponym in *O.Did.* 406 and 430 as 'Aphrodite's Desert', Cuvigny (2018: 125) as 'Aphrodite of the Desert'.

[81] *RES* 3571: Yḏkrʾl ḏ-Ḥyʾl Mʿnyn. Cf. Robin (1994b: 296; 1998: 177–88); Rossi (2014: 111, n. 3); Brun (2018: 9). The Bi'r Minayḥ inscription implies the converging on Coptos of all the caravan roads connecting the Red Sea harbours and the Nile, a phenomenon first attested in 130 BC by *I.Pan* 86, see pp. 47–8. After Aelius Gallus' expedition, the Minaeans seem to disappear: Robin (1998). The epitaph of the Minaean merchant Zydʾl, 'provider of myrrh and calamus to the temples of the gods of Egypt' (*RES* 3427) is dated to the month of Choiak of the twenty-second year of a Ptolemy son of Ptolemy—probably Ptolemy X Alexander (14 December 94/12 January 93 BC), cf. Robin (1994b: 294).

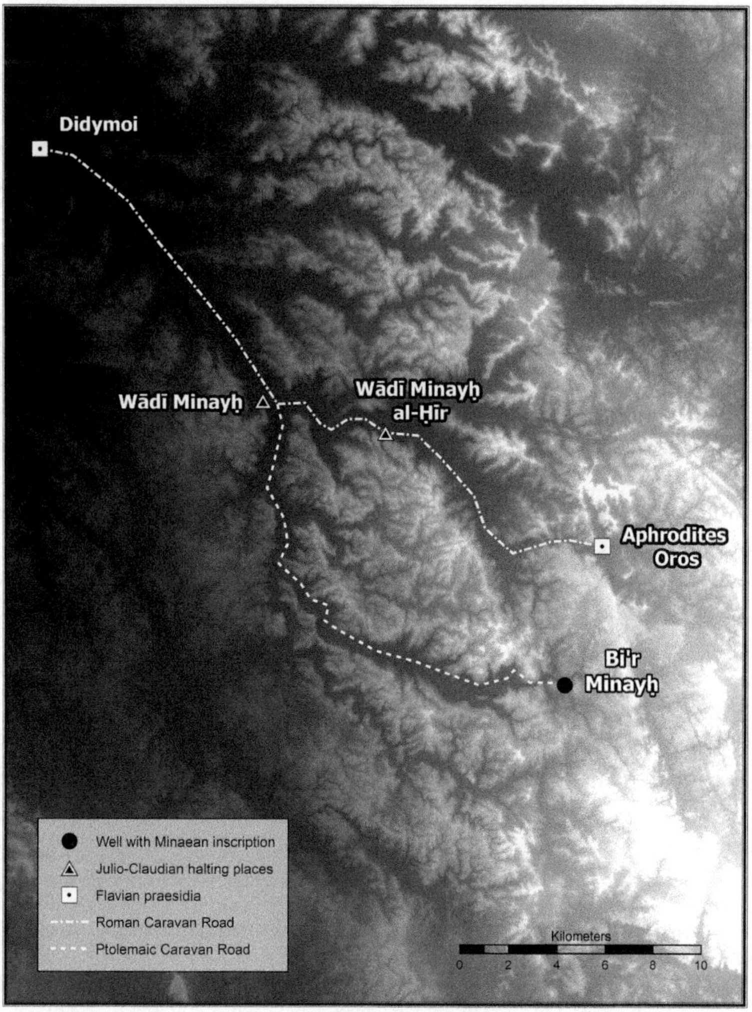

Fig. 1.7 Coptos–Berenice caravan road between Phoinikon and Aphrodites Oros. (©JAXA) ALOS World 3D–30m (AW3D30) Version 2.2 https://www.eorc.jaxa.jp/ALOS/en/aw3d30/index.htm downloaded in August 2019.

the signature of Yḏkr'l is the only inscription datable to Ptolemaic or Roman times that points to Bi'r Minayḫ as a stopover along the Coptos–Berenice caravan route—this despite being engraved next to a well, in a spot that first hosted quarrying activities in the earliest Pharaonic period, and then a village of desert dwellers in Late Antiquity.[82]

A closer look at the region around Bi'r Minayḫ (Figs. 1.7 and 1.8) shows the misalignment of Yḏkr'l's inscription in relation to the layout of the

[82] Luft (2010).

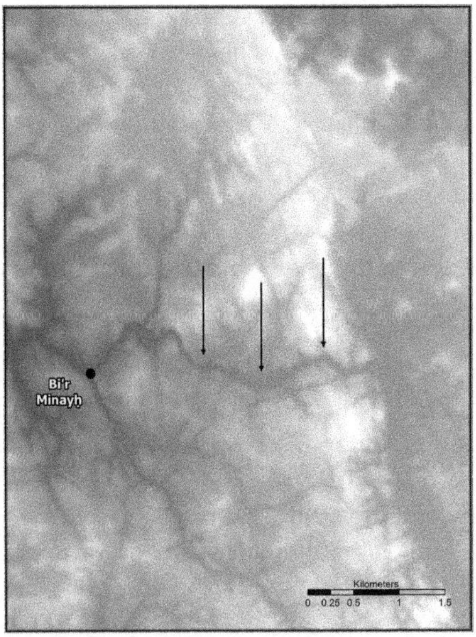

Fig. 1.8 The Bi'r Minayḥ passage.
(©JAXA) ALOS World 3D–30m (AW3D30) Version 2.2 https://www.eorc.jaxa.jp/ALOS/en/aw3d30/index.htm downloaded in August 2019.

Roman caravan road. It also explains why, under Augustus, the Coptos–Berenice caravan road bypassed the watering point of Bi'r Minayḥ to stop in waterless areas like Wādī Minayḥ and Wādī Minayḥ al-Ḥīr. Even a very large caravan can easily approach the well of Bi'r Minayḥ when journeying from Coptos, because up to that point the Wādī Minayḥ has ample room for a comfortable passage. But to proceed from Bi'r Minayḥ on to Berenice, one had to pass through a gorge that was about 4 kilometres long and sometimes as narrow as 10–20 metres. Although smaller caravans with dozens or only a few hundred camels may not have found it too taxing, this portion of the journey would have been extremely time-consuming for a caravan of several thousand camels. The different routes for the Coptos–Berenice caravan road in the Ptolemaic and late Augustan ages reflect the contrast between the relatively low volumes of frankincense and aromatics carried by the few Arab traders that landed at Berenice and the huge pepper cargoes offloaded from the very large ships coming from South India.

Pepper and frankincense were the most voluminous cargoes imported into Roman Egypt via the Red Sea. For the most part, the two items were imported by different traders, with different ships and, in the course of time, through different circuits. During the first decades of Roman rule, both frankincense and pepper entered Egypt mainly through Myos Hormos. The three potsherds with Tamil graffiti found at Myos Hormos, indicating contacts with South India, may belong to this earlier phase.[83] Later, as the South India trade increasingly relied on large pepper carriers, Berenice became the sole terminus for the South Indian ships. The amphora fragment with Tamil graffiti found at Berenice reflects the new arrangement:[84] while Myos Hormos remained the key port for frankincense,[85] Berenice emerged as the sole gateway for pepper. It is not coincidental that peppercorns recovered from the site of Berenice appear to be far more numerous than those recovered from Myos Hormos,[86] whereas the basalt found at Berenice—carried as ballast for lighter frankincense cargoes from Cane—seems to be less abundant than that found at Myos Hormos.[87]

The volume of frankincense that passed through Berenice was minimal compared to the volume of pepper, but it was not entirely absent.[88] In addition to ships from South Arabia or East Africa, which could have preferred, for whatever reason, to dock at Berenice, the pepper carriers bound for South India could import some frankincense to Egypt. When en route from Limyrike, they could call at the South Arabian port of Moscha Limen and still pick up frankincense that had not yet been exported.[89]

1.4. MULTIFACETED COMPLEMENTARITY

The merchant who signed the loan contract of the Muziris papyrus did not intend to make use of either Trajan's Canal or the Babylon–Clysma road. His ship was too large for a secure passage up to Clysma—indeed, it was also too large for a safe passage up to Myos Hormos. It was Berenice, the port of the large pepper carriers, that handled the South India trade. Yet if most of the pepper entered Egypt through Berenice and most of the frankincense through Myos Hormos, it does not follow that Myos Hormos and Berenice, the two 'designated harbours' of Egypt on the Red Sea at the time of the *Periplus*,[90]

[83] For two of the three fragments, a first-century AD chronology has been suggested by Mahadevan (2003: 49); previously, the same Mahadevan, apud Salmon (1991: 734–6), had suggested a second-century AD date; the third fragment would date back to the first century BC: see Mahadevan (2007); Tomber et al. (2011: 8).

[84] The fragment from Berenice, on a Dressel 2–4 amphora, goes back to the (mid-)first century AD: see Mahadevan (1996); (2003: 49); Sidebotham (2011: 75).

[85] Frankincense, however, was also shipped by sea to Leuke Kome and despatched overland to Gaza: *PME* 19; Plin., *NH* 12.63–5. On the location of Leuke Kome, cf. Nappo (2010) and Gawlikowski (2019).

[86] Cappers (2006: 111–19); van der Veen, Cox, and Morales (2011: 41).

[87] Peacock, Williams, and James (2007); Sidebotham and Zych (2010: 12–13 and fig. 13); Sidebotham (2011: 205; 236).

[88] For frankincense unloaded at Berenice, see *O.Did.* 323, ll. 10–13.

[89] *PME* 32.

[90] *PME* 1. For the notion, cf. Casson (1989: 272–4).

were simply the ports of the Red and the Arabian Seas respectively. The ships that sailed to the Indus delta and Barygaza were certainly smaller than the large pepper carriers suited to South Indian trade; they most probably selected Myos Hormos as their home port.[91] Furthermore, if Berenice had nothing special to offer to the Red Sea trade, it would hardly have survived beyond the elephant hunts in the late Ptolemaic period, or re-emerged in the fourth century AD as one of the 'excellent ports' of the Red Sea.[92] Apparently, the southern passage via Berenice suited other ships as well.

For all the sea routes he details—whether to East Africa, South Arabia, or India—the author of the *Periplus* indicates either July or September as the best time to depart Egypt.[93] Dictated by the seasonality of the monsoons and the production of the frankincense, such schedules implied a return voyage in the late autumn or winter, when southerly winds prevail in the southern Red Sea. The only partial exception to this general rule is the route to Adulis—a partial exception, because in theory, the most convenient month to set sail for Adulis would have been September. However, since Adulis was at a relatively short distance from the Red Sea ports of Egypt and its trade was based on non-seasonal goods (ivory, tortoise shell, and rhinoceros horn), the *Periplus* describes a more flexible schedule:

> Most things are exported from Egypt to this emporion [*sc.* Adulis] from January to September, that is, from Tybi to Thoth; but timely (*εὐκαίρως*), they depart from Egypt around the month of September.[94]

The fact that ships bound for Adulis leave Egypt from January to September suggests that theoretically two Egypt–Adulis round trips could be completed within a year. Furthermore, it should be noted that September was also the month for a timely (*εὐκαίρως*) departure for Muza,[95] where, quite remarkably, Adulis' commodities are also recorded as being available:

> Its [*viz.* Muza's] exports consist of local products—myrrh, the select grade and stacte, the Abeirian (?) and Minaean; white marble—as well as all the aforementioned merchandise from Adulis and from the other side [*viz.* the emporia of the north coast of Somalia].[96]

If, in early autumn, Adulis' commodities were available at Muza, but Muza's commodities were not available in Adulis, this is a strong indication that

[91] For a Prakrit ostracon reportedly from Myos Hormos: Salomon (1991: 731–4); (1993: 593).

[92] For Berenice's revival in Late Antiquity, cf. Sidebotham (2011: 259–60).

[93] July: *PME* 14 (Somali coast); 39 (Barbarikon); 49 (Barygaza); 56 (Limyrike). September: *PME* 6 (Adulis); 24 (Muza); 28 (Cane).

[94] *PME* 6. [95] *PME* 24.

[96] *PME* 24; transl. by L. Casson with modifications. For the correction *ἀπὸ τοῦ πέραν* <*καὶ*> *Ἄδουλι*, see De Romanis (2009b: 31–5). The emendations proposed by Fabricius (*ἀπὸ τῆς πέραν Ἄδουλι*) or (in the commentary) by Belfiore (*ἀπὸ τοῦ πέραν Αὐαλίτου*) are less economical.

merchants from Egypt found the emporion of Muza more attractive than that of Adulis. In trying to make sense of the peculiar schedule of the Adulis trade, the appeal of the Muza emporion, and the expediency of the Berenice port, one may then suggest that many Egyptian ships sailed first to Adulis, leaving in January and returning by June, and then to Muza, leaving in September and returning by December (see Fig. 1.9).[97] But while the second round trip, favoured by strong winds in the southern part of the Red Sea, tended to end at Myos Hormos, one could argue that the first round trip, poorly supported even in the southern Red Sea, could have relied more often than not on Berenice.

A similar commercial strategy may also be inferred from a fragment of a private letter apparently sent from Berenice by a slave or an employee of the recipient.[98] The text recounts the recent safe (if troubled) landing at Berenice of ships returning from somewhere unspecified.[99] The sender complains that, despite many letters sent to Oxyrhyncha, he did not get what he asked for.[100] In the left margin are three lines, dated 9 June AD 97, blaming the recipient of the note for not having 'prepared the blankets'.[101] Since it seems unlikely that a slave or an employee addressed his master or employer with these words, one may suggest that the first part of the letter was sent from Berenice by a slave (or an employee) to his master (or employer) dwelling in a place that was not Oxyrhyncha—possibly Coptos. Then the recipient forwarded it, on 9 June AD 97, with the addition of the three lines in the left margin to another slave (or employee) dwelling somewhere else, probably Oxyrhyncha.

The uncertainties regarding the authorship of the lines in the left margin affect the dating of the ships' arrival at Berenice as described at ll. 3–6,[102] which may date back to 9 June if all the lines belong to the same hand, or a few weeks earlier if the lines in the left margin belong to someone else. The most likely explanation for such a return date is that the ships were sailing back from Adulis. In that part of the year, since the winds were contrary throughout the Red Sea (ll. 5–6: *ἄνεμοι γὰρ | ἀντίοι εἰσί*), it could have seemed safer (l. 3 *ἀκινδύνως*) to land at Berenice rather than Myos Hormos.

[97] De Romanis (2009b).

[98] *P.CtYBR* inv. 624, published by Peppard (2009). At l. 8, the sender addresses the recipient with *δέσποτα* (master).

[99] Lines 3–7: *τὰ πλοῖα ἀκινδύνως τὰ ἐν τῆι | ἀνακομιδῆι καθορμισθῆναι εἰς τὴν | ἱερωτάτην Βερενείκην, ἄνεμοι γὰρ | ἀντίοι εἰσί, καὶ τὰ πλοῖα ἔστη ἀπ̣[ὸ] ὡρῶν | πέντε τοῦ εἰσελθεῖν*, 'the returning ships were safely brought into harbour at most-holy Berenice, for the winds are contrary. And the ships stalled from entering for five hours.'

[100] Lines 7–12.

[101] Line 15: *Ὀξύρ]υ̣γχα οὐδὲ τὰς λώδιγας κ̣α̣τεσκεύασας*, 'Oxyrhyncha nor did you prepare the blankets.' The palaeography does not clarify whether they were written by a different hand: Peppard (2009: 194).

[102] Quoted in n. 98.

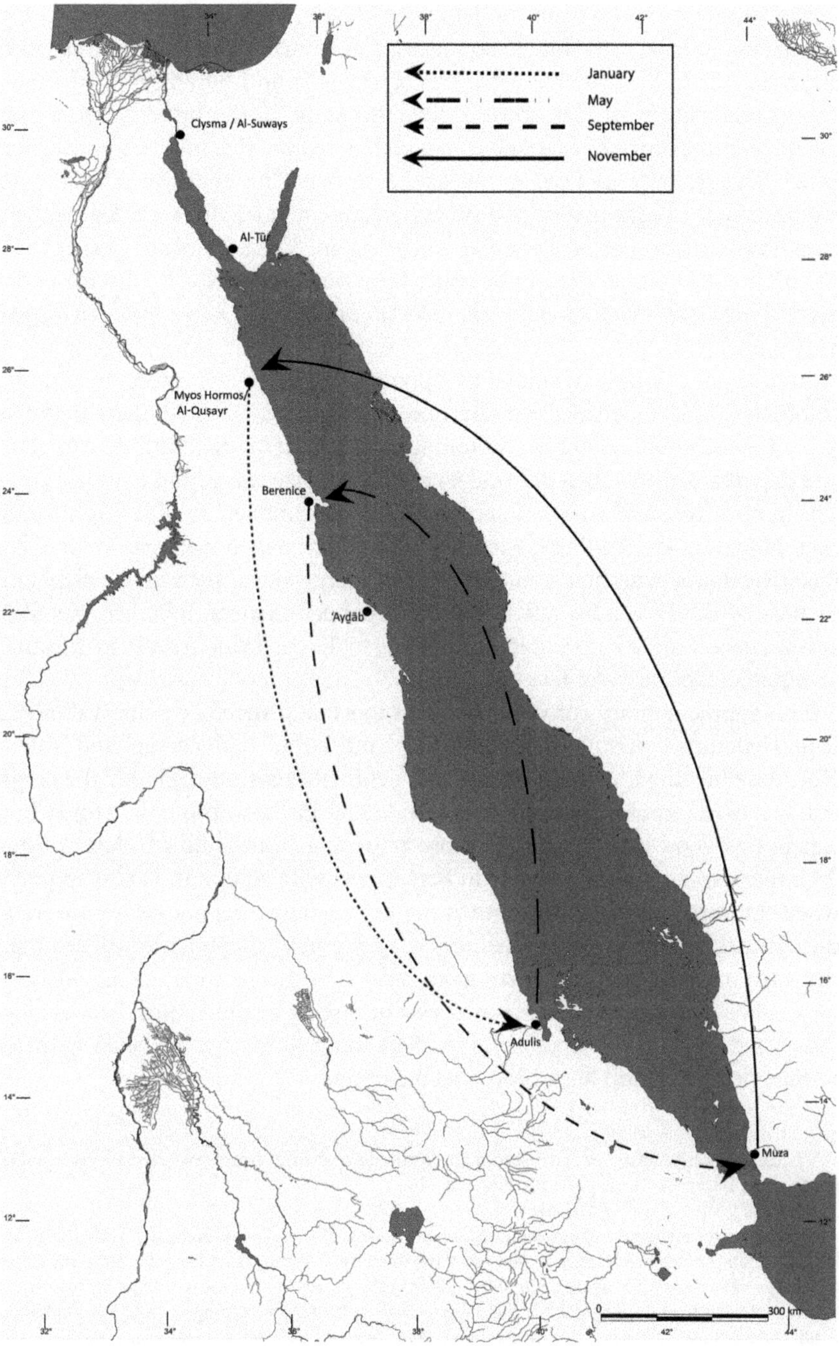

Fig. 1.9 Timetable of the sea routes to Adulis and Muza.

The urgency expressed in the letters to Oxyrhyncha, and the reproach for not having prepared the blankets, suggest the launch (probably months later, given the *c.*900 km distance between Oxyrhyncha and Berenice[103]) of a new commercial enterprise. The most likely destination for the sort of venture that included the export of blankets (*λώδικες*) is Muza, the only emporion for which the author of the *Periplus* attests the export of 'not many blankets'.[104] As mentioned, the best time for a sea voyage from Egypt to Muza was September, even if nothing prevented an earlier embarkation.[105] The (second?) writer of *P. CtYBR* inv. 624 was hoping to be ready for a timely departure: 'with the gods' help, I will set sail timely' (ll. 15–16: *θεῶν ἐπι | τρεπόντων εὐκαίρως ἀ]φήσομαι*).[106]

In sum, the ample window of opportunity for a departure to Adulis, combined with the expedient location of Berenice, allowed merchants to exploit what would have been an idle season. By alternating both destinations and departure points, Red Sea traders could organize two round trips per year. The interlocking and alternating of the sea routes implied by the *Periplus,* and exemplified by *P.CtYBR* inv. 624, reveal an additional convenience offered by Berenice: apart from being suitable for very large ships, such as the elephant carriers of the Ptolemies and the Roman pepper carriers, Berenice was also advantageous for smaller ships returning to Egypt from Adulis in the unfavourable conditions of late spring.[107]

This supplementary convenience helps to explain Berenice's survival in the Late Hellenistic period, when the elephant hunts had ceased and Myos Hormos flourished. Myos Hormos was definitely most suitable for the ships that imported frankincense from South Arabia in the autumn or winter, but was not as good as Berenice for those returning from Adulis in late spring. A similar explanation may apply to Berenice's revitalization in Late Antiquity, when the direct voyages to South India of very large pepper carriers were a distant memory (if remembered at all). In the next chapter, we will see that ships from South India and Sri Lanka arrived in Adulis (or in other ports of the Gulf of Aden) with the late north-east monsoon, around April. Forwarding those cargoes on to Clysma may have been too challenging, but sending them to Berenice could still have been a viable option.

[103] See the computation of the distance and estimate of the travel time between Herakleopolis Magna and Berenice, cf. http://orbis.stanford.edu.

[104] *PME* 24. [105] *PME* 24.

[106] The editor restored and translated *θεῶν ἐπι | τρεπόντων ταχέως ἀ]φήσομαι*, 'With the gods' [help], I shall [go forth quickly?].' However, if the line refers 'to the difficulties of getting the ships ready to leave Berenike again' (Peppard 2009: 198, n. 16), *εὐκαίρως* (timely) seems more appropriate than *ταχέως* (quickly). For *εὐκαίρως* in defining the timings of the sea routes to Adulis and Muza, cf. *PME* 6; 24. In the active voice, *ἀφίημι* is 'to set sail from' in *PME* 57: *τινὲς μὲν εὐθὺς ἀπὸ Κανή, τινὲς δὲ ἀπὸ τῶν Ἀρωμάτων ἀφιέντες κτλ.*

[107] Cf. the South Red Sea wind maps in http://www.punchdown.org/rvb/wind/wmapindex.html, by R. Van Buskirk, K. Garbesi, and K. Rosen.

2

Riding the Monsoons

In the centuries of maritime travel before steam power, it was the regular oscillation between the south-west and north-east monsoons that connected the opposite shores of the Arabian Sea. Very broadly speaking, one can say that the south-west monsoon favoured the voyages from Arabia to India during the spring and summer months, while the north-east monsoon facilitated travel from India to Arabia during the autumn and winter. However, when it comes to defining the precise timetable for a specific transoceanic sea route—from a given point of departure to a given destination—these broad opportunity windows shrink considerably, depending on the departure and arrival points and on the type of commercial enterprise. The precise dates on which ships were launched for each destination represented crucial deadlines that determined many other aspects of the lives of the people involved in the related trade. Therefore, it comes as no surprise that from Antiquity to Early Modernity a considerable corpus of literary and documentary evidence provides specific details about the timings of various Indian Ocean sea routes.[1] To better appreciate the distinctiveness of the trade model reflected in the Muziris papyrus, it will be useful to contrast its peculiarities with those of other trade patterns—both contemporaneous and later—between Egypt and the west coast of India. As often happens, a diachronic perspective will help make sense of the sometimes incomplete, sometimes enigmatic, information concerning Indian Ocean trade in the first centuries AD.

First, however, a cautionary note is in order. When Ancient and Medieval sailing seasons between India and Egypt are compared, we find variances that do not depend so much on different points of departure or arrival, as on the logistics of the trade. From a *longue durée* perspective, the history of trade relations between India and Egypt from Antiquity to the Early Modern era may be divided into periods based on the role played by the emporia in the Gulf of Aden, which over time operated either as stopovers for ships sailing all the way from Egypt to India (a direct sea-route system), or as intermediate meeting

[1] For the timings of Medieval and Early Modern sea routes, Varisco (1994: 215–31; 255–6); Tibbetts (1971: 225–42); Lunde (2013).

The Indo-Roman Pepper Trade and the Muziris Papyrus. Federico De Romanis, Oxford University Press (2020).
 DOI: 10.1093/oso/9780198842347.001.0001

points for vessels sailing from each end of the sea route (a multi-stage sea-route system).

The potential competition between these two modes of trade was envisioned even when one option was much preferred over the other. The author of the *Periplus* explains the origin of the toponym *Eudaimon Arabia* (Aden) by evoking a past in which contacts between Egypt and India resulted from the link between shorter sea routes converging on South Arabia.[2]

One should not infer that in the mid-first century AD anyone recalled a time when Indian and Egyptian ships actually met in South Arabian ports. Rather, the inspiration for the multi-stage model described by the author of the *Periplus* probably arose from the activity at emporia like Muza or Cane, which, while hosting ships coming from Egypt,[3] also cultivated extensive commercial relationships with other regions across the Arabian Sea: Muza with Adulis, the emporia of the northern Somali coast, Rhapta, the island of Socotra, and Barygaza;[4] and Cane with the emporia of the northern Somali coast, the Isle of Sarapis, Barygaza, Skythia, Omana, and Persis.[5] Both Muza and Cane are credited with having commercial links with Barygaza, but those exchanges had little impact on the trade with Egypt. In the *Periplus*, the list of commodities available at Muza includes goods imported from the Somali coast and Adulis, but not from India.[6] The list of commodities available at Cane generically refers to exports 'through its connections with the other ports of trade'.[7] The allusion may be inclusive of commodities from Barygaza, but it is clear that only a minimal fraction of the exchanges between Egypt and India passed through Cane.

The description of Aden's past commercial role outlined by the *Periplus* rests only on a false etymology of the South Arabian toponym Aden (*dhû-'Adan^{um}*), inspired by the old Greek choronymic syntagm *Arabia Eudaimon*.[8] Nonetheless, the passage is noteworthy insofar as it shows that, at a time when most of the commodities exchanged between Egypt and India travelled via direct sea routes, Indian Ocean mariners like the author of the *Periplus* could imagine a multi-stage system for the trade between India and the Mediterranean, with one ship sailing between India and Arabia, another between Arabia and Egypt, and a transhipment point in between. The multi-stage pattern did not exist in the mid-first century AD, but that mythic reconstruction soon became a reality and eventually emerged as the only format for Indo-Mediterranean trade from Late Antiquity to Early Modernity. As we shall

[2] *PME* 26. [3] *PME* 24; 28. [4] *PME* 16; 17; 21; 31. [5] *PME* 27; 33.

[6] *PME* 24. For the correction *ἀπὸ τοῦ πέραν <καὶ> Ἄδουλι*, see p. 55, n. 96.

[7] *PME* 28.

[8] See Schiettecatte (2008: 27–35). *Arabia Eudaimon* is already in Eur., *Bacch*. 16. The author of the *Periplus* has an inclination towards etymologies. The story about the beginning of the open-water sea routes to India in *PME* 57 is also based on a false etymology: see p. 76 n.54.

see, it will entail some alterations both in the timings of the sailing seasons and in the positioning of the Red Sea ports.

2.1. DIRECT SEA ROUTES

The economic sustainability of a long-distance commercial enterprise rests on the ability to balance several factors: the demand of the importing country, the supply of the exporting country, and the suitability of the transport system. The economic sustainability of the Early Roman Empire's South India trade was based on a fondness for pepper that spanned the Roman social spectrum; on a passion for precious stones and ivory peculiar to the upper classes; on an overproduction of pepper, pearls, and ivory in South India; and on the very large pepper carriers that sailed directly between Egypt and India with only an intermediate stopover (but no transhipment of cargo). The Indus Valley and Barygaza trades, which relied on demand for and supplies of different items, used smaller vessels. However, at least until Trajan's Canal was opened, those ships also sailed all the way from Egypt to India.

There is no solid evidence that the direct sea routes to India were ever used before Eudoxus of Cizycus' voyages between 116 and 107 BC,[9] or resumed in Late Antiquity or at any later time before the discovery of the Cape route. The pattern that characterized the late Hellenistic and Early Roman periods remains a unique organizational model in the history of trade between India and the Mediterranean. Nor do we have enough evidence to detail the transition from the direct to the multi-stage sea routes. It seems likely, however, that the evolution of transhipment facilities upon the launch of Trajan's Canal entailed a reduction in Red Sea ship tonnage, which in due course led to the use of multi-stage sea routes to India. Triggered by Trajan's Canal, which was of no use for the South India trade, the evolution may not have been synchronic for all sea routes to India. It seems likely, in particular, that the sea routes to the Indus delta and Barygaza were the first to embrace the new multi-stage system, and that the direct sea route to South India was the last to vanish, some time in the third century AD. At the time of the Muziris papyrus, while the South India trade still retained the old model, the commercial relationships with the Indus delta and Barygaza may have already evolved towards the multi-stage arrangement.

When compared with homologous systems of later ages, the old model has several benefits in terms of economy of means and time efficiency. For instance, the India trade of the Early Roman Empire needed only one ship

[9] Strab. 2.3.4–5 (= Posidonius *FGrH* 87 F 28.4–5 = F 49C E.-K.), cf. Habicht (2013). For the renaming of the *Erythra Thalassa* to *Erythra kai Indike Thalassa*, see p. 48 n.59. Eventually, the notion of *Erythra Thalassa* will encompass both Red Sea and Indian Ocean: *PME* 1; 28; 38; 64.

and delivered Indian commodities to Alexandria right at the start of the Mediterranean sailing season. In Late Antiquity and the Middle Ages, at least two ships were required—one for the Red Sea and one for the Arabian Sea—and the pepper reached Alexandria only by late summer or the dead of winter. In addition, the ships of the Early Roman Empire experienced no idle years, since a single commercial enterprise lasted less than twelve months. By contrast, a Portuguese ship that left from Lisbon in April could return from India only in July of the following year—far too late to sail to India again.

However, the India trade of the Early Roman Empire also had its drawbacks. Its single ships, which had to be large enough to guarantee the profitability of the enterprise, were not suited to the sailing conditions in the northern part of the Red Sea, and they could not have made use of Trajan's Canal. Another drawback (in part also resulting from the size of the ships) concerned the timing of the Arabian Sea crossings. The timings of the direct sea routes were much tighter than those of the multi-stage sea routes, because they had to be synchronized with Red Sea sailing conditions. To reach Myos Hormos and Berenice in the fastest and most comfortable way, ships had to schedule their return voyage so that they could sail the Red Sea before the southerly winds weakened in springtime, which meant catching the early north-east monsoon for the westward return journey and the late south-west monsoon for the eastbound trip.

The multi-stage system of the Middle Ages (and probably Late Antiquity) offered additional options. The westbound trips were also able to benefit from the late north-east monsoon, and the eastbound voyages could use the early south-west monsoon as well. In terms of the pepper trade, this meant that while the pepper carriers of the Early Roman Empire had to leave India by 13 January (around the same time as was advisable for the Portuguese ships that sailed the *Rota do Cabo*), the ships of the Medieval (and probably Late Antique) pepper trade could stay in India for all of February and part of March.

The author of the *Periplus* refers to three sea routes to India (Fig. 2.1): one to Skythia (Barbarikon, on the Indus delta), one to Barygaza, and one to Limyrike.[10] As far as the timing of the outward journey is concerned, the differences between them were not dramatic. Regardless of the port of departure, they are all said to prescribe a July departure from Egypt, corresponding, as the author of the *Periplus* puts it, to the (partially overlapping) Egyptian month Epiphi of the fixed Alexandrian calendar.[11] The vessels were supposed

[10] *PME* 57: *οἱ μὲν εἰς Λιμυρικὴν πλέοντες . . . οἱ δὲ εἰς Βαρύγαζαν οἵ τε εἰς Σκυθίαν κτλ.*

[11] *PME* 39 (Egypt–Indus delta); 49 (Egypt–Barygaza); 56 (Egypt–Limyrike). The days of the month of July that fall in the month Epiphi of the reformed Alexandrian calendar are only the 1st to the 24th.

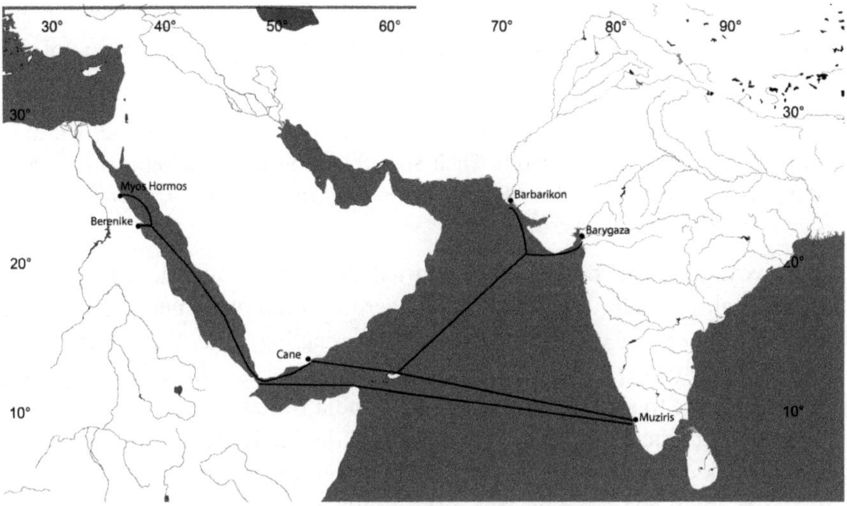

Fig. 2.1 Open-water routes to India.

to sail down the Red Sea in around thirty days,[12] stop in one of the ports on the Gulf of Aden,[13] and then cross the Arabian Sea with the abating south-west monsoon.

The calendric approximation used by the author of the *Periplus* to indicate the timing for the departure from Egypt was certainly sufficient for a readership consisting principally of financiers, whose main concern was to determine the start date of the loan contracts that financed specific commercial enterprises. To this public, the calendric detail makes it clear that maritime loans financing the India trade had to be issued in the preceding month of June/Payni. But this information was not precise enough for prospective ship captains, who would have needed a much narrower window. Of course, the author of the *Periplus* was well aware that marginally different sea routes implied slightly but critically different schedules. For instance, he knows that the ships bound for Cane set sail a little earlier than those for Muza.[14] As for the sea routes to India, a South India-bound ship had to leave from Berenice either before or immediately after the Dog Star rising (20 July).[15] The other sea routes would have required similarly precise, though probably different, deadlines.

[12] Around thirty days from Berenice to Ocelis or Cane for the large pepper carriers: Plin., *NH* 6.104. It may not have taken more time for the smaller ships that departed from Myos Hormos.

[13] While Pliny mentions only Ocelis and Cane (*NH* 6.104), the author of the *Periplus* refers to Ocelis as the first (that is, farthest west) stopping place for those who are about to cross the Arabian Sea (*PME* 25). Other stopping places were *Eudaimon Arabia*, which had 'suitable harbours and sources of water much sweeter than Ocelis' (*PME* 26), Cane, and the Promontory of Aromata (*PME* 57).

[14] *PME* 28. [15] Plin., *NH* 6.104.

It is worth noting that, while setting the timing of the departure for the Indus region, the author of the *Periplus* also points to a peculiar feature of the Indus delta trip:

> They leave around July, that is Epiphi, likewise sailing with the Indian (*sc.* winds, that is the south-west monsoon). Their voyage is dangerous, but benefits from a very favourable wind, and is shorter (δυσεπίβολος μὲν, ἐπιφορώτατος δὲ ἐκείνων καὶ συντομώτερος ὁ πλοῦς).[16]

How a voyage that is shorter and supported by a very favourable wind (which, in fact, is almost astern) can also be dangerous is not explained. At any rate, the wording καὶ αὐτοὶ οἱ πλέοντες (*likewise* sailing) and the comparative συντομώτερος (shorter) make it clear that the author is implicitly comparing the Indus route to the Barygaza and South India routes, the risks of which he also does not elucidate. In all likelihood, the distinctiveness of the sea route to the Indus delta depended on the slightly (but decisively) different timing for the Arabian Sea crossing. Since the south-west monsoon ends earlier in the more northern latitudes—as early as 1 September at the Indus delta (Fig. 2.2)—we may assume that the ships bound for Skythia left Myos Hormos at the very beginning of July and crossed the Arabian Sea in July/August, when the south-west monsoon was at its most intense.

By contrast, ships headed for Limyrike, at around 10° N, could benefit from the protracted (until late November) south-west monsoon in these latitudes. They could cross the Arabian Sea between approximately the last ten days of August and the beginning of October, when the south-west monsoon was much milder. The Indus delta voyage was thus shorter, since the wind was both more favourable and stronger, but at the same time riskier, since the same strong wind could become a hazard.

In another passage, the author of the *Periplus* clearly contrasts the sea route to South India with those to Barygaza and the Indus region. The manuscript tradition of this passage is corrupt, and the exact wording has been variously restored. Nonetheless, the meaning of the passage is clear:

> Since then right up to the present, with some leaving directly from Kane and some from the Promontory of the Aromata, those bound for Limyrike hold out sailing with the wind on the quarter for most of the way; those bound for Barygaza or Skythia do the same only three days and no more: for the rest of the run they are more or less pushed to follow their own proper course and, away from the shore on the high seas, they bypass the aforementioned bays.[17]

[16] *PME* 39. Here also αὐτοὶ οἱ = οὗτοι, cf. Frisk (1927: 65–6).

[17] *PME* 57: ἀφ᾽ οὗ μέχρι καὶ νῦν τινὲς μὲν εὐθὺς ἀπὸ Κανή, τινὲς δὲ ἀπὸ τῶν Ἀρωμάτων ἀφιέντες οἱ μὲν εἰς Λιμυρικὴν πλέοντες ἐπὶ πλεῖον τραχηλίζοντες (τραχηλίζονται *vel* τραχηλίζουσι *Frisk in comm.*), οἱ δὲ εἰς Βαρύγαζαν οἵ τε (*Müller*: οἱ δὲ) εἰς Σκυθίαν οὐ πλεῖον ἢ τρεῖς ἡμέρας ἀντέχουσι καὶ τὸ λοιπὸν † παρεπιφέρον (παρεπίφορον *Müller*, ἐπίφορον *malit Frisk*, παρεπιφέρον<ται> *Casson in comm.*) πρὸς ἴδιον δρόμον † (<ἔχοντες ἄνεμον> *Müller in comm.*, <καὶ> *Casson in*

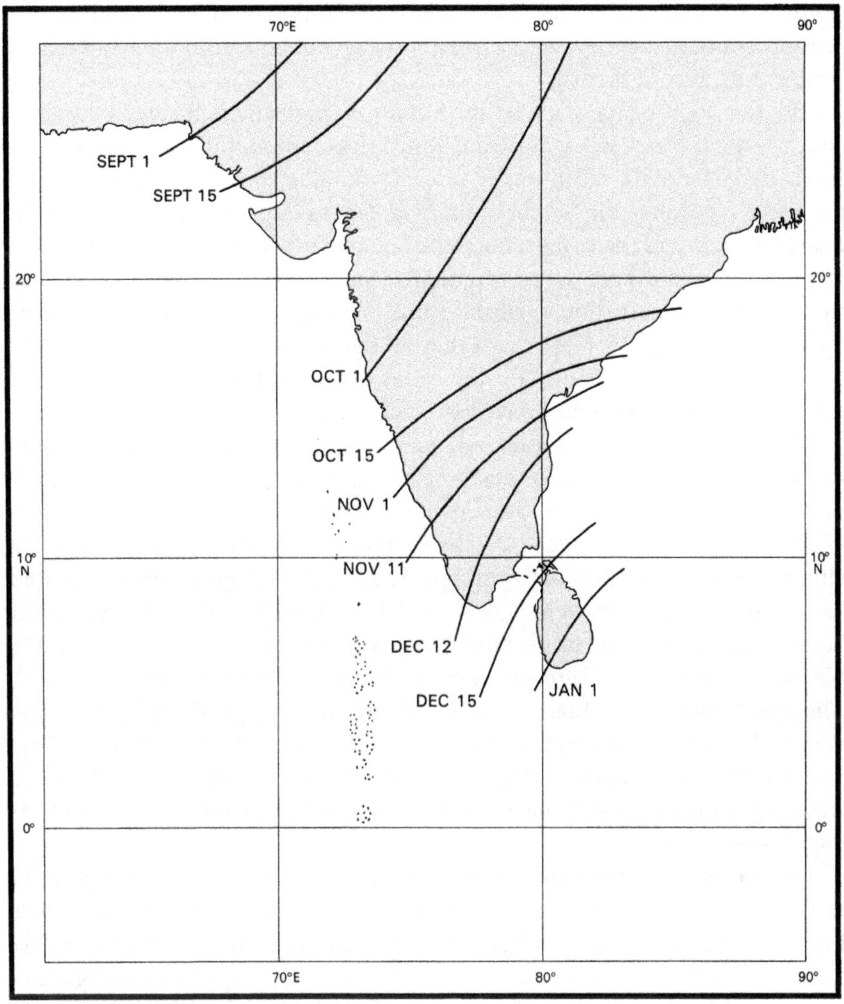

Fig. 2.2 Normal end dates for the southwest monsoon.

Whether the participle *τραχηλίζοντες* is to be kept or corrected to an indicative, the correspondence between *οἱ μὲν—ἐπὶ πλεῖον τραχηλίζοντες* and *οἱ δὲ—οὐ πλεῖον ἢ τρεῖς ἡμέρας ἀντέχουσι* ensures that the two verbs *τραχηλίζειν* and *ἀντέχειν* basically refer to the same nautical manoeuvre. As L. Casson has rightly pointed out, the expressions cannot mean that the ships sailed facing a headwind. In keeping with the angle resulting from the main direction of the

comm.) *ἐκ τῆς χώρας ὑψηλοὶ διὰ τοῦ* (*Müller*: *τῆς*) *ἔξωθεν* [*γῆς*] (*Frisk*) *παραπλέουσι τοὺς προειρημένους κόλπους*. Cf. Frisk (1927: 34; 88; 118); Casson (1984); De Romanis (1997: 680–2).

south-west monsoon and the course set by the ships bound for South India, he sensibly translated ἐπὶ πλεῖον τραχηλίζοντες as 'hold out with the wind on the quarter for most of the way'.

Still, the point being made by the author is that, although ships bound for South India did not sail against the wind, ships bound for Barygaza and the Indus delta certainly sailed under more favourable conditions. In fact, while the vessels heading for South India held out sailing with the wind on the quarter for most of the voyage, the ships bound further north did the same, but for no more than three days. Apparently, for the very first part of their trip from South Arabia to India, all the ships heading to any Indian destination took the same trajectory—perhaps they all sighted Socotra.[18] Eventually, their course split: the ships bound for the Indus delta and Barygaza steered north-east, and those en route to Limyrike continued heading south-east.

Whether with Müller's (καὶ τὸ λοιπὸν παρεπίφορον πρὸς ἴδιον δρόμον <ἔχοντες ἄνεμον> ἐκ τῆς χώρας ὑψηλοὶ κτλ.) or Casson's (καὶ τὸ λοιπὸν παρεπιφέρον<ται> πρὸς ἴδιον δρόμον <καὶ> ἐκ τῆς χώρας ὑψηλοὶ κτλ.) emendations, the sentence conveys the sense that the south-west monsoon was either 'almost favourable', or—perhaps more aptly—'more or less favourable' for the sea routes to the Indus delta and Barygaza. On the contrary, for the South India route the south-west monsoon was neither 'very favourable' (ἐπιφορώτατος),[19] nor 'almost/more or less favourable' († παρεπιφέρον).[20] The ships bound for Muziris sailed with the wind approximately forty-five degrees from the stern for most of the way. Since they did not start the Arabian Sea crossing earlier than 20 August (by which time the south-west monsoon was weakening), their passage was both slower—Pliny states that it lasted forty days[21]—and safer.

The author of the *Periplus* thought it unnecessary to detail the timings of the return voyages from the three Indian destinations. Pliny states that the return journey from South India to Egypt had to start between 9 December and 13 January,[22] but such a schedule cannot apply to the voyage from Barygaza or the Indus delta. In fact, the north-east monsoon does not begin simultaneously all along the west coast of India: the wind starts earlier in the northern latitudes, and then proceeds southwards.[23] Therefore, the ships sailing to Skythia would have been the earliest to return and those going to South India the latest.

[18] For Socotra as a landmark on the sea routes between South Arabia and India, see also p. 76 and Arunachalam (2008: 212–9).

[19] As for the Indus delta: *PME* 39.

[20] As for the Indus delta and Barygaza: *PME* 57.

[21] Plin., *NH* 6.104.

[22] Plin., *NH* 6.106; see p. 145.

[23] The beginning of the north-east monsoon follows the end of the south-west monsoon (see Fig. 2.2); it is alluded to with the words καταρχὴν [---| ἀνέμου in the *Charition* (*P.Oxy.* 3.413, ll. 213–4).

Table 2.1 Timetable of the direct Egypt–India sea routes.

	Outward voyage		Return voyage	
	Departure	Arrival	Departure	Arrival
Egypt–Indus delta	1 Jul?	15 Aug?	19 Oct/21 Dec	Dec/Jan?
Egypt–Barygaza	10 Jul?	15 Sept?	1 Nov/31 Dec?	Dec/Jan?
Egypt–Limyrike	20 Jul	1 Oct	9 Dec/13 Jan	Feb/Apr?

The timing of the return trip from the Indus delta may be inferred from information collected by Macedonians at the time of Alexander's fleet's departure:

> It was reported that there the sea was fit for navigation after the beginning of winter, from the setting of the Pleiades until the winter solstice; for at that season mild breezes usually blow from the land drenched as it has been with great rains; and these winds are convenient on a coasting voyage both for oars and sails.[24]

Since in the Indus delta in 325 BC the Pleiades set around 19 October,[25] the return journey from the mouths of the Indus had to begin between 19 October and 21 December. Therefore, since the return sea voyage from Barygaza must have occurred between those of the Indus delta and Limyrike, we may tentatively fix the schedules of the three sea routes as shown in Table 2.1.

2.2. MULTI-STAGE SEA ROUTES

For quite some time in the centuries immediately before and after the beginning of the Christian era, the South Arabian and East African ports close to the straits of Bab el-Mandeb were also variously involved in the India trade. In particular, on the Arabian side, Muza carried on its own trade with Barygaza;[26] Ocelis and Aden (*Eudaimon Arabia*) served as watering places for the vessels sailing between Egypt and India;[27] Cane was both an emporion that traded with Skythia and Barygaza and a waypoint en route to India;[28] and Moscha Limen was a port where the ships from Barygaza or Limyrike could stop and conduct some additional trade or even winter, if they were too late to continue on to their destination.[29] On the African side, Adulis and the other emporia of

[24] Arr., *Anab.* 6.21. Alexander's fleet set sail on 20 Boedromion of the Attic calendar (Arr., *Indic.* 21), at the rising in the evening (that is, before the setting) of the Pleiades, when the winds were not yet favourable (*κατὰ πλειάδος ἐπιτολὴν ἑσπερίαν . . . μήπω μὲν τῶν πνευμάτων οἰκείων ὄντων*): Nearchos *BNJ* 133 F 1a = Strab. 15.2.5.

[25] Cf. *Planetary, Lunar and Stellar Visibility 3.1*, where Alcyone is 0.7 degrees above the horizon at 17:40 of 19 October 325 BC.

[26] *PME* 21.

[27] *PME* 25; 26.

[28] *PME* 27; 57; Plin., *NH* 6.104. Cf. Cuvigny (2010b).

[29] *PME* 32.

the Somali coast hosted Egyptian and Arabian ships on their way back from India. During these layovers, they exchanged Indian commodities for East African goods.[30] However, even when they carried on their own trade with India, these ports or emporia never functioned as commercial *relais* in the trade between the Mediterranean and India. Rather than Indian commodities, the ships from Egypt imported regional products from them.[31] Thus the multi-stage pattern outlined for Aden by the author of the *Periplus* did not exist in the mid-first century AD: the trade between Egypt and India was carried out via direct sea routes.

Eventually, direct voyages to India would be replaced by a system in which the sailing route was broken into two legs, with one set of ships sailing the Red Sea and another crossing the Arabian Sea, linked by a transhipment of goods at a port near the strait of Bab el-Mandeb. The new sailing pattern can be inferred from a variety of historical references: by the travel of the Theban *scholasticus* who reaches the pepper country via Adulis;[32] by the Adulis ship that would bring the Roman merchant Sopatros to Taprobane (Sri Lanka);[33] and by Justinian's request that the Aethiopians (that is, Adulis merchants) purchase silk from India and sell it to the Romans.[34] Transhipment of Indian commodities may also be suggested for Aden, which Philostorgius describes as a Roman emporion lying out towards the Ocean.[35] However, by far the most vivid description of the new sailing pattern comes from a passage of the *Martyrium Arethae* describing the Indian and Red Sea ships—noted by provenance and number—that anchored at Adulis in winter AD 524/5 (Fig. 2.3):

> For an arrangement of our saviour Jesus Christ, ships of the Roman, Persian, Indian, and Pharsan islands' merchants came: from Ila fifteen, from Clysma twenty, from Berenice two, from Iotabis seven, from Pharsan seven, from India nine. Having gathered them together in an anchorage called Gabaza, under the territory of the city of Adulis on the sea, king Elesbas ordered that they were hauled on land. He himself made ten Indian ships and in that winter of that third *indictio* seventy ships were prepared.[36]

[30] Indian commodities exported to Adulis include iron, steel, cotton cloth, girdles, cloaks, fine cotton garments, and lac: *PME* 6; grain, rice, ghee, sesame oil, cane sugar, cotton cloth, and girdles were exported to the emporia of the Somali land: *PME* 14.

[31] *Κασία* too was one such regional trade item. Exported from Malao, Mundu, Mosyllon, Tabai, and Opone (*PME* 8; 9; 10; 12; 13), the shrub (whose bark was sought) was native to the Horn of Africa. The contention that it was either a central or a south or a south-east Asian product, secretly (and pointlessly) imported to the Somali coast to be re-exported to the Roman Empire (e.g. Casson (1989: 122–4); Amigues (1996)), is science fiction.

[32] Palladius, *De gentibus Indiae et Bragmanibus* 1.7. Cf. Desanges (1969).

[33] Cosmas Indic. 11.17.

[34] Procop., *Pers.* 1.20.9. Although unable to divert the silk trade from its traditional Indo-Persian circuits (Procop., *Pers.* 1.20.12), the Adulis merchants were nonetheless the main intermediary in the Egypt–India trade in Late Antiquity.

[35] Philostorg. 3.4.

[36] *Martyrium Arethae* 29, on which see Christides (2013: 75).

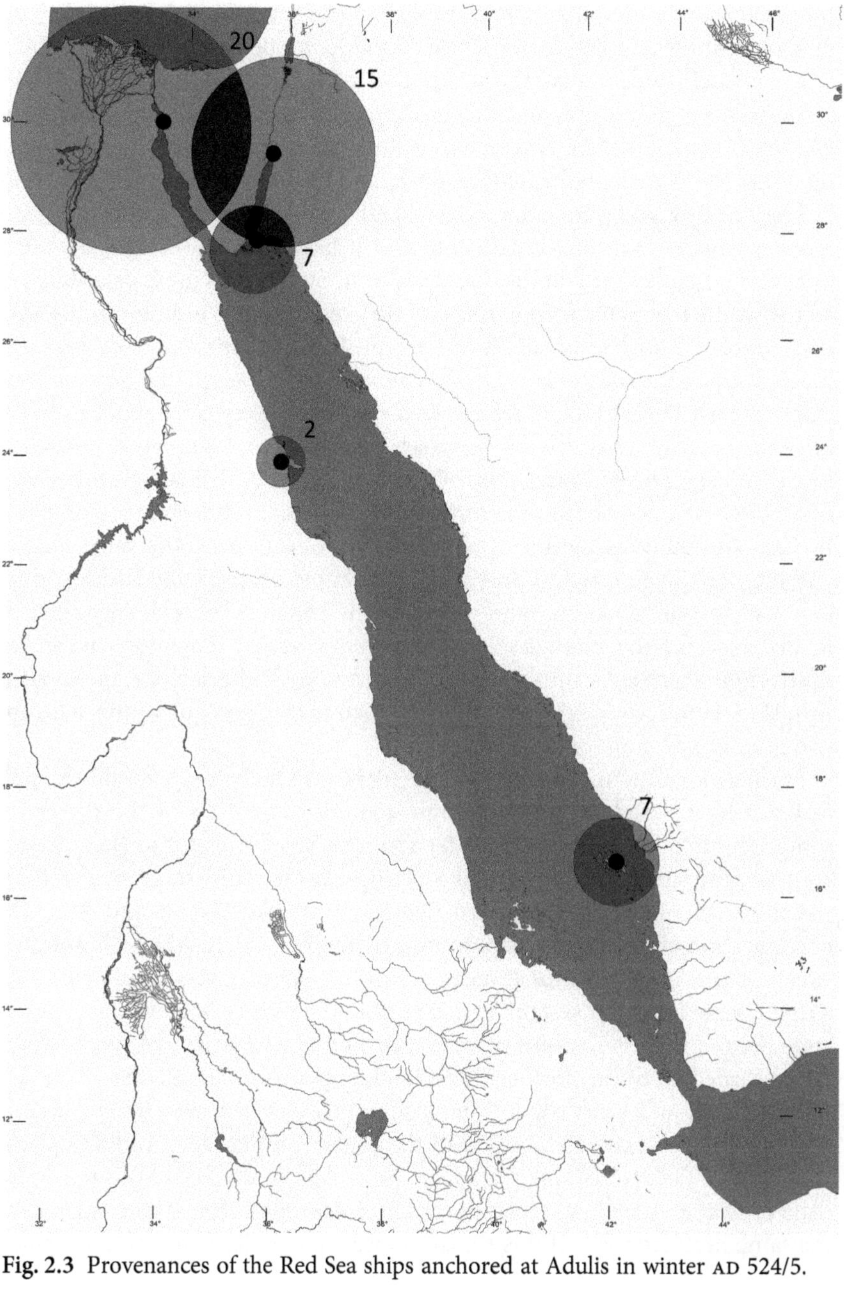

Fig. 2.3 Provenances of the Red Sea ships anchored at Adulis in winter AD 524/5.

It goes without saying that part or probably most of the cargo brought by the nine Indian ships would be transferred to and forwarded on by Red Sea ships. It is equally self-evident that the promotion of Adulis and the Gulf of Aden emporia from simple stopovers to indispensable meeting points between the two legs of the Indo-Mediterranean route introduced modifications to the size of the ships, the location of the Red Sea ports, and the timings of the sailing season.

The multi-stage arrangement was overall more elaborate and presumably more expensive than the direct route. Yet it had some advantages. As mentioned, the Achilles' heel of the direct sea route system was the impossibility of adjusting the size of the ship to the very different sailing conditions of the Red and Arabian Seas. By breaking the Egypt–India voyage into two legs, the multi-stage sea route system allowed merchants to adapt the size of their ships to the different legs. Early Modern evidence is very clear about it. In the fifteenth century, relatively large vessels of 1,000- to 1,200-*bahar* (166–199 tons) tonnage moved spices from Calicut to Aden or Jeddah, whereas very small *ǧilāb* of a few dozen tons forwarded (some of) those spices to al-Ṭūr.[37] In Late Antiquity, while the Arabian Sea was crossed by the huge *'adawlī* (Adulitan) ships referred to in Arabic pre-Islamic poetry,[38] the Red Sea ships that had to sail to Clysma and Aila were as small as the size suggested by R. Pedersen for the Black Assarca Island shipwreck.[39] Therefore, when the *Martyrium Arethae* lists nine Indian and fifty-one Red Sea ships anchored at Adulis in winter AD 524/5, we can safely assume that the total tonnage for the two groups was more or less even.

Furthermore, the multi-stage arrangement also had an impact on the port facilities in the Red Sea. The medium-to-very-large ships of the direct sea routes required the use of ports as far south as Myos Hormos or Berenice. By contrast, the small size of the Red Sea ships in the multi-stage arrangement magnified the role of the northern Red Sea ports like Clysma and Aila. The configuration of Red Sea ports described by Epiphanius, in which Clysma and Aila replaced Myos Hormos and Leuke Kome, respectively, is clearly viable for a multi-stage transport system. In such a plan the Indian cargoes, conveyed on large oceanic vessels to South Arabia (Adane) or East Africa (Adulis), would be forwarded on to the northernmost landing points on the Red Sea by a fleet of very small and swift ships. The decline of Myos Hormos (in the second century AD[40]) and the distribution of the 'Aqaba amphorae in India (Fig. 2.4) suggest that the multi-stage sea routes from Aila (and Clysma) to the Indus delta or Deccan ports had replaced earlier direct routes from Myos Hormos to the same destinations.[41] If this transition was not similarly lethal to Berenice,

[37] See pp. 45-6; 261–2. [38] Agius (2008: 292–4). [39] Pedersen (2008: 90).

[40] See p. 201, n.54.

[41] Tomber (2005); (2007: 978); (2008: 166); Raith et al. (2013). Here, Fig. 2.4 records also the sporadic occurrence at Pattanam, on which see p. 97 n.47.

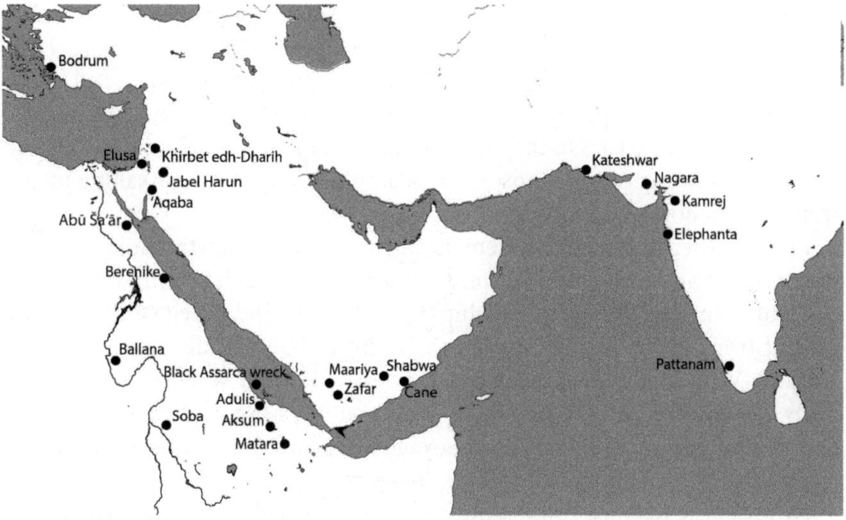

Fig. 2.4 Distribution of the find spots for ʿAqaba pottery (based on a map by P. Yule).

which enjoyed a Late Antique revival, it is probably because the multi-stage sea routes to South India or Sri Lanka continued to require a port at that latitude—and in medieval times, a port even further south. We will return to this point later.

The transition from a direct to a multi-stage sea voyage to India also meant modifications to the sailing timetable. In fact, while the schedule for the Arabian Sea crossing for a direct passage would have been determined by sailing conditions on the Red Sea, it was the reverse for a multi-stage sea route: the timing of the Red Sea sailing had to adapt to the schedules of the Arabian Sea crossing. In practice, this meant that while the direct sea routes could use only the late south-west monsoon to reach India and the early north-east monsoon to return to Egypt, the multi-stage option could exploit (albeit differently for northern and southern India) both the early and late monsoons winds.

The timings of the Late Antique multi-stage sea routes between Egypt and India may be approximated by drawing on the timings of the sea routes to and from Aden, as recorded in the AD 1271 almanac by the Yemeni sultan al-Malik al-Ašraf ʿUmar b. Yūsuf.[42] Beginning with the Arabian Sea leg, it notes two different sailing seasons between India and Aden: the *dīmānī* and the *tīrmāh*. In the *dīmānī* season, ships were supposed to leave India by 16 October, arrive at Aden between 6 November and 21 December, and leave again for India

[42] Varisco (1994: 23, 25, 27, 31, 33 (English translation); 42, 43, 45, 50, 52 (Arabic text)). The timings attested in Early Modern sources are basically in agreement with the Yemeni almanac: Tibbetts (1971: 240); Lunde (2013: 79–80).

between 26 March and 6 May. In the *tīrmāh* season, ships reached Aden by 15 April and left for India by 21 August.[43]

Therefore, the *tīrmāh* season, which took advantage of the very end of the monsoon, would be appropriate only for ships sailing to and from the ports of the South Indian coast. On the other hand, the *dīmānī* season, which exploited the very beginning of the monsoon winds, suited only the ships sailing to and from India's northern latitudes.[44]

In sum, the multi-stage system meant a voyage to north India that was much earlier and a return from South India that was much later than the direct sea routes. In the old system, the ships bound for the Indus delta and Barygaza set sail from Egypt in July and those sailing to South India returned by 13 January. With the new arrangement, the vessels heading to north-west Indian ports could leave Aden between 26 March and 6 May, and those returning from South India could start their voyage as late as 22 March—allowing two extra months for pepper collection.

How did the Red Sea routes adjust to these timetables? For the Red Sea leg, 'Umar's almanac keeps records of no fewer than three different routes between Egypt and Aden: *kārim*, *lāḥiq*, and *ṣā'iḥ*.

For the sea routes scheduled during the early monsoons, we may observe that both the *ṣā'iḥ* and the *kārim* Red Sea routes shared the same departure deadline from Aden (21 November), which is chronologically compatible with the early arrival of the *dīmānī* ships in Aden (1 November). It may be suggested that what distinguished the *ṣā'iḥ* and the *kārim* sea routes was the

Table 2.2 Timetable of the India–Aden sea routes.

	Departure from India	Arrival at Aden	Departure from Aden	Arrival in India
dīmānī	16 Oct.	1/2 Nov.	26 Mar./6 May	Apr/Jun?
tīrmāh	[2 to 22 March]	15 Apr.	20 Aug.	Sept/Oct?

Table 2.3 Timetable of the Egypt–Aden sea routes.

	Departure from Egypt	Arrival in Aden	Departure from Aden
kārim	30 Jun		21 Nov
lāḥiq	6 May	16 May	17 Apr; 26 May
ṣā'iḥ			16 Oct/21 Nov

[43] The deadline for the departure from India is provided by Ibn Māǧid, 231: 'He who leaves India on the 100th day (2 March) is a sound man, he who leaves on the 110th (12 March) will be all right. However, he who leaves on the 120th (22 March) is stretching the bounds of possibility and he who leaves on the 130th (1 April) is inexperienced and an ignorant gambler.'

[44] Cf. Vallet (2010: 546).

Egyptian destination and the type of ship: the Kārim merchants may have employed the large *marākib al-kārim* and landed at ʿAydẖāb (22° 19' N),[45] whereas the merchants who chose the *ṣā'iḥ* sea route sailed with the small *ğilāb* up to al-Quṣayr al-Qadīm (26° 9'15" N) and al-Ṭūr (28° 14' N) (see Fig. 2.5).

As for the sea routes scheduled during the late monsoons, the *lāḥiq* Red Sea route correlates with the early arrival of the *tīrmāh* ships at Aden. The South Indian cargoes, reaching Aden starting from 15 April, could be forwarded to Egypt by 26 May (see Fig. 2.6). The fact that the Yemeni almanac records two deadlines—17 April and 26 May—for the *lāḥiq* voyage from Aden to Egypt suggests that the *lāḥiq* sea route allowed not one but two round trips between Aden and Egypt's southernmost medieval port, ʿAydẖāb,

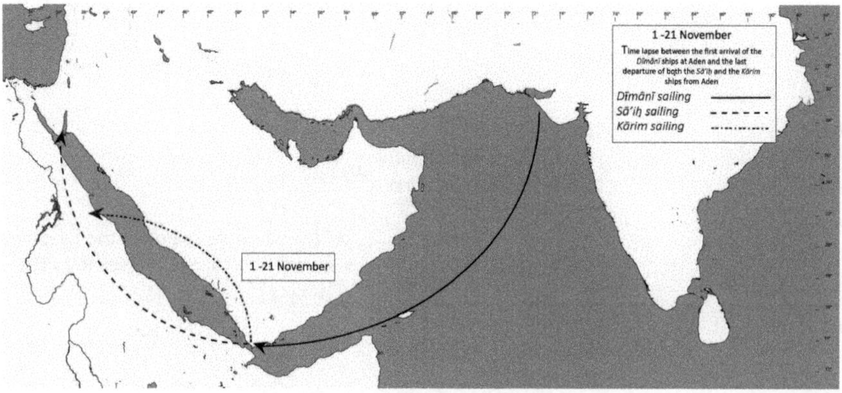

Fig. 2.5 Timing of the *dīmānī, ṣā'iḥ,* and *kārim* sailing seasons.

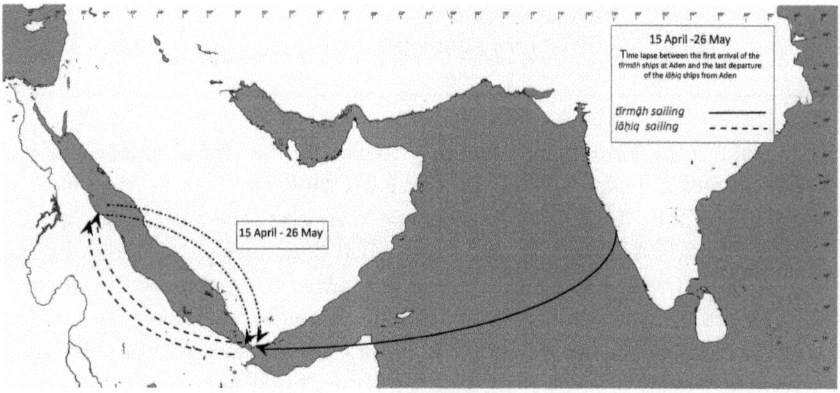

Fig. 2.6 Timing of the *tīrmāh* and *lāḥiq* sailing seasons.

[45] Fischel (1958: 163, n. 1).

Table 2.4 North Indian direct and multi-stage sea routes.

	Direct sea route	Multi-stage sea route	
		Arabian Sea	Red Sea
Jun			**30**: Departure of Egyptian *kārim* [ships] from Egypt to Aden
Jul	(Early) July: Departure from Egypt to India (*Periplus*)		
Oct	**19**: (Pleiades setting): Sailing season from the Indus' mouths (Arrian)	**16**: Departure of the Indian *dīmānī* ships for Aden at the 'First' of the Season	**16**: Sailing of the Egyptian *ṣā'iḥ* [ships] from Aden
Nov		**1**: Arrival of the Indian [ships] called first *dīmānī* to Aden during the First of the Season	**21**: End of the sailing of the Egyptian *kārim* [merchant ships] as the *sā'iḥ* [sailing]
Dec		**21**: End of the last arrival of Indian *dīmānī* [ships] as First of the Season	
Mar		**22**: First sailing of the *dīmānī* [ships from Aden] **26**: Beginning of the *dīmānī* sailing of Indian [ships] from Aden at the First of the Season	

The data in the Yemeni almanac help to explain the arrival schedule of the pepper cargoes in Egypt in Medieval and Early Modern times. For instance, in June AD 1183, Ibn Ğubayr saw many pepper-carrying caravans travelling from 'Aydāb to Qūṣ.[46] Apparently, that pepper had been brought to Aden by the vessels of the *tīrmāh* sailing season and forwarded to 'Aydāb by the ships of the *lāḥiq* sea route. By contrast, in 1561 the Venetian merchant Alessandro Magno and his shipmates decided not to wait for the caravan from al-Ṭūr to arrive in the dead of winter; instead, they purchased pepper that was then (19 October) available in Alexandria. The pepper they bought had been

[46] Ibn Ğubayr, 67 (Engl. transl. 61).

Table 2.5 South Indian direct and multi-stage sea routes.

	Direct sea route	Multi-stage sea route	
		Arabian Sea	Red Sea
Jul	20: Departure from Berenice		
Aug	20: Departure from South Arabia	21: This time is the *tīrmāh* sailing from Aden to India at the Last of the Season, or the Great Season	
Sep	30: Arrival in India		
Dec	9 Dec to 13 Jan: Beginning of the sailing from India		
Feb	Arrival at Berenice		
Mar			
Apr		15: First arrival of the Indian [ships] in Aden during the Last Season . . . this is the *tīrmāh* or Great Season	17: Last of the *lāḥiq* sailing to Egypt
May			6: Beginning of the *lāḥiq* sailing of Egyptian [ships] to Aden 16: End of the *lāḥiq* of Egyptian [ships] 26: Last of the *lāḥiq* sailing from Aden

unloaded at ʿAydẖāb in June by the *lāḥiq* ships; the shipment they did not wait for would arrive at al-Ṭūr by the *ṣāʾiḥ* ships.[47]

Further, the Yemeni almanac helps us to make sense of the simultaneous presence in Adulis of the nine Indian and fifty-one Red Sea ships attested by the *Martyrium Arethae* for the winter AD 524/5.[48] The timetables that directed those ships to Adulis were synchronized to ensure that the ships from the northern Red Sea would receive the Indian cargoes at the beginning of the north-east monsoon, not much later than the *dīmānī* ships from North India were expected to reach Aden (1 November). We may therefore suggest that the ships from Clysma left Adulis early enough (in December? January?) to find Trajan's Canal still navigable.

Trajan's Canal was of no use for the sea routes to the pepper emporia of South India and Sri Lanka. Since those ships returned with the *tīrmāh* sailing season, they could hardly reach Adulis before April/May. Given the weakness of the southerly winds in the Red Sea during these months, those cargoes were probably directed to Berenice, Egypt's southernmost port in Antiquity.

[47] Magno, 660–3. [48] *Martyrium Arethae* 29.

2.3. HEADING FOR INDIA

How did ancient captains manage to guide their ships across the Arabian Sea? The navigation from India towards the strait of Bab el-Mandeb was relatively easy: as long as a storm did not drive the ship south of Cape Guardafui,[49] one had only to enter the Gulf of Aden and keep sailing westwards along the Arabian or African coast. The usual trajectories—different depending on the port of departure—are suggested by the locations of the waypoints: the ships returning from Barygaza could stop either at the emporia along the Somali coast, or at the island of Socotra, or even at Moscha Limen, whereas vessels sailing back from Limyrike visited only Moscha Limen and Socotra.[50] Sailing in the other direction, from Bab el-Mandeb to a specific emporion of the west coast of India, was far more challenging.

The author of the *Periplus* contends that the three open-water routes to Skythia, Barygaza, and Limyrike resulted from a discovery by the ship captain Hippalus, who plotted both the locations of the destinations (that is, calculated their latitudes) and the extent of the sea (that is, determined the longitudinal distances from the South Arabian or East African coast).[51]

Quite interestingly, the author of the *Periplus* imagines that Hippalus developed new sea routes based on geographic estimates. Speculations about new navigational possibilities may also be found in Juba, whose estimate of the distance between Lepte Acra and the Adanu islands is linked to his claim that one could sail from India all the way to Gades,[52] and in Seneca, who maintains that the sea between Spain and India can be sailed in only a few days, if a favourable wind bears the ship along.[53] Yet Hippalus' story cannot be taken at face value,[54] nor is there evidence that the navigation between South Arabia and India was guided by the knowledge of the latitudes of the Indian emporia. As mentioned earlier, for most of the ocean crossing, the approximate trajectories to Skythia, Barygaza, and Limyrike (at around 25°, 22°, and 10° N,

[49] It happened to a certain Diogenes: Ptol., *Geog.* 1.9.1; for the storms off Cape Guardafui, see *PME* 12.

[50] *PME* 14; 31; 32.

[51] *PME* 57.

[52] Plin., *NH* 6.175 = *BNJ* 275 F 35; Solin. 56.4–6. Cf. Roller (2003: 242–3). Juba II contradicted both the theory that the heat prevented any navigation there and the idea—later accepted by Ptolemy (*Geog.* 7.5.2)—that the Atlantic and Indian Oceans did not communicate. The implications of his statement should be appreciated in the light of his exploration of the Canary Islands (Plin., *NH* 6.202–5 = *BNJ* 275 F 44), his duovirate of the Atlantic emporion of Gades (Avien., *Or. Mar.* 273–9 = *BNJ* 275 T 12c), and his dedication of the work *On Arabia* to Gaius Caesar (Plin., *NH* 12.56 = *BNJ* 275 F 2).

[53] Sen., *QNat.* 1.pr.13.

[54] Mazzarino (1982/7) has shown that Hippalus is just an imaginary figure generated by a corruption of the original name for the south-west monsoon—*Hypalos*, that is 'Submarine' (sc. wind)—which was distorted into the personal name *Hippalos*. Eventually, the distortion produced the spurious story of the ship captain Hippalus. See also De Romanis (1997); *contra* Desanges (1996); Habicht (2013).

respectively) were suggested by the steadiness of the south-west monsoon: the vessels heading for South India held out sailing with the wind on the quarter for most of the way, and the ships bound for Skythia and Barygaza did the same, but for no more than three days.[55]

Under these circumstances, sailing some extent off course would not be unusual. A vessel travelling along the sea routes to Skythia and Barygaza (which were basically in the same direction for most of the voyage), could end up landing as far south as Kalliena.[56] According to the *Periplus*, when the ships were about to reach India, particular markers could offer a sense of where the ship was headed. The coasts west of the Indus were heralded by snakes called *graai*, and the sea off the Indus delta by other types of sea snakes and whitish water. Enormous black sea snakes signalled the coasts east of the Indus, and the sighting of smaller greenish sea snakes meant the coasts around and beyond Barygaza.[57] More often than not, western ships bound for Barygaza approached Syrastrene (Kathiawar Peninsula), and were then towed to Barygaza by local fishermen in the king's service, since the mouths of the Narmadā (the river near Barygaza) were not easy to find or navigate.[58]

The Limyrike coast was also announced by the presence of a particular type of snake, black in colour but shorter, with a dragon-shaped head and blood-red eyes.[59] It is likely, however, that what guided the very last part of that sea route (which also happened to be infested with pirates) was the sight of the Lakshadweep Islands. If this possibility is not suggested by modern commentators, it is because they usually refrain from identifying the islands of that archipelago with the islands mentioned at chapter 53 of the *Periplus*:

> Then come the Sesekreienai Islands as they are called, the Isle of the Aigidioi, the Isle of the Kaineitoi near what is called Chersonesos (Peninsula), around which places there are pirates, and next White Island. Then come Naura and Tyndis, the first ports of trade of Limyrike.[60]

In the *Barrington Atlas of the Greek and Roman World*, the Sesekreienai Islands appear as rocks off of Vengurla, the Island of the Aigidioi as Goa, the so-called Chersonesos as Karwar, the Island of the Kainetoi as an islet in front of Karwar, and Leuke Island as Pigeon (Netrani) Island (Fig 2.7).[61] These

[55] *PME* 57. [56] *PME* 52. [57] *PME* 38; 40. [58] *PME* 43–4. [59] *PME* 55.

[60] *PME* 53; transl. by L. Casson, with modifications.

[61] Talbert (2000: Map 5; and, by U.E. Erdosy, 2.60 (Island of the Aigidioi); 2.62 (Chersonesos); 2.65 (Leuke Island); 2.69 (Sesekreienai Islands)). In the directory, I do not find the Island of the Kainetoi, but since in the map it is marked in front of Chersonesos, and since Chersonesos is identified with Karwar, its identification with Oyster Rock (or any other islet in front of Karwar) seems implied.

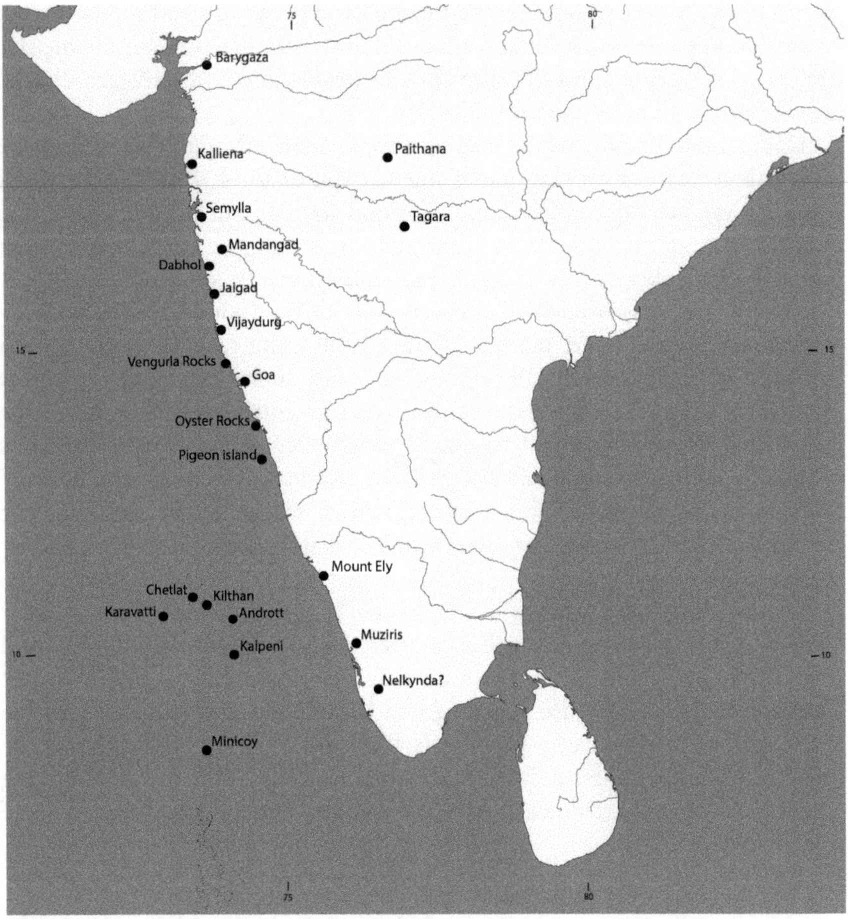

Fig. 2.7 Islands of the Arabian Sea and places mentioned by the *Periplus*.

identifications have been established, minor differences aside, by almost two centuries of scholarship.[62] They are based on the implicit assumption that, since the islands are mentioned after Semylla, Mandagora, and Byzantion, but before the Limyrike emporia, they must have been lying in a row along the coast south of Chaul (definitely Semylla), Mandangad (most probably Mandagora or very close to it), and Vijaydurg (possibly Byzantion), and north of Ponnani (most probably Tyndis or very close to it).[63]

[62] Vincent (1807: 2.432–5); McCrindle (1879: 129–30); Müller (1855: 1.296); Schoff (1912: 200–1); Casson (1989: 297); Belfiore (2013: ad loc.).

[63] Shinde, Gupta, and Rajgor (2002: 78) argue that Mandagora, Melizeigara, and Palaipatmai (and Hippokura, cf. Ptol., *Geog.* 7.1.6–7) lay about or near the Jainjira creek.

Three objections can be raised to these identifications. First, they locate the Island of the Kainetoi and Chersonesos, both occupied by pirates, some 550 kilometres away from Muziris, yet Pliny the Elder claims the pirates are close to Muziris.[64] Second, in evaluating Ptolemy's coordinates for the Isle of the Aigidioi and Leuke Island (the only two nesonyms that are mentioned in both the *Periplus* and Ptolemy), one has to consider that after Semylla, located at 14° 45' of latitude, Ptolemy turned the coastline 90° anticlockwise, making it run west–east.[65] Therefore, Ptolemy's latitudes for the Isle of the Aigidioi and Leuke Island (8° 30' N and 12° N, respectively) should be taken instead as indications for the *longitudes* of those islands.[66] The distances from a coastline approximately aligned to 14° N strongly suggest that the islands were considerably further from the coast than Goa or the Pigeon Islands. Moreover, since Ptolemy locates the same islands at longitude 118°, one should infer that they were actually south, not north, of Muziris (located at longitude 117°).[67]

The Lakshadweep Islands were certainly visible to the crews approaching Limyrike and are generically alluded to in the *Periplus* as the islands lying off Limyrike.[68] It seems inconceivable that none was identified and used as a landmark for directing ships to Muziris or Nelkynda. Suggesting precise identification for the nesonyms mentioned by the author in chapter 55 is risky, and probably not worth the trouble. But it seems possible and worthwhile to suggest an identification for the so-called Chersonesos (peninsula), which must have been a landmark on the coast.

Along the coast of India, Ptolemy locates Chersonesos at 114° 20', 14° 30'; the Nitra emporion (likely Pliny's Nitriae) at 115° 30', 14° 40'; Tyndis at 116°, 14° 30'; and Muziris at 117°, 14°.[69] On his map, this segment of coastline runs west to east, but in reality it goes from north to south. Since Muziris is in the Pattanam area (10° 09' N) and Tyndis is in the Ponnani area (10° 46' N), it seems reasonable to identify the so-called Chersonesos with Mount Ely (Delly, Ezhimala 12° 01' N, 75° 12' E). Visible in fine weather at a distance of 43.5 km and marked in many of the earliest Portuguese maps,[70] it was a prominent landmark for Medieval and Early Modern seafarers, as pointed out by Abū al-Fidā᾿ and by Duarte Barbosa.[71] Mount Ely was most probably the *terra alta* sighted by Vasco da Gama on 18 May 1498 at the end of his voyage from Malindi to Calicut.[72]

Incidentally, it may be noted that the identification of the islands mentioned in chapter 53 of the *Periplus* with islands of the Lakshadweep archipelago proves crucial for understanding how the account of India's west coast was

[64] Plin., *NH* 6.104. [65] See pp. 152–3. [66] Ptol., *Geog.* 7.1.95; 4.11.

[67] Ptol., *Geog.* 7.1.8. *Pace* Müller (1855: 1.296), the argument is compelling. [68] *PME* 56.

[69] Ptol., *Geog.* 7.1.7–8.

[70] Hunter (1885–7: 4.197). Mount Ely is marked, for instance, in the map of Bartolomeu Velho reproduced at p. 263, Fig. 11.2.

[71] Abū al-Fidā᾿, 354 (Fr. transl. 2.116); Barbosa, 162 (Engl. transl. 2.79).

[72] For Mount Ely as da Gama's Indian *terra alta*, Ames (2009: 69, n. 6).

pieced together by the author. In the related section of his work (chapters 38–58), one can discern the various segments of geographic information that were assembled:

1) The description of the Barbarikon/Minnagar emporion and its surroundings (chapters 38–40).
2) The description of the Barygaza emporion and its hinterland (chapters 41–9), plus the Southward Road (*Dachinabades*) Barygaza–Paithana–Tagara (chapters 50–1) and, on the coast, the local emporia around Kalliena and Semylla (chapters 52–3).
3) The description of Limyrike and the islands off its west coast (chapters 53–6; 58).

The author of the *Periplus* knew that a long distance separated Semylla and Limyrike, but this segment of the west coast of India was unfamiliar to him. It follows that he would have compiled data from three separate groups of sea captains and merchants, each of whom had expert knowledge about one set of ports and their environs.

2.4. THE PLEIADES IN THE MIDDLE OF THE YARD

Nowhere does the author of the *Periplus* say that a star was used as a signpost for any of the sea routes to India. Until the ship neared the Indian coast, it was the wind itself that ensured the course direction. The lack of reference to celestial navigation between South Arabia and India is in sharp contrast to a passage by Diodorus of Samos, quoted by Marinus of Tyre and repeated by Ptolemy. A translation of the Greek text as it stands in the best manuscripts should be: 'He [sc. Marinus] says: The people who sail from India to Limyrike, (as Diodorus of Samos says in the third [book]) have Taurus in mid-heaven and the Pleiades in the middle of the yard.'[73]

The oddity of a voyage 'from India to Limyrike' led scholars either to postulate a corruption of the manuscript tradition or to propose interpretations that are not obvious. In particular, A. Letronne suggested the deletion of *ἀπό* (the translation would be 'The people who sail to Limyrike of India'),[74] and Müller, in the commentary, the correction of *Ἰνδικῆς* to *Ζιγγικῆς* (the sailing would be from East Africa to Limyrike).[75] According to Dihle, in this

[73] Ptol., *Geog.* 1.7.6: *φησὶ* [*sc.* Marinus] *γάρ, ὅτι καὶ οἱ μὲν ἀπὸ τῆς Ἰνδικῆς εἰς τὴν Λιμυρικὴν πλέοντες, ὥς φησι Διόδωρος ὁ Σάμιος ἐν τῷ τρίτῳ, ἔχουσι τὸν Ταῦρον μεσουρανοῦντα καὶ τὴν Πλειάδα κατὰ μέσην τὴν κεραίαν*; transl. by J. L. Berggren and A. Jones, with modifications.

[74] Letronne (1831: 243–4, n. 6). Letronne's emendation has been adopted by Wilberg and Müller and rejected by Nobbe and Stückelberger/Graßhoff.

[75] Müller (1883–1901: 1.18–9).

passage Ἰνδική would designate the Indus delta rather than India as a whole,[76] whereas Berggren and Jones take ἀπὸ τῆς Ἰνδικῆς as an indication of the origin of the mariners.[77]

In my view, Diodorus could not be referring to a navigation from the mouths of the Indus (or from anywhere in India) to Limyrike; he must be describing a west-to-east navigation that used the Pleiades—that is, the latitude indicated at their rising or setting—as the bearing.[78]

In order to infer the latitude of the ship's position using Taurus and the Pleiades, those who sail southwards from the Indus' mouths should observe their azimuth at rising in relation to the keel of the ship, not to its yard, as Diodorus writes.[79] If these mariners were supposed to have the Pleiades in the middle of the yard (ἔχουσι . . . τὴν Πλειάδα κατὰ μέσην τὴν κεραίαν) while they were sailing (πλέοντες) to Limyrike, this means that they were sailing from west to east, because only by sailing in that direction can one keep the Pleiades as they rise in that position.

In addition, most readers are unlikely to see in ἀπὸ τῆς Ἰνδικῆς an indication of the seafarers' origin, especially given the parallelism with the subsequent ἀπὸ τῆς Ἀραβίας ἀναγόμενοι. Müller's correction inserts a choronym (Ζιγγική), which is never attested. Letronne's interpretation seems the most plausible: ἀπό must be a spurious insertion, apparently suggested by the parallelism with the subsequent οἱ δ'εἰς τὴν Ἀζανίαν ἀπὸ τῆς Ἀραβίας ἀναγόμενοι.

But one may question whether Letronne was correct in assuming τῆς Ἰνδικῆς as a specification of εἰς τὴν Λιμυρικὴν. While it is quite common in Greek to specify a toponym with a choronym in genitive (especially when the same name may refer to several places),[80] it is not often the case that a choronym clarifies another choronym that designates only one region, as it would be if οἱ μὲν τῆς Ἰνδικῆς εἰς τὴν Λιμυρικὴν πλέοντες is read.

A *locus parallelus* not mentioned by Letronne and perhaps too hastily dismissed by Müller suggests a different correction of the text. In the Armenian text of the *Geography* of Ananias of Širak (Pseudo-Moses of Khoren), Diodorus' quotation (probably reached via Pappus) runs as follows: 'as Diodorus of Samos says about India, that on the journey to Limyrike, one sees

[76] Dihle (1974: 11). Limyrike appears as a region distinct from the southern parts of Indike (*Dakṣiṇāpatha*) in *PME* 47: καταλιπὼν τήν τε Λιμυρικὴν καὶ τὰ νότια τῆς Ἰνδικῆς.

[77] Berggren and Jones (2000: 66 n. 25).

[78] The Pleiades (*al-Ṯurayyā*, *Kartik*) appear also in Arab and Gujarati stellar compasses of later ages, where, due to the precession of the equinoxes, they indicate Indian locations further north: Tibbetts (1971: 296–8); Arunachalam (1993, 123–7; 1996, 270–5; 2008, 212–9); Constable (2013: 2–5); Shihab (2013).

[79] For κεραία as 'yard', see Casson (1986²: 232). For the navigational practice of checking the route with the position of a star at its rising or setting against a part of the ship, cf. de Saussure (1928: 175).

[80] Letronne (1831: 243–4, n. 6) referred to Thuc. 2.18.1: ἀφίκετο τῆς Ἀττικῆς ἐς Οἰνόην.

Taurus in the middle of the sky and the Pleiades in the middle of its yard.'[81] On that basis, one might ask whether Ptolemy's original reading was actually *καὶ οἱ μὲν εἰς τὴν Λιμυρικὴν πλέοντες ὥς φησι Διόδωρος ὁ Σάμιος ἐν τῷ τρίτῳ περὶ τῆς Ἰνδικῆς κτλ.*, 'and the people who sail to Limyrike, as Diodorus of Samos says in the third [book of the work] *About India*, et cetera'.

Whatever the case, by keeping the Pleiades right at the middle of the yard, where at the time of Diodorus would a ship be expected to land in India? The bearing of a star at its rising or setting is determined by its declination, which changes over time due to the precession of the equinoxes. In the *Almagest*, Ptolemy gives three values for the declination of the middle of the Pleiades: it was 14° 30' when measured (probably around 298 BC) by Timocharis; 15° 10' when measured (probably around 128 BC) by Hipparchus; and 16° 15' when measured (probably in AD 57) by someone whom Ptolemy, given the rhythm of the drifting of the stars, could consider his contemporary.[82]

The fact that Ptolemy located Tyndis, the first port of Limyrike, at latitude 14° 30' N—exactly the declination of the middle of the Pleiades measured by Timocharis—and drew its coastline between latitudes 13° 30' N (Komaria) and 15° N (Kolchoi) and between longitudes 116° E (Tyndis) and 123° E (Kolchoi),[83] strongly suggests that he considered Diodorus of Samos chronologically closer to Timocharis than to Hipparchus, and accepted his location of Limyrike at the zenith of the Pleiades. In fact, Ptolemy does criticize Marinus' quotation of Diodorus, but only because Marinus argued, also on that basis, that the latitudinal dimension of the known world had to be increased to the south.[84] Ptolemy did not challenge Diodorus' authority; he only observed that Diodorus still located Limyrike north of the equator.[85]

If this conclusion is correct, we may posit that Diodorus of Samos was the same Diodorus who is hailed as a great glory among the experts in sundials in an epigram of the Greek Anthology, and is referred to by Proclus as one of the first writers on sundials.[86] Whether Diodorus' statement was based on real, if not really accurate, observations during navigations between the two shores of the Arabian Sea, or mere speculations about the latitudinal extension of the Indian peninsula, it is remarkable that already at such an early stage (third century BC?) Hellenistic culture had a notion of Limyrike and its approximate location.

[81] Matenagirk' Hayoc' edition, 2137 par. 4 (long recension): *orpēs Diodoros Samiac'i asē zHndkac', et'ē i Limirikon nawelov, unelov zTawřon mijnerkneay ew zPławda ənd mēj Keřeay.* Cf. 2162 par. 7 for the short recension. The Armenian *keřiay* corresponds to the Greek *keraia* and should be translated as 'yard' (see above n.79); for different translations cf. Hewsen (1992: 42; 79, n. 13).

[82] Ptol., *Alm.* 7.23 (= vol. 1,2 p. 19 Heiberg). The observation dates are those suggested by Brandt, Zimmer, and Jones (2014: especially 329–34).

[83] Ptol., *Geog.* 7.1.8–10. [84] Ptol., *Geog* 1.7.1–3. [85] Ptol., *Geog* 1.7.7.

[86] Anth. Gr. 14.139.1: *γνωμονικῶν—μέγα κλέος*; Procl., *Hypotyp.* 4.54: *οἱ τὰ ἀναλήμματα πρῶτοι γράψαντες*. On him, see Edwards (1985: 157–64; 171–82).

Diodorus' positioning of Limyrike was far less inaccurate than the location chosen by those whom Eratosthenes followed, who had aligned the southernmost part of India with Meroe at 16° 50' N.[87] However, even Diodorus of Samos, as well as Marinus and Ptolemy who follow him, was wide of the mark: Tyndis, which Ptolemy takes as the northernmost port of Limyrike, locating it at 14° 30', was probably in the Ponnani area (10° 46' N); Muziris, positioned by Ptolemy at 14°, included (or was close to) the site of modern-day Pattanam (10° 09' N). In sum, Diodorus located Limyrike at least four degrees further north than it really was, and this misplacement greatly affected Ptolemy's map of India, as we will see.[88]

[87] Strabo 2.1.2 = Eratosth. F III A 2 Berger (= 50 Roller). Berger (1880: 176–7) infers that the latitude of southern India had been approximated by many authors before Eratosthenes (*contra* Shcheglov 2005: 378–9).

[88] See pp. 150–3.

3

Pepper Lands

Broadly speaking, from Antiquity up to the Early Modern Age, South India was the only source of black pepper exported to the West. But within South India the precise geographical loci of pepper appear to have been subject to local intraregional shifts over time. A first shift occurred during the transition to Late Antiquity, when the pepper trade centres (at least those from which pepper was exported to the West) moved from Muziris up to the Mangalore region. In the transition to the Late Middle Ages and then to Early Modernity, the focus of the pepper trade shifted again, but this time in the opposite direction, from Mangalore down to Calicut, and then from Calicut down to Cochin (Fig. 3.1).

Although geographically close, these South Indian sub-regions achieved differing levels of pepper productivity in the Early Modern period. If similar disparities may also be assumed for Antiquity, we can infer a remarkable degree of variation in the volume of trade, which ultimately enables us to identify distinct economic cycles over the *longue durée*. It is not clear whether the shifts were also sensitive to the vagaries of local politics, but whatever the local dynamics, they certainly mirror the shifting balance between the two macro regions that were the primary consumers of South Indian pepper: west Asia and the Mediterranean regions on one side, and the Bay of Bengal and China on the other.

3.1. KOTTANARIKE, THE SOUTHERN PEPPER-PRODUCING LAND

Information derived from multiple sources—Greek and Latin authors, ancient Tamil poetry, and archaeological evidence—helps us locate the major pepper trade centres and production areas in the first and second centuries AD. In the *Periplus*, all the pepper emporia are included in a region called Limyrike:

The Indo-Roman Pepper Trade and the Muziris Papyrus. Federico De Romanis, Oxford University Press (2020).
 DOI: 10.1093/oso/9780198842347.001.0001

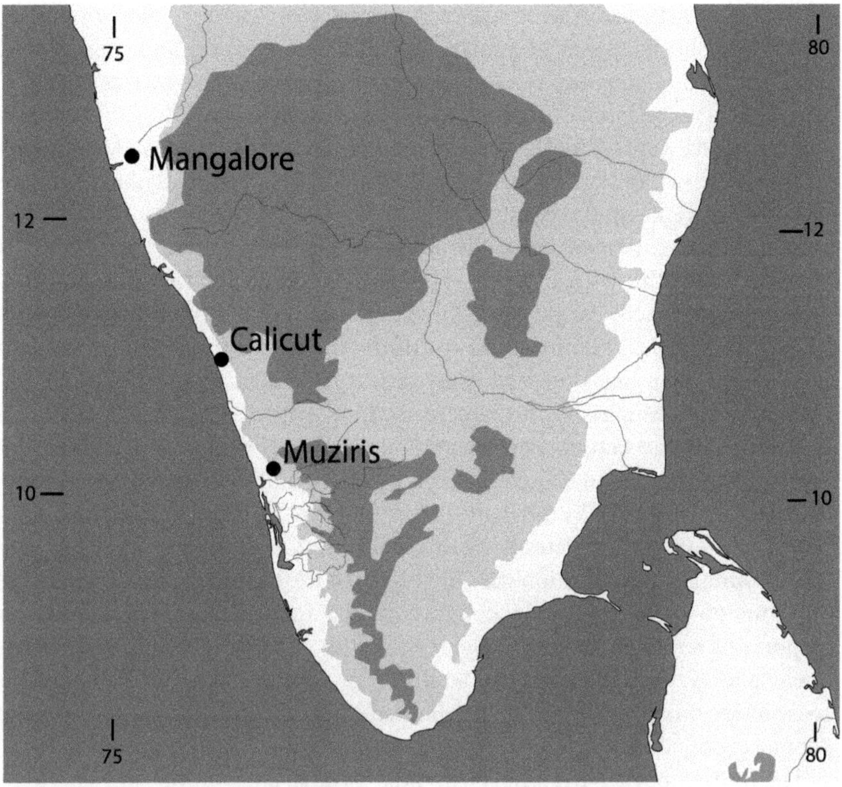

Fig. 3.1 The major Early Roman (Muziris), Late Antique (Mangalore), and Late Medieval (Calicut) pepper emporia.

Then come Naura and Tyndis, the first ports of trade of Limyrike, and, after these, Muziris and Nelkynda, which are now the active ones. Tyndis, a well-known village on the coast, is in the kingdom of Keprobotos. Muziris, in the same kingdom, owes its prosperity to the shipping from Ariake that comes there as well as to Greek shipping. It lies on a river 500 stades distant from Tyndis by river and sea, and from <the river mouth> to it is 20 stades. Nelkynda is just about 500 stades from Muziris, likewise by river and sea, but it is in another kingdom, Pandion's. It too lies on a river, about 120 stades from the sea. Another settlement lies at the very mouth of the river, Bakare, to which vessels drop downriver from Nelkynda for the outbound voyage; they anchor in the open roads to take on their cargoes because the river has sandbanks and channels that are shoal. The kings themselves of both ports of trade dwell in the interior.[1]

[1] *PME* 53–5; transl. by L. Casson.

The spatial relations between the emporia are clear enough. The core of the commercial business was at Muziris and Nelkynda; Naura and Tyndis were peripheral. The same rough distance of 500 stades, measured 'by river and sea', separated Tyndis from Muziris and Muziris from Nelkynda. Both Muziris and Nelkynda were beside a river, but neither was on the seacoast: Muziris was 20 stades inland, and Nelkynda was 120. Only Bakare, Nelkynda's loading site, was situated right on the coast.

Muziris' river, named the Cuḻḻi in an ancient Tamil verse,[2] is commonly identified with the Periyar River. The exact location of Muziris is approximated, if not exactly pinpointed, by the Roman pottery found at the site of Pattanam (some 25 kilometres north of the modern city of Kochi),[3] and the Roman gold coin hoard of Valluvally (a few kilometres south of Pattanam).[4] By combining Muziris' approximate location with the 500-stade distances mentioned by the *Periplus*, one would locate Tyndis north, near the modern town of Ponnani,[5] and Bakare/Nelkynda south, along a river emptying into the southern end of Vembanad Lake.[6] Moreover, since Naura was most probably south of the pirates lying in wait on the Chersonesos (here identified with Mount Ely),[7] its location may have been in the region of Chale (Chaliyam) or Cannanore (Kannur).[8] In conclusion, the mid-first-century AD pepper emporia of South India may have been scattered between Cannanore to the north and Kayamkulam to the south (Fig. 3.2). Approximately the same coastline segment will later be highlighted by Tomé Pires for his estimate of pepper production.[9]

The four emporia—Muziris, Nelkynda, Tyndis, and Naura—are said to be 'of Limyrike'. As a Western interpretation of an Indian geographic concept, the Limyrike of the *Periplus* may be compared with the Tamil choronym *Tamiḻakam*, designating the Tamil-speaking region of South India. In ancient Tamil texts, it is simply identified by the landmarks of the Vēṅkaṭam hill to the north and Cape Comorin to the south.[10] Understandably in a periplographic account proceeding eastwards, the *Periplus* makes Limyrike 'begin' with its 'first' emporia, Naura and Tyndis—the north-western tip of *Tamiḻakam*—and continue along the coast at least up to Nelkynda.[11] From the text as it stands, it is unclear how far Limyrike extended beyond that point: it

[2] *Akanāṉūru* 149.6.
[3] Shajan, Tomber, Selvakumar, and Cherian (2004); Tomber (2015).
[4] See p. 96, n. 44.
[5] Tyndis is located at Ponnani also by Casson (1989: 297–9).
[6] The distances indicated by the *Periplus* advise against locating Bakare near Varkala as Banaji (2015: 116) suggests.
[7] See p. 79.
[8] A location at Mangalore (argued by Casson (1989: 297–9)) is unlikely.
[9] See p. 99.
[10] *Pūṟanāṉūṟu* 168.18; *Cilappatikāram* 3.37; 8.1–2; *Tolkāppiyam*, Pāyiram, 1–7.
[11] By contrast, Ptolemy's Limyrike ended already with the mouths of the Baris River, leaving Nelkynda out; see p. 154.

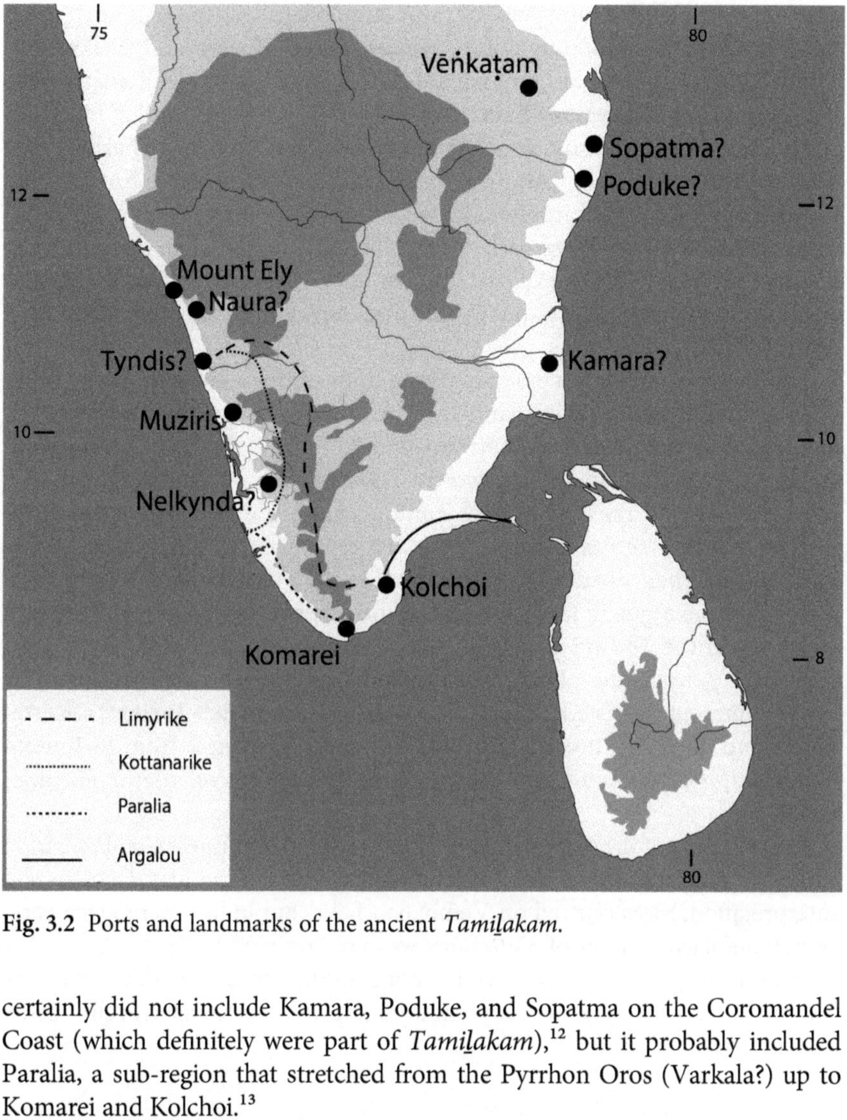

Fig. 3.2 Ports and landmarks of the ancient *Tamiḻakam.*

certainly did not include Kamara, Poduke, and Sopatma on the Coromandel Coast (which definitely were part of *Tamiḻakam*),[12] but it probably included Paralia, a sub-region that stretched from the Pyrrhon Oros (Varkala?) up to Komarei and Kolchoi.[13]

Within the Limyrike region, levels of pepper productivity were not even, and one sub-region stood out. As he lists the commodities available for export in the emporia of Limyrike, the author of the *Periplus* specifies that black pepper

[12] Cf. *PME* 60. Quite understandably, Western merchants excluded from their own notion of Limyrike the section of Indian *Tamiḻakam* that was least familiar to them.

[13] The lacuna at *PME* 58 is probably to be restored *ἄλλη παρήκε<ι> χώρα τῆ<ς αὐτῆς Λιμυρι>κῆς ἥ Παραλία λεγομένη*: see De Romanis (2012b: 337–8).

grew massively 'in the only place of these emporia, called Kottanarike'.[14] Since the demonstrative pronoun points exclusively to Muziris and Nelkynda,[15] which are also emporia of Limyrike, it has to be inferred that Kottanarike was perceived to be a sub-region of Limyrike. Pliny, who does not mention Limyrike, writes that 'the region, from which pepper is conveyed to Becare (Bakare) with dugout canoes, is called Cottonara (Kottanarike)'.[16] Therefore, Kottanarike/Cottonara served as the hinterland for both major coastal emporia, which were 500 stades away from each other. The exceptional pepper productivity of this hinterland region explains the commercial pre-eminence of Muziris and Nelkynda over Naura and Tyndis and, needless to say, any other local coastal sites.

The Kottanarike/Cottonara sub-region draws from a geographical subdivision of the Tamil-speaking land that has its own linguistic markers. The ancient Tamil grammar *Tolkāppiyam* alludes to twelve districts characterized by the use of particular dialectal words. The geographic relationship between these districts and the land of pure Tamil (*centamiḻ*) is not clear. The crucial phrase *centamiḻ cērnta paṉṉiru nilattum* can mean that the land of the *centamiḻ* is either 'divided in' or 'surrounded by' twelve districts. Medieval commentators argue in favour of one or the other interpretation.[17] Although unnamed in the *Tolkāppiyam*, the twelve districts are identified (not always consistently) by medieval commentators. One of the districts mentioned by every commentator is *Kuṭṭam* or *Kuṭṭanāṭu*, from which *Periplus*'s Kottanarike and Pliny's Cottonara apparently derive. 'The people from *Kuṭṭanāṭu* (*Kuṭṭanāṭṭār*), a commentator says, 'call *tāi* (mother) as *taḷḷai* and *nāi* (dog) as *ñeḷḷai*'.[18]

The meaning of the word *kuṭṭam* in Tamil (depth, profundity, tank, pond[19]) makes it certain that the homonymic district (as well as its Greco-Roman interpretations) was centred on Vembanad Lake. But unlike its modern version, the ancient notion of *Kuṭṭanāṭu* was not confined to the lowlands that surround the lake.[20] In fact, while none of the other districts listed by the medieval *Tolkāppiyam* commentators appear to refer specifically to the

[14] *PME* 56: *φέρεται δὲ πέπερι, μονογενῶς ἐν ἑνὶ τόπῳ τούτων τῶν ἐμπορίων γεννώμενον πολύ, λεγομένῃ Κοτταναρικῇ.*

[15] 'These' emporia of *PME* 56 (*τὰ ἐμπόρια ταῦτα . . . τούτων τῶν ἐμπορίων*) are the two emporia of *PME* 55 (*ἀμφοτέρων τῶν ἐμπορίων*), that is, 'Muziris and Nelkynda, which are now the active ones' of *PME* 53 (*Μούζιρις καὶ Νελκύνδα, αἵ νῦν πράσσουσαι*).

[16] Plin., *NH* 6.105.

[17] *Tolkāppiyam* 2.9.883. Cfr. Chevillard (2008); Subbarayalu (2008).

[18] *Tolkappiyum- Collatikaaram- nachinaarkiniyam*, 359–60 Venugopalappillai.

[19] University of Madras Tamil Lexicon, p. 960.

[20] The current notion of *Kuṭṭanāṭu* is basically restricted to the lowlands of the districts of Alappuzha, Pathanamthitta, and Kottayam: Kuttanad Enquiry Commission (1972: 5).

foothills of the Western Ghats east of Vembanad Lake,[21] a few formulae of ancient Tamil poetry show that pepper did commonly grow in the mountains.[22] Moreover, Pliny characterizes pepper as a woodland product (*silvestre*),[23] and specifies that the canoes that conveyed it to Bacare were dugout canoes, which suggests a journey through turbulent upriver currents.[24] Therefore, if pepper grew abundantly only in Kottanarike/Cottonara, then the district must have included the mountainous forests east of Vembanad Lake.

Since pepper collection remained a characteristic of the economy, ecology, and culture of the Western Ghats from ancient times up to the Early Modern era, it may be useful to consider the geography of its production as drawn from a few Early Modern sources.[25] In its review of the different waterways of the Cochin hinterland, the AD 1548 *Livro que trata das cousas da Índia e do Japão* identifies several places that sent pepper to Cochin or elsewhere (Fig. 3.3). They are:

a. Putamguale, which is six or seven leagues up a waterway identified as the Chalakudi River, northeast of Cochin.[26]
b. Belur, on a river that may be identified as the Muvattupuzha River. At the mouth of the river, on the Vembanad Lake, is an island belonging to the lord of Vadakkenkur, significantly (if unceremoniously) called 'the Pepper king'.[27] The river is said to go up towards the highlands for ten or twelve leagues.[28]
c. The customs house of Jumquão Telhado, where several rivers traversing the Thekkenkur kingdom emptied into the southern shore of Vembanad Lake.[29]

[21] Adjoining *Kuṭṭanāṭu* on the west were the districts of *Teṉpāṇṭināṭu* and *Paṉ ṟināṭu*, on the other side of the Western Ghats: see Chevillard (2008); Subbarayalu (2008).

[22] *kaṟi vaḷar aṭukkattu, kaṟi vaḷar cilampin, kaṟi ivar cilampin* (in the mountain side where the pepper grows, the mountain side covered by pepper): *Aiṅkurunūru* 243.1; *Akanāṉūṟu* 2.6; 112.14; *Kalittokai* 52.17; *Kuṟuntokai* 90.2; 288.1; *Naṟṟiṇai* 151.7; *Puṟanāṉūṟu* 168.2. Cf. also *Maturaikkāñci* 289–90: *iñci mancaḷ paiṅkaṟi piṟavum/palvēṟu tāramoṭu kallakattu īṇṭi* (ginger, turmeric, green pepper, and other things, with many kinds of goods do grow luxuriant in the mountain). Black pepper can grow from sea level to 1,200 m: Morrison (2002: 119).

[23] Plin., *NH* 12.29.

[24] I owe this remark to Sundeep Abraham. The dugout canoes (*monoxylae lintres*) mentioned at Plin., *NH* 6.105 seem to be different from the simple *lintres* that bring cargoes to and from the ocean-going vessels (Plin., *NH* 6.104). The latter are called 'backwater boats' (*kaḻittōṇi*) at *Puṟanāṉūṟu* 343.6.

[25] Cf. Malekandathil (2001: 40–7).

[26] *Cousas da India* 45–6.

[27] As far as I know, the earliest document to mention the formulae *rey de Pimenta* and *reyno da Pimenta* is dated 1546: *DUP* VII 289–91.

[28] *Cousas da India* 46.

[29] *Cousas da India* 46. The word *jumquão* means 'customs house', cf. *giunconi* in Sassetti, 476.

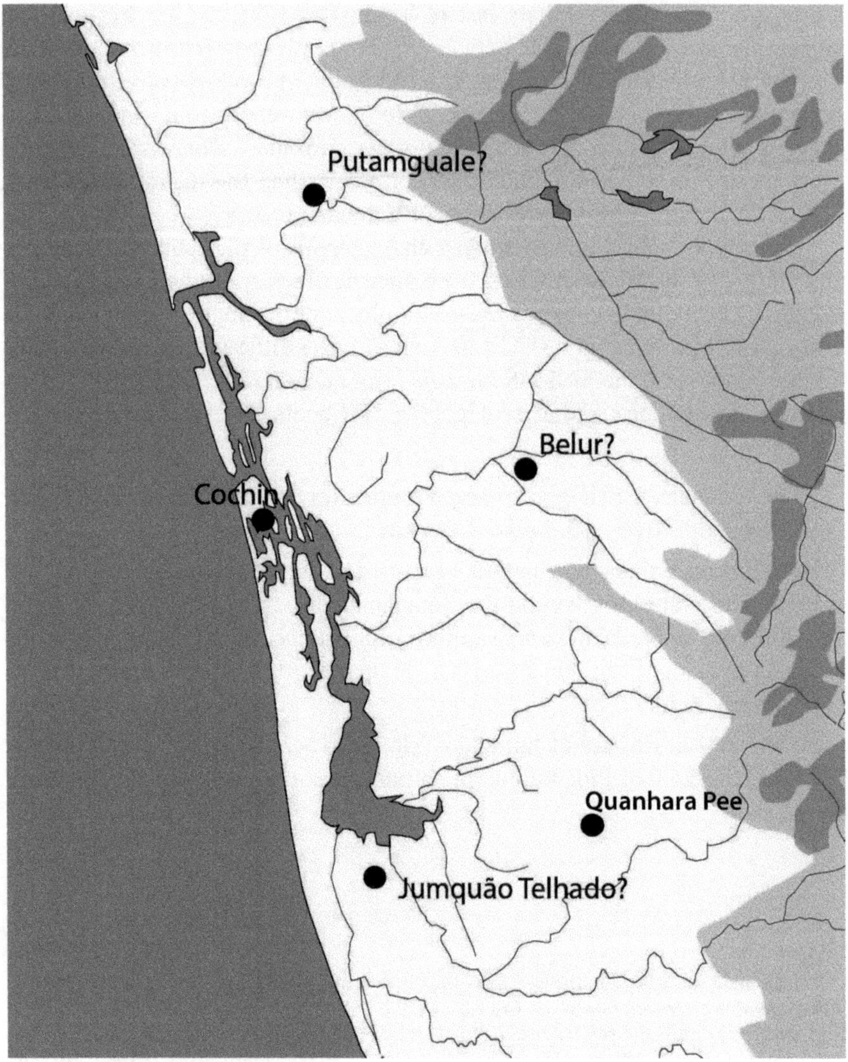

Fig. 3.3 Pepper trade centres according to *Cousas da India e do Japão* (AD 1548).

d. Quanhara Pee (Canharapely, Kanjirappally), in the Thekkenkur kingdom, 22 or 23 leagues from Cochin, at whose monthly fair considerable quantities of pepper were sold and transported inland by oxen.[30]

Other precious, if partial, indications come from a notation added in a margin of a page of Francisco da Costa's manuscript *Relatório sobre o trato da pimenta* (1607). It lists six toponyms (Fig. 3.4), which are followed by weight

[30] *Cousas da India* 47.

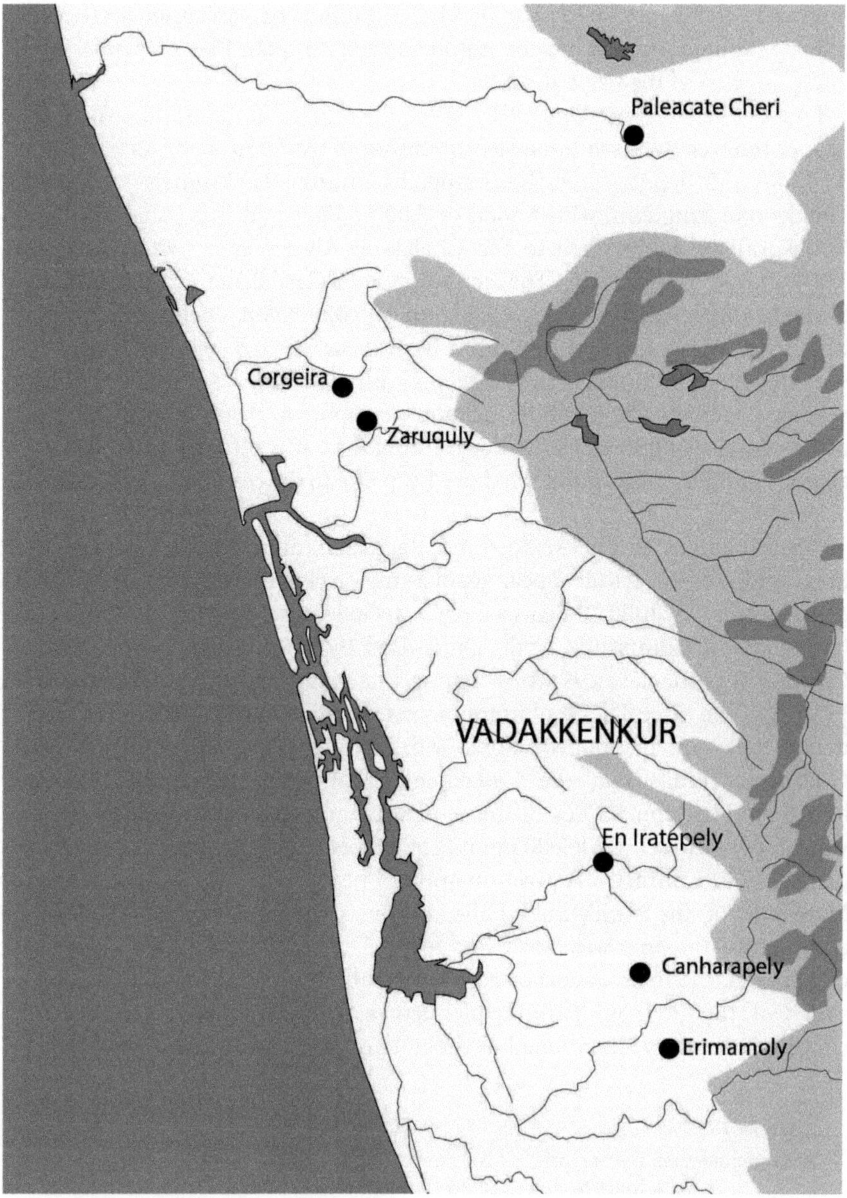

Fig. 3.4 Pepper collection/trade centres according to a note in da Costa's *Relatório* (AD 1607).

numbers totalling 19,000 *bahar* or 61,453 *quintais de pezo pequeno* (*c.*3,158 tons).[31] Apparently, the weight numbers refer to quantities of pepper produced in each of the listed districts.

Five of the six toponyms either coincide with or are close to two of the pepper trade centres mentioned by the author of the *Livro que trata das cousas da Índia e do Japão*: three (Kanjirappally, Erattupetta, Erumely) are in the Thekkenkur kingdom, with a total of 8,000 *bahar*, and two (Chalakudi and Kodakara) are in or close to the Chalakudi River Valley, with 5,000 and 3,000 *bahar,* respectively. The sixth toponym—Palakkad Churam, in the Ponnani River Valley, with a production of 3,000 *bahar*—belongs to an area which was not connected to Cochin by waterways, and for this reason was probably not mentioned in the *Livro que trata das cousas da Índia e do Japão*. Strangely enough, the notation includes no toponym from the Vadakkenkur principality, also known as the Pepper kingdom. It is difficult to explain this absence, but it is most unlikely to have been due to the cessation of production or collection.

The kingdoms of Thekkenkur and Vadakkenkur and the Chalakudi and Ponnani River Valleys all appear again as major pepper producers in the 1743 *Memorandum* by Julius Valentyn Stein Van Gollenesse, the VOC's (Vereenigde Oost-Indische Compagnie, or the Dutch East India Company) commander of Cochin. In particular, it is worth noting that Kanjirappally, Erattupetta, and Erumely—the three Thekkenkur toponyms recorded in the note on da Costa's manuscript—are mentioned, along with Irruny, as pepper bazaars.[32] Van Gollenesse recalls that the Vadakkenkur kingdom, whose 'well-known' bazaar of Thodupuzha lies in the upper valley of the Muvattupuzha River, was supposed to sell 1,000,000 pounds of pepper to the company each year, as per the 1740 contract.[33] A great quantity of pepper was also produced in the highlands of the Anjikaimal Hills, in the Chalakudi River Valley area, although that pepper was never sold to the Dutch, allegedly due to logistical constraints.[34] Pepper was exported from Peratbiddy (Perattuviti) in the upper valley of the Ponnani River, which corresponds to the Paleacate Cheri (Palakkad Churam) mentioned in the note on da Costa's manuscript.[35]

[31] Costa 315:

'Nos tecanqutes em Canharapely	4,000 bares; (Kanjirappally)
En Iratepely	1,000 » (Erattupetta)
Erimamoly	3,000 » (Erumely)
Zaruquly	5,000 » (Chalakudy)
Corgeira	3,000 » (Kodakara)
Paleacate Cheri	3,000 » (Palakkad Churam)
	19,000

São 61 mil 453 quintaes de pezo pequeno.'

[32] Gollenesse 57. Already by 1548, Kanjirappally hosted a monthly pepper fair; see p. 90.

[33] Gollenesse 58–9. [34] Gollenesse 61. [35] Gollenesse 60.

The comparison between the *Livro que trata das cousas da Índia e do Japão*, the notation in da Costa's *Relatório*, and Van Gollenesse's *Memorandum* reveals that the geographic scope of Kerala's pepper production remained basically unchanged from the sixteenth to the eighteenth century. The production that supplied the emporia of Limyrike in the mid-first century AD may have had a similar geography. While the minor emporion of Tyndis received the pepper harvested in Palakkad, Muziris served as the collection point for pepper coming via the Chalakudi and Muvattupuzha Rivers, and Nelkynda/Bakare was the terminus for pepper arriving from Thekkenkur via the rivers further south (Meenachil, Manimala, Pamba, and Achankovil).

3.2. MALE, THE NORTHERN PEPPER-PRODUCING LAND

The phrase used by the author of the *Periplus* to characterize pepper production in the Kottanarike sub-region (*πέπερι μονογενῶς ἐν ἑνὶ τόπῳ τούτων τῶν ἐμπορίων γεννώμενον πολύ*) may be properly translated: 'the pepper that grows *in abundance uniquely* in this one place of these emporia, called Kottanarike.'[36] The recognition that production was nowhere as substantial as in Kottanarike carries the obvious implication that limited quantities of pepper were available outside this sub-region. It seems unlikely that the less copious pepper was long pepper exported from Barygaza, or black pepper exported from Indian regions not mentioned in the *Periplus*. It is more likely that the pepper production of Kottanarike was compared to that of other sub-regions of Limyrike, such as the hinterlands of Naura and Tyndis. The contrasting potential of Naura and Tyndis with respect to Muziris and Nelkynda may be estimated by drawing on details from the above-mentioned marginal note in da Costa's *Relatório*. The note assigns 3,000 *bahar* to Paleacate Cheri (the hinterland of Tyndis), 8,000 *bahar* to Zaruquly and Corgeira (part of the hinterland of Muziris), and 8,000 *bahar* to Kanjirappally, Erattupetta, and Erumely (part of the hinterland of Nelkynda). Moreover, Muziris and Nelkynda were also largely supplied by the Muvattupuzha River region (the Pepper kingdom), whose production the note does not calculate. In conclusion, one may suggest that at the time of the *Periplus* the total production of Limyrike was between 4,000 and 5,000 tons, and that 80 per cent of whatever was exported passed through Muziris and Nelkynda, the remaining 20 per cent through Naura and Tyndis.

[36] Casson's translation ('grown for the most part in only one place connected with these ports of trade, that called Kottanarikê') overstates *πολύ*.

By the sixth century AD and for several centuries afterwards, the western pursuit of black pepper shifted further north, to a section of India's west coast that was unknown to either the author of the *Periplus* or Ptolemy. Since their earliest appearances, the forms of the choronym that eventually resolved as 'Malabar' have been closely interwoven with the history of the pepper trade. The connection is so close that not only was the notion of Malabar often glossed in Arabic geographical literature as *bilād al-fulful* (the Pepper Country), but even its northern boundary shifted southwards, in keeping with the southern relocation of pepper emporia from Late Middle Ages to Early Modern times.

While listing the Christian communities of India or the commercial partners of Taprobane (Fig. 3.5),[37] Cosmas Indicopleustes characterizes Male (one of the forms that preceded the name Malabar) as the region in 'which pepper grows'. More specifically, in presenting the 'splendid' emporia of India, he refers to Male as the region having the five emporia that 'pour' pepper (*πέντε ἐμπόρια ἔχουσα βάλλοντα τὸ πέπερι*):

> The splendid emporia of India are as follows: Sindu, Orrotha, Kalliana, Sibor, Male, with five emporia exporting pepper: Parti, Mangaruth, Salopatana, Nalopatana, Pudapatana. From there about five full days' sail from the mainland in the Ocean lies Sielediba, i.e. Taprobane (Sri Lanka). Then further on from there towards the interior on the mainland lies the port of Marallo, which exports shells, and Kaber, exporting alabandine; then, next after that, the clove country, and finally Tzinista which exports silk. Beyond this, there is no other country.[38]

Cosmas' overview tabulates the emporia in periplographic order—that is, as they came into sight to a ship sailing along the coasts of India, starting from the Indus delta (Sindu) and ending with the Kaveri delta on the Coromandel coast. Quite understandably, Taprobane is inserted between the emporia of the west and east coasts, whereas the clove country and Tzinista (China) are added after Kaber.[39]

Several differences may be noted between the geography of the trade presented by the *Periplus* and that outlined by Cosmas. For instance, Cosmas does not mention Barygaza, which was a thriving transoceanic emporion in the *Periplus*. Conversely, Kalliena, which was merely a local emporion in the

[37] Cosm. Indic. 3.65; 11.15.

[38] Cosm. Indic. 11.16; transl. by D. P. M. Weerakkody, with modifications. In Cosm. Indic. 11.22, the king of Male is mentioned among the rulers of India who own 500–600 captive elephants.

[39] Kalliana (the Kalliena of *PME* 52–3) is Kalyāṇa (for its bishop, Cosm. Indic. 3.65); Orrotha is Sorath, Suraṭh(ṭh)a, Suraṣṭra, (cf. Syrastrene in *PME* 41, 44). Sibor (the Sindābūr of the Arab geographers) is Chandrapura/Chandor, south of Goa: see Moraes (1931). Of the other emporia, Sindu is at the Indus' mouths; Taprobane is Sri Lanka; Marallo (the Malāyūfatan of the *Nūr al-ma'ārif*, cf. Lambourn 2008: 90) is Maraikayar Paṭṭinam, in the Gulf of Mannar; Kaber (Ptolemy's *Χαβηρὶς ἐμπόριον Geog.* 7.1.13, Pukār/Kāviripūmpaṭṭinam), is at the mouth of the Kaveri River.

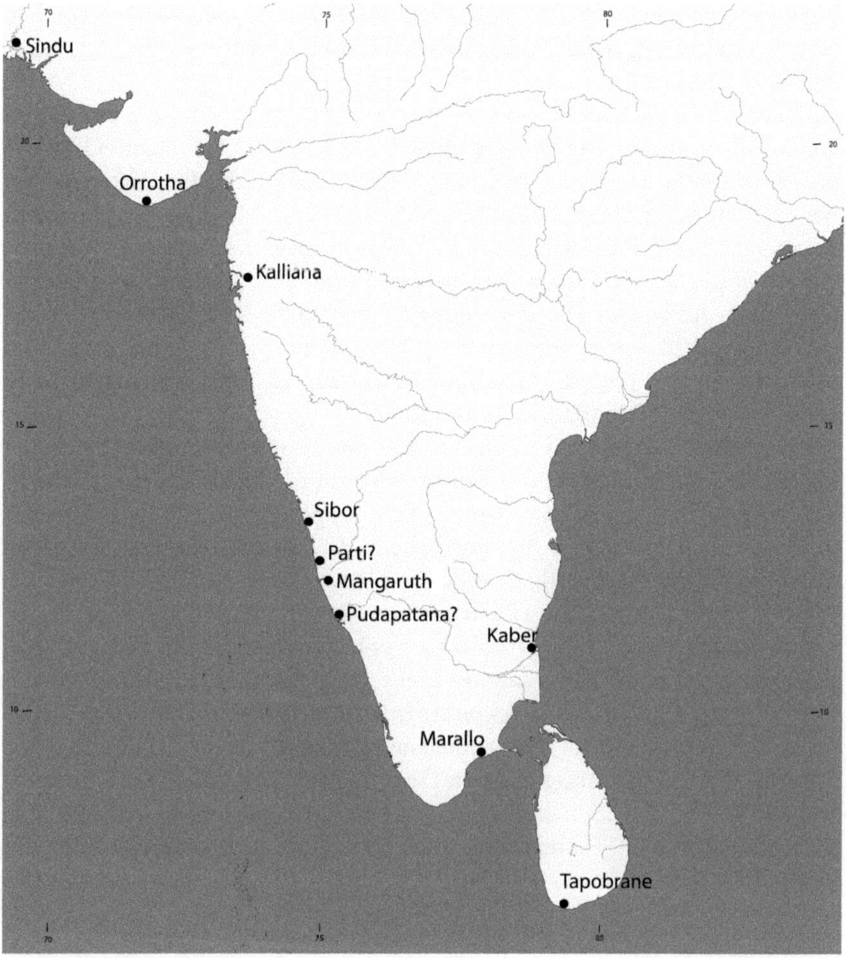

Fig. 3.5 Cosmas Indicopleustes' splendid emporia of India.

Periplus, is in Cosmas the only splendid emporion between Orrotha and Sibor, and the seat of a Christian bishop. This discrepancy is not difficult to explain. Geographically speaking, Barygaza and Kalliena related to different hinterlands and inland trade networks: the former was naturally connected with the upper valley of the Narmadā, Ujjayinī, and the Himālayas, whereas the latter was linked, through the Nānāghāṭ pass, to Paiṭhan and *Dakṣiṇāpatha*. However, as far as maritime trade was concerned, the two ports were in competition with one another. At the time of the *Periplus*, Sandanes, apparently a local ruler subservient to Nahapāna, banned all transoceanic trade from

Kalliena—every western ship that landed there was escorted to Barygaza.[40] In Late Antiquity, the growth of the splendid emporia Orrotha and Kalliana led to Barygaza's decline.

Other discrepancies between the *Periplus* and Cosmas' work are more striking. Cosmas positions the Male region between Sibor and Taprobane. Of its five pepper emporia, the first mentioned, Parti, could be the Bārahakanyāpura/Barakanur/Fāknūr of the Arab geographers, or near it.[41] Mangaruth, the second mentioned, is certainly Mangalore (Manğūr/Manğarūr/Manğalūr).[42] The last emporion mentioned, Pudapatana, may be confidently identified with Budfattan.[43] It is likely that the five *emporia* were listed sequentially along the coastline, just like other trade centres. Thus we may assume that the coastal extent of Cosmas' Male began around 60 kilometres north of Mangalore and ended roughly 130 kilometres to the south.

Male's pepper emporia were around 200–400 kilometres north of the region that at the time of the *Periplus* (and probably of the Muziris papyrus as well) was considered the only place where black pepper grew abundantly. Cosmas mentions no emporion on the coast where Muziris and Nelkynda had been. The obvious inference is that, some time between the second and the sixth centuries AD, there was a drastic reconfiguration in the Roman pepper trade.

Future archaeological investigations may help clarify the chronology of this turn. For the time being, we can just point out that while the Valluvally hoard (terminus post quem AD 155) confirms Muziris' pre-eminence in the mid-second century AD,[44] the new arrangement centred on the Canarese region (and based on a multi-stage sea route) seems to be mirrored by the (presumed) location and composition of the Akki Alur and Mangalore hoards.[45] Although the solidi found at Puthenkavu show that ancient Kottanarike was still

[40] *PME* 52. [41] Nainar (1942: 33–4); Lambourn (2008: 88).

[42] Nainar (1942: 61); Lambourn (2008: 88).

[43] Nainar (1942: 29); Lambourn (2008: 87). There is little ground for the identification of Pudapatana with the site of Pattanam, cf. Malekandathil (2015: 360–1, n. 69). The ending -*patana* of the place name (<Dravidian *paṭṭiṉam*, maritime town, small town) is hardly significant, given its ubiquity along the South Indian coasts. Nor can Cosmas' Pudupatana be identified with Palaipatmai of *PME* 53. Besides, it is difficult to decide whether Palaipatmai of the *Periplus* has to be identified with Ptolemy's Balepatma (*Geog.* 7.1.6), with the consequence that either the former or the latter has been misplaced with respect to Mandagora.

[44] The hoard may have comprised more than 1,000 aurei. Of the 314 specimens seen by Berghaus (252 were recovered by the police: Sathyamurty (1992); Berghaus (1992: 231–2; 241; 1994)), six were of Nero, seven of Vespasian, two of Domitian, two of Nerva, twenty-seven of Trajan, ninety-six of Hadrian, 172 of Antoninus Pius, and two were imitations combining two different emissions of Antoninus Pius: Berghaus (1994: 33–4).

[45] For the Akki Alur hoard, three Severan aurei and forty-three solidi (latest emperor, Justin I), some of them Indian imitations: Gupta (1984); Turner (1989: 48); Berghaus (1991: 110); (1993: 307); Day (2012); Darley (2013: 409–36). The twenty-one solidi (latest emperor, Anastasius) and twenty-three Axumite gold coins (latest king, Ezanas) sold in Mangalore were probably found not far from the place where they were bought: Nawartmal and Nawartmal (1998: 52). For single finds of solidi at Kulathupalayam, Mercara, and Shimoga, see Walburg (2008: 276–7).

somehow integrated in the network of the transoceanic trade at the beginning of the sixth century,[46] the scarcity of Late Antique ʿAqaba pottery at Pattanam suggests that its position was now peripheral.[47] The main pepper supplier for the West was Male, the region around Mangalore.

After Cosmas, the connection between a region called anything close to 'Male' and the pepper trade recurs throughout the Middle Ages. The sources are not, however, unanimous regarding the geographic extent of the choronym. The Malay of the *Ḥudūd al-ʿālam*, the Maliyār of Yāqūt, and the Melibar of Marco Polo all coincide with Cosmas' limited notion of Male.[48] But while it is not clear whether Mulay in Ibn Ḫurradāḏbih and 'Munaybar, the pepper country' in a Genizah papyrus, have the same restricted notion,[49] we can be certain that the region named Malī in the *Aḫbār al-Ṣīn wa 'l-Hind*, Malībār in al-Bīrūnī (Rashīd al-Dīn Ṭabīb) and Wassaf, and Manībār in al-Dimašqī, Abū al-Fidāʾ, and Ibn Baṭūṭah extend as far as Kūlam (Quilon, Kollam).[50]

Whether they restrict Malabar to the Mangalore region or extend it down to Kūlam, the Arab geographers mention no transoceanic emporion in the region of the Periyar delta and Vembanad Lake.[51] Situated in that area,[52] Šinkli and Kunjākarī may have hosted merchants as distinguished as Īssuppu Irappān (Joseph Rabban), honoured in the eleventh century AD by the Muyirikkōḍe ruler Bhāskara Ravivarma,[53] but these sites did not acquire the same prominence as Muziris in Ancient or Cochin in Early Modern times. They never functioned as transoceanic emporia. Their commercial function was to forward to other South Indian emporia a portion of the pepper harvested in ancient Kottanarike. This was the situation witnessed by the Chinese Ma Huan during his visit to Cochin in AD 1433.[54] The 'foreign merchants' who came there to buy 'the pepper stored by the big pepper collectors' were mostly traders based in Calicut, because it was from Calicut that ten to

[46] Aravamuthan (1942: 47) mentions a batch of six solidi (out of a hoard of about fifty) which closes with Justinus I; for a Theodosius' solidus found near Kottayam, see Walburg (2008: 276).

[47] Tomber (2015: 384); Tomber (2017b: 324; 375).

[48] *Ḥudūd al-ʿālam* 10.13; Yāqūt, 1.506; 4.639; Polo, *Divisament* 180; 183 (= *Milione* 176; 179) where Coilun is distinct from Melibar.

[49] Ibn Ḫurradāḏbih, 62 (Engl. transl. 5); Goitein and Friedman (2008: 172). The merchants of the Genizah papyri did business in Manǧarūr and nearby ports such as Sindābūr, Fandarayna, Dahbattan, Fāknūr, and Jurbatan: Goitein (1987: 457; 459); Goitein and Friedman (2008: 332; 337; 564; 477; 598–9; 623–5; 633; 636; 642); as well as in Kūlam: Goitein and Friedman (2008: 127; 160; 382).

[50] *Aḫbār al-Ṣīn wa 'l-Hind* 1.4.2; al-Bīrūnī quoted by Rašīd al-Dīn Ṭabīb apud Elliot and Dowson (1867/1877: 1.68); Wassaf apud Elliot and Dowson (1867/1877: 3.31); al-Dimašqī, 173; Abū al-Fidāʾ, 354–5 (Fr. transl. 115–6); Ibn Baṭūṭah, 4.71; 99–100 (Engl. tr. 181; 193).

[51] Ducène (2016).

[52] Rašīd al-Dīn Ṭabīb and al-Dimašqī, above n. 50; Abū al-Fidāʾ, 355; Ibn Baṭūṭah, 4.99.

[53] Hultzsch (1894/1895); Narayanan (2013: 88; 152; 277; 451–2). Muyirikkōḍe = Muyiri (< Muciṟi, Muziris) + kōḍe (fort).

[54] Ma Huan, 135.

fifteen ships with 1,000–1,200 *bahar* (*c.*170–200 tons) of cargo, mainly black pepper, were sent annually to Aden or Jeddah.[55] The Portuguese were quick to notice the geographic disconnect between the major pepper-trade centre—the port of Calicut—and the major pepper production area. A short visit to Cochin during the voyage of Pedro Álvares Cabral (1500/1) revealed that the pepper exported from Calicut actually came from Cochin.[56] The hinterland of Cochin—ancient Kottanarike—appeared once again to be the only region of India where black pepper grew abundantly.

The pivotal role thereafter assumed by Cochin reshaped the geographic notion of Malabar. The choronym, which up until then had designated either the Mangalore region or the entire south-western coast of India from Hannaur (Onor) to Kūlam, came to mean the coast from Cumbola (north of Cannanore) to Cape Comorin, ironically excluding Cosmas' Male.[57]

3.3. EARLY MODERN QUANTITATIVE DIMENSIONS

The emphasis placed by the author of the *Periplus* on Kottanarike's pepper production may be better understood if we compare it to Early Modern estimates of South Indian pepper productivity.

We may set aside the startling amounts of 300,000 *quintais* (15,420 tons) reported by Ferdinand Cron as the export to Tartaria, Arabia, Persia, the Mughal Empire, Pegu (Bago, Myanmar), the Strait of Malacca, and China,[58] and the 100,000 *bahar* (16,620 tons) that, according to Francisco da Costa, was the production of all South India, from Onor to Travancor, estimated by unspecified *Malavares*.[59] There is no need to emphasize the fact that nobody could have had comprehensive knowledge of what was produced or exported from such vast geographic contexts. Moreover, both figures seem to have been generated by the same round weight number (one lakh *bahar*) that was apparently repeated by the locals in their boastful claims. More circumscribed and reliable estimates never indicate anything less than 10,000 *bahar* (1,662 tons) as the quantity theoretically exportable from the Cochin hinterland (which broadly corresponds to ancient Kottanarike), nor do they point to an overall production for Kerala greater than 30,000 *bahar* (4,986 tons).[60]

[55] Barbosa, 160–1 (Engl. transl. 2.76–7).

[56] Letter of D. Manuel, 16. Cf. also Quirini, 9–10; *CAA* 2.41.

[57] Barbosa, 118, (Engl. transl. 2.1–2).

[58] Letter dated 26 December 1587 from Cochin, mss.cod. 46.1, f. 51v in Fürstlich und Gräflich Fuggersches Familien und Stiftungs Archiv.

[59] Costa, 350–1.

[60] In the sixteenth-century Portuguese documents, pepper is measured either in the *bahar* of Cochin and Quilon (166.272 kg) or in *quintais do peso velho* (51.4 kg): Lima Felner (1868: 47); Bouchon (1977: ix).

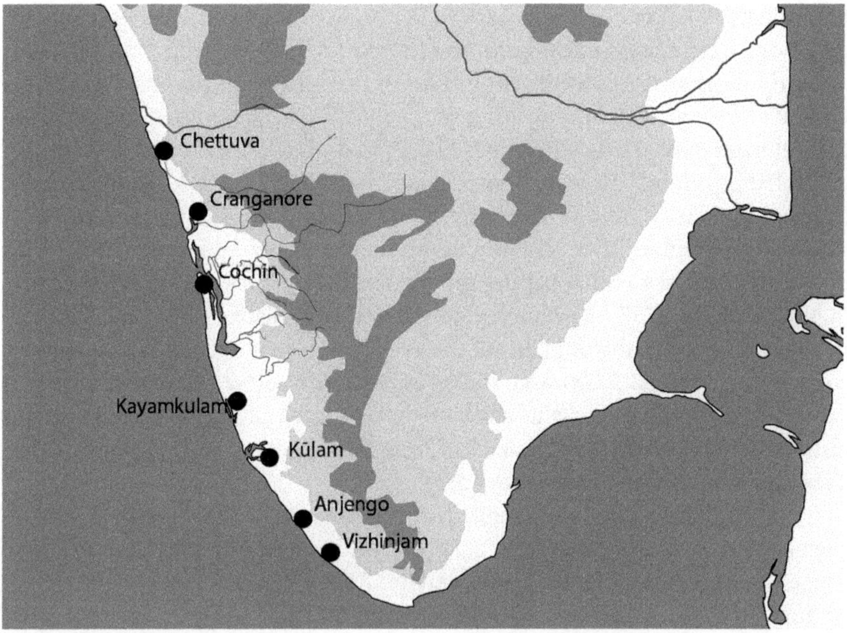

Fig. 3.6 Landmarks for Portuguese pepper productivity estimates.

In 1504, Álvaro Vaz estimated that as many as 30,000 *quintais* (1,542 tons) could be exported from Cochin and Kūlam together (20,000 and 10,000 *quintais*, respectively).[61] Basically the same quantity is indicated in 1506 or a little later by Leonardo da Ca' Masser (10,000 *bahar*, or 30,000–35,000 *cantara* exportable from Cochin) and Vincenzo Quirini (35,000 *cantara* harvested in the mountains east of Cochin).[62] In 1511, Tomé Pires, overseer of drugs (*feitor das drogarias*) in Cannanore, estimated that 20,000 *bahar* (3,324 tons) of pepper was produced annually between Chettuva and Kayamkulam (Fig. 3.6).[63] In 1520, Nuno de Castro gives as his own estimate 15,000–16,000 *bahar* (2,493–2,695 tons) collected from the region between Vizhinjam and Cranganore, apart from 2,000–3,000 *bahar* left over from the previous year's haul. But he adds that local merchants maintained that not 16,000

[61] *CAA* 3.258.

[62] Ca' Masser, 33; Quirini, 9–10. However, it should be noted that neither da Ca' Masser nor Quirini mentions Kūlam as a centre for pepper export.

[63] Pires 2.362 (Engl. transl. 1.82). Probably directly inspired by Pires' are the estimates by Francisco de Albuquerque in 1518 (Aubin 1974: 194) and the anonymous author of a 1568 *relação* (Wicki 1961: 155).

but in fact 20,000 *bahar* was produced.[64] It may be noted that the year before de Castro's estimate, 56,000 *quintais* (*c.*17,300 *bahar*) of pepper and 20,000 *quintais* of other spices were sent to Lisbon in fourteen ships—two loaded in Calicut, three in Kūlam, and nine in Cochin.[65] The quantities recorded in the notation to da Costa's *Relatório* (1607) add up to a total of 19,000 *bahar*, or 61,453 *quintais.*[66] However, since the un-estimated Vadakkenkur production could hardly be less than the 8,000 *bahar* assigned to the adjacent Thekkenkur region, it is fair to assume that whoever added that note was estimating central Kerala's pepper production to be no less than 27,000 *bahar* (4,487 tons). In 1757, the Dutch Commission of Malabar estimated that the pepper produced in the domains of the Travancore Raja Martanda Varma was somewhere between 8,000 and 10,000 *candies* (*c.*2,150–2,700 tons).[67] In the same year, John Spencer, the chief of the English trading post at Anjengo, claimed to have ascertained that 11,752 *candies* of pepper were bought by the Travancore administration—about 3,200 tons.[68]

If central Kerala could be credited with a potential of more than 3,000 or even 4,000 tons of pepper (Fig. 3.7), the indications for Canarese exports suggest a much lower level of productivity. At the beginning of the sixteenth century, da Ca' Masser and Quirini estimated the pepper that could be exported from Batac(h)ala at 1,000 *bahar* and 3,000 *cantera*, respectively (*c.*166 tons)—only 10 per cent of the quantity they predicted could be exported from Cochin.[69] During the last decades of the sixteenth century, the Portuguese exploited the Canarese resources more systematically.[70] Yet the volumes estimated or actually exported remained far below Cochin's potential. Jan Huyghen van Linschoten, who was in India between 1583 and 1589, wrote that the Portuguese had only recently started to export 7,000 or 8,000 *quintais* (*c.*360 or 411 tons) from Onor every year.[71] The quantity is more than double the 1,000 *bahar*/3,000 *cantara* estimated by da Ca' Masser and Quirini as the Batachala export at the beginning of the century, but it is still dramatically smaller than the 61,453 *quintais* recorded in da Costa's *Relatório* as the total combined production from six places in central Kerala—none of which

[64] *CAA* 7.175–6. Unlike De Romanis (2015a: 128–9; 137), I now consider as parts of the estimated total production (15,000 to 16,000 *bahar*) the quantities itemised as consumed in the same land (2,000–2,500 *bahar*), as exported either overland (3,000 *bahar*) or by sea (500–600 *bahar*), and as remnants (9,000 *bahar*). On the other hand, I consider as not included in that amount the 2,000–3,000 *bahar* that are set apart to become old.

[65] 'A mór carga que se nunqua fez': Correa, 2.2.561.

[66] See p. 92 n. 31.

[67] Nationaal Archief, Den Haag, Verenigde Oostindische Compagnie (VOC), nummer toegang 1.04.02, inventarisnummer 2928, Scans 341–2 (25 October 1758). I assume that the *candy* referred to is the one of 597 lbs. 8 oz. For the metrology of Travancore's Sircar, cf. Kelly (1832: 143).

[68] Buchanan, 2.457. Again, I assume a *candy* of 597 lbs. and 8 oz.

[69] Ca' Masser, 35 (308 r); Quirini, 9.

[70] Godinho (1982–1983: 3.33–7).

[71] Linschoten, 1.66.

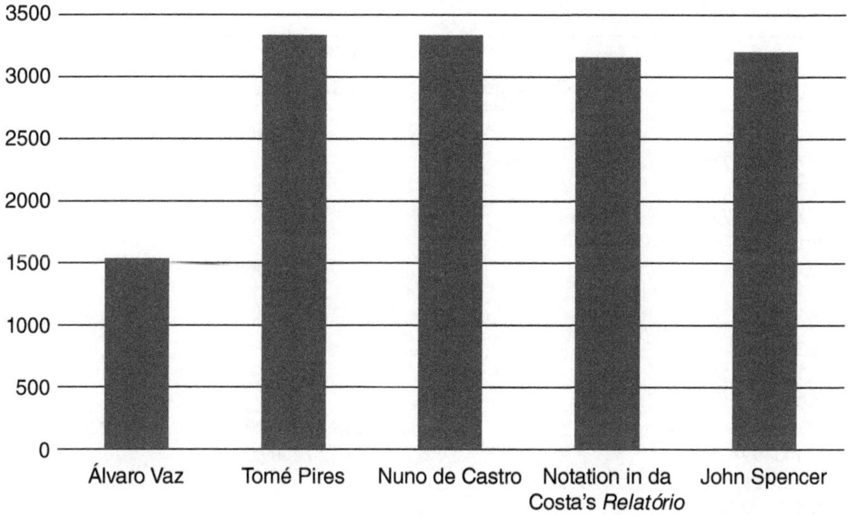

Fig. 3.7 Early Modern estimates or partial data regarding South Malabar's pepper productivity (in tons).

belonged to the 'Pepper Kingdom' (Vadakkenkur). The export from the Canarese region never reached the magnitudes of the Cochin hinterland: from 1612 to 1634, it never surpassed 12,000 heavy quintals (*c.*705 tons), and sometimes was even less than 2,000 (*c.*117 tons).[72]

A detail suggests that the two regions showed the same disparity in ancient times: while pepper was conveyed to Kottanarike's emporia with the typical dugout canoes,[73] Cosmas' reference to buffaloes loaded with saddlebags full of pepper signals the more laborious logistics of the Male emporia.[74]

3.4. ANCIENT PRICES

Over a time span that ranges from the first to the sixth centuries AD, two different patterns emerge in the history of the pepper trade. In the first and second centuries AD, pepper was exported from Kottanarike on very large pepper carriers that sailed all the way from Egypt to India and back. In Late Antiquity, the supply region was the less productive Male area, and the logistics were characterized by a multi-stage sea route travelled (especially in the Red Sea leg) by smaller ships. Did this change have any impact on the way

[72] Disney (1978: 162). [73] Plin., *NH* 6.105. [74] Cosm. Indic. 11.3.

Table 3.1 Gold : pepper ratios.

	Pepper (drachmae per lb.)	Gold (drachmae per lb.)	Ratio gold: pepper
Plin., *NH* 12.28	16	4,500	1 : 281.25
P. Oxy. 54.3731 AD 310/1	6,000		≥ 1 : 288
P. Oxy. 54.3733 AD 25.5.312			
P. Oxy. 43.3121 AD 316–8		1,728,000	
PSI 7.825 AD 325–30		14,400,000	≈ 1 : 200
P. Oxy. 54.3766 AD 329	72,000		
P. Oxy. 51.3628–33 AD 400–99		10,944,000,000 11,520,000,000	≈ 1 : 228 / 1 : 240
CPR 7.42 AD 400–99	48,000,000		≈ 1 : 288
P.Thomas 26 AD 450–75?		13,824,000,000	

pepper circulated inside the Roman Empire? In other words, did pepper grow more expensive in Late Antiquity?

The ratio of pepper to gold in Late Antiquity may be approximated through the few data related to market prices in fourth- and fifth-century Egypt tabulated in Table 3.1.[75] The prices declared by the *myropolai* of Oxyrhynchus in AD 310/1 and 312 (*P. Oxy.* 54.3731; 3733), combined with the market price for gold of 316–17 (*P. Oxy.* 43.3121), give the ratio 1 : 288; this may be taken as the lowest limit, because it is likely that the pepper price went up between AD 312 and 317. The price declared by the same *myropolai* in AD 329, compared with the market price for gold sometime between AD 325 and 330, suggests a ratio of around 1 : 199.5. The fifth-century price of *CPR* 7.42 gives a ratio fluctuating between 1 : 228 and 1 : 240 with the gold prices recorded in *P.Oxy.* 51.3628–33, and 1 : 288 in combination with the gold price attested in *P.Thomas* 26. In conclusion, it seems that, in Egypt, during the fourth and fifth centuries AD, the price for a pound of pepper fluctuated between one-third and one-fourth of a solidus.

The Late Antique ratios for gold to pepper are either slightly lower or remarkably higher than that implied by Pliny's price of four denarii per

[75] I leave aside the gold-to-pepper ratio that may be inferred from Diocletian's Price Edict, because the price of gold is artificially low: see Bagnall (1989: 69–70); Lo Cascio (1993: 160–4). On the price in *PSI* 7.825, see Bagnall (1985: 34, n.23). The fiscal values of the Muziris papyrus and the Coptic papyrus *B.M. Or.* inv. 8903 will be considered later on, see pp. 291–4.

pound (1 : 281.25).[76] However, since Pliny is probably referring to the usual price in Rome, which included the customs duties and the transport costs from Egypt to Rome, as well as the profit margins along the road, it may be suggested that the general level of the pepper prices inside the Roman Empire was considerably lower in the first than in the fourth or fifth centuries AD. In Julio-Claudian Rome, only in extraordinary circumstances did the cost of a pound of pepper correspond to that of five *modii* of wheat;[77] in Late Antique Egypt, with one-third or one-fourth of a solidus one could have bought two to four artabas (nine to eighteen *modii*) of wheat.[78]

The replacement of Kottanarike with Male as the source of pepper and the transition from the direct to the multi-stage trade route rank high on the list of the factors that may have determined the higher level of pepper prices in Late Antiquity. Significant, in this perspective, is a comparison with the prices of South Arabian and East African commodities, whose trade was less affected by the Late Antique restructuring of the maritime connections between India and Egypt (Table 3.2).

Quantitatively speaking, black pepper and frankincense were the most important spices imported into the Mediterranean from the outer world. This is suggested by a variety of references: the expression *libanotika phortia*

Table 3.2 Prices and fiscal values for some commodities imported from the Indian Ocean.

	Pepper	Frankincense	*Κασία*	Ivory	Malabathron
Pliny den. per lb.	4	6, 4, 3	5–50		60
Muziris pap. dr. per mina	6			100/70	12
PSI 15.1558 dr. per mina					150
Edict. de pret. den. per lb.	800	100		150	
P.Oxy. 54.3731den. per lb. (AD 310/1)	1,500	200	375		1,500
P.Oxy. 54.3733 den. per lb. (AD 312)	1,500	200	500		3,000
P.Oxy. 54.3765 tal. per lb. (*c.*AD 327)			6		
P.Oxy. 54.3766 tal. per lb. (AD 329)	12	2			50

[76] Plin., *NH* 12.28. Pliny gives 15 denarii per pound as the price for *piper longum*, 7 denarii per pound as the price for *piper album*, and 4 denarii per pound as the price for *piper nigrum*. However, there is no doubt that the *myropolai* of Oxyrhynchus meant the *piper nigrum*, also known as πέπερι κοινόν (Paulus, *Epit. med.* 7.8.2). Whenever in Greek or Latin texts the simple word πέπερι/*piper* occurs, the *piper nigrum* is intended. *Piper longum* and *piper album*—the former a fruit of a different plant, the latter just *piper nigrum* with the outer layer removed—were much rarer commodities.

[77] Tac., *Ann.* 15.39: see Rathbone (2009: 304).

[78] Carrié (1997: 126).

(meaning spices in general) in Ptolemaic papyri and inscriptions;[79] by the *vici thurarii* ('frankincense seller streets') in Rome and Puteoli;[80] by the label *horrea piperataria* for the 'warehouses of Egyptian and Arabian wares';[81] by the half-pounds of frankincense and pepper presented as *Saturnalia* gifts in Rome;[82] by the sacks of pepper and frankincense represented in a spice seller's funerary monument in Madauros;[83] and by the fourth-century AD declarations of the Oxyrhynchus *myropolai*, in which the prices of black pepper and frankincense are always the first and second prices recorded respectively.[84]

The largest quantities of frankincense mentioned by literary sources include: 1,000 talents sent annually by the Arabs to Darius; 1,000 talents burnt by the Chaldaeans in Babylon; 300 talents burnt by Datis at Delos; 1,000 talents (and 200 talents of *stacte*) given to Antiochus III by the Gerrhaeans; 500 talents (and 100 of myrrh) sent by Alexander to his teacher after the conquest of Gaza; and 50 talents granted to the sophist Hermocrates by Septimius Severus.[85] The largest quantities attested in epigraphic and papyrological evidence are: 10 talents of frankincense (and 1 of myrrh) sent by Seleucus I to the temple of Apollo Didymaeus; 4 talents of Minaean frankincense, 5 of Gerrhaean frankincense, and 1 of myrrh in one of Zenon's commercial papyri; and 30 pounds used at Pompeii for the funeral of M. Obellius Firmus.[86] If pepper was imported in several tens of thousands of talents per year in the first and second centuries AD, the volume of imported frankincense was probably lower, but not dramatically so.

Pliny gives six, five, and three denarii per pound as the price for the frankincense of first, second, and third quality, respectively.[87] We do not know how the three types were selected or in what proportions. We can say, however, that at the time of Pliny frankincense was generally a little more expensive than black pepper or, at the very least, not much less expensive. In Late Antiquity, pepper appears enormously more expensive than frankincense. In Diocletian's Price Edict, 800 denarii is the maximum price for a pound of pepper, whereas only 100 denarii is the maximum price for a pound of frankincense.[88] In the declarations of the Oxyrhynchus *myropolai*, the price of pepper is always considerably higher than that of frankincense: one talent (=1,500 denarii) per pound as opposed to 200 denarii per pound in AD 310/1 and 312, and 12 talents per pound as opposed to 2 in AD 329.[89]

[79] *SB* 3.7176, l.3; 6.9090, *r.* ll.1–2; *v.* l.2; *I.Pan* 86, l.11; cf. also *PSI* 6.628, ll. 3–4: παρὰ Διοδώρου τοῦ ἐπὶ τῆ[ς]|λιβανωτικῆς.

[80] [Ascon.], *ad Cic. II Verr.* 1.154, p. 170 Stangl; Porph., *ad Hor.*, *epist.* 1.20.1; 2.1.269; *ILS* 1224b.

[81] Cass. Dio 72.24.1. [82] Mart. 4.46.7; 7.72.3; 10.57. [83] *ILAlg* 1.2236.

[84] *P.Oxy.* 54.3731; 3733; 3766.

[85] Hdt. 1.183.2; 3.97.5; 6.97.2; Polyb. 13.9.4–5; Plut., *Alex.* 25.6–8; Philostr., *VS* 2.611.

[86] *OGIS* 214; *P.Cair.Zen.* 4.59536; De Franciscis (1976). [87] Plin., *NH* 12.65.

[88] *Edictum de pretiis* 34.10; 68. [89] *P.Oxy.* 54.3731, ll. 9–10; 3733: 9–10; 3766, 84–5.

A similar trend is shown by a comparison with the prices of the East African product κασία.[90] At the time of Pliny, its price varied between 5 and 50 denarii per pound—definitely more expensive than pepper.[91] In the fourth century it was the opposite: the *myropolai* of Oxyrhynchus declare a price of probably 375 denarii per pound in AD 310, 1,500 denarii per pound in AD 312, and 6 talents in *c.*AD 327.[92]

The same can be surmised for ivory. We will see that in the Muziris papyrus the fiscal values for ivory (100 drachmas per mina for the tusks and 70 drachmas for the cuttings) were considerably higher than that for pepper (6 drachmas per mina). While these fiscal values may not be in a fixed ratio with the respective market prices, they certainly imply a hierarchy that sets a higher market price for a mina of ivory than for one of pepper. On the other hand, the Price Edict gives 150 denarii as the maximum price for a pound of ivory and, as mentioned, 800 for a pound of pepper.[93]

Equally affected by the reconfiguration of the trade relationships between the Mediterranean and India, the prices of Indian malabathron tended to remain higher than those of pepper in the fourth century AD. Pliny gives 60 denarii per pound as the price of malabathron leaves, and in third-century AD Egypt, they reached the price of 150 drachmas per mina. The Oxyrhynchus *myropolai* declare prices of 1,500 denarii, 3,000 denarii, and 50 talents per pound in AD 310/1, 312, and 329, respectively.[94]

In retrospect, the relatively low price for pepper in the first and second centuries AD is a testament to the organizational efficiency of the trade system exemplified in the Muziris papyrus. Conversely, the prices of Late Antiquity reflect the reduced supply of the Mangalore region and the indirect connections between Egypt and South India. A reduction in the pepper import also seems to be suggested by the contrasts between the *mation* (3.88 lt = *c.*1.6 kg) sent to an individual in the fort of Didymoi in the first century AD,[95] and the two ounces (53.8 g) requested by a certain Capitolinus from his 'brother'

[90] See p. 68, n. 31. [91] Plin., *NH* 12.97.

[92] *P.Oxy.* 54.3731, l. 18; 3733, l. 17; 3765, l. 37.

[93] *Edictum de pretiis* 16.10a; 34, 68. However, there may have been specific factors that coalesced to determine the low price of ivory in Late Antiquity. If Pliny (*NH* 8.7) is right in claiming that in his own time India was the major supplier of ivory, neither the excellent Adulis (*PME* 6) ivory, nor the abundant, if inferior, Rhapta ivory (*PME* 16; 17), nor any other East African ivory (Ptolemais *ton theron*: *PME* 3; Aualites: *PME* 7; Mosyllon: *PME* 10) was a major Mediterranean import in the mid-first century AD. The potential of the African continent, where both male and female elephants have tusks, was then only marginally exploited. By Late Antiquity, however, the export of African ivory may have substantially increased: *Expositio totius mundi et gentium* 18; Cosm. Indic. 11.23. In general, for ivory sources and availability in Antiquity, see Cutler (1987: 431–3).

[94] Plin., *NH* 12.129; *PSI* 15.1558; *P.Oxy.* 54.3731; 3733; 3766.

[95] *O.Did.* 364, ll. 7–10. Only half a *mation* of salt in *O.Did.* 320; 381.

Sarapammon in the early fourth century;[96] or between the half pounds (161.5 g) casually donated as *Saturnalia* gifts to ordinary *clientes* in Martial's Rome,[97] and the 3,000 pounds that the senatorial households of the city could offer in AD 410 (along with 5,000 pounds of gold, 30,000 pounds of silver, 4,000 silk tunics, and 3,000 scarlet-dyed skins) to appease Alaric and turn him and his Visigoths away.[98] In Pliny's time, senatorial households could definitely have offered much more.

[96] *P.Oxy.* 34.2728, ll. 32–3. For the chronology, see Bagnall (1985: 57, 66). Three ounces of pepper in *P.Ross.Georg.* 3.9, ll. 15–16 (late fourth century); four ounces in *CPR* 7.42 (fifth century); ten peppercorns in *O.Frangé* 101 (eighth century).

[97] Mart. 4.46.7; 10.57.

[98] Zos. 5.41.4. If in early fifth-century Rome the price for pepper was half a solidus per pound (approximately twice the Egyptian price), the value of 3,000 pounds of pepper (1,500 solidi, that is 20.8 pounds of gold) would have been 0.416 per cent of the 5,000 pounds of gold. In the time of Pliny, it would have been 0.21 per cent.

4

South Indian Perspectives

From Antiquity to Early Modernity, South India's pepper trade was built on the geographical and cultural diversity of the communities who made the pepper available for overseas export: the gatherers in the upland forests of the Western Ghats, and the lowland peoples who brought it to the emporia. The otherness of these two groups of people and their relationships are a fascinating, but also extremely difficult, subject of investigation, because the lives of the pepper gatherers have remained almost inaccessible to our sources, whether Indian or foreign, and whether Ancient, Medieval, or Early Modern.[1]

Among the multitude of authors who reported on South Indian pepper, it would be incorrect to claim that no one bothered to explain how the spice was grown and by whom it was gathered. To assert, however, that the documentary corpus clearly explains how a pluri-secular hyper-production of pepper was achieved would be equally inaccurate. Our sources reflect an array of production/collection techniques, which can be confusing. The ecological, cultural, and socio-economic variability within South India gave rise to different patterns of production in different micro-contexts. Travellers who had short-term experiences with a single production style described only the specific realities they encountered. But not all forms of pepper production and collection were associated with transoceanic trade, so it is imperative to discriminate among the different forms reflected in the available sources and to identify the primary productive system.

In addition, it is necessary to investigate how pepper passed from its gatherers to its traders. In a recent book, R. Gurukkal reacted to the widespread tendency to categorize the range of exchanges that produced the transfer of commodities between India and the Roman Empire as 'Indo-Roman trade'.[2] In Gurukkal's view, the term 'Indo-Roman trade' is a misnomer. The complex historical phenomenon to which it usually refers would not be pure 'trade,' if one accepts the comprehensive 'Indo-Roman' qualifier, nor would it be 'Indo-Roman,' if the notion of 'trade' is retained, rather than

[1] Kieniewicz (1986); Prange (2011).   [2] Gurukkal (2016).

The Indo-Roman Pepper Trade and the Muziris Papyrus. Federico De Romanis, Oxford University Press (2020).
 DOI: 10.1093/oso/9780198842347.001.0001

the broader concept of 'exchange.' According to Gurukkal, the contribution from the Indian side was so negligible in terms of trade that even renaming it 'Roman-Indian' would be a misrepresentation. It could not have been proper trade, because the social formations within ancient India—especially in the Tamil south, the focus of Gurukkal's interest—would not have been capable of formalized commercial trade, but only of informal exchanges, at most.

Is this position justified, at least as far as South India is concerned?[3] Did South India provide only natural resources via informal reciprocal exchange systems that never reached the level of trade? Should we talk only of importation from India by Roman traders?

4.1. GATHERERS

From the Middle Ages to Early Modernity, different travellers have left varying reports regarding the means by which Western merchants acquired black pepper. Marco Polo and Giovanni de' Marignolli, for instance, saw pepper vines planted and watered by cultivators in the countryside and in the woods around Kūlam.[4] Ludovico da Varthema reports that pepper grew spontaneously in the vicinity of Calicut and was gathered by the lowly Poliar caste.[5] The late-sixteenth-century English traveller Ralph Fitch writes that around Cochin, pepper grew 'in the fields among the bushes without any labour'.[6] In the hinterland of Battacala, a pepper garden planted within a 'great grove of tall, smalle betelnutt trees, which are orderly sett in ranckes', is described (and drawn) by the seventeenth-century British traveller Peter Mundy (Fig. 4.1).[7] While visiting Calicut's countryside at the very beginning of the nineteenth century, the Scottish physician Francis Buchanan saw homesteads that grew dozens of pepper vines as a complementary crop.[8]

Coming from eyewitnesses, these descriptions are certainly trustworthy. But since they do not refer to the primary source regions for pepper, their value in our quest—to understand how most of the pepper exported in Antiquity was produced—is limited. The small-scale production in Calicut's hinterland made only a modest contribution to the pepper export. The same can be said for the lowlands around Cochin. By contrast, pepper cultivation in Kūlam

[3] The Socotra inscriptions, for which see Strauch (2012), show that Gurukkal's theory does not apply to Barygaza and Hastakavapra.

[4] Polo, *Divis.* 180 = *Mil.* 176; Marignolli, 496. Kūlam's pepper production was estimated at 10,000 *quintais* by Álvaro Vaz in 1504: see p. 99. For Kūlam's pepper woods in the eighteenth century, see p. 111 n.10.

[5] Varthema, li^{v}; lvi^{v}-lvii^{r} (= Engl. transl.142; 157).

[6] Fitch, 188.

[7] Mundy, 3.1.79.

[8] Buchanan, 2.463–5.

Fig. 4.1 Pepper garden drawn by Peter Mundy.
From *The Travels of Peter Mundy in Europe and Asia, 1608–1667*. Courtesy of the Biblioteca della Società Geografica.

was not insignificant,[9] but may have intensified in the Middle Ages, when the port became a favoured waypoint on the sea route between Persia and China. As shown in the preceding chapter, it was the upper valleys of the Ponnani and Chalakudy Rivers and the Early Modern kingdoms of Thekkenkur and Vadakkenkur (that is, the hinterlands of Tyndis, Muziris, and Bakare/Nelkynda) that were the main producers and suppliers, in Antiquity as well as in Early Modernity.

Pepper production in the foothills of the Western Ghats is not often described in the literary sources, precisely because the environmental and cultural peculiarities of the area did not encourage visits by foreigners. A partial exception to this pattern is provided by the Barefoot Carmelite Fra Paolino da San Bartolomeo (Johann Philipp Wesdin), whose thirteen-year service as a missionary in Kerala (1776–89) recommends him as an exceptionally informed witness. His claim that there were entire woods with pepper

[9] In 1504, Álvaro Vaz estimated Kūlam's production at 10,000 quintais (= *c.*500 tons): see p. 99.

vines near Aragoshe (Arakuzha), Porròta (Piravom), Palàya (Pala), Vaypur (Vaipur), Collam (Kūlam), Muhatuge (Muvattupuzha?), Ràamapurata (Ramapura), and everywhere else along the foothills of the Western Ghats is remarkable both for its wide geographic scope and for the assertion that pepper was cultivated in the wooded regions of all these places (Fig. 4.2).[10] Forests with pepper vines seem to have been a long-term primary feature of the Western Ghat landscape, as suggested by Pliny's characterization of pepper as a woodland product[11] and by the Tamil verses connecting pepper and mountain slopes.[12]

Fra Paolino does not say who planted the vines next to the supporting trees. He does say, however, that pepper is among the products gathered by the Maler, the highlanders who have little contact with other natives, who wander naked in the woods and sleep in huts in the trees. Fra Paolino was able to see some of them in villages close to the pepper wood regions.[13] The list of products gathered by the Maler—aside from pepper, Fra Paolino mentions honey, wax, cardamom, medicinal herbs, and bezoar—shows that the pepper woods were just one of the forest resources they exploited.

In ancient Tamil poetry, the mountain slopes where pepper grew were also home to the communities of the Kāṉavar and Kuṟavar, whose

[10] Fra Paolino, 116: 'Il pepe nero piccolo è una elera che si pianta appiè de grand'alberi. Vi sono boschi intieri di pepe in Aragoshe, a Porròta, a Palàya, a Vaypur, a Collam, e da per tutto appiè delle montagne Ghattes, ove il terreno è grasso, nero, argillaceo, focoso'; 356: 'La pianta del pepe è un ellera, o vime, che si pianta presso gli alberi grandi per farla salire, come le viti nella Marca. In Aragoshe, Muhatuge, Ràamapurata, Vaipur, ed altri luoghi del Malabar si trovano boschi interi di ellere di Pepe.' In the English edition (London 1800), only the first passage is found, 163: 'The small black pepper is a kind of ivy, planted for the most part at the bottom of trees, the trunks of which are tall. Large forests of it may be found at Aragoshe, Poròtta, Valaya, Vaypur, and every where at the foot of the Gauts, where the soil is black, rich, argillaceous, and hot.' On 'the pepper forests' (*menasukans*) of the Western Ghats, see Subash Chandran (1997: 150).

[11] Plin., *NH* 12.29. [12] See p. 89 n.22.

[13] Fra Paolino, 182: 'I *Maler*, che abitano le montagne di *Ghattes* sono uomini silvestri, che non comunicano cogli altri Malabari, se non una volta l'anno, quando vengono a comprare le provisioni. Io ne vidi varj a *Maleatur*, a *Codamangalam* e a *Vaypur*. Essi vanno ignudi uomini e donne, ma queste si coprono le parti con un solo foglio di *Banana*, attaccato ad un cordone, che fa il giro delle reni. Si dice, che esse si vergognano più nella loro società di mostrare il seno che in questa parte, perchè dicono, che il petto cresce tardi, e che colli altri membri uno nasce dal ventre della sua madre: Quindi girano affatto ignude nei boschi, e il foglio sudetto si attacca quando vengono alli borghi sulle pianure. Gli uomini raccolgono il mele, la cera, il cardamomo, il pepe, varie erbe medicinali, il *Bezoar* dell'Antilope. Essi dormono sopra gli alberi, per non essere assaliti dalle tigri quando girano per le montagne. Le donne partoriscono sole senza assistenza delle Commari. Nei loro tugurj hanno una pietra, che rappresenta l'anima dei loro parenti defunti, hanno un Re o Capitano che chiamano *Malenragiava*, cioè, *Re dei Montagnoli.* Essi non hanno nè culto pubblico nè Sacerdoti.' I was not able to find this passage in the German (Berlin 1798), English (London 1800), or French (Paris 1808) editions of Fra Paolino's work. More than a century earlier, another Barefoot Carmelite, Vincenzo Maria Murchio, described the same highlanders in approximately the same terms, except for the details about their activity as gatherers: Murchio, 134.

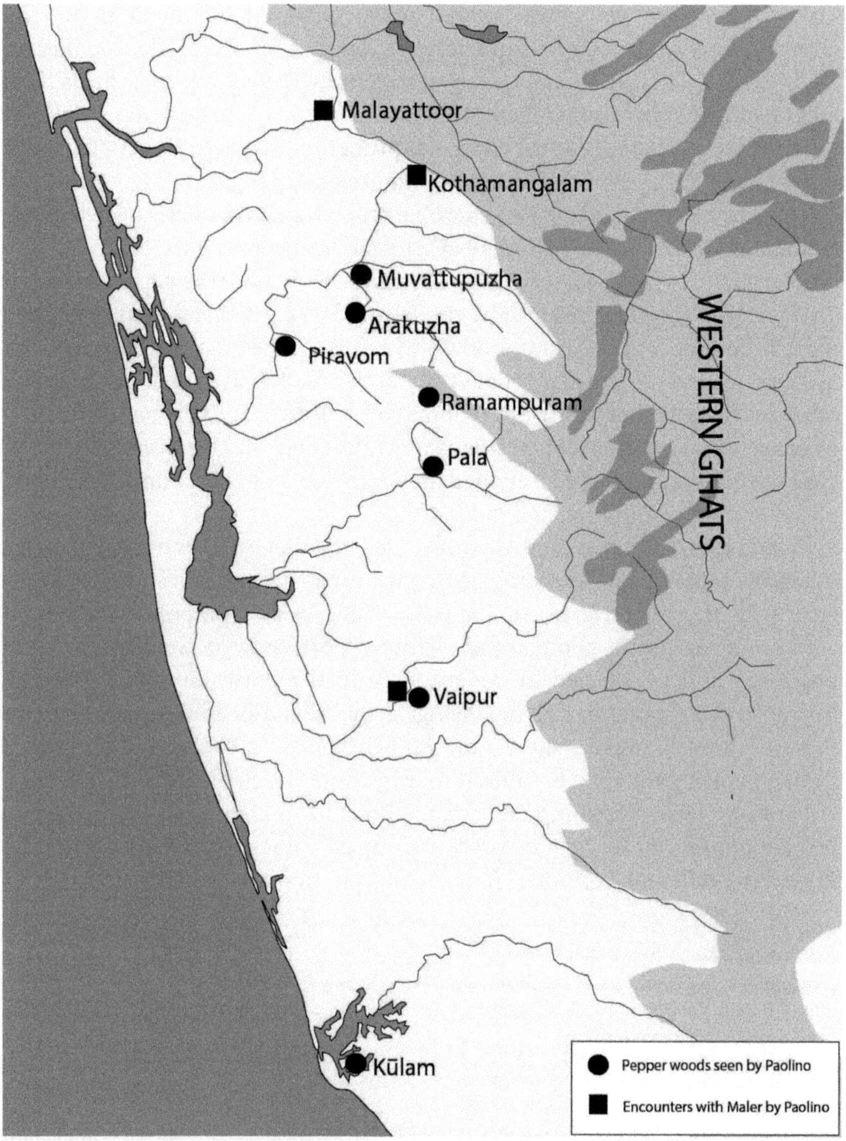

Fig. 4.2 Places mentioned by Fra Paolino as venues for pepper woods and encounters with the Maler.

subsistence economy combined hunting, tropical agriculture, and exploitation of the forest's natural resources.[14] They hunted hares, porcupines, and boars for their meat, and elephants mainly for their

[14] But *Naṟṟiṇai* 276.1–4 contrasts hunters and *Kuṟavar* millet cultivators.

tusks.[15] They dug up yams,[16] sowed millet and wild mountain rice,[17] and collected jackfruits, mangoes, and honey.[18] They processed sandalwood leaves and timber.[19] They dwelt in huts 'on stilts'[20] and watched over their fields from 'high platforms', protecting them from elephant raids.[21] In addition to all this, the Kuṟavar appear once—just once!—as pruners of fragrant creeper vines (*koṭi naṟai pavar*) that grow around sandalwood trees.[22]

This last piece of evidence is somewhat troubling. It is not clear whether the expression *koṭi naṟai pavar* refers specifically to pepper vines or just to any creeper plant, or else to a specific creeper plant that—like the pepper vine, but distinct from it—grew around the sandalwood tree.[23] Whatever the case, one must note that ancient Tamil poetry, which magnifies the role of pepper in Muziris' trade with Yavaṉar,[24] does not portray the Kāṉavar or Kuṟavar or any other mountain community as predominantly dedicated to pepper cultivation or collection. The likely conclusion is that, although vital for overseas trade at coastal emporia, pepper represented only one slice of the economic livelihood of the Western Ghat highland communities.

What, if anything, is known from ancient Western literature about the upland populations of South India? Greco-Roman culture had some acquaintance with the inland areas of Limyrike. The *Periplus* pinpoints the region where pepper grows abundantly;[25] Pliny reports how it would have been processed and transferred from Cottonara to the coast emporia.[26] Ptolemy lists a series of place names belonging to the inland of Limyrike.[27] None of these authors, however, shows any knowledge of or theories about South Indian pepper gatherers. For this, it may be more profitable to look elsewhere.

Fantastic tales describing unusual methods for procuring exotic goods are not uncommon in western classical literatures.[28] For pepper we have at least three very different accounts. A Late Antique tradition posited that pepper

[15] *Akanāṉūṟu* 21.24 (elephants); 132.4–5 (elephants); 82.10–11 (boars); *Malaipaṭukaṭām* 300–1 (porcupines); *Naṟṟiṇai* 65.5–6 (elephants); 82.7–11 (boars); 276.1–4 (animals); 285.3–4 (porcupines); *Perumpāṇāṟṟuppaṭai* 106–17 (boars, hares); *Tirumurukāṇāṟṟupaṭai* 194 (animals).

[16] *Aiṅkuṟunūṟu* 208.1–2.

[17] *Aiṅkuṟunūṟu* 268.2; 270.2; 283.1–2; 284.2–4; *Akanāṉūṟu* 348.8–11; *Kuruntokai* 214.1–2; 335.2–6; *Naṟṟiṇai* 44.6–8; 102.8–9; 108.1–5; 209.1–4; 306.4–5; 386.2–3; *Puṟanāṉūṟu* 143.1–5; 159.15; 168.5–6.

[18] *Aiṅkuṟunūṟu* 213.1–2; *Akanāṉūṟu* 78.7; 322.12; *Malaipaṭukaṭām* 316–18; *Puṟanāṉūṟu* 236.1–2.

[19] *Akanāṉūṟu* 13.4; *Naṟṟiṇai* 64.4–5.

[20] *Akanāṉūṟu* 88.5; 102.2.

[21] *Malaipaṭukaṭām* 203–10; 297–8; *Naṟṟiṇai* 108.1–5.

[22] *Naṟṟiṇai* 5.3–4: 'The *naṟai* vines—which the foresters /Had cut short earlier, have sprouted afresh/And entwined the cool, fragrant sandal trees' (transl. A. Dakshinamurthy).

[23] *Akanāṉūṟu* 2.6: *kaṟi vaḷar cāntam,* 'sandal that fosters pepper'.

[24] *Akanāṉūṟu* 149.7–11.

[25] *PME* 56. See pp. 84–89.

[26] Plin., *NH* 6.105; 12.26–28.

[27] Ptol., *Geog.* 7.1.85–6. However, no reference is made to either Kottanarike or a pepper production area.

[28] It will suffice to recall Hdt. 3.107–12.

woods were in the custody of snakes, and that local people set fire to the trees in order to make the snakes flee so they could safely collect the berries. Reported by both the *Letter to Hadrian on the Wonders of the East* and Isidore of Seville, this story emphasizes the great value of pepper, guarded by snakes in the very same woods where it grew. Moreover, it celebrates a practice that would not only enable the collection of the prized spice but also, conveniently, explain the darkened colour of the berries.[29]

Another Late Antique story, reported by a *scholasticus* from Thebes in Palladius' *De gentibus Indiae et Bragmanibus*, names the Bisades as the protagonists of pepper collection:

> He [sc. the *scholasticus*] came close to the so-called Bisades, who collect the pepper. These people are absolutely small and feeble. Living in rock caves, they are good at climbing precipices because of the twisted place and so they collect pepper from the shrubs: they are small little plants, as the *scholasticus* said. The Bisades are little men with big heads, weak, and with plain hair.[30]

The ethnonym and the physical description of the Bisades pepper collectors recall both the Sesatai of the *Periplus* (who live on the Indian border with China and are involved in the malabathron trade) and the Saesadai (Ξ)/Besadai (Ω) of Ptolemy (located in a Himalayan region).[31] However, unlike the *Periplus*' Sesatai and Ptolemy's Saesadai/Besadai, Palladius' Bisades are specialists in pepper collection, which hints at another source of inspiration, modified to include the features of the Sesatai/Saesadai/Besadai.[32]

An earlier story on pepper collection is given by Philostratus in his *Life of Apollonius*. In this version, pepper grew in the Caucasus near the *Erythra Thalassa*. The mountains were covered with woods with aromatic plants (*ξυνηρεφὲς ἴδαις ἀρωμάτων*) like cinnamon. In their cliffs, next to frankincense trees and many other species, pepper was cultivated by monkeys (*τὰ δένδρα αἳ πεπερίδες, ὧν γεωργοὶ πίθηκοι*).[33] Philostratus explains in detail the curious way by which the Indians trained the monkeys to harvest the pepper:

> The Indians go up to the lower trees and pluck off the fruit, and they make little round shallow pits around the trees, into which they collect the pepper, carelessly tossing it in, as if it had no value and was of no serious use to mankind. Then the

[29] Faral (1914: 205); Isid., *Etym.* 17.8.8.

[30] Palladius, *De gentibus Indiae et Bragmanibus* 1.7. Cf. [Ambrosius] *de moribus Brachmanorum*, *PL* 17.1170. John Lydus attributes a similar account to 'the ancients and Ctesias of Cnidus': Ioann. Lyd., *de mens.* 4.14 = FGrHist 688 F 63. Generally, the fragment is not considered authentic: Hansen (1965); Lenfant (2004: 331–2); Nichols (2011: 161); Marcotte (2017: 57).

[31] *PME* 65; Ptol., *Geog.* 7.2.15. On the relationship between the texts of Palladius, the *Periplus*, the two recensions of Ptolemy's *Geography*, and the Sosaeadae of Plin., *NH* 6.78, see Marcotte (2017: 56–7).

[32] Note that Palladius' description of pepper plants as *δενδρύφια—κολοβά* mimics the physical peculiarities of the Bisades, *ἀνθρωπάρια κολοβά*.

[33] Philostr., *VA* 3.4.

> monkeys mark their actions from above out of their fastnesses, and when the night comes on they imitate the action of the Indians, and twisting off the twigs of the trees, they bring and throw them into the pits in question; then the Indians at daybreak carry away the heaps of the spice which they have thus got without any trouble, and indeed during the repose of slumber.[34]

Of course, Philostratus has freely reimagined both the life of Apollonius and the India to which he sends him.[35] The 'Caucasian' setting for pepper and the coexisting patchwork of mismatched elements like cinnamon, frankincense, and lions are further evidence of his creative license.[36] In addition, the characterization of the pepper collectors as monkeys, and the tactic that the Indians used to get the pepper, are clearly products of an imagination—but perhaps not of Philostratus' own imagination. The fact that in the ancient Tamil poetry the 'mountainsides where pepper grows' are also inhabited by monkeys may be irrelevant.[37] Less irrelevant is the recognition that, in South Asian folklore, the distinction between forest-dwelling people and monkeys sometimes seems ambiguous. Under the entry Kāṉavar (the name of a hill community in the Western Ghats), the seventeenth-century Tamil lexicon *Uriccolnikaṇṭu* also records the meaning *kuraṅku* (monkey);[38] and the Malay word *orangutan* etymologically means 'man of the forest'.[39] No evidence exists to substantiate such a hypothesis, but one may wonder whether fragmented elements of Indian mythology and folklore, for instance Hanumān and his Vānaras,[40] somehow became ingredients in Philostratus' creative alchemy, inspiring his zoomorphization of the pepper collectors.

Consistent with the distortion of the Kottanarike pepper gatherers as a community of monkeys (δῆμος πιθήκων) is Philostratus' depiction of the essentially non-economic relationship between the 'monkeys' who collect the pepper and the Indians who simply take the spice for their own gain. In fact, his 'monkeys' neither expect nor receive anything in return for the pepper. Indeed, they do not even consider their act a gift. The dramatic overreach of Philostratus' tale may actually be a metaphor for the cultural divide between the highland communities of the Western Ghats and the pepper merchants of the lowland towns. We will see that a comparable story circulated about malabathron, pointing to a similar gulf between the Himalayan foothill collectors and the lowland traders of the Ganges Valley.

[34] Philostr., *VA* 3.4, transl. by F.C. Conybeare.

[35] Meyer (1917: 373–80); Charpentier (1934); Bernard (1996); Jones (2001); Reger (2015).

[36] However, a Caucasian setting for pepper had already been suggested and denied long before: Plin., *NH* 12.26.

[37] *Akanāṉūṟu* 2.5–6; 182.14–8; *Kuṟuntokai* 90.2–4; 288.1–2; *Naṟṟiṇai* 151.7–8.

[38] *UMTL* 912, s.v. *kāṉavaṉ*. On the *Uriccolnikaṇṭu* see James (2000: 71; 112; 119; 146; 281; 370; 669; 682–3).

[39] Mahdi (2007: 170–82).

[40] Lutgendorf (2007).

4.2. TRADERS

Gurukkal's argument regarding the nature of Indo-Roman 'trade' has its merits. At the very least, he is justified in calling for a more accurate definition of the complex chain of exchanges so far conventionally labelled as Indo-Roman trade. He is correct, for instance, in pointing out that passages like *Puṟanāṉūṟu* 126.14–16[41] and the pottery fragments with Tamil graffiti found at Khor Rori, Myos Hormos, and Berenice, although otherwise significant, do not justify the theory that South Indian traders crossed the ocean on South Indian ships to trade in South Arabia or Alexandria.[42] On balance, the testimony of both the *Periplus* and *Akanāṉūṟu* 149, 7–11 carries much greater weight and provides unequivocal evidence that Muziris' prosperity was due to visits from Western (and North Indian) ships, not to Indian ships returning from Egypt.[43] But does that prove that the boundaries between formal commercialized trade and informal reciprocal exchanges coincided with boundaries between Roman and Indian actors?

Ancient Tamil poetry attests to the presence of foreign merchants—in particular Westerners (*Yavaṉar*)—in Pukār, on the Coromandel Coast.[44] Muziris, where the *Tabula Peutingeriana* marks the presence of a *templum Augusti*, may have hosted communities of foreign traders as well.[45] However, that does not make Pukār or Muziris mere encampments of foreign traders, much less encampments of solely Roman traders. Apart from the glamorous findings of Roman amphorae, *sigillata*, turquoise-glazed pottery, and torpedo jars, the overwhelming majority of the pottery excavated at Pattanam has been local, and the local coins found there suggest the strong presence of local people with a monetized economy of their own.[46] Even if Pattanam were not inside the Muziris area, but belonged to another settlement very close to it, we should wonder: how could an emporion like Muziris regularly and reliably make available thousands of tons of pepper, hundreds of tons of malabathron, and hundreds of ivory tusks—not to mention pearls, diamonds, Gangetic

[41] 'it is impossible to go behind the gold-giving ship sailing in the western sea of the Cēra king.' One could add *Akanāṉūṟu* 152.4–7: 'the fine ships that bring wealth/gold in the large port on the sea-shore of the vast roaring ocean, in the land of Tittan Veḷiyan famous for his ferocious army.'

[42] However, considering not specifically South India, but India as a whole, it should be recognized that the Prakrit ostracon from Egypt (Salmon (1991)) and Dio Chrys. 32.40 provide proof of Indians sojourning in Egypt.

[43] *PME* 54: 'Muziris, in the same kingdom, owes its prosperity to the shipping from Ariake that comes there, as well as to Greek shipping' (transl. by. L. Casson); *Akanāṉūṟu* 149.7–11: 'the rich Muciṟi, where the ships, the perfect and wonderful constructions of the Yavaṉar, having come with gold, returned carrying pepper, churning the white surf of the great Cuḻḻi river which belongs to the Cēralar.'

[44] *Paṭṭinappālai* 213–8; *Cilappatikaram* 5.9–10.

[45] *Tab. Peut.*, seg. 11.

[46] Foreign ceramic is only 1.427 per cent of the total ceramic assemblage so far found at Pattanam: Cherian (2015: 41–2). For the local coins, see Majumdar (2015).

nard, Chinese silk, and tortoise shell—without a complex local economic system that at least in part may be characterized as 'formal trade'? How could such a network function without the participation—indeed outside the control—of the local populace?

It is easy to acknowledge the role of Indian traders in the supply of non-local commodities such as malabathron, Gangetic nard, silk, and tortoise shell. Decisive in this respect are the emporia of Kamara, Poduke, and Sopatma. There is no reason to assume that the ships of the Coromandel Coast emporia—either the local boats that sailed along the coast as far as Limyrike, or the so-called *sangara*, or the very big vessels that sailed across to Chryse and the Ganges region[47]—belonged to Roman traders. It was these local ships that re-exported the commodities imported from the Bay of Bengal on to Limyrike, and goods traded in Muziris and Nelkynda on to the Coromandel Coast—including 'cash exported over time from Egypt'.[48] Their quantitative bulk (malabathron was the second most voluminous of the commodities exported on the Roman Indiamen), and the use of money as a medium (confirmed by Roman coins, or their imitations, found at the coastal sites of the Bay of Bengal[49]), support the argument that these exchanges are far better defined as trade than as informal reciprocity.

Less conspicuous in this complex intra-regional web of exchange are the pepper dealers. Pepper was gathered in the foothills of the Western Ghats by the forest peoples and exchanged for gold at Muziris.[50] How and by whom was pepper moved to the emporia of the coast? The notion that non-resident merchants acquired pepper directly from the upland gatherers via reciprocal exchanges should be rejected—wasn't pepper carried away by Indians in Philostratus' tale? Nor is there reason to suppose that the dugout canoes that brought pepper to the coast or the pepper warehouses in Muziris belonged—or belonged only—to Roman dealers.[51] The hypothesis that caravans of salt traders could have been sufficient to transfer pepper, ivory, gems, and other items from inland regions to the coast should also be ruled out.[52] Itinerant retailers who distributed salt in the inland regions by cart were poorly equipped to convey huge volumes of pepper from the foothills to the coast.[53]

[47] *PME* 60. [48] *PME* 60.

[49] Cf. Turner (1989); Berghaus (1992; 1994); Suresh (2004); De Romanis (2012a).

[50] *Akanāṉūṟu* 149.9–10.

[51] *Puṟanāṉūṟu* 343.3. From *PME* 56, Gurukkal (2016: 191) infers that overseas vessels had to supply staple grains for the overseas merchants at the ports. However, the text says that the ships bound for Limyrike had to export enough grain for the crew (*nauklerion*), since the (obviously local) merchants (*emporoi*) 'did not use it', that is, did not sell it: cf. Casson (1989: 221, 264). Grain was not grown in Limyrike, whereas it was produced in Ariake (*PME* 41). In their return voyage from Barygaza, Egyptian ships could export Indian grain to East Africa: *PME* 14.

[52] Gurukkal (2016: 222–3).

[53] On salt traders (*umaṉar, umaṉaccāttu*), cf. *Akanāṉūṟu* 119.8; 140.5; 169.6; 191.4; 257.17; 295.9; 303.17; 310.14; 329.5; 337.5; 390.3; *Kuṟuntokai* 124.2; *Naṟṟiṇai* 4.7; 138.3; 183.5; 254.6;

Unquestionably, the Muziris pepper export was supplied by a chain of exchanges between locals, but it is not easy to determine what form these intermediate steps took. It is easier to track down patterns for the local trade in ivory:

> In the rich-in-gold market of the village with scanty fields surrounded by mountains, the hunters wearing glory lily garlands carry murderous bows and slaughter wild cattle with perfect horns. They give away as price for liquor both the white tusks of the wild elephants of the forest and the flesh.[54]

The village in question belongs to the kingdom of the Cēralar and is close to the mountains where the Vēṭṭuvar (hunters of the forest) live. Elephant tusks are exchanged for toddy in a part of the village called *niyamam* (< Skt. *nigama* 'a town, a city, a market-place, a road, a caravan or company of merchants'[55]). The cognate form *nikamam* occurs in early Tamil Brahmī inscriptions. In a text from Māṅkuḷam, a donor presents himself as '*kāviti* (collector of revenues?) of the *nikamam* of Veḷḷaṟai', and 'superintendent of pearls' (*kāḻitika*).[56] 'Members of the *nikamam* of Veḷḷaṟai' are mentioned in another inscription from the same place.[57]

The term *niyamam* occurs nine more times in the *Caṅkam Ilakkiyam*: it refers to 'the two big markets' of Maturai,[58] the market east of Cellūr,[59] the 'excellent big market of the ancient town of Naṉṉaṉ',[60] the commercial area of an ancient town,[61] the 'faultless shopping district where the goddess of wealth resides',[62] a rich-in-toddy market (*kaḷ uṭai niyamattu*),[63] and, again in praise of a Cēra king, to a rich-in-gold market (*poṉ uṭai niyamattu*):

> In your prosperous huge country, goods arrive from oceans, mountains, rivers and elsewhere, unending festivals are celebrated, drums reverberate happily in ancient towns announcing victories and gifts, and banners fly in the rich-in-gold market.[64]

Several times in ancient Tamil poetry, toddy appears as the commodity for which tusks, elephants, and possibly pearls are exchanged.[65] The

331.2; *Puṟanāṉūṟu* 84.6; 102.4; 116.7; 307.7; 313.5; *Perumpāṇāṟṟuppaṭai* 65. At *Naṟṟiṇai* 183.5 and 254.6, they barter for white paddy.

[54] *Patiṟṟuppattu* 30.9–13.

[55] Monier Williams (1899: s.v).

[56] Mahadevan (2003: n. 3, 319; cf. 141, 318, 548–50). Cf. Champakalaksmi (1996: 195–6); Gurukkal (2016: 224). On the term *kāviti* (< Skt. *gṛhapati*?), see *UMTL* 903. The praise of *kāviti mākkaḷ* (*kāviti* men) in *Maturaikkāñci* 493–9 demonstrates their high social status but does not clarify their functions.

[57] Mahadevan (2003: n. 6, 323; cf. 320; 551–2).

[58] *Maturaikkāñci* 365.

[59] *Akanāṉūṟu* 90.12.

[60] *Malaipaṭukaṭām* 480.

[61] *Akanāṉūṟu* 83.7; *Naṟṟiṇai* 45.4.

[62] *Tirumurukāṇāṟṟuppaṭai* 70.

[63] *Patiṟṟuppattu* 75.10.

[64] *Patiṟṟuppattu* 15.16–19 (transl. by V. Herbert, with modifications).

[65] *Akanāṉūṟu* 61.9–10 (tusks); 245.9–11 (tusks); *Patiṟṟuppattu* 30.9–13; 68.9–11 (for tusks). *Akanāṉūṟu* 83.4–8 describes a young male elephant, captured and tied in front of the toddy

characterizations 'rich-in-toddy' and 'rich-in-gold' allude to different forms of exchange, the former rooted in the modalities of reciprocal exchange, the latter moving towards more commercialized trade. However, the polarization of toddy and gold hardly clarifies two distinct types of *niyamam*: in the 'rich-in-gold' market described in *Patiṟṟuppattu* 30.9–13, elephant tusks are exchanged for toddy; conversely, at Muziris, where pepper is exchanged for Roman gold, the Cēra king, lord of the *Kuṭṭanāṭu*, gives toddy unreservedly:

> like Muciṟi (Muziris) of the sea which roars like a drum, which belongs to the Kuṭṭuvaṉ with the golden garland, who offers toddy as if it were water to those who come to pour there the goods from the mountains and those from the sea, to those who bring ashore in the lagoon boats the gifts of gold brought by the ships, to those who crowd the port in the turmoil created by the sacks of pepper piled up in the houses, and to those who return home having sold the fish and having heaped the paddy on the boat.[66]

Muziris was the venue for exchanges of varying nature and scale. The business of the dealers who pile up sacks of pepper in their houses and eventually exchange it for gold coins cannot be equated to the small-time barter between fishermen and farmers. On the other hand, it is likely that, before and besides being exchanged for gold coins, pepper was exchanged the same way as fish and paddy. It is worth noting that in three medieval inscriptions, pepper is valued in terms of quantities of paddy. In a twelfth-century-AD set of copper plates from Thiruvalla, ten *nāḻi* of paddy equals one *nāḻi* of pepper.[67] In an eleventh-century AD inscription from the Thanjavur temple, while the prices of (overseas?) cardamom seeds, *campaka* buds, and *khaskhas* roots are expressed in gold coins (*kāśu*), one *āḻākku* and 1.75 *cevidu* of pepper equal five *nāḻi*, one *ūri*, and one *āḻākku* of paddy (ratio $\frac{39}{32}$: 42).[68] A close ratio may be inferred from an eleventh-century AD inscription from Chidambaram, where one measure of pepper equals five *nāḻi* of paddy and five *ūri* (= 2.5 *nāḻi*) of *āli* (another spice).[69] It is remarkable but not entirely surprising that in Thiruvalla, within the pepper-producing area of Thekkenkur, the ratio of pepper to paddy is 1 : 10, while in Thanjavur and Chidambaram, in the paddy-producing Kaveri delta, the ratio was almost 1 : 40.

In conclusion, it is important to recognize that more than one step of the long process that brought pepper and ivory from the foothills of the Western Ghats to Alexandria occurred within India itself, and that the nature of these exchanges ranged from informal to formal. A broader and more inclusive perspective is therefore necessary to capture both the commercial activities

shop. The abundant toddy enjoyed by the fishermen of Koṟkai is probably part of the reward for the pearls for which they dive: *Maturaikkāñci* 136–8.

[66] *Puṟanāṉūṟu* 343.1–10. [67] Narayanan (2013: 310). [68] Hall (1980: 117; 119).
[69] Hall (1980: 117).

reflected in the Muziris loan contract and the transactions between the Western Ghat forest communities and the Muziris-based dealers. We must be wary of presuming that the Indian participants engaged only in informal transactions, and that commercialized trade was the sole purview of Roman actors.

4.3. KINGS

It may be wondered whether the theory that South India's socio-economic system was unable to produce 'real' trade is based on an accurate reconstruction. For instance, as far as the apex of the South Indian political structure is concerned, it is questionable whether the distinction between *vēntar* and *vēḷir*—crucial in the Tamil sources—is effectively captured by the translations 'major chieftains' and 'minor chieftains', or whether 'there is no evidence to show that the chieftains had governed the ports'; or that 'systematic governance was not within the capability of chiefdom-level political formations precluding bureaucracy'.[70]

Questionable in itself, this minimizing approach to the Tamil evidence is not supported by ancient Western sources, which consider at least two and possibly all three *vēntar* (Cēra, Pāṇṭiya, and Cōḻa) to have been 'kings',[71] while ignoring the impact of the *vēḷir*.[72] This evidence echoes the perception of the merchants from Alexandria, who were certainly able to gauge the power of these polities, just as they were able to acknowledge more marginal political entities. For instance, the author of the *Periplus* labels the rulers of several East African emporia as chiefs (*tyrannoi*), and makes it clear that their dominions are not kingdoms: 'The region [sc. north Somali coast] is not ruled by a king but each port of trade is administered by its own chief.'[73] The distinction has a purpose as well as practical commercial consequences. For one, the Cēra king had an army with several hundred war elephants. Neither the East African chiefs nor the South Indian *vēḷir* had anything comparable. It was an elephant contingent of this proportion that enabled the Cēra king to control the hinterland of an emporion like Muziris—and to harvest hundreds of kilograms of ivory tusk fragments.[74]

[70] Gurukkal (2016: 280).

[71] *PME* 54–5; Plin., *NH* 6.104–5; Ptol., *Geog.* 7.1.86; 89. It is doubtful whether Ptol., *Geog.* 7.1.68: *Ἀρκατοῦ βασίλειον Σῶρα ρλ° κ° δ′* refers to the Cōḻa king.

[72] A partial exception could be the Āy, after whom the land of the Aioi is named in Ptol., *Geog.* 7.1.9; 87.

[73] *PME* 14: *οὐ βασιλεύεται δὲ ὁ τόπος, ἀλλὰ τυράννοις ἰδίοις καθ' ἕκαστον ἐμπόριον διοικεῖται.* Cf. *PME* 16: *κατὰ τὸν τόπον ἕκαστος ὁμοίως τιθέμενοι τυράννοις*, 'depending on the place, each equally subject to chiefs'.

[74] See pp. 217–22.

Both Western and Indian sources point out that the South Indian kings *owned* the coastal emporia.[75] Details regarding the governance of Muziris remain encrypted in the poetic image of the Cēra king who gives toddy to visitors, but it is significant that in the same context Roman gold coins are alluded to as ‘the golden gifts’ (*poṟ paricam*). The expression hints at redistributive exchanges made by the ruler in favour of his ‘gift-seekers’ (*paricilar*), and would hardly be comprehensible if the political power did not take for himself, one way or another, a good portion of those coins.[76]

Another example of governance exercised by a South Indian king over a transoceanic emporion is offered by a passage in the *Paṭṭinappālai*, which describes the customs duties officials and the watchmen of the Cōḻa king deployed in Pukār, on the Coromandel Coast:

> In the pure sandy banks brought up by the great river Kaveri, rest the respected officials who, like the horses tied to the chariot of the red, scorching Sun every day collect the customs duties [*ulku* < Skt. *śulka*, ‘toll, tax, duty, customs (esp. money levied at ferries, passes, and roads)’[77]] with relentless energy and protect the treasure of the good lord in the vast sea shore streets lined by *tālai* plants, with flat leaves and clusters of white flowers. As in the rainy season the water drawn by the sky showers the mountain and joins the ocean, many commodities, impossible to measure, are imported from the sea to the land or conveyed from the land to the sea. They come in unlimited quantities and are stockpiled in the safe and strong warehouses, where the strong watchmen stamp the emblem of the tiger [symbol of the Cōḻa kings] on the sacks full of expensive commodities.[78]

The conclusion that the Cōḻa kings governed the port and profited from the trade activities therein seems inescapable.

4.4. THE PEPPER PENDULUM

Apart from exaggerating the role of Roman traders, minimizing early South India’s oversight of its own intra- and inter-regional commerce weakens our ability to understand later developments in the pepper trade. Indeed, proper recognition of the role of Indian economic players is essential for appreciation of the dynamics of Indian Ocean history in both ancient and later times.

[75] *PME* 54–5; Plin., *NH* 6.104–5; *Akanāṉūṟu* 149.7–11; *Puranāṉūru* 343.9–10.

[76] De Romanis (2006b: 69–82).

[77] Monier Williams (1899: s.v.).

[78] *Paṭṭinappālai* 116–39.

Sometime between the mid-second and sixth centuries AD, Muziris waned and ultimately vanished as a transoceanic trade centre.[79] It may be tempting to correlate its decline with the scarcity of post-Severan specimens among the Roman coins found in India, and then to conclude that Muziris' purpose was simply to connect Indian suppliers of raw materials with Roman traders—thus implying that the end of Muziris as a transoceanic emporion was a direct consequence of the third-century AD crisis in the Roman Empire. Such a conclusion would not be entirely baseless, insofar as it seems plausible that Roman demand for Indian commodities suffered a certain drop in the course of the third century AD. But several additional lines of evidence suggest that Muziris' demise demands a more nuanced explanation.

The most significant sign that Muziris' decline was not a simple by-product of Rome's crisis is the fact that, at least between the sixth and the sixteenth centuries AD, no transoceanic emporion was ever noted along the shores of ancient Kottanarike on the south-west coast.[80] By contrast, at that time Cosmas lists no fewer than three splendid emporia along India's south-eastern coast. Cosmas' silence regarding the west coast south of Male and his emphasis on the relevance of Marallo, Taprobane, and Kaber suggest that in the sixth century AD Kottanarike's black pepper was being exported eastward across the Bay of Bengal rather than westward across the Arabian Sea. So too in later ages: the export of black pepper from the south-eastern emporia is attested in the tenth (Ūr.shfīn), thirteenth (Devipattinam), and sixteenth (Keelakarai) centuries AD (Fig. 4.3).[81] Cosmas' hint of a sea route linking Persia to Sri Lanka and China,[82] and the depiction of pepper as a Persian product in sixth- and seventh-century Chinese texts,[83] adds some weight to the theory that in Late Antiquity pepper was 'brought in by Persian traders across the Indian sea and around the Malay Peninsula to China'.[84]

From this perspective, the rise of the ninth-century pepper emporion Kūlam cannot be seen as a counterbalance to the new eastward orientation

[79] The occurrences of Muziris and Limyrike (*Maziris, Dymirice, Damirice, Dimirica*) in the Peutinger Table (seg. 11) and the *Geographus Ravennas* (5.41; 5.58; 8.29;15.34; 15.64 Schnetz) may prove nothing more than the persistence of the old information in the Late Antique geographic culture.

[80] See chapter three, pp. 94–8.

[81] Large quantities of pepper at Ūr.shfīn: *Ḥudūd al-ʿālam* 10.12 (cf. Minorsky (1970: 87–8; comm. 243–4)); customs duties on pepper at Devipattinam: *SII* 8.403; 405 (cf. Murugeswari (2008: 216; 294)); conveyance of pepper to Keelakarai (Cale care): *CAA* 7.175.

[82] Cosm. Indic. 2.45; 11.15. On Sri Lanka's widespread western and eastern trade relationships in Late Antiquity, see de Saxé (2016).

[83] *Wei-shu* 102.12[a]; *Sui-shu* 83.16[a]. Pepper is labelled as a north-west Indian product in *Hou-Han-shu* 118.12[b] (second century AD) and as a Magadha product in *Yu-yang tsa-tsu* 18.9[b] (ninth century AD).

[84] Hirth and Rockhill (1911: 223); Yung-Ho (1982: 222); *contra* Laufer (1919: 374, n. 1). In general, on the trade between India, South East Asia, and China in Antiquity, see Wolters (1967: 31–85).

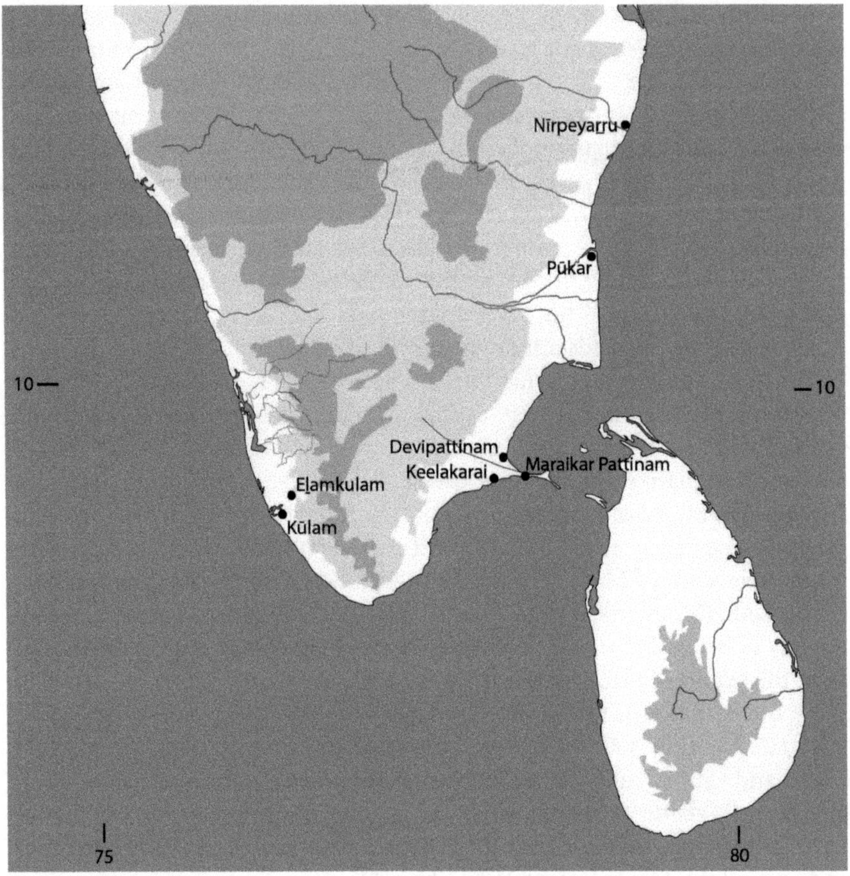

Fig. 4.3 Southern Indian emporia that exported pepper eastward from Ancient to Medieval times.

of South Indian commerce. Despite its location on the south-west coast, Kūlam was not Muziris' successor. It was instead a stopover on the sea routes between Persia and China,[85] and in all likelihood, most of its pepper went to China rather than Persia.[86]

[85] *Aḫbār al-Ṣīn wa 'l-Hind* 1.4.2. The Tharisappalli Copper Plates (AD 849) also provide evidence for Kūlam's links with Persia: Gopinatha Rao (1920: 60–85). On the other hand, it is dubious whether Chalach, mentioned by the Patriarch Isho'yahb (AD 647–59) as an Indian port 1,200 *parasang* distant from the coasts of Persia (Assemani (1719–28: 3.XXVII–VIII)), refers already to Kūlam. The identification is accepted by Padmanabha Menon (1924: 1.270–1); rejected by Yule and Burnell (1886: 752) and Narayanan (2013: 86–7, n. 111).

[86] As suggested by Marco Polo's report of the enormous quantity imported to Zayton: Polo, *Divis.* 157 = *Mil.* 153. Later, an export of Malabar pepper to China is attested by Barbosa, 218–9. In 1548, D. João De Castro's plan to divert a quota of South Indian pepper to the markets

It is important to emphasize that the first signs of this directional shift in South India's pepper export predate the third-century crisis of the Roman Empire. In fact, while the *Akanāṉūṟu* 149 still mentions Yavaṉar's vessels coming to Muziris with gold and sailing back with pepper,[87] later Tamil poems refer to black pepper being transferred to the emporia of the Coromandel Coast.[88] In particular, the *Paṭṭiṉappālai* mentions sacks of black pepper that arrived overland among the foreign commodities lying in the streets of the Coromandel port of Pukār, ready to be sent across the Bay of Bengal:

> The borders of the city with great fame are protected by the celestials. Swift horses with lifted heads arrive on ships from abroad, bags of black pepper arrive overland, gold comes from northern mountains, sandalwood and *akil* wood come from the western mountains, pearls which come from the southern seas, coral which comes from the eastern seas. The commodities from the Ganges, the yield of the Kāviri River, food items from Lanka, products made in Myanmar, and many rare and precious things are piled up on the wide streets.[89]

The *Perumpāṇāṟṟuppaṭai*, attributed to the same bard as the *Paṭṭiṉappālai*, minutely describes the armed merchants who convey pepper to Nīrpeyaṟṟu (Mamallapuram):

> As a protection to those who travel during the day, there are merchants who trade with rare things that are from the mountains and oceans. They are men of firm mind who wear body shirts and sandals that cover their feet. They have scars on their chests, caused by taking arrows from foes. Adept in archery, they carry bright swords with white hilts on the cloth tied around their chests, which resemble snakes crawling on mountains. They have daggers on their tight clothing. Their arms that held black bows are strong. Their strength is like that of Murukan in *kaṭampam* trees. They have large hands carrying spears and do not back off. They travel on wide toll roads with their donkeys with lifted ears and backs with deep scars, that carry loads of pepper sacks, well balanced, resembling jackfruits with small segments that grow on the low trunks of curved trees. The forked forest paths used by merchants are protected by those with bows.[90]

There is no reason to believe that pepper ever ceased to grow and be gathered in the Western Ghats between the third and fifteenth centuries AD. Ancient Kottanarike was always the main pepper-producing area of South India. But, as a result of a gradual process that started in the second century AD

of Bengal, Pegu (Bago, Myanmar), and China probably intended to enhance existing commercial connections: Thomaz (1998).

87 *Akanāṉūṟu* 149.7–11.

88 For a late second-century AD chronology of *Paṭṭiṉappālai* and *Perumpāṇāṟṟuppaṭai*, see Zvelebil (1974: 22–3).

89 *Paṭṭiṉappālai* 184–93.

90 *Perumpāṇāṟṟuppaṭai* 66–82. For Mamallapuram's archaeological evidence, see Badhreenath (2016: 275–87). For ancient land routes of South India, see Selvakumar (2016).

and was accelerated (rather than triggered) by the third-century crisis of the Roman Empire, Kottanarike's pepper export just changed direction. It was the more vibrant trade of the Bay of Bengal—carried out, first and foremost, by Indian traders—that prompted Kottanarike's pepper merchants to turn their backs (literally) on the Arabian Sea.

The growing appeal of the eastern sea routes gradually reoriented the focus of Western merchants as well. Already Marinus of Tyre could refer to a certain Alexander, who sailed from the Golden Chersonese to Kattigara.[91] Dionysius Periegetes mentions the Ganges as the destination of the merchants from Egypt.[92] In AD 166, a self-styled embassy from the Roman emperor reached the Chinese court via Vietnam.[93] While the Yavaṉar merchants of *Akanāṉūṟu* 149 traded at Muziris on the Arabian Sea, their descendants, represented in the later *Cilappatikaram*, built a settlement at Pukār and plied their goods in the Bay of Bengal and further east.[94]

At one time, the quantities of South Indian pepper exported to the West far surpassed those sent across the Bay of Bengal, and pepper was rightly branded as the *yavanapriya*, the 'beloved of the Westerners (*Yavana*)'.[95] But from the second century AD on, the balance of trade tilted progressively to the east, such that by the sixth century AD virtually all of Kottanarike's pepper was going to the Coromandel Coast and the Bay of Bengal. As a consequence, Western demand for pepper had to be met by the relatively modest output from Male, a region that was largely peripheral to the sea routes linking India to South East Asia and China. As discussed earlier, Male played no role in the first- and second-century AD trade between India and the Roman Empire: to the Western traders of Ptolemy's time, Cosmas' eastern pepper emporia were *terra incognita* (or at least *anonyma*). Kottanarike's pepper would travel west again only in the fourteenth century, with the emergence of the Calicut spice trade.

[91] Ptol., *Geog.* 1.14.1. On the location of Kattigara, cf. Sheldon (2012: 55–6).

[92] Dionys. Per. 709–12.

[93] Hirth (1885: 40–3); Leslie and Gardiner (1996: 153–8); Hill (2009). The reports about Seria (the Silk Island) heard by Pausanias (6.26.6–10) probably came from Indian Ocean seafarers.

[94] *Cilappatikaram*, 5.9–10.

[95] Hemacandra, *abhidhāncintāmaṇi* 420.

5

Supporting Sources

Before considering the texts of the Muziris papyrus, we must first discuss literary sources that are critical for understanding the extant parts of the texts and for reconstructing those parts that are lost. Written several generations before the Muziris papyrus, certain passages from Strabo, Pliny, and the *Periplus* give precious information on what were probably still standard features of the South India trade during the first two centuries of the Roman Empire: the items traded, the size of the vessels, the sailing timetables, and the structure of the customs duties. Ptolemy's *Geography* was written at a time close to that of the papyrus; despite the poor placement of South India on its world map, its relevant paragraphs are important, as they provide a more or less contemporaneous perspective of the region's political landscape.

5.1. STRABO: THE CUSTOMS DUTIES ON INDIAN COMMODITIES

Strabo visited Egypt soon after the Roman conquest, when his friend Aelius Gallus was prefect—sometime between 27 and 24 BC.[1] Although what he learnt about the recent developments of the India trade had basically no impact on his description of India in the fifteenth book of the *Geography*, his passing remarks on the subject—coming from a man who was privy to the operation of the Roman government of Egypt and well versed in the historical and geographic literature—are extremely interesting and command close attention. For instance, Strabo notes: that while he was accompanying Aelius Gallus on his voyage to Syene (probably in 26 BC), as many as 120 ships had left from Myos Hormos;[2] that in recent years (*νυνί*) Indian and Arabian commodities reached the Mediterranean via the Myos Hormos–Coptos–Alexandria route

[1] Bastianini (1988: 515); Faoro (2016: 16–17).

[2] Strab. 2.5.12. In Strabo's work, the adverbs *νῦν* (now) and *νεωστί* (recently) may refer to dates as early as 31 (8.6.23) or 26 (2.5.12) BC or as late as AD 18 (12.3.29): see Dueck (1999: 469).

The Indo-Roman Pepper Trade and the Muziris Papyrus. Federico De Romanis, Oxford University Press (2020).
 DOI: 10.1093/oso/9780198842347.001.0001

rather than via the Leuke Kome–Petra–Rhinokoloura route;[3] that in his time (νῦν), large fleets used to set sail to India and the remotest parts of East Africa;[4] and that some merchants from Egypt of his own time (*οἱ νῦν δὲ ἐξ Αἰγύπτου πλέοντες ἐμπορικοί*) had reached the Ganges.[5]

Unsurprising for a man of his generation, connections, and learning, Strabo was inclined to take a historical perspective that aligned the Roman present with the Ptolemaic past—a tendency that occasionally misled him. We have for instance seen him oversimplify the history of the caravan roads between Berenice and the Nile, erroneously assuming that Ptolemy Philadelphus opened one from Berenice to Coptos.[6] At other times, however, he appropriately emphasized the innovations of his own age, such as the new reservoirs for groundwater (*ὑδρεῖα*) and rainwater (*δεξαμεναί*) built in the Eastern Desert of Egypt.[7]

In another passage, Strabo alludes to the increase in Egyptian revenues during his time, resulting from the striking growth in the volume of the India trade:

> As for the revenues of Egypt, Cicero tells about them in a certain speech, saying that a tribute of twelve thousand five hundred talents was paid annually to Auletes, the father of Cleopatra. If, then, the man who administered the kingdom in the worst and most careless way obtained so large a revenue, what should one think of the present revenues, which are managed with so much diligence, and when the commerce with the Indians and the Troglodytes has been increased to so great an extent? In earlier times, at least, not so many as twenty vessels would dare to traverse the Arabian Gulf far enough to get a peep outside the straits, but at the present time even large fleets are despatched as far as India and the extremities of Aethiopia.[8]

One wishes that Strabo had written more—for example, that he had also recorded Egypt's total revenues at the time, and that he had specified the extent to which customs duties on commodities imported via the Red Sea contributed to that total. Instead, he simply invites his readers to imagine the magnitude of the revenues' upturn, taking into account that Cicero maintained (in a lost speech, probably the *De rege Alexandrino* of 65 BC[9]) that Ptolemy Auletes' annual revenues amounted to 12,500 talents, and that under the Ptolemies not even twenty ships would dare to sail beyond Bab el-Mandeb.[10]

[3] Strab. 16.4.24. [4] Strab. 17.1.13. [5] Strab. 15.1.4. [6] See p. 46.
[7] See p. 49. [8] Strab. 17.1.13.
[9] Strab. 17.1.13 = Cic., frg. XVI 13 Schoell = IX 13 Puccioni.
[10] The revenues claimed by Cicero are more than double the 6,000 talents reported in Diod. Sic. 17.52.6. Wilcken (1899: 1.415–16) understands Diodorus' 6,000 talents as related only to revenues from the Egyptian properties of the 300,000 free inhabitants of Alexandria; Manning (2007: 454–5) considers Diodorus' figure more realistic. Weiser (in Weiser and Cotton (1996: 286)) assumes that the two figures were equivalent, and infers that Cicero was referring to

The rhetorical question ('what should one think of the present revenues... when the commerce with the Indians and the Troglodytes has been increased to so great an extent?') implies the conviction—not substantiated by any statistical data, but apparently shared by both the writer and his readers—that the growth in Indian and East African commerce had an appreciable impact on Egypt's annual revenue, which was allegedly on the scale of 300,000,000 sestertii at the time of Ptolemy Auletes.

Although vague about actual returns, Strabo is specific in pointing to trade with India and East Africa beyond Bab el-Mandeb as the major cause of revenue growth. The emphasis on trade beyond the straits and the omission of trade with South Arabia seem noteworthy. It suggests that trade with emporia on this side of Bab el-Mandeb, or South Arabia in general, was already in full swing by the late Ptolemaic age, and that its volume did not change much in the transition to the Roman age. Late Ptolemaic trade on the 'Indian and Red Sea', as they came to call it,[11] was apparently strong, but still mainly confined to the Red Sea.

On the other hand, Strabo's reference to 'the large fleets despatched as far as India and the extremities of Aethiopia' sounds vague when compared to his statement that he learned that as many as 120 vessels were sailing from Myos Hormos to India at the time of Aelius Gallus' prefecture.[12] Here too, his reticence seems significant. At the time he was writing 17.1.13, Strabo was no longer in the privileged position he had been in 26 BC, when he had visited Coptos following Aelius Gallus. About the latest developments of the Indian (and East African) trade, he knew more or less what his readers had heard—hence his generic hint at 17.1.13, written in the late Augustan or early Tiberian age. Still, this does not diminish the importance of his emphasis on the recent growth of the India trade, which finds significant external corroboration.

It is well known that among the Roman coins found in India—and especially South India—the late Augustan and Tiberian issues by far predominate.[13] The distribution of pendants and moulds imitating the reverse of Tiberius' PONT MAX coins (Figs. 5.1–5.3) further confirms the impact of their export to the Indian subcontinent and beyond.[14]

Of course, this does not mean that the late Augustan and Tiberian coins found in India were *all* exported between 2 BC and AD 37. The Augustan denarius with Vespasian's countermark in the Budinathan hoard (1,398 denarii, of which 369 were Augustan CL CAESARES, and 1,029 Tiberian PONT

Ptolemaic talents worth 2,880 denarii. However, in Cic., *Rab. Post.* 22; 30–1 (54 BC), the 10,000 talents supposedly promised by Ptolemy Auletes to Gabinius are explicitly equated to 240,000,000 sesterces. The revenues of Ptolemy Philadelphus are quantified as 14,800 talents and 1,500,000 artabas of grain in Jer., *Comm. in Dan.* 11.5.

[11] *I.Portes* 49, l.5; *I.Philae* 52, ll.4–5; 53, l.3; 56, ll. 8–9; *SB* 1.2264, ll.4–6.

[12] Strab. 2.5.12.

[13] Turner (1989); Berghaus (1992); Suresh (2008: 160–77); Johrden and Wolters (2008); De Romanis (2012); Nappo 2017.

[14] Borell (2014: 22–5).

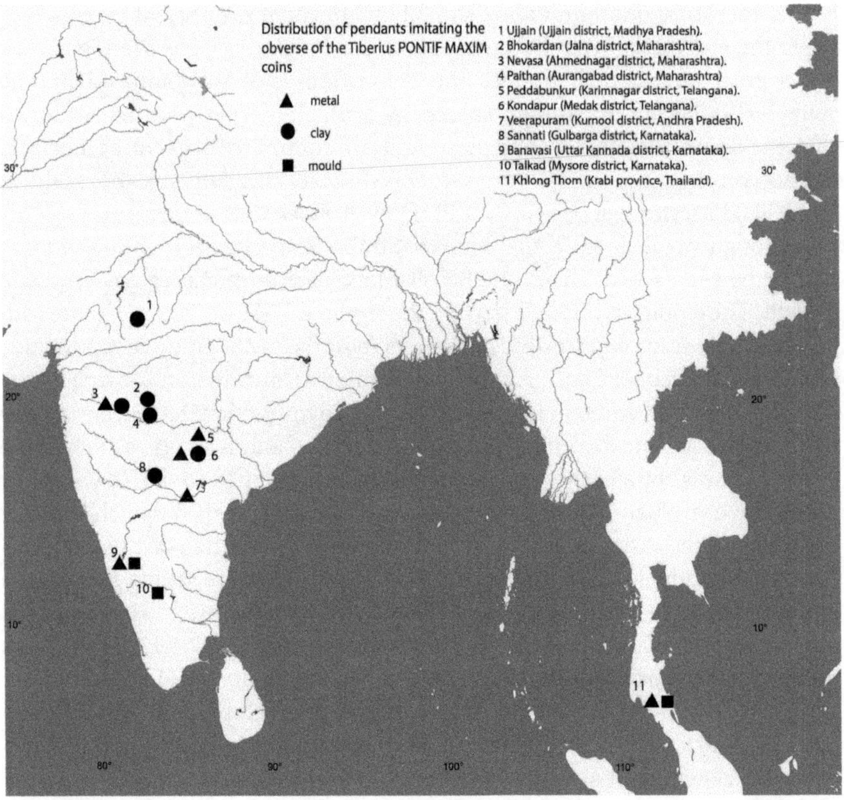

Fig. 5.1 Distribution of pendants and moulds imitating the reverse of Tiberius' PONT MAX.

Courtesy B. Borell.

MAX) demonstrates that many of these coins may have been exported much later than their emission dates.[15] But arguing that little or none of that coinage was exported before AD 37 would be unwarranted. The outflow of Roman coins to India was not a by-product of Nero's monetary reform.[16] In fact, the weight alteration of aurei and denarii only discouraged the export of post AD 64 issues as long as the heavier types were still available. Apart from the passage in Tacitus' *Annals* in which, as early as AD 22, Tiberius laments the haemorrhaging of Roman coinage to alien or hostile nations,[17] there is additional evidence to support the idea that a considerable quantity of late

[15] Berghaus (1998: 126); Johrden and Wolters (2008). Dividing the value of the Roman coins found in India by the years of reign of each emperor does not give any safe indication regarding the intensity over time of the export of coins to India: Nappo (2017: 570–1).

[16] *Contra* MacDowall and Wilson (1970: 234–5); Nappo (2017: 573).

[17] Tac., *Ann.* 3.53. Export of denarii under Claudius: Plin., *NH* 6.85.

Fig. 5.2 Denarius of Tiberius *RIC* I² 95, no. 30. British Museum number 1988,0917.50.
© The Trustees of the British Museum.

Fig. 5.3 Stone mould from Khlong Thom (southern Thailand), Wat Khlong Thom Museum.
Courtesy B. Borell.

Augustan and Tiberian coins had already been exported in the first decades of the Christian Era.

The process by which Julio-Claudian aurei and denarii were exported to India requires some clarification. One must emphasize that the importation and circulation of Indian commodities also provoked money transfers *inside* the Roman Empire. Indeed, the internal transfers were much larger than the outflow beyond the borders, since the prices of imports increased as the commodities penetrated more widely and deeply within the empire. For obvious reasons—Alexandria was the major Mediterranean bridgehead of the India trade, and Puteoli was the major hub for the western redistribution of eastern goods—the internal money transfers from Puteoli to Alexandria were particularly substantial.[18] Moreover, since central Italy was itself a major consumer and distributor of Indian (and, in general, Alexandrian) commodities, and since merchants and financiers from Campania were directly involved in the India trade,[19] it makes sense that aurei and denarii, not commonly used in Egypt, would be exported to India first and foremost from central Italy.

Therefore, to explain the fact that the most popular coin types in Indian hoards are virtually absent in hoards from central Italy and especially from the Vesuvian area, we do not need to infer 'a severe constriction before AD 64 in the flow of precious-metal coin to Italy as compared with the western provinces'.[20] It is not likely, for instance, that the CL CAESARES denarii played no part in the *congiarium* of 2 BC (60 denarii each were distributed to just over 200,000 plebeians resident in Rome).[21] The most obvious explanation for the paucity of Augustan CL CAESARES and Tiberian PONT MAX aurei and denarii in central Italian hoards is that they were used to buy commodities in the East.[22] Their extreme rarity in the Vesuvian sites may be explained by the substantial number that had left the peninsula for Alexandria, and to a lesser extent for India, before AD 79. The forty aurei given by Augustus to each of his companions at Puteoli in AD 14 for the purchase of commodities from Alexandria suggest that monetary transfers from Puteoli to Alexandria and then to India began not later than the first decades AD.[23]

Most of the time, the transfer of the CL CAESARES and PONT MAX specimens from Italy to India was the result of a multi-stage process characterized by different timetables for the Puteoli–Alexandria and Alexandria–India legs. Due to the disparity in the value of Indian commodities in their homeland and in Alexandria, a coin could wait many years, even decades, before being re-exported from Alexandria to India. Therefore, it comes as no surprise that the transfer of the Augustan and Tiberian specimens to India persisted for several decades after their issue, nor can it be surprising that the

[18] For the imbalanced trade between Alexandria and Puteoli, see Strabo 17.1.7.

[19] De Romanis (1996a; 1996b).

[20] Duncan-Jones (1994: 122). On the distribution of the pre-AD 64 coinage in Italy and the Western provinces, Butcher and Ponting (2014: 207–10).

[21] *RG* 15. [22] De Romanis (2012); *pace* Nappo (2017: 572).

[23] Suet., *Aug.* 98.2. *Contra* MacDowall (1991: 151–2; 1996, 92–4). Cf. also Cobb (2015: 379–89).

inflow of coins to Alexandria triggered by the India trade had an impact on the credit market in Egypt.

F. Lerouxel has shown that, in Egypt, loans in kind virtually disappeared after AD 15, and that the interest rate gradually dropped from 24 per cent (which had been typical in the Ptolemaic age and was still attested at Alexandria in 5 BC[24]) first to 18 per cent,[25] and then to 12 per cent (which was already attested in AD 18, 23, and 26 at Soknopaiu Nesos, and in AD 29 at Tebtynis[26]). It is important to point out that all this was happening while the high interest rate was fanning the flames of Florus' and Sacrovir's AD 21 revolt in Gallia.[27] This turnaround in Egypt's credit market, comparable to what happened in Italy upon the arrival of Octavian's Egyptian spoils,[28] can hardly be ascribed to the emission of Tiberius' silver tetradrachms. A far more significant contribution to the monetary mass circulating in Alexandria (with consequences for the whole of Egypt) would have been provided by the exchange of aurei and denarii in return for Indian commodities.[29] The effect of this influx was softened only in part by the less substantial export of the same coins to India: figuratively speaking, Julio-Claudian Alexandria was like a funnel that received more liquid than it released.

Another piece of evidence suggests that a sizable number of late Augustan and Tiberian aurei and denarii were exported in the first decades AD. The isotopic signature of a Tiberian denarius found at Woodham Mortimer (Essex) indicates a provenance from ores that are radiogenically much older than those in the Mediterranean area, and similar to lead isotope signatures from India.[30] One may posit that at some time during Tiberius' reign, there was an import of silver from India large enough to help supply the imperial mint. This surprising conclusion may be bolstered by the fact that at the time of the *Periplus* (a few years or, at most, a few decades later), Roman aurei and denarii were exchanged for local coinage (most probably, silver punch-marked coins) in Barygaza at a profit. The denarius found at Woodham Mortimer

[24] *BGU* 4.1175 (see *BL* 5.16, Alexandria, BC 5).

[25] *BGU* 1.189 (Soknopaiu Nesos, AD 7); *SB* 1.5243 (Soknopaiu Nesos, AD 7); *P.Corn.* 6 (Oxyrhyncha, AD 17); *P.Mich.* 5.336 (Tebtynis, AD 27); *P.Lond.* 3.1273 (Soknopaiu Nesos?, AD 28–9).

[26] *BGU* 3.911 = *P.Dime* 3.7 (Soknopaiu Nesos, AD 18); *P.Lond.* 2.277 (Soknopaiu Nesos, AD 23); *PSI* 9.1051 (Soknopaiu Nesos, AD 26); *P.Mich.* 5.328 (Tebtynis, AD 29). The legal maximum interest rate fixed by the Gnomon of the Idios Logos is 12 per cent: *BGU* 5.1210, ll.235–6. On all this, see Lerouxel (2016: 55–6; 79–84).

[27] Tac., *Ann.* 3.40. For the *gravitas faenoris* as a 'high interest rate', see Lo Cascio (1978: 244). The variability of the interest rate inside the Roman Empire is pointed out by Gaius, *Dig.* 13.4.3.pr.

[28] The interest rate dropped from 12 to 4 per cent: Suet., *Aug.* 41.1; Cass. Dio 51.21.5; Oros. 6.19.19; cf. Billeter (1898: 165–7); Lo Cascio (1978: 250–1).

[29] For Alexandria's permeability for aurei and denarii, cf. Andreau (2005: 331–2); Van Minnen (2008: 238–40).

[30] Butcher and Ponting (2014: 177; 186; 199).

strongly suggests that such exchanges were already underway in the age of Tiberius.[31]

In sum, although many of the Augustan and Tiberian coins found in India left Italy only after Caligula squandered the huge cash reserves left by his predecessor,[32] and were exported to India several decades after they reached Alexandria, the preponderance of Augustan CL CAESARES and Tiberian PONT MAX types in Indian hoards cannot be entirely dissociated from the increase in the volume of the India trade mentioned by Strabo. As a consequence, Tacitus can hardly be accused of an anachronism when he depicts Tiberius as lamenting the loss of Roman coinage to alien or hostile nations in AD 22. In fact, the growing India trade revives the debate on the *luxus mensae* in Rome's senate in AD 16 and 22,[33] and contributes to the increase of the fiscal revenues from Egypt. Tiberius' famous dictum that he wanted his sheep (the taxpayers) shorn, not flayed, is reported by Cassius Dio-Xiphilinus as a reaction to the increase of Egyptian revenues announced by a prefect of Egypt, perhaps at the very beginning of his principate.[34] It is worth noting that it was probably the prefect of Egypt who farmed out the collection of the Red Sea tax and sent the accounting of the Indian customs duties to the central imperial administration.[35]

In addition to the emphasis on the parallel growth of the India trade and Egyptian revenues—and even more relevant for understanding the Muziris papyrus texts—we have the following lines from Strabo, with their valuable details about the mechanics of the customs duties collection from Indian commodities:

> At the present time even large fleets are despatched as far as India and the extremities of Aethiopia, from which the most valuable cargoes are brought to Egypt, and thence sent forth again to the other regions; so that double duties are collected, on both imports and exports; and on goods that cost heavily the duty is also heavy.[36]

The geographer points out two peculiar features regarding the taxes on goods imported via the Red Sea. First, the duties were subject to double customs

[31] See pp. 327 n.2; 331–2.

[32] Suet., *Calig.* 37.3; Cass. Dio 59.2.6. Cf. Cavallaro (1984: 162, n. 9; 187, nn. 106, 107).

[33] Tac., *Ann.* 2.33; 3.53–5.

[34] Cass. Dio 57.10.5. However, the existence of an Aemilius Rectus prefect of Egypt in the first years of Tiberius is controversial, cf. Bastianini (1988: 504); Cazzaniga (1992: 7 n. 14); Gambetti (2009: 275, n. 14); Faoro (2016: 30). Nonetheless, even if Cassius Dio-Xiphilinus mistook the name of the prefect, it is significant that the tradition he accepted indicated Egypt as the source of the increase of fiscal revenues. The geographical detail is missing in Suet., *Tib.* 32.2.

[35] See pp. 302 n.20; 317–8.

[36] Strab. 17.1.13: *νῦν δὲ καὶ στόλοι μεγάλοι στέλλονται μέχρι τῆς Ἰνδικῆς καὶ τῶν ἄκρων τῶν Αἰθιοπικῶν, ἐξ ὧν ὁ πολυτιμότατος κομίζεται φόρτος εἰς τὴν Αἴγυπτον, κἀντεῦθεν πάλιν εἰς τοὺς ἄλλους ἐκπέμπεται τόπους, ὥστε τὰ τέλη διπλάσια συνάγεται τὰ μὲν εἰσαγωγικὰ τὰ δὲ ἐξαγωγικά· τῶν δὲ βαρυτίμων βαρέα καὶ τὰ τέλη.*

duties (*τέλη διπλάσια*), due first when the Indian commodities entered Egypt (*εἰσαγωγικά*), and then again when they left (*ἐξαγωγικά*) for other regions of the empire. Second, since they related to high-value commodities, the *τέλη* were heavy. Taken by itself, this second remark is ambiguous, because the words *βαρέα καὶ τὰ τέλη* may allude to the tax rate, implying that high-value commodities are as a rule taxed at a high rate, or they may refer to the revenues, emphasizing the obvious—that customs duties on high-value commodities generate high(er) revenues (compared to low-value commodities). The first interpretation seems preferable. We will show that the two texts of the Muziris papyrus indicate that, as they moved from the Red Sea to the Mediterranean, Indian commodities were subject to double customs duties, and that their rate was an unusually high 25 per cent.

In describing the structure of customs duties on Indian commodities, Strabo displays the same degree of accuracy as when he specifies the number of ships that set sail for India from Myos Hormos.[37] It is probable that this precision was learnt during the geographer's Egyptian sojourn, when his friend Aelius Gallus was prefect. This raises the question of whether the structure of the duties on commodities imported via the Red Sea was inherited from the Ptolemies or designed anew by the Romans. The fact that Strabo refrains from highlighting these duties as an example of Roman administrative diligence supports the notion that the tax structure was to some extent a Ptolemaic legacy.[38]

Strabo's comment may be better appreciated when juxtaposed with his remarks about duties levied on commodities from the English Channel. In Strabo's eyes, this region and the Indian Ocean were poles apart in more than one sense. While the fabulous wealth of the Arabs had inspired Augustus' plans for the conquest of Arabia Felix,[39] Britain's poverty had discouraged any prospect of occupying the island.[40] The cheap trinkets exchanged between Gaul and Britain were no match for the exotic items from India and East Africa. Consistently, the 'not at all heavy' customs duties on the cross-channel trade form a striking contrast with the definitely 'heavy' duties on Indian Ocean imports.[41]

[37] Other passages in which Strabo refers to customs duties, either of his own time or of the past, are not as accurate: Strab. 4.1.8 (*fossa Mariana*, Massaliotai); 4.3.2 (Arar); 8.6.20 (Corinth); 9.3.4 (Krisaioi); 12.8.19 (Meander); 13.3.6 (Kyme); 14.1.26 (Ephesus); 16.1.27 (Skenitai).

[38] The Ptolemies applied the same steep rate to unguents (*τετάρτη τοῦ μύρου/ τῶν μύρων*): *SB* 3.7176 [247 BC]; 6.9090 [248 BC]; 6.9416 [244 BC]; *O.Cair.* 20 [244 BC]; cf. Raschke (1978: 658, 951–2, n. 1199; 982, n. 1350).

[39] Strab. 16.4.22.

[40] Strab. 2.5.8.

[41] Strab. 4.5.3: *τέλη τε οὔπως* (Xylander: *οὔτως* mss.) *ὑπομένουσι βαρέα τῶν τε εἰσαγομένων εἰς τὴν Κελτικὴν ἐκεῖθεν καὶ τῶν ἐξαγομένων ἐνθένδε . . . ὥστε μηδὲν δεῖν φρουρᾶς τῆς νήσου*. On the passage, cf. De Laet (1949: 127–9). I accept Xylander's correction. Madvig's defence of *οὔτως* (1871: 538) garbles the meaning of the sentence: the consequence of *ὑπομένουσι* is that not the tributes, but the garrisons are unnecessary (*ὥστε μηδὲν δεῖν φρουρᾶς τῆς νήσου*). H. L. Jones's

Since they were given no military assistance and had to provide for their own safety, the tax farmers who levied customs duties on the English Channel trade probably paid a flat sum in advance. The collectors of the duties on Indian Ocean imports, on the other hand, who were protected by military garrisons, sent the revenues to the treasury while keeping a portion for themselves.[42]

This disparity is made even more striking by an additional asymmetry. For cross-channel trade, Strabo mentions customs duties in both directions. For Red Sea trade, he considers only customs duties on Indian and East African commodities that are imported into and then re-exported from Egypt. Customs duties on commodities exported from Egypt to other Indian Ocean emporia are not mentioned. This is not simply an oversight. A similar focus on import-only duties can be found in the description of the Red Sea port of Leuke Kome in the *Periplus.*[43] Whether the 'collector of the quarter-tax on incoming merchandise' (παραλήπτης τῆς τετάρτης τῶν εἰσφερομένων φορτίων) worked on behalf of the Roman Empire or the Nabataean kingdom, the wording of the passage makes it clear that the 25 per cent tax applied only to the imported items. A system in which import duties are not balanced by reciprocal duties on exports is also implied by the list of *species pertinentes ad vectigal*, attached to a rescript of Marcus Aurelius and Commodus.[44] Since the itemized commodities are all exotic goods brought into the Roman Empire via Syria or Egypt, and none is native to the empire, the *vectigal* concerned imports only. So, when the emperor Theodosius stated in AD 381 that foreign ambassadors had to pay a 12.5 per cent tax on commodities they imported from home, but not on the goods they took out of the Roman Empire, he was following a very old fiscal tradition, whereby taxation on Eastern imports had no reciprocal counterpart for Roman exports.[45]

Goods exported to Indian Ocean regions were also exempt from the *quintana*, a tax on commodities and services offered locally, for which ostraca from Berenice provide evidence.[46] Let-passes addressed to the officials at the town gate (*quintanenses*) imply that jars of wine and oil brought from Coptos were subject to the *quintana* if meant for sale in Berenice, but exempt if they were to be loaded on a ship. One may speculate whether commodities

translation ('they submit so easily to heavy duties') would require a different word sequence; as it stands, the text makes it clear that the adverb goes with βαρέα, not with ὑπομένουσι. On the connection between heavy customs duties and garrisons, cf. *PME* 19, and below, p. 318.

[42] It may be suggested that the revision of the Zarai customs duties, implied by the *lex portus post discessum coh(ortis) instituta* (*CIL* 8.4508, ll. 4–5, cf. recently France (2014)), aimed to compensate tax farmers for the additional expenses and risks following the removal of the cohort.

[43] *PME* 19.

[44] Marcian., *Dig.* 39.4.16.7.

[45] *Cod. Theod.* 4.13.8= *Cod. Iust.* 4.61.8.

[46] Bagnall, Helms, and Verhoogt (2000); (2005); Cuvigny (2006: 689–90); Nappo and Zerbini (2011); Vandorpe (2015: 100).

exported from Egypt to Indian Ocean regions were subject to some other as yet unknown tax. Even so, Strabo's emphasis on import duties and his corresponding silence on export duties suggest that—with regard to the Eastern trade at least—the fiscal burden rested primarily if not exclusively on imported commodities.

5.2. THE *PERIPLUS*: THE SHIPS AND CARGOES OF THE SOUTH INDIA TRADE

Authorship of the *Periplus* is falsely assigned to Arrianus by the extant manuscript tradition. When Marcianus of Heraclea read it,[47] the work may have gone under the name of a ship captain known as Sosandros.[48] Whatever the case, its author is certainly an insider knowledgeable about navigational techniques on the Red Sea and the Indian Ocean.[49]

Anchored to the decades between AD 40 and 70 by the mention of the Nabataean king Malichus,[50] the timeframe of the *Periplus* is further confirmed by the identity and approximate chronology of two other rulers. The first is Charibael, labelled the legitimate king of two nations, the Homerite and the Sabaean.[51] Charibael is Karibī'l Watār Yuhan'im, grandfather of Karibī'l Bayān, who was king around AD 80/90.[52] The description of Charibael as 'a friend of the emperors thanks to continuous embassies and gifts' implies that diplomatic relations occurred over many years and under several emperors. The second ruler is Manbanos, mentioned as the king of Ariake and other regions.[53] Manbanos is the Kṣaharāta king Nahapāna, whose reign preceded that of Caṣṭana and the beginning of the Śaka era (AD 78).[54] Nahapāna's reign was in part contemporary with those of the Indo-Scythian Satavastres and the Sātavāhana Gautamīputra Śiva Sātakarṇi.[55] Since the latter, the predecessor of

[47] Marcotte (2012: 19–20).

[48] De Romanis (2016: 105–6).

[49] Cf. especially *PME* 20; 57.

[50] *PME* 19. The end of Malichus' reign is inferred from *CIS* 2.161, cf. Wenning (1993: 36 n. 98); cf. also Bowersock (1983: 70 n. 37); Casson (1989: 7). For a confutation of the third-century chronology, cf. Dihle (1965: 9–35); Robin (1991).

[51] *PME* 23.

[52] Robin (1991). Cholaibos, the lord of the Mapharitis (*PME* 22), is Kulayb Yuha'min: Robin (1994a).

[53] *PME* 41.

[54] The identification of Manbanos with Nahapāna goes back to Boyer (1897) and is generally accepted—doubts, however, in Fussman (1991). Nahapāna's inscriptions are dated with regnal years: Pauli (1986); Cribb (1992: 132); (2000: 41–3); Shimada (2006: 125–7).

[55] Nahapāna's overstrikes on the coins of Satavastres and Gautamīputra Śiva Sātakarṇi show that the beginning of the reign of the latter two preceded the end of the reign of the former. On the other hand, overstrikes on Nahapāna's coins show that a part of his reign preceded the end of the reigns of the Indo-Scythian kings Satavastres and Saves (Sasan) and the Sātavāhana kings

Gautamīputra Śrī Sātakarṇi,[56] is named by the author of the *Periplus* as the elder Saraganos,[57] former lord of Kalliena, we may infer that the *Periplus* was written sometime between AD 40 and 70, coinciding with the second part of Nahapāna's rule and the first part of Gautamīputra Śrī Sātakarṇi's rule.[58]

The purpose of the *Periplus* is to provide both a comprehensive description of the Indian Ocean coastline and an account of the trade opportunities within its many emporia. In previous chapters, we analysed the *Periplus*' geographic reconstruction of the west coast of India and Limyrike.[59] Now, we will consider its portrayal of the commercial opportunities in those regions.

Amounting to roughly 20 per cent of the entire text, the meticulous lists of commodities exported from and imported to each of the Indian Ocean emporia visited by Egyptian merchants are a conspicuous and distinctive feature of the *Periplus*. Like the information on departure times for different sea routes, these lists establish that the author was also writing for a readership of financiers. It is worth repeating that if there is any area in which the *Periplus* is absolutely reliable, it is these lists. The knowledge of the Indian Ocean trade they display is hardly the outcome of a single trader's experience. Since the cargo of every ship returning from any Indian Ocean destination had to be scrutinized and inventoried by fiscal authorities and financial investors when it was unloaded at Berenice and then warehoused and sold in Coptos and Alexandria, one may surmise that, as far as imported commodities are concerned, each list in the *Periplus* was based on and crosschecked against a variety of contemporaneous documents, such as fiscal declarations from returning ships and papers belonging to private investors. By contrast, since the commodities exported from Egypt to the Indian Ocean emporia do not seem to have been subject to any customs duties, inventories of the outgoing shipments would be drawn up only by the merchants themselves or by the investors, whose credit may have been used for (and secured by) the commodities to be exported.[60]

The list of commodities exported to Limyrike (*PME* 56) may be better appreciated when compared to the lists of goods sent to Barbarikon-Minnagar

Gautamīputra Śiva Sātakarṇi and Gautamīputra Śrī Sātakarṇi: Cribb (1992: 133); Turner and Cribb (1996: 313–18); Bhandare (2006: 27–30).

[56] Bhandare (2006: 26–9). [57] *PME* 52.

[58] Different hypotheses have been put forward regarding the precise chronology of Nahapāna's reign. Cribb (1998: 157) suggests the beginning of the era of Gondophares (AD 20); Falk (2008: 143, n. 23) the beginning of the era of Sphujiddhvaja (March 21, AD 22) as the base of the time-reckoning in Nahapāna's inscriptions; Bhandare (1999) argues for AD 32 and 79 as the beginning and the end of Nahapāna's reign.

[59] See pp. 76–80; 84–88.

[60] Cf. [Dem.] 35.10–11: *ἐδάνεισαν . . . ἐπὶ οἴνου κεραμίοις Μενδαίοις τρισχιλίοις ὃς πλεύσεται ἐκ Μένδης ἢ Σκιώνης ἐν τῇ εἰκοσόρῳ ἣν Ὑβλήσιος ναυκληρεῖ*; Scaev., *Dig.* 45.1.122.1: *Callimachus mutuam pecuniam nauticam accepit . . . sub pignoribus et hypothecis mercibus a Beryto comparatis.*

(*PME* 39) and Barygaza (*PME* 49), either for the market or for the king. The three lists have in common money, wine, peridots (?),[61] coral,[62] and clothing. The limited quantities of wine sent to Barygaza for the king are said to be of excellent quality. The same was probably true of the equally limited exports to Limyrike. At any rate, it was good enough for a Tamil poet to invite the Pāṇṭiya king to enjoy 'the sweet, cool wine brought by the perfect ship of the Yavaṉar'.[63]

Copper, tin, lead, raw glass, sulphide of antimony, and realgar appear only in the Barygaza and Limyrike lists (Barbarikon has glassware); multi-coloured textiles are only in the Barbarikon and Limyrike lists (Barygaza has multi-coloured girdles); storax and silverware appear in the Barbarikon and Barygaza lists (since it is destined for the king, Barygaza's silverware is 'very costly'). Only a few items are peculiar to a single emporion: frankincense to Barbarikon; yellow sweet clover (? μελίλωτον), unguent, dancers, and beautiful girls for concubinage to Barygaza; and trisulphide of arsenic to Limyrike. The equally singular inclusion in the Limyrike list of 'grain in sufficient quantity for the *nauklerion*', along with the explanation that the merchants do not 'use' it, means that grain was available at Barbarikon and Barygaza,[64] but not in Limyrike. Unlike the ships headed for Barbarikon and Barygaza, vessels bound for Limyrike had to carry grain from Egypt for both the outward and return voyages.

In sum, although they include many of the same items, the lists of commodities exported to the various Indian emporia reflect some differences among the destinations. Most notable, though, is the difference in how one export—money—is recorded in each of the three lists. In the Barbarikon list it is recorded with the simple entry χρῆμα; in the Barygaza list, the mention of δηνάριον χρυσοῦν καὶ ἀργυροῦν (Roman aurei and denarii) is followed by the note that they were exchanged for the local coinage at a profit.[65] By contrast, the entry in the Limyrike list (προηγουμένως χρήματα πλεῖστα) emphasizes that the value of the coins stood out both in relation to the other items exported to the same ports (προηγουμένως) and to the money exported to other Indian Ocean emporia (πλεῖστα).[66]

It is important to underline that in Limyrike's emporia the volumes of the incoming and outgoing cargoes were not even. The author of the *Periplus* explains that Nelkynda and Bakare lay on the banks of the same river, and while the former (120 stades upriver) was the place where the Western ships

[61] For the *chrysolitha* as possible peridots, cf. Casson (1989: 190).
[62] For coral export to India, De Romanis (2000).
[63] *Puṟanāṉūṟu* 56, 18–21.
[64] The author records abundant production of grain both in the land of the Parsidai and in Ariake: *PME* 37; 41.
[65] See Appendix 1.
[66] In addition to Barbarikon and Barygaza, cf. *PME* 6: δηνάριον ὀλίγον (Adulis); 8: δηνάριον οὐ πολὺ καὶ χρυσοῦν δὲ καὶ ἀργυροῦν (Malao); 24: χρῆμα ἱκανόν (Muza).

unloaded and wintered, the latter, which was right on the coast, was the port where they loaded their heavy return cargoes. The presence of sandbanks and narrow passages discouraged any loading at Nelkynda.[67] The unstated but obvious implication is that the western ships arrived in India comparatively light in weight and that a substantial bulk of Indian commodities was exchanged for Roman coins.

The list of the commodities acquired in Limyrike—much longer than the list evaluated in the Muziris papyrus—shows a remarkable mix of both typical South Indian products (pearls, ivory, and pepper) and goods from elsewhere on the subcontinent and beyond (tortoise shell from Lakshadweep and Chryse Island; jacinth from Sri Lanka; diamonds, possibly from Andhra Pradesh; malabathron and Gangetic nard from the Ganges Valley; and silk from China). This unusual assortment is absent from any other commodity list in the *Periplus*, supporting the conclusion that the cargo evaluated in the Muziris papyrus (which includes both ivory and Gangetic nard) originated from a Limyrike emporion.

Even more important, however, is that at *PME* 56 the lists of exported and imported goods are preceded by a remark about the unusual size of the ships that travel there, and the rationale for their size. Both in the Heidelberg manuscript (Codex Palatinus Graecus 398) and its copy (Brit. Mus. Add. Ms. 19319 ex Vatopedinus 655, L in Frisk's edition), the text runs as follows:

> πλεῖ δὲ εἰς τὰ ἐμπόρια ταῦτα μεστὰ πλοῖα διὰ τὸν ὄγκον καὶ τὸ πλῆθος τοῦ πιπέρεως (πεπ- L) καὶ τοῦ μαλαβάθρου.

The first scholar to suggest that μεστὰ—then read as μετὰ—resulted from a corruption of the original reading was J. W. Stuck, who in his edition (1577) replaced με(σ)τὰ with πολλὰ in the text and added in a footnote: 'Forsan πολλὰ vel μεγάλα legendum.'[68] The first option (πολλὰ) was accepted by B. Fabricius (1849); the second (μεγάλα) was preferred by K. W. L. Müller (1855), Fabricius (1883) and H. Frisk (1927). Frisk, however, pointed out that the manuscripts do not have μετὰ, but μεστὰ,[69] a reading that was defended by E. Drakonaki-Katantzaki (1982) and retained by L. Casson (1989) and M.D. Bukharin (2007).[70]

I do not think that the author of the *Periplus* could have written μεστὰ—διὰ τὸν ὄγκον καὶ τὸ πλῆθος τοῦ πιπέρεως καὶ τοῦ μαλαβάθρου to mean μεστὰ πιπέρεως καὶ μαλαβάθρου.[71] Nor can I see how, after πλεῖ, εἰς τὰ ἐμπόρια ταῦτα

[67] *PME* 55. [68] Stuck (1577: 81).

[69] Mayer (2018: 564, n. 13) takes μετὰ as the manuscript's reading and μεστὰ as Casson's conjecture. His revival of Stuck's emendation μεγάλα is baseless.

[70] Drakonaki-Katantzaki (1982: 50–1); Casson (1989: 264). Casson's translation runs as follows: 'Ships in these ports of trade carry full loads because of the volume and quantity of pepper and malabathron.'

[71] Cf. e.g. Plut., *Nic.* 18.7: πλοῖα μεστὰ σίτου.

can be taken as ἐν τοῖς ἐμπορίοις τούτοις, and result in a meaningful sentence. In my view, the manuscript's reading cannot be kept as it is: it must be amended to μέ<γι>στα ('very large'), which is palaeographically more economical than the solutions suggested by Stuck.[72] An English translation of the amended text should read:

> Very large ships sail to these emporia because of the volume and quantity of pepper and malabathron.[73]

The adjustment of the ship size to accommodate the volume of the commodities is a basic principle of economic rationalism, which the author of the *Periplus* did not ignore in other contexts. For instance, in his description of the emporion of Mosyllon, on the northern Somali coast, he observes that the huge amount of κασία available there called for bigger ships.[74] In this passage, the comparative 'bigger' (μειζόνων) shows that the author is referring to ships that are larger than the ones usually bound for the emporia of the Somali land, but not 'very large', as in the case of the Limyrike ships. 'Very large' vessels occur only once more in the *Periplus*; they are those sailing from the emporia of the Coromandel Coast to 'Chryse Island' and the Ganges Valley.[75] Therefore, if the above correction is accepted, the *Periplus* singles out the South Indian emporia as the only ones in the western Indian Ocean where 'very large' ships can be loaded. Consequently, the combination of pepper and malabathron emerges as the most voluminous cargo of the Indo-Roman trade.

We do not need the *Periplus* to confirm that pepper was one of the main cargoes—indeed, *the* main cargo—of the Roman Indiamen returning from Muziris. The same is implied by the Tamil verses mentioning the Yavaṉar ships that came with gold and went back with pepper.[76] But what the *Periplus* comment does introduce is the relevance of malabathron.

The Indian origin of the word 'malabathron'—from the Sanskrit compound *tamālapattra* (leaf of *tamāla*)—and the synonymic expression 'Indian leaf'[77] confirm that malabathron refers to the leaves of an Indian plant known as the *tamāla*. *Tamāla* is frequently identified with the *Cinnamomum tamāla*, a tree that grows wild in the (sub-)Himalayan regions from 450 to 2,000 metres

[72] Cf. De Romanis (1996a: 178–80, n. 40). The correction is accepted by Belfiore (2013).

[73] Since pepper and malabathron are mass nouns, reference to both ὄγκος and πλῆθος (volume and quantity) is redundant, strictly speaking. But it is not when it comes to considering the volume and numerical quantity of countable nouns such as atoms (Leucipp. *VSF* 7) or Spartan coins (Plut., *Lys.* 17.2). According to Drakonaki-Katantzaki (1982: 51), it would be a 'figure of speech *hen dia dyoin*'.

[74] *PME* 10: ἐξάγεται δὲ ἀπὸ τῶν τόπων κασίας χῦμα πλεῖστον, <δι>ὁ καὶ μειζόνων πλοίων χρῄζει τὸ ἐμπόριον, 'exports from this area are: a great quantity of cassia (for this reason the port requires bigger ships)' (transl. by L. Casson).

[75] *PME* 60.

[76] *Akanāṉūṟu* 149.7–13.

[77] Hippiatrica, Excerpta Lugdunensia 205.

above sea level.[78] Together with Gangetic nard and Chinese silk, its leaves were exported from the Ganges emporion down to the Limyrike emporia.[79] Apart from the *Periplus*, written sources are virtually silent regarding the trade and consumption of malabathron in ancient India. In the Roman Empire, malabathron leaves (or their oil) were used for unguents[80] and drugs,[81] to oil the hair,[82] flavour wine,[83] or perfume breath or cloth.[84] Greek and Latin texts mention a 'Syrian' and an 'Egyptian' malabathron, which may refer to fake malabathron, or else Indian malabathron leaves that had been processed in Syria and Egypt.

However, none of the Western texts convey the sense that the volume of malabathron imported was in some way comparable to that of pepper—except the author of the *Periplus*, who makes it clear that in the mid-first century AD the production of unguents and medicines required an enormous amount of malabathron oil. Papyrological and literary evidence shows that malabathron continued to be imported up to the fifth or sixth century AD,[85] but it seems likely that in the latter centuries the volume was tapering off. Ultimately, malabathron disappears from the Arabian Sea trade, only to re-emerge, with the new name of *dārčīnī,* along the caravan roads between China and Persia.[86]

Although he fails to specify how it was collected and by whom, the author of the *Periplus* states that pepper grows abundantly only in Kottanarike. For malabathron, however, he offers up a marvellous story about how it passed from the people who collected it to those who traded it. Our understanding of this passage is hindered by several false readings in the manuscript, but it is nonetheless clear that the people who prepared the leaves for trading did not obtain the plant via commercial transactions with the malabathron-collecting community:

> Every year there turns up at the border of Thina a certain tribe, short in body and very flat-faced . . . called Sesatai . . . They come with their wives and children bearing great packs resembling mats of green leaves and then remain at some spot on the border between them and those on the Thina side, and they hold a festival for several days, spreading out their mats under them, and then take off

[78] Miller (1969: 74–7); Raschke (1978: 651–2, 838, 1045, 1489, 1632; Casson (1989: 241–2); *contra* Laufer (1918).

[79] Malabathron and Gangetic nard are mentioned in the lists of the commodities available both in the emporia of Limyrike and the Ganges emporion: *PME* 56; 63. For the silk route China–Ganges Valley–South India, cf. *PME* 56; 64.

[80] Plin., *NH* 12.129; 13.14; 18.

[81] In general, for the medicinal properties of malabathron, see Dsc. 1.12; Plin., *NH* 23.93. There is no point in listing all the occurrences in Scribonius Largus, Soranus, Galen, Oribasius, Aëtius, and Paulus.

[82] Hor., *Carm.* 2.7.7–8. [83] Plin., *NH* 14.108. [84] Plin., *NH* 23.93.

[85] *P.Strasb.* 4.222; *BGU* 1.93; *PSI* 15.1558; *SB* 8.9834; *P.Corn.* 35r; *BGU* 3.953; *P.Ant.* 1.32; *P.Oxy.* 54.3731; 3733; 3766; *PSI* 12.1264; *P.Genova* 1.28; Theophyl. Sim. 7.13.6.

[86] Laufer (1919: 541).

> for their own homes in the interior. The [? locals], counting on this, then turn up in the area, collect what the Sesatai had spread out, extract the fibres from the reeds which are called *petroi*, and lightly doubling over the leaves and rolling them into ball-like shapes, they string them on the fibres from the reeds. There are three grades: what is called big-ball malabathron from the bigger leaves; medium-ball from the lesser leaves; and small-ball from the smaller. Thus three grades of malabathron are produced, and then they are transported into India by the people who make them.[87]

Just as with Philostratus' pepper story,[88] this tale reflects an awareness on the part of the Western merchants that pepper and malabathron—the two commodities which represented, in terms of weight and volume, the bulk of the cargo on the very large ships returning from South India—were goods often exchanged via barter and gift in their home country, rather than through formalized trade.

5.3. PLINY: THE TIMETABLE OF THE COMMERCIAL ENTERPRISES TO SOUTH INDIA

Unlike Strabo, who felt no need to incorporate data from the Alexandrian traders, Pliny opted to include the reports of contemporaneous merchants in his geographical books. A particularly noteworthy example is the brief history of the sea voyages between Arabia and India, which Pliny inserted after the exposition of India, but before describing Carmania, Persis, and Arabia.[89]

Pliny's account begins with a reiteration of Alexander's travels from Patale to Susa.[90] He then records two older sea routes, both of which depart from the South Arabian promontory of Syagrus, and reach Patale and Sigerum, respectively.[91] Finally, he adds the full description of the contemporaneous Alexandria–Muziris–Alexandria sea route.[92] Pliny emphasizes that it was worthwhile chronicling the entire voyage in detail, because it was only in his own time that solid information became public knowledge.[93] In fact, compared to what Strabo had assembled in his fifteenth book, Pliny's chapter on the South India trade seems ground-breaking. The little we know about Juba's *Arabica* and Seneca's *de situ Indiae* does not invalidate Pliny's statement that the nations, ports, and towns mentioned in his work were not to be found in any earlier work.[94] We will see that at least part of Pliny's information

[87] *PME* 65; transl. by L. Casson. [88] See pp. 114–5.

[89] Merchants' reports are referred to also in the chapter regarding the Persian Gulf, Plin., *NH* 6.140; 149.

[90] Plin., *NH* 6.96–100. [91] Plin., *NH* 6.100–1. [92] Plin., *NH* 6.101–6.

[93] Plin., *NH* 6.101. [94] Plin., *NH* 6.105.

about the South India trade goes back to a year between AD 49 and 52, whereas his emphasis on Indian pirates reflects a later development and draws on subsequent updates.[95]

One distinctive feature of Pliny's report on South India (and the one most relevant to an analysis of the Muziris papyrus) is his acute sensitivity to the spatio-temporal aspects of the different segments of the Alexandria–Muziris journey. The river passage, the desert crossing, and the sea voyage, on both the Red and the Arabian Seas, are all timed and sometimes also spatially measured. First the river passage: 'Two miles from Alexandria is the town of Iuliopolis. The voyage up the Nile from there to Coptos is 309 (?) miles, and takes 12 days when the Etesian winds are blowing.'[96]

It has to be emphasized that the river voyage starts from Iuliopolis and ends at Coptos. The relevance of noting the departure point and its distance from Alexandria will be discussed later on, in chapter eight. As for the arrival point, here it will be recalled that while the wadi system of the Eastern Desert makes Coptos one of the few terminal points for the desert caravan roads, the Etesian winds favour upriver navigation only up to the Qena bend.[97] It is not coincidental that in Lucian's *The Lover of Lies* Eucrates is said to have sailed upstream to Coptos, and then proceeded by land to his destination 40 kilometres further on.[98] Like the whole communication system between Lower and Upper Egypt, the river journey that served the Indo-Mediterranean trade was shaped by climate and geography.

Then comes the desert crossing:

> From Coptos the journey is made with camels, stations being placed at intervals for the purpose of watering; the first, a stage of 22 miles, is called Hydreuma; the second is in the desert, a day's journey on; the third at the second Hydreuma, 85 miles from Coptos; the next is in the desert; next we come to Apollo's Hydreuma, 184 miles from Coptos; again a station in the desert; then we get to New Hydreuma, 230 miles from Coptos. There is also another Hydreuma—it is called Old Trogodyticum—where a guard is stationed on outpost duty at a byway of two miles; it is seven miles from New Hydreuma. Then comes the town of Berenice, where there is a harbour on the Red Sea, 257 miles from Coptos. But as the greater

[95] By contrast, it may be noted that the construction of new *praesidia* along the Coptos–Berenice caravan road in AD 77/78 (Bagnall, Bülow-Jacobsen, and Cuvigny (2001)) is not recorded.

[96] Plin., *NH* 6.102. The number of miles between Iuliopolis and Coptos fluctuates in Pliny's manuscripts between CCCIII (*E*^{s}*p*) and CCCVIIII (*reliqui*), the latter being chosen by Ian-Mayhoff. However, the real distance between Alexandria and Coptos is much longer than 309 miles (http://orbis.stanford.edu measures 879 km between Alexandria and Coptos). Moreover, Pliny's remarks about the distance and duration of the desert crossing (see p. 143) strongly suggest that he did not write either of those two numbers. Restoring the genuine reading is a matter of guesswork.

[97] See p. 47, n.56.

[98] Luc., *Philops*. 33. See pp. 37–8.

> part of the journey is done by night because of the heat and the days are spent at stations, the whole journey from Coptos to Berenice takes twelve days.[99]

Pliny records the distances along the Coptos–Berenice caravan road with noteworthy precision.[100] Such a degree of accuracy may be compared to the 461 stades between the Nile and Bi'r 'Iayyan, measured by Ptolemaic officials in 22 August/20 September 257 BC.[101] But the Roman miles recorded by Pliny do not translate measures taken under the Ptolemies in stades. In all likelihood, they derive from official measurements commissioned by the Roman government, on the occasion of the (re)construction of the phreatic water reservoirs mentioned in *ILS* 2483. The distance from Coptos (85 miles) locates Pliny's second *hydreuma* at Compasi; the *laccus* (or *lacci*) of Apollonos Hydreuma could not refer to any watering point other than Pliny's Apollonos Hydreuma, whereas his Novum Hydreuma, only 21 miles from Coptos, was probably the *laccus* or *lacci* built *Berenicide* in *ILS* 2483.[102] Besides, it is worth noting that all these distances refer to Coptos, just as the distances on the *lapis Pollae* and the *miliarium* of ʻAin al-Beida refer to the places where they were erected.[103]

Quite remarkably, Pliny explains that the 257 miles from Coptos to Berenice cannot be covered in less than twelve days, because daytime travel is precluded by the unbearable heat. While this information probably comes from the merchants who actually travelled across the desert in July,[104] the expression of disappointment at the relatively slow speed is apparently prompted by the comparison with the voyage from Iuliopolis to Coptos, which, thanks to the Etesian winds that aided upriver sailing, also lasted twelve days. Pliny's emphasis on the slow pace of the desert crossing reinforces the idea that he did not quantify the distance between Iuliopolis and Coptos as either 303 or 309 miles, and that both the numbers given by the manuscripts at 6.102 are corrupt.

Next, Pliny records the timing of the departure from Berenice and the length of the sea voyages from Berenice to Ocelis (or Cane), and from Ocelis to Muziris:

> Travelling by sea begins at midsummer before the Dog star rises or immediately after its rising, and it takes about thirty days to reach the Arabian port of Ocelis or

[99] Plin., *NH* 6.102–3; transl. by H. Rackham, with modifications. At 102, the reading *XXII* of DFR is to be preferred to *XXXII* of E^{s}pg.

[100] Measurements of the distances along the Coptos–Berenice caravan road, with the inclusion of the later forts, appear in the *Itinerarium Antonini* (171–3) and the *Tabula Peutingeriana* (seg. 11). However, the distances recorded here refer not to Coptos, but to the next station of the road.

[101] *SEG* 46.2120 (= 52.1774).

[102] De Romanis (1996a: 175, n. 23; 2006a: 644–7); *contra* Cuvigny (2003: 300); (2018: 142–3; 192–3).

[103] *ILLRP* 454; *ILS* 5836.

[104] Probably drawn from the same informers is the explanation of how the nitrous and salty-acid waters of the Eastern Desert of Egypt are made sweet: Plin., *NH* 31.36 (cf. 24.3).

> Cane in the frankincense-producing district . . . the most advantageous way of sailing to India is to set out from Ocelis; from that port, with the Hippalus wind, it is 40 days' voyage to the first emporion of India, Muziris.[105]

Pliny does not convert the length of the outward sea voyage into spatial distances, but the deadline and timings are carefully laid out. The deadline for the departure from Berenice is fixed around the rising of Sirius (Dog Star), an astronomical phenomenon of great importance in Egyptian religion and culture.[106] Regarding the length of the sea voyage, Casson has argued that Pliny's calculation of forty days for the Ocelis–Muziris leg is a palpable error, since that would mean that the almost 1,900 nautical miles would have been sailed at an average speed of only 1.97 knots.[107] A similar—indeed even more appropriate—argument could be made for the roughly thirty-day Berenice–Ocelis/Cane voyage.[108] Despite the extremely favourable wind, the average speeds for these distances (800/1,100 nautical miles) are only 1.1/1.5 knots.

Nonetheless, it is unnecessary, in my opinion, to posit errors by Pliny or corruptions in his manuscript tradition. There are several reasons why these schedules are plausible. The extremely slow pace of the Berenice–Ocelis/Cane leg may in part be explained by the fact that night sailing in the Red Sea was to be avoided due to the rocky islands, shoals, and coral reefs.[109] As for the Ocelis–Muziris leg, the timing of this crossing—from the end of August to the end of September, when the southwest monsoon was abating—may have contributed to the modest sailing speed.[110] On top of these factors, however, the slow pace of both the Berenice–Ocelis and Ocelis–Muziris trips can also be attributed to the very large size of the ships involved.

Unlike the author of the *Periplus*, Pliny does not specify the size of the vessels bound for South India, but two details in his account corroborate the statement in the *Periplus* regarding their large size. According to Pliny, the ships bound for South India used to take 'cohorts of archers' on board, and they made a point of departing from Berenice, apparently because it was difficult and dangerous to sail the ships upwind to Myos Hormos.[111]

[105] Plin., *NH* 6.104; transl. by H. Rackham, with modifications.

[106] Pliny is probably referring to the Egyptian celebrations for the heliacal rising of Sirius on 20 July: Censorinus *DN* 21.10. The actual heliacal rising of Sirius could be observed on 16 July at the latitude of Berenice and on 22 July at the latitude of Memphis: Ptol., *Phaseis* 59–60 Heiberg.

[107] Casson (1980: 32–3) = Casson (1984: 190–1); Casson (1989: 289, n. 18).

[108] Casson (1980: 32–3) questions the accuracy of a thirty-day duration for both a Berenice–Ocelis and a Berenice–Cane sea voyage. But Pliny's *circiter* shows that his informants were aware of the distance (*c.*300 miles) between the two harbours: their thirty-day approximation may represent a little overreach for Ocelis and a little shortfall for Cane.

[109] See pp. 44–5.

[110] Since the ships bound for South India set sail from South Arabia around 20 August, it is inaccurate to say that they would have the south-west monsoon on their heels 'just when that strong wind was blowing its hardest' (Casson 1980: 33).

[111] Plin., *NH* 6.101; 103.

By the time Pliny's informers were making their way to South India, decades of travel between Muziris and Berenice had already taught Western sailors that the return voyage had to begin within a very particular time frame. The result of all that experience is evident in the following lines:

> Travellers set sail from India on the return voyage at the beginning of the Egyptian month Tybi, which is our December, or at all events before the sixth day of the Egyptian Mechir, which works out to before 13 January in our calendar—so it happens that they return home in the same year.[112]

The earliest departure date was contingent on the recurrence of the north-eastern monsoon, which begins sometime after the first week of December at the latitude of Muziris/Becare.[113] The latest possible date was based on a thorough calculation of the navigational risks, which recommended departing no later than the sixth day of the Egyptian month of Mechir, which Pliny's informers equate to 13 January.

There is no way to justify the equations Tybi = December and, more precisely, 6 Mechir = 13 January, other than by postulating the use of the old revolving Egyptian calendar, in a year in which 1 Tybi = 9 December and 6 Mechir = 13 January of the Roman calendar. Officially replaced by the fixed Alexandrian calendar, the revolving Egyptian calendar would still have persisted for some time among the more traditional or marginal communities in Egypt.[114] The manner in which Pliny defines this time span thus characterizes (one of) his source(s), both socially and chronologically. His somewhat surprising references to both calendars reflect the partnership between the Egyptian crews, who stuck to their traditional calendar system despite the Augustan reform, and the Italic merchants and financiers, who were comfortable only with Roman calendars.[115] This detail is invaluable, because the correspondence between the Egyptian sixth day of Mechir with the Roman thirteenth day of January was valid only in the years AD 49, 50, 51, and 52. Therefore, Pliny's informers must have been engaged in South Indian business in one of the following sailing seasons: AD 48/49, 49/50, 50/51, or 51/52.[116]

Although the timing of the return journey is not recounted in as much detail as the outward voyage, Pliny's final statement that merchants return

[112] Plin., *NH* 6.106: *ex India renavigant mense Aegyptio Tybi incipiente, nostro Decembri, aut utique Mechiris Aegyptii intra diem sextum, quod fit intra idus Ianuarias nostras. ita evenit ut eodem anno remeent*; transl. by H Rackham, with modifications.

[113] See Fig. 2.2. [114] De Romanis (2001).

[115] By contrast, the author of the *Periplus* refers to the months of the Roman and Egyptian reformed calendars roughly synchronized: *PME* 6, 14, 24, 39, 49, 56. See De Romanis (1988: 5–19) and above p. 62, n. 11.

[116] Unaware of the revolving movement of the Egyptian calendar, Pliny erroneously assumes that 6 Mechir of the Egyptian calendar *always* (*quod fit*) corresponded to the Julian 13 January. The hypothesis that the equivalence was calculated by the naturalist (Desanges 2012: 70) seems extremely unlikely.

within one year makes it clear that Alexandria's trade with South India was an annual enterprise. This suggests an important contrast with the sixteenth-century Portuguese trade with South India. Ships of the *Carreira da Índia* could sail between Portugal and India only in alternate years: therefore, in order to maintain an annual business with South India, Portuguese kings had to manage a fleet whose tonnage was twice the size of the expected annual trade volume. Since Roman ships had no such idle seasons, Roman traders could adjust the capacity of their fleet to accommodate a single year's cargo.

Another contrast, this time with medieval trade practices, concerns the deadline for the departure from India, which Pliny sets as 13 January—considerably earlier than the medieval deadline for the voyage from India to Aden in the *tīrmāh* season.[117] This asymmetry has its consequences. A departure by 13 January allowed Roman ships to make the Arabian Sea crossing in more or less forty days,[118] then to stop somewhere in the Gulf of Aden for fresh water[119] (perhaps also transacting some additional business),[120] and finally to cross the southern part of the Red Sea before the weakening of the southerly Red Sea winds.[121] Roman vessels leaving Muziris by early December could reach Berenice as early as February/March and Alexandria by April–May, well within twelve months of their departure (see Fig. 5.4).[122]

In the multi-stage Egypt–South India sea routes during the medieval period, departures from South India in the *tīrmāh* season could be delayed until March.[123] Pepper merchants had more time to amass their cargoes in India, but they also had more trouble forwarding them from Aden to Egypt. Quite significantly, their Red Sea voyage had to stop at ʿAyd̲āb, and in June their pepper was still travelling through the desert between ʿAyd̲āb and Qūṣ.[124]

Portuguese ships of the sixteenth and seventeenth centuries were supposed to leave South India by about the same deadline recommended for the Roman Indiamen. A departure from South India as early as 13 January required a prompt and efficient loading of export goods—something not always easy to

[117] Ibn-Mājid, 231 (see p. 72, n.43) fixes 2 or, at the latest, 22 March, as the deadline for a voyage from India to Arabia, which obviously relates to the *tīrmāh* season. Barbosa, 161 confirms that Calicut merchants used to leave for Aden in February (Julian) and return from mid-August to mid-October.

[118] The time taken by the Ocelis–Muziris leg on their outward journey: Plin., *NH* 6.104.

[119] Just as during the outward journey, water could be taken at Ocelis, *Eudaimon Arabia*, or Cane: *PME* 25; 26; 27; 57; Plin., *NH* 6.104.

[120] On the island of Socotra: *PME* 31; at Moscha Limen: *PME* 32; at Ocelis, as one may argue based on Plin., *NH* 12.87–8.

[121] Plin., *NH* 6.106. See the wind maps in http://www.punchdown.org/rvb/wind/RSWindex.html.

[122] For the return of C. Numidius Eros, see p. 49.

[123] See above n. 117.

[124] See p. 74.

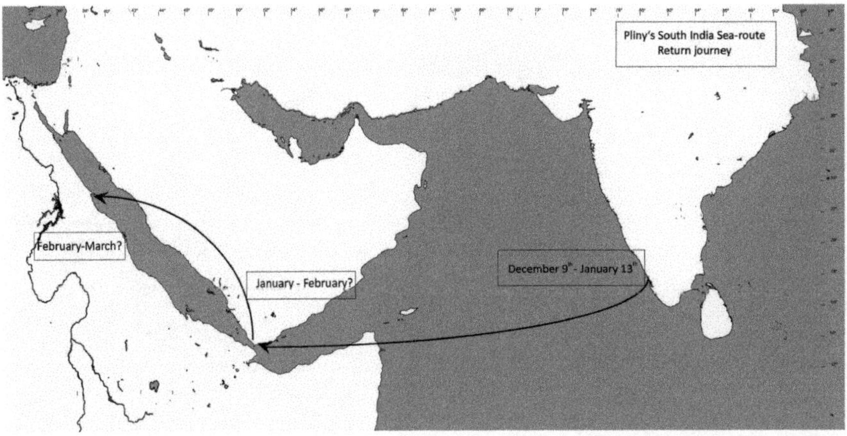

Fig. 5.4 Timing of the South India sea route return journey according to Pliny.

achieve. Ideally, the Portuguese carracks were supposed to leave by 20 December (Julian) or, a little less cautiously, by 10 January (Gregorian).[125] Then they were supposed to reach Mozambique within a month, take on fresh water, and 'turn the Cape of Good Hope before the beginning of the westerly winds'. However, due to delays in the purchase of pepper, they were rarely lucky enough to leave India before 31 December (Gregorian). A departure in January or even February resulted in either a troubled non-stop Cochin–Lisbon voyage passing east of Madagascar, or a wintering in Mozambique, or a shipwreck off the South African coasts (see Fig. 5.5).[126]

In addition to the timing of the Alexandria–Muziris–Alexandria voyage, Pliny provides pertinent details about the South Indian emporia. In particular, he advises against docking at Muziris on three accounts: the neighbouring pirates who occupy Nitriae, the scarcity of the Muziris supply, and the distance between anchorage and shore.[127] Instead, he recommends Becare as a more serviceable port,[128] which suggests that in his informers' time, Muziris was more vulnerable than Becare/Nelkynda to pirate attacks. Pliny fails to clarify

[125] The first date is given by the *Informação a el-rei sobre o comercio da pimenta e do cravo* (*CVR* 95, between AD 1551 and 1557), in de Sá (1954: 333). The second is in a letter from King Philipp II to Martim Affonso de Castro, viceroy of India [1607] *Livros das Monções*, 1.65).

[126] Cf. Bentley Duncan (1986: 14): 'Of the ships that left in December and January, 84% arrived safely in Lisbon, without shipwreck or *invernada*; but of those leaving in February only 50% arrived in Portugal on time. Actually, 15 January seems to have been the critical date. Of the 231 ships that had left by then, 87% arrived in Lisbon without mishap or unusual delay. The percentage drops to 81 for those leaving between 16 and 23 January, and 67 for those leaving 24 January and later. Of the 462 ships with known dates of departures, 69 left in December, 173 during 1–15 January, 172 during 16–31 January, and 46 in February. One-quarter of all known departures had occurred by 5 January, one-half by 15 January, and three-quarters by 23 January.'

[127] Plin., *NH* 6.104.

[128] Plin., *NH* 6.105.

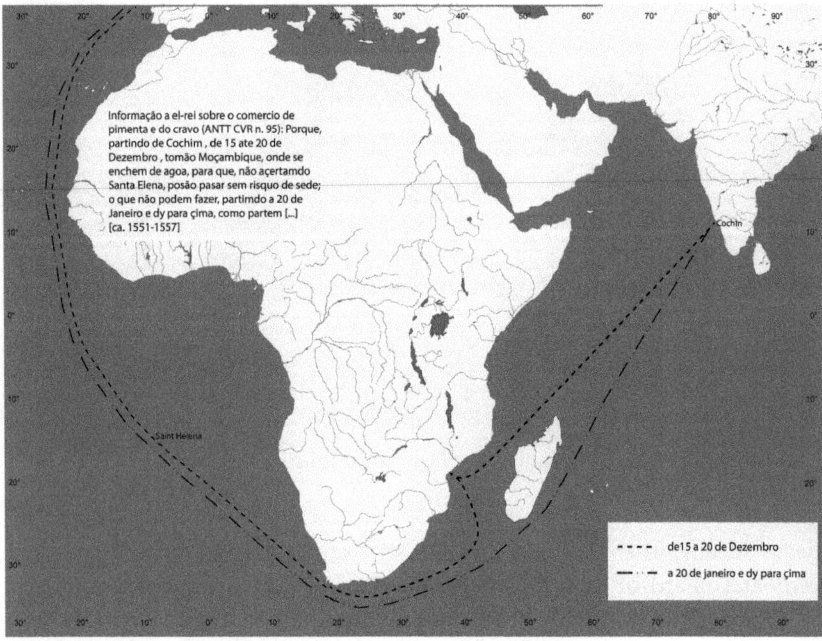
Informação a el-rei sobre o comercio de pimenta e do cravo (ANTT CVR n. 95): Porque, partindo de Cochim , de 15 ate 20 de Dezembro , tomão Moçambique, onde se enchem de agoa, para que, não açertamdo Santa Elena, posão pasar sem risquo de sede; o que não podem fazer, partimdo a 20 de Janeiro e dy para çima, como partem [...] [ca. 1551-1557]
Cochin
Saint Helena
de15 a 20 de Dezembro
a 20 de janeiro e dy para çima

Fig. 5.5 *Carreira da Índia* return voyage according to ANTT CVR n. 95.

that the western ships wintered not at Bakare, but at Nelkynda, 120 stades upriver. He does not even acknowledge the existence of a place called Nelkynda, but only of a *gens Neacyndon*. Based on Pliny's account, one would hardly imagine the complementarity between Nelkynda (where the western ships unloaded their arriving cargo and wintered) and Bakare (where they loaded their returning cargo).[129] On the other hand, Pliny did know, as did the author of the *Periplus*, that Muziris and Becare belonged to two different kings, Caelobothras and Pandion. Furthermore, he writes that the latter dwelled far away from the emporion in the inland town called Modura—which is not mentioned in the *Periplus*.[130] Pliny does not state that Cottonara is the only region of India where pepper grows abundantly, but he knows that it is from there that it is conveyed to Becare in dugout canoes.[131]

Pliny refrains from inserting the new information regarding the South Indian emporia into his description of India (6. 56–80). Probably, he was unaware of their exact location. Apart from Modura, which is vaguely said to lie deep in the interior with respect to Becare, and Nitriae, which is said to be close to Muziris, the relative location of all the other places is not detailed,

[129] *PME* 55, see pp. 137–8.
[130] Plin., *NH* 6.104-5. In *PME* 55, the two kings simply 'dwell in the interior'.
[131] Plin., *NH* 6.105.

either with respect to one another or to other places in India. If no other supporting evidence existed, these towns and regions would float untethered in the imagination of the reader, who would—for instance—wonder why pirates would threaten Muziris more easily than Becare.

Pliny designates Muziris as the 'first emporion of India'. This may be understood either in terms of trade volume or else in a hodological sense, since it could have been the first South Indian port encountered when sailing from some close landmark (one of the Lakshadweep islands or Mount Ely).[132] Even though the first-in-volume sense contrasts with his next sentence about Muziris' undesirability as a port of call, it cannot be completely discarded. In fact, the commercial primacy of Muziris is implied by the approximately contemporaneous *Periplus*,[133] by the ancient Tamil poetry (which, by contrast, does not even mention Bakare/Nelkynda),[134] and, as we shall see, by the Muziris papyrus. The resulting contradiction between Pliny's two statements about Muziris could proceed from two chronologically distinct layers of information reflecting two different phases of Roman trade with South India. The first phase was characterized by the primacy of Muziris, also attested by the *Periplus*. There followed a second phase, in which the pirates (mentioned also in the *Periplus*, but not as menacing) threatened Muziris' trade more directly. The undisputed commercial pre-eminence of Muziris passed, if only temporarily, to the safer port of Becare, which then seemed more convenient and richer in merchandise. An earlier draft of the *Natural History*, where Muziris appeared as the first, viz. the most important, port of India, may have been modified with the dissonant evaluation *non expetendum* etc. The considerable lapse of time between the travel of Pliny's (first?) informers (between AD 48/49 and 51/52) and the *Natural History*'s prefatory letter to Titus *sexies consul* (AD 77 or 78)[135] makes the hypothesis of a chronological stratification of his information on South India not unlikely.

Finally, Pliny's emphasis, both on the scarcity of commodities at Muziris (*neque est abundans mercibus*) and on the imperative (*utique*) to sail back from Muziris by 13 January, strongly suggests that the ancient merchants may have been subject to the same constraints and experienced the same anxieties as the Portuguese officers who struggled to stockpile enough pepper in a timely manner.[136]

[132] See 79. Similarly, Ocelis is in *PME* 25 the 'first halting-place for those who cross (sc. the Arabian Sea) eastwards' (πρώτη καταγωγὴ τοῖς ἔσω διαίρουσι), because, sailing from Egypt to India, it comes before *Eudaimon Arabia* (Aden) and Cane. For the hodological perception of space in classical texts, see Janni (1984).

[133] The *Periplus* presents only Muziris as a flourishing (ἀκμάζουσα) destination for ships coming from north-west India and from Egypt. It is difficult to say whether this description reflects an earlier or later scenario than that depicted by Pliny.

[134] *Akanāṉūṟu* 57.14–17; 149.7–16; *Puṟanāṉūṟu* 343.1–11.

[135] Plin., *NH* praef. 3.

[136] The ships that set sail too late from Barygaza or Limyrike could be forced to winter in Moscha Limen: *PME* 32, see De Romanis (2009a: 646–52).

5.4. PTOLEMY: THE EVOLUTION OF THE SOUTH INDIAN CONTEXT

Chronologically close to the Muziris papyrus, Ptolemy's *Geographia* provides an updated picture of the political geography of South India. However, the correct evaluation of his information requires a clarification regarding his reconstruction of India, especially of its west coast.

In Ptolemy's world map, the Indian subcontinent looks so different from the shape we are familiar with that we would hardly recognize it, if it were sketched without the Indus and Ganges Rivers (Fig. 5.6). By contrast, the Arabian and even the Malay peninsulas are not too badly rendered.

Yet Ptolemy provides an extremely detailed inventory of India's geography, with an extraordinary number of place names and locations. How could such a rich store of information produce such a poor cartographic outcome? In particular, can we clarify why the *Geographia* is so flawed when shaping the west coast of the subcontinent?

In chapter two, we argued that ships bound for Limyrike crossed the Arabian Sea with the south-west monsoon on the quarter most of the time, and used the Lakshadweep archipelago and Mount Ely as landmarks to direct the last part of their course. We also emphasized that the author of the *Periplus* claimed that the open-water routes across the Arabian Sea emerged after Hippalus plotted the locations of the emporia and the extent of the sea.

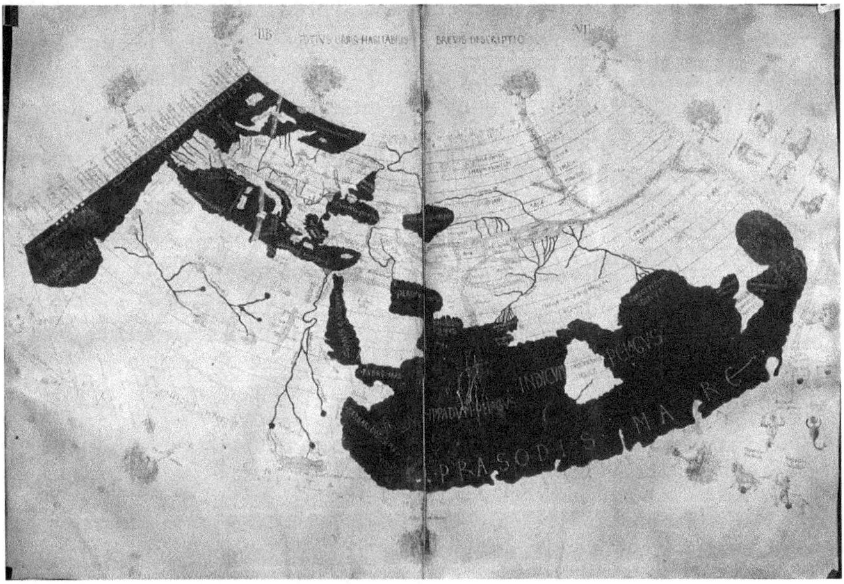

Fig. 5.6 Ptolemy's world map (Harleian MS 7182, ff 58–59).

In the eyes of our author, the sea routes of his day resulted from knowing the exact locations of the emporia on either side of the Arabian Sea.[137] Therefore, it comes as a surprise that Ptolemy locates Muziris at 14° N, nearly four degrees north of the site of Pattanam (10° 9' N).[138] Even more surprising, Muziris is not only placed *north* of Ocelis and Cane (the South Arabian ports from which the pepper carriers set sail, which are more or less correctly located at 12° and 12° 30' N respectively),[139] but it is also only 3° 20' south of Barygaza, and in particular only 45' south of Simylla (Chaul).[140]

Ptolemy's disproportionate latitudinal distances between India's west coast emporia are all the more remarkable in that while Muziris is located almost four degrees *north* of the site of Pattanam, Barygaza and Simylla are approximately four degrees *south* of Bharuch (21° 42' N) and Chaul (18° 33' N), respectively. In sum, as outlined by Ptolemy, the west coast of India between Barygaza and Muziris falls short by more than eight degrees in latitude. While it is not crucial to detail here how the overestimation of continental India led him to set Barygaza four degrees south of where it actually was,[141] it is important to explain why the extent and the direction of the coastline after Barygaza were so badly misrepresented.

Ptolemy's critical remarks on Marinus make it clear that both in Marinus' and in Ptolemy's geographies, the coastline of India after Barygaza was basically shaped by the locations of Simylla and Limyrike.[142] Both Marinus and Ptolemy situated Simylla somewhere south-west of the mouth of the Indus. Between the beginning of the gulf of Barygaza and Simylla, Ptolemy postulated a distance in latitude of 2° 15'.[143] Marinus, who pushed Simylla further west, may have reduced that distance, but not by much. On the other hand, both Marinus and Ptolemy followed Diodorus in positioning Limyrike—apparently perceived as the southernmost region of India—at the zenith of the Pleiades. At least for Ptolemy, that meant that Tyndis, the 'first place' of Limyrike, could not be north of 14° 30' N.

Therefore, Ptolemy shaped the line of the west coast of India by locating the gulf of Barygaza at around 17° N,[144] Simylla at 14° 45',[145] and Limyrike at the

[137] See p. 76. [138] Ptol., *Geog.* 7.1.8; cf. 8.26.4.

[139] Ocelis: Ptol., *Geog.* 6.7.7, cf. 8.22.7; Cane: 6.7.10, cf. 8.22.9. The site of Ocelis was probably at 12° 43' N, 43° 28' E: (Casson 1989: 158); Cane (Ḥiṣn al-Ghurāb) is at 14° N, 48° 19' E: Salles and Sedov (2008).

[140] Barygaza is positioned at 17° 20' N: Ptol., *Geog.* 7.1.62, cf. 8.26.12; Simylla is located at 14° 45' N: 7.1.6, cf. 8.26.3. Ptolemy's manuscripts spell the name as *Σίμυλλα*, whereas in the codices of the *Periplus* it is *Σήμυλλα*.

[141] On Ptolemy's overestimation of continental India, cf. Berthelot (1930: 263).

[142] Ptol., *Geog.* 1.7.6–7; 17.3–4. [143] Ptol., *Geog.* 7.1.5–6.

[144] Kamanei, the first toponym of the Gulf of Barygaza, is located at 17° N: Ptol., *Geog.* 7.1.5.

[145] It is worth noting that Ptolemy (*Geog.* 1.17.3–4) criticizes Marinus for positioning Simylla west of the Indus' mouths, but he too locates the westernmost mouth of the Indus (Sagapa, at 110° 20' 19° 50': Ptol., *Geog.* 7.1.2) 20' northeast of Simylla (110° E 14° 45' N: Ptol., *Geog.* 7.1.6).

zenith of the Pleiades—that is, at 14° 30' N.[146] The 2° 15' between the beginning of the Barygaza gulf and Simylla is certainly less than the roughly 3° 30' between the beginning of the gulf of Khambhat and Chaul, but it is not as distortive as the insignificant 15' in latitude between Simylla and Tyndis. In Ptolemy's terms, 15' in latitude equals 125 stades, that is, *c.*23 kilometres. Between Chaul (Simylla) and Ponnani (Tyndis), there are almost 8° in latitude, or roughly 850 kilometres! On the other hand, while the distance in latitude is minimized, the distance in longitude is overestimated: between Simylla and Tyndis, Ptolemy sets a longitudinal interval of 6°, whereas between Chaul and Ponnani there is only 3°.

It is worth emphasizing that the author of the *Periplus* had envisioned the coastline between Barygaza and Limyrike very differently. First he notes that immediately beyond Barygaza, 'the coast runs from north to south' and that, as a consequence, the region is called Dachinabades, for 'the word for south in their language is *dachanos*.'[147] In addition, he estimates the coastal voyage to Limyrike (probably from Astakapra) as being 7,000 stades—or in Ptolemy's latitudinal degrees, 14°.[148] Whether the 7,000 stades was derived from the Indian merchants who regularly plied between Ariake and Muziris,[149] or was just inferred from the twenty-day journey from Barygaza to Paithana,[150] it is certain that, in the *Periplus* author's mind, the southward direction (πρὸς νότον) of the Barygaza–Paithana road necessarily implied an equivalent southward extension of the coast of India after Barygaza.

The voice of the author of the *Periplus* was presumably not an isolated one. All the Western and Indian merchants reported that Simylla was south of the Indus' mouths.[151] Most probably, they also claimed that from Barygaza it took long southerly journeys to reach Simylla and Limyrike, and long southbound caravan roads to get to Paithana and Tagara. Yet this southward extension of the Indian subcontinent was hardly compatible with the location of Limyrike as established by Diodorus of Samos and accepted by both Marinus and Ptolemy.[152] Therefore, in order to recover some of the distance that their sources claimed existed between the beginning of the Barygaza gulf and Limyrike, Ptolemy (following Marinus) shifted Simylla westwards and

146 Ptol., *Geog.* 7.1.8.

147 *PME* 50; transl. by L. Casson. On *Dachinabades* < *Dakṣiṇāpatha*, the 'Southward Road', cf. De Romanis (2012b: 329–35).

148 *PME* 51. The distance from Barbarikon to Astakapra (Hastakavapra) is given at *PME* 41.

149 *PME* 54.

150 *PME* 51. The author of the *Periplus* may have presumed an average speed of 300 stades per day and added 1,000 stades to account for the distance in latitude between Tagara and Limyrike. Ptolemy assumes 270 stades as the distance covered in a day's journey overland between Leptis Magna and Garama in *Geog.* 1.10.2. Pliny's estimate (*NH* 12.64) of the distance between Thomna and Gaza as 2,437.5 miles (19,500 stades) results from the 65 *mansiones* multiplied per 300 stades. Strabo (16.4.4, from Eratosthenes) equates the distance from Aelana to the Minaean land to seventy days' journey.

151 Ptol., *Geog.* 1.17.4.

152 See p. 82.

bent the subsequent Indian coastline towards the east.[153] From Simylla (long. 110°) up to Poduke (long. 130° 15'), Ptolemy's South India recovered in longitude what it had lost in latitude because of Diodorus' positioning of Limyrike.[154]

Of course, these adjustments have consequences. It is not coincidental that Ptolemy locates Paithana not south, but *north* of Barygaza,[155] or that he fails to mention the hodonym/choronym Dachinabades (< *Dakṣiṇāpatha*, the Southward Road), which is mentioned and explained in the *Periplus*.[156] In Ptolemy's map, there was no room for a twenty-day *Southward* Road from Barygaza to Paithana.

Incidentally, one may note that the author of the *Periplus* directed the Paithana–Tagara road eastward (πρὸς ἀνατολήν),[157] although it may have been oriented even more north–south than the Barygaza–Paithana leg.[158] The distortion may have seemed necessary in order to reconcile the thirty days of the Barygaza–Tagara journey with a plausible location for Limyrike. With Tagara positioned south of Paithana, the author of the *Periplus* should have postulated a distance of at least 9,000 stades between Astakapra and Limyrike (parallel to a thirty-day voyage from Barygaza to Tagara, heading due south at 300 stades per day). The result may have seemed excessive even to him, and thus he turned the Paithana-Tagara leg of the Southward Road eastward. The distortion is even more radical in Ptolemy, who locates Tagara north-east of Paithana.[159]

As for the southernmost part of the subcontinent, Ptolemy extends the coastline between Tyndis and Kolchoi over a longitudinal distance of 7°. As mentioned, its general west–east orientation depends on Diodorus' location of Limyrike. However, its real direction, most familiar to Western merchants, is reflected by some latitudinal variations: Muziris is 30' south of Tyndis, Komaria (Comorin) 30' south of Muziris, and Kolchoi (Eral) 1° 30' north of Komaria.[160]

That said, it has to be emphasized that despite these flaws, the pertinent sections of Ptolemy's *Geography* are the most eloquent testament to (and meagre compensation for) the now-lost geographical works on South India that were written in the first and early second centuries AD.[161] Ptolemy's dry

[153] Berthelot (1930: 323): 'il [sc. Ptolémée] a commis une erreur fondamentale, déplaçant d'à peu près un quart de cercle la ligne du rivage et conséquemment l'arrière-pays; il l'a dirigée d'ouest en est, alors qu'elle va du nord au sud.' Cf. Winkler and Mittenhuber (2009: 301).

[154] Ptol., *Geog.* 7.1.8–14.

[155] Ptol., *Geog.* 7.1.62; 82. Cf. Tchernia (1995: 996).

[156] See n. 147.

[157] *PME* 51.

[158] Although the precise layout of the ancient Barygaza–Paithana–Tagara road is unknown, the longitudes of Bharuch (72° 59' 50.20" E), Paiṭhan (75° 23' 9.92" E), and Ter (76° 8' 31.50" E), combined with the fact that the Southward Road included long roadless (mountainous) tracts (*PME* 51), suggest that the Paiṭhan–Ter leg (difference in longitude between the two ends: *c.*45' 21.50") was more north–south oriented than the Bharuch–Paiṭhan leg (difference in longitude *c.*2° 23' 20").

[159] Ptol., *Geog.* 7.1.82.

[160] Ptol., *Geog.* 7.1.8–10. On the site of Kolchoi/Koṟkai, cf. Arunachalam, Sukumar, and Sukumar (2006).

[161] Ptol., *Geog.* 7.1.8–14; 33–45; 85–91.

lists of place names and geographical coordinates include many more coastal sites than are found in either Pliny or the *Periplus*, and provide an impressive number of inland places. Moreover, they locate the sources, bends, and mouths of the two major waterways—the Pseudostomos and Baris Rivers—that linked the ports of Muziris and Bakare to their hinterlands.

Recorded more or less in the same decades as the Muziris papyrus, Ptolemy's overview delivers an updated look at South India's political and economic landscape. Points to note in particular include the following:

a. The choronym Limyrike survives, but is restricted to a smaller area, extending along the coast from Tyndis to the mouths of the Baris River.[162]
b. The choronym *Kuṭṭunāṭu*/Cottonara/Kottanarike has either disappeared from Ptolemy's map or, if it is to be identified with *Kottiara metropolis*, has been downgraded to a toponym.[163]
c. The royal dwellings of the Cēralar and the Pāṇṭiyar kings—the former at Karura, between the Pseudostomos and Baris Rivers, and the latter at Modura, in the land of the Pāṇṭiyar—are noted.[164]
d. Beyond the Baris River, the land of the Aioi (< Āy) begins.[165]
e. The Aioi and Kareis chiefdoms occupy all the land between the Baris (Pamba?) and Solen (Vaikai?) Rivers.[166]
f. Muziris is the only emporion of Limyrike. The only other South Indian emporia are Nitra, in the land of the Pirates, and Elagkon/Elagkoros (E̲lamkulam?), in the land of the Aioi.[167] It is uncertain whether they represented attractive alternatives to Muziris for Western merchants. The fact that neither port appears in the Peutinger Table suggests that their role remained marginal with respect to Western trade.

When contrasted with the information from the *Periplus*, Pliny, and ancient Tamil literature, these data give a sense of the evolution of South India's political and commercial milieux. In the first century AD, the Pāṇṭiyar competed with the Cēralar for control over the entire *Kuṭṭanāṭu* region,[168] and their emporion of Bakare/Nelkynda—rich, safe, and convenient—challenged Muziris' commercial primacy. By the time of Pliny, Bakare/Nelkynda had

[162] Ptol., *Geog.* 7.1.8; 85.
[163] Ptol., *Geog.* 7.1.9. Cf. *Cotiara* in *Tab. Peut.*, seg.11. Curiously enough, Ptolemy locates the sources and bends of the rivers that crossed Muziris and Nelkynda/Bakare (7.1.33–4), and positions the beryl mines of Punnata (7.1.86), but fails to indicate the area where pepper was grown most abundantly.
[164] Ptol., *Geog.* 7.1.86; 89. The *Periplus* locates them vaguely 'in the interior' (*PME* 55); Pliny knows only about Modura, 'a long way in the interior' (*NH* 6.105).
[165] Ptol., *Geog.* 7.1.9. [166] Ptol., *Geog.* 7.1.9–10; 87–8. [167] Ptol., *Geog.* 7.1.7; 9.
[168] Ancient Tamil poetry alludes to a siege of Muziris by a Pāṇṭiyan̲ king: *Akanān̲ūr̲u* 57; 149.

become so attractive that it was recommended over Muziris. Later on, it was the Cēralar who became the masters of the *Kuṭṭanāṭu* region. Palyāṉaic Celkeḻu Kuṭṭuvaṉ, hero of the third decade of *Patiṟṟuppattu*, may have been the first Cēra king to be hailed as *Kuṭṭuvaṉ* (Lord of *Kuṭṭanāṭu*) by poets.[169] Since some portion of the fifty-year reign of his nephew Kaṭal Piṟakōṭṭiya Ceṅkuṭṭuvaṉ, hero of the fifth decade of *Patiṟṟuppattu*, may have coincided with a part of the twenty-two year reign of Gajabāhu in Sri Lanka in the second half of the second century AD,[170] we may suggest that the twenty years of Palyāṉaic Celkeḻu Kuṭṭuvaṉ's (co-?)reign may date to the first half of the second century AD.[171]

Finally, just as he omits mention of the choronym Kuṭṭunāṭu/Cottonara/Kottanarike, Ptolemy fails to locate the region where pepper is grown. This is rather remarkable, considering that he pinpoints the position of the Limyrike beryl mines, as well as the places in trans-Gangetic India where the best malabathron and much of the nard are collected.[172] However, and most importantly for the appreciation of the Muziris papyrus, Ptolemy attests that Bakare and Melkynda (Nelkynda)—recommended by Pliny as the most convenient trade centres—are no longer emporia in the second century AD, whereas Muziris (threatened by pirates and poor in supplies and infrastructure, according to Pliny) is the sole emporion of Limyrike. All this explains why loan contracts financing the South India trade in this period are called 'the Muziris loan contracts', and why a large second-century AD aurei hoard (*terminus post quem* AD 155) has been found at Valluvally, near Pattanam.[173]

[169] *Patiṟṟuppattu* 22.27; 23.10; 29.14. Other Cēra kings addressed with the same epithet are Kaṭal Piṟakōṭṭiya Ceṅkuṭṭuvaṉ (*Patiṟṟuppattu* 42.8; 43.11; 46.13; 47.1; 49.17; *Patikam* 5.22) and Iḷañcēral Irumpoṟai (*Patiṟṟuppattu* 90.26; *Patikam* 9.1). Other occurrences of *Kuṭṭuvaṉ*: *Aiṅkuṟunūṟu* 178.3; *Akanāṉūṟu* 91.13; 212.16; 270.9; 290.12; 376.17; *Naṟṟiṇai* 14.3; 105.7; *Puṟanāṉūṟu* 343.9; 394.3.

[170] *Cilappatikāram* 30.160; *Dīpavaṁsa* 22.14.28 and *Mahāvaṁsa* 35.115. Cf. Zvelebil (1992: 110–14). On the chronology of the Sri Lankan kings, De Romanis (1988: 45–55).

[171] Each of the eight surviving decades of *Patiṟṟuppattu* is completed by a *patikam* (colophon) specifying the regnal years of the hero. But since the regnal years assigned to Neṭuñcēral Ātan, his brother (Palyāṉaic Celkeḻu Kuṭṭuvaṉ), and his three sons add up to 178, their numbers must at least in part refer to years of co-reign. In general, on *Patiṟṟuppattu* colophons, cf. Marr (1985: 272–303).

[172] Ptol., *Geog.* 7.1.86; 2.16; 2.23.

[173] See p. 96, n.44.

Part II

Let Him Look to His Bond
A Loan Contract for Muziris
(*P. Vindob.* G 40822 Recto)

6

Deadline and Whereabouts

The recto text of the Muziris papyrus is a loan contract signed by a single borrower and a single lender. The borrower speaks most of the time in the first person singular; the lender is mostly addressed using the second person singular. In three instances, however, the parties are referred to using verbs or pronouns in the plural form.[1] In the case of the lender, this may be because at stops along the internal trade route—at the Red Sea port, in Coptos, and in Alexandria—the lender is either assisted or represented by agents or managers. The language of the recto text is fairly clear and does not pose particular problems, per se, but gaining a thorough and proper understanding of this fragmentary document has been a problematic endeavour. We have limited knowledge of ancient maritime loan protocol—especially regarding the loans that financed commercial enterprises to Muziris, which apparently had their own peculiarities. In this unfamiliar context, relatively short lacunae (even a few uncertain letters) and minor semantic ambiguities still generate debates concerning the fundamental nature of the contract. A range of issues continue to be controversial, among them the time and place of loan execution, the manner in which the customs duties and the loan were to be (re)paid, and the relationship between the lender and the cameleer (mentioned at l. 2). Crucial questions remain unanswered, or even unasked. Who was the lender? Who was the borrower? What was the loan for?

6.1. A DEBATED CONTRACT

Our analysis of the recto text will begin with the words at ll. 12–13, 'the time established for the repayment in the *kata Mouzeirin* loan contracts'—a simple formula that has turned out to be extremely puzzling. It will help, first, to

[1] Col. ii, ll. 16; 19; 20: *ἐὰν αἱρῆσθε*; l. 21: *ἐὰν βούλησθε*; l. 24: *ὄντων ἡμῶν*.

The Indo-Roman Pepper Trade and the Muziris Papyrus. Federico De Romanis, Oxford University Press (2020).
 DOI: 10.1093/oso/9780198842347.001.0001

present the context in which that phrase occurs and to review earlier interpretations.[2]

In the extant column, the borrower promises to transport a cargo, first with a camel caravan from the Red Sea to Coptos, then on a ship from Coptos to the customs warehouse of the quarter-tax in Alexandria, where he will put the cargo under the lender's control:

12 *πρὸς τὸ ἐνστάντος τοῦ ἐν ταῖς κατὰ Μουζεῖριν τοῦ δα-*
13 *[νείου σ]υνγραφαῖς τῆς ἀποδόσεως ὡ̣ρισμένου χρόνου ἐὰν μὴ δικαί-*
14 *[ως τότ]ε̣ χρεολυτῶ τὸ προκείμενον ἐν ἐμοὶ δάνειον τότε εἶναι*
15 *[πρὸς σ]ὲ καὶ τοὺς σοὺς ἐπιτρόπους ἢ φροντιστὰς τὴν ἐγλογὴν καὶ ὁλο-*
16 *[σχερῆ] ἐξουσίαν ὡς ἐὰν αἱρῆσθε ποιήσασθαι τὰ τῆς πράξεως χωρὶς*
17 *[διαστ]ολῆς καὶ προσκρίσεως (l.προσκλήσεως) κρατεῖν τε καὶ κυριεύειν τὴν προκε̣ι̣-*
18 *[μένη]ν ὑποθήκην καὶ τεταρτολογεῖν καὶ τὰ λοιπὰ ἐσόμενα μέρη*
19 *[τρία μ]εταφέρειν οὗ ἐὰν αἱρῆσθε καὶ πωλεῖν καὶ μεθυποτίθεσθαι*
20 *[καὶ] ἑ̣τ̣[έ]ρωι παραχωρεῖν ὡς ἐὰν αἱρῆσθε καὶ τὰ καθ' ἑαυτὴν διοικονο-*
21 *[με]ῖσθαι καθ' ὃν ἐὰν βούλησθε τρόπον καὶ ἑαυτῶι ὠνεῖσθαι τῆς ἐπὶ `τοῦ'*
22 *καιροῦ φανησομένης τιμῆς*

so that, if, on the occurrence of the time established for the repayment in the *kata Mouzeirin* loan contracts, I do not properly pay the aforesaid loan in my name, then you and your agents or managers shall have the choice and complete power, if you choose, to carry out execution without notification or summons and to get possession and own the aforesaid security and levy the quarter-tax and transfer the three parts that will remain to whomever you choose and sell and re-hypothecate and cede to another, if you choose, and handle the security whichever way you want and buy for yourself at the then current price.

What should we infer from the words 'on the occurrence of the time established for the repayment in the *kata Mouzeirin* loan contracts'?[3] Why wasn't a calendric date used, which would have been succinct and more precise?

[2] My own observations in De Romanis (1996a: 167–202); (2014a: 78–89) will be restated in the next section.

[3] For the sake of convenience, I transcribe here the translations of other commentators. Harrauer and Sijpesteijn (1985): 'wenn der Augenblick der Darlehensrückgabe, der in den bei Muziris abgeschlossenen Darlehensvertragsexemplaren vereibart ist'; Casson (1986: 75) and Casson (1990: 200): 'on the occurrence of the date for repayment specified in the loan agreements at Muziris'; Thür (1987: 231): 'sobald der in der Darlehenurkunde nach Muziris bestimmte Zeitpunkt der Rückzahlung eingetreten ist'; Rathbone (2000: 40): 'on occurrence of the date for repayment specified in the contracts of lo[an] for (the trip to) Muziris.'

The editors apparently assumed that 'the *kata Mouzeirin* loan contracts' coincided with the contract of the Muziris papyrus, and that the deadline for the repayment was specified in the lost column of the text. Without explaining why the text did not include something like 'by the day established in the present contract', they inferred that the terms of the contract had been agreed upon at Muziris and the co-signatories were a ship owner (the borrower) and a merchant (the lender). In their view, the agreement would have been a sort of 'double' contract, conflating a loan contract (in which the borrower would acquire financing by offering his ship as collateral) with a transport contract (in which the borrower would agree to transport the commodities of the lender).[4]

Independently of one another, L. Casson and G. Thür recognized that the collateral offered by the borrower was not the ship, but the imported cargo. They also understood that the phrase 'in the *kata Mouzeirin* loan contracts' did not refer to the contract preserved in the Muziris papyrus. They disagreed, however, on the identification of these contracts, as well as on the nature of the extant document and the time and place of its execution. Casson claimed that the phrase 'in the *kata Mouzeirin* loan contracts' referred to several copies of a loan agreement signed *at* Muziris. Co-signatories would have been a merchant permanently residing in Muziris (the lender), and an Egyptian merchant (the borrower) sailing between Egypt and India, who carried the commodities of the lender along with his own.[5] The extant contract would have been an update to the prior (Muziris) contract, executed by the borrower and a deputy of the lender in one of the Egyptian Red Sea ports.[6]

For Thür, 'the *kata Mouzeirin* loan contracts' referred to a maritime loan contract signed in Alexandria at the beginning of a commercial enterprise to Muziris. The signatories would have been a financier residing in Alexandria (the lender) and a merchant (the borrower) transporting only his own commodities.[7] The loan would have been granted not *at*, but *for* (a voyage to) Muziris.[8] The text preserved on the recto of the papyrus would not have been the loan contract, but only a security document ('Sicherungsurkunde'). Distinct from the loan contract with which it would be associated, this document would have enabled the lender to seize the collateral.[9]

According to Rathbone, the text on the Muziris papyrus recto was not a real contract, but, as he puts it, only a 'master' contract belonging to a financier who regularly made maritime loans for ventures to Indian ports—a sort of template that contained only 'the standard operational terms', but no specific details. Building on the master contract, the financier's office would regularly

[4] Harrauer and Sijpesteijn (1985: 141; 145).
[5] Casson (1986: 76–7).
[6] Casson (1986: 76–8; 1990: 206).
[7] Thür (1987: 240–1).
[8] Thür (1987: 235, n. 18; 1988: 233).
[9] Thür (1987: 243–4).

draw up specific contracts that incorporated the details relevant to each individual business venture (names, destination, dates, sums, etc.).[10]

Morelli's interpretation argues for the existence of two loan contracts agreed upon by the same parties, a merchant (borrower) and a financier (lender). The first contract would have been signed in Alexandria at the beginning of the commercial enterprise. The second—the one partially preserved in the Muziris papyrus—would have been signed in an Egyptian Red Sea port once the merchant returned from India, in order to set the terms for the last leg of the voyage from the Red Sea to Alexandria.[11] Finally, X. Pérez López proposed that the Muziris papyrus contract was the second and legal version of a contract, signed in an Egyptian Red Sea port, which served to re-affirm the terms of a first, legally defective contract drawn up in Muziris between the lender's agent and the merchant.[12]

All the above interpretations stem from a common view: that the sentence at col. ii, ll. 11–12, *ἐνστάντος τοῦ ἐν ταῖς κατὰ Μουζεῖριν τοῦ δα|[νείου σ]υνγραφαῖς τῆς ἀποδόσεως ὡρισμένου χρόνου* (when the time for the repayment established in the *kata Mouzeirin* contracts has come), does not identify the repayment due date. They assume that the deadline for the repayment was unambiguously specified elsewhere with an explicit calendric date. The exact location varies: in the lost columns of the papyrus (seemingly implied by Harrauer and Sijpesteijn); in another document, either in the 'real' contract (Casson, Thür, and Rathbone) or in a first contract (Morelli); or in the original but legally defective loan contract (Pérez López). Is such an assumption supported by what we know of ancient maritime loan contracts, whether in the Indian Ocean area or in the Mediterranean? Is it realistic to assume that a maritime loan contract—and especially one for a commercial enterprise to Muziris—would express its loan repayment deadline with a calendric date?

6.2. TIME AND MARITIME LOANS

The available evidence for ancient maritime loans consists of only a few contracts, or else of texts that in some manner summarize the terms of a loan. The agreements show differences that are sometimes merely formulaic,

[10] Rathbone (2000: 41). Rathbone characterizes the text as 'a sloppy copy, careless of grammar and syntax, probably penned in haste (and as much from memory as reading an exemplar?) by one of the financier's clerks'. Ultimately, the idea that the text on the papyrus is only an inaccurate copy goes back to the editors, who postulated a lacuna at col. ii, l. 12, implying an erroneous transcription of the original text (Harrauer and Sijpesteijn 1985: 141). However, there is no need to postulate a lacuna. Moreover, the handwriting is elegant and, common spelling errors aside, the grammar is linear.

[11] Morelli (2011: 206). [12] Pérez López (2007: 656; 678).

sometimes consequential. They do, however, share a common feature: they never stipulate the deadline for the loan repayment with an a priori calendric date. In fact, the elusiveness of the repayment deadline (or, to be more accurate, the dependence of the deadline on the date of the ship's return) has been a typical characteristic, throughout antiquity, of 'two-way' (*amphoteropla*) maritime loan contracts. As the Constantinopolitan ship owners explained to the praetorian prefect Ioannes in AD 540, maritime loans were not conceived in relation to a predetermined time period, but rather as contingent on the sea voyage. As a consequence, the total yield agreed upon before the voyage was independent of actual length of the voyage:

> if the creditors did not choose this method, they would receive the eighth part on each gold piece as yield, not figured at a definite time but until the ship returned safely; that under this method, accordingly, it would happen that the time might run for a year or more, if the ship were on the journey for that long, or it might be shortened to a month or two, if the ship returned, and they (the creditors) would have the benefit of the one-eighth whether the time was short or whether the debt remained due from the debtors a longer time.[13]

The ship owners' claim does not mean that the loan terms—and especially the yield rates—were also indifferent to the *presumptive* length or risk of the voyage. Most probably, the flat reward of 12.5 per cent of the capital depended on the sea routes in question, which were presumably of similar length and risk. The yield for a loan financing a voyage that was expected to be longer or riskier was most probably higher than a loan financing a shorter or safer sea route.[14] On the other hand, once it was agreed upon at the start of the venture, the yield would not change if the actual length of the voyage turned out to be longer than anticipated. In fact, the lender took upon himself all the risks of the sea voyage—delayed return included. The yield rates were not affected by either a later or an earlier return.

In the maritime loan contract transcribed in the *Against Lacritus* speech of the Demosthenic corpus, the loan is being issued for a specific voyage, which admitted only a limited number of variations:

> Androcles of Sphettus and Nausicrates of Carystus lent to Artemo and Apollodorus, both of Phaselis, three thousand drachmae in silver for a voyage

[13] Just., *Nov.* 106; transl. F. H. Blume, with modifications. Since the maritime τόκοι did not depend on time, they are better translated as 'yields' rather than 'interests', which are inherently time related, as Cohen (1992: 45–6) pointed out. The law presents this as a second type of maritime loan. In the first type, the yield was 10 per cent of the capital, but the creditor could load a bushel of wheat or barley onto the ship for each gold piece of money lent: Billeter (1898: 323–30); Gofas (2002: 1097).

[14] In the fourth century BC, a maritime loan for a voyage from Sestus to Athens was given with a 12.5 per cent yield rate ([Dem.] 50.17) and a maritime loan for a voyage from Athens to Pontus (Bosporus in Crimea) with a 30 per cent yield rate ([Dem.] 34.6; 23). Different rates for different destinations are implied by Dem. 56.5. Cf. Schuster (2005: 82–5).

> from Athens to Mende or Scione, and thence to Bosporus—or if they so choose, for a voyage to the left parts of the Pontus as far as the Borysthenes—and thence back to Athens, on yield at the rate of two hundred and twenty-five drachmae on the thousand; but, if they should sail out from Pontus to Hieron after the rising of Arcturus, at three hundred on the thousand . . . And, if they do not enter Pontus, but remain in the Hellespont ten days after the rising of the Dog star, and disembark their goods at a port where the Athenians have no right of reprisals, and from thence complete their voyage to Athens, let them pay the yield written into the contract the year before.[15]

Quite remarkably, the rate of the yield would remain 22.5 per cent of the capital whether or not the borrower sailed beyond the Hellespontus, but it would rise to 30 per cent if the return voyage from the Black Sea began after the rising of Arcturus. In other words, the contract specifies a geographic radius for the voyage (from Athens as far as the Borysthenes, maximum) and a deadline for the start of the return voyage (from Pontus to Hieron before the rising of Arcturus). Within these limits, the yield rate did not change, whether the voyage turned out to be longer or shorter. It did change, however, if the voyage was made riskier by sailing out of Pontus after the rising of Arcturus.

In case of failure to repay the loan on time, the borrowers faced basically the same consequences that are foreseen in the Muziris papyrus loan contract:

> And, if they shall not pay it within the time agreed upon, it shall be lawful for the lenders to pledge the goods or even to sell them for such price as they can get; and if the proceeds fall short of the sum which the lenders should receive in accordance with the agreement, it shall be lawful for the lenders, whether severally or jointly, to collect the amount by proceeding against Artemo and Apollodorus, and against all their property whether on land or sea, wheresoever it may be, precisely as if judgement had been rendered against them and they had defaulted in payment.[16]

By contrast, note that the creditors of Justinian's age were more lenient:

> if the debt remained unpaid longer, they would give eight per cent interest to the owners of the money, the loan being placed on the footing of one that is made on land, there being no further danger to the creditors from the perils of the sea.[17]

However, although they differ—and quite remarkably—regarding the penalties for overdue repayment, the two lending patterns agree in not using a calendric date as an a priori deadline for the loan repayment. The *Against Lacritus* contract states only that:

> If the goods are brought safe to Athens, the borrowers are to pay to the lenders the money due in accordance with the agreement within twenty days after they shall

[15] [Dem.] 35.10–13; transl. A. T. Murray, with modifications. I understand *εἰς Βόσπορον* as Thracian Bosporus, not the kingdom of Bosporus in Crimea, cf. Cohen (1992: 54, n. 73).

[16] [Dem.] 35.12; transl. A. T. Murray.

[17] Just., *Nov.* 106; transl. F. H. Blume. Cf. Billeter (1898: 319–21; 325); Gofas (2002: 1096–7).

> have arrived at Athens, without deduction save for such jettison as the passengers shall have made by common agreement, or for money paid to enemies; but without deduction for any other loss.[18]

The clause 'if they shall not pay within the time agreed upon' (12: *ἐὰν δὲ μὴ ἀποδῶσιν ἐν τῷ συγκειμένῳ χρόνῳ*) does not refer to a pre-determined calendric date, but to the twentieth day following the ship's return. Likewise, in AD 540 Constantinople, the yield was 'figured until the ship returned safely' plus a time lapse of twenty days:

> when they (the merchants) would come back from a journey with a safe ship and could no longer make any shipment on account of the season, they would be given twenty days' grace, without any charge of interest, till the cargo would be sold.[19]

In a contract transcribed in a Berlin papyrus, a loan granted to five shipmates (*σύνπλοι*) who are about to sail to the Aromatophoros Land in East Africa is given 'for one year from the present month' (l. 13).[20] If the five shipmates fail to repay their loan at its expiration, the lender is not allowed to seize the pledged goods (as in the *Against Lacritus* contract and the Muziris papyrus), but only to claim interest at the legal rate for ordinary loans, exactly like Justinian's lenders—the only difference is that the legal rate was 24 per cent per year under the Ptolemies and 8 per cent in AD 540.[21]

U. Wilcken and R. Bogaert inferred that the loan to the five shipmates had been issued not for a voyage, but for the time span of one year.[22] Formulaically, the inference is correct, but in substance the difference is almost irrelevant in this case. Since commercial enterprises to the Aromatophoros Land could exploit just one sailing season per year,[23] their one-year loan contracts were virtually equivalent to a loan for a single commercial voyage. Furthermore, the one-year extension is consequential only if the voyage ends much earlier than the repayment deadline. In this case, the borrower may have more than twenty days to sell his commodities. But if the ship returns to its home port later than expected, the two types of contract ultimately lead to very similar procedures. In fact, if, against their will, the shipmates/borrowers returned to the Red Sea port of Egypt too late for repayment within the stipulated year, they would not have owed additional interest from the first day of the next year. They were given enough time (the lacuna and the remaining letters suggest fifty, seventy, eighty, or ninety days) to cross the desert between the Red Sea and the Nile,

18 [Dem.] 35.11; transl. A. T. Murray.

19 Just., *Nov.* 106; transl. F. H. Blume.

20 *SB* 3.7169, l. 13: *εἰς ἐ[νι]α[υ]τ[ὸ]ν [ἀπὸ το]ῦ πρ[ο]κει[μένου] μηνός.*

21 *SB* 3.7169, ll. 15–6. Cf. Bogaert (1965: 148); von Reden (2007: 154). It is uncertain whether the borrowers had to pay a premium of 50 per cent of the capital, as argued and restored by Wilcken (1925: 96).

22 Wilcken (1925: 94); Bogaert (1965: 149).

23 *PME* 14.

sail downriver to Alexandria, sell their aromatics, and repay their debt.[24] In this respect, the only difference from the *Against Lacritus* contract depends on the distance between the Red Sea port and the final emporion, which required a much longer interval between the docking date and the loan repayment deadline—somewhere between fifty and ninety days, as opposed to twenty. Therefore, the repayment deadline of the alleged one-year maritime loan remained contingent on the day the sea-going ship returned—exactly as in mid-fourth-century BC Athens or in AD 540 Constantinople.

Incidentally, it may be noted that in fourth-century BC Athens, loans for commercial enterprises in which Athens was not the final destination were prohibited by law.[25] As a result, maritime loan contracts may have had to include accurate route descriptions that, without exception, terminated in Athens. This condition also determined the length of the loan, since it clearly implied that both the outbound and return journeys had to occur in the same sailing season. If not, it would have been only too easy to circumvent public law by sending the cargo of the return voyage to another city.[26] Except for force-majeure circumstances, any return journey that was deliberately delayed beyond the sailing season would have been deemed a contract violation.

In conclusion, aside from the penalties for overdue repayment and the necessary adaptations to different geographical settings, the procedures for setting the deadline to pay off a maritime loan were basically the same, as reflected in the *Against Lacritus* contract, *SB* 3.7169, and *Nov. Iust.* 106. Maritime loan contracts could establish a deadline for the repayment only with reference to the day on which the sea-going vessel reached its final port. Regardless of the fate of the ship, no penalty was ever imposed for failure to re-pay a loan by a specific calendric date.

The same procedures may be presumed in the contract between the banker Stichus, slave of Seius, and the merchant Callimachus, as summed up by the jurist Cervidius Scaevola:

> Callimachus took a transmarine loan from Stichus, the slave of Seius, at Berytus in the province of Syria, for a voyage to Brentesium. The loan for the full two hundred days of the voyage with security by way of *pignus* and *hypotheca* over the cargo bought at Berytus for transport to Brentesium and that which he would buy at Brentesium for transport by sea to Berytus. It was agreed by the parties that when Callimachus reached Brentesium, he should, before the thirteenth of September next, himself take ship for Syria with other cargo purchased and put on board or, if

[24] *SB* 3.7169, ll. 14–5: ἐὰν δ' ἐκπε[σ]ό[ν]τ[ε]ς τοῦ χρόν[ου] παραγένω[νται ἀπὸ τῆς Ἀ]ρ[ω]-μα[το]φόρ[ο]υ [εἰς] τὴν χώραν ὁμοίως . . . [ ]ηε., ἀφ' ἧς ἂν ἡμέρας παραγένωνται [ε]ἰς τὴν χώραν [ἡμερῶν ---]ήκοντα, 'if, missing the right time, they get back from the Aromatophoros to the land (of Egypt) anyway| . . .]ty [days] from the day they get back to the land'.

[25] [Dem.] 35.50–1. This is why the proposal to finance a voyage from Athens to Egypt and then to Rhodes is rejected in Dem. 56.6.

[26] This was the case argued in *Against Dionysodorus*.

> by the said date he did not buy the cargo or set sail from that *civitas*, he would repay the whole amount at once, as if the voyage ended, and pay all the costs of those persons who recovered the money and took it to the city of Rome.[27]

The loan was granted for the entire 200 days of the sailing season (*in omnes navigii dies ducentos*), as well as for a voyage from Berytus to Brentesion and back. Here also the duration of the loan—the 200 days of the full sailing season—indicates neither the maximum length of the voyage nor a deadline for repayment. Rather, it clarifies that the borrower could use the entire (*omnes*) sailing season for a round-trip voyage from Berytus to Brentesion, on the condition that he would depart from Brentesion to Berytus before 13 September. There can be no doubt that in the part of the contract that was not summed up by Scaevola (because it was irrelevant to the case), Callimachus himself would have pledged to repay his loan a certain number of days—most probably, twenty—after the return of the ship to Berytus, and that clause would have established the legally valid deadline for repayment. If Callimachus, having set sail from Brentesion by 13 September, ended up landing in Berytus after the two hundredth day of the sailing season, he would certainly have still been allowed the agreed-upon time interval to sell his commodities and repay his debt, at no additional cost.

In sum, while the deadline for the repayment of a maritime loan ultimately depended on the day the ship returned, and therefore could not be specified with a calendric date, there is no reason why the maritime loan contracts for round trips could not have expressly required or favoured a timely start for the return voyage using a precise departure date. In order to exploit the most favourable environmental conditions for safe navigation, and thus limit the lender's financial risk, such contracts may have called for the return voyage to commence within a certain deadline, specified by an astronomical phenomenon or a precise calendric date. In the *Against Lacritus* contract, if the borrowers began their return voyage from Pontus after the rising of Arcturus, the yield on the money lent rose from 22.5 to 30 per cent, given the greater risks of winter sailing.[28] In Callimachus' contract, if the merchant could not set sail from Brentesion by 13 September, he would have had to repay his entire debt—both loan and yield for the two-way voyage—immediately, by sending the money from Brentesion to Rome, where Stichus' master probably lived.[29]

The fact that the *SB* 3.7169 contract does not penalize those who were unable to return to Egypt on time does not necessarily mean that they were free to leave the Aromatophoros Land whenever they chose. Although the extant fragments do not confirm it, it is likely that the concession of

[27] Scaev., *Dig.* 45.1.122.1, trans. by A. Watson. For the textual problems, see Lübtow (1976).
[28] [Dem.] 35.10.
[29] Callimachus' case may not be an *exemplum fictum*: De Romanis (2008: 156).

extra time in the event of a late return was balanced by the condition that the return voyage begin before a certain date. A late return to Egypt would then occur only in exceptional and unpredictable circumstances.

This combination of a fixed-time loan, a fixed departure for the return voyage, and a flexible repayment schedule reflects the fact that the lenders expected the commercial venture to be completed within one sailing season, and the relevant loan to be repaid within one year's time, in normal conditions. The borrowers, on the other hand, would have wanted to be protected against an unforeseen delayed return.

Given that maritime loan contracts for shorter and safer commercial voyages foresaw a delay in the repayment deadline if the ship returned too late, is it conceivable that one for a voyage to Muziris would require the borrower to repay his loan by a specific date, with no regard for the imprecise duration of a transoceanic voyage?

6.3. THE DEADLINE FOR THE REPAYMENT OF THE MUZIRIS LOAN CONTRACTS

The protocol followed by *SB* 3.7169 seems particularly suited to our reconstruction of the terms for the loan contracts for commercial enterprises to Muziris. In the mid-first century AD, voyages to the Aromatophoros Land and to South India had approximately the same schedule. Merchants bound for either destination were supposed to leave Egypt's Red Sea ports in the month of 'Epeiph (of the fixed Alexandrian calendar), which is July (of the Julian Roman)',[30] and be back in Alexandria within a year (in all likelihood, merchants bound for the Aromatophoros Land returned earlier than their colleagues bound for South India). As a consequence, it is extremely likely that loans financing those enterprises were all granted for one year from the month they were signed—that is, from June to the following May.[31] Pliny's clause 'it happens that they [sc. the merchants bound for South India] return in the same year' refers neither to the Roman nor to any of the Egyptian calendric years, but rather to a commercial year shaped by the sailing seasons.[32]

In all likelihood, the precise time limit for the start of the return journey from South India (13 January) was established in connection with maritime loan contracts. Just as signatories of Berytus–Brentesion–Berytus contracts were required to leave Brentesion by 13 September, so signatories of

[30] *PME* 14; 56. [31] Cf. *SB* 3.7169 l. 13.

[32] Plin., *NH* 6.106. In the *Against Lacritus* loan contract, a commercial year based on the sailing season is implied by the wording 'the yields written into the contract the year before' (*τοὺς τόκους—τοὺς πέρυσι γραφέντας εἰς τὴν συγγραφήν* [Dem.] 35.13).

Alexandria–Muziris–Alexandria contracts were obliged to leave India by 13 January. The firm deadline for the start of the return voyage determined a time span (February/March?) during which ships sailing back from Muziris were expected to arrive in Egypt.[33] By adding two or three months for the transport of goods from the Red Sea coast to Alexandria, and for the sale of the cargo (a time lapse comparable to the days conceded to the five borrowers of *SB* 3.7169 in case of late arrival in Egypt), we arrive at 'the established time for repayment in the Muziris loan contracts'. The contracts were most likely signed in June, for a one-year loan period, and set to expire on the same day of the following year (Fig. 6.1).

Of course, mishaps and delays during the return voyage were always possible. But in case of late arrival, the Alexandria–Muziris–Alexandria contracts would have certainly tolerated a postponement in the repayment deadline, just as the Aromatophoros Land contracts had done since the Ptolemaic age. For the loan contract of the Muziris papyrus, a similar clause would probably have been located in the missing recto col. iii.

As Thür first realized, the *κατὰ Μουζεῖριν* loan contracts are not 'signed at Muziris', but 'for (a voyage to) Muziris'. However, the expression 'the established time for the repayment in the Muziris loan contracts' does not refer to a previous contract specifying the deadline for repayment with a specific date. Here, the syntagma 'in the Muziris loan contracts' (*ἐν ταῖς κατὰ Μουζεῖριν τοῦ δα|νείου σ]υνγραφαῖς*) does not hint at several copies of a specific contract.[34] The preposition *ἐν* is used in a metaphorical sense, and the plural *σ]υνγραφαῖς* clearly indicates a *category* of contracts—the contracts for (a voyage to) Muziris.[35] Nor does the sentence imply the existence of a previous contract (whether signed in Muziris or in Alexandria), or of a separate document. There is no need to conclude that the loan contract was something other than the document we (partially) have in hand. The way the deadline was specified was customary for the repayment of commercial loans that bankrolled the movement of goods between Alexandria and Muziris. To South India traders, an expression such as 'the established time for the repayment in the Muziris loan contracts' would have been absolutely unambiguous.

[33] On the timing of C. Numidius Eros' return from India, see p. 49; for the envoy of camels 'for the caravans from Berenice', see pp. 200–3.

[34] A plural *συγγραφαί* may well allude to multiple copies of a single contract (cf. [Dem.] 34.32), but when reference is made to the *content* of a single contract, the singular is required, because even if it was written in several copies, the text of the copies was the same: cf. *SB* 6.9571 = 14.11850, ll. 7–8: *κατὰ ναυτικὴν συνγραφὴν ἧς ἡ ἔν|γειος παρ' ἐμοὶ* (according to the maritime loan agreement, of which I have the land copy). If it alluded to different transcriptions of the same loan contract, *ἐν ταῖς—συνγραφαῖς* would be confusing, if not misleading.

[35] For *ἐν* in the metaphorical-spatial sense, to indicate classes and categories of people and things, cf. Mayser (1923–1934: 2.2.394).

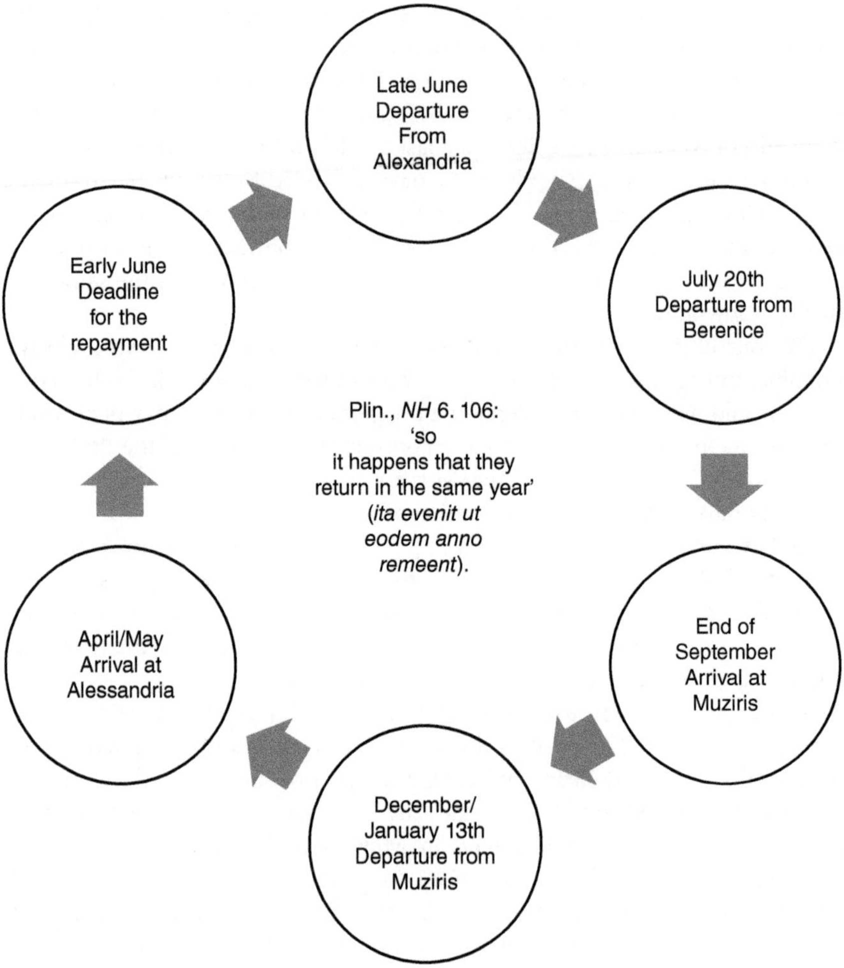

Fig. 6.1 Timing of Roman trade with South India according to Pliny.

6.4. IN THE BEGINNING WAS THE LOAN CONTRACT

As mentioned, Morelli has argued that no reference is made to the outward journey in the extant column of the Muziris papyrus contract, and that two loan contracts would have financed the same commercial enterprise to Muziris. The first contract (signalled by the phrase at col. ii, ll. 11–12) would have been signed in Alexandria at the start of the venture, and the second (partially preserved in the recto) would have been signed in an Egyptian Red Sea port, once the merchant had returned from India.

The idea that an Alexandria–Muziris–Alexandria commercial enterprise was financed in two instalments—one before and one after the sea voyage—makes sense. It would have been logical not to expose the capital financing for the last leg of the voyage, from the Red Sea coast to Alexandria, to the perils of the sea. Yet the assumption that this business deal required two loan contracts is unwarranted. Neither the extant portions of the papyrus, nor inferences regarding the missing portions, suggest that the Muziris papyrus contract supplemented a previous contract between the same parties.

If the contract had been signed in a Red Sea port and concerned only the last Egyptian leg of the voyage, the missing information could hardly have required an entire column (col. i)—especially if the same two parties had already signed another contract for the same venture, and the first contract was explicitly referred to in the second. Rather, the extent of the lost portion on the left of the surviving fragment (at least one entire column, but possibly more) strongly suggests that the preceding text (in addition to presenting the co-signatories and detailing the loan, its aim, and length) described the first part of a round-trip journey and specified the commitments of the borrower during the outward trip and for part of the return journey.

Moreover, it is difficult to imagine the lender signing the alleged second contract in the Red Sea port. In col. ii, ll. 5–6 and 9 show that upon reaching first Coptos and then Alexandria, the borrower could find the lender at either customs duties warehouse.[36] By contrast, what we read in col. ii, l. 1 strongly suggests that the lender was not expected to be in the Red Sea port where the borrower's ship would dock.[37] Whatever action was attached to the phrase *].μένων σου ἑτέρων ἐπ[ι]τρ̣ό̣πων ἢ φροντιστῶν* ('your other agents or representatives'), it is clear that in the place where it occurred—very probably the Red Sea port—the lender himself was not present. And we may also observe that the *ἑτέρων* (other) in the same sentence seems to imply that, before that moment, some other action had been taken by some other agent or representative of the lender.

Based on a controversial reading at col. ii, l. 2 (which will be dealt with in chapter eight), and on the unmistakable plural form *ναύλων* at col. ii, l. 11, Thür argued that the contract took into account more than one shipment across the desert and more than one voyage along the Nile.[38] Despite his reading of col. ii, ll. 10–11 *καὶ φο|ρέτρω]ν̣ ὄρους καὶ ναύλων ποταμίων* (the expenses of the desert transports and the river freights),[39] which makes the text even more consistent with Thür's interpretation, Morelli argued that the plurals *φορέτρων* and *ναύλων* do not necessarily imply more than one desert passage and river voyage.[40] However legitimate an interpretation, a plurality of both desert crossings

[36] Col. ii, ll. 5–6: *ὑ]π̣ὸ τὴν σὴν ἢ τῶν σῶν ἐπιτρόπων ἢ τοῦ παρόντος αὐτῶν| ἐξουσία]ν καὶ σφραγεῖδα*; l. 9: *ὑπὸ τὴν σὴν ἢ τῶν σῶν ἐξουσίαν καὶ σφραγεῖδα.*

[37] Col. ii, l. 1: *].μένων σου ἑτέρων ἐπ[ι]τρ̣ό̣πων ἢ φροντιστῶν.*

[38] Thür (1987: 234, n. 7; 235, n. 14).

[39] Morelli (2011: 200, n. 3).

[40] Morelli (2011: 206, n. 21).

and river passages is consistent with, and supported by, the length of missing col. i, which probably contained more than the few lines sufficient for the names of the co-signatories and the details of the loan.[41]

Besides, given the anticipated size of the incoming cargo, those arranging a commercial venture to Muziris could hardly defer the arrangements for the return desert crossing until the ship's return to its Red Sea port. An improvident merchant sitting on a 600-ton cargo (or even much less than that) in a Red Sea port would have lost precious time organizing the desert journey. Large herds of camels were not to be found so easily. They were probably housed somewhere in the valley, to be summoned when the ships arrived at Berenice. Without preplanning, it would have been nigh impossible for a South India merchant to find a cameleer with access to several thousand animals and to negotiate a fee that was not extortionate.

In sum, there are good reasons to argue that the Muziris papyrus contract anticipated more than the simple transport of goods from the Red Sea to Alexandria, and that it was signed in Alexandria to finance an imminent Alexandria–Muziris–Alexandria commercial venture.

[41] Besides, it should be borne in mind that more than one column may be missing on the left of what we call col. ii.

7

Selling and Repaying

With the restoration of the correct reading $\bar{\gamma}$ at verso col. iii, l. 27, and the subsequent revision of the sentence at ll. 27–9, Rathbone was able to ascertain that the sum at l. 29 represents the value of only three-quarters of the *Hermapollon*'s cargo. How do we make sense of this oddity?

Rathbone offered an appealing theory: that the evaluation of the verso text concerns only three-quarters of the cargo because the quarter-tax repeatedly alluded to in the two texts had already been levied in kind.[1] Pointing out that, despite the huge quantities involved, the goods of the cargo each have only one price, he inferred that the merchant/borrower would sell the tax-free cargo *en bloc* to a single buyer, who would be none other than the lender, at the final price stated at verso col. iii, l. 29.[2]

In Rathbone's view, the calculations on the verso text do not concern the assessment of customs duties, but rather the acquisition of the tax-free cargo by the lender, a procedure anticipated in the contract in case of outstanding loan, as we have seen: 'if, on the occurrence of the time established for the repayment in the loan contracts for Muziris, I do not properly pay the aforesaid loan in my name, then you and your agents or managers shall have the choice and complete power, if you choose, to carry out execution without notification or summons and to get possession and own the aforesaid security and levy the quarter-tax and transfer the three parts that will remain to whomever you choose and sell and re-hypothecate and cede to another, if you choose, and handle the security whichever way you want and buy for yourself at the then current price' (recto col. ii, ll. 14–22).

Rathbone implicitly recognizes that these lines of the loan agreement do not suggest that the merchant could not seek a buyer other than the lender. Quite the contrary, the text makes it clear that he would sell to the lender only after the expiration of the repayment deadline—that is, only after having tried to sell his goods to somebody else. Based on this discrepancy between the terms

[1] Rathbone (2000: 43, 45). The quarter-tax is alluded to at recto col. ii, ll. 8; 10; 18; verso col. ii, l. 7; col. iii, ll. 6, 12, 18, 22.

[2] Rathbone (2000: 43, 45).

The Indo-Roman Pepper Trade and the Muziris Papyrus. Federico De Romanis, Oxford University Press (2020).
 DOI: 10.1093/oso/9780198842347.001.0001

of the agreement and the course of action supposedly taken by the merchant/borrower, Rathbone postulates a kind of inconsistency between the 'fairly traditional' forms of maritime loans and the unequal relationship between a very powerful lender and a cash-poor borrower. He suggests that while the standard legal contract would have been appropriate for 'a merchant planning a venture and seeking capital where he could find it', in this case the format was being used by a financier who had a 'network for distributing and marketing the goods to Rome and other cities' and 'habitually recruited merchants to undertake the annual journey to India'.[3]

Rathbone's argument is elegant and clever, but we will see that the two texts of the papyrus include too many details that do not conform to his theory. I acknowledge that the evaluation of the three-quarter portion has a connection to the quarter-tax—but not, as I will demonstrate, because the merchant/borrower paid it in kind. Hence, Rathbone's assumptions must be re-evaluated. In this and the following chapters, I will argue that:

a. it was common practice to sell Indian commodities both at Coptos and at Alexandria to a variety of buyers;
b. the loan contract on the recto of the Muziris papyrus assumes that the Indian commodities would be sold to multiple customers, some of them in Coptos and the rest in Alexandria;
c. implicit in the contract on the recto is the expectation that the customs duties on Indian commodities could be paid either in money or in kind;
d. the loan granted by the papyrus reflects a more or less balanced relationship between borrower and lender;
e. the verso text suggests that the commodities identified as pepper, malabathron, and possibly tortoise shell would be sold to more than one buyer; and
f. the verso text indicates that the customs duties on the *Hermapollon*'s cargo were supposed to be paid in money.

7.1. REPAYING A MARITIME LOAN IN FOURTH-CENTURY BC ATHENS

One significant question that requires more consideration—not only for the Muziris papyrus contract, but also more generally for classical maritime credit—is how a borrower actually repaid his debt. At first glance, the details

[3] Rathbone (2000: 42–3; 45); (2003: 221).

provided in the loan contract on the Muziris papyrus recto do not help to answer this question. Since determining how the borrower would repay his debt while his cargo was 'under the power and seal' of the lender is critical for understanding the contract as a whole, we may seek clues in distant *comparanda*.

This *escamotage* is not new. Comparison with the loan agreement in *Against Lacritus* has already proved decisive in clarifying details concerning the collateral of the loan.[4] Comparability does not mean absolute uniformity. The available evidence clearly shows that different business conditions can lead to different stipulations in a maritime loan contract. For instance, in both *Against Lacritus* and in the most common type of Constantinopolitan contracts of the Justinianic age, the borrower was supposed to repay his debt within twenty days following his return, whereas a much longer term is allowed in the Aromatophoros Land loan contract of the Hellenistic age, apparently because of the distance between the Red Sea port (Myos Hormos?) and the emporion (Coptos? Alexandria?).[5]

The South India trade of the Roman age had conditions of its own. For one, Indian commodities were usually sold not in one, but in two emporia—Coptos and Alexandria—that were several hundred kilometres apart, and also rather distant from the Red Sea docking port. Since the repayment schedule had to accommodate this peculiar scenario, it is reasonable to expect some procedural differences. Still, we may wonder whether the procedure for loan repayment shared any similarities with what went on in fourth-century BC Athens.

How was a maritime loan repaid in fourth-century BC Athens? This question stems from a procedural riddle raised by the terms of the contract included in *Against Lacritus*. Once the goods were brought safely to Athens,

> the borrowers are to pay to the lenders the money due in accordance with the agreement within twenty days after they shall have arrived at Athens, without deduction save for such jettison as the passengers shall have made by common agreement, or for money paid to enemies; but without deduction for any other loss. And they shall deliver to the lenders in their entirety the goods offered as security to be under their absolute control until such time as they shall themselves have paid the money due in accordance with the agreement.[6]

How can a borrower sell his commodities and repay his debt, if they are under the lender's 'absolute control' from the moment of the borrower's arrival? To reconcile the rights of the lender with the needs of the borrower, U. E. Paoli

[4] Casson (1986: 77); Thür (1987: 229). [5] See pp. 165–6.

[6] [Dem.] 35.11: *σωθέντων δὲ τῶν χρημάτων Ἀθήναζε, ἀποδώσουσιν οἱ δανεισάμενοι τοῖς δανείσασι τὸ γιγνόμενον ἀργύριον κατὰ τὴν συγγραφὴν ἡμερῶν εἴκοσιν, ἀφ' ἧς ἂν ἔλθωσιν Ἀθήναζε, ἐντελὲς πλὴν ἐκβολῆς, ἧς ἂν οἱ σύμπλοι ψηφισάμενοι κοινῇ ἐκβάλωνται, καὶ ἄν τι πολεμίοις ἀποτείσωσιν· τῶν δ' ἄλλων ἁπάντων ἐντελές. καὶ παρέξουσι τοῖς δανείσασι τὴν ὑποθήκην ἀνέπαφον κρατεῖν, ἕως ἂν ἀποδῶσι τὸ γιγνόμενον ἀργύριον κατὰ τὴν συγγραφήν*; transl. A. T. Murray.

imagined that the borrower would find a buyer for his items, receive payment, and use that money to free his goods from the financier's control.[7] But it is unlikely that the standard practice was like this. What makes it improbable is not so much that all the steps would have had to occur simultaneously, as Paoli recognized, but the fact that it would have required a first single sale that repaid the entire loan. The imperative to make a first big sale would have severely restricted the borrower's options, compelling him to reject any partial sale that did not entirely repay his loan. Conversely, it would have unnecessarily increased the first buyer's leverage, allowing him to bargain down the price. None of the contract co-signatories stood to gain from such a procedure.

Equally unsatisfactory is W. Schwahn's interpretation that the lender could at any time take away the mortgaged commodities, even before the twenty-first day after the arrival.[8] L. Gernet is certainly correct when he notes that the verb *kratein*, both in this passage and in another one of *Against Timotheus*,[9] cannot mean that the borrower no longer owned the security and was prevented from paying his debt by selling it.[10] To Gernet, however, the verb implied nothing more than a supervision of the sale: 'Il ne faut pas trop presser ce mot *kratein* et lui faire signifier une prise de possession . . . Il faut entendre que la vente sera suivie par les créanciers (cf. *C. Phorm.* 8; *C. Timothée* 35).'[11]

It is difficult to concur with Gernet's conclusion. The pairing of the passages from *Against Phormio* ([Dem.] 34. 8) and *Against Timotheus* ([Dem.] 49.35) is misleading. The two texts do both describe how the lender—through agents—supervised the sale of mortgaged goods, but the situations are different, as is the intent of the supervision. The passage from *Against Phormio* concerns an intermediary sale within a round trip financed with a two-way maritime loan contract. Phormio received a loan of 2,000 drachmas for a voyage to the kingdom of Bosporus and back to Athens, on the condition that he would export a cargo worth 4,000 drachmas.[12] At Bosporus, Phormio was supposed to sell his commodities and buy another cargo under the supervision of lender's agents (one of his slaves and a partner), who, however, did not take control (*κρατεῖν*) of the goods offered as security; they only had to inspect and keep an eye on them (*ἐξετάζειν καὶ παρακολουθεῖν*).[13] The reason is clear: since the loan was to be repaid in Athens, the slave and the lender's partner were

[7] Paoli (1930: 85–6). Schuster (2005: 122) considers it quite possible that the creditors collect the money directly from the buyer's hands; but, like Paoli, conceives only a collection of the entire sum from a single transaction.

[8] Schwahn (1935: 2039); followed by Schuster (2005: 121).

[9] [Dem.] 49.11: *ἡ μὲν γὰρ οὐσία ὑπόχρεως ἦν ἅπασα, καὶ ὅροι αὐτῆς ἕστασαν, καὶ ἄλλοι ἐκράτουν.*

[10] Gernet (1954: 173, n. 5).

[11] Gernet (1954: 173, n. 5); cf. Schuster (2005: 122, n. 534).

[12] [Dem.] 34.6.

[13] [Dem.] 34.8.

only required to take note and report on what the borrower sold and bought, nothing more.

By contrast, the sale imagined in *Against Timotheus* would have been the *final* sale from a round trip financed with a loan contract and, as in the final sale of the *Against Lacritus* contract, the proceeds would repay the loan. Let us briefly recall this part of the dispute between Timotheus and Apollodorus. Apollodorus' father Pasion gave Philondas, a trusted aide of Timotheus, 1,750 drachmas to pay the freight for some timber imported from Macedonia.[14] Apollodorus argues that this sum was actually requested by and lent to Timotheus, to whom the timber belonged and on whose behalf it was imported. In fact, the records of Pasion's bank identify Timotheus as the debtor.[15] The defendant Timotheus, who was not even in Athens when the sum was delivered, contends that the 1,750 drachmas had been given to Philondas, who on his own initiative imported the timber 'for the sake of trade' (*ἐμπορίας ἕνεκα*).[16]

After presenting the testimony of his father's clerks, Apollodorus makes his case with circumstantial evidence. His key arguments are the storage of the timber on Timotheus' premises, its use for building Timotheus' house—but first and foremost the contention that his father would have acted differently, had the money been lent to Philondas:

> For do you suppose, men of the jury, that, if the timber had not been the property of Timotheus, and if he had not begged my father—at the time he introduced Philondas to him, when he was about to set sail to join the king's generals—to provide the freight, *my father would ever have allowed Philondas to carry the timber away from the harbour, seeing that it was pledged as security to him for the freight, and would not rather have set one of his servants to keep watch and to receive the price as the timber was sold, until he had recovered his money, if we suppose that the timber was the property of Philondas and was brought in for the sake of trade*? Then, besides this, does it seem to anyone likely, that if Timotheus had not bidden my father to supply the freight for the timber given to him by Amyntas, my father would have trusted Philondas, and have suffered him to deliver the timber to the defendant's house? Or, how is it possible that Philondas, as is stated by the defendant, brought in the timber for the sake of trade, and yet that the defendant on his return used this timber for the building of his house?[17]

[14] [Dem.] 49.25–8. [15] [Dem.] 49.29–30; 60–1. [16] [Dem.] 49.35–36; 59.

[17] [Dem.] 49.35–6: *οἴεσθε γάρ, ὦ ἄνδρες δικασταί, τὸν πατέρα τὸν ἐμόν, εἰ μὴ Τιμοθέου ἦν τὰ ξύλα καὶ ἐδεήθη οὗτος αὐτοῦ συστήσας τὸν Φιλώνδαν, ὅτε ἀνήγετο ὡς τοὺς στρατηγοὺς τοὺς βασιλέως, παρασχεῖν τὸ ναῦλον, ἐᾶσαι ἄν ποτε ὑποκειμένων αὐτῷ τῶν ξύλων τοῦ ναύλου ἀνακομίσαι τὸν Φιλώνδαν τὰ ξύλα ἐκ τοῦ λιμένος, ἀλλ᾽ οὐκ ἂν παρακαταστήσαντά τινα τῶν οἰκετῶν φυλάττειν καὶ τιμὴν λαμβάνειν πωλουμένων τῶν ξύλων, ἕως ἐκομίσατο τὰ ἑαυτοῦ, εἴπερ Φιλώνδου ἦν τὰ ξύλα καὶ ἐμπορίας ἕνεκ᾽ ἤχθη; ἔπειτα πρὸς τούτοις τίνι ὑμῶν εἰκὸς δοκεῖ εἶναι, μὴ κελεύσαντος τούτου τὸ ναῦλον παρασχεῖν τῶν ξύλων τῶν δοθέντων τούτῳ ὑπὸ Ἀμύντου, πιστεῦσαι τὸν πατέρα τὸν ἐμὸν Φιλώνδᾳ καὶ ἐᾶσαι ἀνακομίσαι τὰ ξύλα ἐκ τοῦ λιμένος εἰς τὴν οἰκίαν τὴν τούτου; ἢ πῶς οἷόν τ᾽ ἐστὶ τὸν μὲν Φιλώνδαν ἐμπορίας ἕνεκ᾽ ἀγαγεῖν τὰ ξύλα, ὡς οὗτός φησιν, καταχρήσασθαι δὲ τοῦτον ἥκοντα εἰς τὴν οἰκοδομίαν τὴν αὑτοῦ τοῖς ξύλοις τούτοις;* transl. A. T. Murray.

Apollodorus explains here what would have been the expected procedure, if Pasion and Philondas had really agreed on a loan 'for the sake of trade'. Admittedly, the arrangement that Timotheus claims occurred between Pasion and Philondas was not a real maritime loan contract (*ναυτικὴ συγγραφή*). In fact, the 1,750 drachmas covered only the freight and, more importantly, it was delivered upon the arrival of the timber at Athens, thereby bypassing the risks associated with the sea voyage.[18] Still, as an agreement on a loan 'for the sake of trade', it would have required a repayment procedure and a collateral similar to a maritime loan contract. Apollodorus argues that neither Philondas nor Pasion acted as if he had signed the alleged contract. If 1,750 drachmas had been lent for the sake of trade, he points out, the timber would have remained in the port, pledged to the lender until the loan was fully repaid.

Precisely because the procedure presented by Apollodorus is fictional, it must have been one that the jury would have recognized as standard practice in a loan contract for the sake of trade. The phrasing 'would not rather have set one of his servants to keep watch and to receive the price as the timber was sold' clearly shows that, while it is the borrower who makes the sale (that is, decides what to sell, to whom to sell, and for how much), it is the lender's agent who—unlike the supervisors of the intermediary sale—collects the money (*τιμὴν λαμβάνειν*). This is the reason for the lender's control (*κρατεῖν*) over the security: both at [Dem.] 35.11 and [Dem.] 49.11 the debtor sold the cargo, but it was the creditor who collected the proceeds of the sale.

Moreover, what is most important, adding the phrase 'until he had recovered his money' (*ἕως ἐκομίσατο τὰ ἑαυτοῦ*) makes it clear that the borrower could repay his debt over time, with a series of non-simultaneous sales. The borrower was thus free to sell any portion of the cargo, to whichever customer he chose, at the best price possible. On the other side, the lender was the first to reap the profits of the enterprise. Far more practical than the scenario imagined by Paoli, this procedure freed the borrower and gave him maximum flexibility to respond to the fragmentations and fluctuations of demand. It also afforded maximum assurance to the lender, who got the speediest return on his investment.

Whether to Timotheus or to Philondas, Pasion's loan did not cover the purchase of the timber, but only the freight. The sum that was lent was relatively modest. It amounted to only slightly more than half of the 3,000 drachmas lent in the *Against Lacritus* contract. Yet Apollodorus envisioned a plurality of non-simultaneous sales to repay the loan (*τιμὴν λαμβάνειν τῶν πωλουμένων ξύλων, ἕως ἐκομίσατο τὰ ἑαυτοῦ*). A fortiori, the possibility of repayment through several sales should have been anticipated when the commercial enterprise was more substantially financed. As a consequence, it

[18] It will be argued that a similar procedure was anticipated in the *ναυλωτική* (sc. *συγγραφή*) referred to at *TPSulp.* 78, see pp. 194–7.

can be suggested that the maritime loan contracts of fourth-century BC Athens implicitly assumed that the loan would have been repaid via multiple sales, and that the lender would have been collecting the proceeds from each transaction until the loan was repaid.

Before leaving this passage, I would like to draw attention to the construct *ὑποκειμένων αὐτῷ τῶν ξύλων τοῦ ναύλου*, translated by Murray as '[timber] pledged as security to him for the freight'.[19] We may classify the genitive *τοῦ ναύλου* either as a *genitivus relationis* or a *genitivus pretii*.[20] The meaning of the sentence is that the timber should have been pledged as collateral *for the price* of the freight—that is, until the 1,750 drachmas lent for the freight were reimbursed.

7.2. UNDER THE LENDER'S POWER AND SEAL

A curious detail in the loan contract of the Muziris papyrus is that the Indian commodities are *intermittently* placed under 'the power and seal' of the lender, or of his agents or representatives. This procedure occurs first when the goods are stored in the 'public fiscal storehouses of Coptos' until they are loaded on the ship. Col. ii, ll. 3–6:

3 *καὶ ἀνοίσω διὰ τοῦ ὄρους μετὰ παραφυλακῆς καὶ ἀσ̣φ̣αλε̣ίας*
4 *[εἰς τὰ]ς̣ ἐπὶ Κόπτου δημοσίας παραλημπτικὰς ἀποθήκας καὶ ποι-*
5 *[ήσω ὑ]π̣ὸ τὴν σὴν ἢ τῶν σῶν ἐπιτρόπων ἢ τοῦ παρόντος αὐτῶν*
6 *[ἐξουσία]ν καὶ σφραγεῖδα μέχρι ποταμοῦ ἐμβολῆς*

and I will bring [the cargo] through the desert with vigilance and precaution up to the public customs warehouses in Coptos and I will put [*sc.* the cargo] under the power and seal of yourself or your trustees or whoever of them is there up to the loading [*sc.* of the cargo] on the river.

Then, the lender's 'power and seal' appears again when the commodities are stored in Alexandria. Col. ii, ll. 6–9:

6 *καὶ ἐμβαλοῦμαι*
7 *[τῶι δέ]οντι καιρῶι εἰς ποτάμ̣ιον ἀσφαλὲς πλοῖον καὶ κατοίσω εἰς τὴν*

[19] Scafuro (2011: 376) translates: 'Do you think, on this hypothesis, that my father would ever have allowed Philondas to carry the timber away from the harbor, seeing that the timber was secured to him for the transport money?' The genitive *τοῦ ναύλου* is missing in Gernet's translation (1954: 23): 'Croyez-vous, juges, que mon père aurait laissé Philondas enlever du port les bois sur lesquels il avait un droit de gage?'

[20] Cf., e.g., Is. 6.33: *οἰκίαν . . . τεττάρων καὶ τετταράκοντα μνῶν ὑποκειμένην ἀπέλυσε*; [Dem.] 49.11: *ἑπτὰ μνῶν . . . ἡ ἄλλη οὐσία ὑπέκειτο*. *Genitivus pretii*: Schwyzer (1950: 125–8); *genitivus relationis*: Schwyzer (1950: 130–1).

8 [ἐν Ἀλεξ]ανδρείᾳ̣ τῆς τετάρτης παραλημπτικὴν ἀποθήκην καὶ ὁ-
9 [μοίω]ς̣ ποιήσω ὑπὸ τὴν σὴν ἢ τῶν σῶν ἐξουσίαν καὶ σφραγεῖδα

and I will load in due time in a safe ship and I will convey [*sc.* the cargo] downstream up to the customs warehouses of the quarter-tax in Alexandria and likewise I will put [*sc.* the cargo] under your or your people's power and seal.

Misled by the assumption that the signatories were a ship owner and a merchant, the editors argued that the alleged ship owner had to put the cargo under the seal of the supposed merchant, because, as owner of the cargo, the merchant, and not the ship owner, would be responsible for its customs duties.[21] The correct identification of the parties led Thür to interpret the seal of the lender as a sign of the lender's power of disposal (Verfügungsmacht).[22] Other commentators have posited that the imported commodities were sealed at the Red Sea port by clerks in the tax collector's office and travelled as bonded goods up to Alexandria.[23]

These interpretations fail to convince for reasons both external and internal to the recto text. To begin with, the idea that Indian commodities were sold only in Alexandria, as well as the claim that Indian goods in general (and the *Hermapollon*'s cargo in particular) were not also intended for the internal market, is hardly correct.[24] Certainly these notions are not supported by Strabo, Pliny the Elder, or Aelius Aristides, all of whom cite Coptos as an emporion for Indian and Arabian (and East African, according to Strabo) goods.[25] In all likelihood, the purchases at Coptos were mostly intended for Egypt's internal market.[26] In fact, the wholesale emporion of Coptos saved the Upper Egyptian retailers from having to travel all the way to Alexandria to acquire Indian, Arabian, and East African merchandise. Why would a retailer from Syene go up to Alexandria, if the same commodities were also available at Coptos? Why not pay even a little more, if it saved him the hassle of a much longer journey and the cost of a much longer *naulon*?

Moreover, a closer look at the recto text does not support the theory that the commodities were sealed to ensure the lender's power of disposal. In fact, it should be noted that the goods are put under 'the power and seal' only in

[21] Harrauer and Sijpesteijn (1985: 139).

[22] Thür (1987: 234, n. 10). Thür argues that the seal of the lender would have been applied after a seal of the customs officer.

[23] Rathbone (2000: 43); (2002, 183–4); Burkhalter in Cuvigny (2006: 16); Jördens (2009: 368).

[24] Morelli (2011: 232).

[25] Strab. 17.1.45; Plin., *NH* 5.60; Ael. Ar., *Orat.* 48.361. Pepper purchases at Coptos are alluded to by Pers. 5.136. Malabathron and other spices acquired at Coptos: *PSI* 15.1558.

[26] The spices purchased at Coptos in *PSI* 15.1558 are for Egyptian customers. *WChr* 273 gives evidence for the peddling along the Nile of Arabian and East African goods. Egyptian peddlers are more likely to buy wholesale at Coptos rather than Alexandria.

specific circumstances—first, when they are stored in the public fiscal warehouses at Coptos, before being loaded onto a river ship;[27] and second, when they are stored in the fiscal warehouse of the quarter-tax in Alexandria, before the loan has been repaid or the repayment period has expired. Furthermore, the commodities are put under 'the power and seal' of the lender *or*, if he is not present, of one of his agents who *is* present. Such an alternative demonstrates that the act of putting the cargo under the power and seal of the lender or his people is not just a simple reminder of the lender's 'Verfügungsmacht'. The cargo needs to be supervised by someone—whether the lender or one of his agents—who is physically present and can perform some essential duties. It is also apparent—and, we will see, confirmed by recto col. ii, ll. 22–5—that the act of putting the cargo under the seal and power of the lender or his agents was indeed a recognition of the lender's power over unloaded mortgaged cargo (to be 'under the seal' of some entity means to be under its control[28]), but it did not prevent the borrower from selling those items. Just as in fourth-century BC Athens, it only allowed the lender to collect the proceeds of the sales until his loan was repaid. Consequently, parts of the *Hermapollon*'s cargo could be sold either at Coptos or at Alexandria not *despite* being under—but *because* they were under—the power and seal of the lender or his representatives. Of course, the lender or his representatives would provide receipts for those proceeds to the borrower, who in turn was expected to carefully keep them until the loan was repaid and the contract was destroyed.

7.3. EARNINGS AND BENEFIT OF ASSUMPTION

The loan contract of the Muziris papyrus accounts for the possibility that the borrower may be unable to repay his debt on time. In this case, the borrower agrees that the lender can levy the quarter-tax and (apart from other options) also:

ἑαυτῶι ὠνεῖσθαι τῆς ἐπὶ \`τοῦ´
καιροῦ φανησομένης τιμῆς καὶ ἐκκρού[ει]ν καὶ ἐνλογεῖν τὰ πεσούμενα
[- - -]ọụ δανείου τῆς πίστεως τῶν πεσουμένων

[27] Of course, the commodities were also stored in the now epigraphically attested 'spice warehouse' (*ἀποθήκη ἀρωματική*, cf. p. 304) in Berenice. But the contrast between ll. 4–5 *καὶ ποι|[ήσω ὑ]π̣ὸ τὴν σὴν* and ll. 8–9: *καὶ ὁ|[μοίω]ṣ ποιήσω ὑπὸ τὴν σὴν* shows that they were not put 'under the power and seal' of the lender or his agents there.

[28] In *BGU* 1.98 the grain artabas left *ἐν [κ]έλλῃ οὔσῃ ἔν τε τοῦ ἀνδρός| μου καὶ τοῦ ἐπιτρόπου οἰκίᾳ ἐπὶ σφραγί|δων ἐμοῦ τε καὶ τοῦ ἐπιτρόπου* (ll. 14–16) are nonetheless taken out: *μ[ετ]ὰ τὰς χωρού|σας αὐτοῖς εἰς τροφ[ά]ς* (ll. 17–18).

24 [οὔσης π]ερὶ σὲ καὶ τοὺς ἐπιτρόπους ἢ φροντιστάς, ὄντων ἡμῶν ἀσυκοφαν-
25 [τήτ]ω̣ν κατὰ πάντα τρόπον τοῦ δὲ περ̣ὶ̣ τὴν̣ ἐνθήκην ἐνλείμματός
26 [τ]ε καὶ πλεονάσματος πρὸς ἐμὲ τὸν δεδανεισμένον κα̣ὶ̣ ὑποτεθει-

Col. iii:
1 [μένον ὄντος ---]

buy for yourself at the then-current price and subtract [*sc.* its value] and include the future proceeds (*τὰ πεσούμενα*) . . . of the loan, with the benefit of assumption (*πίστις*) regarding the future proceeds being on you and your trustees or agents, and us being absolutely free from misrepresentation; the shortfall or surplus with respect to the capital will be on me, the borrower and mortgager.

Since earlier commentators did not envision the cargo sale in the form of multiple small transactions, they found it necessary to contort the most common meaning of either *ἑαυτῶι ὠνεῖσθαι* ('to buy for yourself') or *πεσούμενα* ('future earnings') or *πίστις* ('benefit of assumption'). Thus, the exact meaning of the sentence—further obscured by the lacuna at col. ii, l. 23—has been lost.[29]

Thür should be given credit for understanding that, at col. ii, ll. 23–4, the clause *τῆς πίστεως—οὔσης περὶ* clarifies who has the burden of proof in the case of a legal dispute: when one of the two parties has the benefit of assumption (*πίστις*)—that is, is under no obligation to provide evidence to support a claim—it is the other party that bears the burden of proof—that is, is responsible for providing the evidence to support the claim.[30] As for the *πεσούμενα*, for which the lender has the benefit of assumption, the editors had translated it as 'proceeds' (Einnahmen). Thür claimed that the term may

[29] Some of the translations: Harrauer and Sijpesteijn (1985: 133): 'und dir selbst zu verkaufen zu dem dann üblichen Marktpreis und einzubehalten und abzuziehen von oben erwähnten Darlehen die Einnahmen. Die Verantwortung der Einnahmen liegt bei dir und deinen Vicechefs oder Geschäftsführern'; Thür (1987: 231): '(sie) auf eigene Rechnung zu übernehmen (‚kaufen') zu dem dann gültigen Tagepreis und (bei all dem) die für das gegenständlichen Darlehen anfallenden (Aufwendungen) abzuziehen und in Rechnung zu stellen, wobei wir unter Zugrundelegung der von dir und deinen Vertretern glaubwürdig gemachten Aufwendungen in jeder Hinsicht klagfrei gestellt sein sollen'; Casson (1990: 200): 'sell them for your account at the then prevailing market price, and deduct and include in the reckoning whatever expenses occur on account of the aforementioned loan, with complete faith for such expenditures being extended to you and your agents or managers'; Rathbone (2000: 40): 'and to buy them for yourself at the price current at the time, and to subtract and reckon in what falls due [on account of the aforesai]d loan, on terms that the responsibility for what falls due [lies] with you and your administrators or managers.'

[30] Thür (1987: 237, n. 30). The implications of the clause *τῆς πίστεως οὔσης περὶ* in a loan contract had been inferred from *P.Oxy.* 3.506 = *MChr* 248 by Mitteis (in Mitteis and Wilcken (1912: 2.2, 283 n. 15)). *Contra*, Schmitz (1964: 71–80).

indicate either 'future proceeds' or 'future expenses',[31] but argued that the reference here is to supplementary expenses, and consistently translates the term as 'anfallenden (Aufwendungen)'.[32] In this version, the lender would have had the benefit of assumption not for the proceeds he received, but for the expenses he would have incurred on behalf of the borrower.

I find it difficult to agree with such a conclusion. First of all, it is questionable whether the verb πίπτω also conveys the meaning of 'spending'. When it is used in the sense of 'to fall to one', the verb regularly refers to *income* falling into someone's fund.[33] Therefore, 'things that will fall' should be either proceeds from sales or income from revenues. Moreover, in a loan contract the benefit of assumption cannot be given to either of the two parties, regardless of the mechanism of the contract. In particular, it cannot be given to a lender who claims money for undocumented expenses.

The τῆς πίστεως—οὔσης περὶ clause occurs in eight (or possibly nine) other loan contracts on papyrus. In six cases, the contracts do not foresee an increase in the loan amount resulting from additional expenses incurred by the lender: the benefit of assumption is given to the lender in five cases, to the borrower in only one.[34] Obviously, when the benefit of assumption is given to the lender, the borrower would expect receipts for his partial repayments, which would protect him from illegitimate claims. In the case in which the benefit of assumption—regarding only the interest!—was given to the borrower, the sentence 'I will repay to you the interest every month (the benefit of assumption being on me) and the capital in 30 Mesore of the present second year' strongly suggests that the interest for all nine months of the loan was actually deducted in advance. In fact, 1 per cent per month interest on 84 drachmas comes to less than one drachma per month. Such a small amount of money was hardly worth a monthly payment and meeting. A single comprehensive deduction of 7.5 drachmas would have been more practical. Finally, there are cases (two, or possibly three) in which the τῆς πίστεως—οὔσης περὶ clause occurs in loan contracts that do foresee an increase in the loan amount because of the lender's additional expenses.[35] In these cases, the benefit of assumption is indeed given to the lender, but only if the expenses are

[31] Thür (1987: 236, n. 29): 'Mit dem neutralen Ausdruck τὰ πεσούμενα können sowohl künftige Einnahmen . . . als auch Ausgaben gemeint sein.'

[32] Thür (1987: 236, n. 29): 'Vom Erlös, den der Gläubiger bei der Verwertung der verpfändeten Waren erzielt, wird es gewiss seine Aufwendungen abziehen durfen.'

[33] Cfr. *LSJ* s.v. πίπτω B.V. 3, but *IPE* 1².32, B 75 does not require a different meaning: see Austin (2006²: 221).

[34] Benefit of assumption given to the lender: *P.Genova* 2.62, ll. 4–23 (AD 98); *P.Oxy.* 3.506 = *MChrest* 248, ll. 13–19 (AD 143); *P.Oslo* 2.40, ll. 30–5 (AD 150); *SB* 14.11599, ll. 1–8 (AD 155); *P.Oxy. Hels.* 36, ll. 4–10 (AD 167); benefit of assumption given to the borrower: *P.Rend.Harr.* 85, ll. 7–15 (AD 117).

[35] *P.Mich.* 11.605, ll. 23–5: (AD 117); 3.188 (AD 120), ll. 16–17; cf. 3.189, ll. 32–4 (AD 123).

demonstrated first (*ἐὰν φανῇ*): in substance, for the additional expenses, the burden of proof rests with the lender.

A clause that gave the lender the benefit of assumption for any undocumented expense made in favour of the borrower would be a departure from the basic principle that the burden of proof always lies with the person who lays charges.[36] The unfortunate borrower would have been at the mercy of his lender, and could never hope to challenge an illegitimate claim. We may therefore conclude that in the Muziris papyrus loan contract both the meaning of the verb and the structure of the clause show that the *πεσούμενα* of col. ii, ll. 22 and 23, are not 'future expenses', but 'future proceeds'.

Since the only 'future proceeds' we can imagine are those from the partial sales of the cargo, we may infer: 1) that the cargo was meant to be sold to multiple purchasers, each one buying a small batch of commodities at his/her own convenience; and 2) that the lender or his agents collected the proceeds from each sale and provided receipts to the borrower as proof of partial debt repayment, until such time as the loan was completely paid off. If the borrower failed to repay his debt by the customary deadline of the loan contracts for Muziris, the lender was allowed to take for himself the three-quarter portions of the unsold commodities at the current price. The lender would then deduct (*ἐκκρούειν*) that value from the amount due and factor in what would have been collected from the earlier partial sales (*ἐνλογεῖν τὰ πεσούμενα*).

If the above argument is correct, the lacuna at col. ii, l. 23 could be tentatively restored as *καὶ ἐνλογεῖν τὰ πεσούμενα|[ἀπ' ὠνίων εἰς ἔκτεισιν τ]οῦ δανείου* (and reckon the proceeds from the goods for the payment in full of the loan).[37] Of course, in order to prove that the lender or his agents collected the proceeds of those sales, the borrower would have to produce the necessary receipts. Should the borrower fail to do so, and should a legal dispute arise, the benefit of assumption (*πίστις*) would be granted to the lender and his agents.

7.4. OUTSTANDING LOANS

Constant anxiety—whether about securing or repaying a loan—was a quintessential feature in the life of the maritime trader. In a passage of Philostratus' *Life of Apollonius*, the philosopher is imagined dissuading a young Spartan nobleman from his indecorous passion for ship-owning and seafaring. Apollonius' argument displays a good knowledge of both the economic and

[36] Marcian., *Dig.* 22.3.21.pr.

[37] Cfr. *P.Fam.Tebt.* 24 col. ii, ll. 19–20: *ὧν τὴν σύνοψει̣[ν] οὐκ ἐνλογήσηι εἰς τὸ διδόμενον| δαπάνημα.*

psychological conditions of a maritime trader, which is consistent with a character who recalls being the captain of an Egyptian ship in a previous life:[38]

> Well, and can you mention any rabble of people more wretched and ill-starred than merchants and ship-owners? In the first place they roam from sea to sea, looking for some market that is badly stocked; and then they sell and are sold, associating with brokers ['patrons' in the manuscripts] and retailers, and they subject their own heads to the most unholy yields in their hurry to get back the principal; and if they do well, their ship has a lucky voyage, and they tell you a long story of how they never wrecked it either willingly or unwillingly; but if their gains do not balance their debts, they jump into boats and dash their ships on to the rocks, and make no bones as sailors of robbing others of their substance, pretending in the most blasphemous manner that it is an act of God.[39]

In this dreadful description, maritime merchants—regardless of whether they were also ship owners—were by default condemned to an endless spiral of burdensome loans and difficult repayments, interrupted only by deliberate or unplanned disasters. In this Sisyphean task, merchants had to contend with two partly symbiotic, partly parasitic partners: brokers and retailers. This is why I believe a small textual correction is needed in the passage above. The manuscripts' reading *προξένοις* should, I believe, be emended to *προξενηταῖς*. It is the *proxenetai* (brokers), not the *proxenoi* (patrons), who interacted with maritime merchants (*emporoi*),[40] and it is the pair *proxenetai* and *kapeloi* (brokers and retailers) who were active participants at the beginning (the brokers) and at the end (the retailers) of a transmarine commercial enterprise.

Philostratus' wording betrays the sense of superiority that men like Apollonius or his noble listener were supposed to feel towards such men. But the low birth and presumably unrefined manners of brokers and retailers alone do not explain the distress of the *emporoi* who dealt with them. The truth is that the *emporoi* needed the *proxenetai* to secure the loans, and then the *kapeloi* to repay them. The leverage held by *proxenetai* and *kapeloi* over the *emporoi* who were in need of a loan or desperate to repay one could make for extremely unpleasant interactions. It could be challenging, for instance, especially for a novice ship owner, or even an experienced one who had a record of wreckages, to get a loan from a cautious *proxenetes*. On the other hand, driven by a looming loan expiration date, the effort to sell a cargo in time could end in a psychological battle with the *kapeloi*, who were always ready to exploit the *emporoi*'s panic. In the time between securing and repaying a loan, the *emporos* must constantly reappraise rising costs and prospective profits. The

[38] Philostr., *VA* 3.23.

[39] Philostr., *VA* 4.32; transl. by F.C. Conybeare, with modifications. On this passage, cf. Tchernia (2016: 23 n. 65).

[40] Sen., *Ep.* 119.1.

fear that, at the end of the day, he would not break even is second only to the alarm caused by a storm while at sea.[41]

The recto text of the Muziris papyrus clarifies the procedure in case the borrower does not repay his debt on time. Like the maritime loan contract in *Against Lacritus* (and unlike the one for the voyage to the Aromatophoros Land, and most of those signed by the Constantinopolitan *naukleroi* in AD 540),[42] the loan contract of the Muziris papyrus foresaw that, should the borrower fail to repay his debt at the expiration of the loan schedule, the collateral became the property of the lender: 'then be to you . . . to get possession and own the aforesaid security and levy the quarter-tax, and transfer the remaining three-quarters to where you wish, and sell, and re-hypothecate, and cede to another as you wish, and decide in the way you want, and buy for yourself at the current price' (col. ii ll. 14–2002), (col. ii ll. 14–22).

The lender—now the new owner of the outstanding portion of the cargo—may use the cargo in different ways—*all* on the condition, however, that the goods will be evaluated at the current market price (Fig. 7.1).

Once the ship safely returned to its final port, it was the lender, not the borrower, who was protected from the fluctuations in market prices. If the goods originally mortgaged were to be sold off cheaply, the borrower would

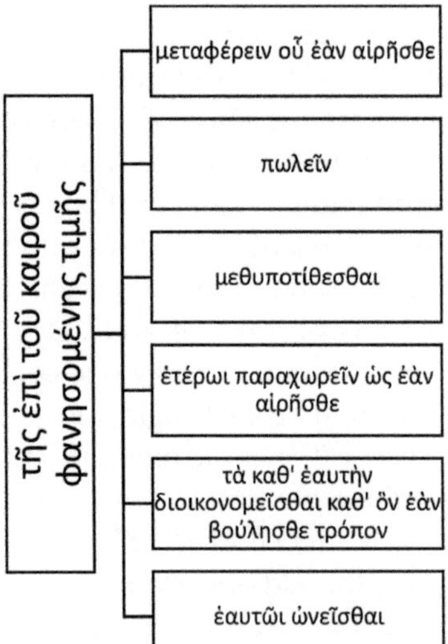

Fig. 7.1 Lender's options in case of an outstanding loan.

[41] *CIL* 9.60 (= *CLE* 1533), ll. 7–8: *sidera non timeo hic nec nimbos nec mare saevom | nec metuo sumptus ni quaestum vincere possit.*

[42] See pp. 163–5.

have to refund the lender using his other assets.[43] Thus whenever a cargo was not expected to break even—*εἰ δὲ ἡ ἐμπορία πρὸς τὰ χρέα μὴ ἀναφέροιτο*, in Apollonius' words—it could become financially convenient for merchants to dash their ships onto the rocks.[44]

In the Muziris papyrus loan contract, after the lender has appropriated the three-quarter portions of the unsold commodities and valued them at the current rates, the borrower is expected to pay or receive the difference between the market value of the seized security and his debt, as described in recto, col. ii, ll. 25–6:

> 25 *τοῦ δὲ περ̣ὶ τὴ̣ν ἐνθήκην ἐνλείμματός*
> 26 [τ]ε *καὶ πλεονάσματος πρὸς ἐμὲ τὸν δεδανεισμένον κ̣α̣ὶ ὑποτεθει-*
>
> Col. iii
>
> 1 [*μένον ὄντος* ---]
>
> the shortfall and surplus with respect to the capital will be on me, the borrower and mortgager.

Col. ii, l. 26 makes it clear that another column followed to the right. In all likelihood, col. iii contained clauses concerning possible unfortunate events en route: perhaps a change in the itinerary,[45] the loss of the ship,[46] or the death of the borrower.[47] Certainly, and most crucially, it would have included a clause regarding the failure to assemble enough cargo before 13 January.[48] The text may have ended with the statement that the contract was binding, and the names of the witnesses.[49]

[43] [Dem.] 35.12; Paul., *Dig*. 22.2.6.pr. [44] Dem. 32.5; Philostr., *VA* 4.32.
[45] [Dem.] 35.13. [46] [Dem.] 35.13. [47] Labeo, *Dig*. 22.2.9.pr.
[48] See pp. 145; 168–70. [49] Cf. [Dem.] 35.13.

8

Loan and Logistics

In his vehement warning to the unconventional Spartan nobleman, Philostratus' Apollonius emphatically deplores the condition of the merchants who 'mortgage their own heads to the most unholy yields' of the maritime loan.[1] Yet the overall relationship between maritime traders and financiers was not always so bleak. Expensive for the borrowers and hazardous for the financiers, the maritime—or, better, transmarine—loan (*pecunia traiecticia* or *mutua pecunia nautica*) was not the only way maritime trade could be financed.[2] Maritime merchants could also resort to cheaper loans that were carried across the sea, but not at the creditor's risk,[3] or to loans that were carried only in part, or not carried at all, across the sea.[4]

The loan of the Muziris papyrus was not used to buy commodities either in Egypt or in India. It was meant for transport costs in Egypt—across the Eastern Desert, and along the Nile—for both the outward and the return journeys. As such it was only to some extent vulnerable to the risks of the sea voyage, and so can only in part be considered a maritime loan. Most of the money was delivered on shore, once the Indian commodities were safe from the dangers of the sea, but supplementary resources were needed to transfer the cargo to Alexandria. In addition to the financial support, the river and desert transport required a safe environment and special infrastructures, which, if necessary, were guaranteed by the imperial administration.

8.1. WHAT THE LOAN WAS ALL ABOUT

The surviving part of the Muziris papyrus loan contract reveals which expenses the loan was supposed to cover. Setting aside the controversial restoration of l. 10 (to be discussed later), the text of recto col. ii, ll. 8–16 runs as follows:

[1] Philostr. *VA* 3.23, see p. 185.
[2] *Pecunia traiecticia*: Mod., *Dig.* 22.2.1.pr.; *mutua pecunia nautica*: Scaev., *Dig.* 45.1.122.1.
[3] Papin., *Dig.* 22.2.4.pr.: *traiecticia pecunia sine periculo creditoris.*
[4] Mod., *Dig.* 22.2.1. pr.: *si eodem loci consumatur.*

The Indo-Roman Pepper Trade and the Muziris Papyrus. Federico De Romanis, Oxford University Press (2020).
© Federico De Romanis. DOI: 10.1093/oso/9780198842347.001.0001

καὶ ὁ-
[μοίω]ς̣ ποιήσω ὑπὸ τὴν σὴν ἢ τῶν σῶν ἐξουσίαν καὶ σφραγεῖδα ταῖς
[- - -]ί̣ου ἀπὸ τοῦ νῦν μέχρι τεταρτολογίας δαπάναις πάσαις καὶ φο-
[ρέτρω]ν̣ ὄρους καὶ ναύλων ποταμίων καὶ τῶν ἄλλων κατὰ μέρος ἀνα-
[λωμά]τ̣ων πρὸς τὸ ἐνστάντος τοῦ ἐν ταῖς κατὰ Μουζεῖριν τοῦ δα-
[νείου σ]υνγραφαῖς τῆς ἀποδόσεως ὡ̣ρισμένου χρόνου ἐὰν μὴ δικαί-
[ως τότ]ε̣ χρεολυτῶ τὸ προκείμενον ἐν ἐμοὶ δάνειον τότε εἶναι
[πρὸς σ]ὲ καὶ τοὺς σοὺς ἐπιτρόπους ἢ φροντιστὰς τὴν ἐγλογὴν καὶ ὁλο-
[σχερῆ] ἐξουσίαν ὡς ἐὰν αἱρῆσθε ποιήσασθαι τὰ τῆς πράξεως χωρὶς
[διάστ]ολῆς καὶ προσκρίσεως (l. προσκλήσεως) κτλ.[5]

and similarly I will put (*sc.* the cargo) under your or your people's power and seal... all the expenses... from now up to payment of the quarter-tax the costs of the desert transports, the river freights and the other due outlays, so that, if I [*sc.* the borrower] do not correctly repay the aforementioned loan in my name within the time established for the repayment in the Muziris loan contracts, you [*sc.* the lender] will be fully authorized to carry out the execution without notification or summons, etc.

It is unquestionable that the words 'all the expenses... from now to the payment of the quarter-tax' (ll. 9–10) refer to expenses incurred from the signing of the agreement to the payment of the quarter-tax, which marks the end of the lender's obligations. Furthermore, the sentence 'if I do not correctly repay the aforementioned loan in my name' (l. 14) makes it clear that the borrower is expected to repay a loan. Owing to the critical lacuna at l. 10 ([- - -]ί̣ου), and to the ambivalence of the dative (ταῖς—δαπάναις πάσαις), the interpretation of these lines—and therefore the relationship between the 'loan' and 'all the expenses from the beginning to payment of the quarter-tax'—has been controversial. In general, opinions differ regarding:

1) the lacuna at l. 10, which has been restored as [τοῦ πλο]ί̣ου by Harrauer and Sijpesteijn and by Thür; as [τοῦ λοι]π̣οῦ by Casson; as [ἐκ τοῦ δανε]ί̣ου by myself; and as [ἐκ τοῦ ἰδ]ί̣ου by Morelli;
2) the meaning of the dative ταῖς—δαπάναις πάσαις, which is taken as causal by Thür ('I will put [the cargo] under your power and seal *because* of all the expenses'),[6] and as circumstantial-modal by Harrauer and Sijpesteijn, Casson, and Morelli ('I will put [the cargo] under your power and seal *assuming* all the expenses').[7]

[5] At l. 12, the editors (Harrauer and Sijpensteijn 1985: 141, followed by Rathbone 2000: 41), postulated a long haplography, which is actually unnecessary: see Thür (1987: 235, n. 16). The insertion ἐνστάντος – τὸ προκείμενον ἐν ἐμοὶ δάνειον may look clumsy (N. Lewis apud Casson 1990: 197), but the syntax is nonetheless straightforward.

[6] Thür (1987: 234, n. 11); De Romanis (1998: 20–1).

[7] Harrauer and Sijpesteijn (1985: 133); Casson (1986: 75; 1990: 200); Morelli (2011: 201–4).

Regarding the lacuna at l. 10, while Casson's restoration ([τοῦ λοι]π̣οῦ) seems palaeographically impossible,[8] the reading by the editors ([τοῦ πλο]ί̣ου) turns out to be inconsistent with the complement ἀπὸ τοῦ νῦν μέχρι τεταρτολογίας, if, as Thür contends, [τοῦ πλο]ί̣ου refers to the sea-going vessel and ἀπὸ τοῦ νῦν μέχρι τεταρτολογίας indicates the beginning and the end of an Alexandria–Muziris–Alexandria enterprise.[9] The sea-going vessel neither left from nor returned to Alexandria.[10] By contrast, Morelli's proposal ([ἐκ τοῦ ἰδ]ί̣ου) is both palaeographically apt and formulaically very plausible, if ταῖς—δαπάναις πάσαις is to be taken as a circumstantial or modal dative: 'with all the expenses from now until the payment of the quarter-tax on me.'[11]

Incidentally, it may be noted that Morelli's restoration and interpretation seem incompatible with his theory that the Muziris papyrus recto text is a second loan contract signed in a port on the Red Sea coast of Egypt.[12] Since the rationale for the alleged second loan is to enable the borrower to meet the expenses of the journey from the Red Sea to Alexandria, it would be awkwardly redundant to specify that the borrower had to cover the cost of those expenses for which he had sought the loan. A lender may want to ensure that the borrower did not or would not pledge his assets elsewhere,[13] but he should have no objection if someone else were to bear costs in the borrower's stead. In a loan contract, stating that the borrower is expected to pay the expenses for which the loan was secured would be a legally irrelevant truism.

Morelli's restoration would be less problematic if we assumed that the contract had been signed in Alexandria and concerned a single loan, to be delivered in one instalment at the beginning of the commercial venture. After all, this is the manner in which the loan was granted to the five shipmates bound for the Aromatophoros Land.[14] The complement ταῖς [ἐκ τοῦ ἰδ]ίου ἀπὸ τοῦ νῦν μέχρι τεταρτολογίας δαπάναις πάσαις would clarify that the borrower was expected to repay his loan in Alexandria without receiving any other financial support up to that point. The clause καὶ φο[ρέτρω]ν̣ ὄρους καὶ ναύλων ποταμίων καὶ τῶν ἄλλων κατὰ μέρος ἀνα[λωμά]τ̣ων would be only partially explanatory of ταῖς—δαπάναις πάσαις, and the complete

[8] Palme apud Thür (1988: 229, n. 2).

[9] Thür's (1987: 231) translation is: 'und ich werde (sie) in gleicher Weise unter dein oder deiner Leute Vefügungsrecht und Siegel stellen für alle Ausgabe für das Seeschiff vonjetzt an bis zur Erhebung der *Tetarte* und für Frachtlĭhne an Flußschiffer und für die sonstigen anteiligen Aufwendungen.'

[10] Rightly, Morelli (2011: 203): 'come è possibile parlare di "tutte le spese della nave da adesso fino alla *tetartologia*", se su questa nave il mercante si imbarca solo a Berenice—o in altro porto sul Mar Rosso—per sbarcare al ritorno nello stesso porto, mentre tanto il νῦν della redazione del contratto quanto la *tetartologia* sarebbero da collocare in Alessandria?'

[11] Circumstantial or modal datives with δαπάναι and ἀναλώματα occur very often in the papyri, when it comes to determining which party must bear certain expenses; cf. Morelli (2011: 203).

[12] Morelli (2011: 206). For my objections, see above.

[13] Cf. [Dem.] 35.11: ὑποτιθέασι δὲ ταῦτα, οὐκ ὀφείλοντες ἐπὶ τούτοις ἄλλῳ οὐδενὶ οὐδὲν ἀργύριον, οὐδ' ἐπιδανείσονται.

[14] See p. 165.

sentence would run: 'taking on myself all the expenses from now [*sc.* beginning of the commercial enterprise] to the payment of the quarter-tax [*sc.* end of the same], *including* [*sc.* besides other, more obvious expenses] the transports across the desert, the river fares, and the other particular expenditures.'

Still, as appealing as Morelli's restoration is, I do not think that the words *ταῖς— ἀνα[λωμά]τ̣ων* describe the borrower's promise to bear all the expenditures of the voyage from start to end. The reason for my disagreement lies in the position of the clause in the general syntax of the sentence. The sequence is shown in Fig. 8.1:

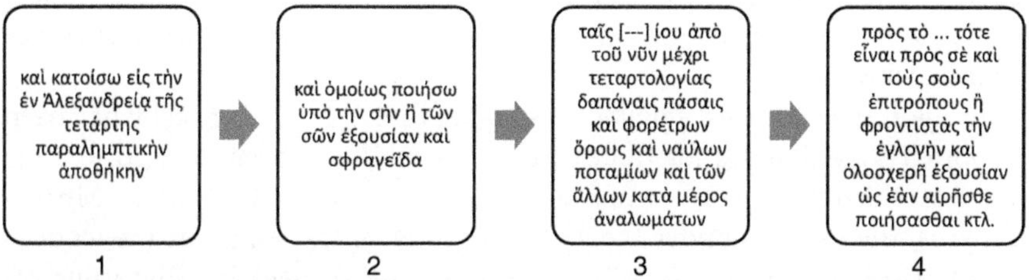

Fig. 8.1 The sequence of the phrases at recto col. ii, ll. 8–16.

Sandwiched between the main clause *ὁμοίως ποιήσω ὑπὸ τὴν σὴν—σφραγεῖδα* (2) and the subordinate clause *πρὸς τὸ—εἶναι* (4), the dative *ταῖς—δαπάναις πάσαις* (3) must mean something that is logically connected with the premise *ὁμοίως ποιήσω κτλ.* (2) and the possible consequence *πρὸς τὸ—εἶναι* (4). Therefore, the dative *ταῖς—δαπάναις πάσαις* can be understood as circumstantial or modal only if the implementation of *ποιεῖν ὑπὸ τὴν σφραγῖδα* implied an expenditure—that is, only if it were one of the *ἄλλα κατὰ μέρος ἀναλώματα*. If this is not the case (and I believe it is not), one has to conclude that the dative *ταῖς—δαπάναις πάσαις* cannot be circumstantial/modal. To put it another way: if these lines really meant that the borrower had to bear all the expenditures from the beginning to the end of the commercial venture, the words *ταῖς* [—] *ἰ̣ου—ἀναλωμάτων* (3) should have been positioned after *καὶ κατοίσω εἰς τὴν—ἀποθήκην* (1), and before *καὶ ὁμοίως ποιήσω* (2), like in Fig. 8.2:

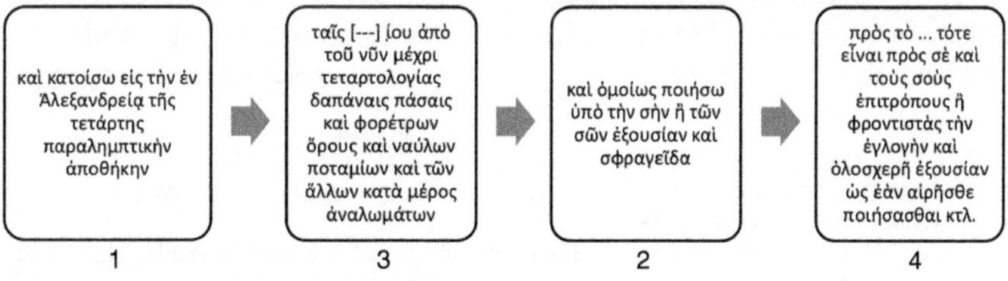

Fig. 8.2 The sequence of the phrases at recto col. ii, ll. 8–16 as it should be, if the borrower meant to assume the desert and river transport expenses.

With the syntax as it is, the only possible way I see to make sense of the dative *ταῖς—δαπάναις πάσαις* as a complement of *ποιήσω ὑπὸ τὴν σὴν—σφραγεῖδα* is to interpret it as the value at which the commodities are placed 'under the power and seal' of the lender, so that the dative *ταῖς—δαπάναις πάσαις* expresses the *measure* of the lender's rights. The commodities would stay under the lender's control as long as all the loan-related expenses remain unpaid. Admittedly, the value for which something is pledged, denoted by the genitive case in classical Greek,[15] is normally expressed by *πρός* + accusative in papyri.[16] In this case, however, a shift to a simple dative—either a sort of instrumental dative or a *dativus relationis*[17]—may be explained by the two occurrences of *πρός* + accusative that follow (*πρὸς τὸ—εἶναι πρὸς σὲ κτλ.*), which would probably make a third occurrence sound awkward.[18]

In *Against Timotheus*, Apollodorus argues that if the timber really had been imported by Philondas for trade's sake, it would have been pledged for (the value of) the freight: *ὑποκειμένων αὐτῷ τῶν ξύλων τοῦ ναύλου*.[19] In the Muziris papyrus, the cargo is under the seal and power of the lender or the lender's people (*ὑπὸ τὴν σὴν ἢ τῶν σῶν ἐξουσίαν καὶ σφραγεῖδα*) for (the value of) expenditures incurred between the beginning and the end of the commercial enterprise.

From this perspective, at l. 10 something like *ἐκ δανε]ί̣ου* or *τοῦ δανε]ί̣ου* or *ἐκ τοῦ δανε]ί̣ου* or *διὰ τοῦ δανε]ί̣ου* may be restored,[20] and at ll. 10–11 the words *καὶ φο|ρέτρω]ν̣ ὄρους καὶ ναύλων ποταμίων καὶ τῶν ἄλλων κατὰ μέρος ἀνα|λωμάτων* can be taken as *fully explanatory* of *ταῖς—δαπάναις πάσαις*. The translation of recto col. ii, ll. 8–12 should run: 'I shall place [*sc.* the commodities] under your or your people's power and seal for (the value of) all the expenditures covered by the loan from now to the payment of the quarter-tax, both those for the transport costs across the desert and the river freights and the other due outlays.'

Thus, the financier did not grant a fixed sum in a single instalment at the beginning of the enterprise, nor did he give a loan at the beginning of the voyage and pay for all the expenses projected for the return journey, from the Red Sea to Alexandria. He granted a loan that *exactly coincided* with the specified expenditures.

The syllogism seems compelling to me. The borrower is expected to repay only a loan (*δάνειον*).[21] On the other hand, the cargo is 'under the lender's or the lender's people's power and seal' for all the expenses from the beginning to

[15] Cf. p. 179 n.20.

[16] E.g. *P.Oxy.* 10.1269, ll. 24, 26, 28, 30, 31. Cf. Mayser (1923–1934, 2.2.2: 506–7).

[17] Mayser (1923–1934, 2.2.1: 283; 285).

[18] The link between the expenses and the right of disposal is acknowledged by Thür (1988: 231), who understands *ταῖς—δαπάναις πάσαις* as *dativus causae*.

[19] [Dem.] 49.35.

[20] Cf. De Romanis (1998: 20–1).

[21] Recto, col. ii, l. 14.

the end of the enterprise, which include the transport costs between Alexandria and the Red Sea for both the outward and return journeys, as well as other minor expenditures, presumably including the loading and unloading operations at Alexandria, Coptos, and in the Red Sea port, and rental space in the Coptos and Alexandria *paralemptikai* storehouses.[22] It follows that the loan and those expenses are one and the same. If the loan covered anything else, the cargo would have been put under the lender's seal 'for the loan and all the expenses' (τῷ δανείῳ καὶ ταῖς—δαπάναις πάσαις).

8.2. PRUDENT LOANS FOR MARITIME TRADE

Modestinus defines the transmarine loan (*pecunia traiecticia*) as money or cargo that is carried over sea at the risk of the creditor:

> A "transmarine loan" consists of money carried overseas. If it is spent where lent, it is not "transmarine". But are goods bought with the money in the same position? It depends on whether they are carried at the lender's peril. If so, the loan is transmarine.[23]

Risky for financiers and onerous for merchants, transmarine loans were only one of several options for financing maritime trade. Another option, in which the loan is lent, expended, and repaid in the same place, is suggested by the passage in *Against Timotheus* considered above.[24] In Timotheus' version, Philondas would import timber for the sake of trade, on the promise that, on his arrival at Athens, Pasion would lend the money for the freight (ναῦλον). Apollodorus objected that if the timber had been imported 'for the sake of trade' (ἐμπορίας ἕνεκα), his father would have 'set one of his servants to keep watch and to receive the price as the timber was sold, until he had recovered his money'. By piecing together Timotheus' claim and Apollodorus' objection, we envision a scenario in which a financier based in the destination port guarantees the payment of the freight to a merchant chartering transport space on someone else's ship. In return, the merchant will offer his goods as security, so that the financier can collect the proceeds of their sale until the debt is repaid.

Given his personality and his past relations with the lender, Timotheus did not need a written pledge from Pasion promising the payment of the freight. Nor—being away from Athens when the timber arrived—could he

[22] Recto, col. ii, ll. 8–12.

[23] Mod., *Dig.* 22.2.1.pr.; trans. by A. Watson (A. M. Honoré) with modifications. However, the money financing maritime trade without lender's risk (*sine periculo creditoris*) is equally called *pecunia traiecticia* by Papinianus: Papin., *Dig.* 22.2.4.pr.

[24] [Dem.] 49.35–6, see p. 177.

acknowledge receipt of the 1,750 drachmas. In many other contracts of the same type, it is likely that the parties signed a written agreement in which the financier promised to pay the freight upon arrival of the commodities and the merchant agreed to pledge the commodities for the value of the freight and to repay the loan under certain conditions. Thus, when the sum was actually delivered, the merchant would acknowledge receipt and promise to repay the loan as agreed.

I suggest recognizing such an agreement in the controversial ναυλωτική referred to in one of the two *chirographa*, the first in Greek, the second in Latin, written in the *TPSulp*. 78 tablets.[25] In this document dated 11 April AD 38, Menelaos from Keramos acknowledges receipt, in Puteoli, of 1,000 denarii 'in the terms established in a sealed freight contract' (Tab. I, pag. 2, l. 9: ἐκ ναυλωτικῆς ἐκσφραγισμένης). The lender is Primus, slave of P. Attius Severus.[26] Menelaos then promises to repay the money according to the terms established in the same freight contract and indicates M. Barbatius Celer as guarantor for the full payment. In the second *chirographum* (by hand of Q. Aelius Romanus because M. Barbatius Celer was illiterate) Barbatius confirms his *fideiussio*.

The circumstances and conditions of the lost ναυλωτική are not known, and they have been imagined in very different ways. H. Ankum argued that the term corresponds to the Latin *traiecticius*, and the ναυλωτική contract was just a maritime loan contract for a round-trip voyage; Menelaos would have been either a ship owner or a merchant who chartered transport space.[27] G. Purpura also interpreted the contract as a maritime loan.[28] D. C. Gofas contended that the contract was for a fictive loan attached to a transport contract, and it aimed to insure the cargo against the maritime risks. The 1,000 denarii would thus represent the value of (a part of) the cargo entrusted by Primus to the alleged ship owner Menelaos to be transported elsewhere from Puteoli. Should Menelaos fail to deliver the cargo, he would have had to return that sum to Primus.[29] Basically the same context is assumed by Thür, who differs from Gofas on the legal definition of the contract; to Thür, it was an agreement on the value of the cargo.[30] Suggesting a parallel with the agreement referred to in Ulp., *Dig*. 19.2.15.6, É. Jakab sees Menelaos as a ship owner who received the 1,000 denarii formally as a loan, but in fact as a freight pre-payment: an *exceptio* in the ναυλωτικὴ συγγραφή would have allowed Menelaos to keep the money in case of regular delivery.[31] According to J. G. Wolf, the 1,000 denarii represented the cargo to be transported to another port by the alleged

[25] *TPSulp*. 78.

[26] The name of P. Attius Severus appears also in the *tituli picti CIL* 15.3642; 3644; 3645; 4748; 4749; cf. Rovira Guardiola (2007: 1264–5).

[27] Ankum (1978; 1988).

[28] Purpura (1984: 1245–53).

[29] Gofas (1993: 264–5). The medieval parallels suggested by Gofas (1993: 261, n. 46) correspond less closely than those indicated by Tchernia (2016: 270, n. 13).

[30] Thür (1993).

[31] Jakab (2000). On Ulp., *Dig*. 19.2.15.6, see Zwalve (2013).

ship owner Menelaos.[32] D. F. Jones argues that the 1,000 denarii was a loan to allow Menelaos to pay the customs duties at the destination port.[33]

Some weaknesses in the above interpretations have already been highlighted. It has been observed that a *ναυλωτική* (*sc. συγγραφή*) is properly a transport contract, not a maritime loan contract (*ναυτικὴ συγγραφή*);[34] that a fictive loan to ensure a cargo is unparalleled in ancient evidence;[35] and that if the 1,000 denarii was supposed to be delivered to a third person, at Tab. I p. 2, l. 10 *παραδώσω* would have been more appropriate than *ἀποδώσω*.[36] More generally, we may further remark:

1. None of the above interpretations explains why M. Barbatius Celer would give his *fideiussio* to Menelaos. Although Puteoli's bustling economy may have generated intercultural partnerships, it is difficult to see why an illiterate local would have been guarantor for a transmarine venture of an alleged ship owner from Keramos, who could not write in Latin.
2. None of the above interpretations explains why Menelaos acknowledges receipt of 1,000 denarii 'resulting from sealed *ναυλωτική*' and promises to repay that money 'according to the *ναυλωτική*' in a document which is not the *ναυλωτική*. If the freight contract concerned Menelaos' impending voyage, why two separate documents?[37]

In *DDbDP*, the adjective *ναυλωτική* occurs in seven documents, whose chronology ranges from the second to the seventh centuries AD. Apart from three cases, in which the context is either too fragmentary or concerns payments for various purposes,[38] all the others are contracts in which a ship owner or captain transports something for a fee. Other contracts may be defined *ναυλωτικαὶ συγγραφαί*, even if the adjective *ναυλωτική* may not have occurred. In all these contracts, the fee may be received either entirely at the delivery,[39] or entirely upon signing of the contract,[40] or only partly at the signing and partly at the delivery.[41] When all or part of the fee is given in advance, the contracts never comprise two separate documents (one for the conditions of the agreement and another for the receipt of the money), nor is the money expected to be repaid.

[32] Wolf (1979; 2001).

[33] Jones (2006: 103–17). On the document, see further Camodeca (1999, 177–80); (2000, 188–90); (2001: 86–8); (2003, 88–90); Pontoriero (2011: 13–16); Tchernia (2016: 269–73).

[34] Gofas (1993: 258–9); Wolf (2001: 437–9).

[35] Jakab (2000: 253).

[36] Ankum (1978: 160); Jakab (2000: 250); Wolf (2001: 453).

[37] More creative than convincing are the explanations suggested by Ankum (1978: 162).

[38] *P.Iand.* 8.150v col. ii, ll. 1–2; *P.Oxy.* 3.643; *P.Lond.* 5.1851.

[39] *P.Wisc.* 2.65; *T.Varie* 3, on which Morelli (2010).

[40] *P.Oxy.* 43.3111.

[41] *P.Oxy.* 45.3250; 49.3484; *P.Lond.* 3.948r; *P.Ross. Georg.* 2.18.6.24–34; 29.125–34; 40.175–83; 51.188–97; *SB* 14.11552.

It is therefore evident that the ναυλωτικαὶ συγγραφαί on the Nile are differently engineered from the ναυλωτική of *TPSulp*. 78. They also differ from the agreement that allegedly occurred between Pasion and Philondas. In fact, the Nilotic freight contracts are between a ship owner and a charterer, whereas the Athenian agreement would have been between a merchant and a banker who promises to pay the freight for a voyage that is longer and riskier than a Nile voyage. In the ports of the Mediterranean, it may have been customary for a merchant to require the assurance of a banker for the payment of a transmarine freight, so as not to be compelled to sell too hastily upon his return. As far as terminology is concerned, since contracts of this type aimed to guarantee the payment of a freight (ναῦλον), it is not unlikely that they were called ναυλωτικαὶ συγγραφαί.

For the ναυλωτικὴ συγγραφή agreed upon by Primus and Menelaos to be similar to the alleged agreement between Pasion and Philondas, we would have to conjecture that Menelaos was an *emporos*, and Primus a banker. This is not problematic, because the two *chirographa* do not compel us to see Menelaos and Primus as a *naukleros* and a charterer, respectively. We would also need Menelaos not to have been about to leave Puteoli, but to have just arrived there on 11 April AD 38. At first glance, this seems to be more difficult, because that date falls in a period—between 11 March and 15 May—that is no longer *mare clausum*, but is not yet safe for sailing.[42] But we should bear in mind, first, that energetic merchants were not shy about exploiting less safe sailing opportunities (as Vegetius points out) and, second, that ships that left late from the Eastern Mediterranean could winter en route and arrive at Puteoli at the beginning of the next sailing season.[43]

The most likely explanation for all the clues provided in the two *chirographa* is that, in the previous sailing season, Menelaos and Primus had signed a contract in Puteoli—the ναυλωτική referred to in *TPSulp*. 78 t.p.2, ll. 9, 11—in which Primus pledges to lend Menelaos 1,000 denarii to cover the freight costs for his next voyage to Puteoli. Menelaos then arrives in Puteoli on 11 April AD 38. Based on what has been agreed in the ναυλωτικὴ συγγραφή, Primus gives 1,000 denarii to pay the freight and Menelaos offers his commodities as security, acknowledging the receipt of the loan. Eventually, Menelaos sells part of his cargo to a local retailer, M. Barbatius Celer, for the value of at least 1,000 denarii. As (partial?) payment for the goods acquired, M. Barbatius Celer, indicated by Menelaos as *fideiussor* for the received 1,000 denarii, acknowledges the *fideiussio*, as set down by Q. Aelius Romanus. The 1,000 denarii are paid to Primus by C. Sulpicius Faustus, who keeps the two tablets with Menelaos' receipt and Celer's *fideiussio*.

[42] Veg., *Mil.* 4.39.

[43] NT, *Acts* 27.6–28.13; Luc., *Navigium* 7–9. Based on Cic., *Att.* 4.10.1, Casson (1971: 298, n. 5) argues that in 55 BC, ships from Alexandria arrived at Puteoli before 22 April.

If this interpretation is correct, the covenant between Primus and Menelaos replicates the steps of the agreement that purportedly occurred between Pasion and Philondas, according to Timotheus' claim and Apollodorus' counterargument:

1. As Pasion promises to pay Philondas' freight before Philondas leaves Athens for Macedonia, so Primus and Menelaos sign the ναυλωτικὴ συγγραφή before Menelaos leaves Puteoli in the AD 37 sailing season.
2. As Pasion pays the freight of 1,750 drachmas upon the arrival of the timber, so Primus delivers, per the ναυλωτικὴ συγγραφή, the 1,000 denarii when Menelaos lands in Puteoli.
3. As Pasion should have taken control of the sale of the timber, if the money had been given 'for the sake of trade', so Primus takes control of Menelaos' cargo per the ναυλωτικὴ συγγραφή.
4. As Pasion should have collected the proceeds of the sale until the 1,750 drachmas was repaid, so Primus collects the 1,000 denarii owed by the buyer/*fideiussor* M. Barbatius Celer.

If such were the terms of the agreement between Menelaos and Primus, it appears that the rationale for this kind of contract was to finance maritime trade yet still avoid the 'unholy yields' of the transmarine loan, because money that is spent where it is lent (*pecunia quae eodem loci consumatur*) costs less than money that is carried overseas (*pecunia quae trans mare vehitur*). Contracts of this type may have been common practice for the bankers of Puteoli, and may have contributed, for instance, to the popularity of L. and C. Calpurnii among the merchants active in Asia, Syria, and Alexandria.[44]

A loan that covers marginal expenses when the goods are safely ashore and a transmarine loan that finances an entire commercial enterprise from beginning to end are the two theoretical extremes of the maritime trade-financing spectrum. In between, many degrees of liability exist and even hybrid contract forms. The loan of the Muziris papyrus financed neither the sea voyage nor the purchase of Indian commodities. It covered only the desert and river transport in Egypt, plus other minor disbursements. When viewed through the lens of Modestinus' distinction, only the lender's financing for the outward journey could be considered a 'transmarine loan' (*pecunia traiecticia*), since it was vulnerable to the risks of the round-trip sea voyage. This did not apply to the financing for the return journey, making it a hybrid loan—and, moreover, one that was mostly non-transmarine, since the cargo volume and the transport costs between Alexandria and the Red Sea were far lower on the outward than on the return journey.

[44] *ILS* 7273. Jaschke (2010: 129–30).

The borrower of the Muziris papyrus loan contract is more financially circumspect than the five shipmates who borrow a lump sum at the beginning of their Aromatophoros Land venture: while the shipmates' entire loan applies to goods travelling by sea at the lender's risk, such that they must eventually pay the 'unholy yields' of the transmarine loans, only a fraction of the Muziris papyrus loan is exposed to the risk of the sea: therefore, it must have been less expensive, for the merchant, than a full transmarine loan. The remarkably cautious behaviour shown by the borrower in this contract characterizes the lender as well. At the end of the day, the lender's financial support was pertinent only within the borders of Egypt and, more substantially, after the cargo was safely on land. Such prudent borrowing and funding seems absent in the borrower/lender relationship imagined by Rathbone, in which a destitute borrower is desperate to repay his debt and a super-rich lender is ready to buy three-quarters of a South Indian cargo for almost 7,000,000 drachmas. Instead, the loan agreement of the Muziris papyrus describes a merchant who has the resources to pay for both the sea voyage and the purchase of Indian commodities, and a lender who provides limited financial support, which was perhaps vitally important when the merchant returned to the Red Sea port of Egypt. True, the borrower also opts to get a loan for the transport costs within Egypt on the outward journey; this, in the abstract, may have been neither necessary nor financially convenient. However, in the context of the borrower/lender relationship, such a decision may have been sensible, given the lender's role, assets and connections.[45]

The lender had a network of agents all along the route between Alexandria and the Red Sea, so it seems improbable that this setup was in place only for the enterprise financed with the Muziris papyrus loan contract. It is likely that in the same year the lender underwrote other loan contracts with other Indian Ocean merchants, always restricting his financial support to the transport costs within Egypt. It is equally likely that this was not the only year in which he had transacted such business. Thus, one may wonder whether the lender had ongoing relationships with the Eastern Desert cameleers and the owners of the Coptos river ships. Does the loan contract of the Muziris papyrus offer any information on this point?

8.3. CARAVANS FROM BERENICE

A few uncertain readings at recto col. ii, l. 2 make it difficult to clarify how the borrower intended to organize the transport of the cargo from the Red Sea port to Coptos. At recto col. ii, ll. 2–3, the editors read the lines as:

[45] They will be further elucidated in chapter thirteen, pp. 308–12.

2 [δώσω τ]ῷ̣ σῷ̣ καμηλείτηι ἄλλα (τάλαντα) ρ̣ο̣ (δ̣ρ̣α̣χ̣μ̣ὰ̣ς̣) ν̣ πρὸς ἐπίθ̣εσιν τῆς εἰς Κόπτον

3 [εἰσόδο]υ̣ κτλ.

As a result of these readings and restorations, it has generally been inferred that, in the preceding lost part of the contract, the borrower had already promised to give another sum of money (presumably for an outward transport from Coptos to the Red Sea), and here is once again promising to give another 170 talents and 50 drachmas to a cameleer in some way affiliated with the lender for a transport from the Red Sea back to Coptos.

While other alterations to the editors' text have had little impact on the general interpretation,[46] the reading of l. 2 proposed by Morelli,]δ̣ώσω καμηλείτηι ἀξ̣ι̣οχρ̣έωι πρὸς ἐπίθεσιν, completed by the restoration παρα]δ̣ώσω suggested by N. Gonis,[47] has more consequential implications. It eliminates both the connection between the lender and the cameleer and the sums of money to be given to the cameleer for the outward and the return journeys. The borrower would promise only to hand the cargo over to a reliable, though unspecified, cameleer. The cost of that transport would not be predetermined.

Morelli's elegant reading is formulaically impeccable and fits the context very well—not least because the resulting sentence would be a perfect parallel to col. ii, ll. 6–7, concerning the navigation from Coptos to Alexandria. There, the borrower does not promise to put the cargo on the lender's ship at a predetermined price. He simply promises to load it on a safe ship (ἀσφαλὲς πλοῖον).[48]

I would accept Morelli's ἀξ̣ι̣οχρ̣έωι without hesitation, if only I could be persuaded that his reading -ξ̣ι̣- is correct. But, to me, the -λλ- read by the editors (or -δδ- or even -βδ-) seems more likely.[49] Right before πρός, there are dots that may be remnants of a vertical stroke. This would lead either to a problematic ν (as read by the editors), or to an ι (Harrauer and Morelli), or, theoretically, to a φ, compatible with a number of drachmas.

I cannot say whether the character preceding ρ is the abbreviation for talent, as the editors read, or a stained χ, as Morelli sees it. Morelli rightly emphasizes that the abbreviation for talent is completely different in the verso text. Conversely, it may be observed that in every other instance on the recto side χ looks different from the alleged one at l. 2. Ultimately, given the uncertainty

[46] So, at l. 2, Harrauer's subsequent reading (apud Casson 1990: 204) ἄλλα (τάλαντα) ε̣[ἴ]κ̣ο̣σ̣ι̣; and, at l. 3, the alternative restorations (συνόδο]υ̣) and (ἀνόδο]υ̣), respectively by Thür (1987: 234, n. 8) and N. Lewis (apud Casson (1990: 197)).

[47] Morelli (2011: 200–1). A translation could be: 'I will hand (the cargo) over to a reliable cameleer for the shipment to Coptos.'

[48] Col. ii, ll. 6–7: καὶ ἐμβαλοῦμαι |τῶι δέ]οντι καιρῶι εἰς ποτάμιον ἀσφαλὲς πλοῖον.

[49] The possibility of an αβδ- reading has been suggested to me by M. R. Falivene.

of what precedes and follows, the interpretation of the sentence hinges on the reading of that character. Taking it as the abbreviation of talents, we would have to accept the idea (and the implications) that the price for the transfer of Indian commodities from the Red Sea to the Nile was agreed upon between borrower and lender at the beginning of the enterprise.[50] Reading it as a χ, we would have to assume that between *καμηλείτηι* and *πρός*, there was either an adjective related to *καμηλείτηι* (*ἀξ̣ιοχρ̣έωι* as read by Morelli or something similar to it) or the proper name of the cameleer.[51] In turn, these two possibilities have different implications: the latter suggests that the agreement between borrower and lender included an arrangement for both trips across the desert; the former merely binds the borrower to select a fit candidate for the desert transport.

The question of the exact reading of the characters between *καμηλείτηι* and *πρός* at l. 2 is better left open. Nonetheless, the few words safely read in this line, combined with the data from the verso text and some other external pieces of evidence, still enable us to reconstruct crucial aspects of the desert transport. First of all, it should be pointed out that the text refers to a single cameleer (*καμηλείτηι*) and a single trip (*ἐπίθ̣εσιν*) from the Red Sea to Coptos. The transhipment of a cargo weighing—as we will see—more than 600 tons required more than 3,000 camels. How many single cameleers would be available to deliver such a service at a particular time?

Eastern Desert transport conditions in the mid-second century AD are illuminated by a camel declaration from Soknopaiu Nesos, dated 29 January AD 163:

> Of Soknopaiu Nesos camel number one. To Stephanos, the *strategos*, and to Zoilos, royal scribe of the Arsinoite nome, Herakleides division, from Harpagathes son of Satabus son of Harpagathes, from the village of Soknopaiu Nesos. Of the two camels and one estimated foal now full-grown, total camels three, I handed one over for the imperial services of the caravans from Berenice in the past month of Tybi by command of the most splendid prefect Annius Syriacus (*παρέσ|χον εἰς κυριακὰς χρείας τῶν ἀπὸ| Βερνείκης γεινο(μένων) πορ<ε>ιῶν τῷ | διελη̣λ(υθότι) μηνὶ Τῦβι κάμηλον ἕνα | ἐξ ἐνκελεύσεως τοῦ λαμπροτάτου | ἡγεμόνος Ἀ̣ν̣νίου Συριακοῦ*). I declare the remaining two camels for the present third year of Antoninus and Verus the lords Augusti in the same village. Of these, one was sent on hire for the service of transporting the porphyry column on the orders of the most splendid prefect (*ἐκ δὲ τούτων ἐπέμφθη | ἐπὶ μισθοφορᾷ πρὸς χρείαν τοῦ κα|θελκομένου κείονος πορφυρειτικοῦ | ἐξ ἐ̣ν̣κελεύσεως τοῦ λαμ(προτάτου) ἡγεμ(όνος) κά|μηλος εἷς*).[52]

[50] I cannot see how the character could refer to talents of weight (Casson (1990: 204)) rather than talents of money.

[51] Proper names more often precede, but sometimes follow, the word *καμηλ(ε)ίτης* (e.g. *O.Claud.* 1.27; 28; 29; 30; 31; 32; 33?; 34).

[52] *P.Lond.* 2.328, ll. 1–22.

No other camel declarations on papyrus offer an instance of a camel being sent from elsewhere in Egypt to join the caravans from Berenice, so it is difficult to say whether this single piece of evidence represents a routine procedure or an extraordinary measure adopted in exceptional circumstances.[53] While the construction of Trajan's Canal and the subsequent gradual decline of Myos Hormos in favour of Clysma may have caused a structural reduction in the number of cameleers operating between Coptos and the Red Sea,[54] in AD 162/3 preparations for the Parthian war may have put special pressure on the Egyptian transport system to ship grain to the front.[55] The coincidence that in the same year, from the same village, two camels were sent 'for the service of transporting the porphyry column' adds to the plausibility that this was a year unlike any other.[56]

Whatever the case, the camel sent 'for the imperial services of the caravans from Berenice' specifically contributed to the transhipment of South Indian pepper cargoes. A. Bülow-Jacobsen has rightly remarked that the wording of the declaration is at odds with the suggestion that the animal was meant to serve the desert guards protecting the route or to transport supplies for the soldiers based at Berenice and the desert stations.[57] In fact, the expression 'caravans *from* Berenice' is incompatible with the task of supplying Berenice itself or any of the intermediate stations between the Nile and the Red Sea with provisions from the valley. Instead, the camel was meant to help a *plurality* of caravans, *all* of which travelled from Berenice.

The wording of *P.Lond.* 2.328, l. 11 and the date of the requisition (ll. 11–12) suggest three inferences. First, the transport to which the camel was supposed to contribute was always in only one direction—from the Red Sea to the Nile. Second, the caravans the camel joined travelled from Berenice, the Egyptian port that hosted the very large pepper carriers.[58] Third, the requisition itself occurred in the month of Tybi (between 27 December and 25 January), about the same time pepper carriers departed from South India. No other fleet was expected at Berenice in springtime. No other fleet could have commanded requisitions from so far away. In all likelihood, the order was scheduled to ensure that the

[53] For the camel declarations on papyrus, see Kruse (2002: 1.181–212); *P.Berl.Cohen* 10; 11; *P. Louvre* 2.108; *P.Gen.*4.161; Malouta (2014).

[54] Archaeological evidence suggests this site declined during the second century AD: Peacock and Blue (2011: 67–94); Cobb (2015: 403–7); Tomber (2017: 538); Nappo (2018: 189).

[55] Birley (2001: 123–6); De Romanis (2007: 203); McLynn (2009: 154).

[56] The next day, 30 January AD 163, in the same village, a Satabus, son of Satabus, son of Harpagathes (seemingly a brother of the Harpagathes of *P.Lond.* 2.328) declares four camels, one of which was also sent on hire for the service of transporting a porphyry column: *BGU* 3.762. For a socio-economic appreciation of the camel trade and ownership in Soknopaiu Nesos, see Jördens (1995: 76–9).

[57] Bülow-Jacobsen (2013: minute 52 ff). Contra Lewis (2000: 431). Cf. also Adams (2007: 151; 215; 234); Jördens (2009: 220, n. 210).

[58] See pp. 46–54.

camels reached Berenice (more than 900 kilometres away from Soknopaiu Nesos) just before the arrival of the pepper carriers[59]—that is, when they were most needed.

The thousands of tons of South Indian commodities offloaded each spring in Berenice had to be sold within 'the established time for the reimbursement of the maritime loans for Muziris'. Since their transfer to the Nile could not be spread out over the entire year, it must have required several thousand camels. For instance, the transfer of a 600-plus ton cargo in just one trip would require at least three thousand camels.[60] Therefore, from around February to April, the Coptos–Berenice road would have been traversed by caravans that were at least as large as those that operated between Leuke Kome and Petra in the early Augustan age.[61] During the other months of the year there was no need for such a large number of animals. Since the cargoes heading to Berenice and South India were considerably lighter in volume, even at the time of the departure (July), the constraint was not that critical.[62]

How many of these transfers were necessary at the time of the Muziris papyrus? The plural *πορ<ε>ιῶν* at P.Lond. 2.328, l. 11 makes clear that in AD 162/3 there were more than one. On the other hand, Early Modern data on South India's black pepper productivity limit the number of pepper carriers plying between Berenice and South India to a maximum of eight or nine.[63] In all likelihood, at the time of the Muziris papyrus, their real number was closer to two than to nine. Thus, it is unlikely that, upon his return, the merchant would choose a trustworthy cameleer among dozens of candidates. Not many options were available. Two herds of camels make sense only if four or more pepper carriers were operating. With fewer than four South Indian cargoes to tranship, it would have been more economical to have just one herd move back and forth for two or three months.

We do not know how often camels were requisitioned throughout Egypt 'for the imperial services of the caravans from Berenice'. Nor do we know how many were ordered each time, although a requisition as far away as Soknopaiu Nesos suggests the occasional need for a considerable number. We do know, however, that the transfer of South Indian commodities from Berenice to Coptos by caravan was considered an imperial service. We also

[59] For an approximation of the distance, see the computation of the distance and estimate of the travel time between Herakleopolis Magna and Berenice, cf. http://orbis.stanford.edu.

[60] Assuming 600 Roman pounds as the maximum weight carried by each camel: *Edictum de pretiis* 17.4.

[61] Camel-traders travel back and forth between Petra and Leuke Kome 'in such numbers of men and camels that they differ in no respect from an army': Strab. 16.4.23. A text from Krokodilo (*O.Krok.* 1.4), along the Myos Hormos–Coptos road, contrasts a *πορία* and a *μεικρὰ πορία*.

[62] The ships bound for Limyrike sailed light in weight on their outward journey: see pp. 137–8.

[63] See pp. 98–101; 252–6.

know that the prefect of Egypt had to ensure its proper functioning with camel requisitions, if necessary. Incidentally, it may be noted that while the camels sent for 'the service of transporting the porphyry column' were on hire (ἐπὶ μισθοφορᾷ), the camel sent 'for the imperial services of the caravans from Berenice' was not. Just as the maintenance of Trajan's Canal was ensured by the requirement that Egyptian villages produce forced labour,[64] the effectiveness of the land transport across the Eastern Desert was guaranteed, if necessary, with camel requisitions by the prefect of Egypt.

It is legitimate to have varying opinions—or none at all—about the exact reading at recto col. ii, l. 2. But even if the terms of agreements for desert transports were vague (such as 'I will hand the cargo over to an adequate cameleer'), we should not doubt the state's supervision, if not control, of this vital stage of the South India trade. The large caravans from Berenice could hardly have been arranged without a system that guaranteed both the merchant and the cameleer. Asking a cameleer to wait for an only roughly predictable return would have been extremely costly for a merchant on his own, and landing in Egypt with no prearranged transport to Coptos would have been financial suicide. The state, which secured the imperial service of synchronized caravans from Berenice, and the lender, who covered the transport expenses of the merchant, were critical for the successful functioning of the system.

8.4. THE COPTOS SHIPS

After being transported across the desert in a single journey, the Indian commodities brought back by the borrower of the Muziris papyrus loan contract were loaded onto a single ship for the downriver voyage to Alexandria. Unless the loan contract on the recto of the Muziris papyrus relates only to a portion of the *Hermapollon* cargo, we have to infer that the carrying capacity of the Nile ship equalled that of the very large pepper carriers sailing between Berenice and Muziris. Yet the inference finds no corroboration in the contemporaneous papyrological evidence. Among those whose size is known, only very few Nile ships (and none from the second century AD) come close to a carrying capacity of *c.*650 tons.[65] But rather than conclude that the recto text does not concern the entire cargo of the *Hermapollon*, it seems preferable to suggest that the available evidence, which is basically restricted to grain carriers from some nomes, fails to record the entire range of Nile-sailing vessels, and certainly not the specific type that sailed between Coptos and

[64] Cf. p. 36, n. 13.

[65] Thompson (1983: 72); Poll (1996); Arnaud (2015: 105-108); Adams (2017: 195–7).

Alexandria. As further analysis of the verso text will confirm, the idea that the pepper cargoes reached Alexandria scattered in multiple independent lots is best rejected. In fact, one may argue that the ships moving the Indian Ocean trade cargoes between Coptos and Alexandria in the mid-second century AD had to be significantly larger than contemporaneous grain transporters.

Although unattested in Roman times, grain ships of very large tonnages (up to 18,000 artabas = *c.*700 cubic metres = *c.*540 tons) are recorded in Ptolemaic Egypt.[66] However, the striking contrast between the huge carrying capacities of the largest Ptolemaic *kerkouroi* and the small volumes they loaded at each port (a few hundred artabas) suggests slow downriver journeys, and long final stoppages to unload the cargo. Apparently, speed was not a priority then.[67] Once it became vital for Rome's supply, Egyptian grain needed to move more expeditiously. Large carriers of 10,000 artabas or more that made dozens of stops on their way to Alexandria were replaced by a fleet of smaller ships with capacities of 5,000 artabas or less that made few or no stops. The new system certainly required more ships and crews, but it offered speedier and more flexible service: handling more loading points simultaneously, reducing loading and unloading times, and shortening voyage times up and down the Nile.

Transporting Indian commodities from Coptos to Alexandria required a different strategy. The huge caravans from Berenice discharged enormous quantities of goods into Coptos' only port all at once. Except for what was sold in Coptos, these cargoes were forwarded on to Alexandria with no intermediate stops. The relatively long distance between Alexandria and Coptos (*c.*870 km) and the timetable for the South India trade (the goods were in Coptos no earlier than March and the loans had to be repaid by June) limited the number of trips up and down the Nile. In these circumstances, it would have been cost-effective to use vessels that were even larger than the largest *kerkouroi* of the Ptolemaic age.

In the mid-second century AD, when Myos Hormos was declining or had declined, such ships may have been used only for the purpose of conveying South Indian cargoes to Alexandria, and returning to Coptos with merchants and commodities headed to South India.[68] Consequently, we should not infer from the promise 'I will load [sc. the cargo] at the required time in a safe river ship' that there were dozens of adequate ships available. Just as there may have been only one or two herds of several thousand camels carrying the

[66] *P.Tebt.* 3.2 856. [67] *P.Tebt.* 3.2 856, l. 112.

[68] Assuming the *via nova Hadriana* from Berenice to Antinoupolis, inaugurated 25 February AD 137 (*I.Pan.* 80; Sidebotham and Zitterkopf (1997; 1998)), was intended to serve the transhipment of Indian commodities from Berenice to the Nile, the large Coptos ships would have been replaced with ships from the Heptanomia. If this was the *via nova Hadriana*'s rationale, the excessive extension of the land transport (more than 600 km, compared to *c.*380 km) explains why Coptos remained the terminal point for the large South Indian cargoes coming from Berenice.

South Indian cargoes from Berenice to Coptos, so too there might have been just one or two very large riverine ships for the South Indian cargoes going to Alexandria. This may be why the borrower promises to load the ship at the *required* time (τῶι δέ]οντι καιρῶι):[69] he may have had to wait in Coptos until the ship came back from Alexandria, to load up his cargo. But once the ship was available, he could no longer wait.

Ships of this size could not sail just anywhere in the delta. In the Muziris papyrus loan contract the borrower commits himself to 'convey [sc. the cargo] downstream up to the customs warehouse of the quarter-tax in Alexandria', but the expression 'in Alexandria' is approximative, topographically speaking. In all likelihood, 'the customs warehouse of the quarter-tax' was in Iuliopolis, from where, in Pliny's age, the South India traders departed.[70] Pliny's Iuliopolis is the same as the Nicopolis mentioned by Strabo and Flavius Josephus.[71] Strabo remarks on Nicopolis' large settlement on the sea—he refers to its amphitheatre and *stadion*, its quinquennial games, and its recent building activity—but fails to mention a fluvial port or a customs warehouse.[72] The only customshouse he mentions is at Schedia.[73] By the time of Pliny's informants, however, Iuliopolis was the port for the river ships sailing to Coptos, and Josephus reports that Titus' army was loaded onto long ships in Nicopolis and sailed from there up to Thmuis.[74] One is tempted to infer that the Iuliopolis port and customs warehouse of the quarter-tax emerged in the period between Strabo and Pliny's informants, precisely to accommodate the cargoes of the growing South India trade.

While the grain ships and the ships that supplied Alexandria reached the Lake Mareotis harbour via the Schedia canal,[75] the Coptos ships carrying South Indian commodities went to Iuliopolis through another waterway. The use of a separate route for the commodities that were subject to the *maris Rubri vectigal* (as opposed to the supplies for Alexandria) is reflected by the designation of the supervisor of Alexandria's customs areas as 'assigned to the office of superintendent over Schedia and Iuliopolis'(ἀσχολούμενος ἐπιστατείαν Σχεδίας καὶ Ἰουλιοπόλεως).[76] Past Schedia, the Coptos ships kept travelling downriver on the Canopic branch and entered the Canopic canal, on which Iuliopolis/Nicopolis was situated.[77] Although the Canopic canal continued on to the Canopic gate of Alexandria, the port of Iuliopolis/Nicopolis was situated 2 miles (Pliny) or 20 stades (Josephus) away from the city.[78] Most

69 Recto col. ii, ll. 6–7. 70 Plin., *NH* 6.102.

71 On Nicopolis/Iuliopolis, cf. Hanson (1980). 72 Strab. 17.1.10.

73 Strab. 17.1.16. 74 Joseph., *BJ* 4.659. 75 Strab. 17.1.7.

76 *P.Diog.* 13, ll. 3–4; 14, ll. 5–6 (AD 141/142). Cf. *SB* 6.9210, ll. 2–4: δημοσιώναις | καὶ ἐπιτηρηταῖς Σχεδίας | [καὶ Ἰ]ουλοπόλεως (c.AD 151/155: Beutler (2007: 76)). See Jördens (2009: 371–2).

77 Strab. 17.1.16.

78 On the discrepancy between the distances given by Strabo (30 stades), Pliny (2 miles) and Josephus (20 stades), cf. Bingen (1944: 278, n. 3); Hanson (1980: 249, n. 2). The difference

probably, it could not be located closer, because the Coptos ships were unable to manoeuvre further.

8.5. LATE MEDIEVAL *COMPARANDA*

The mid-second-century AD system for transferring Indian commodities from the Red Sea to the Mediterranean may be better appreciated when compared to the description by the Venetian Emmanuel Piloti of the fifteenth-century spice cargo transfers from al-Ṭūr to Cairo:

> But when their adventure allows them to complete their (sea) voyage, and they reach al-Ṭūr (this is the name of the Saint Katherine of Mount Sinai harbours), and when they arrive at the said harbours, immediately messengers are sent to Cairo to announce that the said spice ships from Mecca arrived at the said port. Instantly officers and evaluators are informed, and they go to the said ships, because they are not allowed to unload (and they would not dare to), until the abovementioned officers arrive. And immediately they unload and weigh the said quantity of spices. And once they are unloaded, the said officers return to Cairo. And at the news of the arrival of the said spice ships, everybody from the Arab country and equally from Cairo moves with great numbers of camels, and they go to the said port; and there they make agreements with the said spice merchants, and they load two sacks for each camel, and they transport them by land for seven or eight days, until they arrive to the Nile River, where they find a huge quantity of boats waiting for the said spices; and there they agree at the usual price and as they can. And they load the said spices and sail on the river and they arrive at Cairo and pass to Babylon, where there is the customhouse (*doana*), that is the spice tax (*gabella des epices*), and the warehouse where the spices are unloaded and stored. The next day, each merchant is compelled to pay the tax on his spices. The rate is 10 per cent—which is more than fifteen (because of both?) the unfair estimate, and the weight that they make without reason.[79]

The comparison reveals some similarities, but many more differences:

a. Piloti refers to a fleet of very small sea-going ships (the overall carrying capacity may not have been larger than the second-century pepper carrier) that sailed from Jeddah to al-Ṭūr. The *Hermapollon* is a very large vessel that stopped at a southern Red Sea port, most likely Berenice.
b. Both in the Roman and the Mamluk ages the cargoes were weighed as soon as they were unloaded. However, in Mamluk Egypt the customs

between the three authors would be less striking if Pliny's text was affected by a slight corruption (MMM>MM). But the shorter distances given by Pliny and Josephus refer to the port of Iuliopolis/Nicopolis, which may have been built as close as possible to the city of Alexandria.

[79] Piloti, 46–7.

officers and evaluators did not reside at al-Ṭūr. They had to be summoned from Cairo, and they returned to Cairo once their job was done. At the time of the Muziris papyrus, the customs officers resided permanently at the Red Sea ports, controlling the coming and going of ships and ensuring the prompt unloading of the cargoes.[80]

c. In Piloti's account, many cameleers 'from the Arab country and equally from Cairo' went to al-Ṭūr upon learning about the arrival of ships at the port. In the Muziris papyrus, the transfer of the *Hermapollon*'s entire cargo assessed in the verso was taken care of by a single cameleer, who most probably waited in the valley—where water and fodder were more easily available—for the arrival of the pepper carriers. The time required to unload the cargo from the ship would have given him enough time to convey the camels to Berenice.

d. When they arrived at al-Ṭūr, the Mamluk merchants had no pre-agreement for the transport to the Nile. The cameleers arrived unsolicited and made agreements—in all likelihood, one by one—with the spice merchants. At the time of the Muziris papyrus, the transfer of South Indian cargoes from the Red Sea to the Nile was most probably arranged at the beginning of the enterprise, and entrusted to a single cameleer who had the resources to transfer the cargo of a large pepper carrier. Moreover, the imperial administration ensured that a sufficient number of camels were available for what was considered an 'imperial service'.

e. When the Mamluk cargoes reached the Nile, presumably somewhere in the Eastern delta, the merchants found 'a huge quantity of boats waiting for the said spices'. Again, the Nile navigation was not pre-arranged, and the cargoes of the many merchants were loaded onto many ships. Upon bringing his cargo to Coptos and storing it in the local customs warehouses, the merchant of the Muziris papyrus waited for a free 'safe ship'. However, the ship had to be large enough to carry all his cargo in one voyage. While waiting, he could start to sell some of his cargo to Upper Egyptian customers.

f. The Mamluk spice cargoes were sent to Babylon, where they were stored at the customshouse. The Roman cargoes were stored first in the customs warehouses of Coptos and then in the quarter-tax warehouses of Alexandria.

g. The Mamluk merchants paid their customs duties the day after their cargo was stored at the customs warehouse. The Roman merchants paid their customs duties (and the loan financing their travel expenses in Egypt) as they sold their cargo.

[80] See pp. 306–7.

h. Piloti claims that the nominal rate of the Mamluk customs duties was 10 per cent. We will argue that at the time of the Muziris papyrus, Indian commodities passing from the Red Sea to the Mediterranean were subject to double customs duties, whose nominal rate was 25 per cent. The first dues applied to 100 per cent of the cargo, the second only to 75 per cent of it.

i. In Mamluk Egypt, the dues could only be paid in money, and were calculated in a way that was not favourable to the merchants. Piloti's complaints about the unfair estimates and the unreasonable weights that caused the tax rate to rise, in real terms, from 10 to 15 per cent may refer to fiscal values higher than the market price, and to lower weight standards. We will show that, at the time of the Muziris papyrus, customs duties on Indian commodities could be paid either in kind or in money, in theory. However, a fiscal policy characterized by low fiscal values and the practice of weight-standard manipulation in favour of the taxpayer encouraged payment in money, as it was more convenient for the taxpayer.

j. We do not know whether the Mamluk traders took out loans in order to carry out their business. The merchant of the Muziris papyrus did, and during his voyage from the Red Sea to Alexandria, he was helped and monitored by his lender and his lender's agents.

Part III

The Assessment of a Cargo from Muziris (*P. Vindob.* G 40822 Verso)

9

Three Minor Cargoes

Col. iii is the only column of the verso text that has come down to us almost in its entirety. As we will see, it is the last part of a section of the text that began at the bottom of the lost col. i and continued through the mostly lost col. ii. The last three lines of col. iii (ll. 27–9) reveal the aim of the section: to evaluate the three-quarter portions of the items imported by a ship named the *Hermapollon*.

The preceding lines of col. iii (ll. 1–26) record the evaluation process of the portions of three items in that cargo: Gangetic nard, entire tusks of sound ivory, and *schidai* (the trimmings of ivory tusks). The manner in which these commodities are evaluated is not the same. While the value of the Gangetic nard cargo is calculated simply by multiplying the price per container by the number of containers, the assessment of the two types of ivory—the tusks of sound ivory and the *schidai*—is more complex. Understanding the rationale for this convoluted procedure will reveal the purpose of the entire text.

9.1. THREE-QUARTERS OF AN INDIAMAN'S CARGO

Our analysis of the Muziris papyrus verso text begins with col. iii, ll. 27–9:

> 27 ἐπὶ τὸ αὐτὸ τιμῆς μερῶν γ̄ τῶν ἐκπεπλευκότων
> 28 ἐν τῷ̣ ⟦εμ⟧ Ἑρμαπόλλωνι πλοίῳ̣ φορτίων ἀργυ-
> 29 ρίου (τάλαντα) Ἀρνα (δραχμαὶ) Ἑωνβ

'Grand total of the value of the 3 (*sc.* out of four) parts of the cargo shipped out on the vessel *Hermapollon*: 1,151 talents of money 5,852 drachmas'.

The above transcription incorporates three improvements to the editors' reading. Two concern the amount of money recorded at l. 29, correctly read by Morelli as 1,151 talents and 5,852 drachmas.[1] The third correction, by

[1] Morelli (2011: 214). The editors' reading had been 1,154 talents of money and 2,852 drachmas.

The Indo-Roman Pepper Trade and the Muziris Papyrus. Federico De Romanis, Oxford University Press (2020).
© Federico De Romanis. DOI: 10.1093/oso/9780198842347.001.0001

Rathbone (at l. 27 μερῶν γ̄ instead of μερῶν (ϛ̄) read by the editors), profoundly affects the meaning of the sentence (ll. 27–8) that states what the huge sum at l. 29 represents.

According to the editors, that sum would be the 'total value of the six parts of the cargo exported on the ship of (a merchant named) Hermapollon'.[2] Several misinterpretations shaped their understanding of this crucial sentence. One, quickly detected by Thür, was that the dative Ἑρμαπόλλωνι (l. 28) is better explained as the name of the ship, rather than that of the ship owner with an incorrect case ending.[3] Other more consequential inaccuracies took longer to identify.[4] By claiming that the sum at l. 29 represented the entire value of six commodities exported on the ship, the editors mistook a very regular 3 (γ̄) at l. 27 for a badly made 6 (ϛ̄), and twisted the meaning of μερῶν (parts) at l. 27 and φορτίων (cargoes) at l. 28.

By establishing the correct reading as 3 (γ̄), Rathbone demonstrated that the words μερῶν γ̄ τῶν ἐκπεπλευκότων | ἐν τῷ ⟦εμ⟧ Ἑρμαπόλλωνι πλοίῳ φορτίων (ll. 27–8) instead specified the portion (three-quarters) of the cargoes that had been assessed.[5] Rathbone's translation is: 'Makes the price of the 3 parts of the cargoes shipped out on the ship *Hermapollon*.' In addition, Rathbone pointed out that the number of containers and the weights of the three items evaluated in the preceding lines (1–26) are all divisible by three: 60 containers of Gangetic nard (col. iii, l. 1), 78 talents and 54.75 minas of 'sound' ivory (col. iii, l. 4), and 13 talents and 9.75 minas of *schidai* (col. iii, l. 16). He therefore suggested that they represent three-quarters of what had been 80 containers of Gangetic nard, 105 talents and 13 minas of 'sound' ivory, and 17 talents and 33 minas of *schidai*.[6] As we will see in the next chapter, his suggestion has been confirmed by Morelli's readings and interpretation of col. ii, ll. 4–13.

That said, one more point still needs to be clarified regarding verso col. iii, ll. 27–9. At ll. 27–8, the commodities are said to have 'sailed out (ἐκπεπλευκότων) on the ship *Hermapollon*'. On the question of where the *Hermapollon* sailed from, opinions have differed. According to the editors, the perfect participle ἐκπεπλευκότων would point to a voyage from Alexandria to some other Mediterranean destination, probably Rome.[7] In Thür's interpretation, it would refer to the voyage from South India to Egypt.[8] According to Morelli, who argued

[2] Harrauer and Sijpesteijn (1985: 134): 'Insgesamt von dem 6 (Fracht)teilen, die im Schiff des Hermapollon exportiert worden sind'.

[3] Thür (1987: 233, 239 n. 45).

[4] They were not recognized by Thür (1987); Casson (1990); or De Romanis (1998).

[5] Rathbone (2000: 45).

[6] Rathbone (2000: 45).

[7] Harrauer and Sijpesteijn (1985: 149–50).

[8] Thür (1987: 239, n. 45): 'Aus dem Perfekt ἐκπεπλευκότων (Z. 27) wird klar, daβ die Aufstellung den Export aus Indien, also den Import in das Imperium Romanum betrifft' (Thür's emphasis).

that the verb ἐκπλέω could not be used for a voyage from India to Egypt,[9] it would describe a downriver shipment along the Nile from Coptos to Alexandria.[10]

As Morelli points out, the choice between ἐκπλέω and εἰσπλέω is subjective, the first term emphasizing the place of departure, the second focusing on the destination of the voyage. Notwithstanding, we may wonder whether in a circumscribed social context like the community of Indian Ocean seafarers from Egypt, such subjectivity implied a shared linguistic convention. It is worthwhile to explore whether, within that circle, sea voyages from Egypt to India and from India to Egypt were consistently referenced using one of the two verbs. But first the implications of the perfect tense of the participle ἐκπεπλευκότων must be considered. The basic meaning of ἐκπλέω is 'to sail out' or 'to sail away'.[11] The verb can definitely mean 'to leave by ship', but not in the perfect tense, where it denotes a completed voyage and not just a completed departure (so to speak).[12] If the text was referring to commodities that had just left their port of departure, but had not yet arrived at their destination, it would have used the aorist tense, ἐκπλευσάντων.[13] As pointed out by Thür, the perfect ἐκπεπλευκότων shows instead that the voyage had concluded. Therefore, the commodities have 'arrived by ship' rather than 'left by ship'.

Moreover, while a καταπεπλευκότων would have been more appropriate for a downriver voyage,[14] the assumption that ἐκπεπλευκότων cannot be used for voyages from India to Egypt is unwarranted.[15] Literary and papyrological evidence directly related to Indian Ocean traders and their voyages shows that the reciprocal pair εἰσπλέω/ἐκπλέω (sail in/sail out) refers to voyages *from* and *to* Egypt, respectively. Examples of the use of εἰσπλέω for voyages from Egypt to other countries of the Red Sea/Indian Ocean area include the following:

a. *O.Berenike* 2.198, l. 11–2: ἤκουσα γὰρ ὅτ{ε}ι καὶ σὺ εἰσπλ̣(ε)ῖ̣ς̣. The recipient is in Berenice, and he is about to depart.

b. *PME* 1: *μετὰ δὲ αὐτὸν* [*sc. Μυὸς ὅρμον*] *εἰσπλεόντων ἀπὸ χιλίων ὀκτακοσίων σταδίων ἐν δεξιᾷ ἡ Βερνίκη*. Sailing from Myos Hormos to Berenice is expressed by the verb εἰσπλεῖν.

c. *PME* 20: διὸ καὶ εἰσπλεόντων <τὸν> μέσον πλοῦν κατέχομεν [εἰς τὴν Ἀραβικὴν χώραν] <καὶ> μᾶλλον παροξύνομεν ἄχρι τῆς Κατακεκαυμένης νήσου. Again, sailing southwards on the Red Sea is expressed by the verb εἰσπλεῖν.

[9] Morelli (2011: 230). [10] Morelli (2011: 233). [11] *LSJ* s.v.

[12] E.g. Plut., *Cim.* 14: καταφρονοῦντες τοῦ Κίμωνος μετ' ὀλίγων παντάπασι τριήρων Ἀθήνηθεν ἐκπεπλευκότος, 'despising Cimon, who had arrived from Athens with absolutely few triremes'.

[13] E.g. Diod. Sic. 20.32.4: τῶν Καρχηδονίων τριάκοντα ναυσὶν ἐκπλευσάντων ἐπ' αὐτοὺς τὸ μὲν πρῶτον ἐπεβάλοντο ναυμαχεῖν κτλ, 'when the Carthaginians sailed out against them with thirty ships, they first tried to fight at sea'.

[14] Cf. κατοίσω, at recto col. ii, l. 6. [15] Morelli (2011: 230).

d. *I.Portes* 67, l. 18–19: (γ)υναικῶν εἰσπλεουσῶν δρα|χμὰς εἴκοσι. The 'women who navigate' are charged 20 drachmas for the ἀποστόλιον; this must refer to women who board ships at Red Sea ports bound for overseas destinations.[16]

e. Ptol., *Geogr.* 1.17.4: μόνον γὰρ μεσημβρινώτερον ὁμολογεῖται τῶν στομάτων εἶναι τοῦ ποταμοῦ παρά τε τῶν ἐντεῦθεν εἰσπλευσάντων καὶ χρόνον πλεῖστον ἐπελθόντων τοὺς τόπους καὶ παρὰ τῶν ἐκεῖθεν ἀφικομένων πρὸς ἡμᾶς, καλούμενον ὑπὸ τῶν ἐγχωρίων Τίμουλα. Ptolemy's criticism of Marinus of Tyre's location of Semylla is also based on the opinion of those who sailed to India from Egypt (τῶν ἐντεῦθεν εἰσπλευσάντων).

f. Procop., *Pers.* 1.19.3–5: καὶ αὐτὸν ἐνθένδε ἐσπλέοντι ἐν δεξιᾷ μὲν ὄρη τὰ Αἰγυπτίων πρὸς νότον ἄνεμον τετραμμένα ἐστὶν . . . καὶ γῆν μὲν τὴν ἐν δεξιᾷ οἱ ταύτῃ ἐσπλέοντες οὐκέτι ὁρῶσιν. Procopius indicates a southward voyage in the Gulf of ʿAqaba and in the Red Sea with ἐσπλεῖν.

Conversely, examples of the use of ἐκπλέω for voyages from overseas to Egypt may also be cited:

a. *O.Berenike* 2.129, ll. 7–9: μό|νον ἐρτο (l. ἐρωτῶ) σε καὶ παρακαλῶ καὶ ἐξορκίζῳ σε τού[τ]ου ουσε..ην.|κες καὶ τὴν μνήαν (l. μνείαν) σου το(ῦ) γεν(ν)ήσαντος [ἐ]ὰν ὑγια[ίνῃς] | ἐκπλε(ῦ)σ(α)ι. From Berenice (l. 2), a mother begs her son, who is somewhere overseas (ll. 1–2)—possibly in Arabia (l. 6)—to sail back to Egypt.

b. *PME* 30: εἰσὶν δὲ ἐπίξενοι καὶ ἐπίμικτοι Ἀράβων τε καὶ Ἰνδῶν καὶ τινα μὲν Ἑλλήνων τῶν πρὸς ἐργασίαν ἐκπλεόντων. Greeks who 'sail back' for trade contribute to the particular ethnic mix on Socotra Island. Admittedly, this occurrence is ambiguous per se, but it is clarified by the next example.

c. *PME* 31: συνεχρήσαντο δὲ αὐτῇ καὶ ἀπὸ Μούζα τινὲς καὶ τῶν ἐκπλεόντων ἀπὸ Λιμυρικῆς καὶ Βαρυγάζων ὅσοι κατὰ τύχην εἰς αὐτὴν ἐπιβάλλοντες. Apart from traders from Muza, Socotra is approached by those who, bound for Egypt from Limyrike and Barygaza, happen to stop there.

The use of the verbs εἰσπλέω and ἐκπλέω for Indian Ocean voyages has a simple psychological explanation. Seafarers from Egypt would have viewed commercial voyages in the Red Sea/Indian Ocean area as round trips that began and ended in Egypt's Red Sea ports. Since the destination of an Indian Ocean voyage mattered more than the departure point, the outward journey was perceived as an εἰσπλεῖν ('sailing into'), and the return as an ἐκπλεῖν ('sailing from').

[16] Despite Boyaval (2004: 263–5).

Actually, this use of *εἰσπλέω/ἐκπλέω* is not exclusive to Red Sea/Indian Ocean merchants. It can be observed in the Mediterranean Sea as well, where it indicates the outward and return voyages of a round trip. In contrast with the occurrences of *ἐκπλέω* cited by Morelli as indicating departures from Egypt (referring to voyages that are perceived as one-way without an immediate return), fourth-century BC Athenian traders would also use *ἐκπλέω* for voyages *towards* Athens, if it referred to part of a round trip that started from and ended in Athens. Unsurprisingly, *ἐκπλέω* indicates part of the return journey to Athens in the round-trip maritime loan contract in *Against Lacritus*.[17] Incidentally, the perception, in the eyes of an Egyptian seafarer, that a voyage on the Indian Ocean is more of a voyage toward a specific destination than a departure from Egypt explains why at *PME* 26 the manuscript's reading *εἰς τοὺς ἔσω τόπους* (towards the inside places), alluding to navigations towards India, must be retained (as per Müller, Wistrand, Casson, and Belfiore), and not corrected (as per Fabricius and Frisk) to *εἰς τοὺς ἔξω τόπους* (toward the outside places).[18]

In conclusion, the sum recorded at col. iii, l. 29 represents the value of three-quarters of the cargo of a ship named the *Hermapollon*. The *Hermapollon* had returned from an Indian port—most probably Muziris, as we will see. The assessed value of the three-quarter portions of the imported commodities was 1,151 talents and 5,852 drachmas.

9.2. GANGETIC NARD

The first commodity whose value is calculated in col. iii, ll. 1–3 is sixty containers of Gangetic nard. It is extremely important that it is not just simple nard, but Gangetic nard, the qualification being diagnostic on several counts.

The word *nardos* entered the Greek lexicon before Theophrastus, whose sources classified it as a plant from Media or from India.[19] Since William

[17] [Dem.] 35.10: *ἐὰν δὲ μετ' Ἀρκτοῦρον ἐκπλεύσωσιν ἐκ τοῦ Πόντου ἐφ' Ἱερόν κτλ.*, 'if they should sail out from Pontus to Hieron after the rising of Arcturus'. Otherwise, *ἐκπλέω* refers to trips *from* Athens perceived as one-way voyages, cf. e.g. Thuc. 5.4.2.

[18] *PME* 26: *μηδὲ ἀπὸ Αἰγύπτου τολμώντων εἰς τοὺς ἔσω τόπους διαίρειν*. Cf. Wistrand (1946: 20–1), who points to the consistent wording of *PME* 25: *πρώτη καταγωγὴ τοῖς ἔσω διαίρουσιν*, 'first stopover for those who sail further inside'; and to the twice occurring expression (*PME* 6; 14) *ἀπὸ τῶν ἔσω τόπων τῆς Ἀριακῆς*, 'from the inside places of the Ariake'.

[19] Hippoc., *Nat. Mul.* 34; *Mul.* 45; Antiph., *CAF* ii, frg. 35 Kock; Theophr., *Hist. pl.* 9.7.2; 3; 4. Greek *νάρδος* is an indirect loanword from ancient Indian (pā. *narada*, skt. *nalada*): Mayrhofer (1996: 2.23). The Babylonian nard in Alexis *CAF* ii, frg. 308 Kock suggests that the word may have found its way into the Greek language in circumstances similar to *πέπερι* (see p. 48). Western pseudo-nards—Thracian, Gallic, Cretan, and possibly Syrian nard, if it has to be

Jones—indeed, since Jacopo de Orta—all nard has been identified with *nardostachys jaṭāmānsi,*[20] a plant that grows all along the Himalayan belt between 3,200 and 5,000 metres above sea level.[21] From its rhizomes, an essential oil is distilled that is credited with the same virtues and employed for the same purposes as malabathron oil:[22] as an ingredient for unguents[23] and medical remedies,[24] and as a wine-flavouring additive.[25] The first documented notice of Gangetic nard may belong to the Augustan poet Grattius.[26] It is at any rate mentioned by both Servilius Damocrates and Dioscorides.[27] Dioscorides lists Gangetic nard as a subspecies of Indian nard,[28] whereas Pliny distinguishes between simple and Gangetic nard.[29]

Both Dioscorides and Pliny rate Gangetic nard as being of inferior quality, albeit for spurious reasons. Dioscorides claims that it is weaker because it would grow in humid places; Pliny assumes its low value based on the additional label *ozaenitis*. Making an inference from the adjective 'Gangetic', Dioscorides incorrectly asserts that the plant grew next to the river. Pliny construes the adjective *ozaenitis* as a reference to the stinking sea polyp (*ozaena*, ὄζαινα), but it is far more likely to derive from the Indian city of Ujjayinī (Ὀζήνη)—a hub for the nard (though not the Gangetic nard) trade.[30] The author of the *Periplus* includes simple nard in the list of commodities available at Barbarikon and Barygaza,[31] and explains how four types of nard (three of them—Kattyburine, Patropapige, and Kabalite nard—brought 'through Proklais', another 'through the adjacent Skythia') are conveyed to Ujjayinī and then to Barygaza.[32]

The commercial circuits of Gangetic nard were different from those of simple nard, and this is why the specification 'Gangetic' is extremely important in our text. The *Periplus* mentions Gangetic nard among the commodities exported from the emporia of Limyrike and, unsurprisingly, the Ganges

distinguished from the Syrian/Indian nard in Dsc. 1.7.2—are attested in Theophr., *Hist. pl.* 9.7.4; Plin., *NH* 12.45–6.

[20] Orta, 2.291–7; Jones (1790; 1795); Steier (1935). However, neither Dioscorides' (Dsc. 1.7) nor Pliny's (Plin., *NH* 12.42–3) description of the nard seems to tally with the *Nardostachys jaṭāmānsī* that is still collected in Nepal: Steier (1935: 1706).

[21] Lama, Ghimire, and Aumeeruddy-Thomas (2001); Olsen (2005); Fortier (2009: 20; 105).

[22] Although belonging to different species, nard and malabathron have a similar smell and similar medicinal properties: e.g. Dsc. 1.12; Gal., *simpl. med. temp. fac.* 12.66; 153.

[23] E.g. Antiph. *CAF* ii frg. 35 Kock; Polyb. 30.26.2; Hor., *Carm.* 2.11.16; 4.12.16–7; *Epod.* 5.59; 13.9; Tib. 2.2.7; 3.6.63; Ov., *Ars am.* 443; Marc. 14.3; Joh. 12.3; Sen., *Herc. f.* 469; Petron. 78; Plin., *NH* 12.42; 13.15; Mart. 3.65.8.

[24] It would be too long to list all the passages in Aurelius Celsus, Scribonius Largus, Soranus, Galenus, Oribasius, Aëtius, and Paulus.

[25] E.g. Plaut., *Mil.* 824, see also Steier (1935: 1705–14).

[26] Grat., *Cyn.* 314.

[27] Democrates apud Gal. 13.1057.

[28] Dsc. 1.7.2.

[29] Plin., *NH* 12.42, not counting, of course, the western nards: Plin., *NH* 12.45.

[30] *PME* 48. Cf. Warmington (1928: 196).

[31] *PME* 39; 49.

[32] *PME* 48.

emporion.[33] Since the Ganges emporion was inaccessible to merchants making the year-long round-trip journey between Egypt and India, and since Muziris was the only active Limyrike emporion in the mid-second century AD, the presence of Gangetic nard in the *Hermapollon*'s cargo confirms that Muziris was the Indian trade centre from which the vessel had returned.

The *Periplus*' catalogue of Limyrike's trade goods includes two more items that actually came from the Ganges emporion: silk and malabathron.[34] In all likelihood, silk was not part of the *Hermapollon*'s cargo. Whether the absence reflects the demise of this alternative silk route is unclear,[35] but it certainly does not signify the collapse of the trade networks linking the Ganges Valley and Limyrike. Col. iii, ll. 1–3 show that the *Hermapollon* had imported eighty containers of Gangetic nard, and we will see that the remnants of verso col. ii, ll. 17–19 strongly suggest that the second most important item on the *Hermapollon*, both in terms of weight and value, was malabathron. At the time of the *Periplus*, malabathron was Limyrike's second most important export—at least in terms of weight and volume, if not also of value.[36] In sum, while the absence of silk remains to be explained, the combined evidence of the *Periplus* and the Muziris papyrus demonstrates continuous and robust trade relationships between the Ganges Valley and South India from the mid-first to the mid-second century AD.

9.3. *SCHIDAI*

The two other commodities whose three-quarter portions are evaluated in verso col. iii are 'sound' ivory (ll. 4–15) and *schidai* (ll. 16–25). For convenience's sake, a proper discussion of the sound ivory entry is deferred until chapter ten, after the analysis of verso col. ii. For the time being, it is enough to note that it refers to ivory tusks of good quality. Here, we will focus instead on *schidai*.

The *schidai* are the last item evaluated, as well as the least valuable and probably the least heavy of all the *Hermapollon*'s cargoes. But what exactly is a *schida*? The term does not occur in the *Periplus* and, among papyrological documents, is mentioned only on the verso of the Muziris papyrus at col. iii, ll. 16 and 25. Inspired by an entry in Hesychius' lexicon,[37] the editors understood

[33] *PME* 56; 63. [34] *PME* 56.

[35] *PME* 64. The major silk trade centres in the Arabian Sea were Barbarikon and Barygaza: *PME* 39; 49.

[36] *PME* 56.

[37] Hesych., vol. III p. 399, Σ 3010 Hansen: entry <σχίδα>· *σχίδος σινδόνος, πῆγμα* (*schida*: division of a garment, fabric). Frisk and Chantraine suggest a correction of *πῆγμα* in *ῥῆγμα* 'breakage'.

schida as 'a detached piece of a larger whole σινδών, a bale of cloth',[38] pointing out that 'very excellent σινδόνες, called the Gangetic ones', are listed among the exports from the Ganges emporion in the *Periplus*.[39] The implicit suggestion was that excellent Gangetic lengths of fabric were exported from the Ganges emporion to Muziris and from there to Egypt, just like Gangetic nard, malabathron, and silk at the time of the *Periplus*. Moreover, Harrauer and Sijpesteijn considered the possibility that at verso col. ii, ll. 16 and 25, σχιδῶν could be a misspelling of σχιζῶν,[40] but they rejected the idea that it could have meant 'piece of wood'.[41] They also rejected a connection with Hesychius' entry σχίδια· ὠμόλινα, on the grounds that 'raw flax' (ὠμόλινα), a typical Egyptian product, is unlikely to have appeared among imports from India.[42]

This interpretation was challenged by Rathbone. Considering σχίδα as only a variant of σχίζα (piece of wood cut off, lath, splinter), he suggested that *schidai* were fragments of elephant tusks and thus distinct from the 'sound ivory' (ἐλέφας ὑγιής) mentioned at col. iii, l. 4, which were *entire* tusks (cf. ὀδόντων col. iii, l. 12).[43] Rathbone buttressed his interpretation by observing that 1) the μέν at col. iii, l. 4 and the δ[έ] at col. iii, l. 16[44] structured the phrase so as to contrast sound ivory and *schidai*; and 2) the value of the unspecified ivory (ἐλέφας), lost in the lacuna at col. iii, l. 26, must have merged the value of sound ivory with that of the *schidai*.[45] To me, Rathbone's argument seems decisive on this point. If *schidai* were not ivory, the μέν at col. iii, l. 4 would be a very strange *μέν solitarium*. Moreover, it would be difficult to explain (except as an error) why the clerk chose to record the value of an unspecified ivory a second time at l. 26, after having already calculated the value of sound ivory (ll. 4–15) and *schidai* (ll. 16–25).[46] Although it seemed reasonable at the time, the editors' interpretation does not fit the context as neatly as does Rathbone's.

That said, the nature of the contrast between the two ivory types remains to be properly understood. The difference in price between sound ivory (100 drachmas per mina) and *schidai* (70 drachmas per mina) makes it clear that *schidai* were less valuable. Rathbone posited that they were pieces of ivory tusk, more precisely 'accidental fragments rather than sawn pieces'.[47] By contrast, for reasons that will be discussed in the next section, Morelli argued

[38] Harrauer and Sijpesteijn (1985: 148). Followed by Thür (1987: 233): 'Ballen Stoff'; Casson (1990: 201): 'lengths of fabric'; De Romanis (1998: 14): 'tessuti'.

[39] *PME* 63.

[40] Gignac (1976: 75–6).

[41] Harrauer and Sijpesteijn (1985: 149). *LSJ* s.v. translates σχίζα as 'piece of wood cut off, lath, splinter'.

[42] Harrauer and Sijpesteijn (1985: 149).

[43] Rathbone (2000: 45).

[44] Rathbone (2000: 44; 45); see also Morelli (2011: 213, 44).

[45] Rathbone (2000: 45).

[46] Morelli (2011: 221–2) offers further support for the argument that *schidai* were a particular kind of ivory by observing that the entry σχιδῶν (col. ii, l. 16), unlike those of Gangetic nard and sound ivory (col. ii, ll. 1; 4), is not in *ekthesis*.

[47] Rathbone (2000: 45). Etymology in Frisk (1973^2: 838–9); Chantraine (1968–1980: 1081).

that they must have been entire tusks, only imperfect in some way—spoiled, cracked, or slightly broken.

It should be recognized that if the classification of the tusks as delineated in the Muziris papyrus was intended to distinguish entire tusks from fragments, then entries such as 'ivory tusks' (ἐλέφαντος ὀδόντων) or 'entire ivory tusks' (ἐλέφαντος ὀδόντων ὅλων) would have been more appropriate than 'sound ivory' (ἐλέφαντος ὑγιοῦς). The emphasis on soundness seems to point to qualities that characterize an easy-to-carve material. In this context, it may be worthwhile to recall that in a passage of the *Life of Apollonius*, Philostratus outlines a taxonomy of the Indian elephants in which each type—marsh, mountain, and plain elephant—is characterized by tusks of different quality: the tusks of the marsh elephants (dark, fibrous, with cavities and knots) are difficult to work; the tusks of the mountain elephants (smaller but very white) are not at all difficult to work; and the tusks of the plain elephant are the best—largest, whitest, easy to split, such that 'they become whatever the hand desires'.[48]

On the other hand, the fact that the entry 'sound ivory' implies a qualitative assessment is not enough reason to reject Rathbone's translation of *schidai* as 'fragments', which is firmly supported by the undeniable connection with the verb σχίζω (split, divide, cut out, tear) and by the parallelism with terms like σχίζα and σχίδαξ (piece of wood cut off). The fact that in the Muziris papyrus verso col. iii 'sound ivory' and *schidai* appear opposed to each other does not guarantee that any tusk deemed 'not sound' was by default a *schida*, or that a *schida*, as such, could not be defined as 'sound'. It may be observed that if the restoration ὀδ]ọῦσι suggested by Morelli at col. ii, l. 5 is correct, the distinction between sound ivory and *schidai* would have been defined differently there from how it appears at col. iii. At col. ii, the same entry ['Ελέφαντος ὑγιοῦς] (l. 5) may have been differentiated in terms of tusks (l. 5: ἐν μὲν ὀδ]ọῦσι) and *schidai* (l. 10: [ἐν δὲ σχίδαις?]).

Nor can the *schidai* of the Muziris papyrus be considered *débitage* from the shop floors of ivory carvers.[49] The difference between the price of tusks (100 drachmas per mina) and of *schidai* (70 drachmas per mina)

[48] Philostr., *VA* 2.13. Philostratus' classification of the elephants echoes the contrast, in the Sanskrit sources quoted below (p. 220), between 'river elephant' or 'humid place elephant' (*nadījāna*, *anūpacarāṇāṃ*) and 'mountain elephant' (*parvata-okasa* and *giricāriṇāṃ*). The 'soundness' of a tusk was evaluated in sixteenth-century trade as well: noteworthy is the 1530 *Informacão de Jordão de Freitas para el-rei*, in *DPMAC* 6.428: 'marfym... bom grande são e linpo'. The criteria of the evaluation implied by the 'Adulis standard' (*PME* 3; 17) are unknown. Morelli (2011: 213, 41) refers to *Merck's Warenlexikon*, Leipzig 1920[7], 107, where the value of a tusk is said to be diminished by its weakness, its curving, its fractures, and the extension of its cavity from the root.

[49] Called περιπρίσματα or παραπρίσματα in *IG* II/III^2 2 1408, ll. 13–4; 1409, ll. 6–7; 1412, ll. 32–3; 1414, ll. 17–18; *IDélos* 298 A, l. 181; 300 B, l. 30.

is too slight to reflect the gap in value between entire tusks and small scraps.[50] In order to justify his translation of the term *schidai*, Rathbone referred to a passage by Pliny the Elder, in which elephants are said to deliberately break their tusks in order to 'ransom themselves at the price of the desired booty'.[51] Ancient Tamil poetry does offer examples of tusk fragments lost in battle by war elephants,[52] but these literary elaborations could not account for the more than half a ton of ivory fragments exported from Muziris. Another explanation seems more likely. I propose identifying *schidai* as those fragments that are regularly trimmed from the tusks of captive elephants.[53] Elephant-tusk trimming is a standard practice in Kerala today, but it was also common in ancient India, as is shown in some Sanskrit classical texts: 'Leaving the double length of the circumference of the tusk at the root, he should cut [sc. the rest], every two years and a half in the case of those [*sc.* elephants] from river-banks, every five years in the case of those from mountainous regions.'[54] Or: 'Having left the double length of the circumference of the tooth at its root, cut the rest; more (often) in those elephants that live in humid places, a little less often in those that live in the mountains.'[55] If we turn to Greek authors, the sawing of Indian elephant tusks is also noted by Cosmas Indicopleustes, although limited to a few war elephants with unusually big tusks: 'The Indian elephants are not provided with large tusks, but should they have such, they saw them off, that their weight may not encumber them in war.'[56]

Thus, the roughly 538.5 kilograms of *schidai* shipped out by the *Hermapollon* could very well have been trimmings taken from captive elephants. As the tusks had to be trimmed leaving 'a length of double the circumference of the tusk at the root', a *schida* could not weigh much more than one-third of an entire tusk. More precisely, since captive elephant tusks had to be trimmed either every two and a half or every five years, the weight of a *schida* could have

[50] The 3 talents and 60 drachmae of ivory sold for 1,309 drachmae in *IG* I^3 449, 392–4 is taken to be waste by *Lapatin* (2001: 14).

[51] Plin., *NH* 8.8. A comparable tactic is ascribed to beavers: cf. Devecka (2013: 88–91). Other defensive strategies are mentioned by Philostr., *VA* 2.16 (= *BNJ* 275 F 47b). Pliny's passage belongs to a section (Plin., *NH* 8.1–8.) comprising several other *mirabilia* testifying to the quasi-human affective and cognitive capacities of the elephant—a rather popular topic in Western classical literatures: Wellmann (1905: 2252).

[52] *Akanāṉūṟu* 1.4; 24.11.

[53] In De Romanis (2014b), pictures show the method of trimming and reshaping the tusks of captive elephants.

[54] *Arthaśāstra* 2.32.22.

[55] Varāhamihira, *Bṛhat Saṃhitā*: 78, 20 ab = 93, 1 ab. Cf. Sukumar (2011: 66). The practice of leaving 'the double length of the circumference of the tooth at its roots' addresses the need to avoid cutting into the tusk's live pulp; another method is to replicate the distance between the beginning of the exposed tusk and the elephant's eye.

[56] Cosm. Indic. 11.23.

been anything between 1 and 7 kilograms.[57] An export of 538.5 kilograms must therefore have numbered between 75 and 540 pieces.[58]

In ancient India, captive male elephants with big tusks were the prerogative of the highest political authorities, and essential for military strength.[59] According to Megasthenes, only the king has the right to own horses and elephants,[60] and in the *Arthaśāstra*'s words, the 'king's victory is mainly a matter of elephants'.[61] In the protocol laid down by the *Tolkāppiyam*, the ownership of war elephants is a distinctive feature of the *aracar* (kings).[62] It is likely that this term, a Tamilization of the Sanskrit *rājan*,[63] is meant to be inclusive of both *vēntar*—'kings' of the highest rank—and *vēḷir*—secondary kings or dependent chieftains.[64] It is reasonable to assume, however, that the regional pre-eminence of the *mūvēntar*—the three major powers of the Cēralar, Pāṇṭiyar, and Cōḻar—was sustained by the ability to lay claim to a significant number of war elephants.[65] This must have been especially true of the Cēralar, who controlled both the emporion of Muziris and the inland forests rich in wild elephants.[66] The conspicuous presence of elephants in the

[57] The weights of the four fragments of tusk reported in *The Hindu* article of 9 June 2012, were 5.4, 5.6, 4.3, and 2.54 kg, respectively. The average weight is 4.46 kg. The lengths of the trimmings were 44, 43, 47, and 43, cm respectively—approximately double those indicated as the norm by Dr Cheeran after 18–20 months.

[58] At col. ii, l. 16 the editors read *σχιδῶν* ͵*νδ* ('of 54 *schidai*'), accepted by Thür (1989); Casson (1990); De Romanis (1998). The reading has been rightly rejected by Rathbone (2000: 44) and Morelli (2011: 213).

[59] Trautmann (2015). Small-tusk elephants are not supposed to be captured, cf. *Arthāśastra* 2.31.10.

[60] *BNJ* 715 F 19b = Strab. 15.1.41. Cf. Nearchus *BNJ* 133 F 11 = Arr., *Indic.* 17.1–2; F 22 = Strab. 15.1.43.

[61] *Arthaśāstra* 2.2.13: *hastipradhāno vijayo rājñaḥ.*

[62] *Tolkāppiyam* 3.9.72: 'weapon (*paṭai*), flag, umbrella, drum, horse of studied pace, elephant, car, garland, crown, and such others be-fitting the kings (*aracar*) of sceptre, well-versed in judgment'; transl. S. V. Subramanian. However, the term *paṭai* may here have the alternative meaning of 'army'. In the ancient Tamil poetry, captive elephants are almost by default war elephants: see Varadarajaiyer (1945: *passim*).

[63] Burrow and Emeneau (1961: 15, n. 167).

[64] Cf. Thirunavukarasu (1994: 33–5). In ancient Tamil poetry, many *vēḷir* are said to have (or to donate) captive elephants: Varadarajaiyer (1945: 4–6).

[65] See e.g. a few lines in praise of the Cēra king Celvakkaṭuṅkōv Āḻiyātaṉ, *Puṟanāṉūṟu* 387.5–13: 'You free the poets from poverty with the tribute that you receive from the inimical *maṉṉar* ('kings', but not of the highest rank)! The many male elephants perfect in action, who with their large rugged trunks and lifting tusks were stationed near the guarded forest of the *vēntu* (kingdom of a *vēntaṉ*, a 'king' of the highest rank), with their big necks with flower-like spots and fragrant cheeks smeared with dust, they moved, dispersed here and there and destroyed the ramparts of the enemy.' Since they were stationed 'near the guarded forest of the *vēntu*', the war elephants must belong to a *vēntaṉ* (the Cēra king), not to the *maṉṉar*, as the translation by Hart and Heifetz (1999: 227) posits. Moreover, it would be strange if such extensive praise addressed the enemy's war elephants. The interpretation accepted here is also in the Italian translation of Panattoni (2002: 331).

[66] Remarkable is how one of these kings is hailed in *Puṟanāṉūṟu* 5.1–3: 'Are you the king of the forests where elephants spread to graze like cows amidst buffalo-like rocks?'

Muziris hinterland is also reflected in the Peutinger Table caption near *Mons Lymodus*, a mountain range that could be the Western Ghats: *in his locis elephanti nascuntur*, 'in this place elephants are native'.[67] It is not a coincidence that Cēra coins—also found at the site of Pattanam—bear an elephant on their obverse.[68]

The export of 538.5 kilograms of *schidai* most likely would not have been possible without including the trimmings from the large elephant troupe belonging to the Cēra king. If the quantity exported by the *Hermapollon* did not represent an exceptional peak but was in fact the routine annual export from Muziris, then this export had to be sustained by a population of at least 380 captive adult male elephants.[69] This number is not far from the 500–600 elephants that Cosmas Indicopleustes attributes to several kings of the west coast of India of his time—among them, the king of Male.[70]

9.4. STRAIGHTFORWARD AND CIRCUITOUS EVALUATIONS

As mentioned, col. iii, l. 29 records the total monetary value of the three-quarter portions of the *Hermapollon*'s cargo. But the portions recorded at col. iii were not all calculated in the same manner.

Gangetic nard apparently arrived in containers (*kistai*) that precluded ascertainment of its net weight, so its value was reckoned based on the number of containers and evaluated at 4,500 drachmas per container. In the text, this evaluation takes up only three lines of col. iii (ll. 1–3):

1 *Νάρδου Γαγγιτικῆς κιστῶν ξ ὧν ὁμοίως*
2 *τιμὴ λογίζεται ὡς τῆς κίστης (δραχμῶν) ᾿Δφ ἀργυρί-*
3 *ου (τάλαντα) με*

1 Of **Gangetic nard**, 60 containers, of which likewise
2 the value is reckoned per container at 4,500 drachmas:
3 45 talents of money.

67 *Peutinger Table* seg. 11.

68 De Romanis (2014b).

69 For elephants between ten and thirty years of age, the average growth pace of ivory is 1.4 kg per year per elephant. Before and after, the pace is slower: Sukumar (1989: 82; 225).

70 Cosm. Indic. 11.22. Greek and Latin authors often number the elephants of the Indian kings or nations: Diod. Sic., 2.37.3; 17.93.2; Curt. 9.2.4; Plut., *Alex.* 62; Plin., *NH* 6.66–8. The size of Porus' elephant wing in the battle against Alexander varies according to author between 130, 85, and 200: Diod. Sic. 17.87.2; Curt. 8.13.6; Arr., *Anab.* 5.14.4. In general, for the armies of ancient India, cf. Thapar (2002: 25–37). For the Indian elephants in the Seleucid army, cf. Bar-Kochva (1976: 76–84).

Table 9.1 Layout of verso col. iii.

1	3/4 portions of Gangetic nard	
2	3/4 portions of Gangetic nard	
3	3/4 portions of Gangetic nard	45 talents
4	3/4 portions of sound ivory	
5	3/4 portions of sound ivory	
6	3/4 portions of sound ivory	
7	3/4 portions of sound ivory	
8	3/4 portions of sound ivory	
9	3/4 portions of sound ivory	
10	3/4 portions of sound ivory	
11	3/4 portions of sound ivory	
12	3/4 portions of sound ivory	
13	3/4 portions of sound ivory	
14	3/4 portions of sound ivory	76 talents,
15	3/4 portions of sound ivory	5,275 drachmas
16	3/4 portions of *schidai*	
17	3/4 portions of *schidai*	
18	3/4 portions of *schidai*	
19	3/4 portions of *schidai*	
20	3/4 portions of *schidai*	
21	3/4 portions of *schidai*	
22	3/4 portions of *schidai*	
23	3/4 portions of *schidai*	8 talents,
24	3/4 portions of *schidai*	5,882 drachmas,
25	3/4 portions of *schidai*	3 obols
26	Total of the ivory 3/4 portions	
27	Total of the 3/4 portions	
28	Total of the 3/4 portions	1,151 talents,
29	Total of the 3/4 portions	5,852 drachmas

The calculation of the three-quarter portion of this cargo could not be simpler. At the price of 4,500 drachmas (three-quarters of a talent) per container (l. 2), 60 containers of Gangetic nard (l. 1) makes 45 talents (l. 3).

By contrast, the evaluation of the three-quarter portions of sound ivory tusks and *schidai* occupies twelve (ll. 4–15) and ten (ll. 16–25) lines (Table 9.1), respectively, and takes a more complicated path. These are the lines concerning the sound ivory tusks:

4 Ἐλέφαντος ὑγιοῦς μὲν ὁλκ(ῆς) (ταλάντων) οη μν(ῶν) νδ Ḷʹδ̣ʹ
5 ὧν ὁμοίως τιμὴ λογίζεται ὁλκ(ῆς) μὲν (ταλάντων) οη μν(ῶν) μγ̣
6 τῶν γινομένων σταθμίοις τῆς τετάρτης τοῦ
7 ταλάντου λογιζομένο̣υ̣ πρ̣ὸς λί(τρας) ϙ̅ε̅ λι(τρῶν) ͵Ζυοη
8 ἐξ ὧν αἱρεῖ λογιζομ̣ε̣ν̣ων εἰς τὸ τάλαντον λι(τρῶν) ϙ̣̅[ζ Lʹ
9 ὅσῳ συνήθως πρὸς τοὺς ἐμπόρους λογίζεται ὁλ[κ(ῆς)
10 (τάλαντα) ος μν(αῖ) μα ὡς τῆς μν(ᾶς) (δραχμῶν) ρ (τάλαντα) ος (δραχμαὶ) ͵Δρ

11 *τῶν δὲ λοιπῶν ὑπὸ τῶν ἀραβαρχῶν πλείω ὑπὲρ*
12 *τῆς τεταρτολο̣γ̣ίας ἀρθέντων ἐν ἀ̣ριθμῷ ὀδόντων*
13 *παρὰ τὸ αἱροῦν [- - -]λων ὀδόντων μν(ῶν) ια Ḷ′[δ̣′*[71]
14 *ὡς τῆς μν(ᾶς) τῶ̣ν̣ ἴ̣σω̣ν̣ (δραχμῶν) ρ (δραχμαὶ) Ἀ̣ροε̣*
15 *γίν(εται) ἐπὶ τὸ α̣ὐ̣τ̣ὸ̣ (τάλαντα) ος (δραχμαὶ) Ἐσο̣ε̣*

4 Of **sound ivory**, 78 talents of weight 54 ½ ¼ minas,
5 of which likewise the price is reckoned thus: *a)* Of the 78 talents of weight 43 minas
6 which—since, for the weight standard of the quarter-tax,
7 the talent is reckoned at 95 lbs.—is 7,478 lbs.;
8 from which, being likewise reckoned 97.5 pounds to talent
9 as it is usually reckoned for the merchants, is derived
10 76 talents of weight 41 minas. At 100 drachmas per mina: 76 talents 4,100 drachmas;
11 *b)* Of the remaining (sc. tusks), taken in addition by the arabarchs for
12 the payment of the quarter-tax, in the sum of tusks
13 together with the result [- - -] tusks, 11¾ minas
14 At the same 100 drachmas per mina: drachmas 1,175.
15 Makes the total 76 talents 5,275 drachmas.

And these are the lines regarding the *schidai*:

16 *σχιδῶ̣ν̣ δ̣’ ὁλκ(ῆς) (ταλάντων) ιγ μν(ῶν) θḶ′δ′*
17 *ὧν ὁμοίως τιμὴ λογ̣ί̣ζ̣εται ὁλκῆς μὲν (ταλάντων) ιβ μν(ῶν) μ[ζ*
18 *τῶν ὡς πρόκ̣ε̣ιτ̣α̣ι̣ ὁ̣μ̣οίοις̣ σταθμί̣ο̣ι̣ς μὲν τετάρτης*
19 *λι(τρῶν) Ἀσιδ καθὼς ⟦καὶ⟧ δὲ πρὸς τοὺς ἐμπόρους λογί-*
20 *ζεται ὁλκ(ῆς) (ταλάντων) ιβ μν(ῶν) κζ ὡς τῆς μν(ᾶς) (δραχμῶν) ο*
21 *ἀργ(υρίου) (τάλαντα) η (δραχμαὶ) Ἀσϙ*
22 *τῶν δὲ λοιπῶν πλείω ὑπὲρ τῆς τεταρτολογίας ἀρθει-*
23 *σῶν ὡς πρόκειται μν(ῶν) κβ* <L′> *δ′ ὡς τῆς μνᾶς τῶν*
24 *ἴσων (δραχμῶν) ο ἀργ(υρίου) (δραχμαὶ) Ἀφϙβ⸓*
25 *γίν(εται) σχιδῶν (τάλαντα) η̣ (δραχμαὶ) Ἐωπβ⸓*

[71] At l. 13, the reading *καὶ τεταρτολογουμένων*, proposed by the editors and generally accepted, has rightly been rejected by Morelli, who reads *διπ̣ή̣χ̣ε̣ω̣ν̣ ὅ̣λων* (entire, two-cubit-long tusks) Morelli (2011: 213), with reference to the 2,000 three-cubit-long tusks paraded by L. Aemilius Paullus in his triumph of 167 BC: Diod. Sic. 31.8.12. Of the letters read by Morelli, I consider safe the ending *-λων*, certainly belonging to an adjective qualifying *ὀδόντων*, whereas the initial *διπ-* seems doubtful to me. I confess I have entertained the possibility of *ἐ̣κ̣ τ̣ῶ̣ν̣ ἄ̣λ̣λων*: *παρὰ τὸ αἱροῦν ἐ̣κ̣ τ̣ῶ̣ν̣ ἄ̣λ̣λων ὀδόντων* would nicely echo *ἐξ ὧν αἱρεῖ* of l. 8. However, the traces of the vanished letters do not seem to support the reading. The meaning of the sentence is nonetheless clear: the shares taken in addition by the arabarchs are 'in the number of the tusks' (*ἐν ἀ̣ριθμῷ ὀδόντων*), along with the portion of the goods recalculated and evaluated in the preceding section (*παρὰ τὸ αἱροῦν* referring to *αἱρεῖ* of l. 8).

16 Of *schidai*, 13 talents of weight 9 ½ ¼ minas,
17 of which likewise the value is reckoned thus: Of the 12 talents of weight 47 minas,
18 which, as above, for the same weight standard of the quarter-tax,
19 is 1,214 lbs., in the way they are reckoned for the merchants,
20 12 talents of weight 27 minas. At 70 drachmas per mina:
21 8 talents of money 4,290 drachmas
22 Of the remaining (sc. *schidai*), taken in addition for the payment of the quarter-tax,
23 as above, 22 <½ >¼ minas. At the
24 same 70 drachmas per mina: 1,592 m. drachmas 3 obols
25 Total for *schidai*: 8 talents 5,882 drachmas 3 obols.

The valuations for the three-quarter portions of sound ivory tusks and *schidai* are carried out in the same intricate manner. The entire process may be broken down into five steps (Figs. 9.1 and 9.2):

a. A small share—11.75 minas of sound ivory and 22.75 of *schidai*—is subtracted from the weights of the three-quarter portions of each commodity (ll. 7–10; 16–17). The share is said 'to be taken (by the arabarchs) in addition for the payment of the quarter-tax' (ll. 11–12; 22–3).[72]
b. The remaining weight of each imported item is converted twice—from talents to pounds, and then back again from pounds to talents: the first conversion (ll. 5–7; 17–19) uses the ratio 1 talent = 95 pounds; the second (ll. 5–7; 19–20) uses the ratio 1 talent = 97.5 pounds.
c. The weight number obtained in step 'b' is multiplied by the price per unit —100 drachmas per mina for sound ivory (l. 10) and 70 drachmas per mina for *schidai* (ll. 20–1).
d. The weight of the shares 'taken by the arabarchs in addition for the payment of the quarter-tax' is multiplied by their price per unit—again, 100 drachmas per mina for sound ivory (ll. 11–14) and 70 drachmas per mina for *schidai* (ll. 22–4).
e. Finally, the monetary values obtained in steps 'c' and 'd' are added together (l. 15, for the ivory tusks; l. 25, for the *schidai*).

How do we explain the rationale for such a convoluted procedure? Rathbone and Morelli based their interpretations on three (or four) assumptions, as follows:

1. The monetary evaluation of the three-quarter portions occurs after the payment in kind of a quarter-tax on imported commodities—in other

[72] For the arabarchs as contractors of the Red Sea tax, see pp. 298–303.

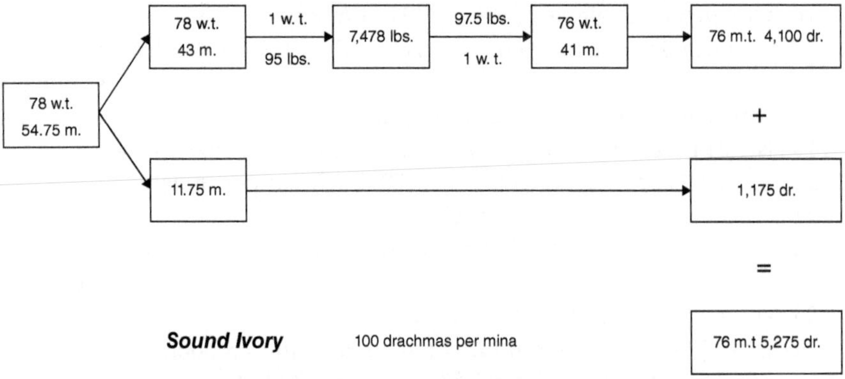

Fig. 9.1 Evaluation of the sound ivory cargo's three-quarter portion.

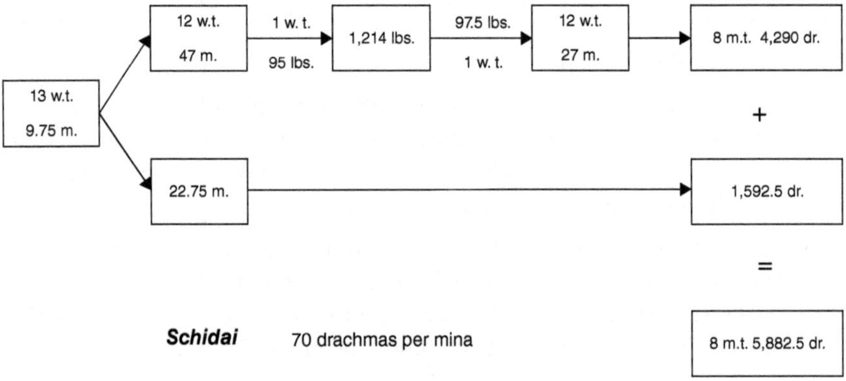

Fig. 9.2 Evaluation of the *schidai* cargo's three-quarter portion.

words, after one-quarter of the *Hermapollon*'s cargo has been taken by the arabarchs as payment of the quarter-tax.[73]

2. The monetary evaluation is not meant to be used to calculate the tax, but either to establish the price for an *en bloc* sale (Rathbone) or to evaluate the collateral of the loan (Morelli).[74]
3. The additional shares taken by the arabarchs for the payment of the quarter-tax are random extra weights taken from commodities like ivory tusks and *schidai* (which, they argue, may have been impossible to divide safely into precise shares of predetermined weight).[75]

[73] τετάρτη mentioned both at recto col. ii, l. 8 and at verso col. ii, l. 7; col. iii, ll. 6; 18; cf. τεταρτολογεῖν at recto, l. 18; τεταρτολογία at recto col. ii, l. 10; verso ll. 12; 22: Rathbone (2000: 43; 45); Morelli (2011: 220).

[74] For the first hypothesis, Rathbone (2000: 45); for the second, Morelli (2011: 233).

[75] Rathbone (2000: 46); Morelli (2011: 219).

4. There was a 'correct' weight talent of 97.5 Roman pounds used by the merchants, as opposed to the 'artificial' weight talent of 95 Roman pounds used by the tax collectors.[76] The double conversion of the weight unit was an accounting artifice devised by tax collectors to return only 950/975 of the total due to the merchant.[77]
5. Moreover, Morelli suggests that the values of the arabarchs' shares were included in the final assessment of the three-quarter portions of the entire cargo, because those shares were eventually repaid to the merchant.[78]

For several reasons, I find it difficult to adopt these assumptions. First of all, the assumption that it was impossible to divide *c.*3,200 kilograms of ivory tusks or *c.*538 kilograms of *schidai* into two shares of predetermined weight is unwarranted. We will see in the next section that in verso col. ii, l. 5 the entire cargo of sound ivory tusks is quantified by both the number of tusks (167) and the total weight (105 talents and 13 minas). Extracting one-quarter of that weight from the 167 tusks of sound ivory should not have been more difficult than, for example, separating out 750 grams of cherries from a 3-kilogram heap. A sixteenth-century Portuguese document shows how 385 tusks weighing 4,828.68 kilograms could be divided into thirteen lots of six *quintaes* each, plus a fourteenth lot of 4 *quintaes* and 24 *arrateis.*[79] Extracting one-quarter of the roughly 538 kilograms of *schidai* should have been equally unproblematic.

Second, the weights of the arabarchs' shares are not random, but seem to be arithmetically determined: 11.75 minas represent one-six hundredth (*hexakosioste*) of the total shipment of sound ivory tusks, and 22.75 minas one-fiftieth (*pentekoste*) of the *schidai.*[80] Third, the shares taken by the arabarchs could not represent some final rounding off of the quarter-tax paid in kind, if they were determined at the *beginning* of the calculation, before the double conversion of the remaining weight. Fourth, if the *schidai* are ivory trimmings weighing a maximum of 7 kilograms each, as argued earlier, then the 22.75-mina (*c.*11.6 kg) share taken by the arabarchs must correspond to more than one *schida*, also contradicting the idea that the shares taken resulted from a rounding off and were reimbursed. In all likelihood, the arabarchs' additional shares were arithmetically determined surcharges.

[76] Rathbone (2000: 46); Morelli (2011: 218).

[77] Rathbone (2000: 46); Morelli (2011: 217–18).

[78] Morelli (2011: 218).

[79] *DPMAC* 3.572–9.

[80] The quota of sound ivory (11.75 minas) results from charging 1 mina for every 10 weight talents (1/600, ἑξακοσιοστή) of the total amount (105 talents and 13 minas, rounded up to 110 talents), plus the fraction of mina of the three-quarter portion (0.75). Similarly, the quota of the *schidai* (22.75 minas) results from charging 120 drachmae for every weight talent (1/50, πεντηκοστή) of the total amount (17 talents and 33 minas, rounded up to 18 talents, which makes 21.6 minas, rounded up to 22), plus the fraction of mina of the three-quarter portion (0.75).

The question of the quarter-tax payment will be discussed in chapter twelve, but here I would like to draw attention to the fact that the three-quarter portions of the cargo and the additional shares taken by the arabarchs are considered notional quantities. It should be noted that while at verso col. ii, l. 5, the entire cargo of sound ivory is quantified by both the number of tusks (167) and the total weight (105 talents and 13 minas), at col. iii, ll. 4, 5, and 14, the three-quarter portion is referred to using only the weight, and at col. iii, ll. 11–13, the 11.75 minas of sound ivory 'taken by the arabarchs' are referred to as 'tusks' (plural!), even though such a small weight cannot correspond to an entire tusk, let alone more than one. This disparity among the three labels—total number of tusks and weight number at col. ii, l. 5; weight number of the three-quarter portion only at col. iii, ll. 4, 5, and 14; and plural 'tusks' at col. iii, ll. 11–13 for the small arabarchs' share—confirms that while the first entry measures a real cargo with a specific number of tusks and a specific weight, the second and third entries are nothing more than arithmetically determined abstractions.

As for the double conversion of the weight unit, the wording at col. iii, ll. 5–7 shows that the unit used by the customs officials was a talent set at the standard of 1 talent = 95 official Roman pounds. This is why the 78 talents and 43 minas of sound ivory equals 7,478 official Roman pounds. It is only at a second stage that the 7,478 official Roman pounds is converted (ll. 8–9) into 76 talents and 41 minas—based on a conversion rate in which 1 talent equals 97.5 official Roman pounds.

The sentences at col. iii, l. 9 'as it is usually reckoned for the merchants' (*ὅσῳ συνήθως πρὸς τοὺς ἐμπόρους λογίζεται*) and ll. 19–20 'in the way they are reckoned for the merchants' (*καθὼς* ⟦*καὶ*⟧ *δὲ πρὸς τοὺς ἐμπόρους λογί|ζεται*) do not refer to a merchant metrology that is distinct from the one employed by customs officials.[81] The sentences refer instead to a practice whereby a reduction of the nominal weight was granted to the merchants. The double conversion generates smaller nominal weight numbers of the *very same amounts* of sound ivory and *schidai*.

A reduction of the value through a reduction of the nominal weight also appears in *P.Oxy.* 31.2580, where the price of 61 lumps of pitch weighing 100 talents and 8 minas is reduced from 1 talent and 1,100 drachmas to a final value of 1 talent and 1,012 drachmas, because the measuring weight unit was 1/80 lighter (ll. 4–6: *τοῦ σταθμοῦ |ἐνδέοντ(ος) ὡ̣ς τοῦ (ταλάντου) α |μνᾶς* L′δ′).[82] It is unclear whether this reduction of the nominal weight and value is

[81] In the letter *PSI* 15.1558, l. 4, reference is made to the Coptos weight standard, which seems to be heavier than another weight standard, familiar to the recipient of the letter. Of course, this does not hint at a difference, in Coptos, of the weight standard of the tax-collectors from that of the merchants.

[82] *P.Oxy.* 31.2580, ll. 1–8.

tax-related,[83] but we do know that in medieval Aden reductions in the customs duties for several commodities (coincidentally, including pepper and ivory) were calibrated through reductions in the nominal weight (*ḥaṭīṭ*).[84]

Odd as it may seem, the assessment of the three-quarter portion of sound ivory foresees that 1/600 of the total sound ivory cargo (the arabarchs' additional share) will be evaluated at the price of 100 drachmas per 95 lbs., and that 449/600 of the total quantity will be evaluated at the price of 100 drachmas per 97.5 lb. Similarly, the evaluation of the three-quarter portion of *schidai* anticipates that 2/100 of the total quantity (again, the arabarchs' additional share) will be evaluated at the price of 70 drachmas per 95 lbs., and that 73/100 of the total quantity will be evaluated at the price of 70 drachmas per 97.5 lb. Such a peculiar system cannot be associated with customary mercantile transactions; only a bureaucratic procedure related to customs duties could account for all these eccentricities.

9.5. CARGOES, QUARTERS, AND THE ARABARCHS' ADDITIONAL SHARES

The evaluation of the three-quarter portions of Gangetic nard, sound ivory, and *schidai* at col. iii, ll. 1–26 was based on the calculation of the quarter portions and the arabarchs' additional shares recorded at col. ii, ll. 4–13. This section of the text had been an enigma for a long time, until it was correctly read and understood by Morelli. With his emendations, ll. 4–13 run as follows:

4 [ ]ṭạị κ
5 [Ἐλέφαντος ὑγιοῦς ἐν μὲν ὀδ]ọῦσ̣ι ρξζ ὁλ(κῆς) (ταλάντων) ρε μν(ῶν) ιγ
6 [ ] . . (τάλαντα) κϛ μν(αῖ) λ
7 [ ]ṿṭω τῆς τετάρτης
8 [ὁμ]οίως ὁλ(κῆς) μν(αῖ) ια L'δ'
9 [ ] . (τάλαντα) κϛ μν(αῖ) ιη δ'
10 [ἐν δὲ σχίδαις] ọ̣λ̣κ̣(ῆς) (ταλάντων) ιζ μν(ῶν) λγ
11 [ ] (τάλαντα) δ μν(αῖ) μ̣ϛ
12 [ ] . . . . . π . . ικω
13 [ ] (τάλαντα) δ μν(αῖ) κγ δ'

[83] It is worthwhile to note that in the last part of the text (*P.Oxy.* 31.2580, ll. 9–16), apart from other expenses, money for a φόρος ζυγ(οστασίας) καὶ σταθ(μοῦ) and a φόρος ζυγ(οστασίας) ἀγορανόμ(ου) ἀντὶ συν|κρίσεως σταθ(μοῦ) is recorded.

[84] Vallet (2010: 181–2): 'Il n'est pas question ici de taxes, mais bien plutôt de 'réductions' (*ḥaṭīṭ*) du poids des marchandises exprimées en *raṭl*... L'ivoire connaît une baisse d'un *raṭl* pour 50, ou de 25 *raṭl* pour 800. Mais il n'est pas le seul: le poivre, l'encens, la cannelle, le beurre clarifié sont affectés aussi d'une baisse du dixième de leur poids... Enlever une partie du poids revenait à alléger la taxe d'importation.'

4	[Of **Gangetic Nard** 80 containers, quarter-tax] 20 containers	
5	[Of **Sound Ivory** in] 167 **Tusks** of 105 talents of weight 13 minas	
6	[	] 26 talents of weight 30 minas
7	[	] of the quarter-tax
8	[	] likewise 11 ½ ¼ minas of weight
9	[	] 26 talents [of weight] 18¼ minas
10	[in x **Fragments**	] 17 talents of weight 33 minas
11	[	] 4 talents [of weight] 46 minas
12	[	]
13	[	] 4 talents [of weight] 23¼ [minas]

The new readings enabled Morelli to recognize that these lines record numbers and weights related to the cargoes of Gangetic nard, sound ivory tusks, and *schidai*. In particular, he ascertained that:

1) At l. 4, the number 20 refers to the containers of Gangetic nard corresponding to the quarter rate;
2) Lines 5–9 list:
    a. the entire quantity of sound ivory tusks imported by the *Hermapollon* both in number and weight: 167 tusks, for a weight of 105 talents and 13 minas (l. 5);
    b. the weight of sound ivory tusks corresponding to the sum of the base quarter rate, plus the arabarchs' additional share: 26 talents and 30 minas (l. 6);
    c. the weight of sound ivory tusks corresponding to the arabarchs' additional share: 11.75 minas (l. 8); and
    d. the weight of sound ivory tusks corresponding to the base quarter rate: 26 talents and 18.25 minas (l. 9).
3) Lines 10–13 record:
    a. the weight of the entire *schidai* cargo: 17 talents and 33 minas (l. 10);
    b. the weight of *schidai* corresponding to the sum of the base quarter rate and the arabarchs' additional share: 4 talents and 46 minas (l. 11); and
    c. the weight of *schidai* corresponding to the base quarter rate: 4 talents and 23.25 minas (l. 13).

Morelli's explanation of col. ii, ll. 4–13 confirmed Rathbone's interpretation that the verso col. iii, ll. 27–9 referred to the value of the three-quarter portions of the cargo, and therefore that the quantities of Gangetic nard, ivory tusks, and *schidai* evaluated at verso col. iii, ll. 1–25 were just three-quarter portions of the original shipment. Does this also confirm, as both Rathbone and Morelli maintain, that the quarter-tax was paid in kind?

10

The Other Cargo Items

Apart from the almost fully preserved third column, the Muziris papyrus also retains the ends of most of the lines of verso col. ii (the far right side). Because of several misreadings by the editors and a fragment positioned incorrectly at the time of the first edition,[1] for quite some time almost nothing could be inferred from the few weight numbers or sums of money that could be discerned.[2] Eventually, Morelli improved on several earlier readings and, most importantly, brilliantly succeeded in understanding the rationale of ll. 4–13. His breakthrough has had an enormous impact both on the understanding of the overall structure of the text and on the reconstruction of the *Hermapollon*'s cargo. We now know that the evaluation of the three-quarter portions of the cargo began at col. ii, l. 14, and that the commodities (whose three-quarter portions' value represented 88.64 per cent of the total at col. iii, l. 29) were evaluated in col. ii, ll. 14–30. We also know that the text did not begin with what was previously labelled col. i, and is here called col. ii.

My analysis of col. ii is divided into three sections: the first presents a general overview; the second focuses on ll. 20–30 and 1–3, which, I will argue, pertain to pepper; the third examines ll. 14–19, which, I will suggest, refer to two items—one of which is most probably malabathron (ll. 17–19), and the other (ll. 14–16) possibly tortoise shell.

10.1. COL. II, LL. 14–30: AN OVERVIEW

Gangetic nard, sound ivory, and *schidai*, the three cargoes whose three-quarter portions are evaluated in col. iii, ll. 1–26, were just minor cargo items. Their combined weight may have been around five tons, and the subtotal of the

[1] For the previously overturned position of the fragment preserving col. ii, ll. 19–20, cf. Morelli (2011: 207, n. 24).

[2] However, Rathbone (2000: 43) understood that col. ii, ll. 5–9 were pertinent to one and the same commodity.

The Indo-Roman Pepper Trade and the Muziris Papyrus. Federico De Romanis, Oxford University Press (2020).
 DOI: 10.1093/oso/9780198842347.001.0001

Table 10.1 Cargoes and values evaluated on verso col. iii.

Item	Quantity	Value
Gangetic nard	60 containers	45 talents
Sound ivory	78 talents, 54¾ minas	76 talents 5,275 drachmas
Schidai	13 talents 9¾ minas	8 talents 5,882 drachmas 3 obols
Total	60 cont., 92 talents, 4½ minas	130 talents, 5,157 drachmas, 3 obols

values of their three-quarter portions equalled 130 talents, 5,157 drachmas, and 3 obols (Table 10.1)—only 11.36 per cent of the 1,151 talents and 5,852 drachmas that are the total value of the three-quarter portions of the *Hermapollon*'s cargo (col. iii, l. 29).

How many commodities contributed to the remaining 1,021 talents, 694 drachmas, and 3 obols? Based on an inaccurate reading (μερῶν ϛ̄) at col. iii, l. 27, the editors had inferred that the cargo comprised six items.[3] With the establishment of the correct reading, μερῶν γ̄, and the appropriate understanding of the whole sentence provided by Rathbone, any certainty about the number of items contained in the cargo based on col. iii became unwarranted. It is therefore a great stroke of luck that Morelli was able to show that col. ii, ll. 4–13 prepare, so to speak, the evaluations of the three-quarter portions of Gangetic nard, sound ivory, and *schidai* in col. iii, ll. 1–26. This finding has an extremely important implication: the three-quarter portions of all the other commodities of the cargo, worth 1,021 talents, 694 drachmas, and 3 obols, were evaluated in the lines that run from 14 to the end of column ii (Table 10.2). The analysis of that section will show that, although based on faulty assumptions, the editors nevertheless reached the correct conclusion: the cargo of the *Hermapollon* included only six items.

My interpretation of the crucial section in ll. 14–30[4] is based on the sequence of the preserved numbers along the far right end of the lines. In many cases, either the signs or the numeric values identify the entries as weight numbers or monetary values:

14 --- μν(ῶν)] λα̣ L´
15 ---] . . κ̣α
16 ---]η
17 ---] . . [---μν(ῶν)---]. δ´
18 --- ὁλκ(ῆς)(ταλάντων)] Ἀωξ [? μν(ῶν) ??] Ḷ´δ´
19 --- ἀργ](υρίου) (τάλαντα) σ̣κ[---
20 ---] ’Τφ [---

[3] Harrauer and Sijpesteijn (1985: 134; 149–50).

[4] It will be shown that below col. ii, l. 28, two lines are lost. The blank space (at least 5 cm) below col. iii l. 29 (a little lower than col. ii, l. 28) allows for them. My readings of ll. 14, 17, 18, 19 differ from those by Morelli: see p. 22.

Table 10.2 Layout of verso coll. ii–iii.

	Col. ii		Col. iii	
1	Other item(s)		¾ portion of Gangetic nard	
2	Other item(s)		¾ portion of Gangetic nard	
3	Other item(s)		¾ portion of Gangetic nard	45 tal.
4	Gangetic nard		¾ portion of sound ivory	
5	sound ivory		¾ portion of sound ivory	
6	sound ivory		¾ portion of sound ivory	
7	sound ivory		¾ portion of sound ivory	
8	sound ivory		¾ portion of sound ivory	
9	sound ivory		¾ portion of sound ivory	
10	*schidai*		¾ portion of sound ivory	
11	*schidai*		¾ portion of sound ivory	
12	*schidai*		¾ portion of sound ivory	
13	*schidai*		¾ portion of sound ivory	
14	¾ portion of the other item(s)		¾ portion of sound ivory	76 tal.,
15	¾ portion of the other item(s)		¾ portion of sound ivory	5,275 dr.
16	¾ portion of the other item(s)		¾ portion of *schidai*	
17	¾ portion of the other item(s)		¾ portion of *schidai*	
18	¾ portion of the other item(s)		¾ portion of *schidai*	
19	¾ portion of the other item(s)		¾ portion of *schidai*	
20	¾ portion of the other item(s)		¾ portion of *schidai*	
21	¾ portion of the other item(s)		¾ portion of *schidai*	
22	¾ portion of the other item(s)		¾ portion of *schidai*	
23	¾ portion of the other item(s)		¾ portion of *schidai*	8 tal.,
24	¾ portion of the other item(s)		¾ portion of *schidai*	5,882 dr.,
25	¾ portion of the other item(s)		¾ portion of *schidai*	3 ob.
26	¾ portion of the other item(s)		Total of ivory ¾ portions	
27	¾ portion of the other item(s)		Total of the ¾ portions	
28	¾ portion of the other item(s)	1,021 tal.,	Total of the ¾ portions	1,151 tal.,
29	¾ portion of the other item(s)	694 dr.,	Total of the ¾ portions	5,852 dr.
30	¾ portion of the other item(s)	3 ob.		

21 ---] *'Γσκγ μν(ῶν) β̣*
22 ---]*κα̣ ἐξ ὧν̣ ἀ̣ν̣τ̣ι̣*
23 ---]*ται η . . . υ...*
24 ---] . . . .*ριων*
25 ---] *ἀ̣ρ̣γ(υρίου) (τάλαντα) ψοα*
26 ---] *(δ̣ρ̣α̣χμ̣α̣ὶ) 'Δχλβ*
27 ---] *μ̣ν̣(ῶ̣ν̣) μδ̣ δʹ*
28 ---] ...*ν*
29 ---
30 ---

14 . . .] 31 ½ [minas]
15 . . .] 21
16 . . .]8

17 . . .]¼ [minas]
18 . . .] 1,86̣? [talents of weight, . . .] ½¼ [minas]
19 . . .] 2̣2? talents of money
20 . . .]3,5?? [talent of weight . . .
21 . . .]3,223 [talent of weight] 2̣ minas
22 . . .]
23 . . .] from which
24 . . .]
25 . . .] 771 talents of money
26 . . .] 4,632 drachmas
27 . . .] 4̣4¼ minas
28 . . .]
29 . . .
30 . . .

The surviving letters show that ll. 14, 17, 18, 20, 21, and 27 end with weight numbers, whereas ll. 19, 25, and 26 end with sums of money. Line 25 ends with 771 talents (more than two-thirds of the total at col. iii, l. 29); l. 26 ends with 4,652 drachmas. At least one other sum is lost after l. 28, because the weight number at l. 27 requires a corresponding monetary value, which is not recognizable at the end of l. 28. The last letters of ll. 15 and 16 may be numerals that represent the endings of either a weight number or a sum of money. By contrast, ll. 22, 23, 24, and 28 have no figures at the end.

My reasoning is as follows. Since the weight numbers at ll. 17 and 18 relate to the monetary value at l. 19, the number at l. 16 must be a sum of money, which requires at least one weight number at ll. 14 or 15. Therefore, I assume that ll. 14–19 reported the same sequence of two weight numbers (ll. 14–15; 17–18) and one sum of money (ll. 16; 19) twice.[5] As for ll. 20–30, the considerable weight numbers at ll. 20 and 21 (exceeding 3,000 talents) must relate to the monetary value(s) at ll. 25–6. The three lines (ll. 22–4) that separate the weight numbers of ll. 20 and 21 from the monetary value(s) at ll. 25–6 end with no figure, which suggests that the value(s) at ll. 25 and 26 was (were) obtained through a complicated process, comparable to that of the sound ivory tusks and *schidai* evaluated in col. iii. The sequence of weight numbers and sums of money at ll. 14-30 is shown in Table 10.3.

We shall now consider col. ii, ll. 1–3. Since in col. ii, l. 4 refers to Gangetic nard, ll. 5–9 to sound ivory, and ll. 10–13 to *schidai*, and since the order in which the evaluation of the three commodities is first prepared (col. ii, ll. 4–13) and then executed (col. iii, ll. 1–26) is the same (Gangetic nard, then sound

[5] Sequences of two weight numbers are at col. ii, ll. 20–1 and col. iii, ll. 4–5; 16–17. Morelli's assumption (2011: 212) that the weight number at l. 14 represents the sum of the quarter-taxes on both sound ivory and *schidai* is unlikely—such a sum would be useless. The total value of the ivory at col. iii, l. 26 does not require a total of the weight for the base quarter rates.

Table 10.3 Endings of verso col. ii, ll. 14–30.

Verso col. ii, ll. 14–30	
14	Weight number
15	Weight number?
16	Sum of money?
17	Weight number
18	Weight number
19	Sum of money
20	Weight number
21	Weight number
22	No number
23	No number
24	No number
25	Sum of money
26	Sum of money
27	Weight number
28	No number
29	[Sum of money]
30	[Sum of money]

ivory, and finally *schidai*), it is likely that ll. 1–3 refer to the commodity whose three-quarter portion was evaluated in the bottom part of column ii. This is somewhat confirmed by the last parts of the recorded weight numbers:

1 ---] μν(αῖ) νθ
2 ---] μν(αῖ) ι̣δ L´δ´
3 ---]̣ μν(αῖ) νη

1 . . .] minas 59
2 . . .] minas 14.75
3 . . .] minas 58.

As suggested by their mina components, the weight numbers of col. ii, ll. 1 and 2 are likely to relate to each other: the 14.75 minas at l. 2 is one-quarter of the 59 minas at l. 1. Moreover, the weight of col. ii, ll. 27—44.25 minas—is likely to relate to it as well, 44.25 being three-quarters of 59, as Morelli already noted. The fact that the evaluation of Gangetic nard is prepared at col. ii, l. 4 and executed at col. iii, ll. 1–3, combined with the presumption that the order in which the evaluation of the commodities was first prepared and then executed remained the same, supports the working hypothesis that the first (ll. 1–3) and the last (at least ll. 27–30) sections of col. ii concerned the same commodity. Later in this chapter, I hope to demonstrate that the extant weight numbers at ll. 20 and 21 and the monetary values at ll. 25 and 26 show that ll. 1–3 and 20–30 all refer to the same item.

On the other hand, it is unlikely that the five monetary values at col. ii, ll. 16, 19, 25, 26, and 29, all relate to just one commodity—the one referred to at col. ii, ll. 1–3.[6] If they do not, the evaluation of the other commodity or commodities must have been prepared in a preceding column, the existence of which was not recognized by the editors, but is virtually guaranteed by the presumptive width of recto col. iii (Fig. 0.2).

I will show that the remnants of col. ii, ll. 14–19 strongly suggest that two commodities were evaluated therein. The section preparing the assessment of their three-quarter portions most probably occupied six lines of the lost col. i.

10.2. PEPPER: COL. II, LL. 20–30 (AND LL. 1–3)

The interpretation of col. ii, ll. 20–30 has been impeded by several misreadings by the editors and even by the misplacement of a fragment at the time of publication.[7] The text and translation again reproduced below incorporates (ll. 20; 21; 25; 26) several corrections proposed by Morelli and myself.[8]

20 ---] ʼΓφ̣ [---
21 ---] ʼΓσκγ μν(ῶν) β̣
22 ---]κα̣ ἐξ ὧν̣ ἀ̣ν̣τ̣ι̣
23 ---]ται η̣...υ̣...
24 ---]...... ριων
25 ---] ἀ̣ργ(υρίου) (τάλαντα) ψοα
26 ---] (δ̣ρ̣α̣χ̣μ̣α̣ὶ̣) ʼΔχλβ
27 ---] μ̣ν̣(ῶ̣ν̣) μδ̣ δ´
28 ---]...ν
29 ---
30 ---

20 ...]3,5?? [talents of weight]
21 ...]3,223 [talents of weight] 2̣ minas
22 ...] from which...
23 ...]...
24 ...]...
25 ...] 771 talents of money
26 ...] 4,632 drachmas

[6] In col. iii, for only three items, there were nine sums of money (ll. 3, 10, 14, 15, 22, 25, 26 [27]) before the grand total.

[7] Morelli (2011: 207, n. 24).

[8] For Morelli's different readings of ll. 20 and 21, see p. 22 and below.

Fig. 10.1 *P.Vindob.* G 40822 verso col. ii, ll. 25–6.
P.Vindob. G 40822. Austrian National Library. http://data.onb.ac.at/rec/RZ00001642.

27 . . .] 44 ¼ minas
28 . . .
29 . . .
30 . . .

Of the misreadings that hindered the interpretation of col. ii, ll. 14–30, those at ll. 25–6 (Fig. 10.1) were particularly damaging. At l. 25, the first editors read] μ̣ν̣(ῶν) (δραχμῶν) ψ̸οα, 'minas, drachmas, 771'. Such a reading makes little sense: it conjoins a unit of weight with a unit of currency in a single descriptive measure. Moreover, at l. 26 the editors read (ταλάντων)] δ (δραχμῶν) λβ, which is also unsatisfactory.

Independent of one another, both Morelli and I read ἀργ(υρίου) (τάλαντα) ψ̸οα at col. ii, l. 25 and 'Δχλβ at l. 26.[9] What 771 talents of money—more than two-thirds of the total recorded at col. iii, l. 29—must refer to becomes indisputable when the connection of this sum of money with the weight number (more than 3,500 talents) at col. ii, l. 21 is taken into account: in a ship returning from Muziris, such immense value and large volume can mean only pepper. In turn, this conclusion strongly suggests that the 771 talents in col. ii, l. 25 would also be followed by the sign for drachmas and a number. In fact, the possibility of an evaluation in talents that is not followed by drachmas is extremely unlikely in the case of pepper. Granted, we have an evaluation in talents at col. iii, l. 3, for Gangetic nard. But, with a price per container of three-fourths of a talent, there is one chance in four that the resulting value of a cargo of nard would be a whole unfractionated number of talents. Whether measured by containers or by weight, the price of pepper per unit would be a

[9] On the left of 'Δ there are slight traces of ink, which Morelli takes as the remnants of the sign for drachmas.

fraction of a talent with a denominator much higher than four; we will see in fact that it is $\frac{1}{1000}$ of a talent per mina. To have the total value of a pepper cargo expressed with a whole sum of talents with no drachmas attached (although not impossible) would be a remarkable coincidence.

It is also unlikely that the clerk—being unable to squeeze the total value resulting from his calculation into col. ii, l. 25—would decide to write the number of drachmas at the beginning of the following line—and then start a new topic on the same line. Elsewhere in the papyrus, the clerk took care to render the sums of money clearly, either by placing them at the end of a line or by leaving blank spaces before and after them.[10] In col. ii, it seems very likely that he decided to leave the rest of l. 26 blank in order to add, just under *ἀργ(υρίου) (τάλαντα) ψοα* in l. 25, the number of drachmas that went with the 771 talents of money (especially since, in this context, a number like 4,632 can hardly refer to anything other than drachmas).

All this justifies the conclusion, independently drawn by both Morelli and me, that the numbers in ll. 25–6 are a single sum—771 talents and 4,632 drachmas, corresponding to about 66.9 per cent of the total value at col. iii, l. 29—and that this sum refers to the primary commodity from Muziris, pepper.

How much pepper corresponded to 771 talents and 4,632 drachmas? In other words, what was the value of a mina of pepper? Both Morelli and I connect the sum of money in col. ii, ll. 25–6 to the weight number at col. ii, l. 21, but in different ways. By reading the weight at l. 21 as 3,215 talents and 43 minas, Morelli assumes that the amount of money at ll. 25–6 results from the weight at l. 21 being assessed at the price of 24 drachmas per mina. In effect, the sum of money would be a multiple of 24 drachmas, and 3,215 talents and 43 minas × 24 drachmas equals exactly 771 talents of money and 4,632 drachmas. Morelli also pointed out that 24 drachmas per mina is approximately the price for black pepper given by Pliny the Elder.[11]

Straightforward as it seems, this conclusion is far from indisputable. To begin with, Pliny's price, which was most probably the retail price in Rome,[12] would argue against a fiscal value as high as 24 drachmas in Alexandria, or would lead one to postulate a dramatic price rise between the mid-first and the mid-second century AD. Neither of these scenarios seems very likely. But even more crucial is the most obvious and puzzling problem: between the weight number at col. ii, l. 21 and its value at col. ii, ll. 25–6, there are three lines (22–4) with no numbers at the end. If 771 talents and 4,632 drachmas directly resulted from the weight number at l. 21 multiplied by the price per unit, we would expect to find the result of that calculation in l. 22, not three lines later. In all

[10] In col. iii, the monetary values tend to occupy the end of the lines (ll. 10, 14, 15, 21, 24, 25, 26, 29), or in one case, the centre of the line, flanked by blank spaces (l. 3).

[11] Morelli (2011: 212; 222–225); Pliny's price in *NH* 12.28.

[12] Plin., *NH* 33.164.

likelihood, the weight number and price per unit that determined the sum in ll. 25–6 were in the missing part of l. 25. They took up so much space that the clerk was compelled to write the resulting monetary value partly at l. 25 (the number of talents), and partly at l. 26 (the number of drachmas). It is extremely unlikely that l. 21 and l. 25 recorded exactly the same weight number.

Still, I do not think that the remnants of col. ii allow nothing more than guesswork.[13] The reasonable assumption that the weights at col. ii, l. 20 and 21 (the heaviest recorded in the text) and the money value at col. ii, ll. 25–6 (roughly two-thirds of the total recorded at col. iii, l. 29) relate to each other offers a solid base for a logical inference about the size of the pepper cargo and its fiscal value. Morelli was certainly right to try to connect the weight number of l. 21 and the money value of ll. 25–6, but I disagree with his denial that the evaluation of the three-quarter portion of pepper paralleled the evaluations of sound ivory and *schidai*.[14] Quite the opposite: the three-line gap between the weight of l. 21 and the sum of money of ll. 25–6 supports the idea that pepper was evaluated more or less in the same way as sound ivory and *schidai*. The weight number at l. 20 would represent the three-quarter portion of the pepper cargo before the arabarchs' additional share was deducted. The weight in l. 21 would be for the three-quarter portion that remained after the deduction. The same weight would have appeared in the missing part of l. 25, recalculated using a different standard. The relative clause beginning at l. 22 (ἐξ ὧν 'from which') would introduce the recalculation of the weight of pepper recorded at l. 21.[15] The number in l. 27 would convey the weight of pepper in the arabarchs' additional share, which would then be monetarily assessed at ll. 28–9. The last line of the column (l. 30) would have recorded the total monetary value of the three-quarter portion of the pepper cargo.

If this interpretation is correct (and we will show that col. ii, ll. 1–3 and 27 strongly suggest it is), the price of pepper could not be 24 drachmas per mina. In fact, while the subtotal of the evaluations at col. ii must be 1,021 talents, 694 drachmas, *and 3 obols*, the 3 obols do not appear at the end of the sums of money recorded at col. ii, ll. 16 and 25–6, and cannot be restored at the end of l. 19.[16] It is therefore clear that the 3 obols belonged with the sum of money recorded at col. ii, l. 29 (and at col. ii, l. 30, as a result of the sum of the values at ll. 25–6 and 29). But with a price for pepper of 24 drachmas per mina, a weight number ending with a quarter of a mina (44¼ minas) would

[13] Evers (2017: 107).

[14] Morelli (2011: 224–5). The arabarchs' additional shares were surcharges arithmetically determined: see pp. 227; 281.

[15] Cf. col. iii, l. 8 ἐξ ὧν αἱρεῖ κτλ.

[16] We will see (p. 247) that the price of the item evaluated at col. ii, ll. 17–19 is 12 drachmas per mina, so that no sum of money ending with three obols can be obtained from a weight number ending with three-quarters of a mina (l. 18).

have produced a sum ending with a round number of drachmas, no obols required. In col. iii, a money value ending with three obols (ll. 24; 25) is generated by a price with an even number of drachmas that is *not* a multiple of four (70 drachmas per mina: ll. 20; 24). Similarly, in col. ii, l. 29 only a price per mina with an even number of drachmas not in a multiple of four (2, 6, 10, 14, and so on) would produce a sum of money ending with 3 obols.

In conclusion, while the sum of 771 talents and 4,632 drachmas (col. ii, ll. 25–6) was generated by a submultiple of 24 as the price in drachmas per mina, the sum of money lost at col. ii, l. 29 was generated by an even number that was not a multiple of 4. Since a price of 2 drachmas per mina would give a result that does not match the remnants of the weight numbers at ll. 20–1 (and moreover would mean an impossibly huge cargo of more than 1,600 tons), a price of 6 drachmas per mina *is the only option.*

This result is further confirmed by the other data that can be read in col. ii. Only a fiscal price of 6 drachmas per mina can account for both the structure of col. ii, ll. 1–3, 20–30 and the readable weight numbers in those lines. We will see that a price of 6 drachmas leads to a satisfactory restoration of the weight number at col. ii, l. 21, thus accounting for the three-line gap between the weight number and the monetary value. In turn, and most significantly, the restored number at l. 21 sheds light on the otherwise enigmatic sequence of weight numbers at col. ii, ll. 1–3.[17] Thus, there can be no doubt that pepper is the commodity whose three-quarter portion was evaluated at col. ii, ll. 20–30, and a price of 6 drachmas per mina is consistent with all the other remnants of numbers at col. ii, ll. 1–3; 20–8.

A value of 6 drachmas per mina may seem considerably lower than the price of 4 denarii per pound (= 25.33 drachmas per mina) recorded by Pliny. But, as noted, Pliny refers to retail prices in Rome; and, even more important, the monetary values recorded on the Muziris papyrus were not market prices.[18] They were values fixed by the imperial administration to offset the financial burden brought on by the Red Sea tax double customs duties (which, we will see, amounted to a rate of 43.75 per cent). The Muziris papyrus values reflect not the dynamics of the Alexandrian market, but rather the fiscal policies of the imperial administration.

If the price per mina was 6 drachmas, the weight number missing at col. ii, l. 25 was 12,862 talents 52 minas. On this basis, we can restore the weight number at col. ii, l. 21 and reconstruct the entire process that led from that weight to the monetary value in ll. 25–6. Consider the following conditions: the weight at col. ii, l. 21, measured with the official talent of 95 pounds, was 1] 3,200 + x talents and y minas; this weight was recalculated with a heavier

[17] The attempts at explanation by Morelli (2011: 226–7) are at odds with the remnants of ll. 20–8.

[18] See pp. 291–4. The point is missed by Mayer (2018: 575, n. 36).

Table 10.4 Hypotheses of the pepper weight number before recalculation.

Weight after recalculation (col. ii, l. 25)	Recalculation talent	Weight with 95 lb. talent (col. ii, l. 21)
12,862 talents 52 minas	97 lb. 6 oz.	13,201 talents 22 minas
	97 lb. 7 oz.	13,212 talents 12 minas
	97 lb. 8 oz.	13,223 talents 2 minas
	97 lb. 9 oz.	13,235 talents 13 minas
	97 lb. 10 oz.	13,246 talents 3 minas
	97 lb. 11 oz.	13,258 talents 14 minas
	98 lb.	13,269 talents 4 minas
	98 lb. 1 oz.	13,279 talents 54 minas
	98 lb. 2 oz.	13,290 talents 44 minas

talent, calibrated on one using whole numbers of Roman pounds and ounces; the result of the recalculation was 12,862 talents and 52 minas (the missing weight number to be restored at col. ii, l. 25). If these conditions are accurate, then the weight in l. 21 should be one of those indicated in Table 10.4.

Considering what remains visible at col. ii, l. 21 (Fig. 10.2), we can draw the following conclusions:

1. The correct reading at l. 21 is 1]3,223 [talents of weight] and 2̣ minas. Such a reading is compatible with the remnants of the entry: I take the long horizontal stroke and the oblique stroke located after the supposed ϵ as γ.[19] Between the supposed ϵ and what I perceive as the oblique stroke of the γ, I cannot see any sign of—or even sufficient space for—the mina symbol. In my opinion, the symbol for mina is after—not before—the oblique stroke of the γ. The γ, therefore, must be the last digit (3) of the number of talents. The preceding digit, situated between the hundreds (σ) and the units (γ) positions cannot be a 5 (ϵ), as read by the first editors. It must be a multiple of ten, very likely 20 (κ). Under the horizontal stroke and on the right side of the oblique stroke of the γ, I read the symbol for mina, followed by the remnants of a letter compatible with β. My reading for what remains of l. 21 is thus:]’*Γσκγ μν(ῶν) β̣*. The entire line should be restored as follows: [*ὧν ὁμοίως τιμὴ λογίζεται ὁλκ(ῆς) μὲν (ταλάντων) μ(υριάδος) α*] *’Γσκγ μν(ῶν) β̣* (of which likewise the price is reckoned thus: Of the 13,223 talents of weight 2 minas).

[19] Of course, the γ is a little further from the κ and its horizontal stroke extends longer than the usual pattern. I surmise that the clerk, thinking he had to write only 13,323 talents of weight, filled the blank space up to the end of the line with a long stroke, exactly as he does with the υ at col. iii, l. 28. Subsequently, having realized that 2 minas had to be added, he wrote *μν(αῖ) β* under the horizontal stroke of the γ.

Fig. 10.2 *P.Vindob.* G 40822 verso col. ii, ll. 20–21.
P.Vindob. G 40822. Austrian National Library. http://data.onb.ac.at/rec/RZ00001642.

2. The weight of 13,223 talents and 2 minas, first measured using a talent standard of 95 pounds, was then arithmetically recalculated with a talent standard of 97.66 pounds (97 pounds and 8 ounces) through the simple equivalence of 1,028 talents (of 95 pounds) = 1,000 talents (of 97.66 pounds).[20]

The actual weight of the three-quarter portion of the *Hermapollon*'s pepper cargo was recorded at col. ii, l. 20, where Morelli reads either]'*Γ*τ̣η (3,308) or]'*Γ*τ̣ι̣ε̣ (3,315). In a previous paper, I had accepted the first reading,[21] but now, it seems preferable to me to read]'*Γ*φ̣[, (]3,500), and restore μ(υριάδος) α]'*Γ*φ̣[(13,5??).

In order to proceed further with the reconstruction of the monetary evaluation of the three-quarter portion of the pepper cargo, we need to consider col. ii, ll. 1–3:

1 - - -] μν(αῖ) νθ
2 - - -] μν(αῖ) ι̣δ L´δ´
3 - - -]. μν(αῖ) νη

1 . . .] minas 59
2 . . .] minas 14.75
3 . . .] minas 58

As we said, Morelli ascertained not only that ll. 4–13 in col. ii deal with the same commodities evaluated in col. iii, ll. 1–25, but also that they deal with

[20] I wonder whether at col. ii, ll. 22–3 something could be restored like τῶν σταθμῶν ἐνδεόντων ὡς τῶν (ταλάντων) 'Α (ταλάντων)]κ[η] ἐξ ὧν̣ ἀ̣ν̣τ̣ι̣|λημματίζονται ὁλκ(ῆς)(τάλαντα) τξ μν(αῖ) ι—]ται η . . . υ( ).
[21] De Romanis (2011 [2012]: 83; 99).

them in exactly the same order: Gangetic nard (col. ii, l. 4; col. iii, ll. 1–3), sound ivory tusks (col. ii, ll. 5–9; col. iii, ll. 4–15), and *schidai* (col. ii, ll. 10–13; col. iii, ll. 16–25). Since the evaluation of the three-quarter portion of the pepper cargo began at col. ii, l. 20 and continued to the end of the column, the evaluation of Gangetic nard must have been the next item recorded, immediately following the pepper. Such a conclusion strongly suggests that the whole sequence of weight numbers at col. ii, ll. 1–3 relates to the pepper cargo. In other words, just as the monetary evaluation of the Gangetic nard cargo (col. iii, ll. 1–3) followed that of pepper (col. ii, ll. 20–30), the data on the nard (col. ii, l. 4) must have immediately followed the data on the pepper (l. 1–3).

Building on these assumptions, we can attempt to explain the data in col. ii, ll. 1–3. The remaining figures for the three weight values at col. ii, ll. 1, 2, and 3 (59 minas, 14¾ minas, and 58 minas) confirm a connection to the weights we reconstructed at col. ii, ll. 21 and 27. In particular, the 44¼ minas of col. ii, l. 27 is equal to three-quarters of the 59 minas at col. ii, l. 1, while the 14¾ minas of col. ii, l. 2 must be the remaining quarter. Even more significant, however, is the 58 minas of col. ii, l. 3.

I suggest reading col. ii, ll. 1–3 as follows:

1. The weight of l. 1 (**x** talents + 59 minas) is the quantity corresponding to the sum of the base quarter rate plus the arabarchs' additional share;
2. The weight of l. 2 (**y** talents + 14¾ minas) is the quantity corresponding to the base quarter rate;
3. The weight of l. 3 (**z** talents + 58 minas) is the quantity corresponding to a further deduction. We will see that the weights of the three-quarter portions of the three cargo items evaluated at col. ii, ll. 14–30 undergo an alteration (more specifically, a reduction) that is distinct from the subtraction of the additional share taken by the arabarchs.

As mentioned, a base quarter rate ending with 14¾ minas must come from a total quantity ending with 59 minas; the remaining three-quarters must be a quantity ending with 44¼ minas. Recalling the 1]3,5?? talents of weight to be restored at col. ii, l. 20, we may therefore conclude that:

1. three-quarters of the pepper cargo amounted to 13,500 + 3x talents and 44¼ minas;
2. the base quarter rate of the pepper cargo amounted to 4,500 + x talents and 14¾ minas; and
3. the entire pepper cargo was 18,000 + 4x talents and 59 minas.

Because the weight number of the total quantity of pepper ended with 59 minas, and because the sum of all the deductions (the base quarter rate, the arabarchs' share, and the further deduction) amounted to a weight number ending with 57 minas,[22] one can confirm that the weight number at col. ii, l. 21 ends with 2 minas, giving additional—indeed decisive—support to the reading of the weight at col. ii, l. 21 as 1]3,223 talents and 2 minas.

To sum up, the entire process of evaluating the three-quarter portion of the pepper cargo carried on the *Hermapollon* may be reconstructed as follows (Fig. 10.3):

1. From the weight specified at col. ii, l. 20 (13,500 + [3 x talents and 44 ¼ minas], measured with the official talent of 95 pounds), two different amounts (one of which is the arabarchs' additional share) are deducted.
2. What remains, 13,223 talents and 2 minas, is then recalculated using a weight talent of 97.66 pounds. In practice, for every 1,028 official talents, only 1,000 are counted. The result is 12,862 talents and 52 minas.
3. This result is multiplied by 6 drachmas per mina (360 drachmas per talent of weight), now equalling 771 talents and 4,632 drachmas.
4. The quantity corresponding to the arabarchs' additional share is also multiplied by 6 drachmas per mina. The result is a sum of money ending with 5 drachmas and 3 obols.
5. The sum of 771 talents and 4,632 drachmas is added to the monetary evaluation of the arabarchs' additional share.

It is worth emphasizing that the three-quarter portion of the pepper cargo is evaluated in much (but not exactly) the same way as the three-quarter portions of the sound ivory and *schidai* cargoes. Two differences stand out: first, the pepper cargo undergoes not one but two reductions in weight;

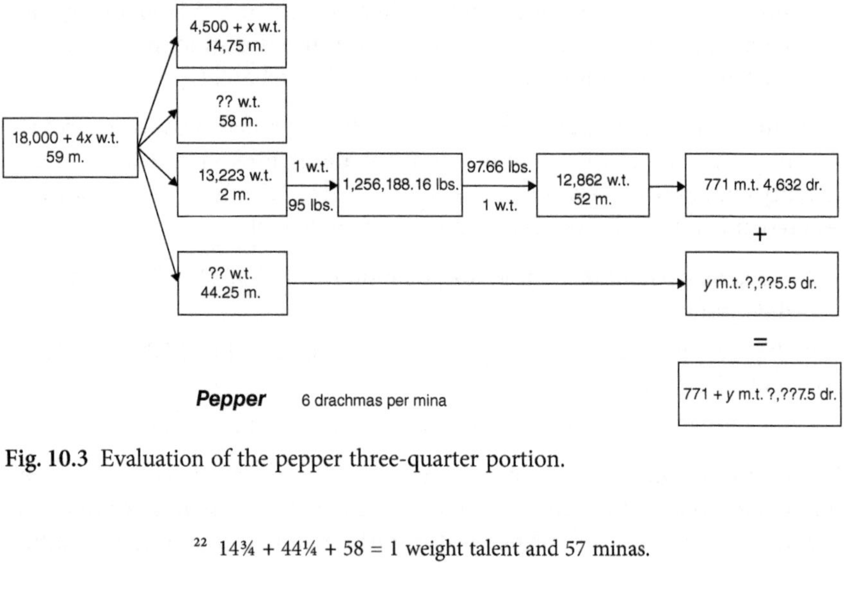

Fig. 10.3 Evaluation of the pepper three-quarter portion.

[22] 14¾ + 44¼ + 58 = 1 weight talent and 57 minas.

second, the remaining weight is recalculated using a talent not of 97.5, but of 97.66 lbs. Therefore, if for sound ivory and *schidai* the value equation was:

$$V = \left\{ [(\frac{3}{4}a - b) \times \frac{95}{97.5}] \times c \right\} + (b \times c),$$

where a is the weight number of the cargo measured with a talent of 95 Roman pounds, b the arabarchs' additional share, c the price per weight unit, and V the resulting value of the item, the same equation for pepper will be:

$$V = \left\{ [(\frac{3}{4}a - b - d) \times \frac{95}{97.66}] \times c \right\} + (b \times c).$$

The reasons for the second deduction (*d*) will be discussed in chapter twelve.

10.3. TORTOISE SHELL (?) AND MALABATHRON: COL. II, LL. 14–19

Incorporating the calculations so far discussed, the values of the three-quarter portions of known and unknown items may be reconstructed as shown in Table 10.5.

The remaining item(s) was (were) evaluated at col. ii, ll. 14–19:[23]

14 - - -μν(ῶν)] λα̣ L´
15 - - -]. . κ̣α
16 - - -]η
17 - - -] [- - -μν(ῶν)]. δ´
18 - - - ὁλκ(ῆς)(ταλάντων)] ᾿Αωξ̣ [? μν(ῶν) ??] Ḷ´δ´
19 - - - ἀργ](υρίου) (τάλαντα) σ̣κ[- - -

14 . . .] 31 ½ [minas]
15 . . .] 21
16 . . .] 8
17 . . .] ¼ [minas]
18 . . .] 1,86̣? [talents of weight ??] ½ ¼ [minas]
19 . . .] 2̣2? talents of money . . .

As mentioned, the fractions at col. ii, ll. 14, 17, and 18 make it clear that a weight number ending with fractions of minas was at the end of each line. On the other hand, the currency symbol for talent at col. ii, l. 19 shows that at the

[23] The fragment with ll. 17–20 was positioned upside-down at the time of publication: see Morelli (2011: 207, n. 24).

Table 10.5 Values of the six cargoes' three-quarter portions.

Items	Value of the three-quarter portion
Pepper[1]	771 talents 4,632 drachmas
Pepper[2]	? talents ?,??5.5 drachmas
Gangetic nard	45 talents
Sound ivory	76 talents 5,275 drachmas
Schidai	8 talents 5,882.5 drachmas
Missing item(s)	≤ 249 talents ?,??7 drachmas
Total	1,151 talents 5,852 drachmas

end of this line was the monetary evaluation of the item whose weight was specified at the end of l. 18.

We can eliminate the idea that ll. 14–19 in col. ii concern one item that was assessed with the same procedures used for the other commodities so far examined. The two weight numbers at the ends of ll. 17 and 18 are inconsistent with those modi operandi. The most satisfactory explanation for what remains in ll. 14–19 is that *two* items are evaluated, both measured by weight: 'missing item **a**' is evaluated in ll. 14–16, and 'missing item **b**' in ll. 17–19. It appears that the evaluation of these two items was done with a procedure that differed from those used for Gangetic nard and for pepper, sound ivory, and *schidai*. It diverges from the nard calculations because the items are measured by weight, and also because the weight numbers of their three-quarter portions, which were apparently recorded at ll. 14 and 17, undergo an adjustment resulting in the weights given at ll. 15 (κα is the number of minas) and 18. Likewise, it differs from that of the pepper, sound ivory, and *schidai* calculations, as it does not include the arithmetic manoeuvres either for the arabarchs' additional share or for the recalculation of weight using a heavier talent. After the adjustment, the weight numbers are immediately multiplied by their respective prices per unit, leading to the amounts of money recorded at ll. 16 and 19. Building on these premises, the remnants of col. ii, ll. 14–19 show the following:

1. The unadjusted weight number of item **a** ends with 31.5 minas (l. 14).
2. The adjusted weight number of item **a** ends with ̣21 minas (l. 15).
3. The monetary value of item **a** includes a number of drachmas ending with the digit 8 (l. 16).
4. The adjusted weight number of item **b** is 1,860 + x talents and y + 0.75 minas (l. 18).
5. The monetary value of item **b** is 220 + z talents (l. 19).

From these clues, we deduce the following:

1. The price per mina of item **a** was a number of drachmas ending with the digit 8.

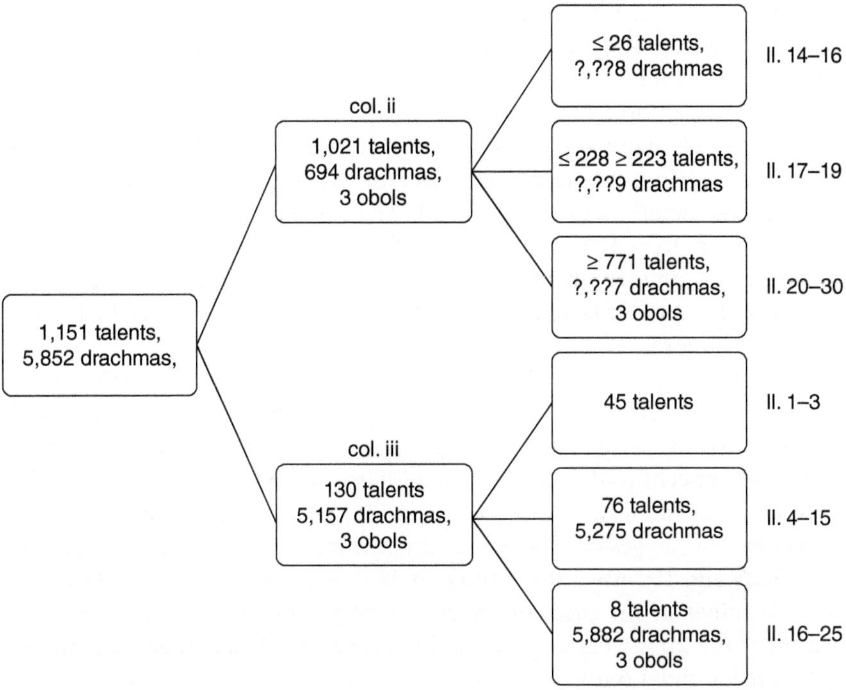

Fig. 10.4 Values of the *Hermapollon* cargo's three-quarter portions.

2. The monetary valuation of item **b** included a number of drachmas ending with the digit 9.
3. The price per mina of item **b** cannot be more than 12.36 or less than 11.76 drachmas.[24]

In turn, we may infer the following:

1. The price per mina of item **b** was 12 drachmas.
2. The monetary valuation of item **b** was somewhere between 223 and 228 talents.[25]
3. The monetary valuation of item **a** was no greater than 26 talents (Fig. 10.4).[26]

Since the price per mina of item **a** is a number of drachmas ending with the digit 8, it is likely that the price was less than 100 drachmas. Given the

[24] The higher limit is obtained assuming that 229 talents and 5,999 drachmas (the highest possible monetary value) was the value of 1,860 talents and 0.75 mina (the lowest possible weight number); the lower limit assumes that 220 talents and 9 drachmas (lowest possible monetary value) was the value of 1,869 talents and 59.75 minas (the highest possible weight number).

[25] The first sum results from 1,860, the second from 1,899 talents of weight.

[26] The lowest possible monetary value cannot be established, since we ignore the exact value of the pepper taken by the tax collectors on top of the quarter-tax (col. ii, ll. 27 ff.).

tendency to assume simple fractions of a talent as prices per unit (container or mina),[27] we may suggest that the price of item **a** was either 18, 48, or 78 drachmas per mina.[28]

If item **a** needs to be identified as one of the Limyrike exports listed in the *Periplus*,[29] not many suitable candidates are at hand. Along with pepper, malabathron, Gangetic nard, and ivory, the *Periplus* lists silk, pearl, translucent stones, jacinth, and tortoise shell. The three-quarter portion of item **a** weighed more than 31.5 minas (*c.*16 kg)[30] and its fiscal value was less than 27 talents. In my opinion, this precludes the identification of item **a** as silk, pearl, translucent stones, or jacinth—all of which would have either weighed less or been worth more.

By contrast, tortoise shell is a plausible option.[31] Since in Diocletian's Edict on Maximum Prices, the price of tortoise shell (100 denarii per pound) is two-thirds the price of ivory (150 per pound),[32] a price of 48 drachmas per mina (48 per cent of the value of sound ivory and 68.5 per cent of the value of *schidai*) or of 78 drachmas per mina (78 per cent of the value of sound ivory) can be suggested. Therefore, the maximum weight figures would be 54 talents and 10 minas at the price of 48 drachmas per mina, or 33 talents and 20 minas at the price of 78 drachmas per mina. In other words, the weight of the three-quarter portion of the cargo would have been somewhere between 1.1 and 1.6 tons.[33]

Both the weight and the value of its three-quarter portion qualify item **b** as the second major item in the *Hermapollon*'s cargo. When compared to the weights of the two main cargoes (pepper $\geq$ 18,000 talents, item **b** $\geq$ 2,480 talents), the weights of sound ivory (105 talents 13 minas) and *schidai* (17 talents 33 minas) appear negligible. The ratio between the weight of item **b**

[27] It is ¾ of a money talent per Gangetic nard container; $\frac{1}{60}$ of a money talent per mina of sound ivory; $\frac{1}{100}+\frac{1}{600}$ of a money talent per mina of *schidai*; $\frac{1}{1000}$ of a money talent per mina of pepper; and $\frac{1}{500}$ of a money talent per mina of item **b**.

[28] That is, $\frac{3}{1000}$, $\frac{8}{1000}$, and $\frac{13}{1000}$ of a talent, respectively.

[29] However, the possibility that item **a** is a commodity taken aboard in Socotra or South Arabia during the return voyage (see p. 146, n.120) cannot be excluded.

[30] Col. ii, l. 15.

[31] The tortoise shell sold in Limyrike came from Chryse Island (Malay peninsula? Sumatra?), as well as the Lakshadweep islands: *PME* 56; 63. The *Periplus* also records tortoise shell as available at Ptolemais *ton theron* (3), Alalaiu Islands (4), Adulis (6), Aualites (7), Mundu (10), Tabai (13), Menuthias (15), Rhapta (16;17), Dioscurides Island (30; 31), Sarapis Island (33), and Taprobane (61).

[32] *Edictum de pretiis* 16.10–1. However, one must note that while black pepper has a much lower value (6 drachmas per mina) than both sound ivory (100 drachmas per mina) and *schidai* (70 drachmas per mina) in the Muziris papyrus, its maximum price in Diocletian's edict (34.68) is much higher (800 denarii per pound) than that of the ivory.

[33] The number of shells should have been between a little less than 2,000 and a little less than 1,000.

Table 10.6 Quantities and values of the six cargoes.

Item	Quantity	Value of the cargo
Gangetic nard	80 containers	60 tal.
sound ivory	105 tal. 13 m. (3.2 t)	105 tal. 1,300 dr.
schidai	17 tal., 33 m. (0.53 t)	12 tal. 1,710 dr.
tortoise shell?	> 72 tal.? > 44 tal.? (> 2.2 t? 1.35 t?)	*c.*34 tal.?
malabathron	≥ 2,480 tal. (≥ 76 t)	≥ 297 tal. 3,600 dr.
pepper	≥ 18,000 tal. 59 m. (≥ 552.3 t)	≥ 1,080 tal. 354 dr.
Total	> 20,603 tal. 45 m. (> 632.2 t)	> 1,555 tal. 964 dr.

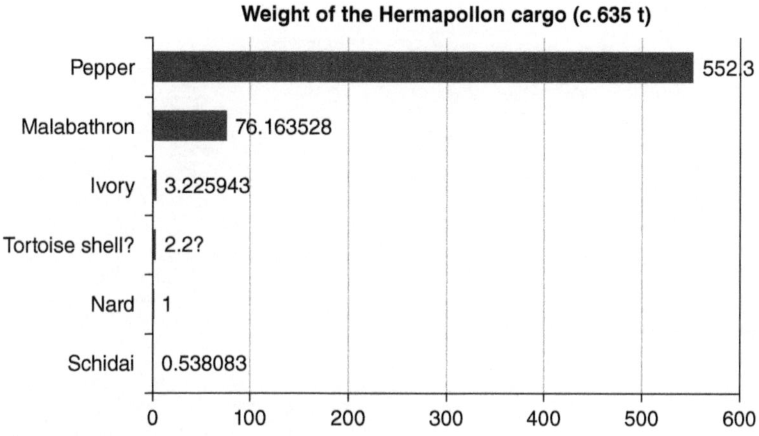

Fig. 10.5 Weight of the *Hermapollon*'s cargo.

and that of the pepper cargo was approximately 1 : 7.25. The ratio between the fiscal values of the two commodities (12 versus 6 drachmas per mina) is 2 : 1.

The eighty containers of Gangetic nard in the *Hermapollon*'s cargo are a testament to the persistence, in the second century AD, of trade relations between the Ganges Valley (whence malabathron was exported) and Limyrike.[34] At the time of the *Periplus*, the ships that sailed the South India sea route were 'very large vessels for the volume and quantity of the pepper and the malabathron'.[35] Pliny the Elder fixes 4 denarii per pound as the price of black pepper, and 60 denarii per pound as the price for malabathron leaves.[36] In Oxyrhynchus, between AD 310/311 and 329, the price ratio

[34] *PME* 56; 63; 64. [35] *PME* 56. See pp. 138–41.

[36] Plin., *NH* 12.129. On the other hand, the price of malabathron oil fluctuated between 1 and 300 denarii per pound.

between malabathron and pepper fluctuates between 1 : 1, 2 : 1, and 50 : 12.[37] The identification of item **b** with malabathron may be considered certain.[38] Quantities and values of the *Hermapollon*'s six cargoes are detailed and represented in Table 10.6 and Fig. 10.5.

[37] *P.Oxy.* 54.3731; 3733; 3766.

[38] *Pace* Evers (2017: 107). Morelli (2011: 226) hesitates to attribute to malabathron the weight and the sum at col. ii, ll. 18 and 19 because the inferable fiscal value would be lower than 24 drachmas per mina, which he assumes as the value for pepper.

11

Contrasts

The reconstruction of the *Hermapollon*'s cargo allows for three pertinent comparisons. The first comparison concerns the size of both the ship and its pepper cargo, and the relationship of ship size and cargo to both the production output of the region from which the spice was exported and the sea route by which it was transported.[1] The pepper trade took different forms over time, and the pattern detailed by the Muziris papyrus proves to be unique in the long history of the South Indian pepper trade. In all likelihood, the Late Antique replacement of Kottanarike with Male as the source of supply and the shift from direct voyages to multi-stage sea routes meant a reduction in both the trade volume and in vessel size. Even if no evidence is available to clarify the size of the ships that exported pepper from the Mangalore region in Late Antiquity and the Middle Ages, it is unlikely that they were larger than the 1,000- to 1,200-*bahar* (*c.*166–200 tons) ships that transferred spices from Calicut to Aden or Jeddah before the arrival of the Portuguese.[2] By contrast, when the Cochin hinterland (roughly corresponding to ancient Kottanarike) started supplying the West with pepper in the Early Modern age, the Portuguese ships of the *Carreira da Índia* eventually equalled the ancient pepper carriers in size (although the challenges of rounding the Cape of Good Hope soon discouraged the use of vessels as large as the *Hermapollon*). Furthermore, during the sixteenth century, another form of pepper trade thrived. In competition with the struggling Cape route, and often in defiance of the Portuguese monopoly, the multi-stage Red Sea route was revived by medium-sized ships and very small *paraos* that crossed the Arabian Sea from India to Arabia, but did not return home.

The second comparison is betweeen the *Hermapollon*'s entire cargo and the *Periplus*' list of commodities available in Limyrike's emporia. In the *Periplus*, pearls stand out for their quantity and quality; a variety of translucent stones, diamonds, and jacinth are also mentioned.[3] Pearls and precious stones also appear on a list of eastern commodities subject to the *vectigal*,

[1] On the preconditions of a large-size-vessel-based trade, cf. the sensitive remarks of Tchernia (2011: 86–7).

[2] Barbosa, 160–1 (Engl. transl. 2.76–7).

[3] *PME* 56.

The Indo-Roman Pepper Trade and the Muziris Papyrus. Federico De Romanis, Oxford University Press (2020).
 DOI: 10.1093/oso/9780198842347.001.0001

which was attached to a rescript of Marcus Aurelius and Commodus.[4] Quite remarkably, none of these items can be identified with any of the commodities evaluated on the Muziris papyrus verso. The question arises whether this discrepancy can be ascribed to a change in the South India trade between the mid-first and mid-second centuries AD or to an incomplete tax declaration, (fraudulently?) omitting high-value and easy-to-hide commodities.

Finally, the third comparison concerns the size of the elephant tusks. When compared with the average weight of certain sixteenth-century East African cargoes, the average weight of the *Hermapollon* tusks reveals the overall fine quality of the batch as well as the distinctiveness of the human–elephant relationship in India compared to East Africa.

11.1. ANCIENT AND EARLY MODERN PEPPER CARRIERS

The *Hermapollon* and its more than 635-ton cargo (roughly 552 tons of which were pepper) are typical of a trade pattern that started in the Augustan age, when Berenice—the former port of the Ptolemaic elephant carriers—flourished once again as the home port of the gigantic pepper carriers. In the years during which South Indian black pepper was consumed in the Roman camp of Oberaden (Germany), the Alexandrian ship industry gave an impressive demonstration of its know-how in terms of large-tonnage ships. Around 10 BC, a vessel ironically called the *Acatus* managed to convey the Circus Maximus obelisk (263 tons, now in Piazzale Flaminio) to Italy,[5] together with 1,200 passengers and a cargo that—in addition to traditional Alexandrian exports like grain, linen, paper, and glass—significantly included pepper.[6]

Remarkable as it was (Augustus put it on display at Puteoli, until a fire destroyed it),[7] the *Acatus* was not an isolated experiment with no connection to the merchant ships of its own time or later. On the contrary, that exceptionally large ship was typical of a context—that of Alexandria—in which the mercantile community did not hesitate to exploit the skills of their naval architects whenever conditions allowed. For more than a couple of centuries, the shipbuilding industry that designed the prodigious obelisk-carrier also constructed both the large grain carriers (*sitegoi*) that transferred the Egyptian

[4] Marcian., *Dig.* 39.4.16.7.

[5] Chron. Min. 1.145 Mommsen. The number of *modii* of grain (400) is probably corrupt. Cf. Felici (2017: 8–11).

[6] For the export of linen, paper, and glass from late Ptolemaic Alexandria: Cic., *Rab. Post.* 40.

[7] Plin., *NH* 37.69–70.

public grain to Rome and the very large pepper carriers for the South India trade.[8] Of course, the grain-carriers of the Mediterranean were far more numerous than the pepper-carriers of the Indian Ocean, but it is nonetheless noteworthy that both the importation of pepper and the transfer of Egyptian public grain required comparable types of ships.[9] Besides, if Gades' very large ships are brought into the picture,[10] the use of very large vessels to ply long-distance routes in the Mediterranean Sea and in the Indian and Atlantic Oceans emerges as a distinctive characteristic of Roman trade in the Augustan age.

Apart from the tale about monkeys as pepper collectors,[11] Philostratus' acquaintance with the South India traders is revealed in another passage of the *Life of Apollonius*. Quite interestingly, the passage is based on an allegory suggested by the Indian sage Iarchas, who is himself presented as being familiar with the Egyptian traders visiting India.[12] Iarchas finds no better way to expound on his conception of the universe than by resorting to a simile using the 'ship, such as the Egyptians construct for our seas and launch for the exchange of Egyptian goods against Indian wares':

> There is an old rule of the Red Sea, which king Erythras once laid down when he ruled that sea, that Egyptians may not enter in a warship, but instead must use a single round-bottomed vessel. So the Egyptians construct a ship equivalent to many of those used by others (*σοφίζονται πλοῖον Αἰγύπτιοι πρὸς πολλὰ τῶν παρ' ἑτέροις*). They seal it with all the joints that hold a ship together, and over these they build hulls and a mast, and make numerous cabins such as those over the benches. There are many captains of this ship, sailing under the command of the eldest and most skilful among them, and many steersmen at the stern, and excellent, nimble sailors who eagerly tend the sails. This ship also carries armed men, since the barbarians of the gulf live on the right side of its entrance, and the ship must do battle with them when they attack and try to plunder it.[13]

Here again, fictional elements intermingle with the realities of the India trade. Iarchas' explanation for the Egyptian use of this kind of ship is clearly fantastical (the king Erythras is a mythical figure, and his law is a product of fantasy). It may be wondered whether Erythras' demand that they use a single ship reflects the declining conditions of direct trade with South India at the beginning of the third century AD. It may also be wondered whether the location of the pirates implies a new geographical setting for either the Indian pirates or the pepper-trade centres.[14] But the description of the ship and its

[8] On large tonnage vessels, cf. Pomey and Tchernia (1978); Tchernia (2011); Nantet (2016: 144–9).

[9] In terms of tonnage, the *Hermapollon* may be compared with the Ostia ship of 22.500-artaba tonnage in *P.Bingen* 77, ll. 9–10: Heilporn (2000: 352–3).

[10] Strab. 3.5.3: *τὰ πλεῖστα καὶ μέγιστα ναυκλήρια*. Cf. Shaw (2006: 26).

[11] See pp. 113–4.

[12] Philostr., *VA* 3.25.

[13] Philostr., *VA* 3.35; transl. by C. P. Jones.

[14] While the *Periplus* refers to pirates occupying islands and places north of Muziris (*PME* 53: see p. 77), Philostratus refers to pirates who are 'on the right' of those who navigate outward

crew is definitely based on reality, as is the notation about the size of the vessel, equivalent to that of several normal ships combined. This recommends the identification of its type with that of the very large ships bound for South India mentioned in the *Periplus*.[15] The verso of the Muziris papyrus shows that these ships could accommodate a cargo of 635 tons.[16]

When the *Hermapollon*'s pepper cargo is compared with estimates or with partial data on the productive capacity of the Cochin region in Early Modern times (Fig. 11.1), it becomes clear that Strabo's number of 120 for ships leaving for India from Myos Hormos refers to much smaller vessels and a very different pattern of trade.[17] Even allowing for cargoes with a smaller proportion of pepper (plausible when silk was also included), eight or nine ships like the *Hermapollon* would have sufficed to export the *c*.4,500 tons that can be inferred as

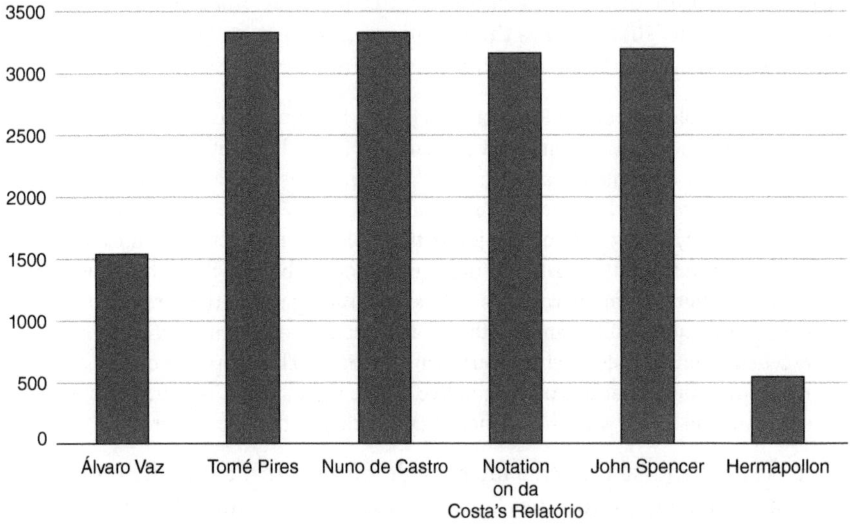

Fig. 11.1 South Malabar's pepper productivity (Early Modern estimates or partial data) and the *Hermapollon*'s pepper cargo (in tons).

(*οἳ ἐν δεξιᾳ̂ τοῦ ἔσπλου κεῖνται*): if he alludes to Indian pirates, they were located south of the emporia for which the merchants were bound.

[15] See p. 138–9.

[16] Evers' (2017: 107) scepticism, as well as his contention that the preferred size of the pepper carriers was around 340 tons cargo capacity (2017: 108), are unwarranted, especially when one postulates, as Evers does, that 'the pepper carriers had to meet much the same basic requirements as the grain freighters on the Alexandria to Rome *annona* route', and admits, again as Evers does, that *P.Bingen* 77 attests to a grain carrier from Ostia of 22,500-artaba tonnage (600–900 tons, according to the editor). Mayer's (2018: 575, n. 36) claim that a price of 6 drachmas per mina would result in an 'improbably large freighter' is probably influenced by his misreading of *PME* 56: see p. 138 n. 69.

[17] Strab. 2.5.12.

the annual output for the entire Cochin hinterland, based on the notation on da Costa's *Relatório* manuscript.[18]

It is unlikely that Roman traders managed to import the entire pepper production of South India. It is also unlikely that, in the first century AD, the import volume from each of the other two Roman trade destinations in India—Barbarikon and Barygaza—equalled that from Limyrike. Therefore, we can assume 12,000 tons as the upper limit for the total import from India in the mid-first century AD and, *a fortiori*, in 26 or 25 BC.[19] If, at the beginning of Roman rule in Egypt, 120 ships were needed for a maximum import of 12,000 tons, then ships of the late Ptolemaic/early Augustan India trade carried, on average, a relatively meagre 100 tons each at most. The technological and organizational leap implied by a ship like the *Hermapollon* is enormous.

A single ship like the *Hermapollon* would allow inhabitants of the Roman Empire (pop. 50,000,000–100,000,000) an annual average consumption between 11 and 5.5 grams per head,[20] whereas an annual production of 4,000 tons would have theoretically made 80 to 40 grams available to the same population. In 1621, Thomas Mun estimated the quantity of pepper imported into Europe at 6,000,000 pounds, and that 'yearely spent in the Realme of England' at 400,000 pounds. The first amount is a little more than four times the *Hermapollon*'s pepper cargo. The second, if referring to a population of approximately 5,000,000 inhabitants,[21] allows for an average consumption of approximately 35 grams per head per year.[22]

It is difficult to estimate the average pepper consumption inside the Roman Empire in the first and second centuries AD.[23] What may be observed is that pepper consumption was geographically ubiquitous—from the Red Sea ports to Hadrian's Wall in Britain[24]—and often crosscut social strata.[25] Moreover, in

[18] See pp. 90–3; 98–101.

[19] The method of Mayer's estimate (Mayer 2018: 583–4) is questionable, and its result (20,000 tons) probably too high; see p. 319, n. 98.

[20] Scheidel (2001: 63–4).

[21] Wrigley and Schofield (1981: 208–9).

[22] Mun, 10–11; 44.

[23] Based on the *Price Edict* data, Cobb's study (2018: 519–59) offers interesting insights that apply better to Late Antiquity than to the Early Empire. For the different value of pepper in the two periods, see p. 101–6.

[24] Findings of peppercorns in Roman archaeological sites: Cappers (2006: 112–19) (Berenice, Shenshef, Qasr Ibrim); Van der Veen (2001) (Mons Claudianus); Van der Veen (2004: 126); (2011, 41–6) (Myos Hormos); Ciaraldi (2007: 102; 114–15; 125; 139); Kučan (1984;1992: 245–6) (Oberaden); Kreutz (1994/5: 70) (Hanau); Küster (1995: 137–8) (Straubing); Drummond-Murray (2002: 246, Table 126) (London); Reddé (2005: 255) (Oedenburg on the Rhine). The findings from Bath in Durrani (2004: 105) have been rejected as a misidentification by Cool (2006: 64, n. 47). Papyrological and epigraphic evidence for trade or consumption of black pepper: *O.Did.* 327; 328; 364; 399 (Didymoi); *P.Quseir* 28 (Myos Hormos); Schwinden (1985: 121-129) (Trier); *VT* 184 col. i, l. 4. 84 (Vindolanda); *ILAlg* 1.2236 (Madauros); for white pepper: *SEG* 37.1019 (Pergamon).

[25] Pepper could equally serve the unrestrained extravagances of the very rich (Petr. 33.8; 36.3), the savoury routines of the affluent (Pers. 3.73–6), the measured luxuries of the middle class (Mart. 7.27), and the occasional feasts of the poor (Pers. 6.19–21).

places that were—for different reasons—privileged, the levels of consumption may have been remarkably high: the *mation* (3.88 lt = *c.*1.6 kg) sent to the fort of Didymoi in Egypt's Eastern Desert and the half-pounds (161.5 g) given or received as a common *Saturnalia* gift by otherwise undistinguished clients in Rome provide significant clues in this respect.[26] Of course, elsewhere consumption levels would have been much lower, but the resulting average may have been no less than that of Early Modern Europe.

The Indiaman described by Philostratus in his *Life of Apollonius* appears a few generations after the Muziris papyrus, some 150 years after the *Periplus*' very large vessels that sailed to Limyrike, and more than 200 years after the voyage of C. Numidius Eros,[27] which may be taken as a *terminus ad quem* for the onset of a trade pattern that characterized Roman trade with South India from the time of Augustus up to the Severans. Such long continuity may be better appreciated when compared to the evolution of the sixteenth-century *Carreira da Índia* ships.

Sixteenth-century sources rarely specify—either in *tonéis* or in *quintais* of pepper—the tonnage of a single ship of the *Carreira da Índia* fleet.[28] More often than not, all one can do is infer the minimum tonnage of a single ship (or the average minimum tonnage of a fleet) from the quantities of spices that were loaded or unloaded.

In Table 11.1, I tabulate the available data and what may be inferred from the total cargoes.

The data indicate two periods during which the Portuguese boosted the capacity of their pepper-carrying ships. The first falls between 1504 and 1518.[29] The tendency towards larger pepper carriers is also discernible in Afonso de Albuquerque's 1512 letter, in which the governor of the State of India promises the king that 38,000 *quintais* of *pimenta e drogoarias* would be sent to Lisbon on only five *new* ships of 7,500/8,000 *quintais* tonnage, while *older* ships, which held no more than 6,000 to 6,500 *quintais*, would be redirected elsewhere.[30] The peak of this trend is represented by the *Nazaré* and the *Santa Catarina de Monte Synay* (the latter built in Cochin in 1511–1513), which in 1518 loaded as much as about 9,500 *quintais* each—1,500 *quintais* more than the new ships of 1512.[31]

[26] See p. 104. [27] See p. 49.

[28] A *tonel* is a cask 1.54 m high and 1.027 m wide at its maximum diameter. A *tonel* of pepper weighs approximately 13.5 *quintais*: Costa (1997: 79).

[29] In these years, the Portuguese estimates of South Indian pepper productivity escalated from the 30,000 *quintais* (almost 10,000 *bahar*) appraised by Álvaro Vaz, to the 20,000 *bahar* assessed by Tomé Pires before 1515; see pp. 98–101.

[30] *CAA* 1.83. Cf. Fonseca (1926: 232–6).

[31] Cf. *CAA* 1.121. The drive towards larger tonnages did not result in the abrupt suspension of smaller ships; on 25 June 1511, D. Manuel ordered the construction of four other ships, again for the Cape route, of only 460 *toneladas*, which makes them more similar to the old *Nazaré* than to the new ships (*ANTT*, *Corpo Cronológico*, P. I, M. 10, D. 53). The relatively high number of ships

Table 11.1 Ships and cargoes of the *Carreira da Índia*, 1501–85 (in *quintais*).

Year	Fleets			Single Ships		Source
	Number of ships	Comprehensive cargo	Average per ship	Estimated tonnage	cargo	
1501	6	2,000	333			1501: Ca' Masser, 15.[32]
1502	4	1,550	387			Ca' Masser, 17.
1503	16	30,000	1,875			Ca' Masser, 17.
1504	3	12,000	4,000			Ca' Masser, 19.
1505	13	24,000	1,846			Ca' Masser, 20. Bouchon (1976).
1505	1				3,430	Bouchon (1976).
1505	1				2,625	Bouchon (1976).
1505	1				1,027	Bouchon (1976).
1505	1				1,203	Bouchon (1976).
1505	1				1,013	Bouchon (1976).
1505	1				2,334	Bouchon (1976).
1505	1				961	Bouchon (1976).
1505	1				2,950	Bouchon (1976).
1505	1				467	Bouchon (1976).
1505	1				1,043	Bouchon (1976).
1505	1				886	Bouchon (1976).
1505	1				1,220	Bouchon (1976).
1505	1				1,479	Bouchon (1976).
1506	1				4,810	Ca' Masser, 23.
1506	1				5,000	Ca' Masser, 23.
1506	1				3,500	Ca' Masser, 23.
1506	1				2,800	Ca' Masser, 23.
1506	1				2,000	Ca' Masser, 23.
1512	5	38,000	7,600			*CAA* 1.83.
1513	3	18,408	6,103			Sanuto, 17.191.
1513/14	1				6,980	Sanuto, 18.143.
1513/14	1				7,301	Sanuto 18.143.
1514	1				7,254	Sanuto 18.143.[33]
1514	1				7,570	Sanuto 18.143.

(continued)

in the 1519 fleet (fourteen) suggests that several ships of lower tonnage had to be used in order to transfer the exceptional cargo of 56,000 *quintais* of pepper and 20,000 of other spices—'a mór carga que se nunqua fez': Correa 2.2.561.

[32] I assume that da Ca' Masser *K(antari)* are *quintais do peso velho* (51.4 kg) when related to pepper and *quintais do peso novo* (58.7 kg) when related to other spices.

[33] I do not take into account the puzzling cargo of the five ships that arrived in June the same year: Sanuto 18.409.

Table 11.1 Continued

Year	Fleets			Single Ships		Source
	Number of ships	Comprehensive cargo	Average per ship	Estimated tonnage	cargo	
1518	1				9,534	For the 1518 fleet, *Caderno* 1518; Sanuto 25.594–5.[34]
1518	1				9,443	
1518	1				8,128	
1518	1				6,307	
1518	1				7,648	
1518	1				7,500	
1519	14	88,815	6,343			Correa, 2.2.561; Sanuto, 27.641.
1526	5	22,053	4,410			Sanuto, 42.453–4.[35]
1527	3	19,298	6,432			*CVR* 16, fol. 1v.[36]
1530	3	18,547	6,182			Sanuto, 54.131.
1531	4	21,980	5,495			Sanuto, 54.599.
1547	6	39,859	6,643			For the 1547 fleet, *Livro das mercês que fez D. João de Castro* (Biblioteca da Ajuda, Lisbon) ff. 59–60v; *ANTT Colecção São Lourenço* iv ff. 329–30; Caminha, 85.
1547	1				7,488	*Livro das mercês*
1547	1				9,069	*que fez D. João de*
1548	4	26,790	6,697			*Castro* ff. 62–4v.

[34] As for the pepper cargo of the *Madanela*, probably the last ship to leave India, the *Caderno* and Sanuto give strikingly different data: only 826 *bahar* (*c.*2,667 *quintais*) the former, 7,500 *cantera* (that is, *quintais*) the latter; cf. Bouchon (1977: VII). I follow Sanuto, who may have known the quantity finally loaded on the ship. In Andrea Corsali's (188) opinion, two ships of the 1518 fleet had a capacity of 2,000 *botte*, and four had capacities of only 800, 900, or 1,000 *botte*. The cargoes recorded in the *Caderno dos ofiçiaes* do not show a similar disparity between the two larger ships—the *Santa Catarina do Monte Sinai* and the *Nazaré*—and three of the other four ships, the *Serra*, the *San António*, and the *Piedade*.

[35] If Sanuto's information is accurate, the relatively modest quantity (22,700 *quintais*) of spices carried by the 1526 fleet (five ships) may reflect supply problems more than they reflect the limited capacity of those vessels: the only ship whose cargo he describes in detail carried a little more than 7,000 *quintais* (of which 6,210 were pepper).

[36] The cargo of 1527 (roughly 19,300 *quintais*) was sent on ships (probably only three) that were very big (*muy grandes*), and two of them were not fully loaded.

1552	1			12,000	Gomes de Brito, 1.5–38.
1551/ 1554	1			12,000	*ANTT Corpo Cronológico* P. I, M. 86, D. 94; Figuêiredo Falcão, 163; 165; Gomes de Brito, 1.41–168; cf. Fonseca (1926: 285–6).
1558	1			10,125/10,800	*ANTT Corpo Cronológico* P. I, M. 103, D. 31.
1558	1			10,125/10,800	*ANTT Corpo Cronológico* P. I, M. 103, D. 31.
1558	1			6,750	*ANTT Corpo Cronológico* P. I, M. 103, D. 31.
1558	1			6,750	*ANTT Corpo Cronológico* P. I, M. 103, D. 31.
1558	1			8,100	*ANTT Corpo Cronológico* P. I, M. 103, D. 31.
1559	1			13,500	Gomes de Brito, 1.221–52, cf. Fonseca (1926: 310–11).
1558	5	36,852	7,370		Seure, 71
1585	6	30,000	5,000		Mathew (1997: 256–7).

The second period to witness an increase in ship tonnage falls in the middle of the sixteenth century, and is revealed by three vessels, whose size is comparable to that of the *Hermapollon*: the *São João* and the *São Bento*, each with a tonnage of 12,000 *quintais* (*c.*620 tons), and the *Garça*, with a tonnage of 1,000 *toneladas* (13,500 *quintais, c.*697 tons).[37] The latter was 'the largest that until then had been in the way of India' (Gomes de Brito), such that it could be loaded only in Cochin. If these tonnages were intended to increase the cost-effectiveness of the Cape route at a time when it faced competition from the Red Sea route,[38] then the effort failed. In fact, the delays in order to fill such large vessels to capacity forced the crews to miss the best departure window and to navigate the Cape passage in unfavourable conditions. In their last voyages, the *São João* and the *São Bento* left

[37] See Table 11.1 under 1552, 1551–4, and 1559.

[38] See pp. 260–2.

Cochin at the beginning of February, and the *Garça* departed almost at the end of January. Their subsequent wreckages off the South African coast—in 1552, 1554, and 1559, respectively—led to the discontinuation of these large-tonnage ships.

The 1558 *Relatório* advocated for a fleet from Cochin which included a couple of rather large ships (750 to 800 *tonéis* = *c.*520/550 tons), plus two much smaller ships (500 *tonéis* = *c.*350 tons), as well as one of intermediate size (600 *tonéis* = *c.*420 tons).[39] Later on, first the requirement and then the suggestion of a more drastic downscaling were simply ignored. Apparently, the opportunity for profit outweighed the risk of shipwreck.[40] In the last decades of the sixteenth century, a tonnage of 600 *tonéis* (*c.*420 tons) seems to have been the norm.[41]

The size of the *Hermapollon* and the chronology of its commercial enterprise are extremely significant data: they show that after approximately two centuries of trade relations between Roman Egypt and South India, Western merchants used ships carrying cargoes of more than 600 tons, which contrasts with the fluctuations and, in the end, the smaller tonnages of the *Carreira da Índia* ships in the sixteenth century. This observation contains two implications. The first is that the Red Sea route was far less challenging than the *Rota do Cabo*. The second is that, since in the first–second centuries AD more than one ship sailed between Egypt and South India,[42] the South Indian emporia were able to supply thousands of tons of pepper every year.

11.2. ANOTHER PEPPER TRADE

Like the moon, the mid sixteenth-century pepper trade had two faces, one visible and one veiled. The visible side was the one carried out by the *Carreira da Índia* through the Cape route, with recorded shipments. But, competing with the pepper monopoly enforced by the Portuguese, a parallel spice trade emerged that exploited the marginal productions and the peripheral emporia

[39] See Table 11.1 under 1558. In all likelihood, the two larger ships were loaded and sent as early as possible, and the smaller ones left last.

[40] In a 1570 law of the king D. Sebastião, prescribed tonnages were between 450 and 300 *tonéis* (*c.*315/210 tons): Sebastião, 81. See Godinho (1981/1983: 3.51): 'A ordenação de 1570 não foi respeitada; era de prever—o máximo admitido parece demasiado baixo.' A tonnage of 300 *tonéis* was advised again in 1581: Santa Cruz, 54.

[41] Santa Cruz, 53 refers to 'cinco viages' made by ships of '600 toneladas de Portugal que hacen mas que 1200 de Castilla'. The 1585 contract projected an import of 30,000 *quintais* of pepper on six ships, five from India and one from Malaca: Mathew (1997: 256–7).

[42] Several ships sailed to the Limyrike emporia in the mid-first century AD (*PME* 56) and several caravans transferred South Indian cargoes from Berenice in AD 163 (*P.Lond.* 2.328). See pp. 138–9; 202.

along the west coast of India. Carried out by *pimenteiros* with or without permission from the Portuguese authorities in India, this shadow trade successfully competed with the *Carreira da Índia* in supplying pepper for European consumption. This side of the pepper trade was visible only from particular view points.

Devoted to the topic of pepper, the forty-sixth chapter of Garcia de Orta's *Colóquios dos simples, e drogas he cousas medicinais da Índia* begins with Ruano emphatically asking de Orta to explain the failure of the Portuguese pepper monopoly, which by then (the *Colóquios* were printed in Goa in 1563) was a long-established fact: 'Is it not unreasonable that, after such labour as the Portuguese have gone through to have all the pepper in their own hands, they should consume the smallest part while Germany and Flanders consume the rest?'[43]

The loss of Aden in 1538 had reopened the Red Sea passage to both authorized and unauthorized pepper traders. As a consequence, Alexandria resumed its role as the supplier of pepper for Venetian trade and north European consumption.[44] By the time of Viceroy D. João de Castro (1545–1548), the falling pepper prices made its trade so unattractive that shrewd bankers like the Florentine Luca Giraldi were reluctant to engage in it.[45] In the attempt to quash the Red Sea route supply line, the Viceroy formed a project to export the Malabar pepper that was not being shipped to Lisbon eastwards—to Bengala, Pegu, and China.[46] But the project was not implemented, and the Red Sea trade continued to prosper. Its covert mechanics and actual volume—unclear to de Orta—are revealed by Lourenço Pires de Távora.[47]

De Távora, who had been fleet captain in India in 1546, was ambassador to the Pope in 1560. Since his arrival at Rome, he had been trying to gather information about the spice trade. As it turns out, the details he forwarded to the king of Portugal on 30 November 1560 did not come from his spies in Cairo and Aleppo, but from his newly appointed secretary, Antonio Pinto, who for a long time had been a spice merchant in India and a broker in Cairo.

In his detailed account, Pinto explains that apart from what was sent through Bassora to the Middle East, 40,000 *quintais* of spices (*c.*2,000 tons), mostly pepper, was shipped annually to Alexandria.[48] The spices arrived in Egypt after transhipment in one of the intermediary ports close to Bab el-Mandeb: Aden, Moca, Boca, Camorão, Jeddah, and Lemba on the Arabian side or Suakim and Quṣayr on the African shore. In particular, from Aden and Jeddah, the spices could also be forwarded to Cairo by caravan (*em cafillas*). More often, they were transferred on very small ships (*em geruas*) to al-Ṭūr

[43] Orta, 2.241; (Engl. transl. 367). [44] Godinho (1981/1983: 3.128–34).
[45] Rau (1965). [46] Thomaz (1998). [47] Pires de Távora, 110–1.
[48] D. Antão de Noronha estimated 20,000–25,000 *quintais* of pepper in 1566: *DPP*, 10.157–8.

(whence they travelled by caravan to Cairo) or to Quṣayr (apparently to be sold in Upper Egypt).

As for the traders involved, Pinto itemizes six different groups of ships or merchants, each exporting spices from specific ports along India's west coast. They are:

1. Khwaja Safar's six or seven ships (*naos*) that export from Surat;
2. the *mercadores mouros* exporting from Baroche to Damão and Baçaim;
3. the *mouros naytias* from Thana to Chaul;
4. the *mouros dacanins* from Danda to Dabul;
5. the *mouros balagatins* of Ancola and Baticala, exporting from Zanguizara Cifardão, Mazagão, and Carapatão up to Banda; and
6. the *paraos* from Cananor, Barcelor, and Chale.

These six sets of merchants may be rearranged in two groups. The first includes the first five, who traded in the emporia from Surat to Banda and imported—in addition to ginger from the same coast, and pepper and cinnamon from Sri Lanka—the pepper called *guari*.[49]

The second group of merchants—the sixth set listed by Antonio Pinto—smuggled black pepper from Cananor, Barcelor, and Chale, and their supply represented a large portion (*muita somma d ella*) of the 40,000 *quintais* of spices sent annually to Alexandria.[50] While the first group of merchants sailed across the Arabian Sea with medium-sized ships (*naos*) authorized with *cartazes* by the Portuguese authorities, the second group used unauthorized large boats (*paraos*) on the outward journey, and returned on authorized ships, having sold their boats at Jeddah.

The numbers of these *naos* and *paraos* are not specified, except for Khwaja Safar's six or seven ships. However, it seems unlikely that the *naos* of the first five groups totalled less than one or more than three dozen. As a consequence, they could have carried (in addition to other commodities?) no less than 20 tons but no more than 100 tons each. Their size may have been similar to the twenty-three ships that in 1564 delivered 21,000 *quintais* of spices (18,000 of which were pepper) to Jeddah, coming from Aceh and Baticala: the average cargo was less than 1,000 *quintais* (*c*.50 tons).[51] In all likelihood, the *paraos* from Cananor, Barcelor, and Chale were even smaller. Therefore, if the black pepper exported from those places was a significant quota of the 40,000 *quintais* of spices sent annually to Alexandria, the number of vessels must have been relatively high.

[49] Cf. *pepe gauro* in Sassetti, 461.

[50] Smuggling from some of these ports was bemoaned already in 1545: Thomaz (1988: 121; 131; 152).

[51] *ANTT, Corpo Cronológico*, P. I, M.107, D. 9: Gaspar e João Ribeiro to D. Sebastião from Venice 27.8.1564.

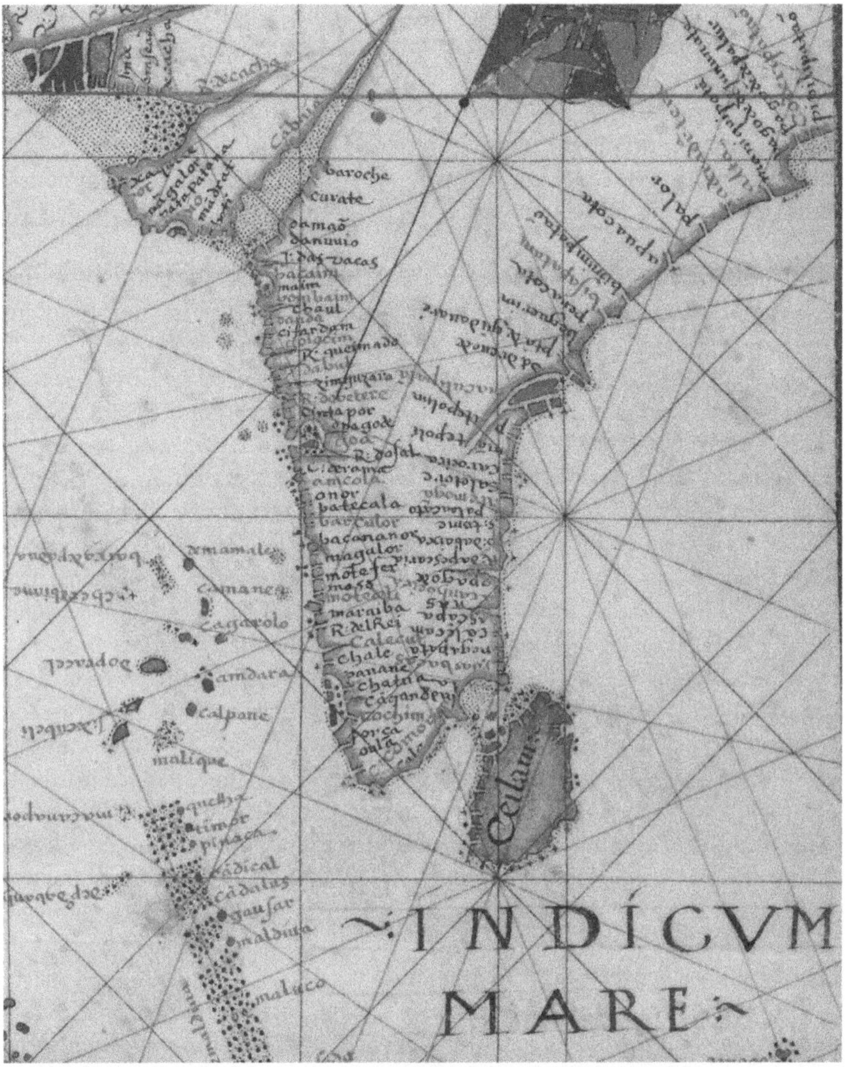

Fig. 11.2 Bartolomeu Velho, Portolan Atlas (ca. 1560) Huntington Library HM 44 f 7.
Courtesy of the Huntington Library, San Marino, California.

11.3. CONSPICUOUS ABSENCES

The analysis of the Muziris papyrus verso text provides a series of factual data, which may be briefly reiterated: col. iii, ll. 27–9 state that 1,151 talents and 5,852 drachmas was the estimated monetary value of the three-quarter portions of the commodities—*all* the commodities, apparently—carried on the *Hermapollon* and inventoried in the declaration (*apographe*) submitted to customs officials; the commodities evaluated at col. iii, ll. 1–26 were Gangetic nard and ivory, also mentioned in the *Periplus* among the commodities available in Limyrike.[52] Two of the three other commodities whose three-quarter portions are evaluated at col. ii, ll. 14–30 may be confidently identified as malabathron (ll. 17–19) and pepper (ll. 20–30), which were the most voluminous commodities imported from South India, according to the *Periplus*. The minimum weight and maximum possible value of the commodity evaluated at col. ii, ll. 14–16 recommend its identification as tortoise shell. At any rate, the weight and value preclude its identification as silk, pearls, diamonds, jacinth, or various translucent stones, all mentioned by the *Periplus* as commodities available in the emporia of Limyrike yet conspicuously absent from the *Hermapollon*'s cargo.

The absence of these commodities on the Muziris papyrus cargo list may stem from different causes. It may be taken for granted that the *Hermapollon* did not carry Chinese silk—either because it was no longer available in the South Indian emporia or because the *Hermapollon* traders simply did not buy it. On the contrary, it is not equally safe to assume that no merchant on board the *Hermapollon* bought any pearls or precious stones. Particularly suspicious is the apparent absence of pearls, which were fished for centuries in the nearby Gulf of Mannar, and at the time of the *Periplus* were abundant and excellent (*ἱκανὸς καὶ διάφορος*) in Limyrike's emporia.[53] Did the *Hermapollon's* merchants decide not to buy—or just not to declare—them? In other words, does the list of the *Hermapollon*'s goods reflect a disinclination to invest in the gemstone trade, or a reluctance to declare high-value, easy-to-hide commodities? More generally, should we infer a change from a trade pattern in which pearls and (semi)precious stones represented a considerable part of the import value (mid-first century AD) to one from which those commodities were totally removed (mid-second century AD)? Was it instead common practice —at least in the mid-second century AD, but possibly also before—to smuggle high-value, inconspicuous Indian items? Only supplementary evidence can help us choose between these two options.

The possibility that the *Hermapollon*'s cargo included undeclared pearls and precious stones raises a more general and far-reaching question: how effectively could such trade goods be taxed? A rescript of Marcus Aurelius and Commodus states that a tax farmer (*publicanus*) was not responsible for allegedly unintentional violations of the law by merchants. In particular, it was not the tax farmer's duty to inform the merchant whether a commodity was subject to customs duties (*vectigal*). At the same time, the tax farmer was not allowed to deceive merchants who wanted to declare, by claiming that a certain commodity was tax-free when it was not.[54] In all likelihood, the rescript settled a dispute on undeclared goods imported from the East: a list

[52] *PME* 56. [53] Cf. De Romanis (1982/7: 184–93); Coelho (1997: 112–56).
[54] Marcian., *Dig.* 39.4.16.6.

of eastern commodities 'subject to the *vectigal*' was attached to the rescript and served to remind the addressee of all the commodities that had to be declared.[55] Apparently, the distinction between taxable and exempt items was not always clear to either merchants or customs officials; the former could fail to declare goods assuming (or pretending to assume) that they were tax-free, whereas the latter could (disingenuously?) consider tax-free in Berenice what their colleagues in Coptos or Alexandria confiscated as taxable and undeclared. In particular, the boundaries must have been blurred by the innumerable variety and the uncertain value of precious and translucent stones (λιθία διαφανὴς παντοία). This may be why, in order to prevent any attempt at circumvention on the part of the merchants, the list attached to the rescript mentions the comprehensive and precautionary entry 'all kinds of stone' (*lapis universus*).

But the taxation of pearls and gemstones was challenging on several accounts. The rather long classification displayed by the list of the rescript (pearl, sardonyx, ceraunium, jacinth, emerald, diamond, sapphire, turquoise, beryl) shows that a thorough taxation of those commodities would require customs officials who were well trained in gem identification and authentication. Moreover, a payment in money would require a fiscal value for each type of stone. But a *fair* evaluation of the imported items must have been extremely problematic, since the actual prices of gemstones—especially of the most expensive ones—were consistently minimised by both sellers and buyers, not least to bypass sumptuary laws.[56]

Therefore, even when these imported goods were declared to customs officials (and the temptation not to declare them at all must have been very strong), their fiscal values may have been quite out of line with the enormous prices at which they were sold within the empire. All this suggests that the Roman tax system was less than successful at either preventing gemstone smuggling or taxing them appropriately. Here, a comparison with Habsburg Portugal may be enlightening. As shown by J. C. Boyajian, in the seventeenth century the kingdom of Portugal failed spectacularly in taxing the *pedraria* trade: the rate of tax evasion proved to be enormous, in the few cases when it was serendipitously discovered, and the overall secrecy concerning the final prices guaranteed a low taxation anyway.[57]

In Antiquity, trading in pearls was an expensive yet potentially highly remunerative venture,[58] and even though the female passion for pearls and gemstones was universally blamed as the cause of a heavy outflow of Roman coinage,[59] no one had a clear idea of the precise scale of the investments in (or of the profits generated by) that trade. When, at an ordinary betrothal party,

[55] Marcian., *Dig.* 39.4.16.7. As it stands in the *Digest*, the list is not complete.

[56] Tac., *Ann.* 3.52. [57] Boyajian (1993: 50–1; 135–9). [58] NT, *MT* 13.45–6.

[59] Plin., *NH* 12.84; Tac., *Ann.* 3.53.

Lollia Paulina averred that she had bought her amazing pearl and emerald *parure* for 40,000,000 sesterces (more than four times the fiscal value of the *Hermapollon*'s cargo), her statement must have shocked even her wealthy fellow diners.[60]

Incidentally, the striking difference between the official valuation and the real market prices of gemstones may help explain the impasse faced by the committee of thirty knights responsible, in AD 69, for the recovery of the 2.2 billion sesterces that had been squandered in gifts by the late emperor Nero. Nero's favourites did not have any land or principal, however, but only 'tools of vices', hardly worth 10 per cent of what they had received. Confiscated and auctioned by the committee, the pearls and gemstones were sold for a tiny fraction of the incredibly high prices they secretly commanded under Nero.[61]

The absence of pearls and precious stones from the cargo manifest of the *Hermapollon* may thus reflect either actual changes in South India trade practices with respect to the mid-first century AD, or else a long-established administrative laxity, facilitated by customs officials who may have found complicity more beneficial than the laborious effort to seize hidden—and sometimes hardly identifiable—objects.

In any case, a comparison of the Muziris papyrus' data with Pliny's famous claim—that at that time Indian trade 'absorbed' at least 50,000,000 sesterces every year and sent back commodities that were sold within the Roman Empire at a price a hundred times higher than the one for which they were bought in India—requires several caveats.[62]

To begin with, there is no doubt that in emphasizing the difference between the initial and final prices of Indian commodities, Pliny has succumbed to the temptation to impress his readers with a large round ratio that cannot be taken literally. It may have been true for some items, in some places, at certain times, but not for all items, in all places, at all times. The mark-up in the price of pepper from India to Rome can only be vaguely approximated. The contrast between the fiscal value assumed by the Muziris papyrus (360 sesterces per weight talent) and the price indicated by Pliny (1,520 sesterces per weight talent), presumably the retail market price in Rome, makes it likely that the wholesale market price in Alexandria fluctuated between 900 and 1,200 sesterces per weight talent, customs duties included. But how much lower the Indian price was is just a matter of guesswork. Apart from Pliny's hyperbolic ratio, no ancient data are available for pepper prices in India.

For the sixteenth century, we are better equipped to gauge Indian pepper prices. Garcia de Orta indicates 2.5 *cruzados* per *quintal* as the usual price for black pepper at Cochin.[63] As evinced by V. M. Godinho based on the 1558 *Orçamento*, the average cost of a pepper cargo rose to about 5.60 *cruzados* per

[60] Plin., *NH* 9.117. [61] Tac., *Hist.* 1.20. [62] Plin., *NH* 6.101.
[63] Orta, 2.246 (Engl. transl. 372).

quintal when losses and other expenses are considered, and to about 9.50 *cruzados* per *quintal*, transport to Lisbon included.[64] A cost of 5.66 *cruzados* per *quintal* is implied by the 1585 contract, which allocated 170,000 *cruzados* to buy 30,000 *quintais* of pepper. In those decades, at the *Casa da Índia* in Lisbon, pepper was sold at 32–34 *cruzados* per *quintal*. While the ratio 1 : 13.6 between the prices in Cochin (not counting losses and supplementary expenses) and in Lisbon is very far from Pliny's hyperbolic 1 : 100, the price of 5.66 *cruzados* per *quintal* is not grossly out of proportion to his claim about the size of the Roman trade deficit with India. In fact, 30,000 *quintais* is less than three times the pepper cargo of the *Hermapollon*, and 170,000 gold *cruzados* of about 3.56 g corresponds to almost 8,000,000 sesterces.[65]

As mentioned, in the first century AD it was commonly believed that the outflow of Roman coins to the East was mainly due to the importation of pearls and gemstones.[66] In fact, although barely conspicuous, pearls and gemstones were absolutely no less valuable than the voluminous cargoes of pepper and malabathron. Here again, Early Modern evidence may be of interest. In 1613 Dom Jeronimo d'Oliveira, viceroy of India, estimated that no less than 400,000–500,000 *cruzados* was invested annually in precious stones for shipment to Lisbon.[67] We do not know how d'Oliveira arrived at that estimate (just as we do not know how Pliny came to assess the Roman deficit in the India trade), but we may presume that he was aware that he was describing a business worth more than two and slightly less than three times the 170,000 *cruzados* set aside to buy 30,000 *quintais* of pepper in the 1585 contract.

A cost of 570,000–670,000 gold *cruzados* weighing 3.56 g each for pepper, pearls, and precious stones is not that far from the minimum of 500,000 aurei weighing 7.8 grams that enabled the import of all Indian commodities in a period that witnessed the intensive exploitation of Spanish gold mines,[68] the large-scale production of gold coinage,[69] the reduction of the interest rate in

[64] Godinho (1981–1983: 3. 20–2), based on the *Orçamento que se fez do que custa a el rei N. Sr. um quintal de pimenta* (1558), *ANTT*, *Corpo Cronológico*, P. I, M. 103, D. 131.

[65] Dias (1998: 273).

[66] Plin., *NH* 12.84; Tac., *Ann.* 3.53.

[67] *HAG*, *Livros das monções*, livro 12 (1613–17), f. 10ʳ, 'Reposta da carta que commessa pella gente da nação hebrea' Dec. 1613: 'Pareceo-me tambem em esta occasião dizer a V. Mag.ᵉ o que se me tem offerecido na matéria de pedraria, que se aqui compra todos os annos, emquanto dá muitas cousas que considerar, porque o emprego que nella se faz chega em cadahu' anno a quatrocentos ou quinhentos mil cruzados.' Cf. Boyajian (1993: 50).

[68] Plin., *NH* 33.78. See Domergue and Sillières (1977: 83); Domergue (1990: 198).

[69] For the quantitative relevance of Tiberius' aurei, cf. Giard (1983: 47; 124–9, where 94 obverse and 93 reverse types of the PONTIF MAX issues are listed); on Claudius' aurei, cf. von Kaenel (1986: 255–8, especially 257, n. 400); Burgers (2001: 99–100). In general, on the proportion of the gold and silver emissions before AD 64, see Butcher and Ponting (2014: 439): 'the coinage of the Julio-Claudian period prior to Nero's reform is characterized by a growing disparity in output of the two precious metal denominations. Gold output had remained

Egypt,[70] the amazing donations to the temple of Jerusalem by Alexander the arabarch,[71] the enormous amounts of money squandered by Caligula (2.7, if not 3.3, billion sesterces) and Nero (2.2 billion sesterces),[72] and the *luxus mensae* that characterized the social life of the Julio-Claudian urban aristocracies.[73]

11.4. INDIAN AND AFRICAN TUSKS

As mentioned, the commodity whose three-quarter portion is evaluated at verso col. iii, l. 4–15 is referred to as 'sound' ivory (ἐλέφας ὑγιής) at l. 4 and as 'teeth, tusks' (ὀδόντες) at ll. 12 and 13. The entry refers to entire tusks removed from dead animals, in contrast with the *schidai*, which are trimmings of ivory taken from captive live elephants. At verso col. ii, l. 5, the weight of 105 talents and 13 minas—definitely related to the same cargo of sound ivory—is preceded by the figure 167. As Morelli suggested, it must represent the actual number of tusks carried by the *Hermapollon*.[74]

The combination of the total number of tusks and their aggregate weight leads to interesting considerations. A total of 167 tusks weighing 105 talents and 13 minas (*c.*3,228.5 kg) results in an average weight of 37.8 minas (*c.*19.332 kg) per tusk.[75] A comparison with other lots of raw ivory shows that the tusks imported by the *Hermapollon* were not only 'sound', but also relatively large. It is true that much smaller collections of tusks bought by or donated to temples show even higher average weight numbers—for instance, 46.3125 minas was the average weight of two tusks sold to Apollo's temple in Delos by a Herakleides of Tyre, and 42.94 minas was the average weight of thirty-four tusks donated by Ptolemy Auletes to the temple of Didyma. But these figures do not undermine the average value of the *Hermapollon*'s cargo—first because those limited lots may have been sold or donated to temples precisely for their exceptional quality, and second, because the talent(s) used to measure them was (were) very probably of lighter standard than the one used by the quarter-tax administrators to weigh the *Hermapollon*'s cargo.[76]

high, while the supply of freshly coined silver had been dwindling since the beginning of the first century AD.'

[70] See p. 131. [71] Joseph., *BJ* 5.201–5. [72] See p. 132 n.32; Tac., *Hist.* 1.20.

[73] Tac., *Ann.* 3.55. Cobb (2015: 388) underestimates, it seems to me, the pertinence of Tacitus' remarks. Moreover, texts like Juv. 1.132–4 ('super-rich eats alone, no parasite sits at his old, large tables') or Juv. 3.177–84 ('no difference in the outfit between aristocrats and *plebs*') confirm rather than contradict Tacitus' periodization.

[74] Morelli (2011: 209).

[75] Asian elephant tusks reach that weight when the animal is around thirty-five years old: Sukumar (1989: 225).

[76] Two tusks weighing one talent and 32.625 minas at Delos: *IG* XI ii 203 A, l. 71; thirty-four elephant tusks, weighing 24 talents and 20 minas: *I.Didyma* 1.394, ll. 16–18. The weight unit used

The large commercial ivory lot carried by the *Hermapollon* is more appropriately compared to commercial cargoes of the sixteenth century. In his *Informação para el-rei* (1530), Jordão de Freitas outlines a classification system for African ivory tusks, distinguishing among three types of ivory based primarily on the size of the tusk. The first type is the 'very big, sound, and clean' ivory, worth 30 to 40 *maticais* per *baar* (*c.*240 kg) in Sofala.[77] The second is the 'small' ivory, 'which does not reach a *faraçola* ($\frac{1}{20}$ of *baar* = *c.*12 kg) each tusk', and is worth half the value of the first type. The third is the 'more minute' ivory, which is not even half a *faraçola* (*c.*6 kg), worth 10 to 12 *maticais* per *baar*.[78]

Several contemporaneous documents show the average weight for some commercial lots of African ivory, apparently (in one case, admittedly) including tusks of very different sizes:

1. In 1506, Pero Ferreira Fogaça, *capitão* of Kilwa records a *zambuco* carrying 570 tusks weighing 92 *quintaes*, 2 *arrobas*, and 31 *arrates* (5,448.95 kg). The average weight is 9.56 kg per tusk.[79]
2. In 1507, Nuno Vaz Pereira, *capitão* of Sofala, orders delivery of 264 tusks and two pieces weighing 73 *quintaes*, 1 *arroba*, and 20 *arrates* (4,312.39 kg). Counting the two pieces as tusks, the average weight is 16.21 kg per tusk.[80]
3. In 1514, Álvaro de Bouro reports a sale of a stock of ivory in Lisbon.[81] The document details not only the number of tusks and their total weight, but also the number of tusks contained in each of the thirteen lots of 6 *quintaes* (352.512 kg), plus one lot of 4 *quintaes* and 24 *arrateis* (246.024 kg) in which the stock has been divided and sold. Since the total weight of the 385 tusks was 82 *quintaes* and 24 *arrateis* (4,828.68 kg), the average weight per tusk was 12.542 kg. However, the different lots have very different average weights: they range from 4.641 kg to 20.736 kg per tusk.
4. In 1515, Francesco Corbinelli, *feitor* in Goa, acknowledges receipt of 193 'big and small tusks' weighing 39 *quintaes* and 3 *arrobas* (2,335.39 kg)

to determine the quarter-tax at the time of the Muziris papyrus is a talent of 95 Roman pounds: col. ii, ll. 6–7. The Delos inscription may refer to the Attic/Euboic standard (1 talent = either 62.5 or 80 Roman pounds). The Didyma inscription may refer either to the same Attic/Euboic standard or to the Egyptian or Ptolemaic standard (1 talent = either 80 or 90 Roman pounds): *MSR* 1.233, 22–234, 3; 236, 23–4.

[77] The weight unit should be the 'baar de marfim' of 4 *quintaes* and 10.5 *arrateis*: *Livro dos pesos* fol. 16, p. 26.

[78] *DPMAC* 6.428. I have assumed that the unit of measure used in this and the following documents is the *quintal* of *peso novo* (= 58.752 kg), which is explicitly mentioned in *DPMAC* 5.184 (below, n. 83).

[79] *DPMAC* 1.618. [80] *DPMAC* 2.64. [81] *DPMAC* 3.572–9.

from Lourenço Moreno, *feitor* in Cochin. The average weight is 12.1 kg per tusk.[82]

5. In 1517, Pero Coresma, *feitor* of Cochin, acknowledges receipt in Sofala of 233 'big and small' tusks weighing 61 *quintais*, 3 *arrobas*, and 28 *arrateis* (3,640.788 kg). The average weight is 15.62 kg per tusk.[83]
6. In 1518, Pedro Jacome dies in Sofala, leaving eight tusks weighing *duas arrobas menos quatros arrates* (27 kg). The average weight is 3.37 kg.[84]
7. In 1518, Joham Afonso da Cunha *allcaide mor* and *feitor* of Mozambique receives 349 big and small tusks weighing 92 *quintais* (5,405.18 kg). The average weight is 15.48 kg.[85]
8. Small tusks made up the overwhelming majority of the ivory received by the Sofala factory in 1547: of the 56 *bahar* (approximately 14,240 kg), 14 (around 3,560 kg) were *grosso* ('large') and 42 (approximately 10,680 kg) *miudo* ('small').[86]

With the possible exceptions of the ivory sold in Lisbon in 1514 and the ivory sent to Goa by Lourenço Moreno in 1515,[87] all these lots were of East African origin. The fact that their average weights are lower than the average weight of the tusks imported by the *Hermapollon* is surprising and significant. It is surprising because the species of elephant predominant in East Africa today is the African savannah elephant (*Loxodonta Africana Africana*), which tends to develop longer and thicker tusks than either the Asian *Elephas maximus* or the even smaller West African forest elephant (*Loxodonta Africana cyclotis*).[88] It is significant because it shows that, aside from the varying growth potential

[82] *CAA* 7.136–7.

[83] *DPMAC* 5.184. This lot of ivory was weighed again with the weights that Pero Coresma brought to Cochin. At a first measurement with the weights of Sofala 'eaten away by rust', this same lot of ivory, plus four tusks that are missing, was declared to weigh 68 *quintaes*, 3.5 *arrobas*, and 4 *arrates*: *DPMAC* 5.182–9.

[84] *DPMAC* 7.68. [85] *DPMAC* 5.536. [86] *DPMAC* 7.175.

[87] The Portuguese quickly recognized the commercial potential of Malabar ivory. As early as 1503, Afonso de Albuquerque was said to be trafficking in ivory in Cananor: Pinto (2010: 253). Two *cartas de quitacão* for *feitores* in Cochin mention ivory lots of unspecified origin: 111 *quintaes*, 2 *arrobas*, and 12 *arrateis* is mentioned in the *quitação* issued for Lourenço Moreno after his first stint as *feitor* in Cochin in the years 1506 and 1507 (*ANTT* Chancel. de D. Manuel I, Liv. III, f. 17^{r}, transcribed in Braamcamp Freire 1906: 288) and 55 *quintaes* and 6 *arrobas* is recorded in the *quitação* for André Dias, *feitor* in Cochin from the end of 1507 to 1509 (*ANTT* Chancel. de D. Manuel I, Liv. III, f. 46^{v}, transcribed in Braamcamp Freire 1903: 278–9). However, these two lots may not be of Indian origin: for a shipment of African ivory from Sofala to Cochin in 1517, see *DPMAC* 5.182–9.

[88] Tusks from a fifty-year-old male African savannah elephant can easily weigh more than 50 kg (Laws 1966: 27–8), while the tusks from an Asian elephant of the same sex, age, and weight barely reach 30 kg (Sukumar 1989: 225).

Table 11.2 Average weight per tusk in the lot in *DPMAC* 3.572–9, first the whole cargo (385 tusks), then its fourteen sublots.

Weight	Tusks	Average weight
82 *quintaes* 24 *arrateis* (4,828.68 kg)	385	12.542 kg
6 *quintaes* (352.512 kg)	17	20.736 kg
6 *quintaes* (352.512 kg)	17	20.736 kg
6 *quintaes* (352.512 kg)	19	18.553 kg
6 *quintaes* (352.512 kg)	20	17.625 kg
6 *quintaes* (352.512 kg)	21	16.786 kg
6 *quintaes* (352.512 kg)	22	16.023 kg
6 *quintaes* (352.512 kg)	22	16.023 kg
6 *quintaes* (352.512 kg)	22	16.023 kg
6 *quintaes* (352.512 kg)	26	13.558 kg
6 *quintaes* (352.512 kg)	26	13.558 kg
6 *quintaes* (352.512 kg)	28	12.589 kg
6 *quintaes* (352.512 kg)	38	9.276 kg
6 *quintaes* (352.512 kg)	54	6.528 kg
4 *quintaes* 24 *arrateis* (246.024 kg)	53	4.641 kg

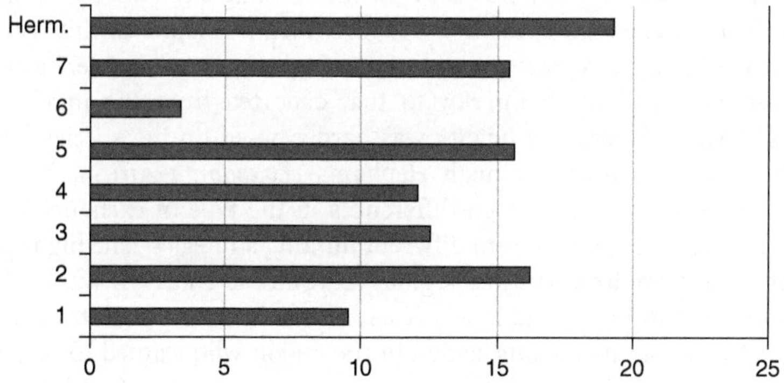

Fig. 11.3 Average weight per tusk of seven sixteenth-century lots and the *Hermapollon*'s cargo (in kg).

of different species, the average weight of the traded tusks depended on the deliberate choices made by both elephant hunters and ivory merchants.

Most of the tusks imported by the *Hermapollon* were probably taken from wild tuskers, killed by forest dwellers who hunted elephants primarily for their ivory (the meat was only a by-product).[89] The ancient Tamil poetry reveals elephant hunters of different types: the 'unkind Kāṉavar' who pursue elephants 'for desire of their white tusks';[90] the inhabitants of the Mount Kolli

[89] Allusions to eating elephant meat: *Akanāṉūṟu* 172.6–14; *Naṟṟiṇai* 114.1–3. See Varadarajaiyer (1945: 22–3).
[90] *Akanāṉūṟu* 21.24.

villages, who make their living by selling tusks;[91] the hunting communities of the Vēṭṭuvar, who exchange elephant tusks for toddy 'in rich-in-gold markets';[92] and the Iḷaiyar, who alternately hunt wild elephants and rob travelling traders.[93]

The high average weight of the tusks carried by the *Hermapollon* shows that the Western merchants carefully selected which ones to import. By extension, it is likely that the South India hunting communities who made their living from the ivory trade were sensitive to the commercial values of different-sized tusks and so carefully selected which animals to kill. By contrast, the small size of the second and third types of tusks in de Freitas' categorization and the low average weight of the East African ivory lots mentioned above suggest that African hunters were only marginally motivated by the ivory trade, and not as influenced by commercial considerations. In other words, in Africa, elephants must have been killed for more than just their tusks, and although savannah elephants may develop bigger tusks than Indian elephants, the African tusks that were traded may not have been *on average* bigger than the Asian ones.

The apparent dissimilarity between ancient African and South Asian elephant hunting strategies offers a clue for interpreting a remark by the author of the *Periplus* concerning the ivory exported from Rhapta. In this 'very last emporion of Azania', a great amount of ivory is said to be available. Its quality, however, was held to be inferior to that exported from the much closer Adulis.[94] The difference in quality was hardly based on the species hunted, which must have been savannah elephants (*Loxodonta Africana*) in both cases.[95] Rather, it resulted from differences in the type of exchange at each emporia, and perhaps also from different hunting strategies. The high-quality Adulis ivory came from faraway regions 'beyond the Nile'.[96] It was conveyed to Axum, then to Koloe, and finally reached Adulis, having been traded down the line by foreign merchants settled in the region who wanted to be paid in Roman currency.[97] From Adulis, the tusks were shipped to Myos Hormos or

[91] *Kuṟuntokai* 100.3–5. Mount Kolli belonged to Ōri, a minor chieftain dependent upon the Cēra kings: see Thirunavukarasu (1994: 49).

[92] *Patiṟṟuppattu* 30.9–13. [93] *Akanāṉūṟu* 245.5–12.

[94] *PME* 16; 17. *PME* 16 locates Rhapta two 'runs' from Menuthias Island (either Pemba or Zanzibar): cf. Casson (1989: 141–2); Fiaccadori (1992: 77–9).

[95] Cosmas Indicopleustes' remark (11.23) that elephants from 'Aithiopia' had bigger tusks than the Indian ones suggests that the elephants who populated East Africa in antiquity were savannah elephants, and is at odds with Scullard's contention (1974: 60–3) that the elephants captured in East Africa by the Ptolemies were actually forest elephants (*Loxodonta Africana cyclotis*).

[96] *PME* 4. Casson (1987: 105–6) takes the expression ἀπὸ τοῦ πέρα<ν> τοῦ Νείλου to refer to the region beyond either the Tekazze or the Mareb.

[97] *PME* 6: δηνάριον ὀλίγον πρὸς τοὺς ἐπιδημοῦντας, 'a little Roman money for the resident foreigners'.

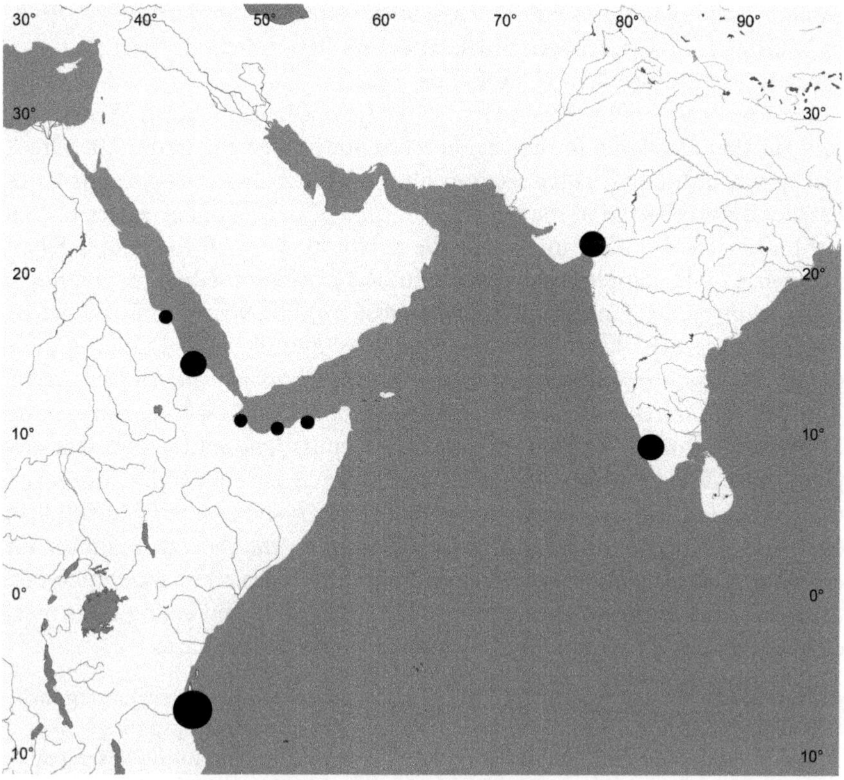

Fig. 11.4 Availability of ivory according to the *Periplus* (small circles 'little ivory', medium circles 'ivory', big circle 'great amount of ivory').

Berenice by merchants from Roman Egypt. Such a commercial circuit necessarily required a deliberate selection of tusks based on their quality, which had to be, quite significantly, of the 'Adulis standard'.[98]

The exchanges at Rhapta had a completely different style. To begin with, the emporion was visited only by small boats from Muza, manned by crews linked through intermarriage with the local population.[99] Together with spears, axes, knives, awls, and glass stones, merchants would bring large quantities of grain and wine to be consumed locally 'not for trade, but because of extravagance, as a courtesy to the barbarians'.[100] It is likely that the Rhapta ivory was 'inferior' to the Adulis ivory because it included—just like the Sofala ivory in the sixteenth century—considerable quantities of 'small' and 'even smaller' tusks. Once it arrived at Muza, the inferior but plentiful ivory from Rhapta was most likely sent to Barygaza.[101] African ivory was exported to India in Late

[98] *PME* 3; 17. [99] *PME* 16. [100] *PME* 17.
[101] For Muza relations with Barygaza, see *PME* 21.

Antiquity and in the sixteenth century, when enormous amounts were sent to India from the coast between Sofala and Malindi—Garcia de Orta estimates 6,000 *quintais* (more than 350 tons) per year.[102]

The low quality of the Rhapta ivory and the idiosyncratic form of exchange confirm that elephants in the region were not hunted for trade. The Greek perception of the particular relationship between humans and elephants in East Africa is reflected in the term *Elephantophagoi* ('Elephant-eaters'),[103] an attribution created at a time when the exploration of Africa beyond Egypt inspired a quite complex diet-based ethnology. Along the lines of the much older *Ichthyophagoi* and the *Chelonophagoi* (re)discovered in Carmania by Alexander's army,[104] other groups were also identified (or imagined), like the *Rhizophagoi, Hylophagoi, Spermatophagoi, Akridophagoi, Struthophagoi, Agriophagoi, Moschophagoi, Ophiophagoi, Pamphagoi, Anthropophagoi*, and *Elephantophagoi.*[105] Greek ethnographic accounts ignored the fact that elephant meat was to some extent also eaten in ancient South India. Moreover, the Greek writings did not consider that African societies may have killed elephants for multiple reasons: in Greek opinion, the African fondness for elephant meat was the sole motivation. In a story repeated by Agatharchides, the *Elephantophagoi* refused to stop killing elephants and eating their meat despite Ptolemy's urging and the promise of splendid rewards:

> Ptolemy, the king of Egypt, urged these hunters to refrain from slaughtering the beasts in order that he might have them alive. Although he promised them many wondrous things, he not only did not persuade them but he heard that their reply was that they would not exchange his whole kingdom for their present way of life.[106]

The task of providing the Ptolemaic army with an Indian-style elephant division had to accommodate African cultural traditions.[107] The story may be fictional, but the perception that human–elephant relations differed in Africa and India was accurate. The inferior African ivory conveyed by Portuguese ships and the heavy ivory tusks carried on the *Hermapollon* support that distinction.

[102] Cosm. Indic. 11.23; Orta, 1.305 (Engl. transl. 181).

[103] Agatharchides 53–6; Strab. 16.4.10; Plin., *NH* 6.191; Ptol., *Geog.* 4.7.34.

[104] Nalesini (2009: 9–18).

[105] Diod. Sic. 3.18–29; *PME* 2–3; Plin., *NH* 6.169; 195.

[106] Agatharchides 56; by transl. by S. M. Burstein. Cf. *Aristophanis historiae animalium epitome* 2.54–5.

[107] Schneider (2009: 310–34).

Part IV

The Red Sea Tax and the Muziris Papyrus

12

Maris Rubri Vectigal

The double (import to and export from Egypt) customs duties on Indian commodities referred to by Strabo[1] and the 'Red Sea tax' (*maris Rubri vectigal*) mentioned by Pliny were one and the same.[2] It was the Egyptian segment of the *vectigal* for eastern commodities, referred to in a rescript of Marcus Aurelius and Commodus,[3] and it paralleled both the quarter-tax on imported commodities collected at Leuke Kome, on the Arabian shore of the Red Sea,[4] and the quarter-tax assessed at Palmyra, in the Syrian desert.[5] These customs duties were one of the major sources of revenue for the Roman Empire. The Muziris papyrus texts provide crucial details regarding how and when they were assessed and paid, in Egypt.

In this chapter, it will be argued that theoretically the customs duties on Indian commodities could be paid either in money or in kind, as the taxpayer wished. However, while some evidence suggests that payments in kind were sometimes chosen in Late Antiquity, the texts of the Muziris papyrus show that the merchant of the *Hermapollon* paid his dues in money, and that in the mid-second century AD, payment in money was the encouraged and preferred option.

12.1. PAYMENTS IN KIND AND PAYMENTS IN MONEY

A few papyri suggest that in Late Antiquity the customs duties on Indian pepper were paid—at least sometimes—in kind. In a fragmentary Coptic papyrus dated 24 October AD 649,[6] representatives of Edfu's professional guilds (the preserved portion mentions potters, fullers, stone carvers, boatmen, cobblers, masons, menders, doctors, oilmen, blacksmiths, and embroiderers)

[1] Strab. 17.1.13. See pp. 132–5. [2] Plin., *NH* 6.84.
[3] Marcian., *Dig.* 39.4.16.7. [4] *PME* 19.
[5] *IGLS* 17.1.196 (=*PAT* 1373); *IGLS* 17.1.197 (=*PAT* 1413); *PAT* 2634, on which De Romanis (2004; 2006b).
[6] *B.M. Or. inv.* 8903. For its chronology: Gascou and Worp (1982: 94).

The Indo-Roman Pepper Trade and the Muziris Papyrus. Federico De Romanis, Oxford University Press (2020).
 DOI: 10.1093/oso/9780198842347.001.0001

Table 12.1 Pepper purchases by guilds at Edfu (AD 649).

Guild	Representatives	Weight (lbs.)	Price (*solidi*)
Potters	1	18	3
Fullers	1	6	1
???	2	18	3
Stone carvers	2	9	1.5
Boatmen	1	36	6
Cobblers	1	12	2
Masons	1	12	2
Menders	1	6	1
Doctors	1	6	1
Oilmen	1	15	2.5
Blacksmiths	2	12	[2]
Embroiderers	1	6	[1]
Total	15	156	26

declare that they have received from the pagarch their own share of the 600 pounds of pepper assigned to the town. For each pound received, the guilds would pay one-sixth of a solidus, so for the whole 600 pounds, 100 solidi would be paid. The text records the quantities of pepper delivered, the guilds that received them, and the prices that were paid (Table 12.1). Only a little more than a quarter of the total 600 pounds is recorded in the extant fragment.

In turn, the shares assigned to each guild would be divided amongst its members, presumably in proportion to their wealth. The recipients would agree to pay a price in proportion to their quota of pepper. The editor of the papyrus, W. E. Crum, thought that the background of the Edfu pepper sale could be further elucidated by Ibn ʿAbd el-Ḥakam's anecdote on the origin of the Old Cairo 'Pepper House':

> It was named 'Pepper House' (*Dār al-fulful*) for the [following] reason. When Usāma b. Zayd al-Tanūḫī was in charge of the collection of Egypt's land tax (*ḫarāǧ*), he bought pepper for 20,000 *dīnār* from Mūsā b. Wardān. Al-Walīd b. ʿAbd al-Malik wanted to send it as a gift to the Byzantine emperor (*ṣāḥib al-rūm*). [Mūsā] stored the pepper in the *Dār al-fulful*, but eventually [the pepper was not delivered and] Mūsā b. Wardān complained to ʿUmar b. ʿAbd al-ʿAzīz, when the latter became caliph. ʿUmar ordered that the pepper would be given back to him.[7]

Crum contended that both the papyrus and Ibn ʿAbd el-Ḥakam's story provide evidence for a pepper monopoly.[8] But, neither proves that the Umayad administration bought *all* the imported pepper only to sell it eventually with forced sales to legally obligated buyers. In Ibn ʿAbd el-Ḥakam's story it is difficult to separate reality from fiction, but even taking it at face value,

[7] Ibn ʿAbd al-Ḥakam, 99; transl. by C. Intartaglia.
[8] Crum (1925). Cf. Gascou (1983: 101); Schmidt (2018: 99–101).

20,000 *dīnār* would be too small a sum to purchase *all* the pepper imported in one year. At the price of 6 pounds per solidus attested in the Edfu papyrus, they would have bought 120,000 pounds—200 times the quantity sent to be sold at Edfu, and less than 1/14 of the *Hermapollon*'s pepper cargo. Moreover, if 20,000 *dīnār* had really been paid by al-Walid b. 'Abd al-Malik (caliph in AD 705–715), Mūsā's complaint to 'Umar b. 'Abd al-'Azīz (caliph in AD 717) would be hardly comprehensible. As a matter of fact, the 'purchase' and storage of pepper by the director of the land tax, as well as the unexecuted plan to send it as a gift, suggest instead that the pepper came from customs duties that had been paid in kind. The AD 649 sales to predetermined and legally obligated buyers, the AD 715–717 projected diplomatic gift, and the customs duties recurrently paid in kind make it look like the early caliphs did not know what to do with their pepper, as if the pepper import had become superabundant in the restricted Mediterranean horizon of Ummayad Egypt's trade.[9]

On the other hand, the legally obligated purchases attested at Edfu in AD 649 may not have been a recent Arab innovation. The same procedure might be implied in a papyrus from Hermopolis Magna, dated on palaeographical grounds to the fifth–sixth centuries AD.[10] In this document, an individual named Heliodoros asks his 'lord' and 'brother' Annas first to supply 'brother' Phoibammon with 6 ounces of pepper and then to provide ten other people (most probably other 'brothers') with quantities of pepper ranging from 1 ounce to 1 pound, for a total of 51 ounces. By analogy with what happens at Edfu in AD 649, where the city as a whole and each guild individually receives a number of pounds of pepper that is a multiple of 6 (or, in two cases, of 3), it may be suggested that Annas is the representative of a guild obliged to purchase 6 pounds (72 ounces) of pepper: the eleven 'brothers' buy 51 ounces, and Annas takes the remaining 21 ounces for himself.

The practice of customs duties being paid in kind might also be implied in the fourth-century AD records of a 'receiver of aromatics' (*ὑποδέκτης ἀρωματικῶν*) named Palladios. In all likelihood, the 146 pounds of pepper from the Antaeopolite nome as well as the 70 pounds of pepper, 4 of malabathron, 4 of *kasia*, 2.5 of spikenard, 2.5 of aloe, 2.5 of myrrh, 2.75 of costus, 2.75 of [unreadable], 1.33 of *arnabo* (?), and 2.25 of *melan* from the Lykopolite nome result from local customs duties on aromatics paid in kind.[11] Together with the quantities levied on the passage from the Red Sea to the Mediterranean, these may have been sold to legally obligated buyers. The cash

[9] Sijpesteijn (2013: 45–6).

[10] *BGU* 17.2704. The editor remarks that the word *ἀδελφός* (brother) stands here for 'colleague', or member of the same community.

[11] *PSI* 12.1264, ll. 11–21. Smaller quantities of pepper (8.5 and 7.33 lbs.) are included in the *apaitesis* lists of two villages of the Hermopolite nome: *P.Turner* 47.

collected and then received by the *alabarches* would be exchanged for gold by the *zygostatai* and *chrysonai* (money changers).[12]

The Late Antique evidence presented here suggests that customs duties on pepper and other Indian spices were paid in kind at that time, at least in some circumstances. Can the same be said for the cargo whose three-quarter portions are evaluated in the verso text of the Muziris papyrus?

The Red Sea tax was theorized as a tax in kind (a quarter of each cargo) and its payment in kind was certainly allowed. Most conspicuously, the possibility of a payment in kind is evoked at recto col. ii, ll. 17–19:

17 κρατεῖν τε καὶ κυριεύειν τὴν προκε̣ι̣-
18 [μένη]ν ὑποθήκην καὶ τεταρτολογεῖν καὶ τὰ λοιπὰ ἐσόμενα μέρη
19 [τρία μ]εταφέρειν οὗ ἐὰν αἱρῆσθε

'to get possession and own the aforesaid security and levy the quarter-tax and transfer the three parts that will remain to whomever you choose'

However, the payment in kind of the quarter-tax appears here only as an extreme solution, to be adopted at the expiration of the loan, after the borrower has proven unable to repay his debt and the lender seizes the pledged and unsold commodities as compensation. If the payment in kind had been the only way to pay customs duties on Indian goods, it would have made more sense to levy the duties as soon as the cargo entered the quarter-tax warehouse in Alexandria, or even earlier. Since, by contrast, the possibility of a payment in kind is evoked only after the loan has expired, one may conclude that the procedure implied in the text foresaw that the duties were paid in kind only in exceptional circumstances.

The text in fact suggests that this occurred only when it was expedient for the taxpayer—that is, only when market prices sank below the fiscal values fixed by the imperial administration. When the market prices in Alexandria were higher than the fiscal values, the merchant would certainly have preferred to sell the commodities on the market and pay the customs duties in money. Vice versa, when the market prices were lower than the values fixed by the imperial administration, the borrower would have no motivation to sell his under-priced goods on the market. He would be better off leaving the quarter portions to the tax collector, who would have kept them while waiting for better prices. It may also be imagined that sometimes customs dues were paid partially in money (for those commodities whose market price was higher

[12] Just., *Ed.* 11.2; 3, see Hendy (1985: 345). On *zygostatai* and *chrysonai* ('weighers' and 'buyers of gold'), cf. De Groote (2002).

than the fiscal value) and partially in kind (for those commodities whose market price happened to be lower than the fiscal value).

Ultimately, the question of how often the Red Sea tax was paid in kind might become one of how often the market prices were less than the fiscal values. The two texts of the Muziris papyrus suggest that the case was relatively rare. Certainly allowed in theory, payment in kind was discouraged in practice, because the establishment of very reasonable fiscal values made cash payment a more appealing option.

But were the customs duties for the *Hermapollon*'s cargo paid in money? As mentioned, the monetary evaluation of the three-quarter portions of the *Hermapollon*'s cargo on the verso text was explained by Rathbone with the possibility—envisioned in the recto text—that the borrower would (finish to) pay both the quarter-tax and his loan in kind: in his view, the merchant would have paid the quarter-tax in kind and the monetary evaluation of the remaining three-quarter portions would have been instrumental to a sale *en bloc* to a single buyer—the lender—at the current prices in the market of Alexandria.[13]

Rathbone's hypothesis is ingenious, but fails to explain why the value of the arabarchs' additional shares was added to the value of the rest of the three-quarter portions. If they were really taken by the arabarchs, why would they be sold by the borrower to the lender at a slightly higher price? Moreover, Rathbone assumes (and so does Morelli, who contends that the assessment concerned the conflated values of the tax-free cargo and the reimbursed arabarchs' additional shares)[14] that the arabarchs' additional shares were random extra weight taken because it would have been difficult to extract the right amount. As we have pointed out, the assumption is unwarranted: the 22.75 minas of *schidai* were more than one *schida* and corresponded to 1/50 (*pentekoste*) of the total shipment, whereas the 11.75 minas of sound ivory represented 1/600 (*hexakosioste*) of the total sound ivory.[15]

Since they were arithmetically determined fractions of the total cargoes, the arabarchs' additional shares were just surcharges of the quarter-tax and of course were not reimbursed. So again, why was the value of the arabarchs' additional shares added to the value of the rest of the three-quarter portions?

In the wording of the text, the arabarchs' additional shares of sound ivory and *schidai* are '*taken* (ἀρθέντων/ ἀρθεισῶν) by the arabarchs in addition for the payment of the quarter-tax (ὑπὲρ τῆς τεταρτολο̣γίας)'.

For the sound ivory, col. iii, ll. 11–14:

11 τῶν δὲ λοιπῶν ὑπὸ τῶν ἀραβαρχῶν πλείω ὑπὲρ
12 τῆς τεταρτολο̣γίας ἀρθέντων ἐν ἀ̣ριθμῷ ὀδόντων

[13] Rathbone (2000: 45). [14] Morelli (2011: 233). [15] See p. 227.

13 παρὰ τὸ αἱροῦν [- - -]λων ὀδόντων μν(ῶν) ια L'δ'
14 ὡς τῆς μν(ᾶς) τῶṿ ἴσ̣ω̣ν (δραχμῶν) ρ (δραχμαὶ) Ἀ̣ροε̣

Of the remaining [sc. tusks], taken by the arabarchs in addition for the payment of the quarter-tax, [included] in the weight number of tusks, in addition to the result [sc. the weight recalculation] [from the other?] tusks, 11.75 minas, at the same price of 100 drachmas per mina, make 1,175 drachmas.

For the *schidai*, col. iii, ll. 22–3:

22 τῶν δὲ λοιπῶν πλείω ὑπὲρ τῆς τεταρτολογίας ἀρθει-
23 σῶν ὡς πρόκειται μν(ῶν) κβ <L>δ' ὡς τῆς μνᾶς τῶν
24 ἴσων (δραχμῶν) ο ἀργ(υρίου) (δραχμαὶ) Ἀφϙβ𐅵

Of the remaining [sc. *schidai*], taken in addition for the payment of the quarter-tax, as above, 22.75 minas, at the same price of 70 drachmas per mina, make 1,592.5 drachmas.

Although the participles ἀρθέντων/ἀρθεισῶν suggest a levy in kind, and the explanation πλείω ὑπὲρ τῆς τεταρτολογίας clarifies that those shares were added on top of the base quarter rate, the reality is that the action of 'taking' was just notional: the arabarchs' additional share of sound ivory tusks is labelled with a plural (col. iii, l. 11: τῶν δὲ λοιπῶν [sc. ὀδόντων]), as if it consisted of several tusks, but its weight value (11.75 minas = *c*.6 kg) shows that it was just a fraction of a tusk.[16] Therefore, the entry 'of the remaining [sc. tusks]' was an arithmetically determined abstraction functional to an entirely notional process.

In the following pages, it will be shown that the assessment on the verso text points to a payment consistent with the main procedure implied by the loan contract on the recto. It will be shown, in other words, that the arabarchs took neither the base quarter rates nor their additional shares, but only the money corresponding to their fiscal values—that is, the money resulting from the weight (or the number) of the items multiplied by the price per unit fixed by the imperial administration. As a consequence, it will be inferred that the prices attested or implied by the verso text of the Muziris papyrus were the fiscal values established by the imperial administration. It will be also inferred that the merchants preferred to pay in money (12 drachmas for each mina of malabathron, 6 for each mina of pepper, 4,500 drachmas for each container of Gangetic nard, 100 drachmas for each mina of sound ivory, 70 drachmas for each mina of *schidai*), because the market prices in Alexandria were higher. Therefore, while Late Antique evidence suggests that the customs duties on pepper and other commodities from India were often paid in kind,

[16] The average weight of a tusk is 37.8 minas, see p. 268.

the Muziris papyrus shows that in the mid-second century AD the Red Sea tax was most often paid in money.[17]

If the inclusion of the arabarchs' additional shares in the evaluation of the three-quarter portions is ultimately incompatible with a payment in kind of the quarter-tax, and if the bureaucratic precision of the monetary evaluation (most unlikely in a normal business transaction worth several million drachmas) and the clearly fixed character of the prices (slightly and yet significantly different for the arabarchs' additional shares) suggest that the calculation was pertinent to a fiscal procedure, then how do we explain the evaluation of the three-quarter portions of the cargoes?[18]

12.2. DOUBLE CUSTOMS DUTIES ON DIFFERENT TAX BASES

What purpose then did the monetary evaluation of the three-quarter portions of the commodities serve? In order to answer this question, two premises should be recognized. First, the quarter-tax referred to in the papyrus may not have been the only tax levied on the *Hermapollon*'s cargo, since according to Strabo, Indian commodities were subject to double customs duties as they moved from the Red Sea to the Mediterranean.[19] Second, the text on the verso of the Muziris papyrus did not begin and possibly did not end with the evaluation of the three-quarter portions of the *Hermapollon*'s cargoes. What we read may have been just part of a more complex calculation.

Neither the editors nor the subsequent commentators emphasized what a reconstruction of the papyrus' width makes apparent (see Fig. 0.2): that the text on the verso did not begin with what was called 'col. i' (what we now call 'col. ii'). To the left, there was still space for one more column. Our interpretation of verso col. ii, ll. 1–3 and 14–19 confirms that this space was indeed used. In fact:

a. if col. ii, l. 4 relates to the assessment of the three-quarter portion of Gangetic nard (evaluated at col. iii, ll. 1–3);
b. if col. ii, ll. 5–9 relate to the assessment of the three-quarter portion of sound ivory (evaluated at col. iii, ll. 4–15);

[17] It is uncertain whether the seals with inscriptions ἀρωματικῆς τῶν κυρίων Καισάρων (*SB* 5.8843) and ἀρωματικῆς Ἀντωνίνου Καίσαρος (*SB* 5.8844) are pertinent to goods collected in kind as a tax on spice merchants, cf. Raschke (1978: 902, n. 996).

[18] In De Romanis (2004: 469 n. 27), I suggested that 75 per cent of the *Hermapollon*'s cargo belonged to one merchant and the remaining 25 per cent to another. But Morelli's interpretation of the weight numbers at col. ii, ll. 5 and 10 proved this suggestion wrong.

[19] Strab. 17.1.13, see pp. 132–5. Mentions of or allusions to the quarter-tax in recto col. ii, ll. 8; 10; 18; verso col. ii., l. 7; col. iii ll. 6; 12; 18; 22.

c. if col. ii, ll. 10–13 relate to the assessment of the three-quarter portion of *schidai* (evaluated at col. iii, ll. 16–26);
d. if col. ii, ll. 1–3 relate to the assessment of the three-quarter portion of pepper (evaluated at col. ii, ll. 20–30);
e. if a comparison with the preliminary section on sound ivory suggests that the preliminary section on pepper comprised one more line before col. ii, ll. 1–3;[20]
f. and if, at any rate, the two items, whose three-quarter portions are evaluated at col. ii, ll. 14–16 (tortoise shell?) and 17–19 (malabathron), require corresponding preliminary sections;

then it is virtually certain that there was an entire column preceding col. ii, whose last six or seven lines comprised the preliminary sections on tortoise shell (?), malabathron, and possibly the first line of the preliminary pepper section (Table 12.2).

It is unlikely that a text such as the one on the verso included an introduction of some twenty-two or twenty-three lines. It is far more likely that the first part of col. i recorded data related to the same six items that made up the *Hermapollon*'s cargo. From this perspective, it is interesting to note that the sequences of figures reported at col. ii, ll. 5–9 (related to sound ivory) and 10–13 (related to *schidai*) follow a pattern. In both cases, the sums of the base quarter rates and the arabarchs' additional shares *precede* the quantities corresponding to the base quarter rates alone and, in the case of sound ivory, it precedes the arabarchs' additional share as well. The same may also be true for the pepper data, if col. ii, l. 1 refers to the sum of the base quarter rate and the arabarchs' additional share: the weight number at l. 2, ending with 14.75 minas, is apparently the base quarter rate of a cargo whose weight number ends with 59 minas. Table 12.3 shows the sequence of total cargo, the base quarter rate + the arabarchs' additional share, and the arabarchs' additional share and the base quarter rate in col. ii, ll. 1–13.

All this suggests that the base quarter rates and the arabarchs' additional shares were broken down from the aggregate import duties (quarter rates + arabarchs' additional shares) rather than the other way round.

The inference that the aggregate duties had already been mentioned in col. i is supported by the formula ὧν ὁμοίως τιμὴ λογίζεται (col. iii, ll. 1–2; 5–10; 17–20).

[20] The 59 minas that closes col. ii, l. 1 identifies the weight number recorded there as either the weight of the entire pepper cargo or the sum of the base quarter rate plus the arabarchs' additional share. Since the parallel sections of sound ivory and *schidai* take five and four lines respectively, it seems unlikely that the pepper data were squeezed into only three lines. Although the layout of the text is not that rigidly structured (see for instance the differences between the sound ivory and *schidai* sections), it is more likely that the pepper section began with the last line(s) of col. i.

Table 12.2 Reconstructed layout of *P. Vindob.* G 40.822 verso coll. i–iv.

	col. i	col. ii	col. iii	col. iv
1	?	pepper	Gangetic nard	?
2	?	pepper	Gangetic nard	?
3	?	pepper	Gangetic nard	?
4	?	Gangetic nard	sound ivory	?
5	?	sound ivory	sound ivory	?
6	?	sound ivory	sound ivory	?
7	?	sound ivory	sound ivory	?
8	?	sound ivory	sound ivory	?
9	?	sound ivory	sound ivory	?
10	?	*schidai*	sound ivory	?
11	?	*schidai*	sound ivory	?
12	?	*schidai*	sound ivory	?
13	?	*schidai*	sound ivory	?
14	?	tortoise shell?	sound ivory	?
15	?	tortoise shell?	sound ivory	?
16	?	tortoise shell?	*schidai*	?
17	?	malabathron	*schidai*	?
18	?	malabathron	*schidai*	?
19	?	malabathron	*schidai*	?
20	?	pepper	*schidai*	?
21	?	pepper	*schidai*	?
22	?	pepper	*schidai*	?
23	tortoise shell?	pepper	*schidai*	?
24	tortoise shell?	pepper	*schidai*	?
25	tortoise shell?	pepper	*schidai*	?
26	malabathron	pepper	total ivory	?
27	malabathron	pepper	total	?
28	malabathron	pepper	total	?
29	pepper	pepper	total	?
30		pepper		?

In these three sentences, the adverb ὁμοίως (similarly) makes sense *only* if other quantities of Gangetic nard, sound ivory tusks, and *schidai* had already been assessed in col. i, with the same fixed values of 4,500 drachmas per container of Gangetic nard, 100 drachmas per mina of sound ivory tusks, and 70 drachmas per mina of *schidai.*

In sum, my understanding of the text rests on the assumption that Indian commodities were subject—just as Strabo says—to double customs duties, once for entering and then again for leaving Egypt. But while the import duties applied to the value of the entire incoming cargoes, the export duties were levied only on the outgoing three-quarter portions of the cargoes,[21] precisely

[21] Since the unsold commodities stored in the *tetarte* warehouse of Alexandria were subject only to the import quarter-tax (recto col. ii, ll. 18–19), the commodities were subject to export customs duties only if and when they were exported outside Egypt.

Table 12.3 Verso col. ii, ll. 1–13: factorization of the pepper, Gangetic nard, sound ivory, and *schidai* cargoes.

Items	Line	Text
pepper	1	59 minas *(base quarter rate + arabarchs' share?)*
	2	14.75 minas *(base quarter rate)*
	3	58 minas
Gangetic nard	4	20 *(base quarter rate)*
sound ivory	5	105 talents, 13 minas *(total cargo)*
	6	26 talents, 30 minas *(base quarter rate + arabarchs' share)*
	7	11.75 minas *(arabarchs' share)*
	8	26 talents, 18.25 minas *(base quarter rate)*
	9	
schidai	10	17 talents, 33 minas *(total cargo)*
	11	4 talents, 46 minas *(base quarter rate + arabarchs' share)*
	12	
	13	4 talents, 23.25 minas *(base quarter rate)*

because one quarter had already been taken (in the case of payment in kind), or considered taken (in the case of payment in money), to cover the cost of the import duties.

The fine levied on those who did not register themselves and their household members in the census declarations may have been assessed similarly.[22] If they failed to do it once, they were fined a quarter of their property; if they were reported not to have done it twice, they were fined twice a quarter of their property: in all likelihood, the first quarter was on the entire property, the second on the remaining three-quarters. It may be interesting to note that a comparable procedure was followed in the assessment of the *quarto e vintena* tax at the *Casa da Índia* in Lisbon: the first rate (*quarto*, 25 per cent) applied to 100 per cent of the pepper cargo, but the second (*vintena*, 5 per cent) only to 75 per cent of it.[23]

Therefore, col. i, ll. 1–21 could have looked something like this:

1. **Heading**: Accountancy of the *Hermapollon*
2. **Import customs duties:**
3. **tortoise shell** (?) weight number
4. quarter of the above
5. price per mina and quarter rate monetary value;
6. **malabathron** weight number
7. quarter of the above

[22] *BGU* 5.1210, ll. 150–2.

[23] Ruy Mendes, ff. 80v.: 'Tirar o quarto e vintena segundo se tira na Casa da Índia não é outra coisa salvo saber de uma certa quantia o quarto e dos três quartos dela mesma a vintena, quantos serão e tirados dela, quantos ficarão.' Cf. Marques de Almeida (1994: 1.255–7).

8. price per mina and quarter rate monetary value;
9. **pepper** 18,??? talents of weight and 59 minas
10. quarter plus arabarchs' additional share
11. price per mina and monetary value of the above;
12. **Gangetic nard** 80 containers,
13. quarter 20 containers,
14. at the price of 4,500 drachmas per container, 15 talents;
15. **sound ivory** 105 talents of weight and 13 minas,
16. quarter plus 1/600 of the above, 26 talents of weight and 30 minas
17. at the price of 100 drachmas per mina, 26 talents of money and 30 minas;
18. ***schidai***, 17 talents and 33 minas,
19. quarter plus 1/50 of the above, 4 talents of weight and 46 minas,
20. at the price of 70 drachmas per mina, 3 talents of money and 2,020 minas.
21. **total** for the *Hermapollon* cargo import customs duties.

Then col. i, ll. 22–29 could have been something like this:

22. **Export customs duties:**
23. **tortoise shell** (?) weight number
24. base quarter rate
25. minuend
26. **malabathron** cargo weight number
27. base quarter rate
28. minuend
29. **pepper** 18,??? talents of weight and 59 minas

If this was approximately the content of col. i, we have to deduce that the rate for the import customs duties was 25 per cent, and that the purpose of evaluating the three-quarter portions was to determine the tax base for the export customs duties to be paid in money, just like the import duties. Therefore, if the first part of col. i assessed the import customs duties, while the second part of col. i and all of columns ii and iii calculated the tax base of the export customs duties, it is likely that the text did not end with col. iii, l. 29. To the right of col. iii there was certainly space for a fourth column, which may have included:

a. the amount of the export customs duties (inferred from the tax base of 1,151 talents and 5,852 drachmas);
b. the amount of the import customs duties (already reckoned in col. i); and
c. the sum of the import and export customs duties.

Finally, a few remarks about the order in which the commodities of the *Hermapollon*'s cargo are arranged in the text. As mentioned, while the import

Table 12.4 Formulae for the evaluation of the three-quarter portions of the *Hermapollon*'s cargoes.

col. ii, ll. 14–30	col. iii, ll. 1–25
$V = (\frac{3}{4}a - d) \times c$	$V = \frac{3}{4}a \times c$
Tortoise shell?	Gangetic nard
$V = (\frac{3}{4}a - d) \times c$	$V = \{[(\frac{3}{4}a - b) \times \frac{95}{97.5}] \times c\} + (b \times c)$
Malabathron	Sound ivory
$V = \{[(\frac{3}{4}a - b - d) \times \frac{95}{97.66}] \times c\} + (b \times c)$	$V = \{[(\frac{3}{4}a - b) \times \frac{95}{97.5}] \times c\} + (b \times c)$
Pepper	Schidai

customs duties applied to the entire incoming cargo, the export duties applied only to the outgoing three-quarter portions of the cargo: that is, whatever did not leave Egypt was not subject to the export customs duties. If the weight alteration of the three-quarter portions of tortoise shell (?) and malabathron and the weight reduction of the three-quarter portion of pepper occurred for the same reason, then the first three items—unlike the subsequent three—undergo a weight reduction that cannot be attributed to either the removal of the quarter or the deduction of the shares taken in addition by the arabarchs.

The point is made clearer in Table 12.4, where the process of evaluating the three-quarter portions is expressed with a series of mathematical equations. The six items are put in two columns in the same order in which they appear in the papyrus. ***V*** is the monetary value of the three-quarter portion; ***a*** is the quantification of the total cargo; ***b*** is the arabarchs' share; ***c*** is the price per unit; and ***d*** is the quantity subtracted for unspecified reasons.

The ***d*** value appears to be crucial. It distinguishes the first three items from the second three. I suggest identifying ***d*** as the amounts of tortoise shell (?), malabathron, and pepper that were not subject to the second quarter-tax because they were not exported outside Egypt. If this identification is correct, then the order in which the six items are listed becomes clear: first the three items that have been partially sold in Egypt are evaluated, then the three that were entirely exported outside Egypt; within each of the two groups, the items from which the arabarchs do not take their share—tortoise shell (?) and malabathron in the first group, and Gangetic nard in the second—are evaluated before the others.

12.3. RATES

Three factors combine to determine the fiscal burden on Indian commodities on their way from the Red Sea to the Mediterranean: the rate at which the customs duties are set; the fiscal value assigned to each commodity; and the weight standard used for the commodities quantified by weight. Since the imperial administration could always choose to maintain or discontinue the established routine by retaining or altering one or more of these three components, the balance between them defines the imperial fiscal policy.

The verso text of the Muziris papyrus clarifies that the rate of the import customs duties was 25 per cent, but the rate of the export duties is not explicitly disclosed. However, several clues suggest that it was as high as the one for the import customs duties.[24] To begin with, an equal rate is supported by Strabo's comment that 'double customs duties are collected, both when they are imported into Egypt and when they are exported from it'.[25] As Harrauer and Sijpesteijn observed, Strabo's τέλη διπλάσια συνάγεται cannot just mean that customs duties were collected twice.[26] In particular, such wording would be awkward if the import customs duty was a 25 per cent tax applied to the entire incoming cargo, while the export customs duty was only 2.5 per cent, and applied only to the three-quarter portions of the cargo, minus what was not exported.[27]

Furthermore, the Muziris papyrus reveals that the fiscal values by which the commodities were assessed did not change from Coptos to Alexandria.[28] Those values were probably much lower than the usual market prices in either place, so that the actual rate was considerably lower than 25 per cent of the market price when the customs duties were paid in money. Assessed on those low values, a 2.5 per cent rate would have produced very modest revenues: a cargo fiscally valued at 100 would pay 25 as an import customs duty, but only 1.875 as an export customs duty. In this way, the export duties would have hardly been more relevant than the local customs duties in the internal Egyptian markets, which Strabo does not mention.[29]

Moreover, the discount granted by calculating the tax base of the export duties with a heavier talent was meant to compensate merchants for the arabarchs' shares on top of the import duties. Since the rates of the arabarchs' shares may have differed considerably (from 1/600 for tusks of sound ivory

[24] My scepticism (De Romanis (1998: 16) about a double quarter-tax did not take into account the possibility that the fiscal values could be considerably lower than the market prices or the fact that the second quarter-tax applied only to 75 per cent of the cargo. Nappo (2018: 89) suggests a rate of 2.5 per cent for the export customs duties. Duncan-Jones (2006: 2) characterizes the rate of 25 per cent for customs duties as typical of the external frontier, in contrast with the low dues—most often 2.5 per cent—at the entrances to provinces inside the empire.

[25] Strab. 17.1.13. [26] Harrauer and Sijpesteijn (1985: 140).

[27] In the Early Roman Empire, customs duties are often 2.5 per cent: De Laet (1949: *passim*); Duncan Jones (2006: 4–6). For pearls subject to a 2.5 per cent tax (*quadragesima Asiae*? *quadragesima Galliarum*?), cf. Quint., *Decl. min.* 359. In Illyricum, 5 per cent and 12.5 per cent are also attested: De Romanis (1998: 51–4).

[28] See the ὁμοίως at col. iii, ll. 1; 5; 17.

[29] For the internal customs duties, cf. *WChr* 273 col. i, ll. 1–15. The dues seem to be calculated at the rate of 1/40 of the fiscal value, with small reductions for some items.

to 1/50 for *schidai*), an almost flat compensation by a recalculation of the weight with a heavier standard (a talent of 97.5 or 97.66 as opposed to 95 lbs.) could not have proportionally counterweighed their uneven rates. However, if the rate of the export customs duties was only 2.5 per cent, the discount granted to the merchants would never have equalled the arabarchs' shares, even when the latter were as low as 1/600, as in the case of sound ivory tusks.[30] Indeed, in the case of *schidai*, the arabarchs' share (2 per cent of the entire incoming cargo) would have been even higher than the export duties themselves, if they were 2.5 per cent of the three-quarters of the cargo.[31]

Finally, the verso text of the Muziris papyrus proves that the rate of the import customs duties was 25 per cent, and the recto text refers to 'the customs warehouse of the quarter-tax in Alexandria' (ἡ ἐν Ἀλεξανδρείᾳ τῆς τετάρτης παραλημπτικὴ ἀποθήκη).[32] If two different rates applied to import and export customs duties, we would expect the warehouse in Alexandria to be labelled the customs warehouse of the quarter- and (for example) the fortieth-taxes (ἡ ἐν Ἀλεξανδρείᾳ τῆς τετάρτης καὶ τεσσαρακοστῆς παραλημπτικὴ ἀποθήκη).

In conclusion, the Red Sea tax (*maris Rubri vectigal*) could be described either as a single or a double quarter-tax, depending on whether the commodities remained in Egypt or were re-exported to other areas of the Roman Empire. The two quarter-taxes applied to different tax bases—the first on 100 per cent of the incoming cargo, the second on 75 per cent of the cargo minus what was to remain in Egypt. The import duties on certain commodities—sound ivory, *schidai*, pepper—had variable surcharges on top of the quarter base rate. These additional charges were compensated by reductions in the tax base for the export duties. Such reductions were granted to the merchants, but not to the arabarchs, which is why the weight values of the arabarchs' additional shares are not recalculated using the heavier weight unit.

In Late Antiquity, the quarter-tax was replaced by a one-eighth tax (*octava*).[33] When exactly the quarter-tax was reduced to an *octava* is difficult

[30] A cargo of 100 talents of sound ivory would have paid 1,000 drachmas as the arabarchs' share. At the rate of 2.5 per cent, the export customs duties would be 10,961 drachmas with a reduction of 289 drachmas from the sum resulting from a talent of 95 lbs. (11,250 dr). By contrast, at the rate of 25 per cent, the export customs duties would be 109,615 drachmas, with a reduction of 2,885 drachmas from the sum resulting from a talent of 95 lbs. (112,500 dr).

[31] The arabarchs' share of 100 talents of *schidai* would be 8,400 drachmas. The discount resulting from the 97.5 lb. talent would only be 202 drachmas, with customs duties of 2.5 per cent; it would be 2,020 drachmas with a tax rate of 25 per cent. Similarly, the arabarchs' share of 100 talents of sound ivory is 1,000 drachmas. The discount resulting from the 97.5 lb. talent would only be 289 dr with customs duties of 2.5 per cent; it would be 2,890 drachmas with a tax rate of 25 per cent.

[32] Recto col. ii ll. 7–8.

[33] The commodities brought by ambassadors from foreign countries were subject to customs duties levied by the *octava* collectors: *Cod. Theod.* 4.13.8 = *Cod. Iust.* 4.61.8; eunuchs (apparently brought from beyond the borders) were subject to the *octava*: *Cod. Iust.* 4.42.2. (for *spadones Indici* subject to the *vectigal*, cf. Marcian. *Dig.* 39.4.16.7); the *octava* was collected in Alexandria:

to say. The *terminus post quem* for the replacement is AD 174, when the quarter-tax farmer (*manc. IIII merc.*, *τεταρτώνης*, *dy rb*ʿ) L. Antonius Callistratus is honoured in a trilingual inscription from Palmyra.[34] The *terminus ante quem* is given by Valens' law, which styles the *octava* for those who trade in the *commercia* as 'customary'.[35] The consequences of the new arrangement seem nonetheless clear. While the loan contract on the recto of the Muziris papyrus and the low fiscal prices on its verso reflect a preference for payments in money, the Late Antique payments in kind suggest that the 12.5 per cent tax rate was applied to relatively high fiscal values. In other words, it seems that the reconfiguration of the customs duties imposed on eastern commodities consisted of a reduction in the tax rate—from 25 to 12.5 per cent—balanced by a rise in the fiscal values.

12.4. FISCAL VALUES

A double quarter-tax for a total rate of 43.5 per cent would hardly have been tolerable if the duties had to be either paid in kind or converted into money at a fiscal value very close to the market price. Such rates could be affordable only if the merchant was allowed to pay in money according to fiscal values that were much lower than the market price.

Based on round fractions of a talent—6 drachmas ($=\frac{1}{1000}$ of a talent) per mina for pepper, 12 drachmas ($=\frac{1}{500}$ of a talent) per mina for malabathron, 4,500 drachmas ($=\frac{3}{4}$ of a talent) per container for Gangetic nard, 100 drachmas ($=\frac{1}{60}$ of a talent) per mina for sound ivory, and 70 drachmas ($= \frac{1}{100} + \frac{1}{600}$ of a talent) per mina for *schidai*—the values that are attested in (or may be inferred from) the verso of the Muziris papyrus were clearly artificial and certainly lower, although not necessarily evenly so, than the market prices in either Coptos or Alexandria. If Pliny's price for black pepper—4 denarii per pound, which means 25.33 drachmas per mina[36]—is in some way indicative of the price in Rome at the time of the Muziris papyrus, then it is extremely unlikely that the price for pepper assumed by the papyrus (6 drachmas per mina)

Sophronius, *Miracula SS. Cyri et Iohannis* 1–2, cf. Duffy (1984: 78); Gascou (2006: 25–6); Berytus: *Cod. Theod.* 4.13.6 = *Cod. Iust.* 4.61.7; and Caesarea Maritima: *SEG* 39.1620: see De Romanis (1998: 48–55); Nappo (2018: 154–6).

[34] *IGLS* 17.1.197 (= *PAT* 1413).

[35] *Cod. Theod.* 4.13.6 = *Cod. Iust.* 4.61.7. I understand *commerciis—interesse* as 'attend the *commercia*' (markets on the borders). For this meaning of *commercium*, cf. *ILS* 775. According to Seeck (1919: 11, 120, 137), the date and the function of the recipient is corrupt: the law dates to 369 and Archelaus would have been *comes sacrarum largitionum* (cf. also Mommsen, *ad loc.*; *PLRE* I Archelaus 3). Delmaire (1989b: 55–6) sticks to the readings of the manuscripts.

[36] Plin., *NH* 12.28.

represented the market price in Alexandria or Coptos. Even allowing for the double quarter-tax and the transport costs, the disparity would remain too wide.

We may hope one day to have some pepper prices from the Eastern Desert of Egypt. In two ostraca from the fort of Didymoi, along the Coptos–Berenice caravan road, a soldier named Albucius (probably stationed at Phoinikon sometime between AD 77 and 92) enquires about some pepper that his fellow soldiers guarding the next station on the way to Berenice may have bought for him:

> Albucius to Annius his master and brother, greetings. Concerning the pepper, as I asked you and Antonius, if you have bought any, send a message so that I too may know how much and for how much. And if you need anything, write to me. Greet Demetrios. Farewell.

> Albucius to Paulus and Sempronius, greetings. Receive a bunch of asparagus and two radishes. And concerning the pepper, write to me if you have any, how much, and at what price, and tell Annius to send a message to me. 11th. Farewell.[37]

In all likelihood, this pepper had been acquired at Berenice, through privileged and probably not entirely legal channels. As A. Bülow-Jacobsen has rightly remarked, the pepper Albucius asks for is 'of the "tax-free" kind that may have come directly, if unofficially, from the docks at Berenike'.[38] In fact, if Albucius is ready to buy any quantity of pepper at any price, it is because he is sure that it will be a modest quantity at a very good price. As a soldier, Albucius could take advantage of the exemption from customs duties,[39] but it may also be surmised that the pepper was somehow extorted by the commanding officer and then resold to his subordinates at a reasonable price. Whatever the case, Albucius expected to pay a price lower than the market rate at either Coptos or Alexandria.

As a proxy for that pepper price, we have the price of frankincense provided by *O.Did.* 323, ll. 10–16, where Iulius, most probably stationed at Aphrodites Oros, replies to his fellow soldier Antonius, posted at Didymoi (the next station toward Coptos), who had enquired about the frankincense price. After consulting the soldiers posted at Compasi, the next station on the road to Berenice, Iulius writes back to Antonius: 'Concerning the frankincense, I wrote to Compasi and they say "for three staters". If any is brought up, I shall send it to you, for I do not have any here.'[40] Here again, the commodity was (illicitly?) acquired at Berenice and resold to the soldiers stationed along the caravan road to Coptos. Assuming that the price refers to the same mina of the Muziris

[37] *O.Did.* 327; 328; transl. by A. Bülow-Jacobsen.
[38] Bülow-Jacobsen (2012), *ad O.Did.* 327.
[39] Tac., *Ann.* 13.51, on which see De Laet (1949: 434).
[40] *O.Did.* 323, ll. 10–16; transl. by Bülow-Jacobsen.

Table 12.5 Prices and fiscal values of black pepper and frankincense (in drachmas per mina).

	Price to the soldiers of the *praesidia*	Price at Coptos and Alexandria	Fiscal value for the quarter-tax	Pliny's prices (Rome)
Black pepper	9?	15/18?	6	25.33
Frankincense	12	18/21?	6/9?	38 (best quality) 31.66 (second quality) 19 (third quality)

papyrus ($\frac{95}{60}$ of a Roman pound), the Coptos market price must have been higher than 12 drachmas per mina, but most probably lower than 38 per mina, which is the price given by Pliny for frankincense of the best quality.[41]

The comparison of the fiscal value for black pepper attested in the Muziris papyrus, the price for frankincense in *O.Did.* 323, and Pliny's prices for both black pepper and frankincense suggest hypothetical ranges for the market prices in Coptos and Alexandria (Table 12.5).

Established by the imperial administration,[42] the fiscal values for the Red Sea tax were not supposed to change with market fluctuations—much less depend on the subjective judgment of the arabarchs.[43] As a consequence, the Red Sea tax was only in theory a combination of the 25 per cent import duties and the 18.75 per cent export duties. In practice, it was a flexible-rate tax dependent on the ratio between the fiscal values and the dynamics of the market prices in Coptos and Alexandria. In other words, the actual rate of the tax varied according to prevailing economic trends: higher market prices meant lower tax rates, and lower market prices meant higher tax rates. When the market prices fell below the fiscal values, the possibility of a payment in kind limited the tax rate of the two quarter-taxes to a maximum of 25 and

41 Plin., *NH* 12.65. For the Late Antique prices, cf. pp. 103–4.

42 Payments in money based on predetermined values were envisioned for the *quadragesima Galliarum* and *quadragesima Asiae* as well; cf. France (2014: 98). However, it was the treasury, not the tax farmers who determined them.

43 Bang (2008: 205) contends that the customs collector was allowed to make a subjective judgement on the value of goods and that the procedure 'left plenty of discretionary scope to the publican for increasing his intake'. This theory applies neither to the Red Sea tax as described by the Muziris papyrus nor, as I see it, to the customs duties alluded to in Quint., *Decl. min.* 340 (cf. Suet., *rhet.* 1), where the *mango*, who dresses his young slave in the *praetexta*, does not fear an illegal overestimation, but a legitimate estimation of the *pretiosus puer*. Moreover, the law allowing the publican to simply return what had been wrongfully exacted without penal consequences (Ulp., *Dig.* 39.4.1.4) aimed to curb widespread behaviours like the *mango*'s, who pretended that his slave was free-born. In a *Rechtsstaat*, this is a fiscal fraud. Exactions in accordance with custom (for the importance of *consuetudo*/*συνήθεια* in the fiscal procedures, cf. e.g. Paul., *Dig.* 39.4.4.2; *CIS* 2.3.3913; *SB* 18.13315) did not prevent disputes between parties (especially, we may imagine, in times of unstable market prices), but that does not mean that they were executed at the discretion of the tax collector.

Table 12.6 Pepper fiscal values in the Muziris papyrus and in *BM Or.* inv. 8903, approximations for Alexandria market prices in the second and seventh centuries AD, and the ratio between the two data.

	Fiscal Values	Market Prices	Ratio FV: MP
Muziris papyrus	6 drachmas per mina	15 to 18 drachmas per mina	1 : 2.5 to 1: 3
BM Or. inv. 8903	1/6 of a *solidus*	1/4 to 1/3 of a *solidus*	1 : 1.5 to 1 : 2

18.75 per cent, respectively. Moreover, since each commodity had its own price curves, the Red Sea tax rate was not only flexible, but also specific to each item, giving the imperial administration the chance to pursue its fiscal policy by establishing fixed prices that were deliberately more or less distant from the most usual market prices.

If, at the time of the Muziris papyrus, the market price for pepper at Coptos and Alexandria was between 15 and 18 drachmas per mina, a fiscal value of only 6 drachmas represented a strong incentive for a payment in money. The Late Antique evidence for payments in kind suggests that the gap between fiscal value and market price had narrowed (Table 12.6). If the Late Antique fiscal value for a pound of pepper was 1/6 of a *solidus*—the price paid by the legally obligated buyers in AD 649—and the retail price ranged between one-fourth and one-third of a *solidus*,[44] it is plausible that the wholesale market price at Alexandria sometimes fell below the fiscal value, inducing the merchant to pay the customs duties in kind.

12.5. WEIGHT STANDARDS

As mentioned, for pepper, sound ivory, and *schidai*, the second quarter-tax was assessed with different weight standards. While the arabarchs' shares were still assessed with the official talent of 95 Roman pounds, the rest of the three-quarter portions, minus what was not re-exported, was recalculated with talents of 97.66 and 97.5 Roman pounds respectively for pepper and the two kinds of ivory. This change in the weight standard has been interpreted as a trick devised by the tax collectors to take more than they were legally entitled to, but it was nothing of the sort. Quite the contrary, by calculating a lower nominal weight for the same amount of pepper, sound ivory, and *schidai*, the tax base of (and therefore what was owed for) the export customs duties of those commodities was reduced. This reassessment is said to be 'usually

[44] See p. 102.

reckoned for the merchants' (*ὅσῳ συνήθως πρὸς τοὺς ἐμπόρους λογίζεται*) because it was in the merchants' favour and was granted to the merchants alone—that is, it was not applied to the arabarchs' share.[45] The ironic (but logical) consequence was that the merchants, who redeemed the quota of the cargoes owed as import customs duties by paying in money, got a discount on the rest of the three-quarter portions when they paid the export customs duties, but not on the arabarchs' additional shares.

Since it ultimately reduced the income of both the treasury and the arabarchs, it is extremely unlikely that the heavier weight standard was adopted on the initiative of the arabarchs. It was probably the imperial administration that granted the merchants a discount on the export customs duties to balance the surcharges applied to the import customs duties on some commodities.

This legitimate manipulation of the weight standard suggests another way in which the imperial administration regulated the tax burden. W. Kula's famous book demonstrates how the chaotic metrologies of pre-capitalistic societies reflect social conflicts revolving around the definition of the fiscal burden.[46] In the verso text of the Muziris papyrus, the surcharges for the arabarchs on the import customs duties and the talents of different standards —95, 97.5, and 97.66 Roman pounds—reflect the tensions between the imperial administration, the tax farmers, and the taxpayers.

That the Roman administration deliberately manipulated the weight standard in order to adjust the fiscal burden is also proved by two official weights, apparently related to different taxes, dated AD 59/60.[47] They both show the standard of two-thirds of a mina, but one, found at Coptos, sets that measure at $1 + \frac{38}{288}$ of a Roman pound, the other, in Alexandria, fixes the same measure at $1 + \frac{51}{288}$ of a Roman pound.[48] They hint at talents that are heavier than the 95-pound talent of the quarter-tax at the time of the Muziris papyrus.[49] The weight from Coptos implies a talent of 101.875 Roman pounds, the one from Alexandria a talent of 105.9375 Roman pounds. A third standard for the same measure is set by another official weight, dated AD 100/101: two-thirds of a mina are equated to $1 + \frac{40}{288}$ of a Roman pound, which leads to a talent of 102.5 Roman pounds.[50] Even more standards are attested in the literary sources (Table 12.7). In general, all this evidence suggests that the imperial administration often manipulated the weight unit in order to adjust the fiscal burden.

[45] Verso col. iii l. 9: *ὅσῳ συνήθως πρὸς τοὺς ἐμπόρους λογίζεται*; ll. 19–20: *καθὼς [[καὶ]] δὲ πρὸς τοὺς ἐμπόρους λογίζεται.*

[46] Kula (1986). [47] *IGRom* 1.1374; 1379. [48] De Romanis (1998: 37–9).

[49] Verso col. iii, ll. 6–7: *σταθμίοις τῆς τετάρτης τοῦ ταλάντου λογιζομένọụ πρὸς λί(τρας) ϙ̅ε̅*; 18: *ὁμοίοις σταθμịọịs μὲν τετάρτης.*

[50] *SB* 8.10070. The weight was bought in Cairo.

Table 12.7 Weight unit standards in Roman Egypt.

<table>
<tr><th>Pounds per talent</th><th>Source</th></tr>
<tr><td>90</td><td>MSR 1.234 ll. 1–3: ἡ Πτολεμαϊκὴ μνᾶ ἔχει Γ· ιη′, < ρμδ′, γράμματα υλβ′, ὀβολοὺς ωξδ′, θέρμους Ἀσϙς′, κεράτια ͵Βφϙβ′, χαλκοῦς ͵Ϛϡιβ′; cf. MSR 1.228, ll. 25–6; MSR 1.236 ll. 22–3; MSR 1.254, 11. 11–4; MSR 1.256, ll. 15–6.</td></tr>
<tr><td>93.75</td><td>MSR 1.208, ll. 19–20: ἡ Ἀλεξανδρινὴ μνᾶ ἄγει ὁλκὰς ρν′, ἀλλαχοῦ ρνη′</td></tr>
<tr><td>98.75</td><td></td></tr>
<tr><td>95</td><td>verso, col. iii, ll. 6–7: σταθμίοις τῆς τετάρτης τοῦ|ταλάντου λογιζομένọụ πρὸ̣ς λί(τρας) ϙ̅ε̅</td></tr>
<tr><td>97.5</td><td>verso, col. iii, l. 8: λογιζομ̣έ̣ṿων εἰς τὸ τάλαντον λι(τρῶν) ϙ̣̅[ζ̅ L′</td></tr>
<tr><td>97.66</td><td>verso, col. ii, ll. 21–5.</td></tr>
<tr><td>100</td><td>Gal., 13.538–9 K.: ἡ δὲ μνᾶ ἐπὶ τούτου τοῦ φαρμάκου ἔχει ὁλκὰς ρξ′ (= MSR 1.212, ll. 12–3); cf. 13.539 K. (= MSR 1.212, ll. 13–9); 647 K.; 13.749 K. (= MSR 1.213, ll. 13–5); 13.789 K. (=MSR 1.214, ll. 5–10); MSR 1.240, 11. 13–4; MSR 1.248, ll. 23–4.</td></tr>
<tr><td>101.875</td><td>I.Portes 63 = IGRom 1.1379: (ἔτους) ἕκτου Νέρωνος|Κλαυδίου Καίσαρος|Σεβαστοῦ Γερμανικοῦ|Αὐτοκράτορος,|ἐπὶ Λουκίου Ἰουλίου|Οὐηστίνου ἡγεμόν[ος],|λί(τρα) α′, ο(ὐ)γ(κία) α′ (ἥμισυ), γρ(άμματα) β′ (Coptos).</td></tr>
<tr><td>102.5</td><td>SB 8.10070: (ἔτους) δ' Αὐτοκράτορος Καίσαρος|Νέρουα Τραϊανοῦ Σεβαστοῦ|Γερμανικοῦ, ἐπὶ Γαΐου Μινικί|ου Ἰταλοῦ ἡγεμόνος,|λί(τρα) α′, ο(ὐ)γ(κία) α′ (ἡμίσεια), γρ(άμματα) δ′.</td></tr>
<tr><td>105.9375</td><td>IGRom 1.1374: (ἔτους) ἕκτου Νέρωνος|Κλαυδίου Καίσαρος|Σεβαστοῦ Γερμαν[ι]κοῦ|Αὐτοκράτορος,|ἐπὶ Λευκίου Ἰουλίου|Οὐηστίνου ἡγεμόνος,| λ(ίτρα) α′, ο(ὐ)γ(κίαι) β′, γ(ράμματα) γ′ (Alexandria?).</td></tr>
</table>

It is likely, and suggested by the Muziris papyrus, that Indian cargoes were weighed in the Red Sea ports with weights installed there.[51] When cargoes were sold at Coptos, they were measured with weights of the same standard. In a papyrus of the third century AD, a certain Kalleas, while sending small amounts of medical and aromatic substances (among them four minas of malabathron) to a lady, adds that 'the way I received (sc. the goods), (measured) with the Coptos weight (*σταθμῷ Κοπτιτικῷ*), so I supplied to her, like it was not for strangers, but for family'.[52] If the AD 59/60 weight found at Coptos implying a 101.875-pound talent pertained to the Coptos standard and the Red sea tax, the difference from the 95-pound talent of the Muziris papyrus implies an escalation of the fiscal burden by about 7.2 per cent.

[51] At recto col. ii, l. 1, *στήσας* should have the cargo as object, even if commodities like Gangetic nard were not weighed, but counted.

[52] *PSI* 15.1558, ll. 4-5: *καθὼ̣ς παρέλαβọν σταθμῷ Κοπτιτικῷ οὕ|τω καὶ ạ[ὐτ]ῇ παρέστησα οὐχ ὡς ξένοις ἀ<λ>λ' ὡ̣ς| ἰδίοις*. The obvious implication is that the 'Coptos weight' was heavier than another that Kalleas could have used.

In conclusion, the mechanics of the Red Sea tax suggest four ways in which the imperial administration could manage the fiscal burden. First, it could authorize the arabarchs to levy variable surcharges. This measure apparently aimed to ease negotiations between the treasury and the tax farmers: the Muziris papyrus shows that at that time the arabarchs were allowed to levy surcharges on pepper and ivory (both sound ivory and *schidai*). Second, the imperial administration could revise the values established for a single commodity. In this way, it could have made small adjustments to the fiscal policy, by selectively increasing or reducing the fiscal burden on one or another commodity. We have no evidence for such revisions, but it seems reasonable to assume that the fiscal values were updated from time to time. Third, the imperial administration could alter the tax rate, which it did sometime between AD 174 and 369, lowering it from 25 to 12.5 per cent. Late Antique evidence for customs duties paid in kind suggests that in connection with the reduction of the tax rate, the fiscal values were brought much closer to market prices. Fourth, the imperial administration could modify the standard of the weight unit. Such a measure would have had a proportionally undifferentiated impact on all the commodities measured by weight: heavier standards corresponded with lighter dues, and lighter standards with heavier dues. In the Muziris papyrus, heavier talents are used to reduce the tax base of the export customs duties on those commodities (pepper and ivory) that had been subject to surcharges on the import customs duties. The introduction of new weight standards by Nero and Trajan marked relevant turns in imperial fiscal policy. The standards introduced in AD 59/60 and 100/101 were probably heavier than those they replaced. It is not coincidental that Nero's weights go back to the very end of his first five years, when measures favouring taxpayers were put in place and even a general suppression of customs duties was imagined.[53] It is also not coincidental that Nero's first five years were enthusiastically praised by Trajan.[54] Emperors like Vespasian had a very different approach to the level of the customs duties at Alexandria.[55] A talent of only 95 pounds, lighter than Nero's and Trajan's standards, was more in line with a stricter attitude towards taxation.[56]

[53] Tac., *Ann.* 13.50–1. [54] Aur. Vict. 5.2. [55] Cass. Dio 66.8.2–7.
[56] De Romanis (1998).

13

Dramatis Personae

The manager of the department charged with levying customs duties on Indian commodities (*paralemptes*) was also the lender of the loan contract written on the recto of the Muziris papyrus. In all likelihood, the borrower was the owner of the *Hermapollon*. However, the cargo imported from Muziris was so considerable that it could hardly have belonged to a single merchant, as the loan contract—signed by a single borrower—seems to suggest. In all likelihood, the underwriter, a lone Erythraean Sea ship owner (*naukleros Erythraikos*), also represented the Erythraean Sea merchants (*emporoi Erythraikoi*) who chartered transport space on his ship. A polarity between the *naukleros Erythraikos* and the *emporoi Erythraikoi* is recorded in an inscription from Coptos, and may be comparable to that between a Palmyrene caravan leader (*archemporos, synodiarches*) and the traders who joined (*synanabantes*) his caravan.

The Muziris papyrus lays bare the terms of a cooperative arrangement between the *paralemptes* and the *naukleros*, which may have been a structural peculiarity of Roman trade with South India in the first two centuries AD. Above the merchants/borrowers and customs collectors/lenders is the imperial administration, whose officers assist and monitor the arabarchs' work.

13.1. ARABARCHS, *PARALEMPTAI*, AND *GRAMMATEIS*

The identification of the arabarchs mentioned at verso col. iii, l. 11 and implied at col. iii, ll. 22–3 depends on how one interprets the shares of pepper, sound ivory, and *schidai* they took 'in addition for the payment of the quarter-tax'.[1] The hypothesis that the additional shares were small taxes levied in the Red Sea ports—distinct from the quarter-tax levied in Alexandria—led to the theory that the arabarchs were not the super-rich farmers of the Red Sea tax, but subordinate customs officials responsible both for checking imported

[1] Col. iii, ll. 11–13; 22–3.

The Indo-Roman Pepper Trade and the Muziris Papyrus. Federico De Romanis, Oxford University Press (2020).
 DOI: 10.1093/oso/9780198842347.001.0001

commodities upon their arrival in the Red Sea ports and levying minor surcharges.[2] My reconstruction of the Red Sea tax argues for a different explanation: that the shares taken by the arabarchs were appended as surcharges to the base quarter-rates for pepper, sound ivory, and *schidai,* and that the quarter rates and surcharges taken together formed Strabo's import customs duties (τέλη εἰσαγωγικά) for those items. This would explain why, in the section that precedes the reckoning of the three-quarter values (verso col. ii, ll. 1–13), the weight numbers corresponding to the quarter-taxes and to the shares taken by the arabarchs appear merged together at first (verso col. ii, ll. 1 (?), 6, 11), and are only subsequently disconnected (verso col. ii, ll. 2, 8, 9, 13). As a consequence, the arabarchs who levied them would be none other than the Red Sea tax farmers themselves.

A passing remark in Pliny's *Natural History* shows that it was the imperial treasury (*fiscus*) that delegated the task of collecting the customs duties on Red Sea imports.[3] Therefore, it was the treasury that received the net revenues of these duties. But what were the terms of the agreement between the treasury and the tax farmers? It is crucial to note that, unlike the base quarter-rate of the import customs duties, the arabarchs' additional shares were subject to export customs duties. This suggests that these shares went solely to the arabarchs, whereas the base quarter-rate was split between the arabarchs and the treasury. In all likelihood, the contractual agreement between the state and the arabarchs was not such that the latter were expected to pay the state a lump sum, and then retain for themselves whatever they would have levied. Rather, the agreement stipulated that the arabarchs would give the Red Sea tax revenue to the imperial treasury, but keep for themselves a percentage of the base quarter-rates of both the import and the export customs duties, as well as the entire additional shares for arabarchs on the import customs duties.[4] Therefore, Red Sea tax revenues must have been recorded in two separate accounts. One account documented the revenues from the arabarchs' additional shares—the money that belonged only to the arabarchs. The other documented the combined revenues from the base rate of the import and the export customs duties—money that was to be apportioned between the treasury and the arabarchs.[5]

[2] Jördens (2009: 358–60); Kramer (2011: 180–1).

[3] An Annius Plocamus is specified as the one who had contracted with the imperial treasury for the (collection of the) Red Sea tax, Plin., *NH* 6.84: *qui maris Rubri vectigal a fisco redemerat.*

[4] It is uncertain whether the same procedure applied to the ἀποστόλιον, a minor tax on people and things moving back and forth between Coptos and the Red Sea ports, due in Coptos to the *arabarchia*. Its collection, included in the *arabarchia* contract, was farmed out to special tax-farmers: *I.Portes* 67 = *OGIS* 674, ll. 1–8, cf. Burkhalter (2002).

[5] Following Brunt (1990: 384), we may say that that was the count of the *res vectigalis* mentioned in Ulp., *Dig.* 39.4.14.pr.

The correlation between the arabarchs' additional shares and the discount granted by the state suggests that both alterations of the base quarter-rate were the result of negotiations between the state, the arabarchs, and the merchants. At the time of the Muziris papyrus, the arabarchs had succeeded in securing surcharges for the import customs duties on pepper, sound ivory, and *schidai*—and the state in turn compensated the merchants with discounts on the export duties for those very same items. The proceeds of the surcharges went to the arabarchs alone, and the loss of revenue caused by the discount was borne mostly by the imperial treasury.

Most of the arabarchs (or alabarchs)[6] recorded in the literary and epigraphic evidence are notable personages, solidly rooted in Alexandria's highest socio-economic milieux. The two exceptions to this pattern appear to be non-locals of comparable social standing. Here is a list of the arabarchs/alabarchs:[7]

a. As mentioned, the Annius Plocamus who farmed the Red Sea tax may be identified as an arabarch. In Claudius' years, one of his freedmen, caught in a storm while sailing *circa Arabiam*, ended up in Sri Lanka.[8] However, as early as 5 July AD 6, Lysas, slave of a P. Annius Plocamus, stopped in the Paneion of Wadi Minayḥ on his way to Berenice.[9] It is difficult to say whether Annius Plocamus' arabarchy was chronologically closer to the inscription of Lysas or to his freedman's misadventure.
b. Arabarch and administrator of Antonia's properties in Egypt, Alexander was 'first in birth and wealth among the Alexandrians of his time'. Philo and Ti. Iulius Alexander were respectively his brother and his son. His son Marcus married Berenice, the daughter of Herod Agrippa. Alexander's amazing donations to the temple of Jerusalem were most probably contemporary with his arabarchy in Alexandria, held between the last years of Tiberius and the first of Claudius.[10]

[6] Forms in ἀλαβ- (ἀλαβάρχης, ἀλαβαρχέω, ἀλαβαρχία) are phonetic variants of ἀραβ-, mostly occurring in the literary texts. Forms in ἀραβ- largely prevail in inscriptions and papyri: see Kramer (2011: 175–183).

[7] For geographical and chronological reasons respectively, I exclude from my list Manesos, the Parthian *paraleptes*, *strategos* of Mesopotamia and Parapotamia, and *arabarches* mentioned in *P.Dura* 20, l.5, and Ioannes, *arabarches* in Antinoupolis in *P. Cair. Masp.* 2.671666 (AD 568). The occurrence of the term *arabarches* (v.l. *alab-*) in Cic., *Att.* 2.17.3 is not pertinent either.

[8] Plin., *NH* 6.84. A freedman of a P. Annius Plocamus is attested in Puteoli (*CIL* 10.2389). Two water pipe fragments found in Rome bear the inscriptions *An]ni Plocami* (*CIL* 15.798) and *A. Anni Plocami* (*CIL* 15.7391). The hypothesis that the farmer of the Red Sea tax was himself a freedman is unwarranted: De Romanis (1988: 18, n. 30; 1996: 249, n. 28).

[9] *AÉ* 1954, 121 (= *AÉ* 1999, 1720–1), on which De Romanis (2001).

[10] Joseph., *AJ* 18.159; 259; 19.276; 20.100. For the donations to the temple, Joseph., *BJ* 5.201–5. On Alexander, cf. *PIR*² A n. 510; Evans (1995). Representatives of his son Marcus were stationed in the Red Sea ports of Egypt between AD 37 and 44, see n. 46.

c. Demetrius, first in birth and wealth among the Alexandrian Jews, was arabarch in the mid-first century AD and married Mariamne, the daughter of Herod Agrippa and Cypros.[11]

d. Ptolemaeus, the father of Apollonius, *strategos* of the Ombite nome and collector for the Red Sea (*paralemptes tes Erythras thalasses*), is generally supposed to have been an arabarch around AD 60.[12]

e. On 3 May AD 65, Ptolemaeus' son, now a fresh Roman citizen with the name of Ti. Iulius Apollonius, appears as an arabarch himself.[13]

f. Juvenal mocks an Egyptian *arabarches* who, much to the satirist's dismay, had a triumphal statue in Rome.[14] This was certainly Ti. Iulius Alexander, who may well have been an arabarch like his father. However, such a function is not attested by any other source, whereas his father is repeatedly labelled Alexander the Alabarch. It is therefore possible that Juvenal disparagingly transferred the father's service to the son.

g. Two first-century AD vase stoppers mention an arabarch named Claudius Anicetus.[15]

h. The arabarch Ti. Claudius Geminus, also known as Isidorus, was the son of a gymnasiarch of Alexandria. In his career, Geminus was gymnasiarch himself, hypomnematograph, *tribunus militum*, epistrategos of the Thebaid and, at the same time, arabarch (being an arabarch did not prevent one from holding office in Egypt).[16]

i. It is uncertain whether the Claudius Geminus, listener of the Memnon colossi, arabarch and epistrategos of the Thebaid at the same time, is different from the Ti. Claudius Geminus mentioned above.[17]

j. An arabarch named Horus is attested by a mid-first/mid-second-century AD vessel stopper found at Myos Hormos.[18]

[11] Joseph., *AJ* 20.147.

[12] *SB* 5.7951. At l. 2, the restoration [ἀραβάρ]χου is usually accepted, but it is not the only option. For the chronology of the inscription, see Nachtergael (1999: 143).

[13] *SB* 5.7952+7950, on which Nachtergael (1999: 141–3). Denecker and Vandorpe (2007: 122) refer to the same man as the inscription on the stopper Cuvigny (1998: n. 5); Cuvigny (2005: 14) points out that Apollonios has the same *praenomen* and *nomen* as Ti. Iulius Alexander.

[14] Juv. 1.129–31.

[15] Milne 33014; 33015.

[16] *SEG* 50.1563. The gymnasiarch Ti. Claudius Isidorus is identified with the gymnasiarch Isidorus of the *Acta Alexandrinorum* (4 col. iii, ll. 8–11; cf. Philo, *In Flacc.* 20; 126; 135–6; 141–2; *Leg.* 355) by Lukaszewicz (2000), followed by Baslez (2005: 106); distinguished from him by Bingen (2002), followed by Harker (2008: 16); cf. also Jördens (2009: 362–3).

[17] *I.Memnon* 67. The personage is distinguished from Ti. Claudius Geminus *qui et* Isidorus by Bingen (2002: 120), who identifies this Claudius Geminus with the *idiologus* mentioned in *SB* 8.9801 = 8.10044 (AD 89–91).

[18] Thomas (2011: 27, ST 0068; 31, fig. 3.14): Ὧρ̣[ο]ς̣ ἀραβάρχ(ης).

k. The Ephesian M. Aurelius Mindius Matidianus Pollio was also an arabarch. His only connection with Egypt was his late second-century AD service as *dioecetes Aegypti*, a position that was probably held simultaneously with his arabarchy. His long experience (thirty years!) in customs duties collection in the province of Asia explains his interest in duties collection in Egypt.[19]

The examples listed above show that at least in three cases—those of Alexander, Demetrius, and Claudius Geminus—the function of arabarch was discharged by a leading figure in Alexandria. Annius Plocamus' links with Puteoli and Rome do not prevent him from being a relevant participant in the Alexandrian financial business, all the more so since a slave of a P. Annius Plocamus appears to have been somehow involved in Indian Ocean trade in AD 6. All these circumstances, together with the likelihood that M. Aurelius Mindius Matidianus Pollio was at the same time arabarch and *dioecetes Aegypti*, support the theory that the collection of the Red Sea tax was farmed out in Alexandria by the prefect of Egypt.[20]

Moreover, the Matidianus Pollio example shows that in the late second century AD, the Red Sea tax collection was still being outsourced to private tax farmers. If the *procuratio alabarchiae Pelusi* mentioned in an early second-century AD inscription marked any departure from the privatized system,[21] such an innovation must have been restricted to a short period of time and/or to the passage opened by Trajan's Canal.[22]

The plural *ἀραβαρχῶν* at verso col. iii, l. 11 contrasts with the literary formulae that suggest a single arabarch.[23] This fluctuation between singular and plural may reflect the structure of the collaboratives that collected the Red Sea tax.[24] Due to the enormous amounts of money involved, the partnerships of the arabarchs may not have been any different from those of the *societates publicorum* of republican Rome.[25] It is likely, in other words, that when the Red Sea tax contract was allocated, even the bids of extremely wealthy contractors had to be underwritten by associates and guarantors.[26]

[19] *I.Eph* 3.627; 7.3056. Cf. *PIR*² A 1559.

[20] De Laet (1949: 417); Jördens (2009: 369).

[21] *AÉ* 1999, 418. Cf. Sabbatini Tumolesi (1993); Jördens (2009: 363).

[22] See p. 306, n. 39.

[23] Plin., *NH* 6.84: *qui maris Rubri vectigal a fisco redemerat*; Joseph., *AJ* 20.147: *τὴν ἀλαβαρχίαν αὐτὸς εἶχεν*. By contrast, a plural form (*τ[οῖ]ς ἀραβάρχαις*) also occurs in *Act. Alex.* 22 fr 1, col. ii, l. 7.

[24] In Late Antiquity, the same fluctuation seems to depend on a multiplication of the arabarchies. This is suggested by both the 'most glorious (*endoxotatos*) arabarch' Ioannes, who in AD 568 had his office in Antinoupolis (*P.CairMasp* 2.67166), and the wording *οἱ τῶν θείων ἡμῶν προεστῶτες ἀλαβαρχιῶν* in Just., *Ed.* 11.3. But see the singular *τῷ τε νῦν* <*καὶ τῷ*> *κατὰ καιρὸν ἀλαβάρχῃ* in Just., *Ed.* 11.2.

[25] Raschke (1978: 849, n. 808). On the *societates publicorum*, cf. Badian (1972); Cimma (1981); Malmendier (2002).

[26] Polyb. 6.17.

Thus, since the partnership as a whole included many members, one could say that the revenues from the tax went to the arabarchs—that is, to all the members of the partnership that held the tax contract. On the other hand, since legally there was just one *manceps* or *redemptor*, it could also be said that a single man 'obtained the Red Sea tax contract' or 'had the *alabarchia*'.[27]

If the arabarch was the *manceps* of the *societas publicorum* that won the Red Sea tax contract (*arabarchia/alabarchia*),[28] and the arabarchs were the *socii* members of the *societas*, then the *paralemptes tes Erythras thalasses* (receiver of the Red Sea) was the *magister* of the partnership (a sort of executive director), and the *paralempsis* (the department headed by the *paralemptes*) was his operative staff. The *paralemptes* was in charge of registering incoming cargo and collecting the appropriate customs duties, a task performed with the help of many agents deployed along the route from the Red Sea to Alexandria. The Muziris papyrus refers to *paralemptes*' warehouses (*παραλημπτικαὶ ἀποθῆκαι, παραλημπτικὴ ἀποθήκη*) in Coptos and Alexandria.[29] Secretaries (*grammateis*), either of the *paralempsis* or connected to a *paralemptes,* were stationed in the Red Sea ports.[30]

Below are the texts in which the terms *parale(m)ptes* and *paralempsis* refer to people who may have been involved in Red Sea tax collection:

a. *PME* 19: *ἔχει* [sc. Leuke Kome] *δὲ ἐμπορίου τινὰ καὶ αὐτὴ τάξιν τοῖς ἀπὸ τῆς Ἀραβίας ἐξαρτιζομένοις εἰς αὐτὴν πλοίοις οὐ μεγάλοις. διὸ καὶ παραφυλακῆς χάριν καὶ εἰς αὐτὴν παραλήπτης τῆς τετάρτης τῶν εἰσφερομένων φορτίων καὶ ἑκατοντάρχης μετὰ στρατεύματος ἀποστέλλεται;*[31]

b. Ast and Bagnall (2015: 172): *Ἴσιδι τῆι ἐν Βερενείκη*[*ι*]||*θεᾶ*[*ι*] *τροφῷ μεγίστηι|Εἰρηναῖος Ἁρποχρατίων*[*ος*]||*γραμματεὺς παραλήμψεως|ἔτους ἐνάτου Τ*[*ι*]*βερίου Κλαυδίου|Καίσαρος Σεβαστοῦ Γερμανικο*[*ῦ*]|| *Αὐτοκράτορος, Παῦνι* λ̅ [Berenice, 24 June AD 49];

c. *SB* 5.7951: [*Ἀπολ*]*λώνιος, Πτολεμαίου*|[*ἀραβάρ*]*χου υἱός, στρατηγὸς τοῦ*| [*Ὀμβ*]*είτου καὶ τοῦ περὶ Ἐλεφαν*|[*τίνην*] *καὶ Φίλας καὶ παραλήμπτης*| [*τῆς Ἐρ*]*υθρᾶς θαλάσσης, ἦλθον*|[*καὶ προσεκύ*]*νησα τὸν μέγιστον Ἑρμῆν*| [*σὺν* ---]*ιναίωι τῷ ἐμῷ ἑταίρῳ* [Pselkis, before AD 65];

[27] A distinction between a plurality of *conductores* and a single *manceps* is shown in *ILS* 1461.

[28] *Arabarchia*: *I.Portes* 67 = *OGIS* 674, l. 4; *BGU* 2.665, l. 5.

[29] Recto col. ii, ll. 3–4: *εἰς τὰ*]*ς ἐπὶ Κόπτου δημοσίας παραλημπτικὰς ἀποθήκας*; ll. 7–8 *εἰς τὴν* [*ἐν Ἀλεξ*]*ανδρείᾳ τῆς τετάρτης παραλημπτικὴν ἀποθήκην*.

[30] Cuvigny (2005: 14–5; 2014: 171–2); Ast and Bagnall (2015: 172–6).

[31] Thus the codex defended by Roos (1932) and Casson (1989). Fabricius and Frisk transferred *καὶ παραφυλακῆς χάριν* after *φορτίων*.

d. *I.Portes* 70: *ὑπὲρ τῆς Αὐτοκράτορος Καίσαρος Νέρουα Τραιανοῦ Σεβασ(τοῦ)|Γερμανικοῦ Δακικοῦ καὶ τοῦ παντὸς οἴκου αὐτοῦ,*[32] *Ἴσιδος|ἐν ἀτρίωι τὸ ξόανον καὶ τὸν ναὸν καὶ τὰ περὶ αὐτὸ πάντα,|ἐπὶ ἡγεμόνος Οὐιβίου Μα[ξίμου] καὶ ἐπιστρατήγου Πομπη|ίου Πρόκλου καὶ παραλήμπτου καὶ στρατηγοῦ Κλαυδίου|Χρυσέρμου, Δίδυμος Θέωνος ῥήτωρ ἀνέθηκεν|ἔτους ζ′ Αὐτοκράτορος Καίσαρος Νέρουα Τραιανοῦ|Σεβαστοῦ Γερμανικοῦ Δακικοῦ Θὼθ α′.* [Coptos, 30 August AD 103];

e. *O.My.Ho.* inv. 512: (unpublished, see Cuvigny (2014: 171–2); Ast and Bagnall (2015: 180–1)): the *Ichthyophagos* Pakybis seeks permission from the *paralemptes* Avitus to sail a raft to Philotera. [Myos Hormos, *c.* AD 108];

f. *O.Krok.* 1.1, ll. 26–8: *ὁμ(οίως) ὥραν η ἡμέρα{ι}ς δίπλωμα Ἀουείτου π[α]ραλήμπτου κα|θὼς γράφ(ε)ι κουράτορσι πραισιδ(ίων) καταστ[ῆσ]αι Μόδεστον γραμμ(ατέα)|Μυὸς Ὅρμου ἀπὸ πραισιδ(ίου) (ε)ἰς πραισίδ(ιον)* [Krokodilo, AD 108];[33]

g. *O.Krok.* 1.24, l. 8: *παραλήμπτηι ἐξηλθόντα̣;*

h. *O.Krok.* 1.26, l. 17: [- ca.15 -] *παραλήμπτ . . κ̣*[-ca.?-];

i. *O.Did.* 189: *Εἰολιανοῦ|παρ[α]λ̣ήμπτῃ;*

j. Ast and Bagnall (2015: 174): *[Γάι]ο̣ν Ἰούλιον Φαυστεῖν̣ο̣[ν]| παραλήπτην Βερενείκης|Γάιος Ἰούλιος Εὐχάριστος|γραμματεὺς ἀποθήκης|ἀρωματικῆς φιλαγα̣[θίας]|χάριν ν (ἔτους) ιε Τραιανοῦ|Καίσαρος τοῦ κυρίου, Μεσορὴ α̣* [Berenice, 25 July AD 112].

One may wonder whether in these documents the term *paralemptes* always refers to the uppermost management of Red Sea tax collection. It is easy to perceive the distance, in terms of title, status, and responsibilities, between *paralemptai (tes Erythras thalasses)* such as Apollonius and Claudius Chrysermus, who were at the same time *strategoi*,[34] and the *grammateis* who, deployed in Myos Hormos or Berenice, recorded the merchants' declarations (*apographai*) and weighed and inventoried the incoming cargo. Less obvious is the position of *paralemptai* like Avitus, who seems to discharge his duty in Myos Hormos, or C. Iulius Faustinus, who is honoured in Berenice as *paralemptes* of Berenice.

As it stands, the evidence related to these two personae is open to two interpretations. The first is based on the hypothesis that the Avitus mentioned

[32] The stone has *αὐτοῦ* after *οἴκου* (see *IGRom* 1.1175; *SB* 5.8815). The writer confused the formulas: either *τῆς* (l.1) is redundant or a *τύχης* is missing after *αὐτοῦ* (l.2), see Ast and Bagnall (2015: 177, n.5).

[33] For the reading *Μόδεστον γραμμ(ατέα)*, see Ast and Bagnall (2015: 174).

[34] Like the arabarch, a *paralemptes* was not prevented, while in charge, from holding public office in Egypt.

in (e) and (f) and the C. Iulius Faustinus honoured in (j) were officials of the *paralempsis* deployed at Myos Hormos and Berenice respectively. In this case, we would have to postulate a 'percolation' of the title *paralemptes* from the top of the quarter-tax department down to junior officials stationed at the Red Sea ports. Even if this were the case, however, I would not conclude that such a dilution of the term equated the *paralemptai* of Myos Hormos and Berenice to the *paralemptes* of the quarter-tax on imported commodities at Leuke Kome, the Red Sea emporion on the Arabian coast. In fact, the functions of the *paralemptai* supposedly stationed at Berenice and Myos Hormos could hardly have been the same as those of the *paralemptes* on the opposite shore.

The *Periplus* designates Leuke Kome as a harbour (and a fort) that, due to the 'not large' vessels that sailed there from Arabia, had something akin to the status of an emporion (*ἔχει δὲ ἐμπορίου τινὰ καὶ αὐτὴ τάξιν*). For this reason, and for the sake of security, a *paralemptes* of the quarter-tax on imported commodities and a centurion with troops were sent there. By contrast, the same text identifies Myos Hormos and Berenice only as ports (*limenes*).[35] In a port that is not also an emporion, neither the selling of overseas imports nor the collection of customs duties is expected. In fact, the borrower in the Muziris papyrus loan contract was not supposed to put his commodities 'under the lender's power and seal' in the Red Sea port, but only at Coptos and Alexandria.[36] Since Indian commodities were not legally put on sale in the Egyptian ports of the Red Sea and the merchants would not have been able to pay the quarter-tax,[37] stationing a real *paralemptes* of the quarter-tax at Myos Hormos or Berenice would have been pointless. The employees of the quarter-tax department assigned to the Red Sea ports merely weighed and inventoried the unloaded commodities and thwarted smuggling efforts.

Yet it is difficult to argue that C. Iulius Faustinus (j)—*parale(m)ptes* of Berenice, honoured by C. Iulius Eucharistus, the 'secretary of the spice magazine'—either belonged to another tax department or was not a tax collector. Moreover, since the 'secretary of the *paralempsis*' Eirenaios (b) can hardly be imagined discharging a different function from the 'secretary of the spice magazine' C. Iulius Eucharistus (j), we may conclude that the former worked for the quarter-tax department as well, and that the office called 'secretary of the *paralempsis*' in AD 49 was in AD 112 referred to as 'secretary of the spice magazine'.

[35] *PME* 1.

[36] Notice the contrast between recto, col. ii, l.1:]̣ *μένων σου ἑτέρων ἐπ[ι]τρόπων ἢ φροντιστῶν*, ll. 4–6: *καὶ ποι|ήσω ὑ]π̣ὸ τὴν σὴν ἢ τῶν σῶν ἐπιτρόπων ἢ τοῦ παρόντος αὐτῶν|ἐξουσία]ν καὶ σφραγεῖδα*, and ll. 8–9: *καὶ ὁ | μοίω]ṣ ποιήσω ὑπὸ τὴν σὴν ἢ τῶν σῶν ἐξουσίαν καὶ σφραγεῖδα.*

[37] The frankincense and pepper sales in Berenice implied by three ostraca from Didymoi (*O.Did.* 323; 327; 328: see p. 292) were most probably illegal, and restricted to the military at Berenice and along the caravan routes.

That said, was C. Iulius Faustinus, the *paraleptes* of Berenice, permanently stationed in the Red Sea port? Was he a superior of C. Iulius Eucharistus, 'secretary of the spice magazine' in Berenice, and, at the same time, another subordinate of the *paraleptes* of the quarter-tax? The two dedications from Berenice, (b) and (j), suggest that the *grammateus* was the most important official on site, and that no *parale(m)ptes* was usually based there. In fact, it seems unlikely that Eucharistus would honour someone who worked shoulder to shoulder with him in Berenice as another of the many subordinates in the Red Sea tax department. It seems more apt to infer that he was honouring someone much higher in rank—in all likelihood, the principal manager of the entire department.[38]

It is not unlikely that the general manager for the collection of the quarter-tax on commodities imported through Berenice and forwarded to Coptos and Alexandria was then officially or unofficially named *paralemptes Berenikes*. Such a title—more circumscribed than *paralemptes tes Erythras thalasses*—may reflect the arrangement following the opening of Trajan's Canal and the installation of the *procuratio alabarchiae Pelusi*, which may have had an organization of its own based in Clysma and Pelusium, and managed by a *paralemptes Klysmatos*. A decline in Myos Hormos' commercial activity and a reorganization of customs collection on Indian Ocean commodities may have narrowed the scope of the comprehensive *paralemptes tes Erythras thalasses* into the more constrained *paralemptes Beren(e)ikes*.[39] Alternatively, a sort of parallelism with the title 'prefect of Berenice' may be suggested.[40] The 'prefect of Berenice' did not normally dwell *in* Berenice. He was the commander of the military deployed in the Eastern Desert and, although he may have often visited the Red Sea ports and the forts along the caravan roads of the desert, he had his residence at Coptos.[41] Most of the time, the *paralemptes* of the Red Sea tax would have stayed in the *paralemptikai* warehouses of Coptos and Alexandria.[42] Only occasionally, he may have visited Berenice. C. Iulius Eucharistus' inscription may have celebrated C. Iulius Faustinus during one of his rare visits to the Red Sea port.

The residency at Myos Hormos of the *paralemptes* Avitus seems to be more solidly supported. In (e), an ostracon found at Myos Hormos, an

[38] For a comparison, in a trilingual inscription from Palmyra (*IGLS* 17.1.197 = *PAT* 1413), it is none other than the *manc(eps) IIII merc.* (τεταρτώνης, *dy rb*ʿ) L. Antonius Callistratus, who is honoured by his *actor* (πραγματευτὴς ἴδιος, *prgmṭt' dydh*) Galenus.

[39] Trajan's Canal was open, but 'new' on 2 September (and possibly 25 August) AD 112: Jördens, Heilporn, and Duttenhöfer (2007). On Myos Hormos' decline, see p. 201, n. 54.

[40] The title ἔπαρχος Βερνίκης is attested already in AD 11. Equivalent formulae are ἔπαρχος ὄρους Βερ(ε)ν(ε)ίκης, ἔπαρχος ὄρους, *praefectus Bernicidis*, *praef. Beren.*, *praefectus praesidiorum et montis Beronices*: Cuvigny (2003: 295–305); De Romanis (2006a: 644–7); Bülow-Jacobsen and Cuvigny (2007: 11–33); Magioncalda (2012); *SEG* 62.1753; 1754.

[41] Cuvigny (2003: 297–8); Magioncalda (2012: 463–4); Pantalacci (2018: 28).

[42] See n. 29.

Ichthyophagos named Pakybis asks the *paralemptes* Avitus to let a raft sail (from Myos Hormos, apparently) to Philotera. Furthermore, in (f), an ostracon from Krokodilo, the same Avitus is referred to as the issuer of a diploma for the 'secretary of Myos Hormos', Modestus, who in AD 108 was travelling between Myos Hormos and Coptos. In this case, there seems to be no question: if Avitus had to pay individual attention to every small boat leaving Myos Hormos, he would hardly have been simultaneously entrusted with the collection of the Red Sea tax in Coptos and Alexandria. Therefore, either he was a *paralemptes* of taxes other than the Red Sea tax or, if he belonged to the quarter-tax department, his status and responsibilities would have been at a much lower level than that of the *paralemptes* heading the entire department. He may have weighed and inventoried the cargo, but he could not have collected the tax. As H. Cuvigny puts it, he would have been just 'a cog in the complex machinery of Roman taxation of imported commodities'.[43]

Yet here again, one may question whether the evidence is as decisive as it seems at first sight. In fact, one should note that Avitus was important enough to issue a diploma for the *grammateus* of Myos Hormos, Modestus, who was apparently one of his subordinates. Moreover, even if Modestus was travelling from Myos Hormos to Coptos, this does not exclude the possibility that his diploma was issued by Avitus at Coptos.[44] As for the permit granted to Pakybis, the simple existence of a 'secretary of Myos Hormos' suggests that it was not Avitus, but his secretary, who wrote the words πάρες <εἰς> Φιλωτ[έραν, 'let pass to Philotera', with his own hand.[45] Can we also imagine that Pakybis' request was formally addressed to the *paralemptes* Avitus in his capacity as top manager of the Red Sea tax, but received and answered by one of his subordinates in Myos Hormos, such as Modestus, the 'secretary of Myos Hormos'? If a positive answer seems plausible (and barring evidence to the contrary), I see no real objection to the hypothesis that at Coptos, in Red Sea ports, and along the caravan routes connecting the former to the latter, the term *paralemptes*—with or without the specifications *tes Erythras thalasses* or *Berenikes*—always denotes the chief administrator of the Red Sea tax department.

It is likely that the *paralemptes* was appointed by (the majority of) the arabarchs, and his nomination reflected the influence of the leading figure (or the leading group) inside the partnership. In particular, the presumption that the arabarch influenced the *paralemptes*' appointment lends weight to the hypothesis that Ptolemaeus was arabarch while his son Apollonius was

[43] Cuvigny (2005: 15); Cuvigny (2014: 172); Ast and Bagnall (2015: 180–1).

[44] Cuvigny (2005: 14).

[45] Cf. Cuvigny (2014: 172): 'the authorization of the παραλημπτής is reduced to a subscription ("let pass") added in his (a secretary's) hand under Pakybis' request.'

paralemptes tes Erythras thalasses. For the same reason, it is likely that M. Iulius Alexander was *paralemptes tes Erythras thalasses* when, between AD 37 and 44, he had representatives in both Myos Hormos and Berenice, and his father was arabarch.[46]

13.2. A LENDER/CUSTOMS COLLECTOR

Although the personal identities of the loan contract signatories are lost with recto col. i, their socio-economic profiles and institutional roles emerge quite vividly from what is left of the Muziris papyrus. It is abundantly clear that the lender was a man of considerable means, residing in either Coptos or Alexandria. His agents were stationed in Alexandria, Coptos, and the Red Sea port where the *Hermapollon* docked—most probably Berenice. Other agents assisted the borrower before he returned to his home port.[47]

Unnoticed thus far, an important function of the lender may be inferred from the verbal form *τεταρτολογεῖν* at recto col. ii, l. 18.[48] Just like cognate or comparable verbs such as *φορολογέω*, *τελωνέω*, etc., which mean 'to pay or to be subject to a tribute, to a toll' in the passive voice, but 'to levy a tribute, a toll' in the active, *τεταρτολογέω* means 'to pay or to be subject to the payment of the quarter' in the passive voice, but 'to levy the quarter' in the active.[49] The occurrence of the active *τεταρτολογεῖν* at col. ii, l. 18 has been translated by scholars in different ways. Misled by their misconceptions about the co-signers and the collateral for the contract, the editors inferred that the lender was allowed to confiscate one-quarter of the borrower's property.[50] When the general terms of the covenant were properly understood and the parties were identified as a financier and a merchant, the *τεταρτολογεῖν* at col. ii, l. 18 was correctly connected to the quarter-tax repeatedly mentioned or alluded to in the two texts of the papyrus.[51] But, the failure to envision a tax collector who is at the same time a financier to the merchants he is supposed to tax, led

[46] See pp. 300–1. For M. Iulius Alexander's representatives in the Red Sea ports: *O.Petr.Mus.* 130 (AD 43, Myos Hormos); 131 (*c.* AD 43, Myos Hormos); 135 (AD 44, Myos Hormos); 173 (AD 43, Berenice); 194 (AD 37). Marcus' elder brother, Ti. Iulius Alexander, was *epistrategus* of the Thebaid in April AD 42: *I.Portes* 30.

[47] Recto ii, l. 1, 5, and 9 show that the presence of the lender is conceived at Coptos and at Alexandria, but not in the Red Sea port. The same lines show his agents stationed in the Red Sea port, at Coptos and Alexandria. The assistance of other agents is implied by recto ii, l.1.

[48] Col. ii, l. 17–19: *καὶ κυριεύειν τὴν προκει̣|̣[μένη]ν ὑποθήκην καὶ τεταρτολογεῖν καὶ τὰ λοιπὰ ἐσόμενα μέρη|[τρία μ]εταφέρειν.*

[49] For the passive voice, cf. *BGU* 5.1210, ll. 116; 117; 118; 147; 151.

[50] Harrauer and Sijpesteijn (1985: 133): 'ein Viertel des Vermögens zu beschlagnahmen' (cf. 145). The translation of the *τεταρτολογεῖν* at col. ii, l. 18 seems to be based on the meaning recorded in Preisigke (1925–31: 592): 'jmd bestrafen durch Beschlagnahme eines Viertels seines Vermögens.'

[51] Recto col. ii, ll. 8; 10; verso col. ii, l. 7; col. iii, ll. 6; 12; 18; 22. At verso col. iii, l. 13, the *τεταρτολογουμένων* read by the editors has been rightly rejected by Morelli (2011: 208).

to the bending of the meaning of the active τεταρτολογεῖν. While Thür's translation may be seen as ingeniously suspended between an active and a passive sense,[52] others translated τεταρτολογεῖν as if it were passive.[53]

Yet the lender's agents and representatives being stationed both in the Red Sea port and in the *paralemptes*' warehouses of Coptos and Alexandria should have alerted us that the active voice was used for a reason.[54] Moreover, after A. Tchernia's brilliant analysis of Cornelius Senecio's portrait by Seneca,[55] we cannot doubt that it was common practice for the *publicani* (and the *paralemptes* may be considered one of them) to combine the *publica* contracts with every sort of business, maritime loans included. It is most unlikely that in this document the parties did not pay attention to the difference, in correct Greek, between 'levy the quarter-tax' and 'pay the quarter-tax'. A lender who can, in case of an outstanding loan, 'seize the aforementioned security and levy the quarter-tax and transfer the remaining three parts' must be a quarter-tax collector. Since we are referring specifically to the Red Sea tax, he must be, more precisely, a *paralemptes* of the tax.

The lender of the Muziris papyrus loan contract combines the collection of the quarter-tax with the financing of the India trade in a fashion that may be considered typical. Apart from identifying his agents and representatives with the staff of the *paralempsis* (one of them, for instance, was the *grammateus* of the *paralempis* stationed at Berenice), the lender's capacity as *paralemptes* explains his possible presence at the *paralemptes*' warehouses in either Coptos or Alexandria,[56] and explains his control of the cameleer in charge of the caravans from Berenice—an 'imperial service' (κυριακαὶ χρείαι) provided with the aid of compulsory requisitions, if necessary.[57] More importantly, the identification of the lender as a *paralemptes* and the clarifications about how the loan was to be repaid resolve an otherwise frustrating conundrum: how the borrower could delay the payment of his import customs duties.

To date, our understanding of the mechanism of the Red Sea tax and the way it was paid has been hampered by a puzzling contradiction: Strabo claims that Indian commodities were subject to double customs duties, upon entering and leaving Egypt, and the Muziris papyrus loan contract attests the existence of 'public customs warehouses in Coptos' and 'a customs warehouse of the quarter-tax in Alexandria'. The very same loan contract, however, records just one payment of the quarter-tax (τεταρτολογία), to be carried out in

[52] Thür (1987: 231): 'die *Tetarte* erheben zu lassen'; followed by De Romanis (1996a: 188): 'far riscuotere la τετάρτη'. However, the identity of 'Zolleinnehmer' and 'Darlehensgläubiger' is missing in Thür (1987: 236, n. 25).

[53] Casson (1986: 76): 'pay the duty of one-fourth'; Casson (1990: 200): 'pay the duty of one-fourth'; Rathbone (2000: 40): 'pay the quarter-tax'.

[54] Recto col. ii, ll. 1 (Red Sea port); 9 (Coptos); 15 (Alexandria).

[55] Sen., *Ep.* 101.4, on which see Tchernia (2016: 38–42).

[56] Recto col. ii, ll. 5; 9.

[57] Recto col. ii, l. 2. See pp. 198–203.

Alexandria, at the end of the commercial enterprise. The payment of customs duties at Coptos appears nowhere in the contract.[58]

Yet Coptos was, after Alexandria, the most important Egyptian emporion for Indian and Arabian commodities. Once they were sold at Coptos, Indian goods were free to move all over Egypt, subject only to very reasonable local duties.[59] Why then does the loan contract of the papyrus fail to mention the payment of import duties at Coptos?[60] The silence can be explained if the lender was *also* the customs collector: as such, he could postpone the borrower's payment of the import duties by guaranteeing the revenue due to the imperial treasury with the property of the arabarchs and their guarantors. The hypothesis is supported by a rescript by Septimius Severus and Caracalla:

> The deified Severus and Antoninus stated in a rescript that if someone has made a declaration to a tax farmer but fails to pay the *vectigal*, and the tax farmer allows this to pass, as they often do, the property does not become liable to confiscation since, they say, once the declarations are received, the possibility of confiscation lapses because it will be possible to meet the demands of the imperial treasury from the goods of the tax farmers or their verbal guarantors.[61]

It is worth emphasizing that the emperors refer here to the collectors' routine procedure (*ut solent facere*). Since the demands of the imperial treasury are based on declarations to the tax farmer, the imperial rescript cannot apply to those *vectigalia* for which the tax farmers pay the imperial treasury a lump sum, but only to those for which the tax-farmers were supposed to hand over a percentage of the collected duties.[62] Therefore, the publicans sanctioned delays in payment, not remissions.[63]

Incidentally, we may note that these sympathetic publicans do not seem like the fiscal vampires depicted in many other sources.[64] However, the two images do not contradict, but complement, each other, because there are different types of *publicani* and different types of merchants. The publican who paid a flat sum to the Roman treasury, and then collected for himself whatever he

[58] The arabarchs' additional shares cannot be identified, in and of themselves, with the import customs duties, as suggested by Thür (1987: 239, nn. 41; 44; 241); Casson (1990: 199, ad ll. 13; 23); Jördens (2009: 358; 366, n. 45; 368).

[59] They are referred to in *WChr* 273.

[60] Jördens (2009: 358, n. 10).

[61] Marcian., *Dig.* 39.4.16.12: *si quis professus apud publicanum fuerit, non tamen vectigal solverit, hoc concedente publicano, ut solent facere, divi Severus et Antoninus rescripserunt res in commissum non cadere: cum enim, inquiunt, professiones recitantur, commissum cessat, cum poterit satisfieri fisco ex bonis publicanorum vel fideiussorum*; trans. by C. J. Tuplin and A. Watson.

[62] *Contra* Maganzani (2002: 159).

[63] De Laet (1949: 443); Brunt (1990: 430); France (2001: 323); *contra* Maganzani (2002: 159, n. 296).

[64] Cf. Bang (2008: 202–38).

could, had a different approach from the publican who simply notified the treasury of his collateral and guarantors, and kept a share of the revenues for himself. The latter was naturally less inclined to develop predatory attitudes towards the taxpayer and was more interested in reaching an agreement with him, even at the expense of the treasury. Furthermore, while the small merchant who paid modest local dues was not equipped to stand up to the tax collector, the powerful long-distance traders could count on influential political support. The inscriptions from Palmyra in which long-distance merchants thank their upstanding patrons (at least one of whom is a collector of the quarter-tax!), the high social standing of the Indian Ocean traders from Egypt, and the cooperation (and possibly complicity) between taxpayer and tax collector implied by the Muziris papyrus show that these merchants were not the defenceless victims of the tax collectors.[65]

On the other hand, the leniency of the publicans was restricted to very rich merchants who were only temporarily unable to pay their enormous dues. Widely practised, such a modus operandi must have been standard practice for the payment of import customs duties on Indian commodities. The tolerance of the publicans probably came at a price, but it was in the best interest of both parties to ease that crucial passage.

In sum, the import customs duties were theoretically due at Coptos. In practice, they could only partially be paid there, because the proceeds of the commodities sold in the Nilotic emporion could hardly equal the amount due. As a consequence, postponing the payment of the import customs duties was unavoidable—and it required a dispensation that only a *paralemptes* could grant. Given the Red Sea–Alexandria transport infrastructure and the architecture of the Red Sea tax, the *paralemptes*, who had the control of the imperial caravans and could delay the payment of the import customs duties, would have been the most logical choice to bankroll the India traders. Indeed, when the advantages are considered, one may wonder whether it made sense for the South India merchants to borrow from anyone else.

Furthermore, the financiers involved in the collection of customs duties on Indian commodities may have also financially supported the Mediterranean circulation of those commodities. As collectors of the Red Sea tax, the arabarchs were creditors for the Indian Ocean traders, but debtors to the treasury from which they farmed the collection of the quarter-tax. Therefore, since they needed to transfer huge amounts of money from Egypt to Italy, they could have considered it convenient, in view of the additional yields, to finance the import of Eastern items from Egypt to Italy with one-way maritime loan contracts. When, in AD 35, Alexander the Alabarch lent the future king

[65] For Palmyrene merchants honouring a collector of the quarter-tax, cf. p. 316 n.88; for two women from Egypt, who were at the same time Erythraean Sea ship owners and merchants and *matronae stolatae*, cf. pp. 313–4.

Herod Agrippa 200,000 drachmas in two instalments—30,000 handed over in Alexandria and 170,000 to be delivered in Puteoli—the second sum may have come from maritime loans repaid there.[66]

13.3. A BORROWER/SHIP OWNER

When the two texts of the Muziris papyrus are viewed as interrelated documents, two striking contrasts emerge. The first is the gap between the average carrying capacity of the second-century AD Nilotic ships (attested in the available papyrological evidence) and the much larger size of the *Hermapollon*'s cargo. The second is the considerable disparity between the limited extent of the lender's financial support, which covers only the transport costs within Egypt, and the enormous market value of the cargo—well beyond the already impressive fiscal value, especially if there were undocumented pearls, diamonds, jacinths, and gemstones.

A loan contract depicting a borrower who puts all his commodities into a single river ship and needs financial support only for the land and river transports could lead one to question whether the two texts of the Muziris papyrus are actually related to each other. Undoubtedly, the loan contract on the recto financed a commercial voyage to Muziris. It is equally certain that the presence of Gangetic nard and ivory (and the values and weights of those commodities we have identified as pepper and malabathron) confirm that the *Hermapollon*'s cargo came from an emporion in Limyrike, most likely Muziris. It could be suggested, of course, that while the verso text concerned the entire cargo, the loan contract on the recto concerned only a single merchant, whose commodities were just a fraction of a South Indian cargo, but the hypothesis would hardly be convincing.

The verso text of the papyrus demonstrates that the *Hermapollon*'s cargo made its way to Alexandria all together, *en bloc*. Both the first and the second quarter-taxes were assessed not on the shares of individual merchants, but collectively: the first quarter-tax on 100 per cent of the cargo, and the second on 75 per cent, minus what was sold at Coptos. It follows that the entire cargo was transported by a single cameleer from the Red Sea to Coptos, and by a single ship from Coptos to Alexandria. The presumption that this was standard procedure is a strong indication that the two texts of the papyrus do relate to each other, and that the loan contract on the recto did finance the commercial venture that carried the cargo evaluated on the verso.

[66] Joseph., *AJ* 18.159–60. In addition, Alexander was then manager of Antonia's estates in Egypt (Joseph., *AJ* 19.276), the revenues of which could have also reached Italy as credits for imports from Egypt.

Why, then, only one borrower? The contrast with *SB* 3.7169, in which five shipmates co-sign a maritime loan contract for a voyage to the Aromatophoros Land, could lead one to propose that the borrower of the Muziris papyrus loan contract was the sole owner of the *Hermapollon*'s entire cargo. We should envision, then, a man of immense wealth, such as the Firmus fantasized by the *Historia Augusta*.[67] But a review of the epigraphic evidence regarding merchants engaged in the Indian Ocean trade suggests other possibilities.

The editors maintained that the borrower of the Muziris papyrus loan contract was a ship owner, on the assumption that the ship had been pledged as security for the loan. When it was shown that the Indian commodities were in fact the collateral, the idea of the *Hermapollon*'s owner being the borrower was discarded. However, no inference can be drawn from the preference for using the commodities as collateral. Easily marketable Indian goods would have been much more attractive as security than a Red Sea ship, especially if the contract (in the missing portion) also entitled the lender to seize any other property of the borrower, whether on land or on sea, should the security be insufficient to repay his debt.[68] Furthermore, the fact that the loan covered only the land and river transports strongly suggests that the merchant/borrower did not sail on someone else's ship, but was the owner of the seagoing vessel. In other words, he was not a simple *emporos*, but rather the *naukleros* of the *Hermapollon*. Of course, he was also a merchant and owned the cargo—or, more likely, a quota of it.[69]

More often than not, it is a challenge to draw meaningful conclusions from epigraphic evidence about Erythraean Sea ship owners. For instance, determining the circumstances that led the *ναύκληρος* Severus to sign his name at al-Kanā'yis, on the Edfu–Berenice road, is not easy.[70] It is also difficult to say where the *ναύκληρος* Septi(mios) Paniskos was sailing from when he left his *proskynema* at Hoq, on the island of Socotra.[71] Only a little more transparent is the votive gift in the shrine of Dios (between Coptos and Berenice) left by Aurelios Sarapion, a *naukleros* from Alexandria, whose activities in the Indian Ocean were probably connected to the sales of exotic commodities in his home city.[72]

An inscription from Medamut (Upper Egypt) characterizes two women—Aelia Isidora and Aelia Olympias, maybe sisters—as *matronae stolatae* and

[67] SHA, *Quad. Tyr.* 3.2. [68] A similar condition in [Dem.] 35.12.

[69] That the Indian Ocean *naukleroi* were not simple carriers is also suggested by Philostr., *VA* 6.12, where an Indian cargo is imagined to be put on sale by either an *emporos* or a *naukleros*. On *naukleroi* and *emporoi*, cf. Vélissaropoulos (1980: 48–56); Woolmer (2015).

[70] *I.Kanaïs* 57 = *SB* 1.4028.

[71] Bukharin (2012: 494–500). For occasional trade in Socotra while sailing back from either Barygaza or Limyirike, cf. *PME* 31.

[72] SEG 60.1788, see Cuvigny (2010a: 255–6, n. 12).

naukleroi kai emporoi Erythraikai (Erythraean ship owners and merchants).[73] It is not clear whether each woman owned her own ship(s) or whether they shared ownership of a single vessel.[74] Nor is it clear whether the coupling *naukleroi kai emporoi Erythraikai* (a formula that may also characterize a Palmyrene honoured in a Greco-Palmyrene fragmentary inscription from Tentyra[75]) only means that the agents of Aelia Isidora and Aelia Olympias were carriers and co-owners of the cargo they transported. Alternatively, one may suggest that, apart from trading on the ship(s) belonging to their bosses, they joined the commercial ventures of ships belonging to other ship owners. In any case, the high social standing of Isidora and Olympias, obvious from the honorific title *matronae stolatae*,[76] suggests that the size of their business was considerable.

The alleged later chronology of the inscription does not preclude a comparison with the Muziris papyrus. In fact, unless Isidora and Olympias were rather unconventional women, they were likely the descendants of a trading dynasty.[77] Their Red Sea ship(s) and Indian Ocean commercial interests must have been akin to the 'inherited business' (*ἐμπορίη πατρώϊος*) alluded to by Dionysius Periegetes: 'For my life is not on black ships,/ I have no inherited business, nor do I go to the Ganges,/ like others do, through the Erythraean sea,/ not caring for their lives, in order to win indescribable wealth.'[78] It is likely that when Dionysius Periegetes was writing his *Periegesis* and when the Muziris papyrus contract was signed, Isidora and Olympias' ancestors—who acquired Roman citizenship under either Hadrian or Antoninus Pius—were already seasoned Indian Ocean traders.[79]

The characterization of Isidora and Olympias as Erythraean ship owners *and* merchants requires further scrutiny. In other documents related to the Indian Ocean trade, the two categories do not apply to the same persons.[80] In an inscription from Coptos a group of Palmyrene *Erythraikoi emporoi* honour

[73] *SB* 5.7539: *Λητοῖ θεᾷ μεγίστῃ|Αἰλία Ἰσιδώρα καὶ Αἰλί[α]|Ὀλυμπιὰς ματρῶναι|στολᾶται, ναύκληροι κα[ὶ]|[ἔμπο]ροι Ἐρυθραϊκαί, ἅμ[α]| - - - Ἀ]πολιναρίῳ|ἐπάρχ[ῳ - - -]ς Ὀλυμ|πιάδος καὶ [Ἰσιδώρας - - - |ἀμφοτέρων [- - -]|ἀνέθηκαν [ἐπ' ἀγαθῷ]*. A timeframe between the end of the second century and the second third of the third century AD has been suggested on palaeographical grounds: Jouguet (1931: 1–2). On the text, cf. Ruffing (2011: 23–30). At l. 7 a restoration of *ἐπάρχ[ῳ Βερ(ε)νίκη]ς* (or *ἐπάρχ[ῳ ὄρου]ς*) seems to me preferable to Rostovtzeff's *ἐπάρχ[ῳ κλάσση]ς*.

[74] For two brothers from Askalon, co-owners (*συνναύκληροι*) of a ship, see *SB* 6.9571 = 14.11850.

[75] *I.Portes* 39:]ρ[|Μακκ[|καὶ ἐμπο[|τὸν παρακ[|συν[./*mqy*. At ll.2–3 a restoration *ναύκληρον]| καὶ ἔμπο[ρον Ἐρυθραϊκόν* seems likely.

[76] Holtheide (1980).

[77] On trading dynasties in the Roman world, cf. Tchernia (2016: 38–71).

[78] Dionys. Per. 709–12, transl. by E. Ilyushechkina, with modifications.

[79] On the *Periegesis*' chronology, see Jacob (1991); Amato (2003).

[80] An Indian cargo is imagined to be put on sale by *either* an *emporos* or a *naukleros* in Philostr., *VA* 6.12.

a descendant from a dynasty of Palmyrene *naukleroi Erythraikoi* and, most probably, a *naukleros Erythraikos* himself.[81] No doubt, the dedicators and the honorand had cooperated in an Indian Ocean-related commercial venture, which was based, as the provenance and the approximate chronology of the inscription suggest, at the Red Sea port of Berenice. The number of dedicators indicates a commercial enterprise of large proportions (such as one bound for the South Indian emporia), to be carried out with a ship belonging to a *naukleros*, but transporting commodities purchased by both a *naukleros* and *emporoi*.

The hierarchical distinction between the *naukleros* (ship owner and merchant) and the simple *emporoi* (merchants) makes the partnerships headed or joined by the agents of Aelia Olympias and Aelia Isidora similar to the one headed by the Palmyrene ship owner of *SEG* 34.1593, and different from that of the five shipmates (*σύνπλοι*) bound for the Aromatophoros Land, who all appear as cosignatories of the loan contract.[82] While the latter arrangement seems to reflect an association of equals, the former shows the leadership of the ship owner. One may recall Ulpian's contrast between a ship managed personally by several owners with no captain, and one on which the owners appoint one of their number to serve as captain: the former are liable in proportion to their shares in the management, the latter can each be sued for the full amount in the captain's name.[83]

The size of the *Hermapollon*'s cargo suggests that a commercial venture to South India required the combined resources of dozens of merchants. On the other hand, the fact that the loan contract of the Muziris papyrus is signed by a single borrower suggests that the association of merchants had one leader among them. The possibility is thus introduced that the façade of a single-borrower loan contract obscures the reality of an association of merchants and a ship owner who represents them.

If this inference is correct, the organizational structure of the Egypt-based commercial ventures to South India may be compared to that of the

[81] *SEG* 34.1593 (= *I.Portes* 103): ..*ẠΚΤΑΚ· τὸν ἄ*[- - -]|*ọ̈σιον Ζαβδάλα Σαλμά*|*νου καὶ Ἀνείνα Ἀδρια*|*νῶν Παλμυρηνῶν*|*ναυκλήρων Ἐρυθραικῶν,*|*ἀναστήσαντα ἀπὸ θεμελίου*|*τὸ προπύλαιον καὶ τὰς στουὰς*|*τρεῖς καὶ τὰ θυρώμ̣ạτα ἐκ και*|*νῆς, τὰ πάντα ἐκ τῶν ἰδίων*|*αὐτοῦ φιλοκαγαθίας χάριν*| [*Ἀ*]*δριανοὶ Παλμυρηνοὶ Ἐρυ̣(θραικοὶ)*|*ἔ̈μποροι τὸν φίλον*. I understand *Ζαβδάλα Σαλμάνου καὶ Ἀνείνα* as the names of the honorand's ancestors and '*Ἀδριανῶν Παλμυρηνῶν ναυκλήρων* as an apposition. Bernand (translation of *I.Portes* 103) takes it for a partitive genitive related to the honorand ('faisant partie des armateurs de la mer Rouge, originaires de l'Hadrienne Palmyre'). The epithet '*Ἀδριανοί* shows that the inscription is later than Hadrianus' visit to Palmyra in AD 130: cf. Halfmann (1986: 129–35; 193; 206). Other epigraphic and papyrological evidence on Palmyrene presence in Egypt is in Dijkstra and Verhoogt (1999: 207–18).

[82] *SB* 5.7169.

[83] Ulp., *Dig.* 14.1.4.pr.-1: si tamen plures per se navem exerceant, pro portionibus exercitionis conveniuntur: neque enim invicem sui magistri videbuntur. sed si plures exerceant, unum autem de numero suo magistrum fecerint, huius nomine in solidum poterunt conveniri.

Palmyra-based Indian Ocean trade. In AD 157, the outstanding Palmyrene M. Ulpius Iarhai was honoured by the merchants (ἔμποροι) who sailed back from Skythia (Pakistan) on the ship of Honainos, son of Haddudanes,[84] who, although not as prominent as M. Ulpius Iarhai, was nonetheless a distinguished Palmyrene citizen: he is mentioned as a builder in a fragmentary inscription on an architrave found next to the temple of Nabū.[85] Therefore, the inscription reveals a tri-level system of organization for oceanic trade. The first level is that of the associated merchants, who rented space on an Indian Ocean ship belonging to someone else. The second is the owner of the Indian Ocean vessel, who certainly owned a part of the cargo. Above both the associated merchants and the ship owner is a patron, whose actual contribution, although only vaguely referred to, was nonetheless vital. In the Coptos inscription *SEG* 34.1593 (= *I.Portes* 103), the *emporoi* honour only the owner of the ship they travelled on, but that does not mean that the third level was not there—the commercial enterprise could hardly succeed without the support of the *paralemptes* of the Red Sea tax.

The hierarchical distinction between a ship owner (ναύκληρος) and a plurality of merchants (ἔμποροι) in Erythraean maritime trade is symmetrical to the organizational pattern of Palmyrene land-based commerce, where a 'caravan leader' (*rš šyr'*/συνοδιάρχης, ἀρχέμπορος), who probably owned a large herd of camels, supervised the small-time merchants (*tgry'*, συναναβάντες, ἀναβάντες), who joined the caravan.[86] Here, again, there was a patron, with unspecified yet crucial support, who ranked above both the caravan leaders and their followers.

Incidentally, it is worth noting that the powerful Palmyrene patrons could support more than one commercial enterprise per year. Apart from the merchants who had sailed back from Skythia, two other groups of merchants—one returning from Chumana, and the other (a caravan) from Spasinu Charax—thanked M. Ulpius Iarhai in the same AD 157.[87] Moreover, it may be noted that in AD 161 (or 163), the caravan led by Nese Boliades thanked M. Aemilius Marcianus Asclepiades, who was councillor of Antiochia and, more importantly, quarter-tax collector.[88] This suggests that Palmyrene traders in their homeland needed the same kind of support that the lender of the Muziris papyrus loan contract provided to his borrower in Egypt.

The proposed identifications of the lender as the *paralemptes* of the Red Sea tax and of the borrower as the owner of the *Hermapollon* shed new light on the location of the two texts—the loan contract for a commercial enterprise to

[84] *IGLS* 17.1.250 (= *PAT* 1403). [85] *IGLS* 17.1.183.

[86] Will (1957); Yon (2002: 100–6).

[87] *CIS* 3.3960 (= *PAT* 306); *IGLS* 17.1.249 (= *PAT* 1399).

[88] *IGLS* 17.1.196 (= *PAT* 1373). Curiously enough, the Greek text is dated AD 161, the Aramaic 163.

Muziris and the assessment of the Red Sea tax—on either side of the papyrus. Since the dues merge with the loan for travel costs in Egypt and other minor expenses, it should not seem odd that the duties for a cargo were calculated on the back side of a copy of the loan contract that financed that commercial enterprise.

The interpretation that has been proposed in this book fixes the timing of the text on the recto at the beginning of the commercial enterprise, before the borrower left Alexandria on his outward journey. The text on the verso was written at the end of the commercial venture, when all the cargo had been sold—it would have been premature, otherwise, to calculate the tax base of the second quarter-tax. Written on the back side of one copy of the loan contract, the calculation of the Red Sea tax and whatever may have followed in the subsequent column(s) of the verso helped one of the two parties to check and record the math at the end of the transaction. This was something both parties needed. The borrower/ship owner needed to present the final account of the commercial enterprise to his partners. The department presided over by the *paralemptes*—who by the way may not have been in Alexandria when the *Hermapollon*'s cargo was being sold[89]—needed to check, or, at any rate, keep a record of: 1) what had been due as a loan, as the Red Sea tax, and as the arabarchs' additional shares; 2) what had resulted from the sale of the commodities; and 3) what had been given back to the borrower/ship owner as the difference between what was owed and received. Without knowing the archaeological context from which the extant fragment emerged or how the verso text continued in the subsequent column(s), it is fruitless to speculate further on its precise purpose.

13.4. THE IMPERIAL ADMINISTRATION

As the above-mentioned rescript by Septimius Severus and Caracalla shows, the treasury had the right to collect unpaid customs duties from the tax farmers or their verbal guarantors. It may be inferred that the accounting of the arabarchs was subject to several checks by the imperial administration. In Alexandria, the arabarchs' accounts were reviewed, possibly by the *ἐπίτροπος τοῦ ἐν Ἀλεξανδρείᾳ φίσκου*,[90] and certainly by the prefect of Egypt.[91] In Rome, they were checked again by the *procurator fisci Alexandrini* and the minister *a rationibus*.[92] However, the imperial administration's control could be effective

[89] Recto col. ii, ll. 5; 9. [90] Meritt (1931: 56–7, n. 75).

[91] For the responsibilities of the prefect of Egypt on that matter, see Jördens (2009: 355–70).

[92] For the *procurator fisci Alexandrini* in Rome, see *AÉ* 2007, 326; *ILS* 1518; *tabularii fisci Alexandrini*: *AÉ* 1901, 171 (Puteoli); *CIL* 6.8573 (Rome). An *adiut(or) tab(ulariorum) f(isci) Alex (andrini)*: *CIL* 6.5744. A *statio fisci Alexandrini*: *CIL* 6.36779; 15.7974a. For the control of the *a rationibus* on the (customs duties on) Indian commodities: Stat., *Silv.* 3.3.92–5.

only if the correspondence between the arabarchs' accounting and the merchants' declarations could be independently verified. In other words, the monitoring of the arabarchs' accounting required that a copy of the declaration be sent immediately and independently to some office of the prefect of Egypt.[93]

A comparable procedure is implied by *P.Amh.* 2.77, in which the inspector (*epiteretes*) of Socnopaiu Nesos' customhouse, in charge of sending the returns of the imports and exports, is accused by the whistle-blower Polydeuces of cooking the books, in complicity with the customs collector Harpagathes.[94] On the Red Sea's Arabian shore, the centurion sent to Leuke Kome to provide the necessary safeguard (*παραφυλακῆς χάριν*) may have had the additional duty of sending a copy of the declarations to the authorities overseeing the accounting of the *paralemptes*.[95] On the Egyptian side, the returns may have been sent by the military under the prefect of Berenice.

How big were the revenues to the Roman treasury from the Red Sea tax? The fiscal value of the *Hermapollon*'s cargo was roughly 10,000,000 sesterces. Its Red Sea tax, counting both import and export customs duties, surpassed 4,000,000 sesterces. When compared to the 100,000 denarii (400,000 sesterces) that was the annual revenue of the imperial treasury from the customs duties in Lycia under Nero,[96] the *maris Rubri vectigal* paid on the declared cargo of the *Hermapollon* looks impressive and justifies Strabo's emphasis on the importance of the revenues from the customs duties on Indian commodities.

However, we should refrain from a misguidedly straightforward conclusion. Assuming that the number of vessels engaged in the India trade had remained more or less the same since 26 or 25 BC, when Strabo learnt that 120 ships set sail for India, and taking the value of the *Hermapollon*'s cargo as typical of a Roman Indiaman,[97] one could suggest that the fiscal value of the annual Indian imports reached 1,200,000,000 sesterces, and that the revenue from the *maris Rubri vectigal* (both import and export customs duties) was approximately 500,000,000 sesterces.

Such assumptions are better avoided. Early Modern-era estimates of South Indian pepper productivity suggest that the pepper export from Kottanarike did not surpass 5,000 tons in the first centuries of the Christian era. Therefore, even at its zenith the ancient South India fleet could hardly have amounted to a double-digit number of ships like the *Hermapollon*. The number of vessels bound for the other Indian emporia—particularly Barbarikon (Skythia) and Barygaza—may have been higher, but their overall cargo wouldn't have

[93] The Coptos tariff shows the line of communication in the opposite direction, from the prefect of Egypt to the prefect of Berenice: *I.Portes* 67, ll. 1–8.

[94] Mitthof (2007). [95] *PME* 19. [96] Takmer (2007: 174).

[97] This is the basis of the experimental speculation of Rathbone (2000: 48–9) and the exemplification of Wilson (2015: 23); cf. also Wilson and Bowman (2017: 14); Mayer (2018: 583–4).

equalled the overall cargo imported from Limyrike. Even if the fleet engaged in the India trade comprised some seventy ships in the mid-first century AD, an annual Indian import of about 10,000 tons (approximately fifteen times the cargo of the *Hermapollon*) would probably be closer to reality than one of 19,500 (thirty times the cargo of the *Hermapollon*).[98] Apparently, the active fleet in 26 or 25 BC consisted of much smaller ships than the pepper carriers that emerged a few decades later. Even if the annual import from India was already 10,000 tons, Strabo's 120 ships carried an average cargo of less than 100 tons.

Even if the magnitude of the import in terms of volume can be more or less approximated, it remains difficult to estimate the revenues for the Roman state. Two unknowns need to be considered. The first is the share taken by the arabarchs. As mentioned, the assessment, control, and taxation of Indian commodities were entrusted to a private company of tax-farmers (*arabarchia*) headed by an arabarch. It was the *arabarchia* who guaranteed the state the revenues from the import of Indian commodities and provided the necessary staff. The shares 'taken by the arabarchs in addition for the payment of the quarter-tax' ($\frac{1}{600}$ of the sound ivory, $\frac{1}{50}$ of the *schidai*, and a fraction of the pepper imported) were only a minor part of their compensation. For the most part, the *arabarchia*'s returns came from a share of the two quarter-taxes, but we can only guess how big that was: one sixth? One tenth? We have no way of knowing.

The second unknown is even more troubling. It is odd that none of the six commodities evaluated on the verso side of the Muziris papyrus can be identified with pearls or precious stones. As we pointed out, it is difficult to say whether their absence hints at a change in Roman trade patterns with South India between the time of the *Periplus* and that of the papyrus, or whether it simply reflects a persistent failure on the part of the Roman fiscal system to tax high-value, easily hidden commodities. The first hypothesis is supported by *Akanāṉūṟu* 149, which represents the Muziris trade as an exchange of gold for pepper; the second is recommended by the rescript of Marcus Aurelius and Commodus, which hints at the smuggling of precious stones, feeding the suspicion that the Romans faced a situation similar to the Portuguese in terms of their helplessness in taxing the *pedraria*.[99] One may even posit a blend of the two hypotheses: a scenario in which a reduction in the trade in pearls and precious stones would have made it easier for merchants to smuggle in a reduced quantity of small, very expensive items, and for the customs officer to believe that the *Hermapollon*'s merchants imported no pearls from a region once famous for its 'good supply of fine-quality

[98] Mayer's (2018: 583–4) estimate of 20,000 tons is too high. Pepper would represent less than one-fifth of the weight. We would not understand why only the pepper emporia were visited by very large vessels.

[99] See p. 265.

pearls'.[100] Still another possibility must be acknowledged: that the vigilance of the fiscal bureaucracy for assessing certain goods may have been less strict than it should have been. In theory, the fact that the arabarchs were paid with a quota of the Red Sea tax revenues should have led to a concurrence of interests between the treasury, the arabarchs, and the *paralemptes*—all of whom would have favoured an accurate cargo inventory. However, given the double role of the *paralemptes*—as both customs collector and lender—the merchants may have been able to negotiate a loan contract with generous terms in exchange for turning a blind eye to pearls and precious stones.

Only other texts like the one on the verso of the Muziris papyrus could tell us if the cargo of the *Hermapollon* reflects an impoverished trade compared to that of the mid-first century AD, or a perpetual laxity in the fiscal apparatus, or some combination of the two.

However, even if the *paralempsis* often failed to tax pearls and precious stones, it should be recognized, per A. Wilson, that the customs duties on eastern trade produced a strategically significant income for the Roman state.[101] The magnitude of the Red Sea tax base, which included customs duties on trade with South Arabia and East Africa, was a nine-figure sum of sesterces. The same can be said for the trade on the Syrian border, where the Indian Ocean commodities arrived via the gulf and the desert. At the customs house of the quarter-tax in Palmyra, in a month of an unspecified year of the first or second century AD, values of as much as 22,369,641 *zwzym* and 2 *m'yn* (89,478,564 sesterces and 2 obols) were measured.[102] Here again, it would be unwise to infer an annual revenue from this apparently exceptional sum. Nonetheless, incomplete and isolated as they are, these quantitative data show that the customs duties on eastern commodities far exceeded the 20,000,000 or 30,000,000 sesterces produced by the tax on gladiatorial games under Marcus Aurelius.[103]

Finally, it is worth emphasizing that, apart from being vital to the Roman state's budget, the eastern trade was instrumental in cementing social consensus: its commodities gave appropriate visibility to the highest elites of the empire; the collection of its customs duties reinforced the financial and political roles of the upper classes of cities like Alexandria, Palmyra, or Antiochia; and it offered opportunities for upward social mobility to the most enterprising middle classes. As the Alexandrian traders told Augustus in Puteoli, 'it was through him that they lived, through him that they sailed the seas, and through him that they enjoyed their liberty and their fortunes.'[104] It is not coincidental that in the book of *Revelations*, the fall of 'Babylon' is mourned by the merchants, shipmasters, and mariners.[105]

[100] *PME* 56: *μαργαρίτης ἱκανὸς καὶ διάφορος*.
[101] Wilson (2015: 23).
[102] *PAT* 2634, on which see De Romanis (2004); (2006b).
[103] *ILS* 5163, ll. 8–9.
[104] Suet., *Aug.* 98.2.
[105] NT, *Rev.* 18.11–8 (cf. 18.3).

Epilogue

The two texts of the Muziris papyrus shed new light on the commercial workings of the Indian emporion of Muziris, and on the fiscal and entrepreneurial game played by the imperial treasury, the Indian Ocean merchants, and the financiers who contracted with the imperial treasury for the Red Sea tax and financed the India trade.

Behind Muziris' trade is the ecology of the Western Ghats of Kerala and the economy of their people, who, in addition to many other activities, annually collected thousands of tons of pepper and several hundred ivory tusks. These mountain commodities were acquired and transferred to the coastal emporia—of which Muziris, at the mouth of the Periyar River, was the most important in the mid-second century AD—most probably by local traders rather than foreign residents. The geographic radius of their pepper business shaped the regional notion of *Kuṭṭanāṭu*/Kottanarike. This trade was protected, facilitated, and probably, to some extent, exploited by the Cēra kings. All this is reflected by the cargo of the *Hermapollon* as itemized in the papyrus' verso text.

According to the *Periplus*, Muziris' trade was also built on other goods: on pearls fished in the nearby Gulf of Mannar, on beryls from the Punnata caves, on jacinth from Sri Lanka, and on diamonds and other gemstones conveyed from various Indian regions. Quite enigmatically, but hardly accidentally, these other aspects of Muziris' trade have left no trace in the texts of the papyrus.

By contrast, the contributions of mountain people dwelling thousands of miles north of the Western Ghats are very well documented. The cargoes of malabathron and Gangetic nard are a testament to the intercourse between the peoples of the Himalayan regions and the Ganges Valley, and to the efficiency of the routes that connected the Ganges Valley to the southern reaches of the subcontinent. Had one of the six commodities imported by the *Hermapollon* been tortoise shell, then trade relations with the Lakshadweep Islands or South East Asia may have been recorded as well.

The customs collection on Indian commodities going into and coming out of Egypt was entrusted to a private company that could guarantee the

The Indo-Roman Pepper Trade and the Muziris Papyrus. Federico De Romanis, Oxford University Press (2020).
 DOI: 10.1093/oso/9780198842347.001.0001

estimated revenues with assets, but was not required to pay anything in advance. The arabarchs were not direct governmental collectors, but agents of a privatized collection: by providing suitable collateral, they collected the tax, keeping only a quota of the revenues. The terms of their contract with the imperial treasury were renegotiated with each allocation of the tax. The arabarchs' additional shares of pepper and ivory, charged on top of the quarter-rate of the import customs duties, resulted from negotiations with the treasury. The hypothesis that M. Iulius Alexander and Ti. Iulius Apollonius (then only Apollonius son of Ptolemaeus) were *paralemptai*—executive directors of the *arabarchia,* in charge of the registration, evaluation, and taxation of imported goods—while their respective fathers were arabarchs, suggests the possibility that these companies were sometimes under the strong leadership of a single family.

In Egypt, the state guaranteed communication and ease of movement between Berenice and Coptos. Comfort and safety along the Eastern Desert caravan roads were ensured by the wells and forts built and overseen by the Roman army. The large caravans from Berenice were an 'imperial service', and the prefect of Egypt had to intervene if a sufficiently large herd of pack animals was not available. Although there was a large transportation industry based at Coptos, which operated smaller caravans to the Red Sea ports throughout the year and probably provided the bulk of the management for the big caravans,[1] the transhipment of the pepper-carriers' cargoes could entail requisitioning camels from as far away as Socnopaiu Nesos.

The papyrus highlights the key organizational role played by the *paralemptes*, as the operative arm of the arabarchs. The distance between the port where the sea voyage ended (Berenice) and the emporion where most of the commodities were sold (Alexandria), plus the considerable customs duties theoretically due at Coptos, forced the merchants to ensure the support of the *paralemptes.* The mutual interests of the arabarchs and merchants in ensuring the prosperity of the India trade brought all the fiscal, financial, and logistical problems encountered by merchants between Alexandria and Berenice to the *paralemptes'* desk: it was he who financed the travel expenses in Egypt for both the outward and return journeys and sanctioned unavoidable delays in the payment of import customs duties. In all likelihood, it was the *paralemptes* who mediated between the cameleer and the merchants.

Consisting of an import quarter-tax (plus an additional arabarchs' share for certain commodities) on 100 per cent of the incoming cargo and an export quarter-tax on 75 per cent of the departing cargo (with discounts for the commodities subject to the additional arabarchs' shares), the Red Sea tax

[1] Ruffing (1993); (2006).

amounted to a nominal rate of about 43.75 per cent for commodities passing from the Red Sea to the Mediterranean. Such was the rate when the customs duties were paid in kind, but when they were paid in money (and they almost always were, in the first and second centuries AD), the values of the cargoes were estimated with generously low fixed prices, so that the actual dues were much less than 43.75 per cent of the Alexandrian market prices.

Precious as they are, the few data we have do not enable us to determine the final balance of the *Hermapollon*'s enterprise. The best we can do to get a vague idea of its profitability is to extrapolate from the approximations for the fiscal value of the whole shipment and the weight and market price of the pepper cargo, and also from the sixteenth-century pepper prices both at Cochin and Lisbon, factoring in the delivery cost.[2]

What we get is nothing too exciting: only incomplete and tentative approximations to be taken, at best, as broad indicators. Assuming that at the time of the Muziris papyrus:

1. Rome's pepper price was the same as in Pliny's time (four denarii per pound);
2. the ratio between the prices in Muziris and in Rome was not too different from the 1 : *c.*13.6 inferred from the mid-sixteenth-century pepper prices in Cochin and Lisbon;
3. the Alexandrian market price of the *Hermapollon*'s cargo was 2.5 times higher than its fiscal value; and
4. the expenses for sea voyages were approximately 12 per cent of the final cost;

then:

1. the Alexandrian market value of the *Hermapollon*'s cargo would be 4,000 talents (24,000,000 sesterces);
2. the cost of the cargo in India would be around 470 talents (2,820,000 sesterces); and
3. the expenses for the sea transport would be 480 talents (2,880,000 sesterces).

Moreover, if we assume that the import and export customs duties were around 700 talents (4,200,000 sesterces) and the expense for the transports in Egypt was 300 talents (1,800,000 sesterces), the balance of the *Hermapollon*'s cargo would be as presented in Table 13.1.

[2] In the sixteenth century, the Cochin–Lisbon freight was 4 *cruzados* per *quintal*. At Cochin, the price for pepper was 2.5 *cruzados* per *quintal* (5.6 on board). In Lisbon, it was sold for 34 *cruzados* per *quintal*: Godinho (1981/1983: 3.21).

Table 13.1 Hypothetical balance of the *Hermapollon*'s enterprise.

Proceeds	24,000,000	
Cost of the cargo		2,820,000
Sea transport		2,880,000
Customs duties		4,200,000
Transports in Egypt		1,800,000
Total	24,000,000	11,700,000

It goes without saying that each entry of the table is a very rough estimate, and that the whole computation produces a mere approximation. Nonetheless, it may provide some sense of the financial apparatus for one commercial enterprise to South India in the mid-second century AD.

Appendices

APPENDIX 1

Exchanging Coins at Barygaza

Like lists of exports to other emporia in the *Periplus*, the one to the emporion of Barygaza includes Roman coinage.[1] Unlike the other lists, however, this one specifies that Roman gold and silver coinage could be exchanged with local currency for a profit: 'In this port of trade there is a market for.... Roman money, gold and silver, which commands an exchange at some profit against the local currency.'[2] What kind of local currency was exchanged for Roman aurei and denarii? Why did it give 'some profit' to the Roman traders?

When the *Periplus* was written, sometime between AD 40 and 70, Nahapāna/Manbanos had been the king of Ariake for quite some time.[3] At Barygaza, his drachmas circulated together with the old drachmas of Apollodotus and Menander.[4] The weight standard of both the old and the new drachmas was about 2.2./2.3 grams.[5] Were these drachmas—old and new—the 'local currency' exchanged for Roman coins?

The phenomenon hinted at in the *Periplus* may be further clarified by a famous inscription set up in honour of Uṣavadāta, Nahapāna's son-in-law, in one of the caves of the Pandav Lena of Nasik.[6] It is worth pointing out that since Gautamīputra Śrī Sātakarṇi—already the Sātavāhana king when the *Periplus* was written—defeated Uṣavadāta and conquered Nasik in his eighteenth year,[7] the time lapse between the *Periplus* and the inscription from Nasik is less than eighteen years.

The three lines of interest here (4–6) are engraved in smaller characters and seem to be a later addition to the preceding text. They show a more Sanskritized orthography (*kārṣāpaṇa* vs. *kāhāpaṇa*) and describe donations to Hindu gods and Brahmans, whereas the lines above account for donations to Buddhist monks. They refer to an accomplishment achieved in Nahapāna's forty-fifth year: 'Again, the gift given by him

[1] The export of Roman coinage—referred to sometimes with the word *denarion* (*PME* 6, 8, 49), sometimes with the generic term *chrema/chremata* (*PME* 24, 28, 39, 56, 60)—is explicitly attested at Adulis (*PME* 6), Malao, (*PME* 8), Muza (*PME* 24), Barbarikon (*PME* 39), Barygaza (PME 49), and the emporia of Limyrike (*PME* 56) and the Coromandel Coast (*PME* 60). It is also implied at Mundu, Mosyllon, at the emporion of the Aromata, and Cane (*PME* 9, 10, 12, 28).

[2] *PME* 49: *προχωρεῖ δὲ εἰς τὸ ἐμπόριον . . . δηνάριον χρυσοῦν καὶ ἀργυροῦν, ἔχον ἀλλαγὴν καὶ ἐπικέρδειάν τινα πρὸς τὸ ἐντόπιον νόμισμα*; transl. by L. Casson.

[3] See pp. 135–6.

[4] As attested by *PME* 47: *ἀφ' οὗ μέχρι νῦν ἐν Βαρυγάζοις παλαιαὶ προχωροῦσιν δραχμαί, γράμμασιν Ἑλληνικοῖς ἐγκεχαραγμέναι ἐπίσημα τῶν μετὰ Ἀλέξανδρον βεβασιλευκότων Ἀπολλοδότου καὶ Μενάνδρου*, 'Because of this, there are to be found on the market in Barygaza even today old drachmas engraved with the inscriptions, in Greek letters, of Apollodotus and Menander, rulers who came after Alexander.'

[5] Rapson (1908: cviii); Jha and Rajgor (1994: 88–104); Fishman (2013: 5–20).

[6] Senart (1905/1906: no. 12, 82–5); Lüders (1912: no. 1132); Mirashi (1981: no. 38, 95–100). Nasik, Ptolemy's *Νασίκα* (*Geog.* 7.1.63), was a centre not far from the maritime emporia of Suppara and Kalliena and the trans-peninsular route to Masalia.

[7] Bhagwanlal Indraji (1883: 573–5); Senart (1905/1906: n. 4, 71–3); Lüders (1912: n. 1125); Mirashi (1981: n. 11, 23–8).

[sc. by Uṣavadāta] formerly in the year 41 [sc. of the king Nahapāna], on the 15th day of Kārttika, was actually delivered on the 15th day (?) of the year 45 to the holy gods and Brahmans: a capital of 2,000 *suvarṇa*, which makes out, as one *suvarṇa* is worth 35 (*kārṣāpaṇa*), seventy thousand (70,000) *kārṣāpaṇa*. On wooden tablets according to custom.'[8]

No doubt, a *suvarṇa* is a gold coin and a *kārṣāpaṇa* is a silver coin, but which ones? And which gold-to-silver ratio do they imply? E. J. Rapson identified the *suvarṇa* with the Kuṣāṇa gold coin, and the *kārṣāpaṇa* with a silver coin of the same weight standard as the drachmas of Apollodotus and Menander, inferring a 1 : 10 gold-to-silver ratio.[9] D. R. Bhandarkar contended that the *suvarṇa* and the *kārṣāpaṇa* were indigenous coins of 146.4 and 58.5 grains (80 and 32 *rattis*) respectively, positing a gold-to-silver ratio of 1 : 14.[10] A. S. Altekar identified the *suvarṇa* and the *kārṣāpaṇa* with the Kuṣāṇa gold coin and Nahapāna's drachma respectively, and inferred a gold-to-silver ratio of 1 : 10.[11] D. W. MacDowall understood the *suvarṇa* as the Roman aureus and the *kārṣāpaṇa* as the drachma of Nahapāna, and again concluded that the gold-to-silver ratio was 1 : 10.[12]

In my view, any interpretation that univocally deduces a gold-to-silver ratio of 1 : 10 from the Nasik inscription is inconsistent with the information provided by the *Periplus*. With such a ratio, Roman merchants would not have (also) exchanged aurei for local silver currency. With such a ratio, Roman merchants would have been better off exchanging only pre-AD 64 denarii for Indian gold.

It is not coincidental that the scholars who have inferred this ratio and tried to establish a relation between the Nasik inscription and the *Periplus* ended up contorting the intent of the *Periplus*' passage. Altekar, who first realized that the Nasik equivalence had to be consistent with the information provided by the Greek author, understood that Roman silver coinage could be profitably exchanged for Indian *gold*, even though the text clearly says *ἐντόπιον νόμισμα* 'local currency'.[13] MacDowall too postulated that only silver denarii were exchanged. The Roman merchants would have achieved their profit by exchanging pre-AD 64 silver denarii struck at Rome at the 1 : 12 ratio for drachmas from Nahapāna issued at the 1 : 10 ratio.[14] It is difficult to see why a different gold-to-silver ratio between the Roman Empire and India should have had an impact on an exchange of silver for silver. At any rate, MacDowall's interpretation is not supported by the text, which clarifies that both aurei and denarii (*δηνάριον χρυσοῦν καὶ ἀργυροῦν*) were exchanged for local currency.

[8] *bhūyo nena dataṃ vase 41 kātikaśudhe panarasa puvāka vase 45 panarasa niyutaṃ bhagavatāṃ devānaṃ brāhmaṇānaṃca kārṣāpaṇasahasrāṇi satari 70,000 paṃcatriśaka suvarṇa kṛtā dina suvarṇasahasraṇaṃ mūlyaṃ phalakavāre caritratoti* (ll. 4–6). Senart's translation (1905/1906: 83) suggests that 70,000 *kārṣāpaṇa* was actually given, not 2,000 *suvarṇa*. This is recommended neither by the syntax, as *dataṃ* and *niyutaṃ* refer to *dina suvarṇasahasraṇaṃ mūlyaṃ*, nor by Uṣavadāta's epithet *suvarṇadāna* in Lüders (1912: 191, no. 1131); Mirashi (1981: no. 43, 107–13).

[9] Rapson (1908: clxxxiv–v).

[10] Bhandarkar (1921: 191–2).

[11] Altekar (1940: 4–5).

[12] MacDowall (1996: 92); MacDowall (2003: 43–4).

[13] Altekar (1940: 4). Schoff's translation (1912: 42), to which Altekar refers, runs as 'gold and silver coin, on which there is a profit when exchanged for the money of the country'.

[14] MacDowall (1996: 92); MacDowall (2003: 43–4); followed by Nappo (2017: 573).

The problem here is the identification of the currencies mentioned in the Nasik inscription. The *suvarṇa* can hardly be anything other than the Roman aureus, the only contemporary gold coin Uṣavadāta could donate by the thousands.[15] As we now know, the gold coins of Vima Kadphises—the earliest of a Kuṣāṇa ruler—were minted several decades after the end of Nahapāna's reign.[16] However, it was not the misidentification of the *suvarṇa* that botched the interpretation of the Nasik inscription—Kuṣāṇa and Roman gold coins have a relatively close weight standard. What is questionable in most of the above interpretations is the identification of the *kārṣāpaṇa*.

Although an identification with Nahapāna's silver drachmas seems to be supported by the large hoard of Jogalthembi, just a few kilometres from Nasik, which included roughly 13,270 such coins (*c.*9,270 of which have Gautamīputra Śrī Sātakarṇi's overstrikes),[17] the term *kārṣāpaṇa* cannot refer to them. Or, at least, it cannot refer to them *alone*. It is worth repeating: the theory that the ratio of gold to silver was about 1 : 10 in the kingdom of Nahapāna is not consistent with the information delivered by the *Periplus* that *both* aurei and denarii were exported and exchanged at a profit at Barygaza during Manbanos' (Nahapāna's) reign. Exchanging one pre-AD 64 aureus for 35 Nahapāna's drachmas would not give any profit to the Western merchants.

In my view, in the Nasik inscription, the term *kārṣāpaṇa* has to refer (or has to refer *also*) to the Indian punch-marked coins that apparently still circulated in that area in the mid-first century AD. In other words, although with some limitations, what Bhandare has observed regarding the Nāṇāghāṭ inscription of Nāganikā (first century BC) can be repeated for the Nasik inscription: the occurrence of *kāhāpaṇa* as the unit of account attests to 'the continuation and impact of punch marked coins in circulation'.[18]

Since these coins were still heavy enough to guarantee a profit to the Roman merchants who exchanged an aureus for thirty-five of them, and since in the Roman Empire the gold-to-silver ratio was approximately 1 : 12,[19] they must have then weighed more than 2.67 grams (7.8 × 12 : 35). The maximum weight of the punch-marked coins circulating in Nasik under Nahapāna may be inferred by hoards that were deposited in the region, most probably sometime before the first century AD. The roughly 87 per cent of 2,029 silver punch-marked coins from the Barwani hoard (reportedly, of 3,450 specimens) weighed between 3.5 and 3.2 grams.[20] Of the thirty-five punch-marked coins found at Kasrawad, thirty weighed between 3.5 and 3.1 grams.[21] If most of the punch-marked coins circulating in the mid-first century AD in Nasik weighed between 3.5 and 2.8 grams, the exchange of one Roman gold coin for thirty-five silver punch-marked coins would give a weight ratio of between 1 : 15.7 and 1 : 12.5.

It is likely that the profit made by Roman merchants who exchanged Roman aurei for local silver coinage also resulted from a higher value for gold in India, but not only

[15] De Romanis (2006b: 70).

[16] Bopearachchi (2006); Bopearachchi (2008: 3–56); Falk (2014).

[17] Scott (1908); Shastri (1995). [18] Bhandare (1999: 55).

[19] Butcher and Ponting (2014: 426–451; 704–705). Even if the *Periplus* was written between AD 64 and 70 (which is far from certain), the fact that the *actual* content of post-AD 64 aurei and denarii results in a higher gold-to-silver ratio may be considered irrelevant, in this regard.

[20] Only *c.*2.5 per cent weighed 3.6 grams, *c.*10.5 per cent less than 3.1: Gupta (1992: 14).

[21] Diskalkar (1949: 146–53); Errington (2003: 108).

from that. The author of the *Periplus* makes it clear that Roman merchants gained by exchanging silver denarii as well. Hence, aside from the different gold-to-silver ratio, there must have been additional reasons for Indian merchants to exchange their silver currency for Roman coins at a loss. Two possibilities arise here that are not mutually exclusive:

a. the good reputation of the Roman coinage exported to India may have induced Indian merchants active on the subcontinent to give up their currency—any local currency—for better-received coins;[22]

b. the coexistence of local silver currencies with inconsistent ratios between metallic content and nominal values may have prompted Indian merchants to exchange currency that was relatively undervalued. If, for instance, the drachmas of Nahapāna (and by extension the Indo-Greek drachmas) were relatively overvalued compared with the punch-marked coins, the dynamics of Gresham's Law ('bad money drives out good') would have offered a further and probably more compelling incentive for Indian merchants to make use of their undervalued punch-marked coins in the least damaging way. Exchanging them for Roman coins might have been less detrimental than exchanging them for Nahapāna's drachmas.

It is worth pointing out a dissimilarity. In the Aï-Khanoum of the mid-second century BC, the circulation of different types of silver coinage—apparently each with a value of its own—resulted in a rich lexicon that distinguishes not only between drachmas and *kasapana*, but also between *kasapana* from different geographical areas, such as *kasapana taxaena* and *kasapana nandena*.[23] By contrast, the Sātavāhana inscriptions show the persistence of the *kārṣāpaṇa* as a unit of account, despite the replacement of punch-marked coins with drachmas as the most common silver currency. This phenomenon has been understood in different ways. Rapson postulated that the occurrences of the term *kārṣāpaṇa* in inscriptions always referred to the drachma.[24] I. K. Sarma posited that the Sātavāhana drachma (and therefore the Nahapāna drachma as well) were actually worth an *ardha-kārṣāpaṇa*—a half-*kārṣāpaṇa*.[25] Neither of these views can apply to the Nasik inscription. If the *kārṣāpaṇa* of the Nasik inscription referred only to drachmas, it would be difficult to understand how the Roman merchants could achieve a profit by exchanging one aureus for thirty-five of them. Conversely, if the drachma of Nahapāna had been an *ardha-kārṣāpaṇa*, it would have been a severely underrated currency compared both to the punch-marked coins and the Roman aureus. Even if the average weight of the punch-marked coins circulating in the mid-first century AD was still about 3.4 grams (but most probably it was much less), a drachma of 2.2/2.3 grams should have been worth at

[22] The silver coins exported by Roman merchants (carefully selected in the first as well as in the sixth century AD: Cosm. Indic. 11.19) provoked the admiration of the Indians for being 'equal in weight, although the various figures on them showed that they had been coined by several people': Plin., *NH* 6.85. On the ancient Indian art of evaluating coins (*rūpasutta*, 'science of coinage'), see De Romanis (1988: 31–7). The popularity of Tiberius' coins is also attested by the imitations, in India and in South East Asia, of the image on the reverse of Tiberius' PONTIF MAXIM type: Borell (2014: 7–43) and pp. 127–30.

[23] Rapin and Grenet (1983: 315–81). I thank Prof. H. Falk for pointing that reference out to me.

[24] Rapson (1908: clxxxiv–v).

[25] Sarma (1980: 60).

least two-thirds of a *kārṣāpaṇa*,[26] whereas an exchange rate of 70 to 1 with the aureus would imply a gold-to-silver ratio of 1 : 20.

On the other hand, if both the Nāṇāghāṭ inscription of Nāganikā (first century BC) and the Kānherī inscription of Apareṇu (sixth year of Gautamīputra Śrīyajña Sātakarṇi, late second century AD) show the *kārṣāpaṇa* as the unit of account,[27] it is because at some point in time, in part due to the weight loss of the punch-marked coins, and in part because the political authorities may have wanted to increase the nominal value of their own coin output, the value of drachmas was equated to that of the older and generally heavier punch-marked coins and fixed at one *kārṣāpaṇa*. If this happened at the time of Nahapāna, his subjects would have been induced to change their undervalued punch-marked coins for coins that did not suffer such a depreciation.

In conclusion, we suggest three possible factors that may have induced Indian traders to exchange their currency for Roman coinage in ways that generated a profit for Roman merchants: a gold-to-silver ratio more favourable to gold in India than it was in the Roman Empire, the good reputation in India of the Roman coinage exported to the subcontinent, and the possibility that the punch-marked coins were undervalued with respect to the drachmas of Nahapāna. In which proportion these three factors contributed to the phenomenon alluded to in the *Periplus* is difficult to say. It is easier to point out three possible consequences of the process:

1. In other regions of the Indian subcontinent, punch-marked coins were still hoarded at relatively late periods. They appear together with Kuṣāna coins in the hoards of Mir Zakah and Taxila, with Indo-Greek coins in the hoards from Kangra, Thatta, and Bairath, and with Roman coins in the hoards of Malambam (Chennai), Pennar, Tondamanathan, Kondapur, Nasthullapur, Weepagandla, and Eyyal.[28] By contrast, they are absent from the large hoards of Gogha (possibly *c.*5,000 silver coins, both of Indo-Greek kings and Nahapāna) and Jogalthembi (*c.* 13,270 of Nahapāna's drachmas).[29] It seems that by the time the Gogha and Jogalthembi hoards were deposited, punch-marked coins had been driven out of the western Deccan.
2. A Tiberian denarius found in the Woodham Mortimer (Essex, UK) hoard has an isotopic signature which suggests an Indian origin for its silver.[30] The denarius is a *RIC* I² 95, no. 30 type, and cannot be precisely dated within the reign of Tiberius. However, several details on its reverse (legs of chair ornamented, single line below, female figure holding a sceptre) occur in specimens whose obverse often displays a very old emperor.[31] It may be suggested that it was issued in the last years of Tiberius. If the silver of the denarius did come from India, it may have been imported from Barygaza in the form of local currency and *used to pay*

[26] The heaviest of the thirty-four punch-marked coins included in the Eyyal hoard (*terminus post quem* AD 98) weighs 2.73 grams, four specimens weigh between 2.5 and 2.2 grams, and the other twenty-nine less than 2.2 grams: Unnithan (1963: 22–8); Gupta (1965).

[27] Nāganikā's inscription: Bühler (1883a: n. 1–2); Lüders (1912: n. 1112); Sircar (1965: 2, n. 75); Mirashi (1981: nn. 3, 27); Apareṇu's inscription: Bühler (1883b: n. 15); Lüders (1912: n. 1025); Gokhale (1991: n. 25).

[28] Gupta and Hardaker (2014²: 63); Suresh (2004: 163; 167; 169; 170).

[29] For the Gogha hoard, see Deyell (1984: 115–27); for Jogalthembi see n.17.

[30] Butcher and Ponting (2014: 176–7; 187; 199).

[31] Mattingly (1923: cxxx); Sutherland (1987: 219–20; 224).

the customs duties in Egypt. It would be farfetched to suggest that such exchanges decisively contributed to the flow of Roman coins towards India.[32] Exchanging Roman coins with local currency did give a profit to Roman merchants, but only *some* profit (*ἐπικέρδειάν τινα*).[33] In normal conditions, the trade in Indian commodities would have been far more profitable. Roman merchants resorted to exchanging Roman for local coins only for the lack of better options. Still, if imported Indian silver coins were occasionally used for the production of denarii, the phenomenon may not have been insignificant between the years of Tiberius and the year in which the *Periplus* was written—the time lapse may extend from just a few years to several decades.

3. Numismatic findings in the region do not corroborate the information in the *Periplus* about the export of Roman coins to Barygaza. It has been suggested that Roman denarii were melted down to issue Nahapāna's silver coins.[34] I do not see how this hypothesis can be consistent with the information that Roman coins were exchanged with local currency for a profit.[35] Alternatively, it may be proposed that denarii and aurei were used by Indian traders from Barygaza for their trade with Dakṣiṇāpatha and Limyrike.[36] The Augustan (1) and Tiberian (10) aurei found at Adam, the Julio-Claudian denarii found at Akkenpalle (more than 1500, Augustus to Nero, but mostly Augustan and Tiberian) and other Roman coins found in Andhra Pradesh and Kerala may have entered India through Barygaza.[37]

[32] Nappo (2017: 573). Tacitus (*Ann.* 3.53) has Tiberius lamenting, in AD 22, that the trade in precious stones caused a haemorrhage of Roman money towards foreign and hostile nations.

[33] See Casson (1989: 209). [34] Turner (1984) [non vidi].

[35] Other objections in Raschke (1978: 631) and Casson (1989: 209).

[36] Imports to Barygaza from Paithana and Tagara: *PME* 51; trade relationships between Ariake and Limyrike: *PME* 54.

[37] Turner (1989: 46; 47); Berghaus (1992: 240).

APPENDIX 2

Axum and Silis in the *Kephalaia*

Trade and Powers in the Late Antique Indian Ocean

The Western merchants of Late Antiquity had a different experience of the Indian Ocean than did their predecessors of the Early Roman Empire: as shown in chapter two, they travelled via multi-stage sea routes and traded in Sri Lanka more often than on the west coast of India. It comes as no surprise that their vision of the world was affected by the reconfigured logistics of Indo-Mediterranean trade and the growth of trade in the Bay of Bengal.

Commentators have sometimes expressed their amazement at the characterization of the Axumite kingdom as one of the four great kingdoms of the world in a passage of the *Kephalaia*, the Coptic translation of an originally Syriac Manichaean text.[1] Much of the incredulity stems from the identification of the mysterious Silis with China, which makes the inclusion of the Axumite kingdom—remote from the commercial land routes that connected China, Persia, and the Roman Empire—remarkable.[2] It may be wondered whether the author's (or the translator's) world view even encompassed both Axum and China. The association of Axum with Rome and Persia would look less awkward if the passage was offering a maritime-based perspective, in which the glamorous status of Aksum reflected the relevance of Adulis as a bustling transhipment point between Egypt and India. In this maritime-based perspective, the traditional identification of Silis with China seems less attractive than an alternative option: identifying Silis with Sielediba/Selediba[3]—that is, Taprobane (Sri Lanka)—a favourite destination for the Western merchants from Adulis.

This possibility is less odd than it might seem at first sight. Adulis and Taprobane, which were only marginal participants in the direct trade between Egypt and South India at the time of the *Periplus*, had blossomed into major hubs of the Late Antique trade network that connected the Mediterranean and China. Taprobane in particular looms large in Late Antique western world views, the size of the island and the power of its king being greatly overestimated in Egypt. Take for instance Ptolemy's map (p. 150, Fig. 5.6), where the island is considerably outsized in comparison with continental India. Consider also Palladius' tale about the *scholasticus* who travels

[1] *Kephalaia*, 77, 188,30–190,10 Böhlig/Polotsky: 'Mani would say: "There are f[our great kingdoms] in the world. [The first is the kingdom of] the land of Ba[by]lon and of Persia. The s[eco]nd is the kingdom of the Romans. The thir[d is the k]ingdom of the Axumites. The fourth is the kin[g]dom of Silis. These four great kingdoms e[x]ist in the world; there is none that surpasses them."' (transl. by I. Gardner). Cf. Gragg (2008: 211).

[2] The literature on this passage counts several different explanations for how China would have come to be identified as Silis in the *Kephalaia*. For a review, see Metzler (1989: 447–9).

[3] Cosm. Indic. 2.45; 11.13; 16; 22. Cf. *Serendivis* in Amm. Marc. 22.7.10. Obviously, *-diba*, *-diva* > ancient Indian *d(v)īpa* (island).

from Adulis/Axum to Taprobane. Quite significantly, while the king of Aksum, extolled in the *Kephalaia*, is styled as only a minor kinglet (*βασιλίσκος μικρὸς τῶν Ἰνδῶν ἐκεῖ καθεζόμενος*), the king of Taprobane is characterized as a king to whom all the minor kings of the land (of India) are subject, like satraps (*ὁ μέγας βασιλεὺς κατοικεῖ τῶν Ἰνδῶν, ᾧ πάντες οἱ βασιλίσκοι τῆς χώρας ὑπόκεινται ὡς σατράπαι*).[4]

What did Silis mean to the translator of *Kephalaia*? Could the world view of Mani's followers have been shaped by the multi-stage sea routes between Egypt and India and the burgeoning Sri Lankan trade?

[4] Palladius, *De gentibus Indiae et Bragmanibus* 1.3–4.

References

Abudanah, F., Tarawneh, M.B., Twaissi, S., Wenner, S., and Al-Salameen, A. (2016). 'The *Via Nova Traiana* Between Petra and Ayn Al-Qana In Arabia Petraea', *Oxford Journal of Archaeology* 35.4: 389–412.

Adams, C. (2007). *Land Transport in Roman Egypt. A Study of Economics and Administration in a Roman Province.* Oxford.

Adams, C. (2017). 'Nile River Transport under the Romans', in A. Wilson, A. Bowman, *Trade, Commerce, and the State in the Roman World.* Oxford, 175–208.

Agius, D.A. (2008). *Classic Ships of Islam. From Mesopotamia to the Indian Ocean*, Leiden and Boston.

Altekar, A.S. (1940). 'The Relative Prices of Metals and Coins in Ancient India', *The Journal of Numismatic Society of India* 2: 1–13.

Amato, E. (2003). 'Per la cronologia di Dionisio Periegeta', *Revue de philologie, de littérature et d'histoire anciennes* 77: 7–16.

Ames, G.J. (2009). Em nome de deus: *The Journal of the First Voyage of Vasco da Gama to India. Translated and edited*, Leiden and Boston.

Amigues, S. (1996). 'Un cinnamome fantomatique', *Topoi* 6: 657–64.

Andreau, J. (2005). 'Le système monétaire partiellement "fermé" de l'Égypte romaine', in F. Duyrat and O. Picard (eds), *L'exception égyptienne? Production et échanges monétaires en Égypte hellénistique et romaine.* Cairo, 329–38.

Ankum, H. (1978). 'Tabula Pompeiana 13: ein Seefrachtvertrag oder ein Seedarlehn?', *Iura* 39: 156–73.

Ankum, H. (1988). 'Minima de tabula pompeiana 13', *Cahiers d'histoire* 33: 271–89.

Aravamuthan, T.G. (1942). *Catalogue of the Roman and Byzantine Coins in the Madras Government Museum*, Madras.

Arnaud, P. (2015). 'La batellerie de fret nilotique d'après la documentation papyrologique (300 avant J.-C.-400 après J.-C.)', in P. Pomey (éd.), *La batellerie Égyptienne. Archéologie, histoire, ethnographie*, Paris, 99–150.

Arunachalam, B. (1993). 'Socotra in Indian Navigational Traditions', in S. Chandra, B. Arunachalam, and V. Suryanarayan (eds), *The Indian Ocean and its Islands. Strategic, Scientific and Historical Perspectives.* New Delhi, 117–27.

Arunachalam, B. (1996). 'Traditional Sea and Sky Wisdom of Indian Seamen and their Practical Application', in H.P. Ray and J.-F. Salles (eds), *Tradition and Archaeology: Early Maritime Contacts in the Indian Ocean*, New Delhi, 261–74.

Arunachalam, B. (2008). 'Technology of Indian Sea Navigation (c. 1200–c. 1800)', *The Medieval History Journal* 11.2: 187–227.

Arunachalam, B., Sukumar, B., and Sukumar, A. (2006). 'Reconstruction of the ancient Port, Korkai in Tuttukkudi District of Tamil Nadu', *Current Science* 91: 278–80.

Assemani, J.S. (1719–28). *Bibliotheca Orientalis Clementino-Vaticana.* 3 vols. Rome.

Ast, R. and Bagnall, R.S. (2015). 'The Receivers of Berenike. New Inscriptions from the 2015 Season', *Chiron* 45: 171–85.

Aubert, J.-J. (2004). 'Aux origines du canal de Suez? Le canal du Nil à la mer Rouge revisité', in M. Clavel-Lévèque and E. Hermon (eds). *Espaces intégrés et ressources naturelles dans l'Empire Romain: actes du colloque de l'Université de Laval-Québec, 5–8 mars 2003*. Paris, 219–52.

Aubert, J.-J. (2015). 'Trajan's Canal: River Navigation from the Nile to the Red Sea?', in F. De Romanis, M. Maiuro (eds). *Across the Ocean. Nine Essays on Indo-Mediterranean Trade*. Leiden and Boston, 33–42.

Aubin, J. (1974). 'Francisco de Albuquerque. Un juif castillan au service de l'Inde portugaise (1510–1515)', *Arquivos do Centro Cultural Português* 7: 175–202.

Austin, M. (2006^2). *The Hellenistic World from Alexander to the Roman Conquest: A Selection of Ancient Sources in Translation*. Cambridge.

Badhreenath, S. (2016). 'Mamallapuram, the Port City. New Revelations', in M.-F. Boussac, J.-F. Salles and J.-B. Yon (eds), *Ports of the Indian Ocean*. New Delhi, 275–87.

Badian, E. (1972). *Publicans and Sinners. Private Enterprise in the Service of the Roman Republic*. Oxford.

Bagnall, R.S. (1985). *Currency and Inflation in Fourth Century Egypt (Bull. Amer. Soc. of Papyrologists, Suppl. 5)*. Chico.

Bagnall, R.S. (1989). 'Fourth-Century Prices: New Evidence and Further Thoughts, *Zeitschrift für Papyrologie and Epigraphik* 76: 69–76.

Bagnall, R.S., Bülow-Jacobsen, A., Cuvigny, H. (2001). 'Security and Water on Egypt's Desert Roads: New Light on the Prefect Iulius Ursus and Praesidia-building under Vespasian', *Journal of Roman Archaeology* 14: 325–33.

Bagnall, R.S., Helms, C., and Verhoogt, A.M.E.W. (2000). *Documents from Berenike. Volume I. Greek ostraca from the 1996–1998 seasons*. Brussels.

Bagnall, R.S., Helms, C., and Verhoogt, A.M.E.W. (2005). *Documents from Berenike. Volume II. Texts from the 1999–2001 seasons*, Brussels.

Bagnall, R.S. and Sheridan, J.A. (1994a). 'Greek and Latin Documents from 'Abu Sha'ar, 1990–1991', *Journal of the American Research Center in Egypt* 31: 159–68.

Bagnall, R.S. and Sheridan, J.A. (1994b). 'Greek and Latin Documents from 'Abu Sha'ar, 1992–1993', *Bulletin of the American Society of Papyrologists*. 31: 109–20.

Banaji, J. (2015). '"Regions that look seaward" – changing fortunes, submerged histories, and the slow capitalism of the sea', in F. De Romanis, M. Maiuro (eds). *Across the Ocean. Nine Essays on Indo-Mediterranean Trade*. Leiden and Boston, 114–26.

Bang, P.F. (2008). *Roman Bazaar. A Comparative Study of Trade and Markets in a Tributary Empire*. Cambridge.

Bar-Kochva, B. (1976). *The Seleucid Army: Organization and Tactics in the Great Campaigns*. Cambridge.

Baslez, M.F. (2005). 'Les Alexandrins, les Juifs et l'empereur: Le « Nous » et « L'Autre » dans les Actes des Alexandrins (Ier-IIIe s.)', in Y. Perrin (ed), *L'étranger, le barbare: image de l'autre*. vol. 2. Saint-Étienne, 94–109.

Bastianini, G. (1988). 'Il prefetto d'Egitto (30 a.C.–297 d.C.): addenda (1973–1985)', in H. Temporini and W. Haase (eds), *Aufstieg und Niedergang der römischen Welt*. 2.10.1. Berlin-New York, 503–17.

Bazou, Th. (1998). 'La voie romaine en Arabie. Le secteur nord, de Bostra à Philadelphie; corpus des inscriptions relevées sur les bornes milliaire; synthèse historique', in

T. Bauzou, A. Desreumaux, P.-L. Gatier, J.-B. Humbert, and F. Zayadine (eds), *Fouilles de Khirbet es-Samra en Jordanie 1. La voie romaine. Le cimetière. Les documents épigraphiques*. Turnhout, 105–255.

Belfiore, S. (2013). 'Periplus Maris Erythraei (2036)'. *Die Fragmente Der Griechischen Historiker Part V*. H.-J. Gehrke and F. Maier (eds), Brill Reference Online, https://referenceworks.brillonline.com/entries/fragmente-der-griechischen-historiker-v/periplus-maris-erythraei-2036-a2036?s.num=1&s.q=Periplo+del+Mare+Eritreo.

Bentley Duncan, T. (1986). 'Navigation between Portugal and Asia in the Sixteenth and Seventeenth Centuries', in C.K. Pullapilly and E.J. Van Kley (eds), *Asia and the West. Encounters and Exchanges from the Age of Explorations. Essays in Honor of Donald F. Lach*. Notre Dame, 3–25.

Berger, H. (1880). *Die geographischen Fragmente des Eratosthenes, neu gesammelt, geordnet und besprochen*, Leipzig.

Berggren, J.L. and Jones, A. (2000). *Ptolemy's Geography. An Annotated Translation of the Theoretical Chapters*. Princeton.

Berghaus, P. (1991). 'Roman Coins from India and Their Imitations', in A.K. Jha (ed) *Coinage, trade and economy*. Nashik, 108–21.

Berghaus, P. (1992). 'Zu den römischen Fundmünzen aus Indien', *Schweizerische Numismatische Rundschau* 71: 226–47.

Berghaus, P. (1993). 'Indian Imitations of Roman Coins', in T. Hackens, G. Moucharte, et al. (eds), *Proceedings of the XIth International Numsiamtic Congress: organized for the 150th anniversary of the Soci'et'e Royale de Numismatique de Belgique, Brussels, September 8th–13th 1991*. Louvain-la-Neuve, 2.305–10.

Berghaus, P. (1994). 'Two Imitations out of the Valuvally Hoard of Roman Aurei (Kerala) 1983', *Studies in South Indian Coins* 4: 33–42.

Berghaus, P. (1998). 'Republican and Early Roman Imperial Denarii from India', in A.K. Jha and S. Garg (eds), *Ex moneta: essays on numismatics, history and archaeology in honour of Dr. David W. MacDowall*. New Delhi, 1.119–27.

Bernard, P. (1996). 'L'Aornos bactrien et l'Aornos indien. Philostrate et Taxila: geographie, mythe et realité', *Topoi* 6: 475–530.

Berthelot, A. (1930). *L'Asie ancienne centrale et sud-orientale d'après Ptolémée*. Paris.

Beutler, F. (2007). 'Wer war ein *Procurator usiacus*? Die Verwaltung des Patrimoniums in Ägypten in der ersten Hälfte des 2. Jahrhunderts', *Cahiers Du Centre Gustave Glotz* 18: 67–82.

Bhagwanlal, I. (1883). 'Nasik', in *Gazetteer of the Bombay Precidency. XVI*. Bombay, 541–639).

Bhandare, S. (1999). *Historical Analysis of the Sātavāhana Era: A Study of Coins*, Ph.D. thesis, University of Bombay.

Bhandare, S. (2006). 'A Tale of Two Dynasties. The Kshaharatas and Satavahana in the Deccan', in H. Ray (ed), *Coins in India: Power and Communication*. Mumbai, 24–33.

Bhandarkar, D.R. (1921). *Lectures on ancient Indian numismatics*. Calcutta.

Billeter, G. (1898). *Geschichte des Zinsfusses im griechisch-römischen Altertum bis auf Justinian*. Leipzig.

Bingen, J. (1944). 'Les papyrus de la Fondation Egyptologique Reine Elisabeth, X', *Chroniques d'Égypte* 19: 271–80.

Bingen, J. (2002). 'Un nouvel épistratège et arabarque alexandrin', *Zeitschrift für Papyrologie und Epigraphik* 138: 119–20.

Birley, A. (2001). *Marcus Aurelius. A Biography*. 2nd edn. New York.

Blouin, K. (2014). *Triangular Landscapes. Environment, Society, and the State in the Nile Delta under Roman Rule*. Oxford.

Bogaert, R. (1965). 'Banquiers, courtiers et prêts maritimes à Athènes et à Alexandrie', *Chroniques d'Égypte* 40: 140–56.

Bopearachchi, O. (2006). 'Chronologie et généalogie des premiers rois kushans: nouvelles données', *Comptes-rendus de l'Académie des Inscriptions et Belles-Lettres* 1433–47.

Bopearachchi, O. (2008). 'Les premiers souverains kouchans: chronologie et iconographie monétaire', *Journal des Savants* 3–56.

Borell, B. (2014). 'The Power of Images – Coin Portraits of Roman Emperors on Jewellery Pendants in Early Southeast Asia', *Zeitschrift für Archäologie Außereuropäischer Kulturen* 6: 7–43.

Bouchon, G. (1976). 'L'inventaire de la cargaison rapportée de l'Inde en 1505', *Mare Luso-Indicum* 3: 101–25.

Bouchon, G. (1977). *Navires et cargaison: Retour de l'Inde en 1518. Caderno dos oficiaes da India da carreguaçam das naos que vieram o anno mdxviij*, Paris.

Bowersock, G.W. (1983). *Roman Arabia*, Cambridge, MA.

Boyajian, J.C. (1993). *Portuguese Trade in Asia Under the Habsburgs, 1580–1640*. Baltimore and London.

Boyaval, B. (2004). 'Sur un passage controversé du Tarif de Coptos', *Chronique d'Égypte* 79: 263–5.

Boyer, A.-M. (1897). 'Nahapāna et l'ère Çaka', *Journal Asiatique* 9.10: 120–151.

Braamcamp Freire, A. (1903). 'Cartas de Quitacão del Rei D. Manuel', *Archivo Histórico Portuguez* 1: 276–88.

Braamcamp Freire, A. (1906). 'Cartas de Quitacão del Rei D. Manuel', *Archivo Histórico Portuguez* 4: 282–8.

Brandt, J.C., Zimmer, P.C., and Jones, P.B. (2014). 'Declinations in the Almagest: Accuracy, Epoch, and Observers', *Journal of Astronomical History and Heritage* 17: 326–38.

Brun, J.-P. (2018). 'Chronologie des forts des routes de Myos Hormos et de Bérénice durant la période gréco-romaine', in J.-P. Brun, Th. Faucher, B. Redon, and S. Sidebotham (eds), *Le désert oriental d'Égypte durant la période gréco-romaine: bilans archéologiques*. Paris. Available at http://books.openedition.org/cdf/5155.

Brunt, P. (1990). *Roman Imperial Themes*. Oxford.

Bühler, G. (1883a). 'The Nânâghât Inscriptions', in J.A.S. Burgess (ed), *Archaeological Survey of Western India 5*. London, 59–74.

Bühler, G. (1883b). 'The Kaṇheri Inscriptions', in J.A.S. Burgess (ed), *Archaeological Survey of Western India 5*. London, 74–87.

Bukharin, M.D. (2007). *Neizvestnogo avtora «Peripl Jeritrejskogo morja». Tekst, perevod, kommentarij, issledovanija*. Saint Petersburg.

Bukharin, M. (2012). 'The Greek inscriptions at Hoq', in I. Strauch (ed), *Foreign Sailors on Socotra. The inscriptions and drawings from the cave Hoq*. Bremen.

Bülow-Jacobsen, A. (2013). 'Caravan Transportation on the Myos Hormos and Berenike Routes', available at http://www.college-de-france.fr/site/en-jean-pierre-brun/seminar-2013-11-26-10h00.htm.

Bülow-Jacobsen, A. and Cuvigny, H. (2007). 'Sulpicius Serenus, *procurator Augusti* et la titulature des préfets de Bérénice', *Chiron* 37: 11–33.

Burgers, P. (2001). 'Coinage and state expenditure: the reign of Claudius AD 41–54', *Historia* 50: 96–114.

Burkhalter, F. (2002). 'Le "tarif de Coptos". La douane de Coptos, les fermiers de l'"apostolion" et le préfet du désert de Bérénice', in *Autour de Coptos. Actes du colloque organisé au Musée des beaux-Arts de Lyon (17–18 mars 2000), Topoi. Orient-Occident*, suppl. 3, 199–233.

Burrow, T. and Emeneau, M.B. (1961). *A Dravidian Etymological Dictionary*, Oxford.

Butcher, K. and Ponting, M. (2014). *The Metallurgy of Roman Silver Coinage: From the Reform of Nero to the Reform of Trajan*. Cambridge.

Camodeca, G. (1999). Tabulae Pompeianae Sulpiciorum *(edizione critica dell'archivio puteolano dei Sulpici)*. 2 vols. Rome.

Camodeca, G. (2000). 'Per un primo aggiornamento all'edizione dell'archivio dei Sulpicii (TPSulp.)', *Cahiers du Centre Gustave Glotz* 11: 173–91.

Camodeca, G. (2001). 'Nuove testimonianze sul commercio marittimo puteolano', in P.A. Gianfrotta and F. Maniscalco (eds), Forma maris. *Forum internazionale di archeologia subacquea, Pozzuoli 22–24 settembre 1998*. Neapols, 85–94.

Camodeca, G. (2003). 'Il credito negli archivi campani: il caso di Puteoli e di Herculaneum', in E. Lo Cascio, *Credito e moneta nel mondo romano. Atti degli Incontri capresi di storia dell'economia antica (Capri 12–14 ottobre 2000)*. Bari, 69–98.

Cappers, R.T.J. (2006). *Roman Foodprints at Berenike. Archaeobotanical Evidence of Subsistence and Trade in the Eastern Desert of Egypt*. Los Angeles.

Carrié, J-M. (1997). 'L'arithmétique sociale de l'économie agraire: prix de la terre, rente foncière et prix des céréales dans l'Égypte romano-byzantine'; in J.Andreau, P.Briant, and R. Descat (eds), *Économie antique: Prix et formation des prix dans les économies antiques*. St.Bertrand-de-Comminges, 121–46.

Casson, L. (1971). *Ships and Seamanship in the Ancient World*. Princeton.

Casson, L. (1980). 'Rome's Trade with the East: The Sea Voyage to Africa and India', *Transactions of the American Philological Association* 110: 21–36.

Casson, L. (1984). 'The Sea Route to India: *Periplus Maris Erythraei* 57', *Classical Quaterly* 34: 473–79.

Casson, L. (1986). 'P. Vindob. G 40822 and the Shipping of Goods from India', *Bulletin of the American Society of Papyrologists* 23: 73–9.

Casson, L. (1989). *The* Periplus Maris Erythraei. *Text with Introduction, Translation and Commentary*. Princeton.

Casson, L. (1990). 'New Light on Maritime Loans: P. Vindob. G 40822', *Zeitschrift für Papyrologie und Epigraphik* 84: 195–206.

Cazzaniga, L. (1992). 'Osservazioni sulla successione dei prefetti d'Egitto all'epoca di Tiberio', *Analecta Papyrologica* 4: 5–19.

Champakalakshmi, R. (1996). *Trade, Ideology and Urbanization*. Delhi.

Chantraine, P. (1968–1980). *Dictionnaire étymologique de la langue grecque: histoire des mots*. Paris.

Charpentier, J. (1934). *The Indian Travels of Apollonius of Tyana*. Leipzig.

Cherian, P.J. (ed) (2015). *Pattanam Excavation Report 2015 9th Season*, Thiruvananthapuram.

Chevillard, J.-L. (2008). 'The concept of *ticai-c-col* in Tamil grammatical literature and the regional diversity of Tamil classical literature', in M. Kannan (ed), *Streams of Language: Dialects in Tamil*. Pondichéry, 21–50.

Christides, V. (2013). *What went wrong in the long distance Roman naval power*, in S.Kh. Samir and J.P. Monferrer-Sala, *Graeco-Latina et Orientalia. Studia in honorem Angeli Urbani heptagenarii*. Cordoba, 63–85.

Ciaraldi, M. (2007). *People and Plants in Ancient Pompeii. A new approach to urbanism from the microscope room*. London.

Cimma, M.R. (1981). *Ricerche sulle società di publicani*. Milan.

Cobb, M.A. (2015). 'The Chronology of Roman Trade in the Indian Ocean from Augustus to Early Third Century', *Journal of the Economic and Social History of the Orient* 58(3): 362–418.

Cobb, M.A. (2018). 'Black Pepper Consumption in the Roman Empire', *Journal of the Economic and Social History of the Orient* 61: 519–59.

Cohen, E.E. (1992). *Athenian Economy and Society. A Banking Perspective*. Princeton.

Constable, A.R. (2013). 'Basic Ideas of Navigation in Relation to the Early History of Sailing in the Indian Ocean', in A.R. Constable and W. Facey, *The Principles of Arab Navigation*, London, 1–20.

Cool, H.E.M. (2006). *Eating and Drinking in Roman Britain*, Cambridge.

Cooper, J.P. (2009). 'Egypt's Nile-Red Sea Canals: Chronology, Location, Seasonality and Function', in L. Blue, J. Cooper, R. Thomas, and J. Whitewright (eds). *Connected Hinterlands. Proceedings of Red Sea Project IV. Held at the University of Southampton September 2008*. Oxford, 195–209.

Cooper, J.P. (2011). 'No easy option: Nile versus Red Sea in ancient and medieval north-south navigation', in W.V. Harris and K. Iara (eds), *Maritime Technology in the Ancient Economy: Ship-Design and Navigation*. Portsmouth, Rhode Island, 189–210.

Cooper, J.P. (2014). *The Medieval Nile: Route, Navigation and Landscape in Islamic Egypt*. Cairo.

Costa, L.F. (1997). *Naus e galeões na ribeira de Lisboa*. Cascais.

Cribb, J. (1992). 'Numismatic Evidence for the Date of the Periplus', in D. W. MacDowall, S. Shama, and S. Garg, *Indian Numismatics, History, and Culture: Essays in Honour of Dr. P. L. Gupta*. Delhi, 1.131–45.

Cribb, J. (1998). 'Western Satraps and Satavahanas: Old and New Ideas of Chronology', in A.K. Jha and S. Garg (eds), *Ex Moneta (Essays in honor of D. W. MacDowall)*. New Delhi, 151–64.

Cribb, J. (2000). 'Early Indian History', in M. Willis (ed), *Buddhist Reliquaries from Ancient India*. London, 39–45.

Crum, W. (1925). 'Koptische Zünfte und das Pfeffermonopol', *Zeitschrift für Ägyptische Sprache* 60.1: 103–11.

Cutler, A. (1987). 'Prolegomena to the craft of ivory carving in late Antiquity and the early Middle Ages', in X. Barral i Altet (ed), *Artistes, artisans et production artistique au Moyen Age*. Paris, 2.431–75.

Cuvigny, H. (1998). 'Bouchons cachetés des fouilles d'Adolphe Reinach à Coptos', *Bulletin des Musées et Monuments Lyonnais* 4: 2–7.

Cuvigny, H. (2005). *Ostraca de Krokodilô. La correspondance militaire et sa circulation.* Praesidia *du désert de Bérénice II.* Cairo.

Cuvigny, H. (ed) (2006). *La route de Myos Hormos.* 2nd edn. Cairo.

Cuvigny, H. (2010a). 'The Shrine in the *praesidium* of Dios (Eastern Desert of Egypt): Graffiti and Oracles in Context', *Chiron* 40: 245–99.

Cuvigny, H. (2010b). 'Qâni' chez les auteurs grecs et latins', in J.-F.Salles and A. Sedov (eds), *Qâni'. Le port antique du Hadramawt entre le Méditerranée, l'Afrique et l'Inde. Fouilles russes 1972, 1985–1989, 1991, 1993–1994*), Turnhout: 419–36.

Cuvigny, H. (2014). 'Papyrological Evidence on "Barbarians" in the Egyptian Eastern Desert', in J.H.F. Dijkstra, G. Fisher, *Inside and out: interactions between Rome and the peoples on the Arabian and Egyptian frontiers in Late Antiquity.* Leuven, 165–98.

Cuvigny, H. (2018). 'La toponymie du désert Oriental égyptien sous le Haut-Empire d'après les ostraca et les inscriptions', in J.-P. Brun, Th. Faucher, B. Redon and S. Sidebotham (eds), *Le désert oriental d'Égypte durant la période gréco-romaine: bilans archéologiques.* Available at http://books.openedition.org/cdf/4932. ISBN: 9782722604810. DOI: 10.4000/books.cdf.4932.

Cuvigny, H., Bülow-Jacobsen, A., and Bosson, N. (2000). 'Le paneion d'Al-Buwayb revisité. [I. Corrigenda aux I.Ko.Ko. 141–185. II. Graffiti inédits d'Al-Buwayb. III. Graffiti grecs du wadi Minayh. IV. Graffito grec du wadi al-'Atwani]'. *Bulletin de l'Institut français d'archéologie orientale* 100: 243–66.

Cuvigny, H., Bülow-Jacobsen, A., Nehmé, L., and Robin, Ch. (1999). 'Inscriptions rupestres vues et revues dans le désert de Bérénice', *Bulletin de l'Institut français d'archéologie orientale* 99: 133–93.

Darley, R.R. (2013). *Indo-Byzantine Exchange, 4th to 7th Centuries: A Global History.* A Thesis Submitted to the University of Birmingham for the Degree of Doctor of Philosophy, Birmingham.

Davies, E. and Morgan, St. (2002). *Red Sea Pilot.* 2nd edn. St Ives.

Day, R. (2012). 'A tale of "four" hoards (or unpicking Akki Alur)', *Journal of the Oriental Numismatic Society* 211: 5–14.

De Franciscis, A. (1976). 'Sepolcro di M. Obellius Firmus', *Cronache Pompeiane* 2: 246–248.

De Laet, S.J. (1949). Portorium. *Étude sur l'organisation douanière chez les Romains, surtout à l'époque du Haut-Empire,* Bruges.

Delmaire, R. (1989). *Les responsables des finances impériales au Bas-Empire romain,* Brussels.

Denecker, E. and Vandorpe, K. (2007). 'Sealed amphora stoppers and tradesmen in Greco-Roman Egypt: Archaeological, papyrological and inscriptional evidence', *BABesch* 82: 115–28.

De Romanis, F. (1982/7). 'Roma e i *Nótia* dell'India. Ricerche sui rapporti tra Roma e l'India dravidica dal 30 a.C. all'età Flavia', *Helikon* 22(27): 143–210 (= in F. De Romanis and A. Tchernia (eds), (1997). *Crossings: Early Mediterranean Contacts with India,* New Delhi, 80–160).

De Romanis, F. (1988). 'Romanukharaṭṭha e Taprobane. Sui rapporti Roma-Ceylon nel I sec. d.C.', *Helikon* 28: 5–58 (= 'Romanukharaṭṭha and Taprobane: Relations between Rome and Sri Lanka in the First Century AD, in F. De Romanis and

A. Tchernia (eds), (1997). Crossings: Early Mediterranean Contacts with India, New Delhi, 161–237.

De Romanis, F. (1996a). *Cassia, Cinnamomo, Ossidiana. Uomini e merci tra Oceano Indiano e Mediterraneo*. Rome.

De Romanis, F. (1996b). 'Graffiti greci da Wadi Menih el-Her. Un Vestorius tra Coptos e Berenice', *Topoi* 6: 731–45.

De Romanis, F. (1997). '*Hypalos*: distanze e venti tra Arabia e India nella scienza ellenistica', *Topoi* 7: 671–92.

De Romanis, F. (1998). 'Commercio, metrologia, fiscalità. Su P. Vindob. G 40822 verso', *Mélanges de l'École française de Rome. Antiquité* 110: 11–60.

De Romanis, F. (2000). *Esportazioni di corallo mediterraneo in India nell'età ellenistico-romana*, in J.-P. Morel, C. Rondi-Costanzo, and D. Ugolini (eds), *Corallo di ieri, corallo di oggi: atti del convegno, Ravello, Villa Rufolo, 13–15 dicembre 1996*. Bari, 211–16.

De Romanis, F. (2001). 'Lysas e il tempo: ulteriori considerazioni su *AEp*, 1954, 121', *Epigraphica* 63: 9–36.

De Romanis, F. (2002). '*Τραιανὸς ποταμός. Mediterraneo e Mar Rosso da Traiano a Maometto*', in R. Villari (ed), *Controllo degli stretti e insediamenti militari nel Mediterraneo*. Rome-Bari, 21–70.

De Romanis, F. (2004). '"Misura" della tetarte a Palmira. Una rilettura di *PAT* 2634', *La parola del passato* 59: 460–75.

De Romanis, F. (2006a). 'Archeologia e papirologia lungo la hodòs Myshormitiké. A proposito di un libro recente', *Topoi* 14: 619–50.

De Romanis, F. (2006b). Aurei *after the trade: Western taxes and eastern gifts*, in F. De Romanis and S. Sorda (eds), *Dal* denarius *al* dinar. *L'Oriente e la moneta romana. Atti dell'incontro di studio, Roma, 16–18 settembre 2004.* Rome, 54–82.

De Romanis, F. (2007). 'In tempi di guerra e di peste *horrea* e mobilità del grano pubblico tra gli Antonini e i Severi', *Antiquités africaines* 43: 187–230.

De Romanis, F. (2008). '*Cultores huius loci.* Sulle coabitazioni divine del *lucus Furrinae*, in B. Palma Venetucci (ed), *Testimonianze di culti orientali tra scavo e collezionismo*. Rome, 149–57.

De Romanis, F. (2009a). 'Zavorra e commercio 'triangolare': a proposito di un libro recente', *Topoi* 16: 641–53.

De Romanis, F. (2009b). 'Patterns of trade in the Red Sea during the age of the *Periplus Maris Erythraei*', in L. Blue, J. Cooper, R. Thomas, and J. Whitewright (eds), *Connected Hinterlands. Proceedings of Red Sea Project IV. Held at the University of Southampton September 2008.* Oxford, 31–5.

De Romanis, F. (2010/1[2012]). 'Playing Sudoku on the Verso of the "Muziris Papyrus": Pepper, Malabathron and Tortoise Shell in the Cargo of the Hermapollon', *Journal of Ancient Indian History* 27: 75–101.

De Romanis, F. (2012a). 'Julio-Claudian *Denarii* and *Aurei* in Campania and India', *Annali dell'Istituto Italiano di Numismatica* 58: 161–92.

De Romanis, F. (2012b). 'On *Dachinabades* and *Limyrike* in the *Periplus Maris Erythraei*', in M.-Fr. Boussac, J.-Fr. Salles and J.-B. Yon (eds), *Autour du Périple de la mer Érythrée*. Topoi. Supplément 11. Paris, 329–40.

De Romanis, F. (2014a). 'Time to Repay a Maritime Loan: A Note on SB III 7169 and SB XVIII 13167 Recto', *Sileno* 40: 73–89.

De Romanis, F. (2014b). 'Ivory from Muziris', *Institute for the Study of the Ancient World Papers* 8, available at http://dlib.nyu.edu/awdl/isaw/isaw-papers/8.

De Romanis, F. (2015a). 'Comparative Perspectives on the Pepper Trade', in F. De Romanis and M. Maiuro, *Across the Ocean. Nine Chapters on Indo-Mediterranean Trade*, Leiden and Boston, 127–50.

De Romanis, F. (2015b). 'Trajan's Canal and the Logistics of Late Antiquity India Trade', in V. Christides (ed), *Interrelations between the peoples of the Near East and Byzantium in Pre-Islamic times*. Córdoba, 123–34.

De Romanis, F. (2016). 'An Exceptional Survivor and Its Submerged Background: The Periplus Maris Erythraei and the Indian Ocean Travelogue Tradition', in G. Colesanti, L. Lulli (eds), Submerged Literature in Ancient Greek Culture. Case Studies, Berlin and Boston, 97–110.

Desanges, J. (1969). 'D'Axoum à l'Assam, aux portes de la Chine: Le Voyage du "Scholasticus de Thèbes" (entre 360 et 500 après J.-C.)', *Historia* 18: 627–39.

Desanges, J. (1996). 'Sur la mer hippale, au souffle du vent hippale', *Topoi* 6.2: 665–70.

Desanges, J. (2012). 'L'excursus de Pline l'Ancien sur la navigation de mousson et la datation de ses sources', in M.-Fr. Boussac, J.-Fr. Salles et J.-B. Yon (eds), *Autour du Périple de la mer Érythrée*'. Topoi. Supplément 11. Lyon, 63–73.

de Saxé, A. (2016). 'Trade and Cross-cultural Contacts in Sri Lanka and South India during Late Antiquity (6th–10th Centuries)', *Journal of Multidisciplinary Studies in Archaeology* 4: 121–159.

Devecka, M. (2013). 'The Traffic in Glands', *Journal of Roman Studies* 103: 88–95.

Deyell, J.S. (1984). 'Indo-Greek and Ksaharata Coins from the Gujarat Seacoast', *The Numismatic Chronicle* 144: 115–27.

Dias, J.J.A. (1998). 'A moeda', in J. Serrão, A.H. Oliveira Marques, *Nova História de Portugal. Do Rennascimento á Crise Dinástica*. Lisbon, 254–76.

Dihle, A. (1965). *Umstrittene Daten: Untersuchungen zum Auftreten der Griechen am Roten Meer*, Opladen.

Dihle, A. (1974). 'Der Seeweg nach Indien', *Innsbrucker Beiträge zur Kulturwissenschaft. Dies philologici Aenipontani* 4: 5–13 (= id., *Antike und Orient. Gesammelte Aufsätze*, Heidelberg 1984, 109–17).

Dijkstra, M., Verhoogt, A.M.F.W. (1999). 'The Greek-Palmyrene Inscription', in S.E. Sidebotham and W.Z. Wendrich (eds), *Berenike 1997. Report of the 1997 Excavations at Berenike and the Survey of the Egyptian Eastern Desert*. Leiden, 207–18.

Diskalkar, D.B. (1949). 'Kasrawad Hoard of Silver Punch-marked Coins', in *Journal of the Numismatic Society of India* 10: 146–53.

Disney, A.R. (1978). *The Twilight of the Pepper Empire: Portuguese Trade in Southwest India in the Early Seventeenth Century*, Cambridge, Mass.

Domergue, C. (1990). *Les mines de la peninsula ibérique dans l'antiquité romaine*. Rome.

Domergue, C., Sillières, P. (1977). *Minas de oro romanas de la Provincia de León I*, Madrid.

Drakonaki-Katantzaki, E. (1982). 'Textual Problems in the 'Periplus Maris Erythraei', in G. Giangrande, *Corolla Londiniensis*. Amsterdam, 2.47–55.

Drummond-Murray, J. et al. (2002). *Settlement in Roman Southwark*. London.

Ducène, J.-Ch. (2010). 'Rites religieux et crue du Nil en Egypte médiévale', *Acta orientalia belgica* 23: 63–76.

Ducène, J.-Ch. (2016). 'The Ports of the Western coast of India according to Arabic geographers (Eighth-Fifteenth centuries AD): A glimpse into the geography', in M.-F. Boussac, J.-F. Salles, J.-B. Yon, *Ports of the Ancient Indian Ocean*, Delhi, 165–78.

Dueck, D. (1999). 'The date and method of composition of Strabo's *Geography*', *Hermes* 127, 467–78.

Duffy, J. (1984). 'Observations on Sophronius' 'Miracles of Cyrus and John', *Journal of Theological Studies*, n.s. 35: 71–90.

Duncan-Jones, R. (1994). *Money and Government in the Roman Empire.* Cambridge.

Duncan-Jones, R P. (2006). 'Roman Customs Dues: A Comparative View', *Latomus* 65: 3–16.

Durrani, N. (2004). 'Luxury Bath', *Current Archaeology* 195: 105.

Edwards, D.R. (1985). *Ptolemy's περὶ ἀναλήμματος. An Annotated Transcription of Moerbeke's Latin Translation and of the Surviving Greek Fragments with an English Version and Commentary.* Diss. Brown University.

Elliot, H.M. and Dowson, J. (1867/1877). *The history of India as told by its own historians. The Muhammadan period.* 8 vols. London.

Errington, E. (2003). 'A Survey of Late Hoards of Indian Punch-marked Coins', *The Numismatic Chronicle* 163: 69–121.

Evans, K.G. (1995). 'Alexander the Alabarch: Roman and Jew', *Society of Biblical Literature Seminar Papers*, 576–94.

Evers, K.G. (2017). *Worlds Apart Trading Together: The Organization of Long-distance Trade between Rome and India in Antiquity.* Oxford.

Fabricius, B. (1849). *Arriani Alexandrini Periplus Maris Erythraei. Recensuit t brevi annotatione instruxit B. Fabricius.* Dresdae.

Fabricius, B. (1883). *Der Periplus des Erythräischen Meeres von einem Unbekannten. Griechisch und Deutsch mit kritischen und erklärenden Anmerkungen nebst vollständigem Wörterverzeichnisse ven B. Fabricius.* Leipzig.

Facey, W. (2004). 'The Red Sea: The wind regime and the location of ports', in P. Lunde, A. Porter, *Trade and Travel in the Red Sea Region. Proceedings of the Red Sea Project I.* Oxford, 7–18.

Facey, W. (2009). 'Jiddah: Port of Makkah, Gateway of the India Trade', in L.K. Blue, J. Cooper, R. Thomas and J. Whitewright (eds), *Connected Hinterlands. Proceedings of Red Sea Project IV Held at the University IV. Southampton, September 2008.* Oxford, 165–76.

Falk, H. (2008). 'Money can buy me heaven. Religious donations in late and post-Kushan India', *Archäologische Mitteilungen aus Iran und Turan* 40: 137–48.

Falk, H. (2014). 'Kushan Dynasty iii. Chronology of the Kushans' Encyclopædia Iranica, online edition, available at http://www.iranicaonline.org/articles/kushan-03-chronology.

Faoro, D. (2016). *I prefetti d'Egitto da Augusto a Commodo*, Bologna.

Faral, E. (1914). 'Une source latine de l'Histoire d'Alexandre, "La lettre sur les merveilles de l'Inde"', *Romania* 43.170: 199–215; 43.171: 353–70.

Fiaccadori, G. (1992). *Teofilo l'Indiano*, Ravenna.

Fischel, W.J. (1958). 'The Spice Trade in Mamluk Egypt', *Journal of the Economic and Social History of the Orient* 1: 157–74.

Fishman, A.M. (2013). *The Silver Coinage of the Western Satraps in India (50–400 AD): Catalogue and Rarity Guide*, South Carolina.

Fonseca, da Q. (1926). *Os Portugueses no mar. Memorias históricas e arqueológicas das naus de Portugal. 2.ª edição. Elementa histórica das naus portuguesas.* Lisbon.

Fortier, J. (2009). *Kings of the Forest: The Cultural Resilience of Himalayan Hunter-Gatherers.* Honolulu.

France, J. (2001). Quadragesima Galliarum*: L'organisation douanière des provinces alpestres, gauloises et germaniques de l'Empire Romain (Ier siècle avant J.-C.—IIIe siècle après J.-C.).* Rome.

France, J. (2014). 'Normes douanières et réglementation des échanges. Trois questions simples sur le tarif de Zaraï (Numidie)', *Antiquités Africaines* 50: 93–110.

Fraser, P.M. (1972). *Ptolemaic Alexandria.* 3 vols. Oxford.

Frisk, H. (1927). *Le Périple de la mer Érythrée, suivie d'une étude sur la tradition et la langue.* Goteborg.

Frisk, H. (1973). *Griechisches etymologisches Wörterbuch.* 2nd edn. Heidelberg.

Fussman, G. (1991). 'Le Périple et l'histoire politique de l'Inde', *Journal Asiatique* 279: 31–8. (= 'The Periplus and the Political History of India', in A. Tchernia and F. De Romanis (eds), *Crossings: Essays in Early Mediterranean Contacts with India,* New Delhi 1997, 66–71).

Gambetti, S. (2009). *The Alexandrian Riots of 38 C.E. and the Persecution of the Jews: A Historical Reconstruction.* Leiden and Boston.

Garcin, J.-C. (1976). *Un centre musulman de la haute Egypte médiévale: Qūṣ.* Cairo.

Gascou, J. (1983). 'De Byzance à l'Islam, les impôts en Egypte après la conquête arabe', *Journal of Economic and Social History of the Orient* 26: 97–109.

Gascou, J. (2006). *Sophrone de Jérusalem, Miracles des saints Cyr et Jean (BHGI 477–479), traduction commentée par J. Gascou,* Paris.

Gascou, J. (2018). *Nouveautés documentaires et littéraires sur Clysma,* in *Le désert oriental d'Égypte durant la période gréco-romaine: bilans archéologiques* [online]. Paris: Collège de France available at http://books.openedition.org/cdf/5183. ISBN: 9782722604810. DOI: 10.4000/books.cdf.5183.

Gascou, J. and Worp, K.A. (1982). 'Problèmes de documentation apollinopolite', *Zeitschrift für Papyrologie und Epigraphik* 49: 83–95.

Gawlikowski, M. (2019). 'Looking for Leuke Kome', in A. Manzo, C. Zazzaro, D. Joyce De Falco (eds), *Stories of Globalization. The Red Sea and the Gulf from Late Prehistory to Early Modernity.* Leiden and Boston, 281–91.

Gernet, L. (1954). *Démosthène. Plaidoyers Civils. Tome I (Discours XXVII–XXXVIII). Texte établi et traduit.* Paris.

Giard, J.-B. (1983). *Le monnayage de l'atelier de Lyon des origines au règne de Caligula (43 avant J.C.—41 après J.C.).* Wetteren.

Gignac, F.T. (1976). *A Grammar of the Greek Papyri of the Roman and Byzantine Periods. I. Phonology.* Milan.

Godinho, V.M. (1981–1983^2). *Os descobrimentos e a economia mundial.* 4 vols. Lisbon.

Gofas, D. (2002). 'The Byzantine Law of Interest', in A.E. Laiou, *The Economic History of Byzantium: From the Seventh through the Fifteenth Century.* Washington, 1095–104.

Gofas, D.C. (1993). 'Encore une fois sur la Tabula Pompeiana 13 (Essai d'une interprétation nouvelle)', in *Symposion 93: Akten der Gesellschaft für Griechische und Hellenistische Rechtsgeschichte 10 (GrazAndritz, 12–16 September 1993).* Köln, 251–66.

Goitein, S.D. (1987). 'Portrait of a Medieval India Trader: Three Letters from the Cairo Geniza', *Bulletin of the School of Oriental and African Studies* 50: 449–64.

Goitein, S.D. and Friedman, M.A. (2008). *India Traders of the Middle Ages: Documents from the Cairo Geniza ('India Book')*. Leiden and Boston.

Gokhale, Sh. (1991). *Kanheri Inscriptions*. Pune.

Gopinatha Rao, T.A. (1920). *Tamil and Vetteluttu inscriptions on stone and copper-plates*. Trivandrum.

Graf, D.F. (1995). 'The Via nova Traiana in Arabia Petraea', in J. Humphrey, *The Roman and Byzantine Near East. Some recent archaeological research*. Ann Arbor, 241–67.

Gragg, G. (2008). 'Aksum', in R.D. Woodard (ed), *The Ancient Languages of Mesopotamia, Egypt and Aksum*. Cambridge, 211–37.

Guo, L. (2004). *Commerce, culture, and community in a Red Sea port in the thirteenth century. The Arabic documents from Quseir*. Leiden and Boston.

Gupta, P.L. (1965). *The Early Coins from Kerala*. Trivandrum.

Gupta, P.L. (1984). 'Early Byzantine solidi from Karnataka', *Numismatic Digest* 8: 37–43.

Gupta, P.L. (1992). 'Barwani hoard of silver punch-marked coins', *Numismatic Digest* 16: 6–23.

Gupta, P.L. Hardaker, T.R. (2014^2). *Ancient Indian Punchmarked Coins of the Magadha-Maurya Kārshāpana Series*. Nasik.

Gurukkal, R. (2016). *Rethinking Classical Indo-Roman Trade: Political Economy of Eastern Mediterranean Exchange Relations*. New Delhi.

Habicht, Ch. (2013). 'Eudoxus of Cyzicus and Ptolemaic exploration of the sea route to India', in K. Buraselis, M. Stefanou, and D.J. Thompson (eds), *The Ptolemies, the sea and the Nile*. Cambridge, 197–206.

Halfmann, H. (1986). Itinera principum. *Geschichte und Typologie der Kaiserreisen im römischen Reich*. Stuttgart.

Hall, K.R. (1980). *Trade and statecraft in the age of Cōḷas*. New Delhi.

Hansen, G.C. (1965). 'Ein unechtes Ktesiasfragment (FGrHist. 688 F 63)', *Helikon* 5: 159–62.

Hanson, A.E. (1980). 'Juliopolis, Nicopolis, and the Roman Camp', *Zeitschrift für Papyrologie und Epigraphik* 37: 249–54.

Harker, A. (2008). *Loyalty and Dissidence in Roman Egypt. The Case of the* Acta Alexandrinorum. Cambridge.

Harrauer, H. and Sijpesteijn, P.J. (1985). 'Ein neues Dokument zu Roms Indienhandel. P. Vindob. G 40822', *Anzeiger der philosophisch-historischen Klasse der Österreichischen Akademie der Wissenschaften* 122: 124–55.

Hart, G.L. and Heifetz, H. (1999). *The Four Hundred Songs of War and Wisdom*, New York.

Heilporn, P. (2000). 'Registre de navires marchandes', in R. De Smet, H. Melaerts, C. Saerens, *Papyri in hornorem Johannis Bingen octogenarii (P.Bingen)*. Louvain, 339–59.

Hewsen, R.H. (1992). *The Geography of Ananias of Širak. The Long and the Short Recension. Introduction, Translation and Commentary*. Wiesbaden.

Hill, J. (2009). *Through the Jade Gate to Rome: A Study of the Silk Routes during the Later Han Dynasty 1st to 2nd Centuries CE*. Charleston.

Hirth, F. (1885). *China and the Roman Orient. Researches into their Ancient and Mediaeval Relations as Presented in Old Chinese Records*. Leipsic & Munich.
Hirth, F. and Rockhill, W.W. (1911). *Chau Ju-kua: His work on the Chinese and Arab Trade in the Twelfth and Thirteenth Centuries, Entitled Chu-fan-chï*. St. Petersburg.
Hölbl, G. (2000). *A History of the Ptolemaic Empire*. London.
Holtheide, B. (1980). '*Matrona stolata-femina stolata*', *Zeitschrift für Papyrologie und Epigraphik* 38: 127–34.
Houston, G. (2003). 'Galen, His Books, and the *Horrea Piperataria* at Rome', *Memoirs of the American Academy in Rome* 48: 45–51.
Hultzsch, E. (1894/1895). 'Cochin Plates of Bhaskara Ravivarman', *Epigraphia Indica* 3: 66–9.
Hunter, W.W. (1885–7^2). *The Imperial Gazetter of India*. 14 vols. London.
Jacob, Ch. (1991). '*Θεὸς Ἑρμῆς ἐπὶ Ἀδριανοῦ*. La mise en scène du pouvoir impérial dans la Description de la Terre habitée de Denys d'Alexandrie', *Cahiers du Centre Gustave Glotz* 2: 43–53.
Jakab, É. (2000). 'Vectura Pro Mutua: Überlegungen zu TP 13 und Ulp. D. 19, 2, 15, 61', *Zeitschrift der Savigny Stiftung für Rechtsgeschichte (Romanistische Abteilung)* 117: 244–73.
James, G. (2000). *Colporuḷ: A History of Tamil Dictionaries*, Chennai.
Janni, P. (1984). *La mappa e il periplo. Cartografia antica e spazio odologico*. Rome.
Jaschke, K. (2010). *Die Wirtschafts- und Sozialgeschichte des antiken Puteoli*, Rahden/ Westf.
Jha, A. and Rajgor, D. (1994). *Studies in the Coinage of the Western Ksatrapas*, Nasik.
Johrden, K. and Wolters, R. (2008). 'Die römischen Fundmünzen in Indien' in A. Bursche, R. Ciołek, and R. Wolters (eds), *Roman Coins Outside the Empire: Ways and Phases, Contexts and Functions*. Wetteren, 341–54.
Jones, Ch. P. (1986). *Culture and Society in Lucian*. Cambridge, MA.
Jones, Ch. P. (2001). 'Apollonius of Tyana's Passage to India', *Greek, Roman and Byzantine Studies* 42: 185–99.
Jones, D.F. (2006). *The Bankers of Puteoli: Finance, Trade and Industry in the Roman World*. Stroud.
Jones, W. (1790). 'On the Spikenard of the Ancients', *Asiatick Researches* 2: 405–17.
Jones, W. (1795). 'Additional Remarks on the Spikenard of the Ancients', *Asiatick Researches* 4: 109–18.
Jördens, A. (1995). 'Sozialstrukturen im Arbeitstierhandel des kaiserlichen Ägypten', *Tyche* 10: 37–100.
Jördens, A. (2009). *Statthalterliche Verwaltung in der römischen Kaiserzeit: Studien zum* praefectus Aegypti. Stuttgart.
Jördens, A., Heilporn, P., and Duttenhöfer, R. (2007). 'Neues zum Trajanskanal' (with P. Heilporn's and R. Duttenhöfer's *Anhängen*), in J. Frösén, T. Purola, and E. Salmenkivi (eds), *Proceedings of the 24th International Congress of Papyrology. Helsinki, 1–7 August, 2004*. Helsinki, 469–85.
Jouguet, P. (1931). 'Dédicace grecque de Médamoud', *Bulletin de l'Institut français d'archéologie orientale* 31: 1–29.
von Kaenel, H.-M. (1986). *Münzprägung und Münzbildnis des Claudius*, Berlin.
Kelly, P. (1832). *Oriental Metrology, comprising the Monies, Weights, and Measures of the East Indies and Other Trading Places in Asia, Reduced to the English Standard by Verified Operations*, London.

Kieniewicz, J. (1986). 'Pepper gardens and markets in precolonial Malabar', *Moyen Orient et Océan Indien* 3: 1–36.

Kotarba-Morley, A.M. (2015). *The Port of* Berenike Troglodytica *on the Red Sea: A Landscape-Based Approach to the Study of its Harbour and its Role in Indo-Mediterranean Trade.* PhD Thesis, University of Oxford.

Kramer, J. (2011). *Von der Papyrologie zur Romanistik*, Göttingen.

Kreutz, A. (1994/5). 'Landwirtschaft und ihre ökologischen Grundlagen in den Jahrhunderten um Christi Geburt: Zum Stand der naturwissenschaftlichen Untersuchungen in Hessen', in *Berichte der Kommission für Archäologische Landesforschungen in Hessen.* 3: 59–97.

Kruse, T. (2002). *Der königliche Schreiber und die Gauverwaltung: Untersuchungen zur Werwaltungsgeschichte Ägyptens in der Zeit von Augustus bis Philippus Arabs (30 v. Chr.-245 n. Chr.)*, 2 vols. Munich.

Kučan, D. (1984). 'Der erste Römerzeitliche Pfefferfund—nachgewiesen im Legionslager Oberaden (Stadt Bergkamen)', *Ausgrabungen und Funde in Westfalen Lippe.* 2.51–6.

Kučan, D. (1992). 'Die Pflanzenreste aus dem römischen Militarlager Oberaden', in J.-S. Küster, H. (1995). *Postglaziale Vegetationsgeschichte Südbayerns. Geobotanische Studien zur Prähistorischen Landschaftskunde*, Berlin.

Kula, W. (1986). *Measures and Men*, Princeton.

Kuttanad Enquiry Commission. (1972). *Report of the Kuttanad Enquiry Commission, November 1971.*

Lama, Y. Ch., Ghimire, S.K., and Aumeeruddy-Thomas, Y. (2001). *Medicinal Plants of Dolpo.* Kathmandu.

Lambourn, E. (2008). 'India from Aden: *Khuṭba* and Muslim Urban Networks in Late Thirteenth-Century India', in K. Hall (ed), *Secondary Cities and Urban Networking in the* Indian *Ocean Realm, c. 1000–1800.* Lanhman: 55–97.

Lapatin, K.D.S. (2001). *Chryselephantine Statuary in the Ancient Mediterranean World.* Oxford.

Laufer, B. (1918). 'Malabathron', *Journal Asiatique* 11 s. 12: 5–40.

Laufer, B. (1919). *Sino-Iranica; Chinese Contributions to the History of Civilization in Ancient Iran. With Special Reference to the History of Cultivated Plants and Products.* Chicago.

Laws, R.M. (1966). 'Age Criteria for the African Elephant: Loxodonta A. Africana', *East African Wildlife Journal* 4: 27–8.

Lenfant, D. (2004). *Ctésias de Cnide. La Perse, l'Inde, autres fragments.* Paris.

Lerouxel, F. (2016). *Le marché du crédit dans le monde romain (Égypte et Campanie)*, Rome.

Leslie, D.D. and Gardiner, K.H.J. (1996). *The Roman Empire in Chinese Sources*, Rome.

Letronne, J.A. (1831). Review to *Κλαυδίου Πτολεμαίου Ἀλεξανδρέως Περὶ Γεωγραφικῆς Ὑφηγήσεως Βιβλίον πρῶτον* &c. Traité de géographie de Claude Ptolémée d'Alexandrie, traduit pour la première fois du grec en français, sur les manuscrits de la Bibliothèque du Roi, par l'abbé Halma, *Journal des Savants*, 238–48.

Lewis, N. (2000). 'Receipt for Requisitioned Palm Fronds', in H. Melaert, *Papyri in honorem Johannis Bingen Octogenarii (P. Bingen).* Louvain, 431–2.

Lima Felner, R.J. (1868). *O Livro dos Pesos, Medidas e Moedas por Antonio Nunes*, Lisbon.

Lo Cascio, E. (1978). 'Moneta e politica monetaria nel principato: a proposito di due lavori recenti', *Annali dell'Istituto Italiano di Numismatica* 25: 241–61.

Lo Cascio, E. (1993). 'Prezzo dell'oro e prezzo delle merci', in *L'«inflazione» del quarto secolo. Convegno internazionale (Roma 23–25 giugno 1988)*, Rome, 155–88.

Lübtow, U. (1976). 'Das Seedarlehen des Callimachus', in D. Medicus, H.H. Seiler, *Festschrift für Max Käser*. Munich, 329–49.

Lüders, H. (1912). 'A List of Brahmi Inscriptions from the Earliest Times to about A.D. 400 with the Exception of those of Asoka', *Epigraphia Indica* 10: Appendix, 1–203.

Luft, U. (ed) (2010). *Bi'r Minayh. Report on the Survey 1998–2004*, Budapest.

Lukaszewicz, A. (2000). *Some Remarks on the Trial of Isidorus junior, Journal of Juristic Papyrology* 30: 59–65.

Lunde, P. (2013). 'Sailing time in Sulaymān al-Mahrī', in A.R. Constable and W. Facey, *The Principles of Arab Navigation*. London, 75–82.

Lutgendorf, Ph. (2007). *Hanuman's Tale. The Messages of a Divine Monkey*, Oxford.

MacDowall, D.W. (1991). 'Indian Import of Roman Silver Coins', in A.K. JHA (ed) *Coinage, Trade and Economy. January 8th–11th, 1991*, Nashik: 145–63.

MacDowall, D.W. (1996). 'The Evidence of the Gazetteer of Roman Artefacts in India', in H.P. Ray, J.–F. Salles (eds) *Tradition and Archaeology. Early Maritime Contacts in the Indian Ocean*. Lyon and New Delhi, 79–95.

MacDowall, D.W. (2003). 'The Indo-Roman Metal Trade', in D.W. MacDowall and A. Jha (eds), *Foreign Coins Found in the Indian Subcontinent*, Anjeri, 39–44.

MacDowall, D., Wilson, N.G. (1970). The References to the Kuṣāṇas in the *Periplus* and Further Numismatic Evidence for its Date, *The Numismatic Chronicle (1966-)*, 10: 221–40.

Madvig, J.N. (1871). *Adversaria critica ad scriptores Graecos*. vol. 1. Hauniae.

Maganzani, L. (2002). *Pubblicani e debitori d'imposta. Ricerche sul titolo edittale* de publicanis, Turin.

Magioncalda, A. (2012). 'I prefetti di Berenice', in C. Wolff, *Le métier de soldat dans le monde romain: actes du cinquième Congres de Lyon (23–25 septembre 2010)*, Paris: 461–77.

Mahadevan, I. (1996). 'Tamil-Brāhmi graffito', in S.E. Sidebotham and W.Z. Wendrich (eds), *Berenike 1995. Preliminary report of the 1995 excavations at Berenike (Egyptian Red Sea coast) and the survey of the Eastern Desert*. Leiden, 206–8.

Mahadevan, I. (2003). *Early Tamil Epigraphy. From the Earliest Times to the Sixth Century A.D.*, Harvard.

Mahadevan, I. (2007). 'Tamil Brahmi script in Egypt', *The Hindu* 21 Nov 2007 available at http://www.thehindu.com/todays-paper/Tamil-Brahmi-script-in-Egypt/article14879671.ece.

Mahdi, W. (2007). *Malay Words and Malay Things: Lexical Souvenirs from an Exotic Archipelago in German Publications before 1700*, Wiesbaden.

Majumdar, S. (2015). 'Money Matters: Indigenous and Foreign Coins in the Malabar Coast (Second Century BCE -Second Century CE)', in in K.S. Mathew (ed), *Imperial Rome, Indian Oceans Regions and Muziris* New Delhi: 395–423.

Malekandathil, P. (2001). *Portuguese Cochin and the Maritime Trade of India 1500–1663*, New Delhi.

Malekandathil, P. (2015). 'Muziris and the Trajectories of Maritime Trade in the Indian Ocean', in K.S. Mathew (ed), *Imperial Rome, Indian Ocean and Muziris: New Perspectives on Maritime Trade*, New Delhi, 339–68.

Malmendier, U. (2002). Societas publicanorum. *Staatliche Wirtschaftsaktivitäten in den Händen privater Unternehmer*. Wien, Köln, Weimar.

Malouta, M. (2014). 'A New Camel Declaration from Soknopaiou Nesos', *Zeitschrift Für Papyrologie und Epigraphik* 190: 215–18.

Manning, J. (2007). 'Hellenistic Egypt', in W. Scheidel, I. Morris, and R. Saller, *The Cambridge Economic History of the Greco-Roman World*, Cambridge, 434–59.

Marcotte, D. (2012). 'Le *Périple de la mer Érythrée* dans son genre et sa tradition textuelle', in M.-Fr. Boussac, J.-Fr. Salles, and J.-B. Yon (eds), *Autour du Périple de la mer Érythrée*. 'TOPOI- Supplément' 11. Paris: 7–25.

Marcotte, D. (2017). 'Ptolémée ethnographe. Questions de tradition', *Geographia antiqua* 26, 47–60.

Marques de Almeida, A.A. (1994). *Aritmética como Descrição do Real (1519–1679)*, 2 vols. Lisbon.

Marr, J.R. (1985). *The Eight Anthologies. A Study in Early Tamil Literature*, Madras.

Mathew, K.S. (1997). *Indo-Portuguese Trade and the Fuggers of Germany. Sixteenth century*. New Delhi.

Mattingly, H. (1923). *Coins of the Roman Empire in the British Museum, vol.1. Augustus to Vitellius*, London.

Mayer, E. (2018). 'Tanti non emo, Sexte, Piper: Pepper Prices, Roman Consumer Culture, and the Bulk of Indo-Roman Trade', *Journal of the Economic and Social History of the Orient* 61: 560–89.

Mayerson, Ph. (1996). 'The Port of Clysma (Suez) in Transition from Roman to Arab Rule', *Journal of Near Eastern Studies* 55: 119–26.

Mayrhofer, M. (1992–2001). *Etymologisches Wörterbuch des Altindoarischen*, 3 vols. Heidelberg.

Mayser, E. (1923–1934). *Grammatik der griechischen Papyri aus der Ptolemäerzeit*, 1–2, Berlin and Leipzig.

Mazzarino, S. (1982/1987). 'Sul nome del vento *hipalus* ('ippalo') in Plinio', Helikon 22 (27): IVII–XIV (= 'On the Name of the *Hipalus* (Hippalus) Wind in Pliny', in F. De Romanis and A. Tchernia, *Crossings. Early Mediterranean Contacts with India*, New Delhi 1997: 72–9).

McCrindle, J.W. (1879). *The commerce and navigation of the Erythraean sea: Being a translation of the 'Periplus maris Erythraei' by an anonymous writer and of Arrian's account of the voyage of Nearkhos, from the mouth of the Indus to the head of the Persian gulf*. Calcutta.

McLynn, F. (2009). *Marcus Aurelius. A Life*. Cambridge, MA.

Meritt, B.D. (1931). *Greek inscriptions 1896–1927*. Cambridge Ma.

Metzler, D. (1989). 'Über das Konzept der "Vier grossen Königreiche" in Manis Kephalaia (cap. 77)', *Klio* 71: 446–59.

Meyer, E. (1917). 'Apollonios von Tyana und die Biographie des Philostratos', *Hermes* 52 (3): 371–424.

Miller, J.I. (1969). *The Spice Trade of the Roman Empire 29 B.C.-A.D. 641*. Oxford.

Minorsky, V. (1970). *Ḥudūd al-'Ālam 'The Regions of the World'—A Persian Geography 372 A.H.—982 A.D. Translated and Explained by V. Minorsky. Second edition*

with the preface by V.V. Barthold translated from the Russian and with additional material by the late Professor Minorsky edited by C.E. Bosworth. Cambridge.
Mirashi, V.V. (1981). *The history and inscriptions of the Sātavāhanas and the Western Kshatrapas*. Bombay.
Mitteis, L. and Wilcken, U. (1912). *Grundzüge und Chrestomathie der Papyruskunde*. Leipzig.
Mitthof, F. (2007). 'Betrügerische Zollbeamte und der procurator usiacus Bemerkungen zu P.Amh. II 77', *Zeitschrift für Papyrologie und Epigraphik* 159: 256–60.
Monier-Williams, M. (1899). *A Sanskrit-English Dictionary: Etymologically and Philologically Arranged with Special Reference to Cognate Indo-European Languages*. Oxford.
Moraes, G.M. (1931). 'Sindābūr of the Arab writers', *Journal of Indian History* 10: 191–5.
Morelli, F. (2010). 'Vino sul Nilo. T. Varie 3, un viaggio a Costantinopoli in meno e una transazione innovativa', *Zeitschrift für Papyrologie und Epigraphik* 175: 209–23.
Morelli, F. (2011). 'Dal Mar Rosso ad Alessandria: il *verso* (ma anche il *recto*) del "papiro di Muziris" (SB XVIII 13167)', *Tyche* 26: 199–233.
Morrison, K.D. (2002). 'Pepper in the hills: upland–lowland exchange and the intensification of the spice trade', in K.D. Morrison and L.L. Junker, *Forager-Traders in South and Southeast Asia. Long-Term Histories*. Cambridge, 105–28.
Mueller, K. (2006). *Settlements of the Ptolemies. City Foundations and New Settlement in the Hellenistic World*. Leuven, Paris, Dudley MA.
Müller, C. (1855–61). *Geographi Graeci Minores*. 2 vols. Paris.
Müller, C. (1883–1901). *Claudii Ptolemaei Geographia*. v.1, pt. 1–2. Paris.
Murugeswari, B. (2008). *History of Trade and Commerce under the Second Pandyan Empire 12th to 14th Century A.D.*, PhD Thesis, Madurai Kamraj University.
Nachtergael, G. (1999). 'Retour aux inscriptions grecques du temple de Pselkis', *Chronique d'Égypte* 74: 133–47.
Nainar, S.M.H. (1942). *Arab Geographers' Knowledge of Southern India*. Madras.
Nalesini, O. (2009). *History and Use of an Ethnonym:* Ichthyophágoi, in L. Blue, J. Cooper, R. Thomas, J. Whitewright, *Connected Hinterlands. Proceedings of Red Sea Project IV*. Oxford, 9–18.
Nantet, E. (2016). Phortia. *Le tonnage des navires de commerce en Méditerranée du VIIIe siècle av. l'ère chrétienne au VIIe siècle de l'ère chrétienne*. Rennes.
Nappo, D. (2010). 'On the Location of Leuke Kome', *Journal of Roman Archaeology* 23: 335–48.
Nappo, D. (2017). 'Money and Flows of Coinage in the Red Sea Trade', in A. Wilson, A. Bowman, *Trade, Commerce, and the State in the Roman World*. Oxford, 557–78.
Nappo, D. (2018). *I porti romani nel Mar Rosso da Augusto al Tardoantico*. Neapols.
Nappo, D., Zerbini, A. (2011). 'On the Fringe: Trade and Taxation in the Egyptian Eastern Desert', in O. Hekster and T. Kaizer, *Frontiers in the Roman World: Proceedings of the Ninth Workshop of the international network 'Impact of Empire. Durham 16–19 April 2009'*, Leiden and Boston, 61–77.
Narayanan, M.G.S. (2013). *Perumals of Kerala. Brahmin Oligarchy and Ritual Monarchy. Political and Social Conditions of Kerala under the Cēra Perumāḷs of Makōtai*. 2nd edn. Thrissur.

Nawartmal, H. and Nawartmal, L. (1998). 'Spätantikes Handelsgold in Südindien', *Money Trend* 30.11: 52–7.

Nichols, A. (2011). *Ctesias. On India*. London and New York.

Nisbet, R. (2007). 'Horace: life and chronology', in St. Harrison (ed), *The Cambridge Companion to Horace*. Cambridge, 7–21.

Olsen, C.S. (2005). 'Trade and conservation of Himalayan medicinal plants: Nardostachys grandiflora DC and Neopicrorhiza scrophulariiflora (Pennell) Hong', *Biological Conservation* 125.4: 505–14.

Padmanabha Menon, K. (1924). *History of Kerala*. 4 vols. Ernakulam.

Panattoni, E. (2002). Puṟanāṉūṟu. *Quattrocento poesie di guerra*, Milan.

Pantalacci, L. (2018). 'Coptos, porte du désert Oriental', in *Le désert oriental d'Égypte durant la période gréco-romaine: bilans archéologiques* [online]. Paris: Collège de France, 2018 (generated 07 May 2018). Available at http://books.openedition.org/cdf/5140.

Paoli, U.E. (1930). *Studi di diritto attico*, Florence.

Papaconstantinou, A. (2015). 'Fusṭāṭ and its governor: administering the province', in T. Treptow and T. Vorderstrasse, *A Cosmopolitan City: Muslims, Christians and Jews in Old Cairo*. Chicago, 43–7.

Pauli, F. (1986). 'NAHAPĀNA/MANBAN.S vor 78 n.Chr.? Ein epigraphischer Neufund aus Indien und seine Bedeutung für die antike Südasien-Chronologie', in H. Kalcyk, B. Gullath and A. Graeber (eds), *Studien zur alten Geschichte S. Lauffer zum 70. Geburstag dargebracht*. Rome, 2.743–53.

Peacock, D. and Blue, L. (eds) (2006). *Myos Hormos-Quseir al-Qadim. Roman and Islamic Ports on the Red Sea. Volume 1. Survey and Excavations 1999–2003*, Oxford.

Peacock, D. and Blue, L. (eds). (2011). *Myos Hormos – Quseir al-Qadim. Roman and Islamic Ports on the Red Sea 2. Finds from the excavations 1999–2003*. Oxford.

Peacock, D.P.S., Williams, D., and James, S. (2007). 'Basalt as Ships' Ballast and the Roman Incense Trade', in D.P.S. Peacock and D. Williams (eds), *Food for the Gods: New Light on the Ancient Incense Trade*. Oxford, 28–70.

Pedersen, R.K. (2008). 'The Byzantine-Aksumite period shipwreck at Black Assarca Island, Eritrea', *Azania* 43: 77–94.

Peppard, M. (2009). 'A Letter Concerning Boats in Berenike and Trade on the Red Sea', *Zeitschrift für Papyrologie und Epigraphik* 171: 193–8.

Pérez López, X. (2007). 'Pap. Vindob. G 40822: préstamo marítimo y perspectiva romanística', in S. Bello Rodríguez and J.L. Zamora Manzano (eds), *IX Congreso Internacional XII Iberoamericano de Derecho Romano, El Derecho Comercial, De Roma al Derecho Moderno*. Las Palmas de Gran Canaria, 2.635–79.

Pinto, P. (2010). 'Índice analítico das cartas dos governadores de África na Torre do Tombo', in *Anais de história de além-mar* 11: 249–380.

Poll, I.J. (1996). 'Ladefähigkeit und Größe der Nilschiffe', *Archiv für Papyrusforschung* 42: 127–38.

Pomey, P. and Tchernia, A. (1978). 'Le tonnage maximum des navires de commerce romains', *Archeonautica* 4: 233–51.

Pontoriero, I. (2011). *Il prestito marittimo in diritto romano*. Bologna.

Popper, W. (1951). *The Cairo Nilometer. Studies in Ibn Taghrî Birdî's Chronicles of Egypt: I*. Berkeley and Los Angeles.

Potts, D.T. (1990). *The Arabian Gulf in Antiquity.* 2 vols. Oxford.
Prange, S.R. (2011). '"Measuring by the bushel": reweighing the Indian Ocean pepper trade', *Historical Research* 84: 212–35.
Preisigke, F. (1925–31). *Wörterbuch der griechischen Papyrusurkunden mit Einschluß der griechischen Inschriften, Aufschriften, Ostraka, Mumienschilder usw. aus Ägypten.* 3 vols., with updates (IV, 2000) and Supplements (I–III, 1971–2000), Wiesbaden.
Purpura, G. (1984). 'Tabulae Pompeianae 13 e 34: due documenti relativi al prestito marittimo', in *Atti del XVII Congresso Papirologia.* Neapols, 3.1245–66.
Raith, M.M., Hoffbauer, R., Euler, H., Yule, P.A., and Damgaard, K. (2013). 'The View from Ẓafār—An Archaeometric Study of the 'Aqaba Pottery Complex and is Distribution in the 1st Millennium CE', *Zeitschrift für Orient-Archäologie* 6: 320–50.
Rapin, C. and Grenet, F. (1983). 'Inscriptions économiques de la trésorerie hellénistique d'Aï Khanoum. L'onomastique iranienne à Aï Khanoum', *Bulletin de Correspondance Hellénique* 107: 315–81.
Rapson, E.J. (1908). *Catalogue of the Coins of the Andhra Dynasty the Western Kṣatrapas, the Traikūṭaka Dynasty and the 'Bodhi' Dynasty,* London.
Raschke, M.G. (1978). 'New studies in Roman commerce with the East', in H. Temporini and W. Haase (eds), *Aufstieg und Niedergang der römischen Welt,* 2.9.2. Berlin-New York, 604–1378.
Rathbone, D. (2000). 'The Muziris papyrus (SB XVIII): financing Roman trade with India', *Alexandrian Studies II in Honour of Mostafa el Abbadi', Bulletin de la Société d'Archéologie d'Alexandrie* 46: 39–50.
Rathbone, D. (2003). 'The Financing of Maritime Commerce in the Roman Empire, I–II AD', in E. Lo Cascio, *Credito e moneta nel mondo romano. Atti degli Incontri capresi di storia dell'economia antica (Capri 12–14 ottobre 2000).* Bari, 197–229.
Rathbone, D. (2009). 'Earnings and Costs: Living Standards and the Roman Economy (First to Third Centuries AD)', in A. Bowman and A. Wilson (eds), *Quantifying the Roman Economy: Methods and Problems.* Oxford, 299–326.
Rau, V. (1965). 'Um grande mercador-banqueiro italiano em Portugal: Lucas Giraldi', *Estudos Italianos em Portugal* 24: 3–35.
Red Sea and Gulf of Aden Pilot (Admiralty Sailing Directions NP64), 2015[18].
Reddé, M. et al. (2005). 'Oedenburg. Une agglomération d'époque romaine sur le Rhin supérieur: fouilles françaises, allemandes et suisses à Biesheim–Kunheim (haut–Rhin)', *Gallia* 62: 215–77.
Reden, S. von. (2007). *Money in Ptolemaic Egypt: From the Macedonian Conquest to the End of the Third Century BC,* Cambridge.
Redmount, C. (1995). 'The Wadi Tumilat and the "Canal of the Pharaohs"', *Journal of Near Eastern Studies* 54: 127–35.
Reger, G., 'Apollonios of Tyana and the *Gymnoi* of India', in M. Futre Pinheiro and S. Montiglio, *Philosophy and the Ancient Novel,* Eelde 2015, 141–57.
Regourd, A. (2011). *Arabic Language Documents on Paper,* in D. Peacock and L. Blue, *Myos Hormos—Quseir al-Qadim. Roman and Islamic Ports on the Red Sea. Volume 2: Finds from the excavations 1999–2003.* Oxford, 339–44.
Ricketts, L.M. (1982/3). 'The epistrategos Kallimachos and a Koptite inscription. SB V 8036 reconsidered', *Ancient society* 13: 161–5.

Robin, Ch. (1991). 'L'Arabie du Sud et la date du Périple de la Mer Erythrée (nouvelles données)', *Journal Asiatique* 279: 1–30 (= 'The Date of thee Periplus of the Erythraean Sea in the Light of South Arabian Evidence', in A. Tchernia and F. De Romanis (eds), *Crossings: Essays in Early Mediterranean Contacts with India*. New Delhi 1997, 41–65).

Robin, Ch. (1994a). 'Kulayb Yuha'min est-il le *Χόλαιβος* du Periple de la mer Erythrée?', *Raydan* 6: 91–9.

Robin, Ch. (1994b). 'L'Égypte dans les Inscriptions de l'Arabie méridionale préislamique', in *Hommages à Jean Leclant*. Vol. 4. Cairo, 285–301.

Robin, Ch. (1998). 'La fin de royaume de Ma'īn', in R. Gyselen (ed), *Parfums d'Orient*. Bures-sur-Yvette, 177–88.

Romanis, F.D. (2019). 'Book review: Rajan Gurukkal, Rethinking Classical Indo-Roman Trade: Political Economy of Eastern Mediterranean Exchange Relations'. *Studies in History* 35(1), 123–8.

Rossi, I. (2014). 'Minaeans beyond Ma'īn', in O. Elmaz and J.C.E. Watson (eds), *Languages of Southern Arabia. Papers from the Special Session of the Seminar for Arabian Studies held on 27 July 2013*. Oxford, 111–23.

Rovira Guardiola, R. (2007). 'El Archivo Sulpicio y los tituli picti β: circulación de comerciantes en el Mediterráneo', in *Acta XII Congressus Internationalis Epigraphiae Graecae et Latinae. 3–8 September, Barcelona 2002*, Barcelona, 1263–8.

Ruffing, K. (1993). 'Das Nikanor-Archiv und der römische Süd- und Osthandel', in *Münstersche Beiträge zur Antiken Handelsgeschichte* 12: 1–26.

Ruffing, K. (2006), 'Nikanor-Archiv', *Der Neue Pauly*, Herausgegeben von: H. Cancik, H. Schneider, M. Landfester. Consulted online on 24 June 2019 http://dx.doi.org/10.1163/1574-9347_dnp_e822050 First published online: 2006.

Ruffing, K. (2011). 'Militärische und zivile Seefahrt im Roten Meer. Einige Überlegungen zu SEG VIII 703 = *SB V 7539* = AE 1930, 53', in B. Onken and D. Rohde (eds), In omni historia curiosus. *Studien zur Geschichte von der Antike bis zur Neuzeit. Festschrift für Helmuth Schneider zum 65. Geburtstag*. Wiesbaden, 23–30.

Sabbatini Tumolesi, P. (1993). 'Un inedito dazio doganale: l'alabarchia Pelusi', *Mélanges de l'Ecole française de Rome. Antiquité* 105: 55–61.

Salles, J.-F. and Sedov, A.V. (2008). *Qani': Le port antique du Hadramawt entre la Mediterrannee, I'Afrique et I'Inde. Fouilles russes 1972, 1985–1989, 1991, 1993–1994*. Turnhout.

Salomon, R. (1991). 'Epigraphic Remains of Indian Traders in Egypt', *Journal of the American Oriental Society* 111: 731–6.

Salomon, R. (1993). 'Addenda to "Epigraphic Remains of Indian Traders in Egypt"', *Journal of the American Oriental Society* 113: 593.

Sarma, I.K. (1980). *Coinage of the Sātavahana Empire*, Delhi.

Sathyamurthy, T. (1992). *Catalogue of Roman Gold Coins*, Thiruvananthapuram.

de Saussure, L. (1928). 'L'origine de la rose des vents et l'invention de la boussole, in G. Ferrand (ed), *Introduction à l'astronomie nautique arabe*. Paris, 31–127.

Scafuro, A.C. (2011). *Demosthenes, speeches 39–49/translated with introduction and notes* by Adele C. Scafuro, Austin.

Scheidel, W. (2001). 'Progress and problems in Roman demography', in W. Scheidel (ed), *Debating Roman Demography*. Leiden and Boston, Köln, 1–81.

Schiettecatte, J. (2008). 'Ports et commerce maritime dans l'Arabie du Sud préislamique', *Chroniques yéménites* 15: 65–90, available at https://cy.revues.org/1671, 1–22.

Schmidt, S. (2018) '(. . .) und schickte mir zen Körner Pfeffer', in K. Ruffing and K. Droß-Krüpe (eds), Emas non quod opus est, sed quod necesse est. *Beiträge zur Wirtschafts-, Sozial-, Rezeptions- und Wissenschaftgeschichte der Antike. Festschrif für Hans-Joachim Drexhage zum 70.Geburtstag.* Wiesbaden, 85–105.

Schmitz, W. (1964). *'H πίστις in den Papyri. Inaugural-Dissertation zur Erlangung der Doktorwürde einer Hohen Rechtswissenschaftlichen Fakultät der Universität zu Köln.* Köln.

Schneider, P. (2009). 'De l'Hydaspe à Raphia: rois, éléphants et propagande d'Alexandre le Grand à Ptolémée IV', *Chronique d'Égypte* 83: 310–34.

Schoff, W.H. (1912). *The Periplus of the Erythraean Sea. Travel and Trade in the Indian Ocean by a Merchant of the First Century,* New York, London, Bombay and Calcutta.

Schuster, S. (2005). *Das Seedarlehen in den Gerichtsreden des Demosthenes mit einem Ausblick auf die weitere historische Entwicklung des Rechtsinstitutes: dáneion nautikón, fenus nauticum und Bodmerei.* Berlin.

Schwahn, W. (1935). '*Ναυτικὸς τόκος*', *Realencyclopädie der classischen Altertumswissenschaft* 16.2, 2034–48.

Schwinden, L. (1985). 'Römerzeitliche Bleietikette aus Trier', *Trierer Zeitschrift* 48: 121–9.

Schwyzer, E. (1950). *Griechische Grammatik. Zweiter Band: Syntax und Syntaktische Stilistik,* vervollständigt und herausgegeben von Albert Debrunner, Munich.

Scott, H.R. (1908). 'The Nasik (Jogaltembhi) Hoard of Nahapana's Coins', *Journal of the Bombay Branch of the Royal Asiatic Society* 22: 223–44.

Scullard, H.H. (1974). *The Elephant in the Greek and Roman World.* New York.

Seeck, O. (1919). *Regesten der Kaiser und Päpste für die Jahre 311 bis 476 n. Chr.* Stuttgard.

Selvakumar, V. (2016). 'The Routes of Early Historic Tamil Nadu, South India', in M.-F. Boussac, J.-F. Salles, J.-B. Yon (eds), *Ports of the Indian Ocean.* New Delhi, 289–321.

Senart, E. (1905/1906). 'The Inscriptions in the Caves at Nâsik', *Epigraphia Indica* 8: 59–96.

Shajan, K.P., Tomber, R., Selvakumar, V., and Cherian, P.J. (2004). 'Locating the Ancient Port of Muziris: Fresh Findings from Pattanam', *Journal of Roman Arachaeology* 17: 312–20.

Shastri, A.M. (1995). 'Jogalthambi hoard of Nahapana coins: some aspects', *Numismatic Digest* 19: 73–95.

Shcheglov, D.A. (2005). 'Hipparchus on the latitude of Southern India', *Greek, Roman, and Byzantine Studies* 45: 359–80.

Sheldon, J. (2012). *Commentary on George Coedès' Texts of Greek and Latin Authors on the Far East.* Turnhout.

Shihab, H.S. (2013). 'Stellar Navigation of the Arabs', in A.R. Constable, W. Facey, *The Principles of Arab Navigation.* London, 21–34.

Shimada, A. (2006). 'The Great Railing at Amarāvatī: An Architectural and Chronological Reconstruction', *Artibus Asiae* 66: 89–141.

Shinde, V., Gupta, S., Rajgor, D. (2002). 'An Archaeological Reconnaissance of the Konkan Coast from Bharuch to Kanjira', *Man & Environment* 27: 73–82.

Sidebotham, S.E. (2011). *Berenike and the Ancient Maritime Spice Route*. Berkeley, Los Angeles London.

Sidebotham, S.E. and Zitterkopf, R.E. (1997). 'Survey of the Via Hadriana by the University of Delaware: The 1996 Season', *Bulletin de l'Institut Français d'Archéologie Orientale* 97: 221–37.

Sidebotham, S.E. and Zitterkopf, R.E. (1998). 'Survey of the Via Hadriana: The 1997 Season', *Bulletin de l'Institut Français d'Archéologie Orientale* 98: 353–65.

Sidebotham, S.E. and Zych, I. (2010). 'Berenike: Archaeological Fieldwork at a Ptolemaic-Port on the Red Sea Coast of Egypt, 2008–2010', *Sahara* 21: 7–26 and pls. A1–7.

Sidebotham, S.E. and Zych, I. (2012). 'Results of Fieldwork at Berenike: A Ptolemaic-Roman Port on the Red Sea Coast of Egypt, 2008–2010', in M.-Fr. Boussac, J.-Fr. Salles, J.-B. Yon (eds), *Autour du Périple de la mer Érythrée*, Paris: 133–57.

Sidebotham, S.E. and Zych, I. (2016). 'Results of the Winter 2014–2015 Excavations at Berenike Egypt & Related Fieldwork in the Eastern Desert', *Journal of Indian Ocean Archaeology* 12: 1–34.

Sidebotham, S.E., Zych, I., Rądkowska, J.K., and Woźniak, M. (2015). 'Berenike Project. Hellenistic fort, Roman Harbor, Late Roman Temple, and Other Fieldwork: Archaeological Work in the 2012 and 2013 Seasons', *Polish Archaeology in the Mediterranean* 24(1): 294–324.

Sijpesteijn, P.M. (2007). 'The Arab Conquest of Egypt and the Beginning of Muslim Rule', in R. Bagnall, *Egypt in the Byzantine World, 300–700*. New York.

Sijpesteijn, P.M. (2013). *Shaping a Muslim State. The World of a Mid-Eighth-Century Egyptian Official*. Oxford.

Sircar, D.C. (1965²). *Studies in Indian Coins*, Delhi.

Steier, A. (1935). 'Nardus', *Realencyclopädie der classischen Altertumswissenschaft* 16.2: 1705–14.

Strauch, I. (2012). 'The inscriptions from Hoq: texts and context. India and Socotra', in I. Strauch (ed), *Foreign Sailors on Socotra. The inscriptions and drawings from the cave Hoq*. Bremem, 254–360.

Stuck, J.W. (1577). *Arriani historici et philosophi ponti Euxini et maris Erythraei periplus*. Lugduni.

Subash Chandran, M.D. (1997). 'On the ecological history of the Western Ghats', *Current Science* 73.2: 146–55.

Subbarayalu, Y. (2008). 'Appendix I. Note on the Twelve Tamil Dialectal Regions', in M. Kannan (ed), *Streams of Language: Dialects in Tamil*. Pondichéry, 319–23.

Sukumar, R. (1989). *The Asian Elephant: Ecology and Management*. Cambridge.

Sukumar, R. (2011). *The Story of Asia's Elephants*. Mumbai.

Suresh, S. (2004). Symbols of Trade. Roman and Pseudo-Roman Objects Found in India. New Delhi.

Sutherland, H. (1987). 'The *Pontif maxim* aurei of Tiberius', *Numismatica e antichità classiche. Quaderni ticinesi* 16: 217–27.

Takmer, B. (2007), '*Lex Portorii provinciae Lyciae*: Ein Vorbericht über die Zollinschrift aus Andriake von neronischer Zeit', *Gephyra* 4: 1–22.

Talbert, R.J.A. (2000). *Barrington Atlas of the Greek and Roman World. Map-by-Map Directory*. 2 vols. Princeton.

Tchernia, A. (1995). 'Moussons et monnaies: les voies du commerce entre le monde gréco-romain et l'Inde', *Annales. Histoire, Sciences Sociales* 50: 991–1009 (= id., *The Romans and Trade*, Oxford 2016, 229–48).

Tchernia, A. (2011). 'L'utilisation des gros tonnages', in W.V. Harris and K. Iara (eds), *Maritime Technology in the Ancient Economy*. Portsmouth, Rohde Island, 83–88.

Tchernia, A. (2016). *The Romans and Trade*, Oxford.

Thapar, R. (2002). 'Army and Exercise of Power in Early India', in A. Chaniotis and P. Ducrey (eds), *Army and Power in the Ancient World*. Stuttgart, 25–37.

Thirunavukarasu, K.D. (1994). *Chieftains of the Sangam Age*. Madras.

Thomas, R. (2011). 'Roman Vessel Stoppers', in D.P.S. Peacock, L.K. Blue, and J. Whitewright, *Myos Hormos—Quseir al-Qadim: Roman and Islamic ports on the Red Sea*. Oxford, 11–34.

Thomaz, L.F.F.R. (1998). *A questão da pimenta em meados do século XVI: um debate político do governo de D. João de Castro*, Lisbon.

Thompson, D. (1983). 'Nile Grain Transport under the Ptolemies', in P. Garnsey, K. Hopkins, and C.R. Whittaker (eds), *Trade in the Ancient Economy*. Cambridge, 64–75.

Thür, G. (1987). 'Hypotheken-Urkunde eines Seedarlehens für eine Reise nach Muziris und Apographe für die Tetarte in Alexandria', *Tyche* 2: 229–45.

Thür, G. (1988). 'Zum Seedarlehen *κατὰ* Μουζεῖριν. P.Vindob. G 40822', *Tyche* 3: 229–33.

Thür, G. (1993). 'Die Aestimationsabrede im Seefrachtvertrag. Diskussionsbeitrag zum Referat Dimitri C. Gofas', in *Symposion 93: Akten der Gesellschaft für Griech'ische und Hellenistische Rechtsgeschichte 10 (GrazAndritz, 12–16 September 1993)*. Köln, 267–71.

Tibbetts, G.R. (1971). *Arab Navigation in the Indian Ocean before the Coming of the Portuguese, being a translation of Kitāb al-Fawā'id fī uṣūl al-baḥr wa'l-qawā'id*, London.

Tomber, R. (2005). 'Aksumite and other imported pottery from Kamrej, Gujarat', *Journal of Indian Ocean Archaeology* 2: 99–102.

Tomber, R. (2007). 'Rome and Mesopotamia—Importers into India in the First Millennium A.D.', *Antiquity* 81: 972–88.

Tomber, R. (2008). *Indo-Roman Trade. From Pots to Pepper*. London.

Tomber, R. (2015). 'The Roman Pottery from Pattanam', in K.S. Mathew, *Imperial Rome, Indian Ocean Regions and Muziris*. London and New York, 381–94.

Tomber, R. (2017b). 'The late Hellenistic and Roman pottery', in A. Pavan (ed), *A cosmopolitan city on the Arabian coast. The imported and local pottery from Khor Rori. Khor Rori Report 3. (with a contribution by Roberta Tomber)*. Rome, 321–97.

Tomber, R., Graf, D., Healey, J.F., Römer-Strehl, Chr., and Majcherek, G. (2011). 'Pots with Writing', in D.P.S. Peacock, L.K. Blue, and J. Whitewright, *Myos Hormos—Quseir al-Qadim: Roman and Islamic Ports on the Red Sea*. Oxford, 5–10.

Trombley, F.R. (2009). ' 'Amr b. al-'Ās's Refurbishment of Trajan's Canal: Red Sea Contacts in the Aphrodito and Apollōnas Anō Papyri', in L. Blue, J. Cooper, R. Thomas, J. Whitewright, *Connected Hinterlands. Proceedings of Red Sea Project IV*. Oxford, 99–109.

Turner, P.J. (1984). *An Investigation of Roman and Local Silver Coins in South India, 1st to 3rd century A.D.*, Unpublished Ph.D. thesis, University of London.

Turner, P.J. (1989). *Roman Coins from India*. London.

Turner, P.J., Cribb, J. (1996). 'Numismatic evidence for the Roman trade with ancient India', in J. Reade (ed), *Indian Ocean in Antiquity*. London, 309–19.

Unnithan, N.G. (1963). 'Eyyal hoard of Silver Punch marked and Roman Coins', *Journal of Numismatic Society of India* 25: 22–8.

Vallet, E. (2010). *L'Arabie marchande: État et commerce sous les sultans rasūlides du Yemen (626–858/1229–1454)*. Paris.

Van Der Veen, M. (2001). 'The Botanical Evidence', in V.A. Maxfield, D.S.P. Peacock (eds), *Survey and Excavations at Mons Claudianus 1987–1993*. Cairo, 2.174–247.

Van Der Veen, M. (2004). 'The Merchants' Diet: Food Remains from Roman and Medieval Quseir al-Qadim', in P. Lunde, A. Porter (eds), *Trade and Travel in the Red Sea Region*. Oxford, 123–30.

van der Veen, M., Cox, A., Morales, J. (2011). 'Spices—Culinary and Medicinal Commodities', in M. Van der Veen (ed), *Consumption, Trade and Innovation: Exploring the Botanical Remains from the Roman and Islamic Ports at Quseir al-Qadim, Egypt*. Frankfurt am Main.

Van Minnen, P. (2008). 'Money and Credit in Roman Egypt', in W.V. Harris (ed), *The Monetary Systems of the Greeks and the Romans*. Oxford, 226–41.

vander Leest, J. (1985). 'Lucian in Egypt', *Greek, Roman and Byzantine Studies* 26: 75–82.

Vandorpe, K. (2015). 'Roman Egypt and the organization of customs duties', in P. Kritzinger, F. Schleicher, and T. Stickler, *Studien zum römischen Zollwesen*. Duisburg, 89–110.

Varadarajaiyer, E.S. (1945). *The Elephant in the Tamil Land*, Annamalai.

Varisco, D.M. (1994). *Medieval Agriculture and Islamic Science. The Almanac of a Yemeni Sultan*. Seattle and London.

Vélissaropoulos, J. (1980). *Les nauclères grecs. Recherches sur les instituitions maritimes en Grèce et dans l'Orient hellénisé*. Geneva-Paris.

Victor, U. (1997). *Lukian von Samosata. Alexandros oder der Lügenprophet. Eingeleitet, herausgegeben, übersetzt und erklärt von U. Victor*. Leiden, New York and Köln.

Vincent, W. (1807). *The Commerce and Navigation of the Ancient in the Indian Ocean*. 2 vols. London.

Walburg, R. (2008). *Coins and Tokens from Ancient Ceylon*. Wiesbaden.

Warmington, E.H. (1928). *The Commerce between the Roman Empire and India*. Cambridge.

Weiser, W. and Cotton, H.M. (1996). '"Gebt dem Kaiser, was des Kaisers ist . . . " Die Geldwährungen der Griechen, Juden, Nabatäer und Römer im syrisch-nabatäischen Raum unter besonderer Berücksichtigung des Kurses von Sela'/Melaina und Lepton nach der Annexion des Königreiches der Nabatäer durch Rom', *Zeitschrift für Papyrologie und Epigraphik* 114: 237–87.

Wellmann, M. (1905). 'Elefant', *Realencyclopädie der classischen Altertumswissenschaft* 5.2: 2248–57.

Wenning, R. (1993). 'Eine neuerstellte Liste der nabatäischen Dynastie', *Boreas* 16: 25–38.

Whitcomb, D. and Johnson, J. (eds) (1979). *Quseir al-Qadim 1978: Preliminary Report.* Cairo.

Whitcomb, D. and Johnson, J. (eds) (1982). *Quseir al-Qadim 1980: Preliminary Report.* Malibu.

Whitewright, J. (2007). 'How Fast is Fast? Technology Trade and Speed under Sail in the Roman Red Sea', in J. Starkey, P. Starkey, and T. Wilkinson (eds), *Natural Resources and Cultural Connections of the Red Sea.* Oxford, 77–87.

Wicki, J. (1961). 'Duas relações sobre a situação da Índia portuguesa nos anos 1568 e 1569', *Studia* 8: 133–220.

Wilcken, U. (1899). *Griechische Ostraka aus Aegyptend und Nubien.* 2 vols. Berlin und Leipzig.

Wilcken, U. (1925). 'Punt-Fahrten in der Ptolemäerzeit', *Zeitschrift für Ägyptische Sprache* 60: 86–102.

Will, E. (1957). 'Marchands et chefs de caravanes a Palmyre', *Syria* 34: 262–77.

Wilson, A. (2015). 'Red Sea Trade and the State', in F. De Romanis, M. Maiuro (eds). *Across the Ocean. Nine Essays on Indo-Mediterranean Trade.* Leiden and Boston, 13–32.

Wilson, A. and Bowman, A. (2017). 'Introduction. Trade, Commerce, and the State', in A. Wilson, A. Bowman, *Trade, Commerce, and the State in the Roman World.* Oxford, 1–24.

Winkler, G. and Mittenhuber, F. (2009). 'Die Ländkarten Asiens', in A. Stückelberger and F. Mittenhuber, *Ptolemaios Handbuch der Geographie. Ergänzungsband mit einer Edition des Kanons bedeutender Städte.* Basel, 290–304.

Wistrand, E. (1946). *Nach Innen oder nach Aussen? Zum geographischen Sprachgebrauch der Romer.* Goteborg.

Wolf, J.G. (1979). 'Aus dem neuen pompejanischen Urkundenfund: Der Seefrachtvertrag des Menelaos', in *Freiburger Univeritätsblätter* 65, 23–6.

Wolf, J.G. (2001). 'Die ναυλωτική des Menelaos', in Iuris vincula *(Studi in onore di Mario Talamanca).* Neapols, 421–63.

Wolters, O.W. (1967). *Early Indonesian Commerce: A Study of the Origins of Śrīvijaya*, Ithaca, NY.

Woolmer, M. (2015). 'Emporoi kai nauklēroi: redefining commercial roles in Classical Greece', *Journal of Ancient History* 3(2): 150–72.

Wrigley, E.A. and Schofield, R.S. (1981). *The Population History of England 1541–1871: A Reconstruction, with contributions by R. Lee and J. Oeppen*, London.

Yon, J.-B. (2002). Les notables de Palmyre. Beirut.

Yule, H., Burnell, A. (1886). *Hobson-Jobson: A Glossary of Colloquial Anglo-Indian Words and Phrases, and of Kindred Terms, Etymological, Historical, Geographical and Discursive.* London.

Yung-Ho, Ts'ao (1982). 'Pepper Trade in East Asia', *T'oung Pao* 68: 221–47.

Zvelebil, K.V. (1974). *A History of Indian Literature. Vol.X Fac. 1. Tamil Literature.* Wiesbaden.

Zwalve, W.J. (2013). 'The Case for the Lost Captain. A Discussion about D. 19,2,15,6', *Tijdschrift voor Rechtsgeschiedenis* 81: 621–31.

Index of Sources

Greek and Latin Texts

Acta Alexandrinorum
4 col. iii, ll. 8–11 301 n.16
22 fr 1, col. ii, l. 7 302 n.23
Aelius Aristides
Orat. 48.361 180 n.25
Agatharchides
53–6 274 n.103
56 274
81 48 n.59
[Ambrosius]
de moribus Brachmanorum, PL 17.1170 113 n. 30
Antiphanes
CAF ii, frg. 35 Kock 215 n.19, 216 n.23
Anthologia Graeca
14.139.1 82 n.86
Arrianus
Anab. 5.14.4 222 n.70
6.21 67 n.24
Indic. 17.1–2 221 n.60
21 67 n.24
Artemidorus
apud Strab. 16.4.5 48 n.59
[Asconius]
ad Cic. Verr.
2.1.154, p.170 Stangl 49 n.70, 104 n.80
Augustus
RG 15 130 n.21
Aurelius Victor
5.2 297 n.54
Avienus
Or. Mar. 273–9 = *BNJ* 275 T 12c 76 n.52
Cassius Dio
51.21.5 131 n.28
57.10.5 132 n.34
59.2.6 132 n.32
66.8.2–7 297 n.55
72.24.1 104 n.81
Censorinus
DN 21.10 144 n.106
Charition
P.Oxy. 3.413, ll. 213–4 66 n.23
Chronographus CCCLIV
Chron. Min. 1.145 252 n.5
Cicero
Att. 2.17.3 300 n.7
4.10.1 196 n.43
Rab. Post. 22 127 n.10
30–31 127 n.10
40 252 n.6
Frag. XVI 13 Schoell = IX 13 Puccioni 126 n.9
Codex Iustinianus
4.42.2 290 n.33
Codex Theodosianus
4.13.6 = *Cod. Iust.* 4.61.7 291 n.33, 35
4.13.8 = *Cod. Iust.* 4.61.8 134 n.45, 290 n.33
Cosmas Indicopleustes
2.45 121 n.82, 333 n.3
3.65 94 n.37, 39
11.3 101 n.74
11.13 333 n.3
11.15 94 n.37, 121 n.82
11.16 94 n.38, 333 n.3
11.17 68 n.33
11.19 330 n.22
11.22 94 n.38, 222 n.70, 333 n.3
11.23 105 n.93, 220 n.56
Curtius Rufus
8.13.6 222 n.70
9.2.4 222 n.70
Demosthenes/[Demosthenes]
32.5 187 n.44
34.6 163 n.14, 176 n.12
34.8 176 n.13
34.23 163 n.14
34.32 169 n.34
35.10 167 n.28, 215 n.17
35.10–11 136 n.60
35.10–13 164 n.15, 187 n.49
35.11 165 n.18, 175 n.6, 178, 190 n.13,
35.12 164 n.16, 187 n.43, 313 n.68
35.13 168 n.32, 187 n.45, 46, 49
35.50–1 166 n.25
49.11 176 n.9, 178, 179 n.20
49.25–8 177 n.14
49.29–30 177 n.15
49.34
49.35 176, 177 n.15, 16, 192 n.19
49.35–36 177, 193 n.24
49.36 177 n.16
49.59 177 n.16
49.60–1 177 n.15
50.17 163 n.14
56.5 163 n.14
56.6 166 n.25

Digesta
Gaius 13.4.3.pr. 131 n.27
Labeo 22.2.9.pr. 187 n.47
Marcian. 22.3.21.pr 184 n.36
39.4.16.6 264 n.54
39.4.16.7 134 n.44, 252 n.4, 265 n.55, 277 n.3, 290 n.33
39.4.16.12 310 n.61
Mod. 22.2.1.pr. 188 n.2, 4, 193
Papin. 22.2.4.pr. 188 n.3, 193 n.23
Paul. 22.2.6 187 n.43
39.4.4.2 293 n.43
Scaev. 45.1.122.1 136 n.60, 167, 188 n.2
Ulp. 14.1.4.pr.-1 315 n.83
19.2.15.6 194
39.4.1.4 293 n.43
39.4.14.pr. 299 n.5
Diodorus Siculus
2.37.3 222 n.70
3.18–29 274 n.105
17.52.6 126 n.10
17.87.2 222 n.70
17.93.2 222 n.70
20.32.4 213 n.13
31.8.12 224 n.71
Dionysius Periegetes
709–12 124 n.92, 314
Dioscorides
1.7 216 n.20
1.7.2 216 n. 19, 28
1.12 140 n.81, 216 n.22
Epiphanius
Adv. haeres. 66 38
Eratosthenes
F III A 2 Berger (= 50 Roller = Strabo 2.1.2) 83 n.87
Expositio totius mundi et gentium
18 105 n.93
Galen
12.66 216 n.22
12.153 216 n.22
13.538-9 296
13.539 296
13.647 296
13.749 296
13.789 296
13.1057 216 n.27
Geographus Ravennas
5.41 121 n.79
5.58 121 n.79
8.29 121 n.79
15.34 121 n.79
15.64 121 n.79
Grattius
Cyn. 314 216 n.26
Herodotus
1.183.2 104 n.85
3.97.5 104 n.85
3.107–12 112 n.28
6.97.2 104 n.85
Hesychius
vol. III p. 399, Σ 3010 Hansen 217 n.37
Hippocrates
Mul. 45 215 n.19
205 48 n.64
Nat. Mul. 34 215 n.19
Horace
Carm. 2.7.7–8 140 n.82
2.11.16 216 n.23
4.12.16–7 216 n.23
Epist. 1.14.23
Epist. 2.1.269–270 49 n.70
Epod. 5.59 216 n.23
Epod. 13.9 216 n.23
Sat. 2. 4.74–5 49 n.68
2. 8.49 49 n.68
Isaeus
6.33 179 n.20
Isidorus
Etym. 17.8.8 113 n.29
Itinerarium Antonini
169.2 40 n.32
171–3 143 n.100
Jerome
Comm. in Dan. 11.5 127 n.10
Ep. 125, 3 45
Josephus
AJ 18.159 300 n.10
18.159–60 312 n.66
18.259 300 n.10
19.276 300 n.10, 312 n.66
20.100 300 n.10
20.147 301 n.11, 302 n.23
BJ 4.659 205 n.73
5.201–5 300 n.10
Juba
BNJ 275 F 2 (= Plin., *NH* 12.56) 76 n.52
BNJ 275 F 35 (= Plin., *NH* 6.175) 76 n.52
BNJ 275 F 44 (= Plin., *NH* 6.202) 76 n.52
BNJ 275 F 47b (= Philostr., *VA* 2.16) 220 n.51
Justinian
Nov. 106 163 n.13, 164 n.17, 165 n.19, 166
Ed. 11.2 280 n.12, 302 n.22
3 280 n.12, 302 n.22
Juvenal
1.129–31 301 n.14
1.132–4 268 n.73
3.177–84 268 n.73
Leucippus
VSF 7 139 n.73

Lucian
Alex. 44 37 n.19
48 38 n.22
Apol. 4 38 n.23
12 38 n.23
Navigium 7–9 196 n.43
Philops. 33 38 n.21, 142 n.98
Martial
3.65.8 216 n.23
4.46.7 104 n.82, 106 n.97
7.27 255 n.25
7.72.3 104 n.82
10.57 106 n.97
Martyrium Arethae
27 34 n.8
29 68, 70, 75 n.48
Megasthenes
BNJ 715 F 19b (= Strab. 15.1.41) 221 n.60
Metrologicorum Scriptorum Reliquiae
1.208, ll. 19–20 296
1.212, ll. 12–3 296
1.212, ll. 13–9 296
1.213, ll. 13–5 296
1.214, ll. 5–10 296
1.228, ll. 25–6 296
1.233, ll. 22–5 269 n.76
1.234, ll. 1–3 269 n.76, 296
1.236, ll. 22–3 296
1.236, ll. 23–4 269 n.76
1.240, 11. 13–4 296
1.248, ll. 23–4 296
1.254, 11. 11–4 296
1.256, ll. 15–6 296
Nearchus
BNJ 133 F 1a (= Strab. 15.2.5) 67 n.24
BNJ 133 F 11 (= Arr., *Ind.* 17.1–2) 221 n.60
BNJ 133 F 22 (= Strab. 15.1.43) 221 n.60
New Testament
Acts 27.6–28.13 196 n.43
Mt. 13.45–6 265 n.58
*Rev.*18.3 320 n.105
18.11–8 320 n.105
Olympiodorus
in met. 81 39 n.26
Orosius
6.19.19 131 n.28
Palladius
De gent. Ind. et Br.: 1.3–4 334 n.4
1.7 68 n.32, 113
Periplus Maris Erythraei
1 54 n.90, 61 n.9, 213, 305 n.35
2–3 274 n.105
3 105 n.93, 219 n.48, 273 n.98
4 272 n.96
6 33 n.3, 55 n.93,94, 58 n.106, 68 n.30, 105 n.93, 137 n.66, 145 n.115, 215 n.18, 272 n.97, 327 n.1
7 105 n.93
8 68 n.31, 137 n.66, 327 n.1
9 68 n.31, 327 n.1
10 68 n.31, 105 n.93, 327 n.1
12 68 n.31, 76 n.49, 139 n.74, 327 n.1
13 68 n.31
14 33 n.3, 55 n. 93, 68 n.30, 76 n.50, 116 n.51, 119 n.73, 145 n.115, 165 n.23, 168 n. 30, 215 n.18
16 60 n.4, 105 n.93, 119 n.73, 272 n.94, 273 n.99
17 60 n.4, 105 n.93, 219 n.48, 272 n.94, 273 n.98, 100
19 54 n.85, 134 n.41,43, 135 n.50, 277 n.4, 303, 318 n.95
20 61 n.9, 135 n.49, 213
21 60 n.4, 67 n.26, 273 n.101
22 135 n.52
23 135 n.51
24 33 n.3, 55 n.93,95,96, 58 n.104,105,106, 137 n.66, 145 n.115, 327 n.1
25 63 n.13, 67 n.27, 146 n.119, 149 n.132, 215 n.18
26 60 n.2, 63 n.13, 67 n.27, 146 n.119, 215 n.18
27 55 n.93, 60 n.5, 67 n.27,28
28 33 n.3, 55 n.93, 60 n.7, 63 n.14, 327 n.1
30 214
31 60 n.4, 76 n.50, 146 n.120, 214, 248 n.29, 313 n.71
32 54 n.89, 67 n.29, 76 n.50, 146 n.120, 149 n.136, 248 n.29
33 60 n.4
37 137 n.64
38 61 n.9, 77 n.57
39 33 n.3, 55 n.93, 62 n.11, 64 n.16, 66 n.19, 137, 145 n.115, 152 n.148, 216 n.31, 217 n.35, 327 n.1
40 77 n.57
41 94 n.39, 116 n.51, 135 n.53, 137 n.64
43–44 77 n.58
44 94 n.39
47 81 n.76, 327 n.4
48 216 n.30, 32
49 33 n.3, 55 n.93, 62 n.11, 137, 145 n.115, 216 n.31, 217 n.35, 327 n.1
50 152
51 137 n.64, 152 n.148,150, 153 n. 157, 158, 332 n.36
52 77 n.56, 96 n.40, 136 n.56
52–3 94 n.39
53 77, 88 n.15, 96 n.14, 253 n.14
53–55 85

Periplus Maris Erythraei (*cont.*)
54 115 n.43, 148 n.129, 152 n.149, 332 n.36
54–5 119 n.71, 120 n.75
55 77 n.59, 88 n.15, 138 n.67, 148 n.130, 154 n.164
56 33 n.3, 55 n.93, 62 n.11, 79 n.68, 88 n.14,15, 112 n.25, 116 n.51, 136, 140 n.79, 145 n.115, 168 n.30, 217 n.33,34,36, 248 n.31, 249 n.35, 251 n.3, 254 n.16, 260 n.42, 264 n.52, 320 n.100, 327 n.1
57 58 n.106, 60 n.8, 62 n.10, 63 n.13, 64 n.17, 66 n.20, 67 n.27,28, 76 n.51, 77 n.55, 135 n.49
58 87 n.13
60 87 n. 12, 116 n.47, 48, 139 n.75, 327 n.1
63 61 n.9, 140 n.79, 217 n.33, 218 n.39, 249 n.34
64 140 n.79, 217 n.35, 249 n.34
Persius
3.73–76 255 n.25
5.136 180 n.25
6.19–21 255 n.25
Petronius
33.8 180 n.25
36.3 180 n.25
Philo
In Flacc.
20 301 n.16
126 301 n.16
135–36 301 n.16
141–2 301 n.16
Leg.
355 301 n.16
Philostorgius
3.4 68 n.35
Philostratus
VA
2.13 219 n.48
2.16 220 n.51
3.23 185 n.38
3.25 253 n.12
3.35 253
3.4 113–114
4.32 185 n.39, 187 n.44
6.12 313 n.69, 314 n.80
VS
2.611 104 n.85
Pliny the Elder
NH Praef. 3 149 n.135
5.58 37 n.16
5.60 180 n.25
6.66–8 222 n.70
6.78 113 n.31
6.84 277 n.2, 299 n.3, 300 n.8, 302 n.23
6.85 128 n.17, 330 n.22
6.96–100 141 n.90
6.100–1 141 n.91
6.101 141 n.93, 144 n.111, 266 n.62
6.101–6 141 n.92
6.102 142 n.96, 205 n.70
6.102–3 51 n.76, 143 n.99
6.103 144 n.111
6.103–4 48 n.63
6.104 63 n.12,15, 66 n.21, 67 n.28, 79 n.64, 89 n.24, 144, 146 n.118, 168 n.32
6.104–5 119 n.71, 120 n.75, 147 n.127
6.105 88 n.16, 89 n.24, 101 n.73, 112 n.26, 141 n.94, 148 n.131
6.106 66 n.22, 145 n.112, 146 n.121, 170
6.139–40 141 n.89
6.149 141 n.89
6.168 46 n.50
6.169 274 n.105
6.175(= *BNJ* 275 F 35) 76 n.52
6.191 274 n.103
6.195 274 n.105
6.202 76 n.52
8.1–8 220 n.51
8.7 105 n.93
8.8 220 n.51
9.117 266 n.60
12.26 114 n.36
12.26–8 112 n.26, 114 n.36
12.28 102, 238 n.11, 291 n.36
12.29 89 n.23, 110 n.11, 249 n.36
12.42 216 n.23, 29
12.42–3 216 n.20
12.45 216 n.29
12.45–6 216 n.19
12.56 (= *BNJ* 275 F 2) 76 n.52
12.63–5 54 n.85
12.64 152 n.150
12.65 104 n.87, 293 n.41
12.84 265 n.59, 267 n.66,
12.87–8 146 n.120,
12.97 105 n.91
12.129 105 n.94, 140 n.80, 249 n.36
13.14 140 n.80
13.15 216 n.23
13.18 140 n.80
14.108 140 n.83
23.93 140 n.81, 84
24.3 143 n.104
31.36 143 n.104
33.78 267 n.68
33.164 238 n.12
37.59–60 252 n.7
Plutarch
Alex. 25.6–8 104 n.85
62 222 n.70

Cim. 14 213 n.12
Lys. 17.2 139 n.73
Nic. 18.7 138 n.71
Sull. 13.3 48 n.66
Polybius
6.17 302 n.26
13.9.4–5 104 n.85
30.26.2 216 n.23
Porphyrion
ad Hor., epist. 1.20.1 104 n.80
2.1.269 104 n.80
Posidonius
FGrH 87 F 28.4–5 = F 49C E.-K
(= Strab. 2.3.4–5) 61 n.9
Procopius
Pers. 1.19.5 215
1.19.6 144 n.109
1.19.6–7 45
1.20.9 68 n.34
1.20.12 68 n.34
Ptolemy
Alm. 7.23 82 n.82
Geog.
1.7.1–3 82 n.84,
1.7.6 80 n.73
1.7.6–7 151 n.142
1.7.7 82 n.85
1.9.1 76 n.49
1.10.2 152 n.150
1.14.1 124 n.91
1.17.2 151 n.142
1.17.3 152 n.151
1.17.3–4 151 n.145
1.17.4 214
4.8.34 274 n.103
6.7.7 151 n.139
6.7.10 151 n.139
7.1.2 151 n.145
7.1.5 151 n.143,144
7.1.6 151 n.140, 151 n.145
7.1.6–7 78 n.63
7.1.7 154 n.167
7.1.7–8 79 n.69
7.1.8 79 n.67, 82 n.83, 151 n.138, 152 n.146, 154 n.162
7.1.8–10 82 n.83, 153 n.160
7.1.8–11 153 n.161
7.1.8–14 153 n.154
7.1.9 119 n.72, 154 n.163,165,167, 155 n.174
7.1.9–10 154 n.166
7.1.13 94 n.39
7.1.33–34 153 n.161
7.1.62 151 n.140,144, 153 n.155
7.1.68 119 n.71
7.1.82 153 n.155, 153 n.159
7.1.85 154 n.162
7.1.85–6 112 n.27, 153 n.161
7.1.86 119 n.71, 154 n.163, 155 n.172
7.1.86–9 154 n.164
7.1.87 119 n.72
7.1.87–88 154 n.166
7.1.89 119 n.71
7.1.95 79 n.66
7.2.15 113 n.31
7.2.16 155 n.172
7.2.23 155 n.172
7.5.2 76 n.52
8.22.7 151 n.139
8.22.9 151 n.139
8.26.3 151 n.140
8.26.4 151 n.138
8.26.12 151 n.140
Phaseis 59–60 Heiberg 144 n.106
Scriptores Historiae Augustae
Quad. Tyr. 3.2 313 n.67
Seneca
Ep. 101.4 309 n.55
119.1 185 n.40
QNat .pr.13 76 n.53
Herc.f. 469 216 n.23
Solinus 56.4–6 76 n.52
Sophronius
Mir. SS. Cyr. et Ioh. 1–2 291 n.33
Statius
Silv. 3.3.392–5 317 n.92
Strabo
2.1.2 = Eratosth. F III A 2
2.3.4–5 61 n.9
2.5.8 133 n.40
2.5.12 48 n.60, 125 n.2, 127 n.12, 254 n.17
3.5.3 253 n.10
4.1.8 133 n.37
4.3.2 133 n.37
4.5.3 133 n.41
8.6.20 133 n.37
9.3.4 133 n.37
12.8.19 133 n.37
13.3.6 133 n.37
14.1.26 133 n.37
15.1.4 126 n.5
15.1.41 221 n.60
15.1.43 221 n.60
15.2.5 67 n.24
16.1.27 133 n.37
16.4.4 152 n.150
16.4.5 48 n.59
16.4.10 274 n.103
16.4.22 133 n.39
16.4.23 47 n.53, 202 n.61
16.4.24 126 n.3
17.1.7 205 n.75

Strabo (*cont.*)
17.1.10 205 n.72
17.1.13 126 n.4, 8, 9, 132 n.36, 277 n.1, 289 n.25
17.1.16 205 n.73, 77
17.1.26 46 n.49
17.1.44–5 46 n.50
17.1.45 46 n.51, 47 n.53, 48 n.60,61,62, 49 n.74, 180 n.25
Suetonius
Aug. 41.1 131 n.28
98.2 130 n.23, 320 n.104
Tib. 32.2 132 n.34
*Calig.*37.3 132 n.32
rhet. 1 293 n.43
Tabula Peutingeriana
seg. 11 115 n.45, 154 n.163
Tacitus
Ann. 2.33 132 n.33
3.40 131 n.27
3.52 265 n.56
3.53 128 n.17, 265 n.56,59, 267 n.66
3.53–5 132 n.33
3.55 268 n.73
13.50–51 297 n.53
13.51 292 n.39
15.39 103 n.77
Hist. 1.20 266 n.61, 268 n.72
Theophrastus
Hist. pl. 9.7.2 215 n.19
9.7.3 215 n.19
9.7.4 215 n.19, 216 n.19
9.20 48 n.65
Theophylact Simocatta
7.13.6 140 n.85
Thucydides
2.18.1 81 n.80
5.4.2 215 n.17
Varro
Sat. Men. 581 49 n.67
Vegetius
Mil. 4.39 196 n.42
Vitruvius
8.3.13 49 n.69
Zosimus
5.41.4 106 n.98

Ostraka, Papyri, and Tablets

BGU
1.93 140 n.85
1.98 181 n.28
1.189 131 n.25
2.665, l.5 303 n.28
3.762 201 n.56
3.911 131 n.26
3.953 140 n.85
4.1175 131 n.24
5.1210, ll.116 308 n.49
ll.117 308 n.49
ll.118 308 n.49
ll.147 308 n.49
ll.150–2 286 n.22
ll.151 308 n.49
ll. 235–6 131 n.26
17.2704 279 n.10
B.M.Or. 6232 (2) 41 n.33
B.M Or. 8903 102 n.75, 277–9, 294
CPR 7.42 102, 106 n.96
O.Berenike
2.129, ll.7–9 214
2.198, l.12 213
O.Bodl.
2.871 36 n.12
O.Cair.
20 133 n.38
99 *GPW* 36 n.12
O.Claud.
1.27 200 n.51
28 200 n.51
29 200 n.51
30 200 n.51
31 200 n.51
32 200 n.51
33 200 n.51
34 200 n.51
O.Did.
189 304
320 105 n.95
323 54 n.88, 292–3, 305 n.37
327 255 n.24, 292, 305 n.37
328 255 n.24, 292, 305 n.37
364 105 n.95, 255 n.24
381 105 n.95
399 255 n.24
O.Eleph.DAIK 18 36 n.12
19 36 n.12
O.My.Ho. inv. 512 304
O.Krok.
1.1 304
1.4 202 n.61
1.24 304
1.26 304
O.Marb. priv. 36 n.12
O.Petr.Mus.
130 308 n.46
131 308 n.46
135 308 n.46
173 308 n.46
194 308 n.46
O.Wilck.
89 36 n.12
90 36 n.12

91 36 n.12
92 36 n.12
P.Ant.
1.32 140 n.85
P.Berl.Cohen
10 201 n.53
11 201 n.53
P.Bingen
77 253 n.9, 254 n.16
P.Cair.Isid.
81 36 n.13, 40 n.29
P.Cair.Masp.
2.67166 34 n.7, 300 n.7, 302 n.24
P.Cair.Zen.
4.59536 104 n.86
P.Corn.
6 131 n.25
35r 140 n.85
P.CtYBR
inv 624 56–8
P.Dime
7 131 n.26
P.Diog.
13 205 n.76
14 205 n.76
P.Fam.Tebt.
24 184 n.37
P.Gen.
4.161 201 n.53
P.Genova
1.28 140 n.85
2.62 183 n.34
P.Iand.
8.150v 195 n.38
P.Lond.
2.227 131 n.26
2.328 200 n.52, 201, 202, 260 n.42
3.948r 195 n.41
3.1273 131 n.25
4.1341 41 n.35
4.1346 40 n.32, 41
4.1351 41 n.35
4.1379 41 n.35
4.1465 41 n.33
5.1851 195 n.38
P.Louvre
2.108 201 n.53
P.Mich.
3.188 183 n.35
3.189 183 n.35
5.328 131 n.26
5.336 131 n.25
11.605 183 n.35
P.Oslo
2.40 183 n.34
P.Oxy.
1.36 = *Chr.Wilck.* 273
3.413 66 n.23
3.506 = *MChr* 248 182 n.30, 183 n.34
3.643 195 n.38
10.1269 192 n.16
12.1426 36 n.13
31.2580 228, 229 n.83
34.2728 106 n.96
43.3111 195 n.40
43.3121 102
45.3250 195 n.41
49.3484 195 n.41
51.3628–3633 102
54.3731 102–3, 104 n.84,89, 105 n.95, 140 n.85
54.3733 102–3, 104 n.84,89, 105 n.95, 140 n.85
54.3765 103
54.3766 102–3, 104 n.84,89, 105 n.95, 140 n.85
55.3814 36 n.13
60.4070 36 n.13
P.Oxy.Hels.
36 183 n.34
P.Quseir
28 255 n.24
P.Rend.Harr.
85 183 n.34
P.Ross.Georg.
2.18 195 n.41
3.9 106 n.96
4.16 41 n.35
PSI
1.87 36 n.13, 40 n.30
6.628 104 n.79
6.689a 36 n.13, 40 n.30
6.689b 36 n.13
6.689d 36 n.13
7.825 102
9.1051 131 n.26
12.1264 140 n.85, 279 n.11
15.1558 103, 105 n.94, 140 n.85, 180 n.25,26, 228 n.81, 296 n.52
P.Strasb.
4.222 140 n.85
P.Tebt.
3.2 856 204 n.66,67
P.Thomas
26 102
P.Turner
47 279 n.11
P.Wash.Univ.
1.7 36 n.13
P.Wisc.
2.65 195 n.39
SB
1.5234 131 n.25
3.7169 165 n.20,21, 166–9, 313, 315 n.82

SB (*cont.*)
3.7176 104 n.79, 133 n.38
6.9090 104 n.79
6.9210 205 n.76
6.9416 133 n.38
6.9545.32 36 n.12
6.9571 = 14.11850 169 n.34, 314 n.74
8.9834 140 n.85
10.10459 41 n.33,34
14.11552 195 n.41
14.11599 183 n.34
14.11850 169 n.34, 314 n.74
TPSulp.
78 178 n.18, 194–7
T.Varie
3 195 n.39
VT
184 255 n.24
WChr
273 180 n.26, 289 n.29, 310 n.59
435 47 n.52
452 47 n.54

Greek and Latin Inscriptions

AÉ
1901, 171 317 n.92
1954, 121 (= *AÉ* 1999, 1720–1721) 300 n.9
1999, 418 302 n.21
1999, 1722 49 n.72
1723 49 n.72
2005, 1626 51 n.80
1627 51 n.80
2007, 326 317 n.92
Ast and Bagnall (2015: 172) 303
Ast and Bagnall (2015: 174) 304
CIL
6.5744 317 n.92
6.8573 317 n.92
6.36779 317 n.92
8.4508 134 n.42
9.60 (= *CLE* 1533) 186 n.41
10.2389 300 n.8
15.798 300 n.8
15.3642 194 n.26
3643 194 n.26
3644 194 n.26
3645 194 n.26
4748 194 n.26
4749 194 n.26
7391 300 n.8
7974a 317 n.92
Cuvigny (1998: n.5) 301 n.13
De Franciscis (1976: 246–8) 104 n.86
Edictum de pretiis
16.10a 105 n.93
16.10–1 248 n.32
17.4 202 n.60
34.10 104 n.88
68 104 n.88, 105 n.93
IDélos
298 A 219 n.49
300 B 219 n.49
I.Didyma
1.394 268 n.76
I.Eph
3.627 302 n.19
7.3056 302 n.19
IG
I^3 449 220 n.50
II/III^2 2
1408 219 n.49
1409 219 n.49
1412 219 n.49
1414 219 n.49
XI ii 203 A 268 n.76
IGLS
17.1.183 316 n.85
196 (= *PAT* 1373) 277 n.5, 316 n.88
197 (= *PAT* 1413) 277 n.5, 291 n.34, 306 n.38
249 (= *PAT* 1399) 316 n.87
250 (= *PAT* 1403) 316 n.84
IGRom
1.1374 295 n.47, 296
1379 295 n.47, 296
I.Kanaïs
9 46 n.52
9bis 46 n.52
10 46 n.52
57 = *SB* 1.4028 313 n.70
ILAlg
1.2236 104 n.83, 255 n.24
ILLRP
454 143 n.103
ILS
657 40 n.32
775 291 n.35
1224b 104 n.80
1461 303 n.27
1518 317 n.92
2483 51 n.75, 143
5163 320 n.103
5836 143 n.103
7273 197 n.44
I.Memnon
67 301 n.17
I.Pan
80 204 n.68
86 48 n.57, 51 n.81, 104 n.79
IPE
1^2.32 183 n.33
I.Philae
52 48 n.59, 127 n.11

53 48 n.59, 127 n.11
56 127 n.11
I.Portes
30 308 n.46
39 314 n.75
49 127 n.11,
63 = *IGRom* 1.1379 296
67 = *OGIS* 674 214, 299 n.4, 303 n.28, 318 n.93
70 304
103 (= *SEG* 34.1593) 315 n.81, 316
Milne
33014 301 n.15
33015 301 n.15
OGIS
214 104 n.86
674 214, 299 n.4, 303 n.28
SB
1.2264 127 n.11
1.4028 = *I.Kanais* 57 313 n.70
5.7539 314 n.73
5.7950 301 n.13
5.7951 301 n.12, 303
5.7952 301 n.13
5.8036 48 n.59
5.8815 (= *IGRom* 1.1175) 304 n.32
5.8843 283 n.17
5.8844 283 n.17
8.9801 = 8.10044 301 n.17
8.10070 295 n.50, 296
18.13315 293 n.43
SEG
34.1593 (= *I.Portes* 103) 315–6
37.1019 255 n.24
39.1620 291 n.33
44.1435 34 n.6
46.2120 (= 52.1774) 143 n.101
46.2176 51 n.78, 79
48.2035 51 n.79
49.2251 48 n.58
50.1563 301 n.16
60.1788 313 n.72
62.1753 306 n.40
62.1754 306 n.40
Thomas
(2011: 27) 301 n.18

Armenian, Chinese, Coptic, Indian, Syriac literary texts

Aiṅkuṟunūṟu
178.3 155 n.169
208.1–2 112 n.16
213.1–2 112 n.18
243.1 89 n.22
268.2 112 n.17
270.2 112 n.17
284.2–4 112 n.17
Akanāṉūṟu
1.4 220 n.52
2.5–6 114 n.37
2.6 89 n.22, 112 n.23
13.4 112 n.19
21.24 112 n.15, 271 n.90
24.11 220 n.52
57 154 n.168
57.14–17 149 n.134
61.9–10 117 n.65
78.7 112 n.18
82.10–11
83.4–8 117 n.65
83.7 117 n.61
88 112 n.20
90.12 117 n.59
91.13 155 n.169
102 112 n.20
112.14 89 n.22
119.8 116 n.53
132.4–5 112 n.15
140.5 116 n.53
149 123–4, 319
149.6 86 n.2
149.7–11 112 n.24, 115, 120 n.75, 123 n.87, 149 n.134
149.7–13 139 n.76
149.9–10 116 n.50
152.4–7 115 n.41
169.6 116 n.53
172.6–14 271 n.89
182.14–8 114 n.37
191.4 116 n.53
212.16 155 n.169
245.5–12 272 n.93
245.9–11 117 n.65
257.17 116 n.53
270.9 155 n.169
290.12 155 n.169
295.9 116 n.53
303.17 116 n.53
310.14 116 n.53
322.12 112 n.18
329.5 116 n.53
337.5 116 n.53
348.8–11 112 n.17
376.17 155 n.169
390.3 116 n.53
Ananias of Širak
Geography 4, 81–82 n.81
Arthaśāstra
2.2.13 221 n.61
2.31.10 221 n.59
2.32.22 220 n.54
Cilappatikāram
3.37 86 n.10
5.9–10 115 n.44, 124 n.94

Cilappatikāram (*cont.*)
8.1–2 86 n.10
30.160 155 n.170
Dīpavaṁsa
22.14.28 155 n.170
Hemacandra
Abhidhāncintāmaṇi 420 124 n.95
Hou-Han-shu
118.12b 121 n.83
Ishoʿyahb
Letter 122 n.85
Kalittokai
52.17 89 n.22
Kuṟuntokai
90.2 89 n.22
90.2–4 114 n.37
100.3–5 272 n.91
124.2 117 n.53
214.1–2 112 n.17
288.1 89 n.22
288.1–2 114 n.37
335.2–6 112 n.17
Mahāvaṁsa
35.115 155 n.170
Malaipaṭukaṭām
203–10 112 n.21
300–1 112 n.15
316–18 112 n.18
480 117 n.60
Maturaikkāñci
136–8 289–90, 365
Naṟṟiṇai
4.7 117 n.53
5.3–4 112 n.22
14.3 155 n.169
44.6–8 112 n.17
45.4 117 n.61
64.4–5 112 n.19
65.5–6 112 n.15
82.7–11 112 n.15
102.8–9 112.17
105.7 155 n.169
108.1–5 112 n.21
114.1–3 271 n.89
138.3 117 n.53
151.7 89 n.22
151.7–8 114 n.37
183.5 117 n.53
209.1–4 112.17
254.6 117 n.53
276.1–4 111 n.14, 112 n.15
285 112 n.15
306.4–5 112.17
331.2 117 n.53
386.2–3 112.17
Patiṟṟuppattu
15.16–19 117 n.64
22.27 155 n.169
23.10 155 n.169
29.14 155 n.169
30.9–13 117 n.54, 65, 118, 272 n.92
42.8 155 n.169
43.11 155 n.169
46.13 155 n.169
47.1 155 n.169
49.17 155 n.169
Patikam 5.22 155 n.169
68.9–11 117 n.65
75.10 117 n.63
90.26 155 n.169
Patikam 9.1 155 n.169
Paṭṭiṉappālai
116–39 120
184–93 123 n.89
213–8 115 n.44
Perumpāṇāṟṟuppaṭai
65 117 n.53
66–82 123,
106–17 112 n.15
Puṟanāṉūṟu
5.1–3 221 n.66
56.18–21 137 n.63
84.6 116 n.53
102.4 116 n.53
116.7 116 n.53
126.14–16 115
143.1–5 112 n.17
159.15 112 n.17
168.2 89 n.22
168.5–6 86 n.10, 112 n.17
168.18 89 n.22
236.1–2 112 n.18
307.7 116 n.53
313.5 116 n.53
343.1–10 118 n.66, 149 n.134
343.3 116 n.51
343.6 89 n.24
343.9 155 n.169
343.9–10 120 n.75
387.5–13 221 n.65
394.3 155 n.169
Sui-shu
83.16a 121 n.83
Tirumurukāṇāṟṟuppaṭai
70 117 n.62
194 112 n.15
Tolkāppiyam
Pāyiram 1–7 86 n.10
2.9.883 88 n.17
3.9.72 221 n.62

Varāhamihira
Bṛhat Saṃhitā
78, 20 ab = 93, 1 ab 220 n.55
Wei-shu
102.12a 121 n.83
Yu-yang tsa-tsu
18.9b 121 n.83

Egyptian, Semitic, and Indian Inscriptions

CIS
2.161 135 n.50
2.3.3913 293 n.43
3.3960 (= *PAT* 306) 316 n.87
Mirashi (1981: no. 38) 327–8
PAT
306 = *CIS* 3.3960 316 n.87
1373 (= *IGLS* 17.1.196) 277 n.5, 316 n.88,
1399 (= *IGLS* 17.1.249) 316 n.87
1403 (= *IGLS* 17.1.250) 316 n.84
1413 (= *IGLS* 17.1.197) 277 n.5, 306 n.38
2634 277 n.5, 320 n.102
RES
3571 51 n.81
3427 51 n.81
SII
8.403 121 n.81
8.405 121 n.81
Urk.
2.101–2 46 n.48

Medieval and early modern sources

Abū al-Fidā'
354 79 n.71
354–5 97 n.50
355 97 n.52
Aḫbār al-Ṣīn wa' l-Hind
1.4.2 97 n.50, 122 n.85
al-Balāḏurī
216 42 n.37
Barbosa
118 98 n.57
160–1 45 n.45, 79 n.71, 98 n.55, 251 n.2
161 146 n.117
162 79 n.71
218–9 122 n.86
Bouchon (1976) 257
Bouchon (1977) 258
Buchanan
2.457 100 n.68
2.463–5 108 n.8
Livros das Monções
1.65 147 n.125
CAA
1.83 256 n.30, 257
1.121 256 n.31
2.41 98 n.56
3.258 99 n.61
7.136–7 270 n.82
7.175 121 n.81
7.175–6 100 n.64
Castanheda
2.150–151 45 n.47
Correa
2.2.561 100 n.65, 257 n.31, 258
Corsali
188 258 n.34
Cousas da India
45–6 89–90
CVR
16 258
95 147 n.125, 148
Ca' Masser
15 257
17 257
19 257
20 257
23 257
33 99 n.62
35 100 n.69
da Costa
315 350–351
Caminha
85 258
al-Dimašqī
173
DPMAC
1.168 269 n.79
2.64 269 n.80
3.572–9 227 n.79, 269 n.81, 271
5.182–9 270 n.83, 270 n.87
5.184 269 n.78, 270 n.83
5.536 270 n.85
6.428 219 n.48, 269 n.78
7.68 270 n.84
7.175 270 n.86
Fitch
188 108 n.6
Fra Paolino
116 110 n.10
182 110 n.13
356 110 n.10
Gomes de Brito
1.5–38 259
1.41–68 259
1.221–52 259
HAG
Livros das monções
livro 12 (1613–7), f. 10r 267 n.67

Ḥudūd al-ʿālam
10.12 121 n.81
10.13 97 n.48
Ibn ʿAbd al-Ḥakam
99 278
163–6 42 n.37
Ibn Baṭūṭah
4.71 97 n.50
4.99 97 n.52
4.99–100 97 n.50
Ibn Ǧubayr
67 44 n.40, 74 n.46
70 44 n.40
Ibn Ḫurradāḏbih
62 97 n.49
Ibn Māǧid
231 72 n.43
Kephalaia
77 333 n.1
Linschoten
1.66 100 n.71
Magno
660–3 75 n.47
Ma Huan
135 97 n.54
al-Malik al-Ašraf ʿUmar b. Yūsuf (Varisco (1994))
23 71–75
25 71–75
27 71–75
31 71–75
33 71–75
D. Manuel
Letter: 16 98 n.56
Marignolli
496 108 n.4
Mun
10–11 255 n.22
44 255 n.22
Mundy
3.1.79 108 n.7
al-Muqaddasī
44 144 n.109
Murchio
134 110 n.13
Nationaal Archief, Den Haag, (VOC)
1.04.02, inv 2928 100 n.67
Orta
1.305 274
2.241 261 n.43
2.246 266
2.291–7 216 n.20
Piloti
46 44 n.41
46–7 206 n.79
Pires
2.362 99 n.63
Pires de Távora
110–1 261–2
111 45 n.45
Polo
Divis. 157 = *Mil.* 153 122 n.86,
Divis. 180 = *Mil.* 176 97 n.48, 108 n.4
Divis. 183 = *Mil.* 179 97 n.48
Al-Qalqašandī
3.468–70 42–4
Quirini
9 100 n.69
9–10 98 n.56, 99 n.62
Santa Cruz
53 260 n.41
54 260 n.40
Sanuto
17.191 257
18.143 257
25.594–5 258
27.641 258
42.453–4 258
54.131 258
54.599 258
Sassetti
461 262 n.49
476 89 n.29
Sebastião
81 260 n.40
Seure
71 259
al-Ṭabarī
1.2574–7 42 n.37
Van Gollenesse
57 92 n.32
58–9 92 n.33
60 92 n.35
61 92 n.34
Varthema
li^{v} 108 n.5
lvi^{v}-lvii^{r} 108 n.5
Yāqūt
1.506 97 n.48
4.639 97 n.48

Geographical Index

Abū Šaʿār 34
Achankovil 93
Adanu islands 76
Aden (*Eudaimon Arabia*, Adane) 59, 60, 63, 67–8, 70–75, 98, 146 n.117, 149 n.132, 229, 251, 261
Aden, Gulf of 32, 33, 58–9, 63, 76, 146
Adulis 1, 37, 55–8, 60, 67–70, 75, 105, 137 n.66, 219 n.48, 248 n.31, 272–3, 327 n.1, 333–4
Aethiopia 126–7
Aigidioi, Isle of the 77, 79
Aï-Khanoum 330
Aila (Ila) 38–9, 45, 70
ʿAin al-Beida 143
Alappuzha 88 n.20
Alexandria 4–5, 7, 15, 26, 33, 35, 37–9, 62, 74, 115, 118, 119, 125, 126 n.10, 130–2, 136, 141–2, 145–7, 159–62, 166, 168–72, 174–5, 179–81, 188, 190, 192–3, 196 n.43, 197–9, 203–5, 206 n.78, 207–8, 212–13, 238, 240, 252, 254 n.16, 261–2, 265–6, 280–2, 285 n.21, 289–98, 300–3, 305–13, 317, 320, 322–3
Andhra Pradesh 332
Anjengo 100
Anjikaimal Hills 92
Antaeopolite nome 279
Antinoupolis 33–4, 204, 302 n.22
Aphrodites Oros 51, 292
Apollonopolis Magna, *see also* Edfu
Apollonopolis Parva 46
Apollonos hydreuma 51, 143
ʿAqaba 214, pottery 70–1, 97
Arabia 1, 33, 45, 59–60, 98, 141, 146, 214, 277, 305
  South Arabia 37–8, 54–5, 58, 60, 66, 70, 75–6, 80, 115, 127, 144 n.110, 248 n.29, 320
  Eudaimon Arabia see Aden
Arabian Sea 2, 45, 59–60, 62–4, 66, 68, 70–1, 74–6, 78, 82, 121, 124, 140, 146, 149–51, 217 n.35, 251, 262
Aragoshe Arakuzha 109, 110 n.10
Ariake 85, 115 n.43, 116 n.51, 135, 137 n.64, 152, 215, 327, 332 n.36
Aromata
  Emporion 327 n.1
  Promontory 63 n.13, 64
Aromatophoros Land 48, 165–9, 175, 186, 190, 198, 313, 315
Arsinoite nome 200
Askalon 314
Astakapra (Hastakavapra) 108, 152–3
Athens 163 n.14, 164–6, 174–6, 178–9, 181, 193, 197, 213 n.12, 215
Atlantic Ocean 31, 76, 253
Axum 272, 333–4
ʿAyḏāb 42–4, 73–4, 146
Azania 272

Bab el-Mandeb 67–8, 76, 126–7, 261
Babylon (Cairo) 40, 42, 54, 206–7
Babylon (Mesopotamia) 104, 320
Baçaim 262
Bairath 262
Balepatma 96 n.43
Bakare (Becare) 85–6, 88, 93, 109, 137, 145, 147–9, 154–5
Banda 262
Bārahakanyāpura (Barakanur, Fāknūr) 96
Barbarikon 55, 62, 80, 136–7, 216, 217 n.35, 255, 318, 327 n.1
Barcelor 262
Baris River 86 n.11, 154
Barygaza (Bharuch, Baroche) 54–5, 60–2, 64, 66–7, 72, 76–7, 80, 93–6, 108 n.3, 116 n.51, 131, 137, 149 n.136, 151–3, 214, 216, 217 n.35, 255, 262, 273, 313 n.71, 318, 327, 329, 331, 332
Bassora 261
Baticala (Bathacala, Battacala) 100, 262
Becare *see* Bakare
Belur 89
Bengal, Bay of 2, 84, 116, 121, 123–4, 333
Ber(e)nice, Red Sea port 1, 4, 5, 7, 33–4, 38–9, 42, 46–9, 51–6, 58, 62–3, 68, 70, 75, 115, 126, 134, 136, 142–6, 169–70, 172, 181 n.27, 190 n.10, 198, 200–7, 213–14, 252, 255 n.24, 260 n.42, 265, 273, 292, 300, 303–6, 308–9, 313, 315, 318, 322
Berytus 166–8, 291
bilād al-fulful 94
Bi'r 'Iayyan 143
Bisades 113
Black Assarca Island 70
Borysthenes 164
Bosporus 164, 176

Bostra 39
Bouweib 51
Brentesion/Brentesium 167–8
Budfattan *see* Pudapatana
Byzantion (Vijaydurg?) 78

Cairo 36, 40, 42, 44, 206, 207, 261, 262, 278, 295 n.50
Calecare *see* Keelakarai
Calicut 45, 70, 79, 84, 85, 97, 98, 100, 108, 117, 124, 146, 251
Campania 130
Canary Islands 76 n.52
Cane 54, 55, 60, 63, 67, 143, 144, 149, 151, 327
Cannanore (Cananor, Kannur) 86, 98–9
Canopic branch canal gate 205
Cape Guardafui 76
Carapatão 262
Carmania 141, 274
Carystus 163
Caucasus 113
Cellūr 117
Chalach 122
Chalakudi River 89, 92–3
Chale (Chaliyam) 86, 262
Chaul (*see* Semylla) 78, 151–2, 262
Chersonesos, (*see* Mount Ely) 77, 79, 86
Chettuva 99
Chidambaram 118
China (Tzinista) 84, 94, 98, 109, 113, 121–4, 138, 140, 261, 333–4
Chryse Island (Golden Chersonese) 116, 124, 138–9, 248 n.31
Chumana 316
Cifardão 262
Clysma (Qulzum) 36–42, 45, 54, 58, 68, 70, 75, 201, 306
Cochin 84, 89–90, 92, 97–101, 108, 147, 251, 254–6, 259–60, 266–7, 270, 323
Codamangalam 110 n.13
Coilun, Collam *see* Kūlam
Comorin Cape 86, 98, 153
Compasi 51, 143, 292
Constantinople 165–6
Coptos 4–5, 7, 15, 26, 33–5, 37, 41, 46–9, 51–3, 56, 125–7, 134, 136, 142–3, 159–60, 171, 174–5, 179–81, 193, 198–207, 213, 228 n.81, 265, 289, 291–6, 298–9, 303–14, 316, 318 n.93, 322
Corgeira 92 n.31, 93
Coromandel coast 87, 94, 115–16, 120, 123–4, 139, 327
Cottonara (*see also* Kottanarike, *Kuṭṭanāṭu*) 88–9, 112, 148, 154–5
Cranganore 99
Crimea 163 n.14
Cuḷḷi 86
Cumbola 98

Dachinabades (Dakṣināpatha), Southward Road, 80–1, 152–3, 332
Dahbattan 97 n.49
Dār al-fulful 278
Delos 104, 268–9
Dendera 142
Delta of the Nile 36–7, 39
Devipattinam 121
Didymoi 51, 105, 255 n.24, 256, 292, 305 n.37
Dios 313
Dymirice, Damirice, Dimirica 121

East Africa 1, 4, 33, 38, 46 n.52, 54–5, 70, 80, 116, 126–7, 133, 165, 252, 270, 272 n.95, 274, 320
Edfu (Apollonopolis Magna) 9, 33, 46, 277, 313
Egypt, 1, 4, 5, 6, 7, 27, 33, 34, 37, 38, 39, 40, 42, 46, 47, 51 n.81, 53, 54, 55, 56, 58, 59, 60, 61, 62, 63, 66, 67, 68, 70, 71, 72, 73, 74, 75, 101, 102, 103, 105, 115, 116, 124, 125, 126, 130, 131, 132, 133, 135, 136, 137, 140, 142, 143 n.104, 145, 146, 149 n.132, 161, 165, 166 nn.24, 25, 167, 168, 169, 188, 190, 197, 198, 201, 202, 203, 204, 206, 207, 208, 212, 213, 214, 215, 217, 218, 255, 260, 261, 262, 268, 273, 274, 277, 285, 288, 289, 290, 292, 296, 300, 301, 302, 304, 309, 310, 311, 312, 313, 315, 316, 317, 318, 321, 322, 323, 324, 332, 333, 334
Elagkon/Elagkoros 154–5
Ely, Mount (Chersonesos, Delly, Ezhimala) 79, 86, 149–50
Erattupetta 92–3
Erythra Thalassa, Erythraean Sea 113, 314
Erumely (Erimamoly) 92–3
Eudaimon Arabia see Aden

Fāknūr 96, 97 n.49
Fandarayna 97 n.49

Gabaza 68
Gades 31, 76, 253
Galatia 37, 51 n.75
Ganges 114, 116, 123–4, 126, 138–40, 150, 216–18, 249, 314, 321
Gaza 54 n.85, 104, 152
Germany 49, 252, 261
Ghats, Westerns 89, 107, 109–10, 114, 116, 118, 123, 222, 321
Gogha 331

Good Hope, Cape 107, 251
Guardafui, Cape 76

Hadriana, Via 33, 204
Hannaur (Onor) 98, 100
Hastakavapra, *see* Astakapra
Herakleopolis Magna 58 n.103, 202 n.59
Ḥiǧāz 42, 44
Himālayas 95
Hippokura 78 n.63
Horn of Africa 68 n.31

India, *passim,* North India 72–5 South India 1–5, 41, 48–9, 53–4, 58, 61, 63–4, 66, 71–2, 75, 77, 84, 86, 98, 105, 107–8, 112, 115, 117, 123, 125, 127, 135, 140–2, 144–7, 149, 150, 153, 155, 168–70, 172, 175, 201–5, 212, 217, 249, 252–6, 260, 266, 272, 274, 311, 315, 318, 319, 324, 333
Indus River 150
Indus delta, Skythia, (Barbarikon) 55, 61–2, 64, 66–7, 70, 72, 74, 77, 81, 94, 94 n.39, 150–2
Iotabis 68
Iratepely 92
Irruny 92
Italy 130–2, 240, 252, 311–12
Iuliopolis 5, 142–3, 205–6
Iyyal 331

Jeddah 42, 44–5, 70, 98, 206, 251, 261–2
Jumquão Telhado 89

Kaber (Kaber/Kaveri/Kaviri) 94, 94 n.39, 118, 120, 123
Kaineitai, Isle of the 77, 79
Kalliena (Kalliana, Kalyāṇa) 77, 80, 94–6, 136, 327 n.6
Kamara 87, 116
Kanā'yis 46, 313
Kangra 331
Kānherī 331
Kanjirappally (Canharapely) 90, 92–3
Karwar 77
Karura 154
Kasrawad 329
Kathiawar 77
Kattigara 124
Kaveri *see* Kaber
Kayamkulam 86, 99
Keelakarai 121
Keramos 194–5
Khor Rori 1, 115
Kochi 86
Kodakara 92
Kolchoi (Koṟkai) 82, 87, 153
Kolli 271–2
Koloe 272
Komaria (Komarei) *see* Cape Comorin 82, 87, 153
Kondapur 331
Koṟkai *see* Kolchoi
Kottanarike (*see also* Cottonara, *Kuṭṭanāṭu*) 34, 84, 88–9, 93, 96–8, 101, 103, 112 n.27, 114, 121, 123–4, 140, 154–5, 251, 318, 321
Kottayam 88 n.20
Kottiara metropolis 154
Kunjākarī 97
Kuṭṭanāṭu (*see also* Cottonara Kottanarike) 88, 89 n.21, 118, 154–5, 321
Kūlam (Quilon, Coilun, Collam, Kollam) 97–100, 108, 109 n.9, 110, 121–2

Lakshadweep Islands 77, 79, 138, 149–50, 248 n.31, 321
Lemba 261
Lepte Acra 76
Leuke Island 77, 79
Leuke Kome 47 n.53, 54 n.85, 70, 126, 134, 202, 277, 303, 305, 318
Limyrike 3, 54, 55 n.93, 62, 64, 66–7, 76–88, 93, 112, 116, 121 n.79, 136–40, 149 n.136, 150–5, 202 n.62, 214, 216–17, 248–9, 251, 255–6, 260 n.42, 264, 312, 319, 327 n.1, 332
Lisbon 62, 100, 147, 256, 258, 261, 267, 269, 270, 286, 323
Lykopolite nome 279

Macedonia 177, 197
Madauros 104, 255 n.24
Malabar 94, 97–8, 100–1, 110 n.10, 122 n.86, 254, 261, 270
Malambam 331
Malao 68 n.31, 327 n.1
Malay peninsula 121, 150, 248 n.31
Malāyūfatan 94 n.39
Male (Malay/ Maliyār/ Melibar/ Mulay/ Munaybar/Malī/Malībār,Manībār *see* Malabar) 34, 94, 96–8, 101, 103, 121, 124, 222, 251
Maler 110–1
Maleatur 110 n.13
Malichus 135
Malindi 79, 274
Mamallapuram 123
Mandagora (Mandangad) 78, 96 n.43
Mangalore(Mangaruth/Manǧūr/Manǧarūr/ Manǧalūr) 84–6, 96–8, 105, 251

Manimala, River 93
Mannar, Gulf of 95, 264, 321
Mapharitis 135
Maraikayar Paṭṭinam 94 n.39
Marallo 94, 94 n.39, 121
Mareb 272 n.96
Mareotis Lake Harbour 205
Masalia 327 n.6
Maturai 117
Mazagão 262
Mecca 206
Mediterranean Sea 1, 3–5, 31–2, 34–5, 42, 47, 49, 61, 68, 103, 105, 125, 133, 162, 196, 206, 208, 215, 253, 279, 283, 288, 311, 322, 333
Meenachil, River 93
Melizeigara 78 n.63
Mende 164
Menuthias 248 n.31
Mesopotamia 300 n.7
Minayh, Bi'r 51–3,
 Wadi 49, 51, 53, 300
Minayh al-Ḥīr 51, 53
Minnagar (*see also* Barbarikon) 80, 136
Moca 261
Modura (Maturai) 148, 154
Moscha Limen 54, 67, 76, 146 n.120, 149 n.136
Mosyllon 68 n.31, 105 n.93, 327 n.1
Muhatuge 110
Mundu 68 n.31, 139, 248 n.31, 327 n.1
Muvattupuzha River 89, 92–3, 110
Muyirikkōḍe 97
Muza 55–8, 60, 63, 67, 137 n.66, 214, 273, 327 n.1
Muziris (Muciṟi) 3, 4, 6, 15, 26, 34, 66, 79, 83–8, 93, 96–7, 109, 112, 115–16, 118–24, 139, 141–55, 159–62, 164–5, 168–70, 172–3, 184, 189–90, 202–3, 215, 217–18, 220–2, 238, 253 n.14, 298, 312, 316, 319, 321, 323
Myos Hormos 1, 7, 46 n.51, 47–8, 51, 53–6, 58, 62–4, 70, 115, 125, 127, 133, 144, 175, 201–2, 204, 213, 254–5, 272, 301, 304–8

Nalopatana 94
Nānāghāṭ 95, 329, 331
Narmadā 77, 95
Nasik 327–30
Nasthullapur 331
Naura 77, 85–6, 88, 93
Nelkynda (*gens Neacyndon*) 79, 85–6, 88, 93, 96, 109, 116, 137–8, 147–9, 154–5
Nepal 216
Netrani 77
Nicopolis (*see also* Iuliopolis) 5, 205–6
Nile 4–5, 26, 33–42, 46–8, 51, 126, 142–3, 165, 171, 180, 188, 196, 200–4, 206, 207, 213, 272
Nitriae (Nitra) 79, 147–8, 154–5

Ocelis 63 nn.12, 13, 67, 143–4, 146 nn.118, 119, 120, 149 n.132, 151
Omana 60
Onor (*see* Hanaur) 98, 100
Orrotha 94, 96
Oxyrhyncha 56, 58, 131 n.25
Oxyrhynchus 102–5, 249
Ozene (Ujjayinī) 216

Paithana (Paiṭhan) 80, 95, 152–3, 332 n.36
Pala (Palàya) 109, 110 n.10
Palaipatmai 78 n.63, 96
Palakkad Churam (Paleacate Cheri) 92–3
Palmyra 277, 291, 306 n.38, 315–16, 320
Pamba 93, 154
Pandav Lena 327
Paralia 87
Parapotamia 300 n.7
Parti 94, 96
Patale 141
Pathanamthitta 88 n.20
Pattanam 1, 70 n.41, 79, 83, 86, 96 n.43, 97, 115, 151, 155, 222
Pegu (Bago) 98, 123, 261
Pelusium 38–9, 306
Pemba (Island) 272
Pennar 331
Peratbiddy (Perattuviti) 92
Persia (Persis) 60, 98, 109, 121–2, 140–1, 333
Persian Gulf 33 n.2, 141 n.89
Pharsan islands 68
Philotera 304, 307
Phoinikon 51, 292
Pigeon Island 77, 79
Pirates 77, 79, 86, 142, 147, 149, 154–5, 253
Piravom (Porròta) 109
Poduke 87, 116, 152
Pompeii 49, 104
Ponnani River 92, 109
Ponnani (*see also* Tyndis) 78–9, 83, 86, 152
Pontus 163–4, 167, 215
Pseudostomos River 154
Ptolemais *ton theron* 46, 105 n.93, 248 n.31
Pudapatana (Budfattan) 94, 96
Pukār (Kāviripūmpaṭṭinam) 94 n.39, 115, 120, 123–4
Punnata 154 n.163, 321
Putamguale 89
Puteoli 104, 130, 194–7, 205, 300 n.8, 302, 312, 317, 320

Puthenkavu 96
Pyrrhon Oros 87

Qena 33, 47
Qulzum 36, 42, 44
Qūṣ 33, 42, 46, 74, 116
Quṣayr 42–4, 73, 261–2

Ràamapurata (Ramapura) 110
Red Sea 1, 3–5, 7, 31–6, 38–9, 41–9, 51, 53–6, 58, 61–3, 68–75, 126–7, 132–5, 142, 144, 146, 159–62, 165–6, 168–9, 172, 175, 180, 190, 192–3, 197–201, 206–8, 213–5, 251, 253, 255, 259–61, 277, 279, 283, 288, 296, 298–9, 300 n.10, 301, 303, 305–9, 311–15, 318, 322
Rhapta 60, 105 n.93, 248 n.31, 272–4
Rhodes 166
Rome 103–4, 106, 130, 132, 167, 174, 204, 212, 238, 253, 254 n.16, 256, 261, 266, 291, 293, 300–2, 317, 323, 328, 333

Sagapa 151 n.145
Salopatana 94
Sarapis, Isle of 60, 248 n.31
Schedia 5, 205
Semylla (Simylla, Chaul) 78–80, 151–3, 214
Septimius Severus 104, 310, 317
Sesekreienai islands 77
Sestus 163 n.14
Sibor 94, 96
Sielediba, Selediba (*see also* Taprobane) 94, 333–4
Sigerum 141
Silis 333–4
Simylla *see* Semylla
Sindābūr 94 n.39, 97 n.49
Sindu 94
Šinkli 97
Skythia 60, 62, 64, 66–7, 76–7, 216, 316, 318
Socotra 60, 66, 76, 108 n.3, 146 n.120, 214, 248, 313
Sofala 269–70, 273–4
Soknopaiu Nesos 131, 200, 201–2
Somali coast 55, 60, 68, 76, 119, 139
Sopatma 87, 116
Sorath (Suraṭh) 116
South India 125–7
Spain 76
Spasinu Charax 316
Sri Lanka (*see* Taprobane) 58, 71, 75, 94, 94 n.39, 121 n.82, 138, 155, 262, 300, 321, 333
Suppara 327 n.6
Surat (Suraṭh(ṭh)a, Suraṣṭra, Syrastrene) 94 n.39, 262
Susa 141
Suways 44
Syagros 141
Syria 134, 140, 166, 197
Syrastrene, Kathiawar Peninsula 77

Tagara 80, 152–3, 332 n.36
Tamiḻakam 86–7
Taprōbane (*see also* Sielediba, Sri Lanka) 68, 94–6, 121, 248, 333–4
Tartaria 98
Tekazze 272 n.96
Thailand 129
Thanjavur 118
Tharisappalli 122
Thebaid 38–9, 42, 47, 301, 308
Thekkenkur 89–90, 92–3, 100, 109, 118
Thina 140
Thiruvalla 118
Thmuis 205
Thodupuzha 92
Thomna 152 n.150
Timotheus 177–8, 193, 197
Traiana, Via Nova 39
Trajan's Canal 35–42, 54, 61–2, 75, 201, 203, 302, 306
Travancore 98, 100
Troglodytes 126–7
Ṭūr 36, 42, 44–5, 70, 73–5, 206–7, 262
Tyndis (*see also* Ponnani) 77–9, 82–3, 85–6, 88, 93, 109, 151–4
Tzinista (*see also* China) 94

Ujjayinī (Ozene) 95, 216
Ūr.shfīn 121

Vadakkenkur 89, 92, 100–1, 109
Vaipur (Vaypur) 109, 110 n.10
Valluvally hoard 31, 32, 54
Varkala 86 n.6, 87
Vembanad Lake 4, 86, 88–9, 97
Vengurla 77
Vēṅkaṭam hill 86
Vesuvian area 130
Vizhinjam 99

Wajh 1
Woodham Mortimer 131, 331

Yemen 43

Zanguizara 262
Zanzibar 272
Zarai 134
Zaruquly 92–3
Zayton 122 n.86

Subject Index

Aelia Isidora, Erythraean Ship owner and merchant 313–15
Aelia Olympias, Erythraean Ship owner and merchant 313–15
Aelius Gallus, prefect of Egypt 47 n.53, 51 n.81, 125, 127, 133
Aelius Romanus 194, 196
M. Aemilius Marcianus Asclepiades, tax farmer 316
L. Aemilius Paulus 224 n.71
Aemilius Rectus, prefect of Egypt 132 n.34
Aioi (Āy), South Indian chieftains 119 n.72, 154–5
Akridophagoi 274
Albucius, soldier 292
Alcyone 67 n.25
Alexander, Indian Ocean seafarer 124
Alexander, of Abonoteichus 37–8
Alexander, the arabarch 268, 300, 302, 311–12
Alexander, the Great 104, 222 n.70, 327 n.4
Amphorae with Tamil inscriptions 54
  from 'Aqaba 70–1, 96 n.43, 97
Amyntas III king of Macedonia 177
Anastasius 96 n.45
Andreas, Indicopleustes 34 n.6
Annius, soldier 292
P. Annius Plocamus, tax farmer 299 n.3, 300, 302
M. Annius Syriacus, prefect of Egypt 200
Antoninus (Marcus Aurelius) 200
Antoninus (Caracalla) 310
Antoninus Pius 96 n.44, 314
L. Antonius Callistratus, quarter-tax farmer 291, 306 n.38
Apollodorus, merchant of Phaselis 163–4
Apollodorus, son of Pasion 177–8, 192–3, 197
Apollodotus, Indo-Greek king 327–8
Arabarchs (tax farmers of the Red Sea tax) 7, 21, 34, 225 n.72, 226, 268, 281, 298–303, 304 n.32, 307–8, 310–1, 317–20, 322
Arabarchs' shares 7, 224, 225–30, 239, 243–6, 278, 281–4, 286–90, 294–5, 298–303, 310 n.58, 317, 319, 322
Archers (on board of Indiamen) 144
Arcturus 164, 167
Arrianus 135
Artemo, merchant 163–4
P. Attius Severus 194
Augustus 49 n.70, 53, 130, 133, 252, 256, 320
M. Aurelius Mindius Matidianus, tax farmer 302
Avitus, paralemptes 304, 306–7

M. Barbatius Celer 194–7
Basilios, dioiketes at Aphrodito 40–1
Benefit of assumption (in a loan contract) 15, 181–4
Bhāskara Ravivarma 97
Bisades 113
Borrower 4, 5, 7, 15, 159–62, 164–5, 167–9, 171, 173, 174–8, 181–4, 186–92, 198–200, 203, 205, 280–1, 298, 305, 308–10, 312–13, 315–17
Boukoloi 38
Brokers (proxenetai) 185, 261
Burden of proof (in a loan contract) 182, 184

Caelobothras *see also* Keprobotos 148
Calendar Revolving Egyptian 145
  Fixed Alexandrian 62, 145, 168
  Attic 67 n.24
  Roman calendar 145
Caligula 132, 268
Callimachus 136 n.60, 166–7,
L. C. Calpurnii 197
Cameleer(s), camel-traders 172, 198–9, 200–3, 207, 309, 312, 322
Camels 160, 169 n.33, 172, 200–3, 204, 206, 207, 316, 322
Cēra, Cēralar (Caelobothras, Keprobotos) 3, 115, 117, 118, 119, 120, 154, 155, 221, 222, 272 n.91, 321
Charibael (Karibī'l Watār Yuhan'im) 135
Chelonophagoi 274
Cholaibos, lord of Mapharitis 135 n.52
Claudius 128 n.17, 267 n.69, 300
Claudius Anicetus, arabarch 301
Claudius Chrysermus, paralemptes 304
Ti. Claudius Geminus, arabarch 301–2
Ti. Claudius Isidorus 301 n.16
Coins Roman 116, 118, 120–1, 127–9, 131, 132, 137–8, 267, 327, 329–32
  Indian 115, 118, 135 n.55, 222, 327–32
  Axumite 96 n.45
  Spartan 139 n.73
  Punch-marked coins 131, 329–31
Cōḻa, Cōḻar 119–20, 221
Commodus 38, 134, 252, 264, 277, 319

Cornelius Senecio 309
Customs Duties 120, 121 n.81, 134, 136, 195, 207–8, 229, 292, 293
  Warehouse(s) 171
  Red Sea tax 2, 4, 5–7, 27, 103, 125–6, 132–4, 173–4, 180, 207–8, 225 n.72, 240, 264, 277, 279–81, 282–3, 285–97, 300–4, 306–7, 309–11, 317–18, 320, 322–4, 332

Darius 36, 104
Datis 104
Diamonds 115, 251, 264, 312, 321
Diodorus of Samos 80–3, 151–3
Dog star 63, 143–4, 164
Domitian 96 n.44

Eirenaios, secretary of the *paralempsis* 305
Elephants 46, 94 n.38, 105 n.93, 112 n.15, 117, 119, 219–22, 268, 271–2, 274
Elesbas, King of Axum 68
Erythraikos Emporos 298, 314–15
  Naukleros 298, 314–15
Eudoxus of Cizycus 61
Eumedes 46 n.52
Exchange vs trade 107–8, 115–19, 140–1

Fiscal values 6, 101–3, 105, 208, 265, 280–2, 289, 291–4, 297
Frankincense, imported to Egypt via Red Sea 47, 53–5, 58
  imported overland to Gaza 54 n.85
  imported to Barbarikon 137
  in the pepper woods 113–14
  libanotika phortia 103–4, 113–14, 137, 144, 292–3, 305
  presented as *Saturnalia* gift 104
  prices 103–4, 292–3, 305 n.37
  producing district 144
  quantities 104
  vicus turarius 49, 104
Freight contracts 194–6
  expenses 15, 171, 177–9, 189, 192–7, 323

A. Gabinius 127
Gaius Caesar 76 n.52
Gajabāhu 155
Gautamīputra Śiva Sātakarṇi 135, 136 n.55
Gautamīputra Śrī Sātakarṇi 136, 327, 329
Gautamīputra Śrīyajña Sātakarṇi 331
Gerrhaeans, frankincense traders 104

Hadrian 96 n.44, 255, 314–15
Herod Agrippa 300–1, 312
Hippalus 76, 144, 150
Hipparchus 82
Hoards Akki Alur 96
  Barwani 329
  Bairath 331
  Budinathan 127
  Gogha 331
  Iyyal 331
  Jogalthembi 329, 331
  Kangra 331
  Kasrawani 329
  Kondapur 331
  Malamban 331
  Mangalore 96
  Mir Zakah 331
  Nasthullapur 331
  Pennar 331
  Puthenkavu 96
  Taxila 331
  Thatta 331
  Tondamanathan 331
  Valluvally 86, 96, 155
  Weepagandla 331
  Woodham Mortimer 331
Honainos, ship owner 316
Hydreuma, hydreumata 46, 51, 67, 142–3
Hylophagoi 274

Ichthyophagos, -oi 274, 307
Iḷaiyar 272
Iḷañcēral Irumpoṟai 155 n.169
Interest rate in Egypt 131, 163 n.13, 183, 267–8
Ioannes praetorian prefect 163
Ioannes arabarch 302 n.22
M. Iulius Alexander 300, 308, 322
Ti. Iulius Alexander 300–1, 308
Ti. Iulius Apollonius 301, 304, 307, 322
C. Iulius Eucharistus 305–6
C. Iulius Faustinus 304–6
Iulius Florus 131
Iulius Sacrovir 131
Īssuppu Irappān 97
Ivory 3, 5, 6, 116, 220 n.50, 268–72, 272
  from Adulis 55, 105 n.93, 272, 273
  from Aualites 105 n.93
  from Mosyllon 105 n.93
  from Ptolemais ton theron 105 n.93
  from Rhapta 105 n.93, 272, 273–4
  from Sophala 273
  from South India 61, 117–18, 138
  prices/fiscal values 103, 105, 248
  schidai 19, 21, 119, 211–12, 217–22, 239, 243–6, 248–9, 268, 281–2, 284–8, 290–1, 294, 297–300, 319

Ivory (*cont.*)
sound 6, 19, 21, 211–12, 217–19, 223–34, 239, 243–6, 248–9, 268, 281–91, 294, 297, 299, 300, 319–35

Jacinth stone 138, 248, 251, 264–5, 321

Kāṉavar 110, 112, 114, 271
Kareis, South Indian chieftains 154
Karibī'l Bayān 135
Κασία 68 n.31, 103, 105, 139
Kaṭal Piṟakōṭṭiya Ceṅkuṭṭuvaṉ 155
Khwaja Safar 262
Kuṟavar 110, 111 n.14, 112

Lender (creditor) 2, 5, 7, 159–65, 167–8, 171, 173–4, 175–6, 178–84, 186–90, 192–4, 197–200, 203, 208, 280–1, 298, 305, 308–13, 316
Lysas 300

Malabathron (*tamālapattra*) 4, 6, 7, 19, 103, 105, 113–16, 138, 140–1, 140 n.79, 155, 174, 180, 216–18, 231, 245, 248–9, 250, 264, 267, 279, 282, 284–8, 291, 296, 312, 321
Maler, Western Ghats inhabitants 110–1
Malichus, Nabataean king 135
Manbanos 135, 327, 329
Manesos 300 n.7
Marcianus of Heraclea 135
Marcus Aurelius 38 n.22, 134, 200, 252, 264, 277, 319–20
Mariamne, daughter of Herod Agrippa 301
Marinus of Tyre 80, 82–3, 124, 151–2, 214
Martanda Varma 100
Menelaos, merchant from Keramos 194–7
Metrology (weight standards) 100 n.67, 208, 228, 270 n.83, 294–7
Modestus, secretary of Myos Hormos 307
Monkeys, as pepper gatherers 113–14, 253

Nāganikā 329, 331
Nard, Gangetic 6, 19, 21, 115–16, 138, 140, 155, 211–12, 215–18, 222–3, 229–35, 237, 243, 246, 248, 249, 264, 282–3, 285–8, 291, 296 n.51, 312
Syrian 215 n.19
Spikenard 279
Nero 96 n.44, 128, 266, 318
C. Numidius Eros, merchant 49, 146 n.122, 256, 266–8, 297

M. Obellius Firmus 104

Pakybis, Ichthyophagos 307,
Palyāṉaic Celkeḻu Kuṭṭuvaṉ 155
Paṇṭiya, Paṇṭiyar (Pandion) 148, 221
Paralemptes 7, 298, 301, 303–9, 311, 316–18, 320, 322
(*paralempsis*) 303
Paralemptikai apothekai 193, 306
Paricilar, gifts seekers 120
Pasion, 177–8, 193, 196–7
Pearls 61, 115, 117, 118, 123, 138, 251, 264–7, 289 n.27, 312, 319, 320–1, 324
Pepper among the cargo items of the Hermapollon 236–50, 264, 284–8, 290
carriers *see* ships
collection 72, 107–14
consumption in the Roman empire 49, 61, 104–6, 255–6
customs duties in Aden 229
eastward export 120–4, 261
emporia 34, 48, 75, 84–6, 89–90, 92, 94, 96–8, 124
estimated production and export 90–93, 98–101, 254–5, 318
findings in Roman sites 49 n.71, 54, 255 n.24, 319 n.98
gatherers 108–14, 321
guari 262
kingdom (Vadakkenkur) 89, 92, 100–1, 109
local exchanges/trade 115–18, 319
long pepper 48, 93
prices/fiscal values 101–5, 249–50, 266–7, 282, 291–4, 323 n.2
producing lands 68, 84–98, 101, 118, 321
purchased at Coptos 180 n.25
purchased by guilds at Edfu 278–9
purchased at Berenice 305 n.37
transport from the Red Sea to Alexandria 198–208
typologies 34, 48, 53–5, 62, 74–5, 94–6, 101, 146–7, 251, 260–2
Philondas 177–9, 192–3, 196
Phormio 176
Pirates 77, 79, 86, 142, 147, 149, 154–5, 253, 254 n.14
Pleiades 67, 74, 80–2, 151–2
Poliar 108
Polydeuces 318
Ptolemy Auletes 126–7, 268
Ptolemy Philadelphus 36, 46, 126–7

Qurra b. Sharik 40–1

Repayment of a maritime loan contract
Deadline dependent on the day the ship returns 162–9
through multiple partial sales 175–81
Retailers (*kapeloi*) 5, 116, 180, 185
Revenues 42, 117, 126–7, 132–4, 183, 277, 289, 299, 303, 311, 312 n.66, 318, 319–20, 322
Rhizophagoi 274
Rota do Cabo 62, 147–8, 260

Sailing seasons and maritime loans 162–8,
in Athens 166
in Constantinople 165
in the Mediterranean 62, 196–7
in Trajan's canal 36–41, 75
in the Red Sea and Gulf of Aden 55, 58, 71–5, 165
in the Arabian Sea 67, 71–5, 146
of the Berytus-Brentesion sea route 167
of the direct sea routes to India 62–7, 145–6
Ṣalāḥal-Dīn b. ʿArrām 43
Sandanes 95
Saraganos the elder (Gautamīputra Śiva Sātakarṇi) 136
Satavastres 135
scholasticus Late Antiquity traveler 68, 113, 120, 333
Ships/Boats Acatus 252
ʿadawlī Large ship 70
ancient pepper carriers 54–5, 58, 61–3, 101, 138–9, 151, 201–3, 206–7, 249, 251–4, 256, 319, 322
backwater boats 89, 118
Calicut pepper carriers 25, 45, 98
Carreira da Índia ships (Portuguese carracks) 3, 146–8, 256–61
Coptos ships 204–6
Coromandel coast ships 116
Cottonara dugout canoes boats 88–9, 101, 116, 148
Red Sea small ships (Ǧilāb, geruas, marākib al-Yaman) 42–3, 45, 262
Elephant carriers 46–8, 58
Grain carriers 204, 252, 254 n.16
Muza small boats 273
Nile boats 206–7
Paraos 251, 262
Qulzum boats 43
Sangara 116
Ship owner(s) 42, 163, 185, 195–6, 313, 316,
co-signatory of the Muziris papyrus contract as 161, 180, 182, 185, 212–13, 317
of the Erythraean Sea 298, 311 n.65, 313–15
Silk 68, 94, 106, 116, 138, 140, 217–18, 248, 254, 264
Sopatros 68
Sosandros 135
Soterichos 47
Spermatophagoi 274
Struthophagoi 274
C. Sulpicius Faustus 196

Taurus, constellation 80–2
Timocharis 82
Timotheus 177–8, 193, 197
Tortoise shell 6, 19, 55, 116, 138, 174, 231, 245, 248–9, 264–5, 284, 285–8, 321
Tyrannoi (East African chiefs) 119

M. Ulpius Iarhai 316
ʿUmar b. ʿAbd al-ʿAzīz 278–9
Usāma b. Zayd al-Tanūḫī 278
Uṣavadāta 327–9

Vānaras 114
vēḷir 221 n.64
Vēntar 119, 221
Vespasian 51, 96 n.44, 127, 297
Vēṭṭuvar 117, 272
Vima Kadphises 329

Al-Walīd b. ʿAbd al-Malik 278–9
Warehouse(s) 171
Winds around Cape of Good Hope 147
Etesian in the Nile valley 33, 47, 142–3
in the Red Sea 32–3, 44, 55–6, 58 n.107, 62, 75, 146
Monsoons 55, 58–67, 71–3, 75, 76 n.54, 77, 144–5, 150
Wine appreciated by the Indian kings 137
brought to Berenice for export and local consumption 134
brought to Rhapta as a courtesy to the locals 273
exported to India 137
flavoured by nard and malabatrhon 140, 216

Yavaṉar, Westerner in Tamil poetry 112, 115, 124, 137, 139
Yḏkrʾl, Minaean merchant 51–2
Yields (rewards for maritime loans) 4, 163–5, 167, 168 n.32, 185, 188, 197–8

Zydʾl, Minaean merchant 51 n.81